# MyWritingLab™ Online Course (access code required) for

## *The Blair Reader, Ninth Edition* by Laurie G. Kirszner and Stephen R. Mandell

MyWritingLab is an online practice, tutorial, and assessment program that provides engaging experiences for teaching and learning.

MyWritingLab includes most of the writing assignments from your accompanying textbook. Now, students can complete and submit assignments, and teachers can then track and respond to submissions easily—right in MyWritingLab—making the response process easier for the instructor and more engaging for the student.

In the **Writing Assignments**, students can use instructor-created peer review rubrics to evaluate and comment on other students' writing. When giving feedback on student writing, instructors can add links to activities that address issues and strategies needed for review. Instructors may link to multimedia resources in Pearson Writer, which include curated content from Purdue OWL. Paper review by specialized tutors through Smarthinking is available, as is plagiarism detection through TurnItIn.

## Respond to Student Writing with Targeted Feedback and Remediation

MyWritingLab unites instructor comments and feedback with targeted remediation via rich multimedia activities, allowing students to learn from and through their own writing.

## Writing Help for Varying Skill Levels

For students who enter the course at widely varying skill levels, MyWritingLab provides unique, targeted remediation through personalized and adaptive instruction, freeing up more class time for actual writing. The results of the pre-assessment inform each student's Learning Path, a personalized pathway for students to work on requisite skills through multimodal activities. In doing so, students feel supported and ready to succeed in class.

## NEW! Learning Tools for Student Engagement

### Learning Catalytics

Generate class discussion, guide lectures, and promote peer-to-peer learning real-time analytics using Learning Catalytics—an interactive student response tool that uses students' smartphones, tablets, or laptops to engage them in more sophisticated tasks and thinking.

### MediaShare

MediaShare allows students to post multimodal assignments easily—whether they are audio, video, or visual compositions—for peer review and instructor feedback. In both face-to-face and online course settings, MediaShare saves instructors valuable time and enriches the student learning experience by enabling contextual feedback to be provided quickly and easily.

## Direct Access to MyLab

Users can link from any Learning Management System (LMS) to Pearson's MyWritingLab. Access MyLab assignments, rosters, and resources, and synchronize MyLab grades with the LMS gradebook. New direct, single sign-on provides access to all the personalized learning MyLab resources that make studying more efficient and effective.

**Visit www.mywritinglab.com for more informati**

# THE BLAIR READER

## EXPLORING ISSUES AND IDEAS

### NINTH EDITION

EDITED BY

# LAURIE G. KIRSZNER

*University of the Sciences, Emeritus*

# STEPHEN R. MANDELL

*Drexel University*

PEARSON

Boston   Columbus   Indianapolis   New York   San Francisco
Amsterdam   Cape Town   Dubai   London   Madrid   Milan   Munich   Paris   Montréal   Toronto
Delhi   Mexico City   São Paulo   Sydney   Hong Kong   Seoul   Singapore   Taipei   Tokyo

**Senior Acquisitions Editor:** Brad Potthoff
**Program Manager:** Anne Shure
**Development Editor:** Karen Mauk
**Product Marketing Manager:** Ali Arnold
**Content Specialist:** Laura Olson
**Project Manager:** Shannon Kobran
**Project Coordination, Text Design, and Electronic Page Makeup:**
Cenveo® Publisher Services
**Program Design Lead:** Beth Paquin
**Cover Art (clockwise from upper left):** Constantine Pankin/Shutterstock; Danil
Melekhin/Getty Images; Christopher Brewer/Shutterstock; CaracterDesign/Getty
Images; Hande Guleryuz Yuce/Getty Images; Fayek Tasneem Khan/Getty Images;
Dimitri Otis/Getty Images; Shahreen/Shutterstock
**Senior Manufacturing Buyer:** Roy L. Pickering, Jr.
**Printer/Binder:** R. R. Donnelley/Crawfordsville
**Cover Printer:** Lehigh-Phoenix Color/Hagerstown

Acknowledgments of third-party content appear on the appropriate page within
text or on pages 519–524.

PEARSON, ALWAYS LEARNING, and MYWRITINGLAB are exclusive trademarks
owned by Pearson Education, Inc. or its affiliates in the United States and/or
other countries.

Unless otherwise indicated herein, any third-party trademarks that may appear in
this work are the property of their respective owners and any references to third-
party trademarks, logos, or other trade dress are for demonstrative or descriptive
purposes only. Such references are not intended to imply any sponsorship,
endorsement, authorization, or promotion of Pearson's products by the owners of
such marks, or any relationship between the owner and Pearson Education, Inc.,
or its affiliates, authors, licensees, or distributors.

**Library of Congress Cataloging-in-Publication Data**
Names: Kirszner, Laurie G., editor. | Mandell, Stephen R., editor.
Title: The Blair Reader : exploring issues and ideas / Edited by Laurie
   G. Kirszner ; Stephen R. Mandell.
Description: Nineth Edition. | Boston : Pearson, [2016]
Identifiers: LCCN 2015044995 | ISBN 9780134110370
Subjects: LCSH: College readers. | English language—Rhetoric—Problems,
   exercises, etc. | Report writing—Problems, exercises, etc.
Classification: LCC PE1417 .B54 2016 | DDC 808/.0427—dc23 LC record
   available at http://lccn.loc.gov/2015044995

1 2 3 4 5 6 7 8 9 10—DOC—19 18 17 16

Student ISBN-10: 0-13-411037-4
Student ISBN-13: 978-0-13-411037-0
A la Carte ISBN-10: 0-13-411041-2
A la Carte ISBN-13: 978-0-13-411041-7

www.pearsonhighered.com

# CONTENTS

# Topical Clusters

## Conformity and Rebellion

## Costumes and Masks

## Reading and Writing

## Rural Life

## Self-Image

## Social and Economic Class

## Stereotyping

## Suburban Life

## Teenage Wasteland

## Speeches

*Note:* Speeches are listed in alphabetical order.

# Rhetorical Table of Contents

Note: Selections are listed alphabetically within categories.

## Cause & Effect

## Comparison & Contrast

## Classification & Division

## Definition

## Argument & Persuasion

# PREFACE

After many years of teaching composition, we have come to see reading and writing as interrelated activities: if students are going to write effectively, they must first be able to read actively and critically. In addition, we see writing as both a private and a public act. As a private act, it enables students to explore their feelings and reactions and to discover their ideas about subjects that are important to them. As a public act, writing enables students to see how their own ideas fit into larger discourse communities, where ideas gain meaning and value. We believe that students are enriched and engaged when they view the reading and writing they do as a way of participating in ongoing public discussions about ideas that matter to them. From the beginning, our goal in *The Blair Reader* has always been to encourage students to contribute to these discussions in the wider world by responding to the ideas of others.

The core of *The Blair Reader* is, of course, its reading selections. As we selected the readings for this book, our goal was to introduce students to the enduring issues they confront as citizens in the twenty-first century. Many of these readings are contemporary; many are also quite provocative. Whenever possible, however, we also include classic readings that give students the historical context they need. For example, Chapter 4, "Issues in Education," includes "School Is Bad for Children" by John Holt; Chapter 5, "The Politics of Language," includes "Learning to Read and Write" by Frederick Douglass; and Chapter 11, "Making Ethical Choices," includes "Letter from Birmingham Jail" by Martin Luther King, Jr. It was also important to us that the selections in *The Blair Reader* represent a wide variety of rhetorical patterns and types of discourse as well as a range of themes, issues, and positions. In addition to essays and articles from print and electronic sources, *The Blair Reader* includes speeches, short stories, poems, and a short play. It is our hope that exposure to this wide variety of formats, topics, and viewpoints can help students discover their own voices and express their own ideas.

As teachers, we—like you—expect a thematic reader to include compelling reading selections that involve instructors and students in spirited exchanges. We also expect readings that reflect the diversity of ideas that characterizes our society and questions that challenge students to respond critically to what they have read. In short, we expect a book that stimulates discussion and that encourages students to discover new ideas and see familiar ideas in new ways. These expectations guided us as we initially created *The Blair Reader*, and they continued to guide us as we worked on this new ninth edition.

## What's New in the Ninth Edition?

In response to the thoughtful comments of the many instructors who generously shared with us their reactions (and their students' reactions) to *The Blair Reader*, we have made many changes in this new edition, adding two new chapters on the reading and writing processes, new readings, new study questions and writing and research prompts, and new visuals.

- **A new Chapter 1,** "Becoming a Critical Reader," includes updated and expanded guidance for reading and reacting critically to texts (including visual texts) and formulating original responses.

- **A new Chapter 2,** "Writing about Reading," explains and illustrates the process of writing responses and academic essays about a range of texts.

- **New Focus sections** showcase related essays that examine contemporary concerns, zeroing in on questions such as "How Free Should Free Speech Be?" and "Why Are Zombies Invading Our Media?"

- **New readings** have been added to stimulate student interest and to introduce them to some of the challenging issues that they confront as students and as citizens. Among the many essays that are new to this edition are Tao Lin's "When I Moved Online . . .," Zeynep Tufekci's "After the Protests," Sheryl Sandberg and Anna Maria Chávez's "'Bossy,' the Other B-Word," Reza Aslan's "Praying for Common Ground at the Christmas-Dinner Table," Jonathan Safran Foer's "How Not to Be Alone," and Barbara Hurd's "Fracking: A Fable." New literary selections—such as Charles Jensen's "Poem In Which Words Have Been Left Out," Lydia Davis's "Television," and Steven Korbar's *"What Are You Going to Be?"*—have also been added.

- **A new Appendix: MLA Documentation** helps students to incorporate research ethically, offering numerous sample citations for commonly used sources.

- **New learning objectives** at the beginning of each chapter reflect and help students to assess their understanding of the chapter's content.

## Resources for Students

We designed the apparatus in *The Blair Reader* to involve students and to encourage them to respond critically to what they read. These responses can lay the groundwork for the more focused thinking that they will do when they write. In order to help students improve their critical reading and writing skills, we have included the following features:

- An **Introduction** maps out the book's features to help students get the most from *The Blair Reader*.

- **Paired visuals** introduce each thematic chapter. These visuals engage students by encouraging them to identify parallels and contrasts. In addition, they introduce students to the themes that they will be considering as they read the selections in the chapter.

- A brief **chapter introduction** places each chapter's broad theme in its social, historical, or political context, helping students to understand the complexities of the issues being discussed. This chapter introduction is followed by **Preparing to Read and Write**, a list of questions designed to help students focus their responses to individual readings and relate these responses to the chapter's larger issues.

- **Headnotes** that introduce each selection provide biographical and other background information as well as insight into the writer's purpose.

- **Responding to Reading** questions that follow each selection address thematic and rhetorical considerations. By encouraging students to think critically, these questions help them to see reading as an interactive and intellectually stimulating process.

- **Writing about Reading** prompts (after essays and speeches) give students the opportunity to write a short, informal response or a longer essay that may require research. A **Responding in Writing** prompt after each literary selection encourages students to write a brief, informal response.

- A **Focus** section at the end of each chapter is introduced by a provocative question related to the chapter's theme, followed by a visual that is accompanied by **Responding to the Image** questions. The heart of the Focus section is a group of readings that take a variety of positions on the issue, encouraging students to add their voices to the debate and demonstrating that complex issues elicit different points of view. Each reading is followed by "Responding to Reading" questions and "Writing about Reading" prompts.

- At the end of each Focus section, a **Widening the Focus** feature includes a writing prompt ("For Critical Reading and Writing") that asks students to tie the readings together; a list of essays in other chapters of the book that also address the issues raised by the Focus question; an Internet research assignment; and a field research assignment ("Beyond the Classroom").

- **Exploring Issues and Ideas** suggestions at the end of each thematic chapter encourage students to explore the chapter's theme in greater depth.

- A **Rhetorical Table of Contents,** located at the front of the book on pages xx–xxviii, groups the text's readings according to the way they arrange material: narration, description, process, comparison and contrast, and so on.

- **Topical Clusters,** narrowly focused thematic units (pp. x–xix), offer students and teachers additional options for grouping readings.

## Additional Resources for Instructors and Students

### Instructor's Manual (0134110404)

Because we wanted *The Blair Reader* to be a rich and comprehensive resource for instructors, a thoroughly revised and updated *Instructor's Resource Manual* has been developed to accompany the text. Designed to be a useful and all-inclusive tool, the manual contains teaching strategies, collaborative activities, and suggested answers for "Responding to Reading" questions. The manual includes web and/or multimedia teaching resources for almost every reading. It also contains new questions for stimulating classroom discussions of the new chapter-opening images. Contact your local Pearson representative for details.

### MyWritingLab                                    MyWritingLab™

MyWritingLab is an online homework, tutorial, and assessment program that provides engaging experiences to today's instructors and students. By incorporating rubrics into the writing assignments, faculty can create meaningful assignments, grade them based on their desired criteria, and analyze class performance through advanced reporting. For students who enter the course underprepared, MyWritingLab offers a diagnostic test and personalized remediation so that students see improved results and instructors spend less time in class reviewing the basics. Rich multimedia resources, including text-specific writing assignments and eText, are built in to engage students and support faculty throughout the course. Visit www.mywritinglab.com for more information.

## Acknowledgments

*The Blair Reader* is the result of a fruitful collaboration between the two of us, between us and our students, between us and Pearson, and between us and you—our colleagues who told us what you want in a reader.

At Pearson, we want to thank Brad Potthoff, Senior Acquisitions Editor, and Eric Stano, Vice President and Editorial Director. We also appreciate the efforts of Anne Shure, Program Manager, and Amanda Norelli, Editorial Assistant.

Karen R. Mauk, our wonderful developmental editor, spent a great deal of time and effort making this book as good as it is. As always, her patience, professionalism, and hard work are greatly appreciated. At Cenveo Publisher Services, we want to thank Kathy Smith, Senior Project Manager, for seeing this book through to completion.

In preparing *The Blair Reader*, Ninth Edition, we benefited at every stage from the assistance and suggestions of colleagues from across the country: Patricia Bjorklund, Southeastern Community College; Gennean Bolen, Fresno City College; Toni L. D'Onofrio, The Art Institute of New York City; Cynthia Elliott, Clovis Community College Center; Kimberly S. Hall, Harrisburg Area Community College; Tabitha R. Miller, Pitt Community College; Matthew W. Schmeer, Johnson County Community College; Mark A. Smith, Lock Haven University; Brian Walter, St. Louis College of Pharmacy; Andrea J. West, Midlands Technical College; and William A. Wilson, San Jose State University.

We would also like to thank the following reviewers of previous editions for their valuable insight: Jacob Agatucci, Central Oregon Community College; Jesse T. Airaudi, Baylor University; Marlene Allen, Fayetteville State University; Linda A. Archer, Green River Community College; Anthony Armstrong, Richland College; Stephen R. Armstrong, Eastern Carolina University; Patricia Baldwin, Pitt Community College; Lisa Beckelhimer, University of Cincinnati; Chere Berman, College of the Canyons; Charlene Bunnell, University of Delaware; Jason Chaffin, Cape Fear Community College; Gail Charrier, Delaware Technical and Community College; Peggy Cole, Arapahoe Community College; Carla L. Dando, Idaho State University; Rosemary Day, Albuquerque Community College; Emily Dial-Driver, Rogers State University; Janet Eldred, University of Kentucky; Anne Fernald, Fordham University; Robert G. Ford, Houston Community College; Web Freeman, Ozarks Technical Community College; Ruth Gerik, University of Texas at Arlington; Janet Gerstner, San Juan College; Lisa Gordon, Columbus State Community College; Kimberly Greenfield, Lorain County Community College; Judy A. Hayden, University of Tampa; David Holper, College of the Redwoods; Pamela Howell, Midland College; Tara Hubschmitt, Lakeland College; Lu Ellen Huntley, University of North Carolina at Wilmington; Jessica Hyatt, Ozarks Technical Community College; Aura Imbarus, El Camino College; Robert S. Imbur,

University of Toledo; JoAnne James, Pitt Community College; James Jenkins, Mt. San Antonio College; Amanda Jerome, Saddleback College; Terry Jolliffe, Midland College; Alan Kaufman, Bergen Community College; Dimitri Keriotis, Modesto Junior College; Robert Leston, University of Texas at Arlington; John Lucarelli, Community College of Allegheny County; Robert Lunday, Houston Community College; Robyn Lyons-Robinson, Columbus State Community College; Dani McLean, Saddleback College; Camilla Mortensen, University of Oregon; Kathryn Neal, York Technical College; Paul Northam, Johnson County Community College; Marguerite Parker, Eastern Carolina University; Andrea Penner, San Juan College; Angie Pratt, Montgomery College; Jeannette E. Riley, UMass Dartmouth; CC Ryder, West L.A. College; Debra Shein, Idaho State University; Margaret Simonton, East Arizona College; Katie Singer, Fairleigh Dickinson University; Darlene Smith-Worthington, Pitt Community College; Derek Soles, Drexel University; Lori Ann Stephens, Richland College; Sharon Strand, Black Hills State University; Ryan D. Stryffeler, Western Nevada College; Diane Sweet, Wentworth Institute of Technology; Katie Thomas, Community College of Beaver County; Cara Unger, Portland Community College; Jennifer Vanags, Johnson County Community College; Stephen H. Wells, Community College of Allegheny County; Mary Williams, Midland College; Mary Ellen Williams, UC Davis; Nicole S. Wilson, Bowie State University; and K. Siobhan Wright, Carroll Community College.

On the home front, we once again "round up the usual suspects" to thank. And, of course, we thank each other: it really has been a "beautiful friendship."

# INTRODUCTION

*The Blair Reader* is a collection of readings, and it is also a book that encourages you to write about what you read, focusing your ideas and at the same time discovering new ideas. To support this dual process of reading and writing, *The Blair Reader* includes a number of features to help you explore your reactions to the readings and express your ideas in writing.

The readings in *The Blair Reader* (classic and contemporary essays as well as speeches, interviews, fiction, and poetry) are arranged in nine thematic chapters, each offering a variety of different vantage points from which to view the chapter's central theme. Each chapter opens with a brief introduction, which provides a context for the chapter's theme and includes a list of **Preparing to Read and Write** questions to guide you as you read. These questions are designed to sharpen your critical skills so you can apply those skills effectively. Each chapter introduction also includes a pair of contrasting visual images to introduce you to the chapter's theme and encourage you to begin thinking about the fundamental issues related to that theme.

Following each essay are three **Responding to Reading** questions that ask you to think critically about the writer's ideas, perhaps focusing on a particular strategy the writer has used to achieve his or her goals. In some cases, these questions may ask you to examine your own ideas or beliefs. Question #3 in each set, designated **Rhetorical Analysis,** may ask you to comment on the writer's audience and purpose as well as consider rhetorical strategies such as thesis, organization, evidence, and stylistic techniques. Following these three questions are two **Writing about Reading** prompts. The first prompt, which does not require research, is suitable for either a short, informal response or a longer essay; the second prompt, designated **Writing with Sources,** calls for a source-based essay. (Fiction, poetry, and drama selections are followed by three **Responding to Reading** questions as well as a **Responding in Writing** prompt suitable for a brief informal response.)

Following the essays that explore each chapter's general theme is a **Focus** section that zeroes in on a specific issue. The Focus section's central question—for example, "Is a College Education Worth the Money?"

(Chapter 4) or "What Has Happened to Academic Integrity?" (Chapter 11)—introduces a cluster of thought-provoking readings that take different positions on a single complex issue; a related visual image is also included here. The assignments in the Focus sections encourage you to analyze, interpret, or evaluate the ideas explored in the Focus readings as well as in related outside sources. Each Focus essay is accompanied by three **Responding to Reading** questions, one of which is designated **Rhetorical Analysis** and two **Writing about Reading** prompts; **Responding to the Image** questions follow each visual. The Focus sections end with **Widening the Focus**, which includes "For Critical Reading and Writing" (an essay prompt that asks you to draw connections among the three Focus readings, perhaps referring to other sources in your discussion); "For Further Reading" (a list of related readings in other chapters of the book); "For Focused Research" (a comprehensive research assignment that relies on web sources); and "Beyond the Classroom" (a prompt designed to encourage you to write about your own observations and experiences). Each chapter ends with **Exploring Issues and Ideas**, a collection of additional writing prompts that offer you an opportunity to explore a general topic related to the chapter's theme.

As you read and write, you will also be learning how to think about yourself and about the world. By considering and reconsidering the ideas of others, by rejecting easy answers, by considering a problem from many different angles, and by appreciating the many factors that can influence your responses, you will develop critical thinking skills that you will use not just in college but throughout your life. In addition, by writing about the themes explored in this book, you will participate in an ongoing conversation within the community of scholars and writers who care deeply about the issues that shape our world.

# 1

## BECOMING A CRITICAL READER

*In this chapter, you will learn to*
- interpret a text
- analyze a text
- highlight and annotate a text
- analyze a visual text

### Reading and Meaning

Like many readers, you may assume that the meaning of a text is hidden somewhere between the lines and that you only have to ask the right questions or unearth the appropriate clues to discover exactly what the writer is getting at. But reading is not a game of hide-and-seek in which you search for ideas that have been hidden by the writer. As current reading theory demonstrates, meaning is created by the interaction between a reader and a text.

One way to explain this interactive process is to draw an analogy between a text—a work being read—and a word. A word is not the natural equivalent of the thing it signifies. The word *dog*, for example, does not evoke the image of a furry, four-legged animal in all parts of the world. To speakers of Spanish, the word *perro* elicits the same mental picture *dog* does in English-speaking countries. Not only does the word *dog* have meaning only in a specific cultural context, but even within that context it also evokes different images in different people. Some people may picture a collie, others a poodle, and still others a particular pet.

Like a word, a text can have different meanings in different cultures—or even in different historical time periods. Each reader brings to the text associations that come from his or her own cultural community. These associations are determined by readers' experience and education as well as by their ethnic group, social class, religion, gender, and many other factors that contribute to how they view the world. Each reader also brings to the text beliefs, expectations, desires, and biases that influence how he or she reacts to and interprets it. Thus, it is entirely possible

3

for two readers to have very different, but equally valid, interpretations of the same text. (This does not mean, of course, that a text can mean whatever any individual reader wishes it to mean. To be valid, an interpretation must be supported by the text itself.)

To get an idea of the range of possible interpretations that can be suggested by a single text, consider some of the responses different readers might have to E. B. White's classic essay "Once More to the Lake" (p. 37).

In "Once More to the Lake," White tells a story about his visit with his son to a lake in Maine in the 1940s, comparing this visit with those he made as a boy with his own father in 1904. Throughout the essay, White describes the changes that have occurred since his first visit. Memories from the past flood his consciousness, causing him to remember things that he did when he was a boy. At one point, after he and his son have been feeding worms to fish, he remembers doing the same thing with his father and has trouble separating the past from the present. Eventually, White realizes that he will soon be merely a memory in his son's mind—just as his father is only a memory in his.

White had specific goals in mind when he wrote this essay. His title, "Once More to the Lake," underscores that he intended to compare his childhood and adult visits to the lake. The organization of ideas in the essay, the use of flashbacks, and the choice of particular transitional words and phrases reinforce this purpose. In addition, descriptive details—such as the image of the tarred road that replaced the dirt road—remind readers, as well as White himself, that the years have made the lake site different from what it once was. The essay ends with White suddenly feeling the "chill of death."

Despite White's specific intentions, each person reading "Once More to the Lake" will respond to it somewhat differently. Young male readers might identify with the boy. If they have ever spent a vacation at a lake, they might have experienced the "peace and goodness and jollity" of the whole summer scene. Female readers might also want to share these experiences, but they might feel excluded because only males are described in the essay. Readers who have never been on a fishing trip might not feel the same nostalgia for the woods that White feels. To them, living in the woods away from the comforts of home might seem an unthinkably uncomfortable ordeal. Older readers might identify with White, sympathizing with his efforts as an adult to recapture the past and seeing his son as naively innocent of the challenges of life.

Thus, although each person who reads White's essay will read the same words, each will be likely to interpret it differently and to see different things as important because much is left open to interpretation. All essays leave blanks or gaps—missing ideas or images—that readers have to fill in. In "Once More to the Lake," for example, readers must imagine what happened in the years that separated White's last visit to the lake with his father and the trip he took with his son.

These gaps in the text create **ambiguities**—words, phrases, descriptions, or ideas that need to be interpreted by the reader. For instance, when you read the words "One summer, along about 1904, my father rented a camp on a lake," how do you picture the camp? White's description of the setting contains a great deal of detail, but no matter how much information he supplies, he cannot paint a complete verbal picture of the lakeside camp. He must rely on his readers' ability to visualize the setting and to supply details from their own experience.

Readers also bring their emotional associations to a text. For example, the way readers react to White's statement above depends, in part, on their feelings about their own fathers. If White's words bring to mind a parent who is loving, strong, and protective, they will most likely respond favorably; if the essay calls up memories of a parent who is distant, bad-tempered, or even abusive, they may respond negatively.

Because each reader views the text from a slightly different angle, each may also see a different focus as central to "Once More to the Lake." Some might see nature as the primary element in the essay and believe that White's purpose is to condemn the encroachment of human beings on the environment. Others might see the passage of time as the central focus. Still others might see the initiation theme as being the most important element of the essay: each boy is brought to the lake by his father, and each eventually passes from childhood innocence to adulthood and to the awareness of his own mortality.

Finally, each reader may evaluate the essay differently. Some readers might find "Once More to the Lake" boring because it has little action and deals with a subject in which they have no interest. Others might believe the essay is a brilliant meditation that makes an impact through its vivid description and imaginative figurative language. Still others might see the essay as falling between these two extremes—for example, they might grant that White is an accomplished stylist but also see him as self-centered and self-indulgent. After all, they might argue, the experiences he describes are available only to relatively privileged members of society and are irrelevant to others.

## Reading Critically

Many of the texts you read during your years as a student will be challenging. In college, you read to expand your horizons, so it makes sense that some ideas and concepts that you encounter in your assigned reading may be difficult or unfamiliar. When you approach an academic text for the first time, you may feel somewhat intimidated, or even overwhelmed, and you may find yourself wondering where to start and what to look for. This is natural. Fortunately, the reading strategies discussed below can make it easer for you to interpret unfamiliar texts.

Before you begin to read, you should understand the difference between *reading* and *reading critically*. For some students, the act of reading a text is simply a search for facts that must be digested and memorized. For critical readers, however, reading is a much more active and dynamic process.

**Reading critically** means interacting with the text, questioning the text's assumptions, and formulating and reformulating judgments about its ideas. Think of reading as a dialogue between you and the text: sometimes the writer will assert himself or herself; at other times, you will dominate the conversation. Remember, though, that a critical voice is a thoughtful and responsible one, not one that shouts down the opposition. Linguist Deborah Tannen makes this distinction clear in an essay called "The Triumph of the Yell":

> In many university classrooms, "critical thinking" means reading someone's life work, then ripping it to shreds. Though critique is surely one form of critical thinking, so are integrating ideas from disparate fields and examining the context out of which they grew. Opposition does not lead to truth when we ask only "What's wrong with this argument?" and never "What can we use from this in building a new theory, a new understanding?"

In other words, being a critical reader does not necessarily mean arguing and contradicting; more often, it means actively engaging the text by asking questions and exploring your reactions—while remaining open to new ideas.

Asking the following questions as you read will help you to become aware of the relationships between the writer's perspective and your own:

- **Whom is the writer addressing?** Who is the writer's intended audience? Does the writer think that readers will be receptive to his or her ideas? hostile? neutral? How can you tell? What preconceived ideas does the writer expect readers to have? For example, the title of John Holt's essay on early childhood education, "School Is Bad for Children" (p. 78), suggests that Holt expects his readers to have preconceived notions about the value of a traditional education—notions his essay will challenge.

- **What is the writer's purpose?** Exactly what is the writer trying to accomplish in the essay? For example, is the writer's main purpose to explain, to entertain, or to persuade? Does the writer have any secondary purposes—for example, to justify, evaluate, describe, debunk, instruct, preach, browbeat, threaten, or frighten? Or, does the writer have some other purpose (or combination of purposes) in mind? Does the writer appeal to the prejudices or fears of his or her readers or in any other way attempt to influence readers unfairly?

- **What genre is the writer using?** Written texts, such as those in this book, fall into categories called **genres**. Each genre is defined by distinct conventions, structures, and techniques. For example, an academic essay is a genre that has three parts: an introduction, a body, and a conclusion. Its purpose is to convince readers that its statements are reasonable and worth considering. An academic essay deals with ideas—sometimes complex ideas—and discusses them in precise language, which includes discipline-specific vocabulary. In general, it avoids the use of the first person *I*, and it is free of slang and ungrammatical constructions. An academic essay almost always has a thesis statement, which it develops using facts, examples, and material from credible outside sources (all borrowed material is documented). Essays can be *descriptive, narrative, expository* (explanatory), or *argumentative*, and each of these types of writing has its own characteristics. For instance, descriptive essays frequently use subjective language and rely on imaginative comparisons to tell what something looks or feels like.

As you approach any reading in this book, ask yourself what genre the writer is using and how this genre determines the way in which the writer treats his or her subject. In addition to the genres represented in this book—which include essays, editorials, op-eds, speeches, poems, and short stories—you will often encounter other writing genres, all of which have their own distinctive forms and conventions.

Throughout your education, you will become familiar with the genres characteristic of your major as well as those of the other subjects you take. Some of these genres appear in the chart below.

| Narrative Essay | Argument Essay | Research Essay | Rhetorical Analysis | Response |
|---|---|---|---|---|
| **Purpose** | | | | |
| to tell a story or to relate a series of events | to persuade readers to accept (or at least consider) a debatable idea | to locate, interpret, and evaluate sources related to a topic | to examine the way the elements in a text work together | to reflect on a text and discuss it |
| **Characteristics** | | | | |
| Thesis statement identifies the point the narrative is making | Thesis statement identifies the position the writer is taking | Thesis statement identifies the stand the writer will take or asks a question that the writer will answer | Thesis statement identifies the point that is being made about the text selected for analysis | Opens with a statement that expresses the writer's reaction to the text |
| Events are usually (but not always) arranged in time order | Points are supported by facts, examples, and opinions of experts | Weaves together paraphrases and summaries as well as quotations and original ideas to support points | Examines various elements of the text—for example, the writer's use of *logos, pathos,* and *ethos* | Identifies the text's central idea or claim |
| Includes details that help readers visualize events | Refutes opposing arguments by showing that they are inaccurate, incorrect, or misguided | | | Discusses how the writer feels about what he or she is reading |

(*continued*)

| Narrative Essay | Argument Essay | Research Essay | Rhetorical Analysis | Response |
|---|---|---|---|---|
| | | Characteristics | | |
| May be written in first person (*I*) or third person (*he, she, it*), depending on whether or not the narrative is based on personal experiences | Relies on logic<br><br>Uses an appropriate documentation format | May use charts, graphs, infographics, and other visuals to present information<br><br>May use headings to separate sections of the essay<br><br>Uses an appropriate documentation format | Makes points supported by references (quotations, summaries, and paraphrases) to the text being analyzed<br><br>Uses an appropriate documentation format | Identifies points of agreement or disagreement<br><br>May include personal observations or experiences if they are relevant to the reading<br><br>May include questions that need to be answered |

Other genres you may encounter in your reading as well as in written assignments include the following.

Abstracts

Blog posts

Book or film reviews

Emails

Job application letters

Lab reports

Literacy narratives

Literary analyses

Memoirs

Memos

Paraphrases

Résumés

Summaries

Visuals (charts, tables, infographics, photos, and so on)

- **What voice does the writer use?** Does the writer seem to talk directly to readers? If so, does the writer's subjectivity get in the way, or does it help to involve readers? Does the writer's voice seem distant or formal? Different voices have different effects on readers. For example, an emotional tone can inspire; an intimate tone can create empathy; a straightforward, forthright tone can make ideas seem reasonable and credible. An ironic tone can either amuse readers or alienate them; a distant, reserved tone can evoke either respect or discomfort.

- **How does the writer try to influence readers?** Writers use rhetorical strategies—called **appeals**—to influence readers. One such strategy is the appeal to **logos**, or logic. Another type of appeal is the appeal to **pathos**, or emotion. A final type of appeal is the appeal to **ethos**, or the credibility of the writer. For example, in the Declaration of Independence (p. 320), Thomas Jefferson constructs a logical argument to support his point that King George III is not fit to rule a free people. In addition, he appeals to the emotions of readers by describing the indignities that he and other colonists must face every day. Finally, he establishes his credibility by identifying himself and the other signatories of the Declaration of Independence as representatives of the United States of America. By doing so, Jefferson makes it clear that he has authority and that he has something important to say.

When you read, ask some of the following questions: Does the writer appeal to reason? Does the writer supply evidence to support his or her ideas? Is this evidence convincing? Does the writer appeal to emotion? What strategies does he or she use to influence you? Finally, does the writer establish his or her credibility? How does the writer demonstrate that he or she is a convincing, legitimate, and trustworthy source of information?

- **What position does the writer take on the issue?** Sometimes a work's title reveals a writer's position—for example, the choice of the word *war* in Christina Hoff Sommers's title "The War against Boys" (p. 247) clearly reveals her position on society's attitude toward boys. Keep in mind, though, that a writer's position may not always be as obvious as it is in these examples. As you read, look carefully for specific language that suggests the writer's position on a particular subject or issue—or for explicit statements that make that position clear. Also, be sure you understand how you feel about the writer's position, particularly if it is an unusual or controversial one. Do you agree or disagree? Can you explain your reasoning? Of course, a writer's advocacy of a position that is at odds with your own does not automatically render the work suspect or its ideas invalid. Remember, ideas that you might consider shocking or absurd may be readily accepted by many other readers. Unexpected, puzzling, or even repellent positions should encourage you to read carefully and thoughtfully, trying to understand the larger historical and cultural context of a writer's ideas.

- **How does the writer support his or her position?** What kind of supporting evidence is provided? Is it convincing? Does the writer use a series of short examples or a single extended example? Does the writer use statistics, or does he or she rely primarily on personal experiences? Does the writer quote experts or just present anecdotal information? Why does the writer choose a particular kind of support? Does the writer supply enough information to support the essay's points? Are all the examples actually relevant to the issues being discussed? Is the writer's reasoning valid, or do the arguments seem forced or unrealistic? Are any references in the work unfamiliar to you? If so, do they arouse your curiosity, or do they discourage you from reading further?

- **What beliefs, assumptions, or preconceived ideas do you have that color your responses to a work?** Does the writer challenge any ideas that you accept as "natural" or "obvious"? Do you consider yourself a hostile, friendly, or neutral reader? What has the writer done to address possible objections to his or her ideas? Should he or she have done more to address these objections? Do your preconceived ideas make it difficult for you to fairly evaluate the writer's ideas?

- **Does your own background or experience give you any special insights that enable you to understand or interpret the writer's ideas?** Are the writer's experiences similar to your own? Is the writer like you in terms of age, ethnic background, gender, and social class? How do the similarities between you and the writer affect your reaction to the work? What experiences have you had that could help you understand the writer's ideas and shape your response to them?

## Recording Your Reactions

It is a good idea to read any text at least twice: first to get a general sense of the writer's ideas and then to react critically to these ideas. As you read critically, you interact with the text and respond in ways that will help you to interpret it. This process of coming to understand the text will prepare you to discuss the work with others and, perhaps, to write about it.

As you read and reread, record your responses; if you don't, you may forget some of your best ideas. Two activities can help you keep a record of the ideas that come to you as you read: **highlighting** (using a system of symbols and underlining to identify key ideas) and **annotating** (writing down your responses and interpretations in the margins of the text).

When you react to what you read, don't be afraid to question the writer's ideas. As you read and make annotations, you may disagree with or even challenge some of these ideas; when you have time, you can think more about what you have written. These informal responses are often the beginning of a thought process that will lead you to original insights. Later, when you write about the text, you can refine these ideas into the points that you will develop more fully in your essay.

Highlighting and annotating helped a student to understand the passage on page 11, which is excerpted from Brent Staples's essay "Just Walk On By" (p. 313). As she prepared to write about the essay, the student identified and summarized the writer's key points and made a connection with another essay, Judith Ortiz Cofer's "The Myth of the Latin Woman" (p. 271). As she read, she underlined some of the passage's important words and ideas, using arrows to indicate relationships between them. She also circled a few words to remind her to look up their meanings later on, and she wrote down questions and comments as they occurred to her.

*Still applies today?*

*(?)*

The fearsomeness mistakenly attributed to me in public places often has a perilous flavor. The most frightening of these confusions occurred in the late 1970s and early 1980s when I worked as a journalist in Chicago. One day, rushing into the office of a magazine I was writing for with a deadline story in hand, I was mistaken for a burglar. The office manager called security and, with an ad hoc posse, pursued me through the labyrinthine halls, nearly to my editor's door. I had no way of proving who I was. I could only move briskly toward the company of someone who knew me.

*(Fear creates danger)*

*First experience*

*(?)*

Another time I was on assignment for a local paper and killing time before an interview. I entered a jewelry store on the city's affluent Near North Side. The proprietor excused herself and returned with an enormous red Doberman pinscher straining at the end of a leash. She stood, the dog extended toward me, silent to my questions, her eyes bulging nearly out of her head. I took a cursory look around, nodded, and bade her good night. Relatively speaking, however, I never fared as badly as another black male journalist. He went to nearby Waukegan, Illinois, a couple of summers ago to work on a story about a murderer who was born there. Mistaking the reporter for the killer, police hauled him from his car at gunpoint and but for his press credentials would probably have tried to book him. Such episodes are not uncommon. Black men trade tales like this all the time.

*Second experience*

*(?)*

*Compare with Cofer's experience w/ stereotypes*

## Reacting to Visual Texts

Many of the written texts you read—from newspapers and magazines to websites to textbooks such as this one—include visuals. Some of these visuals (charts, tables, maps, graphs, scientific diagrams, and the like) primarily present information; others (fine art, photographs, cartoons, and advertisements, for example) may be designed to have an emotional impact on readers or to persuade them to change their minds or to take some kind of action.

Visuals can be analyzed, interpreted, and evaluated just as written texts are. You begin this process by looking critically at the visual, identifying its most important elements, and considering the relationships of various elements to one another and to the image as a whole. Then, you try to identify the purpose for which the image was created, and you consider your own personal response to the image.

As you examine a visual text, finding answers to the following questions will help you to understand it better:

- **Who is the intended audience of this visual?** Does the visual seem to address a wide general audience or some kind of specialized audience, such as new parents, runners, or medical professionals? Is it aimed at adults or at children? Is it likely to appeal mainly to people from a particular region or ethnic group, or is it likely to resonate with a broad range of people? Often, knowing where a visual appeared—in a popular magazine, on a political blog, in a professional journal, or in a trade publication, for example—will help you to identify the audience the visual is trying to reach.

- **For what purpose was the visual created?** Is the visual designed to evoke an emotional response—fear or guilt, for example? Is it designed to be humorous? Or is its purpose simply to present information? To understand a visual's purpose, you need to consider not only its source but also what images it contains and how it arranges them. (Some visuals contain written text, and if this is the case, you will have to consider this written text as well.)

- **What elements does the visual use to achieve its purpose?** What is the most important image? Where is it placed? What other images are present? Does the visual depict people? What are they doing? How much space is left blank? How does the visual use color and shadow? Does it include written text? How are words and images juxtaposed? For example, a visual designed to be primarily informative may use written text and straightforward graphics (such as graphs or scientific diagrams), while one that aims to persuade may use a single eye-catching image surrounded by blank space.

- **What point does the visual make?** How does it use images to get its message across? What other elements help to convey that message? If the visual is designed to convince its audience of something—for example, to change unhealthy behavior, donate to a charity, vote for a candidate, or buy a product—exactly how does it communicate this message? A photograph of starving children on a charity's website, for example, might convey the idea that a donation will bring them food, but statistics about infant mortality might make the image even more persuasive. Moreover, a close-up of one hungry child might be more convincing than a distant photo of a crowd. Similarly, an ad might appeal to consumers either by showing satisfied customers using a product or by setting a memorable slogan against a contrasting background.

- **What beliefs or assumptions do you have that help to determine your response to the visual?** Is there anything in your background or experience that influences your reaction? Just as with written texts, people react differently to various visual texts. For instance, if you have expertise in economics, you may approach a chart depicting economic trends with greater interest—or greater skepticism—than a general audience would. If you know very little about fine art, your reaction to a painting is more likely to be emotional than analytical. And, as a loyal Democrat or Republican, you may react negatively to a political cartoon that is critical of your party. Finally, if you or a family member has struggled with illness or addiction, you might not respond favorably to a visual that took a superficial, lighthearted, or satirical approach to such a problem.

The following visual is a parody of an ad for Marlboro cigarettes. The visual, which appeared on the website www.adbusters.org, was annotated by a student who was assigned to analyze it. As he examined the ad, he identified its key elements and recorded his reactions in handwritten notes.

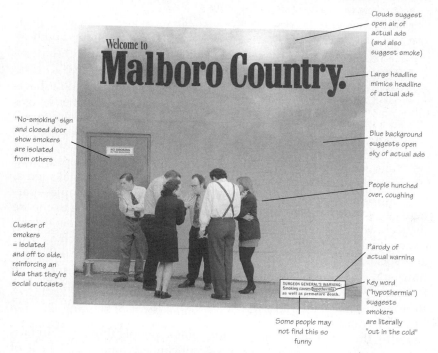

As you now know, reading critically involves more than just skimming a text for its ideas. It involves exploring the ideas of others as well as considering your own responses to those ideas. In the process, it enables you to discover new ideas and new ways of thinking about issues and to discover new things about yourself and your place in the world. In Chapter 2, you will take this process a step farther and examine the **writing process**—an activity that will help you sharpen your thinking and develop your ideas further. Not only will the writing process help you develop a better understanding of your subject, but it will also help you express yourself clearly, concisely, and effectively.

# 2

## WRITING ABOUT READING

*In this chapter, you will learn to*
- recognize the kind of writing you are expected to do
- identify your purpose for writing
- analyze the audience for your writing
- express your responses to a text
- list ideas to write about
- develop a thesis
- arrange your ideas
- draft your essay
- evaluate and revise your essay

For years, journalists, academics, and others have been proclaiming the decline of writing. Because of the rise of social media, such as Facebook and Twitter, the argument goes, people—particularly young people—are writing without taking the time to choose the right word or to craft careful, correct sentences. To a certain extent, of course, this is true: clearly, informal communications such as texts and social media posts are composed quickly, with much less planning and less thought than academic essays or business reports. In fact, many people are probably more accustomed to writing in this informal, spontaneous way than to composing formal, carefully structured pieces of writing.

Still, this situation is not as bad as some people think it is. In fact, when it comes to writing, there is a significant advantage to the rise of social media. Even though much of this writing is not polished or carefully structured, it is still writing, and now that social media has become part of our lives, more and more people are comfortable with expressing ideas in written form. They have also learned the value of concise, efficient communication as well as the need to write for a particular purpose and audience and to pay close attention to content. These valuable skills can be applied to the more formal writing you do in college:

- **Writing concisely** Informal electronic communications often have length restrictions—for example, Tweets are limited to 160 characters—so writers using Twitter learn to express themselves as concisely as possible. Therefore, they tend to be specific and direct.

- **Writing for a particular audience** Informal electronic communications are usually directed at a known audience—a friend or family member, for example, or members of a professional or business network or affinity group. Therefore, writers learn to tailor their messages to their own particular readers.

- **Writing with a purpose** Informal electronic communications are often written with a particular aim in mind—for example, to arrange a meeting or to garner support for a cause. Thus, writers learn to focus on achieving a definite goal.

- **Writing carefully** Informal electronic communications can be forwarded or reposted without the sender's permission. As a result, writers learn to scrutinize their messages more carefully, looking for any content that might have a negative effect on their reputation or on future employment.

- **Writing with images** Informal electronic communications often incorporate images, such as emoticons, emoji, or memes, to achieve particular effects on an audience. As they become accustomed to using images in their writing, writers learn to use them in academic writing as well—for example, adding a chart or a photo to illustrate or support ideas in an essay.

In a sense, then, informal electronic communication prepares you for the more challenging academic writing you will do as a college student (as well as the writing you will do in professional or business situations). As you might expect, however, informal electronic communication and academic writing are very different. For one thing, texts and social media posts are not necessarily grammatically correct or correctly spelled, and they are likely to include slang, abbreviations, emoticons, and shorthand. In addition, sentences are often incomplete or run together, and capitalization is random or even nonexistent. In college writing, this is definitely not the case.

Another difference between informal electronic communications and academic writing is the extent to which careful planning and consideration of rhetorical strategies come into play. When you text a friend or post on Facebook, you write quickly, giving little thought to your message or to the way you are presenting it. In college writing situations, however, instructors expect you to respond to a particular assignment, and to tailor it to the needs and interests of a specific audience.

Moreover, they expect your writing to focus on a single idea, called a **thesis**; to support this thesis with reasons, examples, facts, details, and so on; and to be well organized and coherent. Finally, instructors expect your writing to be clear and grammatically correct, adhering to specific academic conventions of style, structure, format, and documentation. The first step in meeting these standards is to see writing as a process, one that helps you to achieve your purpose, focus your ideas, and express yourself clearly and concisely. The rest of this chapter outlines and illustrates the writing process you will follow as you complete written assignments for your college courses.

The activities discussed below actually overlap and are often repeated. In other words, the writing process is recursive rather than linear, more likely to be characterized by backtracking and repetition than by an orderly forward movement. As you become a more experienced writer, you will discover what works best for you and develop your own approach to this process.

## Understanding Your Assignment

The writing assignment you are given usually specifies the kind of writing—or **genre**—for example, a response, an essay, a proposal, or a report—you are expected to do. Academic genres vary from discipline to discipline and from course to course, and they follow specific stylistic and structural conventions.

The first step in the writing process is identifying the genre in which you are to write and understanding the conventions of that genre. In completing the assignments in this book, you will be writing **responses** and academic **essays**, which often incorporate one or more outside sources—not only print or web texts but also interviews, images, films, music lyrics, and so on. Other academic genres are listed and defined in Chapter 1. In addition to identifying the genre called for in each assignment, you will need to read your assignment very carefully to make sure you know exactly what is expected of you—for example, how many pages to write, when the assignment is due, and whether the use of outside sources is encouraged (or required).

## Understanding Your Purpose

Once you understand your assignment, you should consider your **purpose**—why you are writing. What do you hope to accomplish? For example, do you want to *inform* your audience or to *argue* in favor of a particular position? Your purpose may also be to observe, recall, explain causes or predict effects, describe, analyze, or evaluate—and you may also have other purposes, or more than one purpose.

## Understanding Your Audience

Next, consider who your readers will be. For example, will you be addressing your instructor, your classmates, or a wider audience? Understanding what your readers already know about your topic and what expectations or biases they are likely to have will help you decide what information to include and how to present and develop your ideas.

## Writing a Response

Most of the writing you will do in college will be in response to reading—assigned books and essays, newspapers and journals, research materials, electronic sources, and so on. If you have followed the active reading process described in Chapter 1, you will have highlighted and annotated your reading material. Once you have done this, you can write an informal **response** in which you assess what you have read and record your reactions to it. This process will not only help you to understand what you have read but also suggest ideas to write about.

Amber Lombardi, a student in a first-year writing course, was given the following writing assignment.

---

In the essay "Why We Work," Andrew Curry notes that work today is "hardly the paradise economists once envisioned." In fact, he says, workers are largely discontented, facing long hours and great stress; for many, work has lost the meaning it once had. Do you see this in your own life and in the lives of those you know? Do you agree that work has lost its meaning? Write a one-page response to help you formulate your reactions to the ideas in Curry's essay. Then, referring to Curry's discussion as well as to one or two outside sources, write a two- to three-page essay in which you explore these questions, supporting your points with examples from the experiences of friends and family members. (You can conduct interviews with them in person or by phone or email.) Be sure to explain what you mean by *meaningful work*.

---

Amber began her writing process by reading "Why We Work" and the Responding to Reading questions that follow the essay on page 358. After highlighting and annotating this essay, she wrote the response that appears on pages 18–19.

Lombardi 1

Amber Lombardi

Professor Lieu

English 110

2 October 2015

Response to "Why We Work"

In "Why We Work," Andrew Curry discusses why workers today are dissatisfied with their jobs. He starts by examining the Industrial Revolution and how people's jobs got broken up into parts so that a worker would do one task repetitively on an assembly line for hours on end. According to Curry, workers today feel "crushed"; they are like hamsters in a wheel, running as fast as they can just to stay in one place. If today's workers slow down or think creatively, they risk losing their jobs. It seems pathetic that in a society in which everyone has to work, so many people don't think their jobs have any value.

I can relate to this feeling because of the office job I had the summer between high school and college. One of my routine tasks was to copy and paste reviewer comments from three different versions of the same document into one master document. It was tedious, but that wasn't the problem. The real problem was that I found my job frustrating because I could see that there was a better way to do it, but my supervisor didn't want to hear about it.

At this job, I felt I was being treated like the workers whom Curry describes, almost as if I were a body without a mind. After all, my supervisor made it clear that I wasn't being "paid for thinking," as the factory foreman, Frederick Taylor, was quoted as saying in the Curry essay. (Taylor treated workers as if they were interchangeable, and the

Lombardi 2

tasks he assigned them were uninteresting fragments of the whole.) I was warned to stop thinking creatively about how to improve the process and just do it using the old method. As Curry points out, workers resent being treated in this way because it makes it impossible for them to take pride in what they are doing.

According to Curry, the rise in high technology in the 1990s didn't do much to improve the balance between work and life for most workers. Today, most employees are stressed because their work life invades their private life via cell phones and email and they are essentially working 24/7. But would this situation be a problem if the work was something that actually helped the world—something meaningful? To me, that is the important question that Curry is asking.

## Collecting Ideas

After writing a response to the assigned reading, your next step is to gather ideas to write about. One useful way to find ideas is to **brainstorm** about your assignment by reviewing and then expanding your active reading notes and your written response. At this point, you can also look for outside sources to supplement your own ideas. Later, you will focus on how to develop and structure these ideas in your essay.

After reading Andrew Curry's "Why We Work" and writing a response to his ideas, Amber Lombardi looked online for information about job satisfaction, and she also conducted informal interviews with her brother and sister-in-law and two friends. Then, she composed the following brainstorming notes. Notice that she supplies page or paragraph numbers for information from her sources so that when she writes her essay, she will be able to distinguish others' ideas from her own and document material she borrowed. (See the Appendix for information on MLA documentation style.)

## Brainstorming Notes

In 1930, Kellogg cut the workday by two hours because he believed that the future of work would/should involve more free time, a "workers' paradise," in Curry's words. (pars. 1–2) **But people now work longer and harder to afford the standard of living they want.**

It's harder to get and hold a job; people are willing to accept less just to keep their jobs.

***Employees upset about the reality of their work compared to the ideal. Job satisfaction is going downhill. They feel insecure, overworked, unappreciated, unfulfilled. (Refer to Weber *WSJ* article on job satisfaction, par. 8)

**History:**

- After Industrial Revolution, idea of workers as being interchangeable; Frederick Taylor, factory foreman, broke down work into "component parts." Assembly line; **can't see whole picture**. Repeating small part of process. (pars. 9–11) [Tedious and frustrating, like task I had!]

- Labor unions fought for reduced hours for workers. (par. 14)

- Roosevelt's New Deal encouraged consumerism; new things for people to want and work for. Then, postwar boom of 1950s and 1960s, everyone working, everyone buying. (pars. 17–18)

More work, less satisfaction. Hard work, no spiritual meaning. (Economic downturn in 1970s.) *[But what exactly is "spiritual meaning" when it comes to work?]*

Now can't count on having a job for life, can be fired at any time. Workers feel less valued. (So why get emotionally invested?) **You are replaceable**.

Instead of being offered job security, workers at high-tech firms in the 1990s were offered free food, on-site massages, dry-cleaning services, games. Companies such as Google still do. (par. 22) But people would rather have more time with family than bonuses and backrubs, right?

Technology allows work to invade home life: always on call. *[But maybe that wouldn't be so bad if you really liked the work.]*

***Opposite of assembly-line mentality.

**People I know:**

**Adam:** being a **graduate teaching assistant** is creative, has "huge personal meaning" for him, and he "carries it in his head 24/7." Likes the freedom to make own choices about teaching methods, sees how it helps students.

**Kendra**: job gives her "a community where I am valued." She works with an **international student exchange program** at the college, gets to travel and has "intense friendships" with coworkers, all doing "something we believe in."

Also likes being the "go-to person for certain tasks" and the recognition and responsibility of being in charge of a whole process, being considered an expert who is valuable and unique. (Very different from her high school job, which was a lot like my job between high school and college: no one wanted to hear our ideas! Also like Curry's Frederick Taylor, par. 11.)

**Natalie**: volunteering at a **hospice for people dying of chronic diseases** is "rewarding and fulfilling" because she works directly with clients and sees how what she does—being a companion and helping them be comfortable—comforts them.

**Natalie**: "I don't agree with the statement that work has lost its meaning. I think work is what you make of it, at almost any job." *[Do I agree? Some jobs these days are just demeaning, no matter how much you try to transform them with a positive attitude.]*

**Mario**: as a part-time **grocery bagger**, he's not allowed to chat with coworkers on the job, so he feels like he can't express himself, and he also thinks he isn't paid enough for the physical labor involved.

**Mario's mother**: most meaningful job was **community garden project**. She could see the direct results of what she did and felt like she was part of a process (planting seedlings, seeing them grow, harvesting the vegetables and fruits, selling at farmer's market, etc.).

*[Applying Natalie's view to Mario: he should be getting more out of his work and isn't trying hard enough. But how do you find deep meaning in putting groceries in a bag?]*

Work and life = the same thing? Life doesn't switch off when you start the workday.

***Important for job satisfaction:

* an individual's sense of being an important part of the whole

* contributions being valued

* part of the creative process

* responsible for something worthwhile

[Also: criteria discussed by Schwartz and Porath, chart in *NYT* article]

## Developing a Thesis

Once you have collected ideas to write about and reviewed your notes carefully, you should begin to see a focus for your essay. Now, you need to develop a **thesis statement**, a one-sentence summary of your essay's main idea. The points that you make in your essay should support this central idea. Keep in mind that your thesis statement should be clearly worded and specific, and cover only the points that you will discuss in your essay. (Note that at this stage of the writing process, your thesis is **tentative**; it is likely to change as you write and revise your essay.)

After reviewing her highlighting and annotations as well as her response and her brainstorming notes, Amber drafted the following tentative thesis statement.

> I believe that although work has lost its meaning for many of us because we no longer feel a connection between the tasks we do and their positive results in society, we can regain a sense of meaning by putting ourselves wholeheartedly into every task we take on.

## Arranging Supporting Material

If it is carefully phrased, your thesis statement should suggest a possible arrangement for your ideas. In Amber's case, her thesis statement, although somewhat vague and wordy, suggests that her essay will have a problem/solution structure. That is, she will begin by discussing how and why work has lost its meaning for many people and then move on to discuss how this problem might be solved.

Before you can begin writing, however, you need to review the work you have done so far in order to identify your key supporting points and arrange them effectively. After Amber reviewed her work—particularly her brainstorming notes—she arranged the supporting material for her essay in a logical order. The following informal outline shows how she organized her ideas.

- Workers are unhappy in their jobs (Weber), but they identify some positive aspects (Schwartz and Porath)
- Workers should take part in a whole process
  - Curry's comments
  - Mario's mother's experiences at community garden
- Employees should take responsibility for a significant part of a job
  - My sister-in-law's experiences at Mount Walton College
  - Kendra's experiences in high school job
- Work should benefit society
  - Kendra
  - Natalie
  - Mario

## Drafting Your Essay

Once you have arranged your key ideas into an informal outline, you can use this outline to guide you as you write the first draft of your essay. The opening paragraph of Amber's first draft appears below.

According to Andrew Curry's essay "Why We Work," people's lives are dominated by their jobs, and they are running as fast as they can just to stay in one place. Technology has improved our standard of living in this country, but few of us have time to enjoy it because we have to work so hard just to maintain that standard of living. The problem of being constantly at work is made worse by the fact that few people find their jobs meaningful. It seems pathetic that in a society in which everyone has to work, hardly anyone feels they are doing anything meaningful, or anything of value to society. I believe that although work has lost its meaning for many of us because we no longer feel a connection between the tasks we do and their positive results in society, we can regain a sense of meaning by putting ourselves wholeheartedly into every task we take on.

## Revising Your Essay

A college essay should include an *introduction*, a *body*, and a *conclusion*. The **introduction** identifies the article or essay you are discussing and states your thesis. In the **body paragraphs**, you present the **support** for your thesis—reasons, examples, facts, details, and so on—drawn from your source (or sources) or from your own experiences and observations. Each body paragraph is like a mini-essay, introducing one point in a **topic sentence** (a sentence that states the paragraph's main idea) and then developing that point with facts, reasons, examples, and so on. The **conclusion** reinforces the essay's main idea, ending with a strong concluding statement. As you revise, check to make sure your essay includes all these elements. Only then should you consider questions of style, grammar, mechanics, and punctuation.

---

### Strategies for Revision

- Read and react to your draft, using the same active reading strategies you use when you read an assigned text.
- Outline your work to make sure it conforms to the outline that guided your draft.
- Email a draft to your instructor, and ask for feedback and constructive suggestions for revision.
- Work in a peer-editing group, getting feedback from classmates.
- Work with a writing center tutor.
- Create a **graphic organizer**. Think of your essay as a series of blocks, and try to arrange your paragraphs and sentences within the blocks. This strategy will help you to see if you have arranged ideas logically and effectively.

---

When she revised her essay, Amber used several of the strategies listed in the box. For example, she worked with two other students in a peer-editing group. A body paragraph from Amber's draft, along with two students' comments, appears on page 25.

If you take on responsibility for a job, then you are going to feel excited about it. For example, Kendra Lombardi stated that she finds her current job with Mount Walton College's international student exchange program to be highly satisfying partly because she likes being "the go-to person for certain tasks." In a job she had when she was in high school, she had an idea for improving a process. However, her supervisor told her to keep her ideas to herself, which she found pretty depressing. On the other hand, Adam Lombardi, a graduate teaching assistant at Mount Walton College, says that being given responsibility by his department for creating his own curriculum is very rewarding.

Amber, I'm confused about the second half of your topic sentence. What is actually so good about taking responsibility that you "feel excited" about it? Chris

Amber: How was it rewarding for Adam? You don't really explain this—leaves us hanging. You could add a few quotes from Adam to help us get what was so rewarding about it exactly. Bella

Amber: You switch to a new example with this sentence—kind of abrupt. Not sure where you are going with it. How does it fit with your topic sentence about responsibility being satisfying? You could start the new example with a transition and develop the point more or even leave the whole thing out. Bella

Amber also used the following graphic organizer, filling in revised content from the final draft of her essay (including a revised thesis statement) to help her check its structure before handing it in.

**Opening remarks**: Downside of assembly-line jobs; general background from Curry essay

**Thesis statement**: Although Curry makes it clear that meaningful work is not easy to find, it is still possible for many workers to find meaning—and even joy—in their jobs.

**Topic sentence (background)**: A 2014 study by the Conference Board, discussed in a *Wall Street Journal* article, found that more than half of all American workers were unhappy with their jobs in the previous year.

**Support**: Weber; Schwartz and Porath

**Topic sentence (support for thesis)**: For example, workers who are lucky enough to take part in a whole process from start to finish report being satisfied with what they do.

**Support**: Curry's comments about pre-industrial labor; Mario's mother's experience with community garden

---

**Topic sentence (support for thesis)**: If an employee is allowed to take on responsibility for a significant part of a job, then that employee is going to feel a sense of empowerment and accountability.

**Support**: Kendra's positive experience (contrast with her high school job, comparing it to Curry's comments about Taylor); Adam's positive experience

---

**Topic sentence (support for thesis)**: Finally, many people find satisfaction in their jobs because they see their work benefiting society in some way.

**Support**: Kendra's and Natalie's experiences (contrast with Mario's experience)

---

**Statement that reinforces thesis**: As Curry points out, great numbers of American workers have "a sense that work doesn't satisfy their deeper needs" (358); still, finding meaningful work is an achievable goal for many.

**Concluding statement**: Although most of us do not have the luxury of holding out for the ideal job when there are bills to pay, we should still try to find meaning in our work.

After she made the revisions she thought were necessary, Amber edited her draft, checking to make sure she had used correct grammar and sentence structure and chosen the most appropriate words. She also reviewed her use of punctuation. Then, she proofread carefully, looking for any spelling errors or typos that her spell checker might have missed. She also made sure her essay's format conformed to her instructor's guidelines. Then, she printed out a final draft of her essay. Notice that her essay, which appears below, includes parenthetical references to "Why We Work" and other sources as well as a works-cited page in MLA format that lists the sources she consulted and the informal interviews she conducted. (Marginal annotations provide information about some of the rhetorical choices she made as she developed her essay.)

Lombardi 1

Amber Lombardi

Professor Lieu

English 110

17 October 2015

What Makes Work Meaningful

Drill a hole in a machine part; repeat. Pick up a tub of margarine; put it in a box; repeat. Not all job descriptions are as unappealing as these actual assembly-line tasks, but most American workers today report that their work is similarly uninspiring. According to Andrew Curry's essay "Why We Work," for generations the lives of typical American workers have been dominated by their jobs. As Curry points out, advances in technology have improved the US standard of living, but few of us have time to enjoy our leisure time because we have to work so hard just to maintain that standard. The idea of life being all work and no play is made worse because most people, according to Curry, feel that the work they do lacks meaning. For work to be meaningful, individuals must have a clear sense of themselves as valued participants in a worthwhile collaboration and be able to see the positive results of their efforts firsthand. Although Curry makes it clear that meaningful work is not easy to find, it is still possible for many workers to find meaning—and even joy—in their jobs.

A 2014 survey by the Conference Board, discussed in a *Wall Street Journal* article, found that more than half of all American workers were unhappy with their jobs in the previous year. Workers who responded to the survey were particularly worried about job security (Weber). In a recent

Amber's attention-getting opener attracts readers' interest and draws them in.

Amber's revised thesis statement now tells readers that her essay will suggest that meaningful work is an achievable goal.

This paragraph provides background information from the two sources Amber found online. The paragraph blends summary with brief quotations from one of the sources.

Lombardi 2

*New York Times* article, two management consultants also reported on dissatisfaction in the workplace. A study they conducted revealed that the most important factor in determining job satisfaction is the sense that the jobs workers do are "connected to a higher purpose" (Schwartz and Porath). Other important criteria include "opportunities to regularly renew and recharge at work," "feeling valued and appreciated for their contributions," and being able to "focus in an absorbed way on their most important tasks" (Schwartz and Porath). Interviews with four workers in a variety of jobs, conducted for this essay, seem to confirm these findings, suggesting that while it is difficult for workers to find satisfaction in their jobs, it is still possible if certain conditions are met.

In MLA format, the source of quoted material is given in the text in parentheses. The author's last name in the introductory phrase corresponds to the entry in the works-cited list at the end of the essay. If the author's last name does not appear in the introductory phrase, it appears in the parenthetical reference, with no comma between the last name and the page number.

This paragraph offers Curry's comments and Mario's mother's experience as support for the topic sentence.

For example, workers who are lucky enough to take part in a whole process from start to finish report being satisfied with what they do. This used to be an accepted fact, at least before the Industrial Revolution changed the way people work. In his examination of pre-industrial labor, Curry comments, "For centuries, the household—from farms to 'cottage' craftsmen—was the unit of production. The whole family was part of the enterprise, be it farming, blacksmithing, or baking" (354). In a similar way, Mario Alvarez reports that his mother, when working for a community garden project, was able to feel connected to an entire process. She and her coworkers purchased seedlings, planted them, helped them grow, and then harvested the fruits and vegetables to sell at a farmer's market they set up and promoted. When customers bought the produce and the community organizers were able to reinvest the money into the garden, the process was complete, and taking part in that cycle made the job meaningful.

Lombardi 3

If an employee is allowed to take on responsibility for a significant part of a job, then that employee is going to feel a sense of empowerment and accountability. For example, Kendra Lombardi finds her current job with Mount Walton College's international student exchange program satisfying partly because she likes being "the go-to person for certain tasks." In a job she had when she was a high school student, however, she was not as fortunate. She had an idea for improving a process and would have appreciated being encouraged to implement her plan. However, instead of giving her permission, her supervisor told her to keep her ideas to herself, and her response led Kendra to see her job as pointless. Curry describes a similar situation occurring in the 1930s when factory foreman Frederick Taylor told his workers, "we have other men paid for thinking" (355). In contrast, Adam Lombardi, a graduate teaching assistant at Mount Walton College, reports that being given responsibility by his department for creating his own curriculum gives his job "huge personal meaning." Adam takes pride in devising new ways to reach his students and encourage their success.

Finally, many people find satisfaction in their jobs because they see their work benefiting society in some way. For example, Kendra Lombardi explains that part of the reason she loves her job is that she and her coworkers all feel that they are doing something that helps people. And according to Natalie O'Reilly, a volunteer companion at a hospice for people with chronic diseases, her work is rewarding because she can see firsthand how much her actions comfort others. On the other hand, one of the reasons Mario Alvarez is dissatisfied with his job as a part-time grocery bagger is that

This paragraph offers Kendra's and Adam's recent experiences (in contrast to Kendra's earlier experience and Curry's comments) as support for the topic sentence.

The word *finally* serves as a transition to the essay's discussion of the social impact of work.

This paragraph offers Kendra's and Natalie's experiences (in contrast to Mario's experience) as support for the topic sentence.

Lombardi 4

he has trouble seeing how what he does makes a difference. Without a sense of larger purpose, Mario focuses instead on the negative aspects of his job, such as the low pay and his inability to socialize on the job.

This statement reinforces Amber's thesis about meaningful work.

As Curry points out, great numbers of American workers have "a sense that work doesn't satisfy their deeper needs" (358); still, finding meaningful work is an achievable goal for many. As Natalie O'Reilly would argue, "work is what you make of it." In other words, even if we are stuck temporarily in a dead-end, tedious job, we can try to see the big picture and how what we do fits into it, become an expert at some aspect of the work, and identify the job's benefit to society. Although most of us do not have the luxury of holding out for the ideal job when there are bills to pay, we should still try to find meaning in our work.

This sentence restates the thesis and leaves readers with something to think about.

Lombardi 5

## Works Cited

Alvarez, Mario. Telephone interview. 2 Oct. 2015.

Curry, Andrew. "Why We Work." *The Blair Reader: Exploring Issues and Ideas*. Ed. Laurie G. Kirszner and Stephen R. Mandell. 9th ed. Boston: Pearson, 2017. 353–58. Print.

Lombardi, Adam. E-mail interview. 5 Oct. 2015.

Lombardi, Kendra. E-mail interview. 5 Oct. 2015.

O'Reilly, Natalie. Telephone interview. 6 Oct. 2015.

Schwartz, Tony, and Christine Porath. "Why You Hate Work." *New York Times*. New York Times, 30 May 2014. Web. 5 Oct. 2015.

Weber, Lauren. "U.S. Workers Can't Get No (Job) Satisfaction." *Wall Street Journal*. Dow Jones, 18 June 2014. Web. 7 Oct. 2015.

# 3

# FAMILY AND MEMORY

*In this chapter, you will learn to*
- analyze readings about family and memory
- compose essays about family and memory

The ties that bind us to our families, and to our family history, are like no other human connections. In this chapter, writers explore family dynamics and family values to try to make sense of the gap between children and parents and between past and

E. B. White with his father

present. Some writers search their memories, trying to understand, recapture, or re-create the past, to see across the barriers imposed by time. Other writers examine misunderstandings, miscommunications, or generational conflicts in their current lives, struggling to understand differences in values, find common ground, and work toward reconciliation. In some cases, images and scenes appear in sharp focus; in others, they are blurred, confused, or even partially invented. Many writers focus on themselves; others focus on their parents or other family members, trying to define relationships, to close generational gaps, to replay events, to see through the eyes of others—and, in this way, to understand their families and themselves.

In this chapter's Focus section, "Are 'Tiger Mothers' Really Better?" (p. 59), three writers discuss the pros and cons of a strict, somewhat "old-fashioned" parenting style. First, in the excerpt adapted from *Battle Hymn of the Tiger Mother*, Amy Chua makes her case for her kind of parenting; then, in "Amy Chua Is a Wimp," David Brooks challenges her claims. Finally, in "Why I Love My Strict Chinese Mom," Sophia Chua-Rubenfeld presents a defense of her mother's methods.

Kristin Ohlson (front right) with her mother (third from the left)

## Preparing to Read and Write

As you read and prepare to write about the selections in this chapter, you may consider the following questions:

- What assumptions does the writer seem to have about his or her audience? How can you tell?

- What is the writer's primary purpose? For example, is it to reexamine the past? to discover, explore, or explain family relationships? something else?

- What genre is the writer using? For example, is the reading a reflection? a poem? an argument? a memoir? How do the conventions of this genre influence the writer's choices?

- What appeals does the writer use? For example, does he or she appeal primarily to reason? to emotion? Is this the most effective appeal?

- How does the writer define *family?*

- Does the writer focus on a single person, on a relationship between two people, or on wider family dynamics?

- Does the writer focus on his or her own family members or on family in general?

- How important is the setting in which the events the writer describes take place?

- Do you think the writer's perspective is *subjective* (shaped by his or her emotional responses or personal opinions) or *objective* (based mainly on observation and fact rather than on personal impressions)?

- What insights does the writer have that he or she did not have when the events occurred? What, if anything, has the writer learned—and how?

- Are the memories generally happy or unhappy ones?

- Are family members presented in a favorable, unfavorable, neutral, or ambivalent way?

- Does the writer feel close to or distant from family members? Does the writer identify with a particular family member?

- Does one family member seem to have had a great influence over the writer? If so, is this influence positive or negative?

- What social, political, economic, or cultural forces influenced the family dynamics?

- Do you identify with the writer or with another person the writer describes? What makes you identify with that person?

- Which readings seem most similar in their views of family? How are they similar?

- Which readings seem most different in their views of family? How are they different?

- Which family seems most like your own? Why?

# HERITAGE

## Linda Hogan

### *1947–*

*A Chickasaw Native American, Linda Hogan writes poetry, novels, plays, and essays. She has published numerous works, including, most recently, Dark, Sweet: New & Selected Poems (2014). In the following poem, Hogan explores the complexity of her heritage.*

From my mother, the antique mirror
where I watch my face take on her lines.
She left me the smell of baking bread
to warm fine hairs in my nostrils,
5   she left the large white breasts that weigh down
my body.

From my father I take his brown eyes,
the plague of locusts that leveled our crops,
they flew in formation like buzzards.
10  From my uncle the whittled wood
that rattles like bones

and is white
and smells like all our old houses
that are no longer there. He was the man
who sang old chants to me, the words                                    15
my father was told not to remember.

From my grandfather who never spoke
I learned to fear silence.
I learned to kill a snake
when you're begging for rain.                                          20

And grandmother, blue-eyed woman
whose skin was brown,
she used snuff.
When her coffee can full of black saliva
spilled on me                                                          25
it was like the brown cloud of grasshoppers
that leveled her fields.
It was the brown stain

that covered my white shirt,
my whiteness a shame.                                                  30
That sweet black liquid like the food
she chewed up and spit into my father's mouth
when he was an infant.
It was the brown earth of Oklahoma
stained with oil.                                                      35
She said tobacco would purge your body of poisons.
It has more medicine than stones and knives
against your enemies.

That tobacco is the dark night that covers me.
She said it is wise to eat the flesh of deer                           40
so you will be swift and travel over many miles.
She told me how our tribe has always followed a stick
that pointed west
that pointed east.

From my family I have learned the secrets                              45
of never having a home.

## Responding to Reading

MyWritingLab™

1. What has the speaker inherited from her parents? from her grandparents? from her tribe? Which inheritance does she seem to value
   most? Why?

2. What do you think the speaker means in the poem's last lines when she says, "From my family I have learned the secrets / of never having a home"?
3. What feelings does the speaker have about her family's past? Do you see these as mixed feelings?

## Responding in Writing

MyWritingLab™

In lines 21–38, the speaker describes her grandmother in terms of the colors she associates with her. Write a paragraph in which you describe a family member in this way.

# THOSE WINTER SUNDAYS
## Robert Hayden
### *1913–1980*

*Robert Hayden's work includes poems about slave rebellions and the historical roots of racism as well as about more personal subjects. Hayden's first book of poetry,* Heart-Shaped in the Dust, *was published in 1940. Other works include* Angle of Ascent: New and Selected Poems (1975), *in which "Those Winter Sundays" appeared, and* Complete Poems (1985). *In the following poem, the speaker expresses his ambivalence about his father's sacrifices.*

Sundays too my father got up early
and put his clothes on in the blueblack cold,
then with cracked hands that ached
from labor in the weekday weather made
5　banked fires blaze. No one ever thanked him.

I'd wake and hear the cold splintering, breaking.
When the rooms were warm, he'd call,
and slowly I would rise and dress,
fearing the chronic angers of that house,

10　Speaking indifferently to him,
who had driven out the cold
and polished my good shoes as well.
What did I know, what did I know
of love's austere and lonely offices?

## Responding to Reading

MyWritingLab™

1. Other than having "driven out the cold," what has the father done for his son? To what might "chronic angers" (line 9) refer?
2. What important lessons has the speaker learned? When do you think he learned them? Do you see these lessons as primarily theoretical or practical?
3. In what respects does this poem sound like conversational speech? In what respects is it "poetic"?

## Responding in Writing

MyWritingLab™

What do you now know about your parents' responsibilities and sacrifices that you did not know when you were a child? How has this knowledge changed your feelings about your parents?

# Once More to the Lake

## E. B. White

### 1899–1985

*Well known for his children's stories, Elwyn Brooks White was also a talented essayist and a witty observer of contemporary society. His expansion of Will Strunk's* The Elements of Style *remains one of the most popular and concise grammar and style texts in use today. White wrote for the* New Yorker *and* Harper's *Magazine, and his essays are collected in* Essays of E. B. White *(1977). In 1939, he moved to a farm in North Brooklin, Maine, where he wrote the children's classics* Stuart Little *(1945) and* Charlotte's Web *(1952). As a youth, White vacationed with his family on a lake in Maine. It is to this lake that he returned with his son, and he describes his experience in the following essay.*

One summer, along about 1904, my father rented a camp on a lake in Maine and took us all there for the month of August. We all got ringworm from some kittens and had to rub Pond's Extract on our arms and legs night and morning, and my father rolled over in a canoe with all his clothes on; but outside of that the vacation was a success and from then on none of us ever thought there was any place in the world like that lake in Maine. We returned summer after summer—always on August 1st for one month. I have since become a salt-water man, but sometimes in summer there are days when the restlessness of the tides and the fearful cold of the sea water and the incessant wind which blows across the afternoon and into the evening make me wish for the placidity of a lake in the woods. A few weeks ago this feeling got so strong I bought myself a couple of bass hooks and a spinner and returned to the lake where we used to go, for a week's fishing and to revisit old haunts.

I took along my son, who had never had any fresh water up his nose and who had seen lily pads only from train windows. On the journey over to the lake I began to wonder what it would be like. I wondered how time would have marred this unique, this holy spot—the coves and streams, the hills that the sun set behind, the camps and the paths behind the camps. I was sure the tarred road would have found it out and I wondered in what other ways it would be desolated. It is strange how much you can remember about places like that once you allow your mind to return into the grooves which lead back. You remember one thing, and that suddenly reminds you of another thing. I guess I remembered clearest of all the early mornings, when the lake was cool and motionless, remembered how the bedroom smelled of the lumber it was made of and of the wet woods whose scent entered through the screen. The partitions in the camp were thin and did not extend clear to the top of the rooms, and as I was always the first up I would dress softly so as not to wake the others, and sneak out into the sweet outdoors and start out in the canoe, keeping close along the shore in the long shadows of the pines. I remembered being very careful never to rub my paddle against the gunwale for fear of disturbing the stillness of the cathedral.

The lake had never been what you would call a wild lake. There were cottages sprinkled around the shores, and it was in farming country although the shores of the lake were quite heavily wooded. Some of the cottages were owned by nearby farmers, and you would live at the shore and eat your meals at the farmhouse. That's what our family did. But although it wasn't wild, it was a fairly large and undisturbed lake and there were places in it which, to a child at least, seemed infinitely remote and primeval.

I was right about the tar: it led to within half a mile of the shore. But when I got back there, with my boy, and we settled into a camp near a farmhouse and into the kind of summertime I had known, I could tell that it was going to be pretty much the same as it had been before—I knew it, lying in bed the first morning, smelling the bedroom, and hearing the boy sneak quietly out and go off along the shore in a boat. I began to sustain the illusion that he was I, and therefore, by simple transposition, that I was my father. This sensation persisted, kept cropping up all the time we were there. It was not an entirely new feeling, but in this setting it grew much stronger. I seemed to be living a dual existence. I would be in the middle of some simple act, I would be picking up a bait box or laying down a table fork, or I would be saying something, and suddenly it would be not I but my father who was saying the words or making the gesture. It gave me a creepy sensation.

5    We went fishing the first morning. I felt the same damp moss covering the worms in the bait can, and saw the dragonfly alight on the tip of my rod as it hovered a few inches from the surface of the water. It was the arrival of this fly that convinced me beyond any doubt that

everything was as it always had been, that the years were a mirage and there had been no years. The small waves were the same, chucking the rowboat under the chin as we fished at anchor, and the boat was the same boat, the same color green and the ribs broken in the same places, and under the floor-boards the same freshwater leavings and débris—the dead helgramite,[1] the wisps of moss, the rusty discarded fishhook, the dried blood from yesterday's catch. We stared silently at the tips of our rods, at the dragonflies that came and went. I lowered the tip of mine into the water, tentatively, pensively dislodging the fly, which darted two feet away, poised, darted two feet back, and came to rest again a little farther up the rod. There had been no years between the ducking of this dragonfly and the other one—the one that was part of memory. I looked at the boy, who was silently watching his fly, and it was my hands that held his rod, my eyes watching. I felt dizzy and didn't know which rod I was at the end of.

We caught two bass, hauling them in briskly as though they were mackerel, pulling them over the side of the boat in a businesslike manner without any landing net, and stunning them with a blow on the back of the head. When we got back for a swim before lunch, the lake was exactly where we had left it, the same number of inches from the dock, and there was only the merest suggestion of a breeze. This seemed an utterly enchanted sea, this lake you could leave to its own devices for a few hours and come back to, and find that it had not stirred, this constant and trustworthy body of water. In the shallows, the dark, water-soaked sticks and twigs, smooth and old, were undulating in clusters on the bottom against the clean ribbed sand, and the track of the mussel was plain. A school of minnows swam by, each minnow with its small individual shadow, doubling the attendance, so clear and sharp in the sunlight. Some of the other campers were in swimming, along the shore, one of them with a cake of soap, and the water felt thin and clear and unsubstantial. Over the years there had been this person with the cake of soap, this cultist, and here he was. There had been no years.

Up to the farmhouse to dinner through the teeming, dusty field, the road under our sneakers was only a two-track road. The middle track was missing, the one with the marks of the hooves and the splotches of dried, flaky manure. There had always been three tracks to choose from in choosing which track to walk in; now the choice was narrowed down to two. For a moment I missed terribly the middle alternative. But the way led past the tennis court, and something about the way it lay there in the sun reassured me; the tape had loosened along the back-line, the alleys were green with plantains and other weeds, and the net (installed in June and removed in September) sagged in the dry noon, and the whole place steamed with midday heat and hunger and emptiness. There was a choice of pie for dessert, and one was blueberry and

---
[1]The nymph of the May-fly, used as bait. [Eds.]

one was apple, and the waitresses were the same country girls, there having been no passage of time, only the illusion of it as in a dropped curtain—the waitresses were still fifteen; their hair had been washed, that was the only difference—they had been to the movies and seen the pretty girls with the clean hair.

Summertime, oh summertime, pattern of life indelible, the fade-proof lake, the woods unshatterable, the pasture with the sweetfern and the juniper forever and ever, summer without end; this was the background, and the life along the shore was the design, the cottagers with their innocent and tranquil design, their tiny docks with the flagpole and the American flag floating against the white clouds in the blue sky, the little paths over the roots of the trees leading from camp to camp and the paths leading back to the outhouses and the can of lime for sprinkling, and at the souvenir counters at the store the miniature birch-bark canoes and the post cards that showed things looking a little better than they looked. This was the American family at play, escaping the city heat, wondering whether the newcomers in the camp at the head of the cove were "common" or "nice," wondering whether it was true that the people who drove up for Sunday dinner at the farmhouse were turned away because there wasn't enough chicken.

It seemed to me, as I kept remembering all this, that those times and those summers had been infinitely precious and worth saving. There had been jollity and peace and goodness. The arriving (at the beginning of August) had been so big a business in itself, at the railway station the farm wagon drawn up, the first smell of the pine-laden air, the first glimpse of the smiling farmer, and the great importance of the trunks and your father's enormous authority in such matters, and the feel of the wagon under you for the long ten-mile haul, and at the top of the last long hill catching the first view of the lake after eleven months of not seeing this cherished body of water. The shouts and cries of the other campers when they saw you, and the trunks to be unpacked, to give up their rich burden. (Arriving was less exciting nowadays, when you sneaked up in your car and parked it under a tree near the camp and took out the bags and in five minutes it was all over, no fuss, no loud wonderful fuss about trunks.)

10    Peace and goodness and jollity. The only thing that was wrong now, really, was the sound of the place, an unfamiliar nervous sound of the outboard motors. This was the note that jarred, the one thing that would sometimes break the illusion and set the years moving. In those other summertimes all motors were inboard; and when they were at a little distance, the noise they made was a sedative, an ingredient of summer sleep. They were one-cylinder and two-cylinder engines, and some were make-and-break and some were jump-spark,[2] but they all made a sleepy sound across the lake. The one-lungers throbbed and fluttered, and the

---

[2]Methods of ignition timing. [Eds.]

twin-cylinder ones purred and purred, and that was a quiet sound too. But now the campers all had outboards. In the daytime, in the hot mornings, these motors made a petulant, irritable sound; at night, in the still evening when the afterglow lit the water, they whined about one's ears like mosquitoes. My boy loved our rented outboard, and his great desire was to achieve singlehanded mastery over it, and authority, and he soon learned the trick of choking it a little (but not too much), and the adjustment of the needle valve. Watching him I would remember the things you could do with the old one-cylinder engine with the heavy flywheel, how you could have it eating out of your hand if you got really close to it spiritually. Motor boats in those days didn't have clutches, and you would make a landing by shutting off the motor at the proper time and coasting in with a dead rudder. But there was a way of reversing them, if you learned the trick, by cutting the switch and putting it on again exactly on the final dying revolution of the flywheel, so that it would kick back against compression and begin reversing. Approaching a dock in a strong following breeze, it was difficult to slow up sufficiently by the ordinary coasting method, and if a boy felt he had complete mastery over his motor, he was tempted to keep it running beyond its time and then reverse it a few feet from the dock. It took a cool nerve, because if you threw the switch a twentieth of a second too soon you would catch the flywheel when it still had speed enough to go up past center, and the boat would leap ahead, charging bull-fashion at the dock.

We had a good week at the camp. The bass were biting well and the sun shone endlessly, day after day. We would be tired at night and lie down in the accumulated heat of the little bedrooms after the long hot day and the breeze would stir almost imperceptibly outside and the smell of the swamp drift in through the rusty screens. Sleep would come easily and in the morning the red squirrel would be on the roof, tapping out his gay routine. I kept remembering everything, lying in bed in the mornings—the small steamboat that had a long rounded stern like the lip of a Ubangi, and how quietly she ran on the moonlight sails, when the older boys played their mandolins and the girls sang and we ate doughnuts dipped in sugar, and how sweet the music was on the water in the shining night, and what it had felt like to think about girls then. After breakfast we would go up to the store and the things were in the same place—the minnows in a bottle, the plugs and spinners disarranged and pawed over by the youngsters from the boys' camp, the fig newtons and the Beeman's gum. Outside, the road was tarred and cars stood in front of the store. Inside, all was just as it had always been, except there was more Coca-Cola and not so much Moxie and root beer and birch beer and sarsaparilla. We would walk out with a bottle of pop apiece and sometimes the pop would backfire up our noses and hurt. We explored the streams, quietly, where the turtles slid off the sunny logs and dug their way into the soft bottom; and we lay on the town wharf and fed worms to the tame bass. Everywhere we went I had trouble making out which was I, the one walking at my side, the one walking in my pants.

One afternoon while we were there at that lake a thunderstorm came up. It was like the revival of an old melodrama that I had seen long ago with childish awe. The second-act climax of the drama of the electrical disturbance over a lake in America had not changed in any important respect. This was the big scene, still the big scene. The whole thing was so familiar, the first feeling of oppression and heat and a general air around camp of not wanting to go very far away. In midafternoon (it was all the same) a curious darkening of the sky, and a lull in everything that had made life tick; and then the way the boats suddenly swung the other way at their moorings with the coming of a breeze out of the new quarter, and the premonitory rumble. Then the kettle drum, then the snare, then the bass drum and cymbals, then crackling light against the dark, and the gods grinning and licking their chops in the hills. Afterward the calm, the rain steadily rustling in the calm lake, the return of light and hope and spirits, and the campers running out in joy and relief to go swimming in the rain, their bright cries perpetuating the deathless joke about how they were getting simply drenched, and the children screaming with delight at the new sensation of bathing in the rain, and the joke about getting drenched linking the generations in a strong indestructible chain. And the comedian who waded in carrying an umbrella.

When the others went swimming my son said he was going in too. He pulled his dripping trunks from the line where they had hung all through the shower, and wrung them out. Languidly, and with no thought of going in, I watched him, his hard little body, skinny and bare, saw him wince slightly as he pulled up around his vitals the small, soggy, icy garment. As he buckled the swollen belt suddenly my groin felt the chill of death.

## Responding to Reading

MyWritingLab™

1. How is White's "holy spot" different when he visits it with his son from how it was when he visited it with his father?
2. Why does White feel "the chill of death" as he watches his son? Do you identify more with White the father or White the son?
3. **Rhetorical Analysis** Is White's primary purpose to write about a time, a place, or a relationship? Explain.

## Writing about Reading

MyWritingLab™

1. Write two short paragraphs about a place that was important to you as a child: one from the point of view of your adult self, and one from the point of view of your childhood self. How are the two paragraphs different?
2. **Writing with Sources** Locate a few sources—including some photographs—that focus on a place that was important to you as a child. Write an essay that compares your childhood impression of the place with the impression you get from the sources you find.

# THE GREAT FORGETTING
## Kristin Ohlson
### *1951–*

*A journalist, essayist, and fiction writer, Kristin Ohlson explores topics rang-*
*ing from food and the environment to travel and women's rights. Writing for*
*publications such as* Aeon, Gourmet, Ms., New Scientist, *the* New York
Times, Salon, *and* Utne, *she is also the author of three books, including,*
*most recently,* The Soil Will Save Us *(2014). In the following essay, Ohlson*
*considers the elusive nature of memory.*

I'm the youngest by far of five children. My mother was 35 when she conceived me in 1951, so chagrined by this chronological indiscretion that she tried to hide the pregnancy from her sister. My mortified oldest brother didn't want to tell his high-school friends that a new baby was on the way, but it was a small town. Word spread.

My mother's age and my late arrival in the family felt burdensome to me too, especially when I started school in 1957 and met my classmates' mothers. They were still having babies! Still piling their children into cars and heading off to picnics at the river or hikes into the lava-capped, wild flower-rampant plateau outside town. They still had to mediate hair-pulling and toy-snatching. But by the time I started first grade, my siblings were gone, the oldest three to college and the youngest to a residential school four hours away, and we went from a very noisy household to a very quiet one.

My family has told me stories about those years before everything changed. How my oldest brother nicknamed me "Ubangi" because my hair grew in tight fat curls close to my head. How my other brother liked to ambush me around corners with a toy crocodile because it never failed to make me shriek in terror. How my oldest sister carried me around like a kangaroo with her joey. But I can offer very few stories of my own from those early years.

My strongest recollection is a constant straining to be with my brothers and sisters. I remember having to go to bed when it was still light out, kicking at the sheets as I listened for their voices coming down the hall or through the windows from the back yard. Sometimes I could smell popcorn. The next morning, I'd search the living room rug for their leftovers and roll the unpopped kernels around in my mouth. I do remember that, probably because it was something that played out night after night—our father loved popcorn.

Several years ago, I thought I might have the chance to recover that    5
lost past when we were all tightly clustered together in one house. My brothers had driven to Bucks Lake up in the Sierras of northeastern

This article was originally published in Aeon Magazine [http://www.aeon.co] a digital magazine for ideas and culture. Follow them on Twitter at @aeonmag [https://twitter.com/aeonmag]

California where, until I was around three years old, our family had leased a house every summer to escape the Sacramento Valley heat. They found our old cabin unchanged. Even a table built by a local saw-mill was still in the living room. They knocked on the door and, weirdly enough, my younger brother knew the current lessee. He invited them in and then invited the rest of us back for a look.

With our father, we set off a few months later, up highways that narrowed into dusty roads through dark pines and past bright stony summits. When we got to the cabin, my siblings scattered to claim their favourite outdoor spots, but I was rooted near the car, struck by how much this place differed from what I thought I remembered.

I recalled that the water was a long walk across a sandy beach from the house; I had an image of my mother standing on that wide beach, her dress whipped by the wind, her hand cupped near her mouth. But the pebbled shoreline was just a few feet away. I recalled the spine of a dam jutting from the water not far from the house, a perilous and sudden cliff at the edge of the lake that my siblings had once ventured too close to. But even though the lake is a man-made one, the dam wasn't visible from the house. I followed my father inside, where the tininess of the kitchen fascinated him. He kept opening cabinet doors and laughing as they banged each other in the narrow aisle. "Mother just hated this kitchen!" he said. "She always made big breakfasts— eggs and sausage and pancakes—and as soon as she finished cleaning up, you kids would come running back in the house wanting lunch."

I didn't remember that. I didn't remember the table. I didn't re-member anything about the place. My siblings tugged me through the house, pointing out where everyone had slept—they said I had been in a little alcove in the hallway, though I recalled staying in my parents' room and watching them sleep in the early morning light. They pointed out other features tied to the life that we all lived in the cabin, eager for me to remember, but there was nothing. I even dropped to my knees and circled the living room at toddler level, peering at dusty window-sills and sniffing at the knotholes in the pine walls and running my fingers over the floorboards. Nothing.

I now know that it would have been unusual for me to remember anything from that time. Hardly any adult does. There is even a term for this—childhood amnesia, coined by Sigmund Freud in 1910—to describe the lack of recall adults have of their first three or four years and our paucity of solid memories until around the age of seven. There has been some back and forth over a century of research about whether memories of these early years are tucked away in some part of our brains and need only a cue to be recovered. That's what I was hoping when I revisited our old cabin with my siblings. I intended to jostle out a recalcitrant memory with the sights, sounds, smells and touch of the place. But research sug-gests that the memories we form in these early years simply disappear.

Freud argued that we repress our earliest memories because of 10
sexual trauma but, until the 1980s, most researchers assumed that
we retained no memories of early childhood because we created no
memories—that events took place and passed without leaving a lasting
imprint on our baby brains. Then in 1987, a study by the Emory University psychologist Robyn Fivush and her colleagues dispelled that
misconception for good, showing that children who were just 2.5 years
old could describe events from as far as six months into their past.

But what happens to those memories? Most of us assume that we
can't recall them as adults because they're just too far back in our past
to tug into the present, but this is not the case. We lose them when we're
still children.

The psychologist Carole Peterson of Memorial University of
Newfoundland has conducted a series of studies to pinpoint the
age at which these memories vanish. First, she and her colleagues
assembled a group of children between the ages of four and 13 to
describe their three earliest memories. The children's parents stood
by to verify that the memories were, indeed, true, and even the very
youngest of the children could recall events from when they were
around two years old.

Then the children were interviewed again two years later to see
if anything had changed. More than a third of those age 10 and older
retained the memories they had offered up for the first study. But the
younger children—especially the very youngest who had been four
years old in the first study—had gone largely blank. "Even when we
prompted them about their earlier memories, they said: 'No, that never
happened to me,'" Peterson told me. "We were watching childhood
amnesia in action."

In both children and adults, memory is bizarrely selective about
what adheres and what falls away. In one of her papers, Peterson trots
out a story about her own son and a childhood memory gone missing.
She had taken him to Greece when he was 20 months old, and, while
there, he became very excited about some donkeys. There was family
discussion of those donkeys for at least a year. But by the time he went
to school, he had completely forgotten about them. He was queried
when he was a teenager about his earliest childhood memory and, instead of the remarkable Greek donkeys, he recalled a moment not long
after the trip to Greece when a woman gave him lots of cookies while
her husband showed the boy's parents around a house they planned
to buy.

Peterson has no idea why he would remember *that*—it was a 15
completely unremarkable moment and one that the family hadn't re-
inforced with domestic chitchat. To try to get a handle on why some
memories endure over others, she and her colleagues studied the children's memories again. They concluded that if the memory was a very

emotional one, children were three times more likely to retain it two years later. Dense memories—if they understood the who, what, when, where and why—were five times more likely to be retained than disconnected fragments. Still, oddball and inconsequential memories such as the bounty of cookies will hang on, frustrating the person who wants a more penetrating look at their early past.

To form long-term memories, an array of biological and psychological stars must align, and most children lack the machinery for this alignment. The raw material of memory—the sights, sounds, smells, tastes and tactile sensations of our life experiences—arrive and register across the cerebral cortex, the seat of cognition. For these to become memory, they must undergo bundling in the hippocampus, a brain structure named for its supposed resemblance to a sea horse, located under the cerebral cortex. The hippocampus not only bundles multiple input from our senses together into a single new memory, it also links these sights, sounds, smells, tastes, and tactile sensations to similar ones already stored in the brain. But some parts of the hippocampus aren't fully developed until we're adolescents, making it hard for a child's brain to complete this process.

"So much has to happen biologically to store a memory," the psychologist Patricia Bauer of Emory University told me. There's "a race to get it stabilised and consolidated before you forget it. It's like making Jell-O: you mix the stuff up, you put it in a mould, and you put it in the refrigerator to set, but your mould has a tiny hole in it. You just hope your Jell-O—your memory—gets set before it leaks out through that tiny hole."

In addition, young children have a tenuous grip on chronology. They are years from mastering clocks and calendars, and thus have a hard time nailing an event to a specific time and place. They also don't have the vocabulary to describe an event, and without that vocabulary, they can't create the kind of causal narrative that Peterson found at the root of a solid memory. And they don't have a greatly elaborated sense of self, which would encourage them to hoard and reconsider chunks of experience as part of a growing life-narrative.

Frail as they are, children's memories are then susceptible to a process called shredding. In our early years, we create a storm of new neurons in a part of the hippocampus called the dentate gyrus and continue to form them throughout the rest of our lives, although not at nearly the same rate. A recent study by the neuroscientists Paul Frankland and Sheena Josselyn of the Hospital for Sick Children in Toronto suggests that this process, called neurogenesis, can actually create forgetting by disrupting the circuits for existing memories.

20    Our memories can become distorted by other people's memories of the same event or by new information, especially when that new information is so similar to information already in storage. For instance,

you meet someone and remember their name, but later meet a second person with a similar name, and become confused about the name of the first person. We can also lose our memories when the synapses that connect neurons decay from disuse. "If you never use that memory, those synapses can be recruited for something different," Bauer told me.

Memories are less vulnerable to shredding and disruptions as the child grows up. Most of the solid memories that we carry into the rest of our lives are formed during what's called "the reminiscence bump," from ages 15 to 30, when we invest a lot of energy in examining everything to try to figure out who we are. The events, culture and people of that time remain with us and can even overshadow the features of our ageing present, according to Bauer. The movies were the best back then, and so was the music, and the fashion, and the political leaders, and the friendships, and the romances. And so on.

Of course, some people have more memories from early childhood than others do. It appears that remembering is partly influenced by the culture of family engagement. A 2009 study conducted by Peterson together with Qi Wang of Cornell and Yubo Hou of Peking University found that children in China have fewer of these memories than children in Canada. The finding, they suggest, might be explained by culture: Chinese people prize individuality less than North Americans and thus may be less likely to spend as much time drawing attention to the moments of an individual's life. Canadians, by contrast, reinforce recollection and keep the synapses that underlie early personal memories vibrant. Another study, by the psychologist Federica Artioli and colleagues at the University of Otago in New Zealand in 2012, found that young adults from Italian extended families had earlier and denser memories than those from Italian nuclear families, presumably as a result of more intense family reminiscence.

But it doesn't necessarily take a crowd of on-site relatives to enhance a child's recollection. Bauer's research also points to "maternal deflections of conversation," meaning that the mother (or another adult) engages the child in a lively conversation about events, always passing the baton of remembering back to the child and inviting him or her to contribute to the story. "That kind of interaction contributes to the richness of memory over a long period of time," Bauer told me. "It doesn't predict whether a given event will be remembered, but it builds a muscle. The child learns how to have memories and understands what part to share. Over the course of these conversations, the child learns how to tell the story."

Borrowing Bauer's Jell-O analogy, I've always suspected that my mother had a tinier hole in her Jell-O mould than mine, which allowed her to retain information until it was set into memory. She seemed to remember everything from my childhood, from my siblings' childhoods, and from her own first six years. Intensely, she recalled the fight between her mother and father, when her mother wound up getting knocked out cold and her father forced her to tell visiting neighbours that his wife was sleeping. The day my grandmother packed up my mother and her sister and moved them from Nebraska to Nevada, with their unwanted household goods strewn across their lawn for the townspeople to pick through and haggle over. The day the doctor took out my mother's appendix on the kitchen table. The day she wet her pants at school and the nuns made her walk home in weather so cold that her underwear froze. I wondered if her memories were so sharp because these were all terrible events, especially compared with my presumably bland early years.

25    I now suspect that my mother's ability to tell the story of her early life also came from the constellation of people clustered at the centre of it. Her young mother, bolting from a marriage she was pressured into and retreating to her brother's crowded house, her two girls held close. And her sister, three years older, always the point and counterpoint, the question and response. My mother and her sister talked their lives over to such an extent that it must have seemed as if things didn't really happen unless they had confided them to each other. Thus, "Don't tell Aunt Helen!" was whispered in our house when something went wrong, echoed by "Don't tell Aunt Kathleen!" in our cousins' house when something went amiss there.

I might have a very large hole in my Jell-O mould, but I also wonder if our family's storytelling and memory-setting apparatus had broken down by the time I came along. My brothers and sisters doted on me—I'm told this and I believe it—but it was their job to be out in the world riding horses and playing football and winning spelling bees and getting into various kinds of trouble, not talking to the baby. And sometime between my being born and my siblings leaving, our mother suffered a breakdown that plunged her into 20 years of depression and agoraphobia. She could go to the grocery store only with my father close to her side, steering the cart, list in hand. Even when she went to the beauty salon to have her hair cut and styled and sprayed into submission, my father sat next to her reading his *Wall Street Journal* as she cured under one of those bullet-head dryers. When we were home, she spent a lot of time in her room. No one really knows when my mother's sadness and retreat from the world began—and she's not around to tell us now—but it might have started when I was very young. What I remember is silence.

Our first three to four years are the maddeningly, mysteriously blank opening pages to our story of self. As Freud said, childhood amnesia "veils our earliest youth from us and makes us strangers to it." During that time, we transition from what my brother-in-law calls "a loaf of bread with a nervous system" to sentient humans. If we can't remember much of anything from those years—whether abuse or exuberant cherishing—does it matter what actually happened? If a tree fell in the forest of our early development and we didn't have the brains and cognitive tools to stash the event in memory, did it still help shape who we are?

Bauer says yes. Even if we don't remember early events, they leave an imprint on the way we understand and feel about ourselves, other people, and the greater world, for better or worse. We have elaborate concepts about birds, dogs, lakes and mountains, for example, even if we can't recall the experiences that created those concepts. "You can't remember going ice-skating with Uncle Henry, but you understand that skating and visiting relatives are fun," Bauer explained. "You have a feeling for how nice people are, how reliable they are. You might never be able to pinpoint how you learnt that, but it's just something you know."

And we are not the sum of our memories, or at least, not entirely. We are also the story we construct about ourselves, our personal narrative that interprets and assigns meaning to the things we do remember and the things other people tell us about ourselves. Research by the Northwestern University psychologist Dan McAdams, author of *The Redemptive Self* (2005), suggests that these narratives guide our behaviour and help chart our path into the future. Especially lucky are those of us with redemptive stories, in which we find good fortune even in past adversity.

So our stories are not bald facts etched on stone tablets. They are narratives that move and morph, and that's the underpinning to much of talk therapy. And here is one uplifting aspect of ageing: our stories of self get better. "For whatever reason, we tend to accentuate the positive things more as we age," McAdams told me. "We have a greater willingness or motivation to see the world in brighter terms. We develop a positivity bias regarding our memories." 30

I can't make myself remember my early life with my siblings nearby and my mother before her breakdown, even if I revisit the mountain idyll where the summers of that life unfolded. But I can employ the kinder lens of ageing and the research by these memory scientists to limn a story on those blank pages that is not stained with loss.

I am by nature trusting and optimistic, traits that I've sometimes worried are signs of intellectual weakness, but I can choose to interpret them as approaches to the world developed by myriad, if unrecalled, experiences with a loving family in those early years. I don't remember, but I can choose to imagine myself on my siblings' laps as they read me stories or sang me songs or showed me the waving arms of a crawdad from that mountain lake. I can imagine myself on their shoulders, fingers twined in their curly Ohlson hair.

I can imagine them patiently feeding me the lines to *The Night Before Christmas*, over and over, hour after hour, day after day, because someone had to have done it—my mother told me that I could recite the whole poem when I was two years old. Not that they remember doing this, because most of them were teenagers by then and off having the kinds of encounters with people and culture that would define their sense of self for years to come. But I'll imagine and reconstruct it, both for me and for them. Because our pasts had to have had a lot of that kind of sweetness, given our lucky loving bonds today. We've just forgotten the details.

## Responding to Reading

MyWritingLab™

1. What is childhood amnesia (9)? How does this concept fully explain why Ohlson has no memories of her family's old cabin?
2. What, specifically, does Ohlson learn from her interview with psychologist Patricia Bauer? from the work of psychologist Carole Peterson? from the 2009 study conducted by Peterson and her colleagues? from the writing of psychologist Dan McAdams?
3. **Rhetorical Analysis**   Although Ohlson bases her explanations and conclusions about family and memory on summaries of scholarly research, she also includes her own childhood experiences. Why does she include this material? Do you find it helpful or distracting?

## Writing about Reading

MyWritingLab™

1. What is your earliest childhood memory? Why do you think this particular memory has remained with you while so many others have not?
2. **Writing with Sources**   In a sense, memories are like snapshots: a series of disconnected candid images, often out of focus or gradually fading. Look through your family's photos and videos, and choose five or six key images from your childhood. Then, write an essay analyzing the similarities and differences between these images and your memories of the people, places, and events they capture.

# MY FICTIONAL GRANDPARENTS

## Laila Lalami

### 1968–

*An associate professor of creative writing at the University of California, Riverside, Laila Lalami was born and raised in Rabat, Morocco. The author of three acclaimed novels, she has also published essays in the* Boston Globe, *the* Guardian, *the* Los Angeles Times, The Nation, *the* New York Times, *and the* Washington Post. *In the following essay, Lalami explores the intersection of fiction and reality in family storytelling.*

My mother was abandoned in a French orphanage in Fez[1] in 1941. That year in Morocco, hundreds of people died in an outbreak of the plague; her parents were among the victims. Actually, no, they died in a horrific

---

[1]A city in Morocco. [Eds.]

car crash on the newly built road from Marrakesh[2] to Fez. No, no, no, my grandmother died in childbirth, and my grandfather, mad with grief, gave the baby away. The truth is: I don't know how my mother ended up in a French orphanage in 1941. The nuns in black habits never told.

Growing up in Rabat, I felt lopsided, like a seesaw no one ever played with. On my father's side: a large number of uncles, cousins, second cousins, grandaunts, all claiming descent from the Prophet Muhammad. On my mother's side: nothing. No one. Often I imagined my mother's parents, the man and woman whose blood pulsed in my veins but whom I had never seen.

I would have called them Ba-sidi and Mi-lalla. Like my paternal grandfather, Ba-sidi would have been old but active. He would have retired from a career in the police and spent his days performing El Melhun, Moroccan sung poetry, with his friends. Like my paternal grandmother, Mi-lalla would have worn long, rustling caftans,[3] in which I would have sought refuge every time I got into trouble. She would have taught me all her herbal cures and hennaed my hands before each Eid.[4]

My mother did not take part in these fictions. She spoke little about her childhood in the orphanage. Sometimes she hummed a French lullaby that one of the nuns taught her. I went to sleep on many a night to the sound of *"Au clair de la lune"* or *"Fais dodo, Colas."* But other times, a wave of resentment welled within her, and she would describe being forced to eat on a dirty table from which chickens were allowed to feed. Naturally I developed an early and lifelong affinity for literary orphans, like Oliver Twist and Jane Eyre. Later, when I became a novelist, orphans and abandoned children turned up in my work, unbidden.

On my birthday in February, my husband and I were drinking our morning coffee when he slipped a small box across the kitchen table. Inside was a DNA test kit. "You can use it to find out more about your mom," he said.    5

"But what if this company sells my genetic data?" I asked.

"You can find out more about your mom."

"Like, to an insurance company. Or even a government agency. What about that?"

"You can find out more about your mom!"

Optimism, that peculiar American trait—it was impossible to re- 10 sist it. So I sent a saliva sample, and six weeks later, my results were ready. My health profile listed a series of traits that made me smile with recognition. I had long ago given up drinking milk; now I found out that I was most likely lactose-intolerant. I had always assumed that my strong stomach was attributable to a third-world childhood;

---

[2]A city in Morocco. [Eds.]
[3]Long garments with long sleeves. [Eds.]
[4]A Muslim holiday. [Eds.]

it turned out I had a natural resistance to norovirus. But the profile had sobering news too: I had an elevated risk of coronary heart disease and Alzheimer's disease. No one on my father's side of the family had heart problems or dementia. They might have come from my mother's family.

Finally, I opened the ancestry report. My maternal line was K, a haplogroup[5] commonly found among populations of the Near East, Europe and North Africa. The test also identified relatives on my maternal side: distant cousins in Finland, France and the United States. Their locations intrigued me. How had the descendants of my mother's relatives ended up in such far-flung places?

Or was my mother the one from a far-flung place? After all, she was born in the middle of a world war, when refugees were fleeing in all directions. Perhaps her parents were displaced and ended up in Morocco, where they had to begin new lives. It would have been difficult, in such times, to care for a newborn.

So it was that, in just a few moments, I found myself returning to those childhood days when I used to dream up different families, and different fates, for my mother. What science gave me, in the end, was no different from what my own imagination had fed me for many years—stories. The search was not over. The search would never be over. And not even science could help fill out the abyss I grew up with. Only stories could.

## Responding to Reading

MyWritingLab™

1. In paragraph 3, Lalami speculates about her "fictional grandparents," but in paragraph 4, she notes, "My mother did not take part in these fictions." Why not? How do you explain the different attitudes Lalami and her mother have about their family history?
2. Why does Lalami decide to use the DNA test kit? What does she find out? What doesn't she find out?
3. **Rhetorical Analysis**   Evaluate Lalami's introductory strategy. Why does she include three alternate scenarios here? How is this strategy consistent with the content and structure of her essay's last two paragraphs?

## Writing about Reading

MyWritingLab™

1. In her last paragraph, Lalami concludes that "only stories" (not science) could "help fill out the abyss [she] grew up with." What kind of stories do you think she is referring to? How do such stories "fill out the abyss"?
2. **Writing with Sources**   Research the services of some companies that market DNA test kits. What information do they claim they will provide? What kind of information do they *not* promise to provide? Based on your research, write an essay explaining why you think DNA test kits are (or are not) valuable sources of information for people interested in learning more about their family backgrounds.

---

[5]A genetic family. [Eds.]

# SIXTY-NINE CENTS
## Gary Shteyngart
### *1972–*

*Born in Leningrad (now called Saint Petersburg), Russia, Gary Shteyngart immigrated to the United States when he was seven years old. The author of a memoir and three novels, Shteyngart has also published numerous essays and short stories in publications such as the* New York Times Magazine, *the* New Yorker, Esquire, *and* GQ. *In the following essay, Shteyngart recalls the mixed feelings he had about his family on a childhood trip to Disney World.*

When I was fourteen years old, I lost my Russian accent. I could, in theory, walk up to a girl and the words "Oh, hi there" would not sound like Okht Hyzer, possibly the name of a Turkish politician. There were three things I wanted to do in my new incarnation: go to Florida, where I understood that our nation's best and brightest had built themselves a sandy, vice-filled paradise; have a girl, preferably native-born, tell me that she liked me in some way; and eat all my meals at McDonald's. I did not have the pleasure of eating at McDonald's often. My parents believed that going to restaurants and buying clothes not sold by weight on Orchard Street[1] were things done only by the very wealthy or the very profligate, maybe those extravagant "welfare queens" we kept hearing about on television. Even my parents, however, as uncritically in love with America as only immigrants can be, could not resist the iconic pull of Florida, the call of the beach and the Mouse.

And so, in the midst of my Hebrew-school winter vacation, two Russian families crammed into a large used sedan and took I-95 down to the Sunshine State. The other family—three members in all—mirrored our own, except that their single offspring was a girl and they were, on the whole, more ample; by contrast, my entire family weighed three hundred pounds. There's a picture of us beneath the monorail at EPCOT Center, each of us trying out a different smile to express the déjà-vu feeling of standing squarely in our new country's greatest attraction, my own megawatt grin that of a turn-of-the-century Jewish peddler scampering after a potential sidewalk sale. The Disney tickets were a freebie, for which we had had to sit through a sales pitch for an Orlando time-share. "You're from Moscow?" the time-share salesman asked, appraising the polyester cut of my father's jib.

"Leningrad."

"Let me guess: mechanical engineer?"

"Yes, mechanical engineer.... Eh, please Disney tickets now."

5

---

[1]A shopping street on New York City's Lower East Side, a destination for generations of immigrants. [Eds.]

The ride over the MacArthur Causeway to Miami Beach was my real naturalization ceremony. I wanted all of it—the palm trees, the yachts bobbing beside the hard-currency mansions, the concrete-and-glass condominiums preening at their own reflections in the azure pool water below, the implicit availability of relations with amoral women. I could see myself on a balcony eating a Big Mac, casually throwing fries over my shoulder into the sea-salted air. But I would have to wait. The hotel reserved by my parents' friends featured army cots instead of beds and a half-foot-long cockroach evolved enough to wave what looked like a fist at us. Scared out of Miami Beach, we decamped for Fort Lauderdale, where a Yugoslav woman sheltered us in a faded motel, beach-adjacent and featuring free UHF reception. We always seemed to be at the margins of places: the driveway of the Fontaine-bleau Hilton, or the glassed-in elevator leading to a rooftop restaurant where we could momentarily peek over the "Please Wait to Be Seated" sign at the endless ocean below, the Old World we had left behind so far and yet deceptively near.

To my parents and their friends, the Yugoslav motel was an un-questioned paradise, a lucky coda to a set of difficult lives. My father lay magnificently beneath the sun in his red-and-black striped imita-tion Speedo while I stalked down the beach, past baking Midwestern girls. "Oh, hi there." The words, perfectly American, not a birthright but an acquisition, perched between my lips, but to walk up to one of those girls and say something so casual required a deep rootedness to the hot sand beneath me, a historical presence thicker than the green card embossed with my thumbprint and freckled face. Back at the mo-tel, the *Star Trek* reruns looped endlessly on Channel 73 or 31 or some other prime number, the washed-out Technicolor planets more familiar to me than our own.

On the drive back to New York, I plugged myself firmly into my Walkman, hoping to forget our vacation. Sometime after the palm trees ran out, somewhere in southern Georgia, we stopped at a McDonald's. I could already taste it: The sixty-nine-cent hamburger. The ketchup, red and decadent, embedded with little flecks of grated onion. The up-lift of the pickle slices; the obliterating rush of fresh Coca-Cola; the soda tingle at the back of the throat signifying that the act was complete. I ran into the meat-fumigated coldness of the magical place, the larger Russians following behind me, lugging something big and red. It was a cooler, packed, before we left the motel, by the other mother, the kindly, round-faced equivalent of my own mother. She had prepared a full Russian lunch for us. Soft-boiled eggs wrapped in tinfoil; *vinigret*, the Russian beet salad, overflowing a reused container of sour cream; cold chicken served between crisp white furrows of a *bulka*.[2] "But it's not al-lowed," I pleaded. "We have to buy the food here."

---

[2]Russian bread roll. [Eds.]

I felt coldness, not the air-conditioned chill of southern Georgia but the coldness of a body understanding the ramifications of its own demise, the pointlessness of it all. I sat down at a table as far away from my parents and their friends as possible. I watched the spectacle of the newly tanned resident aliens eating their ethnic meal—jowls working, jowls working—the soft-boiled eggs that quivered lightly as they were brought to the mouth; the girl, my coeval, sullen like me but with a hint of pliant equanimity; her parents, dishing out the chunks of beet with plastic spoons; my parents, getting up to use free McDonald's napkins and straws while American motorists with their noisy towheaded children bought themselves the happiest of meals.

My parents laughed at my haughtiness. Sitting there hungry and all alone—what a strange man I was becoming! So unlike them. My pockets were filled with several quarters and dimes, enough for a hamburger and a small Coke. I considered the possibility of redeeming my own dignity, of leaving behind our beet-salad heritage. My parents didn't spend money, because they lived with the idea that disaster was close at hand, that a liver-function test would come back marked with a doctor's urgent scrawl, that they would be fired from their jobs because their English did not suffice. We were all representatives of a shadow society, cowering under a cloud of bad tidings that would never come. The silver coins stayed in my pocket, the anger burrowed and expanded into some future ulcer. I was my parents' son. 10

## Responding to Reading                    MyWritingLab™

1. This essay contrasts the familiar world of Shteyngart's home and family with the unfamiliar world of Miami. List some of the contrasts he identifies. What other differences would you imagine exist between these two worlds?

2. How do you suppose Shteyngart's memories of this trip differ from his parents' memories?

3. **Rhetorical Analysis**   In paragraph 8, Shteyngart describes in detail the "full Russian lunch" his mother served the family. Why does he include this information? Is it necessary?

## Writing about Reading                    MyWritingLab™

1. Shteyngart's longing for a McDonald's hamburger and a Coke parallels his longing to be "American." What other products and brand names do you see as typically American? Why?

2. **Writing with Sources**   Write an essay in which you discuss some products and brand names that figured prominently in your childhood. Why were they so important to you and to your friends and family? How do they help to define your childhood? Begin by searching online for ads and product descriptions to use as source material in your essay.

# WHEN I MOVED ONLINE...

## Tao Lin

### *1983–*

*An essayist, fiction writer, poet, and graphic artist, Tao Lin is the author of ten books, including, most recently, Taipei (2013). He is also the founder of the small press publisher Muumuu House and the co-founder of the film company MDMAfilms. In "When I Moved Online…," Lin considers the role of the Internet in shaping family relationships.*

I was born in 1983. My parents, in the mid-1990s, briefly knew more than I did about the Internet, I think (the bill from AOL must have required a credit card). But, as adults, with settled understandings of the world, they didn't integrate the Internet into their lives. For around five years, they seemed to use it mostly to check stock prices. The Internet remained nonessential and separate for them, like a vacation destination.

With me it was different. By my second year online, around 1996, I was obsessed with a multiplayer role-playing game called GemStone III, which was set in a virtual world, like Second Life, but without graphics, only text. I'd type "west," and text would appear describing the new surroundings of my character, whom I'd named Esperath Wraithling. Around 1,500 Americans were in the world of GemStone III at any given time.

I was in that world about six hours a day, almost every day, in 9th and 10th grade. Five or six of my friends also played GemStone III. We'd meet at Red Bug park—this was in suburban Florida—to play basketball, but end up talking about GemStone III and returning home to our computers. We called one another addicts.

I'm not sure to what extent, if any, our parents understood GemStone III. None of them ever played, I don't think, even for a minute. I can imagine parents 10 years later playing, but in the mid-1990s there was usually only one computer per household. The Internet was a place you went to alone. Kids, while online, were parentless. Not in the controlled way of summer camp, or the easily monitored way of video games, but in a new, untested, unapparent way.

5      Before the Internet, my parents were privy to most of my world. They saw whom I interacted with, where I was, what I was doing. Being preadolescent, I spent most of my time with them anyway. I had no desire to befriend four to eight strangers and talk to them daily, for hours, in passive secrecy from my parents.

After the Internet, my parents were privy to much less and would only rarely, and with decreasing frequency, ask about what they no longer knew. "What did you do on the Internet today?" was not a question I remember being asked. If my parents, squinting over my shoulder, saw Esperath Wraithling on the screen, they didn't see the dark elf wizard I saw, they saw two meaningless words. If they looked at me—whether I was immersed in GemStone III, on a message board, or in a chat room—I appeared to be sitting in a chair, doing almost nothing.

Far from doing almost nothing, I was socializing in and exploring the metaphysical room that had been quietly connected to millions of houses. The shared, boundless room of the Internet seemed normal, even mundane, in the mid-1990s. I didn't have another childhood for comparison. Only in retrospect—and increasingly, as my memory of a pre-Internet existence became tinier and more conspicuous, like something that glints—does it seem weird and mysterious, almost alien.

I now sometimes imagine the Internet as a U.F.O. that appeared one afternoon in the backyard—to take humankind elsewhere, maybe. My parents noticed it first, but weren't particularly interested. They didn't immediately begin relocating their lives, as if by instinct, into the U.F.O., like my peers and I seem to have done. They remained half-hearted and aloof for around 10 years before finally, slowly beginning (as "lurkers," observing without participating) to learn about the Internet, I feel, in earnest.

Recently, in endearingly impulsive ways, they've become a little interactive. My mother's Twitter account (zero followers, following zero) has one tweet, from 2010: "Tao's birthday is July 2, Happy Birthday, Tao." For at least six years, she has seemed to use Facebook only to look at other people's profiles, until this past summer, when she began "liking" my status updates. Around the same time my father, using a Facebook account I didn't know he had (no profile information, nine friends), "liked" around 10 things on my Facebook wall over a few hours one day. He hasn't "liked" anything of mine since, but about a month ago he e-mailed to say he'd edited my Wikipedia page. He'd added "his father is a retired physics professor" and other details (all of which got deleted within two days) to the "Early and Personal Life" section of my page.

I imagine these interactions wouldn't be so tentative and intermittent, so sheepish and slow to begin—that maybe we'd know one another better—if I had been born in the 1990s, when my parents would have been online when I was a toddler, or 1970s, when we could have learned about the Internet together, to some degree, as adults. 10

As a kid, when I began using the Internet, I was probably most interested in the prospects of solitary exploration. But I'd like to think that I was also compelled by forces outside myself—that, on some level, I might have been dimly aware of the Internet's role in the fulfillment of some ancient, human yearning to externalize our private imaginations into a shared space. Maybe I intuited that the faster the world was relocated into the Internet, the likelier humankind would be returned to an original and undifferentiated oneness, completing what it began around 13,000 years ago with agriculture, which resulted in villages, then cities, finally the Internet.

Maybe some part of me believed that, once we were there, we would know everything about our parents and they would know everything about us—except there wouldn't be a "they," or an "us," only a mind, containing the knowledge of both, that knows itself.

## Responding to Reading

MyWritingLab™

1.  How do the different roles of the Internet in their lives define the generation gap between Lin and his parents?
2.  In paragraphs 5–7, Lin contrasts his life before and after the Internet. What key differences does he identify? How has his parents' use of the Internet changed in recent years? How would you describe his attitude toward those changes?
3.  **Rhetorical Analysis**    Explain how the following statements support Lin's comparison between himself and his parents:
    -   "The Internet remained nonessential and separate for them, like a vacation destination." (1)
    -   "The Internet was a place you went to alone. Kids, while online, were parentless." (4)
    -   "I now sometimes imagine the Internet as a U.F.O. that appeared one afternoon in the backyard—to take humankind elsewhere, maybe." (8)

## Writing about Reading

MyWritingLab™

1.  How is your own use of the Internet and social media different from that of your parents? Do you see the same gap between yourself and your parents that Lin sees between himself and his parents?
2.  **Writing with Sources**    Locate some information about the early years of the Internet. What predictions and warnings did critics make about how the Internet would be used? Were these predictions largely optimistic or pessimistic? How accurate have these early predictions turned out to be? Write an essay that draws some conclusions about how these predictions foreshadowed the generation gap Lin identifies.

---
## FOCUS
---

### Are "Tiger Mothers" Really Better?

Amy Chua and her daughters at home in New Haven, CT

## Responding to the Image

MyWritingLab™

1. The photo above shows writer Amy Chua at home with her daughters, Louisa and Sophia. What message does this photo convey about the family? For example, what can you infer about the family's economic status or educational level?
2. This photograph omits Chua's husband, who lives with the family. Is his absence in any way significant?

# ADAPTED FROM *BATTLE HYMN OF THE TIGER MOTHER*

## Amy Chua

*1962–*

*The John M. Duff, Jr. Professor of Law at Yale Law School, Amy Chua specializes in such topics as ethnic conflict and globalization. She is the author of four books, including* Battle Hymn of the Tiger Mother *(2011), from which the following essay is adapted. In this essay, Chua contrasts two distinct parenting styles.*

A lot of people wonder how Chinese parents raise such stereotypically successful kids. They wonder what these parents do to produce so many math whizzes and music prodigies, what it's like inside the family, and whether they could do it too. Well, I can tell them, because I've done it. Here are some things my daughters, Sophia and Louisa, were never allowed to do:

- attend a sleepover
- have a playdate
- be in a school play
- complain about not being in a school play
- watch TV or play computer games
- choose their own extracurricular activities
- get any grade less than an A
- not be the No. 1 student in every subject except gym and drama
- play any instrument other than the piano or violin
- not play the piano or violin.

I'm using the term "Chinese mother" loosely. I know some Korean, Indian, Jamaican, Irish and Ghanaian parents who qualify too. Conversely, I know some mothers of Chinese heritage, almost always born in the West, who are not Chinese mothers, by choice or otherwise. I'm also using the term "Western parents" loosely. Western parents come in all varieties.

All the same, even when Western parents think they're being strict, they usually don't come close to being Chinese mothers. For example, my Western friends who consider themselves strict make their children practice their instruments 30 minutes every day. An hour at most. For a Chinese mother, the first hour is the easy part. It's hours two and three that get tough.

Despite our squeamishness about cultural stereotypes, there are tons of studies out there showing marked and quantifiable differences between Chinese and Westerners when it comes to parenting. In one study of 50 Western American mothers and 48 Chinese immigrant mothers, almost 70% of the Western mothers said either that "stressing academic success is not good for children" or that "parents need to foster the idea that learning is fun." By contrast, roughly 0% of the Chinese mothers felt the same way. Instead, the vast majority of the Chinese mothers said that they believe their children can be "the best" students, that "academic achievement reflects successful parenting," and that if children did not excel at school then there was "a problem" and parents "were not doing their job." Other studies indicate that compared to Western parents, Chinese parents spend approximately 10 times as long every day drilling academic activities with their children. By contrast, Western kids are more likely to participate in sports teams.

What Chinese parents understand is that nothing is fun until you're good at it. To get good at anything you have to work, and children on their own never want to work, which is why it is crucial to override their preferences. This often requires fortitude on the part of the parents because the child will resist; things are always hardest at the beginning, which is where Western parents tend to give up. But if done properly, the Chinese strategy produces a virtuous circle. Tenacious practice, practice, practice is crucial for excellence; rote repetition is underrated in America. Once a child starts to excel at something—whether it's math, piano, pitching or ballet—he or she gets praise, admiration and satisfaction. This builds confidence and makes the once not-fun activity fun. This in turn makes it easier for the parent to get the child to work even more.

Chinese parents can get away with things that Western parents can't. Once when I was young—maybe more than once—when I was extremely disrespectful to my mother, my father angrily called me "garbage" in our native Hokkien dialect.[1] It worked really well. I felt terrible and deeply ashamed of what I had done. But it didn't damage my self-esteem or anything like that. I knew exactly how highly he thought of me. I didn't actually think I was worthless or feel like a piece of garbage.

As an adult, I once did the same thing to Sophia, calling her garbage in English when she acted extremely disrespectfully toward me. When I mentioned that I had done this at a dinner party, I was immediately ostracized. One guest named Marcy got so upset she broke down in tears and had to leave early. My friend Susan, the host, tried to rehabilitate me with the remaining guests.

The fact is that Chinese parents can do things that would seem unimaginable—even legally actionable—to Westerners. Chinese mothers can say to their daughters, "Hey fatty—lose some weight." By contrast, Western parents have to tiptoe around the issue, talking in terms of "health" and never ever mentioning the f-word, and their kids still end up in therapy for eating disorders and negative self-image. (I also once heard a Western father toast his adult daughter by calling her "beautiful and incredibly competent." She later told me that made her feel like garbage.)

Chinese parents can order their kids to get straight As. Western parents can only ask their kids to try their best. Chinese parents can say, "You're lazy. All your classmates are getting ahead of you." By contrast, Western parents have to struggle with their own conflicted feelings about achievement, and try to persuade themselves that they're not disappointed about how their kids turned out.

---

[1]A Chinese dialect spoken in Southeast Asia. [Eds.]

10    I've thought long and hard about how Chinese parents can get away with what they do. I think there are three big differences between the Chinese and Western parental mind-sets.

First, I've noticed that Western parents are extremely anxious about their children's self-esteem. They worry about how their children will feel if they fail at something, and they constantly try to reassure their children about how good they are notwithstanding a mediocre performance on a test or at a recital. In other words, Western parents are concerned about their children's psyches. Chinese parents aren't. They assume strength, not fragility, and as a result they behave very differently.

For example, if a child comes home with an A-minus on a test, a Western parent will most likely praise the child. The Chinese mother will gasp in horror and ask what went wrong. If the child comes home with a B on the test, some Western parents will still praise the child. Other Western parents will sit their child down and express disapproval, but they will be careful not to make their child feel inadequate or insecure, and they will not call their child "stupid," "worthless" or "a disgrace." Privately, the Western parents may worry that their child does not test well or have aptitude in the subject or that there is something wrong with the curriculum and possibly the whole school. If the child's grades do not improve, they may eventually schedule a meeting with the school principal to challenge the way the subject is being taught or to call into question the teacher's credentials.

If a Chinese child gets a B—which would never happen—there would first be a screaming, hair-tearing explosion. The devastated Chinese mother would then get dozens, maybe hundreds of practice tests and work through them with her child for as long as it takes to get the grade up to an A.

Chinese parents demand perfect grades because they believe that their child can get them. If their child doesn't get them, the Chinese parent assumes it's because the child didn't work hard enough. That's why the solution to substandard performance is always to excoriate, punish and shame the child. The Chinese parent believes that their child will be strong enough to take the shaming and to improve from it. (And when Chinese kids do excel, there is plenty of ego-inflating parental praise lavished in the privacy of the home.)

15    Second, Chinese parents believe that their kids owe them everything. The reason for this is a little unclear, but it's probably a combination of Confucian filial piety[2] and the fact that the parents have sacrificed and done so much for their children. (And it's true that Chinese mothers get in the trenches, putting in long grueling hours personally tutoring, training, interrogating and spying on their kids.) Anyway, the understanding is that Chinese children must spend their lives repaying their parents by obeying them and making them proud.

---

[2]Respect for elders. [Eds.]

By contrast, I don't think most Westerners have the same view of children being permanently indebted to their parents. My husband, Jed, actually has the opposite view. "Children don't choose their parents," he once said to me. "They don't even choose to be born. It's parents who foist life on their kids, so it's the parents' responsibility to provide for them. Kids don't owe their parents anything. Their duty will be to their own kids." This strikes me as a terrible deal for the Western parent.

Third, Chinese parents believe that they know what is best for their children and therefore override all of their children's own desires and preferences. That's why Chinese daughters can't have boyfriends in high school and why Chinese kids can't go to sleepaway camp. It's also why no Chinese kid would ever dare say to their mother, "I got a part in the school play! I'm Villager Number Six. I'll have to stay after school for rehearsal every day from 3:00 to 7:00, and I'll also need a ride on weekends." God help any Chinese kid who tried that one.

Don't get me wrong: It's not that Chinese parents don't care about their children. Just the opposite. They would give up anything for their children. It's just an entirely different parenting model… .

Western parents worry a lot about their children's self-esteem. But as a parent, one of the worst things you can do for your child's self-esteem is to let them give up. On the flip side, there's nothing better for building confidence than learning you can do something you thought you couldn't.

There are all these new books out there portraying Asian mothers 20 as scheming, callous, overdriven people indifferent to their kids' true interests. For their part, many Chinese secretly believe that they care more about their children and are willing to sacrifice much more for them than Westerners, who seem perfectly content to let their children turn out badly. I think it's a misunderstanding on both sides. All decent parents want to do what's best for their children. The Chinese just have a totally different idea of how to do that.

Western parents try to respect their children's individuality, encouraging them to pursue their true passions, supporting their choices, and providing positive reinforcement and a nurturing environment. By contrast, the Chinese believe that the best way to protect their children is by preparing them for the future, letting them see what they're capable of, and arming them with skills, work habits and inner confidence that no one can ever take away.

## Responding to Reading

MyWritingLab™

1. How are Chinese parents different from Western parents? Why, according to Chua, are Chinese mothers better? Does she present sufficient evidence to support her position? If not, what should she add?

2. Explain your reaction to each of the following statements:
   - "What Chinese parents understand is that nothing is fun until you're good at it." (5)
   - "Chinese parents can get away with things that Western parents can't." (6)
   - "Western parents worry a lot about their children's self-esteem. But as a parent, one of the worst things you can do for your child's self-esteem is to let them give up." (19)

How do you think David Brooks (below) and Sophia Chua-Rubenfeld (p. 67) would react to each of these statements?

3. **Rhetorical Analysis**   In paragraph 2, Chua clarifies what she means by the term "Chinese mother." Why do you suppose she feels a need to do this? Do you find her explanation convincing?

## Writing about Reading

MyWritingLab™

1. How are Chua's rules for her children like and unlike the rules your parents set for you? Which set of rules makes more sense to you? Why?

2. **Writing with Sources**   Read the introduction and a few sections of Dr. Benjamin Spock's classic *Baby and Child Care*. (This book, first published in 1946, encourages parents to abandon rigid schedules and strict rules and adopt a parenting style that came to be labeled "permissive.") Then, review some modern-day parenting guides, and identify areas where they reflect or react against Spock's influence. What do you conclude about how parenting has changed since Spock wrote his book? Do you see these changes as positive? Explain your views in an essay.

# AMY CHUA IS A WIMP

## David Brooks

### 1961–

*A* New York Times *columnist and a radio and television political commentator, David Brooks has been an* Atlantic *correspondent, a* Weekly Standard *senior editor, and a* Newsweek *contributing editor. Brooks has published widely on American political and social issues. His latest book is* The Road to Character *(2015). In the following essay, Brooks takes a hard look at Amy Chua's parenting techniques and at her claims about what it takes for a child to succeed.*

Sometime early last week, a large slice of educated America decided that Amy Chua is a menace to society. Chua, as you probably know, is the Yale professor who has written a bracing critique of what she considers the weak, cuddling American parenting style.

Chua didn't let her own girls go out on play dates or sleepovers. She didn't let them watch TV or play video games or take part in garbage activities like crafts. Once, one of her daughters came in second to a Korean kid in a math competition, so Chua made the girl do 2,000 math problems a night until she regained her supremacy. Once, her daughters gave her birthday cards of insufficient quality. Chua rejected them and demanded new cards. Once, she threatened to burn all of one of her daughter's stuffed animals unless she played a piece of music perfectly.

As a result, Chua's daughters get straight As and have won a series of musical competitions.

In her book, *Battle Hymn of the Tiger Mother*, Chua delivers a broadside against American parenting even as she mocks herself for her own extreme "Chinese" style. She says American parents lack authority and produce entitled children who aren't forced to live up to their abilities.

The furious denunciations began flooding my in-box a week ago. Chua plays into America's fear of national decline. Here's a Chinese parent working really hard (and, by the way, there are a billion more of her) and her kids are going to crush ours. Furthermore (and this Chua doesn't appreciate), she is not really rebelling against American-style parenting; she is the logical extension of the prevailing elite practices. She does everything over-pressuring upper-middle-class parents are doing. She's just hard core.

Her critics echoed the familiar themes. Her kids can't possibly be happy or truly creative. They'll grow up skilled and compliant but without the audacity to be great. She's destroying their love for music. There's a reason Asian-American women between the ages of 15 and 24 have such high suicide rates.

I have the opposite problem with Chua. I believe she's coddling her children. She's protecting them from the most intellectually demanding activities because she doesn't understand what's cognitively difficult and what isn't.

Practicing a piece of music for four hours requires focused attention, but it is nowhere near as cognitively demanding as a sleepover with 14-year-old girls. Managing status rivalries, negotiating group dynamics, understanding social norms, navigating the distinction between self and group—these and other social tests impose cognitive demands that blow away any intense tutoring session or a class at Yale.

Yet mastering these arduous skills is at the very essence of achievement. Most people work in groups. We do this because groups are much more efficient at solving problems than individuals (swimmers

5

are often motivated to have their best times as part of relay teams, not in individual events). Moreover, the performance of a group does not correlate well with the average I.Q. of the group or even with the I.Q.'s of the smartest members.

10   Researchers at the Massachusetts Institute of Technology and Carnegie Mellon have found that groups have a high collective intelligence when members of a group are good at reading each others' emotions—when they take turns speaking, when the inputs from each member are managed fluidly, when they detect each others' inclinations and strengths.

Participating in a well-functioning group is really hard. It requires the ability to trust people outside your kinship circle, read intonations and moods, understand how the psychological pieces each person brings to the room can and cannot fit together.

This skill set is not taught formally, but it is imparted through arduous experiences. These are exactly the kinds of difficult experiences Chua shelters her children from by making them rush home to hit the homework table.

Chua would do better to see the classroom as a cognitive break from the truly arduous tests of childhood. Where do they learn how to manage people? Where do they learn to construct and manipulate metaphors? Where do they learn to perceive details of a scene the way a hunter reads a landscape? Where do they learn how to detect their own shortcomings? Where do they learn how to put themselves in others' minds and anticipate others' reactions?

These and a million other skills are imparted by the informal maturity process and are not developed if formal learning monopolizes a child's time.

15   So I'm not against the way Chua pushes her daughters. And I loved her book as a courageous and thought-provoking read. It's also more supple than her critics let on. I just wish she wasn't so soft and indulgent. I wish she recognized that in some important ways the school cafeteria is more intellectually demanding than the library. And I hope her daughters grow up to write their own books, and maybe learn the skills to better anticipate how theirs will be received.

## Responding to Reading

MyWritingLab™

1. In what sense, according to Brooks, is Amy Chua a "wimp"? Do you think Brooks's title is effective, or do you see it as inappropriate—or possibly even offensive? Explain.

2. According to Brooks, what do some critics say is wrong with Chua's child-rearing philosophy? What objections to her practices does Brooks himself have? How do you suppose Chua would defend her family against these criticisms?

3. **Rhetorical Analysis**   In paragraphs 2 through 4, Brooks summarizes some of Chua's key points. Why does he do this? Is his summary accurate? Is it sufficiently detailed, or does he leave out any important pieces of information?

## Writing about Reading

1. Which do you see as more important, the academic success Chua wants for her daughters or the social skills Brooks discusses? Do you think it is possible for a child to excel both academically and socially?
2. **Writing with Sources**   Look online for information about *helicopter parents*. What is a helicopter parent? Do you see helicopter parents as positive influences in their children's lives or as meddlers interfering with their children's development into adults? Write an essay that summarizes the case for and against this kind of parenting and explains your own views on the subject.

# WHY I LOVE MY STRICT CHINESE MOM
## Sophia Chua-Rubenfeld
### *1993–*

*Sophia Chua-Rubenfeld is the daughter of Amy Chua. In the following letter, which appeared in the* New York Post, *Chua-Rubenfeld defends her mother's intense parenting style. According to Chua-Rubenfeld, her mother's strict way of raising her and her sister helped her to learn "that even creativity takes effort."*

Dear Tiger Mom,

You've been criticized a lot since you published your memoir, *Battle Hymn of the Tiger Mother*. One problem is that some people don't get your humor. They think you're serious about all this, and they assume Lulu and I are oppressed by our evil mother. That is so not true. Every other Thursday, you take off our chains and let us play math games in the basement.

But for real, it's not their fault. No outsider can know what our family is really like. They don't hear us cracking up over each other's jokes. They don't see us eating our hamburgers with fried rice. They don't know how much fun we have when the six of us—dogs included—squeeze into one bed and argue about what movies to download from Netflix.

I admit it: Having you as a mother was no tea party. There were some play dates I wish I'd gone to and some piano camps I wish I'd skipped. But now that I'm 18 and about to leave the tiger den, I'm glad you and Daddy raised me the way you did. Here's why.

A lot of people have accused you of producing robot kids who can't think for themselves. Well, that's funny, because I think those people are … oh well, it doesn't matter. At any rate, I was thinking about this, and I came to the opposite conclusion: I think your strict parenting forced me to be more independent. Early on, I decided to be an easy child to raise. Maybe I got it from Daddy—he taught me not to care what people think and to make my own choices—but I also decided to be who I want to be. I didn't rebel, but I didn't suffer all the slings and arrows of a Tiger Mom, either. I pretty much do my own thing these days—like building greenhouses downtown, blasting Daft Punk in the car with Lulu and forcing my boyfriend to watch *Lord of the Rings* with me over and over—as long as I get my piano done first.

5    Everybody's talking about the birthday cards we once made for you, which you rejected because they weren't good enough. Funny how some people are convinced that Lulu and I are scarred for life. Maybe if I had poured my heart into it, I would have been upset. But let's face it: The card was feeble, and I was busted. It took me 30 seconds; I didn't even sharpen the pencil. That's why, when you rejected it, I didn't feel you were rejecting me. If I actually tried my best at something, you'd never throw it back in my face.

I remember walking on stage for a piano competition. I was so nervous, and you whispered, "Soso, you worked as hard as you could. It doesn't matter how you do."

Everybody seems to think art is spontaneous. But Tiger Mom, you taught me that even creativity takes effort. I guess I was a little different from other kids in grade school, but who says that's a bad thing? Maybe I was just lucky to have nice friends. They used to put notes in my backpack that said "Good luck at the competition tomorrow! You'll be great!" They came to my piano recitals—mostly for the dumplings you made afterward—and I started crying when I heard them yelling "bravo!" at Carnegie Hall.

When I got to high school, you realized it was time to let me grow up a little. All the girls started wearing makeup in ninth grade. I walked to CVS to buy some and taught myself how to use it. It wasn't a big deal. You were surprised when I came down to dinner wearing eyeliner, but you didn't mind. You let me have that rite of passage.

Another criticism I keep hearing is that you're somehow promoting tunnel vision, but you and Daddy taught me to pursue knowledge for its own sake. In junior year, I signed myself up for a military-history elective (yes, you let me take lots of classes besides math and physics). One of our assignments was to interview someone who had experienced war. I knew I could get a good grade interviewing my grandparents, whose childhood stories about World War II I'd heard a thousand times. I mentioned it to you, and you said, "Sophia, this is an opportunity to learn something new. You're taking the easy way out." You were right, Tiger Mom. In the end, I interviewed a terrifying Israeli paratrooper whose story changed my outlook on life. I owe that experience to you.

There's one more thing: I think the desire to live a meaningful life is universal. To some people, it's working toward a goal. To others, it's enjoying every minute of every day. So what does it really mean to live life to the fullest? Maybe striving to win a Nobel Prize and going skydiving are just two sides of the same coin. To me, it's not about achievement or self-gratification. It's about knowing that you've pushed yourself, body and mind, to the limits of your own potential. You feel it when you're sprinting, and when the piano piece you've practiced for hours finally comes to life beneath your fingertips. You feel it when you encounter a life-changing idea, and when you do something on your own that you never thought you could. If I died tomorrow, I would die feeling I've lived my whole life at 110 percent. 10

And for that, Tiger Mom, thank you.

## Responding to Reading

MyWritingLab™

1. Given how closely Amy Chua has supervised her children, do you think her daughter's letter in her defense is completely sincere—and completely uncensored? Explain.
2. In paragraph 10, Chua-Rubenfeld asks, "So what does it really mean to live life to the fullest?" How would you answer this question? What is the relationship between this question and Chua-Rubenfeld's defense of her mother's parenting style?
3. **Rhetorical Analysis**   Why do you suppose Chua-Rubenfeld wrote her essay in the form of a letter to her mother? How does this choice affect her writing style? How might it affect her audience's reactions to her defense of her mother's parenting methods?

## Writing about Reading

MyWritingLab™

1. Write a letter to one or both of your parents, explaining why you are (or are not) satisfied with the way you were raised. Be very specific in your explanation of the rules and guidelines that were set for you.
2. **Writing with Sources**   What kind of parenting style did your parents experience? Were they brought up in strict, traditional families, or were their parents fairly free about rules and privileges? Interview your parents (and, if possible, some of your aunts and uncles and your grandparents). Then, write an essay analyzing the parenting styles represented in your family and drawing some conclusions about the pros and cons of the way your parents were brought up.

# WIDENING THE FOCUS

## For Critical Reading and Writing

Referring specifically to the three readings in this chapter's Focus section (and possibly to additional sources as well), write an essay in which you answer the question, "Are 'Tiger Mothers' Really Better?"

## For Further Reading

The following readings can suggest additional perspectives for thinking and writing about different kinds of parent–child relationships.

- Lynda Barry, "The Sanctuary of School" (p. 75)
- Amy Tan, "Mother Tongue" (p. 127)
- Steven Korbar, *"What Are You Going to Be?"* (p. 287)

## For Focused Research

Recent years have seen an increase in the number of afterschool programs designed to improve children's academic performance. One such program is offered by Kumon Learning Centers. Do a *Google* search for afterschool enrichment programs, and select two program websites. Then, write an essay that analyzes these programs. What is their purpose? Why were they developed? Why is their popularity increasing? Are they a good thing for children, or do they create too much pressure for them to excel? Use information from the websites you have chosen to support your conclusions.

## Beyond the Classroom

Conduct an e-mail survey of the friends and classmates whose names are listed in your contacts. After explaining Chua's distinction between Chinese "tiger mothers" and Western mothers, ask each recipient the following questions:

- Which type of mother did you have?
- Did this kind of parenting encourage you to succeed or hold you back?
- Which of these two types of parents do you plan to be, and why?

When you have gathered all your responses, write an essay that summarizes your findings and draws a conclusion about the relative value of each of the two parenting styles.

## EXPLORING ISSUES AND IDEAS

MyWritingLab™
Visit Chapter 3, "Family and Memory," in MyWritingLab to test your understanding of the chapter objectives.

### Family and Memory

Write an essay in response to one of the following prompts, which are suitable for assignments that require the use of outside sources as well as for assignments that are not source-based.

1. What exactly is a family? Is it a group of people bound together by love? by marriage? by blood? by history? by shared memories? by economic dependency? by habit? What unites family members, and what divides them? Does *family* denote only a traditional nuclear family or also a family broken by divorce and blended by remarriage? Define *family* as it is portrayed in several of the readings in this chapter.

2. Leo Tolstoy's classic Russian novel *Anna Karenina* opens with this sentence: "Happy families are all alike; every unhappy family is unhappy in its own way." Write an essay in which you agree with or challenge this statement, supporting your position with references to several of the readings in this chapter.

3. When you think about your childhood and your young adulthood, what music do you imagine playing in the background? Write a musical autobiography that gives readers a sense of who you were at different times of your life. Try to help readers understand the times you grew up in and the person you were (and became). Or, remember the smells and tastes of the food you grew up with, and write a culinary autobiography instead.

4. How do your parents' notions of success and failure affect you? Do you think your parents tend to expect too much of you? too little? Explore these ideas in an essay, referring to readings in this chapter and in Chapter 9, "The American Dream."

5. What traits, habits, and values (positive or negative) have you inherited from your parents? What qualities do you think you will pass on to your children? Read the poem "Heritage" (p. 34) and the essay "Why I Love My Strict Chinese Mom" (p. 67), and then write a letter to your parents in which you answer these two questions. Be sure to illustrate the characteristics you discuss with examples of specific incidents.

6. "Those Winter Sundays" (p. 36), told from the point of view of an adult looking back on his childhood, views the parent–child relationship with a mixture of regret and resignation. Write an essay exploring the similarly ambivalent feelings this work—and others in this chapter—convey about the relationship between child and parent.

# 4

## Issues in Education

*In this chapter, you will learn to*
- analyze readings about issues in education
- compose essays about issues in education

In the nineteenth century, people had little difficulty defining the purpose of education: they assumed it was the school's job to prepare students for the roles they would play in society as adults. To accomplish this end, public school administrators made sure that the elementary school curriculum gave students a good dose of the basics: arithmetic, grammar, spelling, reading, composition, and penmanship. High school students studied literature, history, geography, and civics. At the elite private schools, students studied subjects that would

Nineteenth-century college classroom

prepare them for the leadership positions that they would eventually occupy. They learned physics, rhetoric, and elocution—as well as Latin and Greek so that they could read the classics in the original.

Today, educators seem to have a great deal of difficulty agreeing on what purpose schools are supposed to serve. No longer can a group of school administrators simply proscribe a curriculum. Parents, students, politicians, academics, special interest groups, and religious leaders all attempt to influence what is taught. The result, according to some educators, is an environment in which it is almost impossible for any real education to take place. In fact, in many of today's schools, more emphasis seems to be placed on increasing self-esteem, avoiding controversy, and passing standardized tests linked to Common Core than on challenging students to discover new ways of thinking about themselves and about the world. In this milieu, classic books are censored or rewritten to eliminate passages that might offend, ideas are presented as if they all have equal value, and the curriculum is revised so that teachers can "teach to the test." The result is an educational environment that has all the intellectual appeal of elevator music. Many people—educators included—seem to have forgotten that ideas must be unsettling (or downright disturbing) if they are to make us think. After all, what is education but a process that encourages us to think critically about our world and to develop a healthy skepticism—to question, evaluate, and reach conclusions about ideas and events?

The Focus section of this chapter (p. 102) addresses the question, "Is a College Education Worth the Money?" In "Is College Worth It?"

Contemporary college classroom

David Leonhardt argues for the value of a college education; in "Plan B: Skip College," Jacques Steinberg explores alternatives to college degrees; and in "Is College Worth the Money?" Liz Dwyer examines the answers of six recent college graduates.

───────────── **PREPARING TO READ AND WRITE** ─────────────

As you read and prepare to write about the selections in this chapter, you may consider the following questions:

- What assumptions does the writer have about his or her audience? How can you tell?

- What is the writer's primary purpose? For example, is it to reinforce traditional ideas about education or to challenge them?

- What genre is the writer using? For example, is the reading a reflection? a memoir? an argument? How do the conventions of this genre influence the writer's choices?

- What appeals does the writer use? For example, does he or she appeal primarily to reason? to emotion? to a combination of the two? Is this the most effective strategy?

- How does the writer define *education*? Is this definition consistent with yours?

- What does the writer think the main goals of education should be? Do you agree?

- Which does the writer believe is more important, formal or informal education?

- On what aspect or aspects of education does the writer focus?

- Who does the writer believe bears primary responsibility for a student's education? The student? The family? The school? The community? The government?

- Does the writer use personal experience to support his or her points? Does he or she use facts and statistics or expert opinion as support? Do you find the writer's ideas convincing?

- What changes in the educational system does the writer recommend? Do you agree with these recommendations?

- Are the writer's educational experiences similar to or different from yours? How do these similarities or differences affect your response to the essay?

- In what way is the essay similar to or different from other essays in this chapter?

# THE SANCTUARY OF SCHOOL
## Lynda Barry
### 1956–

*Lynda Barry grew up as part of an extended Filipino family (her mother was Filipino, her father an alcoholic Norwegian-Irishman). The first member of her family to pursue higher education, she majored in art and began her career as a cartoonist shortly after graduation. Barry is known as a chronicler of adolescent angst both in her syndicated comic strip* Ernie Pook's Comeek *and in the semi-autobiographical* One Hundred Demons *(2002). Her latest book is* Syllabus: Notes from an Accidental Professor *(2014). Barry has also written a novel,* The Good Times Are Killing Me *(1988), which was turned into a successful musical. In the following essay, Barry remembers her Seattle grade school in a racially mixed neighborhood as a nurturing safe haven from her difficult family life.*

I was 7 years old the first time I snuck out of the house in the dark. It was winter and my parents had been fighting all night. They were short on money and long on relatives who kept "temporarily" moving into our house because they had nowhere else to go.

My brother and I were used to giving up our bedroom. We slept on the couch, something we actually liked because it put us that much closer to the light of our lives, our television.

At night when everyone was asleep, we lay on our pillows watching it with the sound off. We watched Steve Allen's mouth moving. We watched Johnny Carson's mouth moving. We watched movies filled with gangsters shooting machine guns into packed rooms, dying soldiers hurling a last grenade and beautiful women crying at windows. Then the sign-off finally came and we tried to sleep.

The morning I snuck out, I woke up filled with a panic about needing to get to school. The sun wasn't quite up yet but my anxiety was so fierce that I just got dressed, walked quietly across the kitchen and let myself out the back door.

It was quiet outside. Stars were still out. Nothing moved and no one was in the street. It was as if someone had turned the sound off on the world. 5

I walked the alley, breaking thin ice over the puddles with my shoes. I didn't know why I was walking to school in the dark. I didn't think about it. All I knew was a feeling of panic, like the panic that strikes kids when they realize they are lost.

That feeling eased the moment I turned the corner and saw the dark outline of my school at the top of the hill. My school was made up of about 15 nondescript portable classrooms set down on a fenced concrete lot in a rundown Seattle neighborhood, but it had the most beautiful view of the Cascade Mountains. You could see them from anywhere on the playfield and you could see them from the windows of my classroom—Room 2.

I walked over to the monkey bars and hooked my arms around the cold metal. I stood for a long time just looking across Rainier Valley. The sky was beginning to whiten and I could hear a few birds.

In a perfect world my absence at home would not have gone unnoticed. I would have had two parents in a panic to locate me, instead of two parents in a panic to locate an answer to the hard question of survival during a deep financial and emotional crisis.

10 But in an overcrowded and unhappy home, it's incredibly easy for any child to slip away. The high levels of frustration, depression and anger in my house made my brother and me invisible. We were children with the sound turned off. And for us, as for the steadily increasing number of neglected children in this country, the only place where we could count on being noticed was at school.

"Hey there, young lady. Did you forget to go home last night?" It was Mr. Gunderson, our janitor, whom we all loved. He was nice and he was funny and he was old with white hair, thick glasses and an unbelievable number of keys. I could hear them jingling as he walked across the playfield. I felt incredibly happy to see him.

He let me push his wheeled garbage can between the different portables as he unlocked each room. He let me turn on the lights and raise the window shades and I saw my school slowly come to life. I saw Mrs. Holman, our school secretary, walk into the office without her orange lipstick on yet. She waved.

I saw the fifth-grade teacher Mr. Cunningham, walking under the breezeway eating a hard roll. He waved.

And I saw my teacher, Mrs. Claire LeSane, walking toward us in a red coat and calling my name in a very happy and surprised way, and suddenly my throat got tight and my eyes stung and I ran toward her crying. It was something that surprised us both.

15 It's only thinking about it now, 28 years later, that I realize I was crying from relief. I was with my teacher, and in a while I was going to sit at my desk, with my crayons and pencils and books and classmates all around me, and for the next six hours I was going to enjoy a thoroughly secure, warm and stable world. It was a world I absolutely relied on. Without it, I don't know where I would have gone that morning.

Mrs. LeSane asked me what was wrong and when I said "Nothing," she seemingly left it at that. But she asked me if I would carry her purse for her, an honor above all honors, and she asked if I wanted to come into Room 2 early and paint.

She believed in the natural healing power of painting and drawing for troubled children. In the back of her room there was always a drawing table and an easel with plenty of supplies, and sometimes during the day she would come up to you for what seemed like no good reason and quietly ask if you wanted to go to the back table and "make some pictures for Mrs. LeSane." We all had a chance at it—to sit apart from the class for a while to paint, draw and silently work out impossible problems on 11 × 17 sheets of newsprint.

Drawing came to mean everything to me. At the back table in Room 2, I learned to build myself a life preserver that I could carry into my home.

We all know that a good education system saves lives, but the people of this country are still told that cutting the budget for public schools is necessary, that poor salaries for teachers are all we can manage and that art, music and all creative activities must be the first to go when times are lean.

Before- and after-school programs are cut and we are told that public schools are not made for baby-sitting children. If parents are neglectful temporarily or permanently, for whatever reason, it's certainly sad, but their unlucky children must fend for themselves. Or slip through the cracks. Or wander in a dark night alone.                                                  20

We are told in a thousand ways that not only are public schools not important, but that the children who attend them, the children who need them most, are not important either. We leave them to learn from the blind eye of a television, or to the mercy of "a thousand points of light"[1] that can be as far away as stars.

I was lucky. I had Mrs. LeSane. I had Mr. Gunderson. I had an abundance of art supplies. And I had a particular brand of neglect in my home that allowed me to slip away and get to them. But what about the rest of the kids who weren't as lucky? What happened to them?

By the time the bell rang that morning I had finished my drawing and Mrs. LeSane pinned it up on the special bulletin board she reserved for drawings from the back table. It was the same picture I always drew—a sun in the corner of a blue sky over a nice house with flowers all around it.

Mrs. LeSane asked us to please stand, face the flag, place our right hands over our hearts and say the Pledge of Allegiance. Children across the country do it faithfully. I wonder now when the country will face its children and say a pledge right back.

## Responding to Reading

MyWritingLab™

1.  What information about her school does Barry provide? What information does she not provide? How can you explain these omissions?
2.  In paragraph 22, Barry asks two questions. Why doesn't she answer them? What do you think the answers to these questions might be?
3.  **Rhetorical Analysis** Barry uses her personal experience to support her points about public school. Is this single source enough? Or, would Barry's points be more effective if they were supported by a wide variety of sources?

---

[1] Catchphrase for President George H. W. Bush's plan to substitute volunteerism for government programs. [Eds.]

## Writing about Reading

1. Do you think Barry's assessment of after-school programs is accurate? Are these programs as important to children as she seems to think they are?

2. **Writing with Sources** In her essay, Barry says that before- and after-school programs are being cut regardless of the effect on children. Research the public schools in your community, and determine if their before- and after-school programs are being cut. How cost-effective do both parents and educators think these programs are? Then, write an essay in which you assess the importance of before- and after-school programs in your community.

# SCHOOL IS BAD FOR CHILDREN

## John Holt

### 1923–1985

*John Holt, a teacher and education theorist, believed that traditional schooling suppresses children's natural curiosity about life. In his writings about education, Holt suggests that students be allowed to pursue whatever interests them. Holt worked for an international peace group, traveled in Europe, and then worked at the private Colorado Rocky Mountain School in Carbondale, Colorado, where he taught high school English, French, and mathematics and coached soccer and baseball. His many books include* How Children Fail *(1964),* How Children Learn *(1967),* Education *(1976), and* Learning All the Time *(1989). In the following essay, first published in 1969, Holt makes a plea to free children from the classroom, a "dull and ugly place, where nobody ever says anything very truthful," and to "give them a chance to learn about the world at first hand." Holt was also a major supporter of the Home Schooling movement.*

Almost every child, on the first day he sets foot in a school building, is smarter, more curious, less afraid of what he doesn't know, better at finding and figuring things out, more confident, resourceful, persistent and independent than he will ever be again in his schooling—or, unless he is very unusual and very lucky, for the rest of his life. Already, by paying close attention to and interacting with the world and people around him, and without any school-type formal instruction, he has done a task far more difficult, complicated and abstract than anything he will be asked to do in school, or than any of his teachers has done for years. He has solved the mystery of language. He has discovered it—babies don't even know that language exists—and he has found out how it works and learned to use it. He has done it by exploring, by experimenting, by developing his own model of the grammar of language, by trying it out and seeing whether it works, by gradually changing it and refining it until it does work. And while he has been doing this, he has been learning other things as well, including many of the "concepts" that the schools think only they can teach him, and many that are more complicated than the ones they do try to teach him.

In he comes, this curious, patient, determined, energetic, skillful learner. We sit him down at a desk, and what do we teach him? Many things. First, that learning is separate from living. "You come to school to learn," we tell him, as if the child hadn't been learning before, as if living were out there and learning were in here, and there were no connection between the two. Secondly, that he cannot be trusted to learn and is no good at it. Everything we teach about reading, a task far simpler than many that the child has already mastered, says to him, "If we don't make you read, you won't, and if you don't do it exactly the way we tell you, you can't." In short, he comes to feel that learning is a passive process, something that someone else does *to* you, instead of something you do for yourself.

In a great many other ways he learns that he is worthless, untrustworthy, fit only to take other people's orders, a blank sheet for other people to write on. Oh, we make a lot of nice noises in school about respect for the child and individual differences, and the like. But our acts, as opposed to our talk, say to the child, "Your experience, your concerns, your curiosities, your needs, what you know, what you want, what you wonder about, what you hope for, what you fear, what you like and dislike, what you are good at or not so good at—all this is of not the slightest importance, it counts for nothing. What counts here, and the only thing that counts, is what we know, what we think is important, what we want you to do, think and be." The child soon learns not to ask questions—the teacher isn't there to satisfy his curiosity. Having learned to hide his curiosity, he later learns to be ashamed of it. Given no chance to find out who he is—and to develop that person, whoever it is—he soon comes to accept the adults' evaluation of him.

He learns many other things. He learns that to be wrong, uncertain, confused, is a crime. Right Answers are what the school wants, and he learns countless strategies for prying these answers out of the teacher, for conning her into thinking he knows what he doesn't know. He learns to dodge, bluff, fake, cheat. He learns to be lazy. Before he came to school, he would work for hours on end, on his own, with no thought of reward, at the business of making sense of the world and gaining competence in it. In school he learns, like every buck private, how to goldbrick, how not to work when the sergeant isn't looking, how to know when he is looking, how to make him think you are working even when he is looking. He learns that in real life you don't do anything unless you are bribed, bullied or conned into doing it, that nothing is worth doing for its own sake, or that if it is, you can't do it in school. He learns to be bored, to work with a small part of his mind, to escape from the reality around him into daydreams and fantasies—but not like the fantasies of his preschool years, in which he played a very active part.

5      The child comes to school curious about other people, particularly other children, and the school teaches him to be indifferent. The most interesting thing in the classroom—often the only interesting thing in it—is the other children, but he has to act as if these other children, all about him, only a few feet away, are not really there. He cannot interact with them, talk with them, smile at them. In many schools he can't talk to other children in the halls between classes; in more than a few, and some of these in stylish suburbs, he can't even talk to them at lunch. Splendid training for a world in which, when you're not studying the other person to figure out how to do him in, you pay no attention to him.

In fact, he learns how to live without paying attention to anything going on around him. You might say that school is a long lesson in how to turn yourself off, which may be one reason why so many young people, seeking the awareness of the world and responsiveness to it they had when they were little, think they can only find it in drugs. Aside from being boring, the school is almost always ugly, cold, inhuman— even the most stylish, glass-windowed, $20-a-square-foot schools.

And so, in this dull and ugly place, where nobody ever says anything very truthful, where everybody is playing a kind of role, as in a charade, where the teachers are no more free to respond honestly to the students than the students are free to respond to the teachers or each other, where the air practically vibrates with suspicion and anxiety, the child learns to live in a daze, saving his energies for those small parts of his life that are too trivial for the adults to bother with, and thus remain his. It is a rare child who can come through his schooling with much left of his curiosity, his independence or his sense of his own dignity, competence and worth.

So much for criticism. What do we need to do? Many things. Some are easy—we can do them right away. Some are hard, and may take some time. Take a hard one first. We should abolish compulsory school attendance. At the very least we should modify it, perhaps by giving children every year a large number of authorized absences. Our compulsory school-attendance laws once served a humane and useful purpose. They protected children's right to some schooling, against those adults who would otherwise have denied it to them in order to exploit their labor, in farm, store, mine or factory. Today the laws help nobody, not the schools, not the teachers, not the children. To keep kids in school who would rather not be there costs the schools an enormous amount of time and trouble—to say nothing of what it costs to repair the damage that these angry and resentful prisoners do every time they get a chance. Every teacher knows that any kid in class who, for whatever reason, would rather not be there not only doesn't learn anything himself but makes it a great deal tougher for anyone else. As for protecting the children from exploitation, the chief and indeed only exploiters of children these days *are* the schools. Kids caught in the college rush more often than not work 70 hours or more a week, most of it on paper busywork. For kids who aren't going to college, school is just a useless time waster, preventing them from earning some money or doing some useful work, or even doing some true learning.

Objections. "If kids didn't have to go to school, they'd all be out in the streets." No, they wouldn't. In the first place, even if schools stayed just the way they are, children would spend at least some time there because that's where they'd be likely to find friends; it's a natural meeting place for children. In the second place, schools wouldn't stay the way they are, they'd get better, because we would have to start making them what they ought to be right now—places where children would *want* to be. In the third place, those children who did not want to go to school could find, particularly if we stirred up our brains and gave them a little help, other things to do—the things many children now do during their summers and holidays.

There's something easier we could do. We need to get kids out of the school buildings, give them a chance to learn about the world at first hand. It is a very recent idea, and a crazy one, that the way to teach our young people about the world they live in is to take them out of it and shut them up in brick boxes. Fortunately, educators are beginning to realize this. In Philadelphia and Portland, Oreg., to pick only two places I happen to have heard about, plans are being drawn up for public schools that won't have any school buildings at all, that will take the students out into the city and help them to use it and its people as a learning resource. In other words, students, perhaps in groups, perhaps independently, will go to libraries, museums, exhibits, court rooms, legislatures, radio and TV stations, meetings, businesses and laboratories to learn about their world and society at first hand. A small private school in Washington is already doing this. It makes sense. We need more of it.

As we help children get out into the world, to do their learning there, we get more of the world into the schools. Aside from their parents, most children never have any close contact with any adults except people whose sole business is children. No wonder they have no idea what adult life or work is like. We need to bring a lot more people who are *not* full-time teachers into the schools and into contact with the children. In New York City, under the Teachers and Writers Collaborative, real writers, working writers—novelists, poets, playwrights—come into the schools, read their work, and talk to the children about the problems of their craft. The children eat it up. In another school I know of, a practicing attorney from a nearby city comes in every month or so

10

and talks to several classes about the law. Not the law as it is in books but as he sees it and encounters it in his cases, his problems, his work. And the children love it. It is real, grown-up, true, not *My Weekly Reader*, not "social studies," not lies and baloney.

Something easier yet. Let children work together, help each other, learn from each other and each other's mistakes. We now know, from the experience of many schools, both rich-suburban and poor-city, that children are often the best teachers of other children. What is more important, we know that when a fifth- or sixth-grader who has been having trouble with reading starts helping a first-grader, his own reading sharply improves. A number of schools are beginning to use what some call Paired Learning. This means that you let children form partnerships with other children, do their work, even including their tests, together, and share whatever marks or results this work gets—just like grownups in the real world. It seems to work.

Let the children learn to judge their own work. A child learning to talk does not learn by being corrected all the time—if corrected too much, he will stop talking. *He* compares, a thousand times a day, the difference between language as he uses it and as those around him use it. Bit by bit, he makes the necessary changes to make his language like other people's. In the same way, kids learning to do all the other things they learn without adult teachers—to walk, run, climb, whistle, ride a bike, skate, play games, jump rope—compare their own performance with what more skilled people do, and slowly make the needed changes. But in school we never give a child a chance to detect his mistakes, let alone correct them. We do it all for him. We act as if we thought he would never notice a mistake unless it was pointed out to him, or correct it unless he was made to. Soon he becomes dependent on the expert. We should let him do it himself. Let him figure out, with the help of other children if he wants it, what this word says, what is the answer to that problem, whether this is a good way of saying or doing this or that. If right answers are involved, as in some math or science, give him the answer book, let him correct his own papers. Why should we teachers waste time on such donkey work? Our job should be to help the kid when he tells us that he can't find a way to get the right answer. Let's get rid of all this nonsense of grades, exams, marks. We don't know now, and we never will know, how to measure what another person knows or understands. We certainly can't find out by asking him questions. All we find out is what he doesn't know—which is what most tests are for, anyway. Throw it all out, and let the child learn what every educated person must someday learn, how to measure his own understanding, how to know what he knows or does not know.

We could also abolish the fixed, required curriculum. People remember only what is interesting and useful to them, what helps them make sense of the world, or helps them get along in it. All else they

quickly forget, if they ever learn it at all. The idea of a "body of knowledge," to be picked up in school and used for the rest of one's life, is
nonsense in a world as complicated and rapidly changing as ours. Anyway, the most important questions and problems of our time are not
*in* the curriculum, not even in the hotshot universities, let alone the
schools.

Children want, more than they want anything else, and even after    15
years of miseducation, to make sense of the world, themselves, and
other human beings. Let them get at this job, with our help if they ask
for it, in the way that makes most sense to them.

## Responding to Reading

MyWritingLab™

1. In what specific ways does Holt believe schools fail children?
2. According to Holt, what should schools do to correct their shortcomings?
   Do you think his suggestions are practical? realistic? Why or why not?
3. **Rhetorical Analysis** In paragraph 13, Holt says, "Let's get rid of all this
   nonsense of grades, exams, marks." Do you consider this statement an example of **hyperbole**—the intentional use of overstatement or exaggeration
   to make a point? What point do you think Holt is trying to make? What are
   the advantages and disadvantages of this strategy?

## Writing about Reading

MyWritingLab™

1. What would your ideal elementary school be like? How would it be like
   the schools you attended? How would it be different?
2. **Writing with Sources** Recently, there has been a movement away from the
   unstructured curriculum that Holt supported. Programs such as Common
   Core have been instituted to give curricula more structure and to establish clearer standards. Research Common Core, and then write an essay in
   which you explain your views about how structured (or unstructured) you
   think school curricula should be. What are the advantages and disadvantages of each approach?

# THE GOOD IMMIGRANT STUDENT

## Bich Minh Nguyen

### *1974–*

*Bich Minh Nguyen is an associate professor and the academic director of the
MFA in Writing program at the University of San Francisco and winner
of the PEN American Center's 2005 PEN/Jerard Award in nonfiction for
her memoir,* Stealing Buddha's Dinner *(2007). She has also coedited three
anthologies and written for* Gourmet *magazine, the* Chicago Tribune, *and
other publications. Her latest work is a novel,* Pioneer Girl *(2014). In the
following essay, Nguyen explores the implications of bilingual education for
immigrants in America.*

My stepmother, Rosa, who began dating my father when I was three years old, says that my sister and I used to watch *Police Woman* and rapturously repeat everything Angie Dickinson said. But when the show was over Anh and I would resume our Vietnamese, whispering together, giggling in accents. Rosa worried about this. She had the idea that she could teach us English and we could teach her Vietnamese. She would make us lunch or give us baths, speaking slowly and asking us how to say *water*, or *rice*, or *house*.

After she and my father married, Rosa swept us out of our falling-down house and into middle-class suburban Grand Rapids, Michigan. Our neighborhood surrounded Ken-O-Sha Elementary School and Plaster Creek, and was only a short drive away from the original Meijer's Thrifty Acres. In the early 1980s, this neighborhood of mismatching street names—Poinsettia, Van Auken, Senora, Ravanna—was home to families of Dutch heritage, and everyone was Christian Reformed, and conservative Republican. Except us. Even if my father hadn't left his rusted-through silver Mustang, the first car he ever owned, to languish in the driveway for months we would have stuck out simply because we weren't white. There was my Latina stepmother and her daughter, Cristina; my father, sister, grandmother, and I, refugees from Saigon; and my half-brother born a year after we moved to the house on Ravanna Street.

Although my family lived two blocks from Ken-O-Sha, my stepmother enrolled me and Anh at Sherwood Elementary, a bus ride away, because Sherwood had a bilingual education program. Rosa, who had a master's in education and taught ESL and community ed in the public school system, was a big supporter of bilingual education. School mornings, Anh and I would be at the bus stop at the corner of our street quite early, hustled out of the house by our grandmother who constantly feared we would miss our chance. I went off to first grade, Anh to second. At ten o'clock, we crept out of our classes, drawing glances and whispers from the other students, and convened with a group of Vietnamese kids from other grades to learn English. The teachers were Mr. Ho, who wore a lot of short-sleeved button-down shirts in neutral hues, and Miss Huong, who favored a maroon blouse with puffy shoulders and slight ruffles at the high neck and wrists, paired with a tweed skirt that hung heavily to her ankles. They passed out photocopied booklets of Vietnamese phrases and their English translations, with themes such as "In the Grocery Store." They asked us to repeat slowly after them and took turns coming around to each of us, bending close to hear our pronunciations.

Anh and I exchanged a lot of worried glances, for we had a secret that we were quite embarrassed about: we already knew English. It was the Vietnamese part that gave us trouble. When Mr. Ho and Miss Huong gave instructions, or passed out homework assignments, they did so in Vietnamese. Anh and I received praise for our English, but were reprimanded for failing to complete our assignments and failing to pay attention. After a couple of weeks of this Anh announced to Rosa that we didn't need bilingual education. Nonsense, she said. Our father just shrugged his shoulders. After that, Anh began skipping bilingual classes, urging me to do the same, and then we never went back. What was amazing was that no one, not Mrs. Eunice, my first grade teacher, or Mrs. Hankins, Anh's teacher, or even Mr. Ho or Miss Huong said anything directly to us about it. Or if they did, I have forgotten it entirely. Then one day my parents got a call from Miss Huong. When Rosa came to talk to me and Anh about it we were watching television the way kids do, sitting alarmingly close to the screen. Rosa confronted us with "Do you girls know English?" Then she suddenly said, "Do you know Vietnamese?" I can't remember what we replied to either question.

For many years, a towering old billboard over the expressway downtown proudly declared Grand Rapids "An All-American City." For me, that all-American designation meant all-white. I couldn't believe (and still don't) that they meant to include the growing Mexican-American population, or the sudden influx of Vietnamese refugees in 1975. I often thought it a rather mean-spirited prank of some administrator at the INS, deciding with a flourish of a signature to send a thousand refugees to Grand Rapids, a city that boasted having more churches per square mile than any other city in the United States. Did that administrator know what Grand Rapids was like? That in school, everywhere I turned, and often when I closed my eyes, I saw blond blond blond? The point of bilingual education was assimilation. To my stepmother, the point was preservation: she didn't want English to take over wholly, pushing the Vietnamese out of our heads. She was too ambitious. Anh and I were Americanized as soon as we turned on the television. Today, bilingual education is supposed to have become both a method of assimilation and a method of preservation, an effort to prove that kids can have it both ways. They can supposedly keep English for school and their friends and keep another language for home and family.

In Grand Rapids, Michigan, in the 1980s, I found that an impossible task.

I transferred to Ken-O-Sha Elementary in time for third grade, after Rosa finally admitted that taking the bus all the way to Sherwood was pointless. I was glad to transfer, eager to be part of a class that wasn't, in my mind, tainted with the knowledge of my bilingual stigma. Third grade was led by Mrs. Alexander, an imperious, middle-aged woman of many plaid skirts held safe by giant gold safety pins. She had a habit of turning her wedding ring around and around her finger while she stood at the chalkboard. Mrs. Alexander had an intricate system of rewards for good grades and good behavior, denoted by colored star stickers on a piece of poster board that loomed over us all. One glance and you could see who was behind, who was striding ahead.

I was an insufferably good student, with perfect Palmer cursive and the highest possible scores in every subject. I had learned this trick at Sherwood. That the quieter you are, the shyer and sweeter and better-at-school you are, the more the teacher will let you alone. Mrs. Alexander should have let me alone. For, in addition to my excellent marks, I was nearly silent, deadly shy, and wholly obedient. My greatest fear was being called on, or in any way standing out more than I already did in the class that was, except for me and one black student, dough-white. I got good grades because I feared the authority of the teacher; I felt that getting in good with Mrs. Alexander would protect me, that she would protect me from the frightful rest of the world. But Mrs. Alexander was not agreeable to this notion. If it was my turn to read aloud during reading circle, she'd interrupt me to snap, "You're reading too fast" or demand, "What does that word mean?" Things she did not do to the other students. Anh, when I told her about this, suggested that perhaps Mrs. Alexander liked me and wanted to help me get smarter. But neither of us believed it. You know when a teacher likes you and when she doesn't.

Secretly, I admired and envied the rebellious kids, like Robbie Andrews who came to school looking bleary-eyed and pinched, like a hungover adult; Robbie and his ilk snapped back at teachers, were routinely sent to the principal's office, were even spanked a few times with the principal's infamous red paddle (apparently no one in Grand Rapids objected to corporal punishment). Those kids made noise, possessed something I thought was confidence, self-knowledge, allowing them to marvelously question everything ordered of them. They had the ability to challenge the given world.

10    Toward the middle of third grade Mrs. Alexander introduced a stuffed lion to the pool of rewards: the best student of the week would earn the privilege of having the lion sit on his or her desk for the entire week. My quantity of gold stars was neck and neck with that of my two competitors, Brenda and Jennifer, both sweet-eyed blond girls with pastel-colored monogrammed sweaters and neatly tied Dock-Sides. My family did not have a lot of money and my stepmother had terrible taste. Thus I attended school in such ensembles as dark red parachute pants and a nubby pink sweater stitched with a picture of a unicorn rearing up. This only propelled me to try harder to be good, to make up for everything I felt was against me: my odd family, my race, my very face. And I craved that stuffed lion. Week after week, the lion perched on Brenda's desk or Jennifer's desk. Meanwhile, the class spelling bee approached. I didn't know I was such a good speller until I won it,

earning a scalloped-edged certificate and a candy bar. That afternoon I started toward home, then remembered I'd forgotten my rain boots in my locker. I doubled back to school and overheard Mrs. Alexander in the classroom talking to another teacher. "Can you believe it?" Mrs. Alexander was saying. "A foreigner winning our spelling bee!"

I waited for the stuffed lion the rest of that year, with a kind of patience I have no patience for today. To no avail. In June, on the last day of school, Mrs. Alexander gave the stuffed lion to Brenda to keep forever.

The first time I had to read aloud something I had written—perhaps it was in fourth grade—I felt such terror, such a need not to have any attention upon me, that I convinced myself that I had become invisible, that the teacher could never call on me because she couldn't see me.

More than once, I was given the assignment of writing a report about my family history. I loathed this task, for I was dreadfully aware that my history could not be faked; it already showed on my face. When my turn came to read out loud the teacher had to ask me several times to speak louder. Some kids, a few of them older, in different classes, took to pressing back the corners of their eyes with the heels of their palms while they chanted, "Ching-chong, ching-chong!" during recess. (This continued until Anh, who was far tougher than me, threatened to beat them up.)

I have no way of telling what tortured me more: the actual snickers and remarks and watchfulness of my classmates, or my own imagination, conjuring disdain. My own sense of shame. At times I felt sickened by my obedience, my accumulation of gold stickers, my every effort to be invisible.

Yet Robbie Andrews must have felt the same kind of claustrophobia, trapped in his own reputation, in his inability to be otherwise. I learned in school that changing oneself is not easy, that the world makes up its mind quickly.    15

I've heard that Robbie dropped out of high school, got a girl pregnant, found himself in and out of first juvenile detention, then jail.

What comes out of difference? What constitutes difference? Such questions, academic and unanswered, popped up in every other course description in college. But the idea of difference is easy to come by, especially in school; it is shame, the permutations and inversions of difference and self-loathing, that we should be worrying about.

Imagined torment, imagined scorn. When what is imagined and what is desired turn on each other.

Some kids want to rebel; other kids want to disappear. I wanted to disappear. I was not brave enough to shrug my shoulders and flaunt my difference; because I could not disappear into the crowd, I wished to disappear entirely. Anyone might have mistaken this for passivity.

20          Once, at the end of my career at Sherwood Elementary, I disappeared on the bus home. Mine was usually the third stop, but that day the bus driver thought I wasn't there, and she sailed right by the corner of Ravanna and Senora. I said nothing. The bus wove its way downtown, and for the first time I got to see where other children lived, some of them in clean orderly neighborhoods, some near houses with sagging porches and boarded-up windows. All the while, the kid sitting across the aisle from me played the same cheerful song over and over on his portable boom box. *Pass the doochee from the left hand side, pass the doochee from the left hand side.* He and his brother turned out to be the last kids off the bus. Then the bus driver saw me through the rearview mirror. She walked back to where I was sitting and said, "How come you didn't get off at your stop?" I shook my head, don't know. She sighed and drove me home.

I was often doing that, shaking my head silently or staring up wordlessly. I realize that while I remember so much of what other people said when I was a child, I remember little of what I said. Probably because I didn't say much at all.

I recently came across in the stacks of the University of Michigan library *A Manual for Indochinese Refugee Education 1976–1977.* Some of it is silly, but much of it is a painstaking, fairly thoughtful effort to let school administrators and teachers know how to go about sensitively handling the influx of Vietnamese children in the public schools. Here is one of the most wonderful items of advice: "The Vietnamese child, even the older child, is also reported to be afraid of the dark, and more often than not, believes in ghosts. A teacher may have to be a little more solicitous of the child on gloomy, wintery days." Perhaps if Mrs. Alexander had read this, she would not have upbraided me so often for tracking mud into the classroom on rainy days. In third grade I was horrified and ashamed of my muddy shoes. I hung back, trying to duck behind this or that dark-haired boy. In spite of this, in spite of bilingual education, and shyness, and all that wordless shaking of my head, I was sent off every Monday to the Spectrum School for the Gifted and Talented. I still have no idea who selected me, who singled me out. Spectrum was (and still is) a public school program that invited students from every public elementary school to meet once a week and take specialized classes on topics such as the Middle Ages, Ellis Island, and fairy tales. Each student chose two classes, a major and minor, and for the rest of the semester worked toward final projects in both. I loved going to Spectrum. Not only did the range of students from other schools prove to be diverse, I found myself feeling more comfortable, mainly because Spectrum encouraged individual work. And the teachers seemed happy to be there. The best teacher at Spectrum was

Mrs. King, whom every student adored. I still remember the soft gray sweaters she wore, her big wavy hair, her art-class handwriting, the way she'd often tell us to close our eyes when she read us a particular story or passage.

I believe that I figured out how to stop disappearing, how to talk and answer, even speak up, after several years in Spectrum. I was still deeply self-conscious, but I became able, sometimes, to maneuver around it.

Spectrum may have spoiled me a little, because it made me think about college and freedom, and thus made all the years in between disappointing and annoying.

In seventh grade I joined Anh and Cristina at the City School, a seventh through twelfth grade public school in the Grand Rapids system that served as an early charter school; admission was by interview, and each grade had about fifty students. The City School had the advantage of being downtown, perched over old cobblestone roads, and close to the main public library. Art and music history were required. There were no sports teams. And volunteering was mandatory. But kids didn't tend to stay at City School; as they got older they transferred to one of the big high schools nearby, perhaps wishing to play sports, perhaps wishing to get away from City's rather brutal academic system. Each half semester, after grades were doled out, giant dot-matrix printouts of everyone's GPAs were posted in the hallways.

I didn't stay at City, either. When my family moved to a different suburb, my stepmother promptly transferred me to Forest Hills Northern High School. Most of the students there came from upper-middle-class or very well-to-do families; the ones who didn't stood out sharply. The rich kids were the same as they were anywhere in America: they wore a lot of Esprit and Guess, drove nice cars, and ran student council, prom, and sports. These kids strutted down the hallways; the boys sat in a row on the long windowsill near a group of lockers, whistling or calling out to girls who walked by. Girls gathered in bathrooms with their Clinique lipsticks.

High school was the least interesting part of my education, but I did accomplish something: I learned to forget myself a little. I learned the sweetness of apathy. And through apathy, how to forget my skin and body for a minute or two, almost not caring what would happen if I walked into a room late and all heads swiveled toward me. I learned the pleasure that reveals itself in the loss, no matter how slight, of self-consciousness. These things occurred because I remained the good immigrant student, without raising my hand often or showing off what I knew. Doing work was rote, and I went along to get along. I've never gotten over the terror of being called on in class, or the dread in knowing that I'm expected to contribute to class discussion. But there is a slippage between being good and being unnoticed, and in that sliver of freedom I learned what it could feel like to walk in the world in plain, unself-conscious view.

I would like to make a broad, accurate statement about immigrant children in schools. I would like to speak for them (us). I hesitate; I cannot. My own sister, for instance, was never as shy as I was. Anh disliked school from the start, choosing rebellion rather than silence. It was a good arrangement: I wrote papers for her and she paid me in money or candy; she gave me rides to school if I promised not to tell anyone about her cigarettes. Still, I think of an Indian friend of mine who told of an elementary school experience in which a blond school-child told the teacher, "I can't sit by her. My mom said I can't sit by anyone who's brown." And another friend, whose family immigrated around the same time mine did, whose second grade teacher used her as a vocabulary example: "Children, this is what a *foreigner* is." And sometimes I fall into thinking that kids today have the advantage of so much more wisdom, that they are so much more socially and politically aware than anyone was when I was in school. But I am wrong, of course. I know not every kid is fortunate enough to have a teacher like Mrs. King, or a program like Spectrum, or even the benefit of a manual written by a group of concerned educators; I know that some kids want to disappear and disappear until they actually do. Sometimes I think I see them, in the blurry background of a magazine photo, or in a gaggle of kids following a teacher's aide across the street. The kids with heads bent down, holding themselves in such a way that they seem to be self-conscious even of how they breathe. Small, shy, quiet kids, such good, good kids, *immigrant, foreigner,* their eyes watchful and waiting for whatever judgment will occur. I reassure myself that they will grow up fine, they will be okay. Maybe I cross the same street, then another, glancing back once in a while to see where they are going.

## Responding to Reading

MyWritingLab™

1. What does Nguyen mean when she says that today bilingual education is supposed to be "both a method of assimilation and a method of preservation" (5)? Does she believe this assessment is accurate?
2. What is "the good immigrant student"? How did Nguyen's education reinforce this stereotype? How did it help her move beyond it?
3. **Rhetorical Analysis** Although this essay is primarily narrative, it also deals with cause and effect. Find two passages that include cause and effect and explain what they add to the essay.

## Writing about Reading

MyWritingLab™

1. In paragraph 28, Nguyen says, "I would like to make a broad, accurate statement about immigrant children in schools. I would like to speak for them (us). I hesitate; I cannot." What do you think she means? Why can't she make "a broad, accurate statement"?

2. **Writing with Sources** "The Good Immigrant Student" deals with the issue of bilingual instruction. Research bilingual instruction, focusing specifically on the controversy surrounding it. What do its supporters say about it?
   What do its detractors say? Then, write an essay in which you take a stand
   about whether bilingual instruction actually helps students or hurts them.
   Make sure that you include Nguyen's experiences in your essay.

# ONLINE HIGHER EDUCATION'S INDIVIDUALIST FALLACY

## Johann N. Neem

*A professor of history at Western Washington University, Johann N. Neem
specializes in the history of the early American republic. He is the author of*
Creating a Nation of Joiners: Democracy and Civil Society in Early
National Massachusetts *(2008). In the following essay, Neem argues for
the value of "institutional culture" in higher education.*

There has been much talk of the "online revolution" in higher education. While there is a place for online education, some of its boosters
anticipate displacing the traditional campus altogether. A close reading
of their arguments, however, makes clear that many share what might
be called the "individualist fallacy," both in their understanding of how
students learn and how professors teach.

Of course, individualism has a long, noble heritage in American
history. From the "age of the self-made man" onward, we have valued
those who pull themselves up by their own bootstraps. But, as Warren
Buffett[1] has made clear, even the most successful individuals depend
heavily on the cultural, economic, legal, political, and social contexts
in which they act. This is as true for Buffett as it is for other so-called
self-made men, such as Bill Gates. And it is certainly true for students.

But many advocates of online learning ignore this simple point. The
economist Richard Vedder, for example, believes that being on campus
is only useful for "making friends, partying, drinking, and having sex."
Anya Kamenetz, in her book *DIY U*, celebrates the day when individuals
are liberated from the constraints of physical campuses, while Gates antici-
pates that "five years from now on the Web for free you'll be able to find
the best lectures in the world. It will be better than any single university."

These advocates of online higher education forget the importance
of *institutional culture* in shaping how people learn. College is about
more than accessing information; it's about developing an attitude toward knowledge.

---

[1] Investor and philanthropist (1930–). [Eds.]

5      There is a difference between being on a campus with other students and teachers committed to learning and sitting at home. Learning, like religion, is a social experience. Context matters. No matter how much we might learn about God and our obligations from the Web, it is by going to church and being surrounded by other congregants engaged in similar questions, under the guidance of a thoughtful, caring pastor, that we really change. Conversion is social, and so is learning.

Like all adults, students will pursue many activities during their time on campus, but what distinguishes a college is that it embodies ideals distinct from the rest of students' lives. If we take college seriously, we need people to spend time in such places so that they will leave different than when they entered.

Some argue that large lecture courses make a mockery of the above claims. Admittedly, in a better world, there would be no large lecture courses. Still, this argument misleads for several reasons. First, it generalizes from one kind of course, ignoring the smaller class sizes at community colleges and the upper-division courses in which students interact closely with each other and their professors. Second, it dismisses the energy of being in a classroom, even a large one, with real people when compared to being on our own. Even in large classes, good teachers push their students to think by asking probing questions, modeling curiosity, and adapting to the class's needs. Finally, it disregards the importance of the broader campus context in which all classes, large and small, take place.

The goal of bringing students to campus for several years is to immerse them in an environment in which learning is the highest value, something online environments, no matter how interactive, cannot simulate. Real learning is hard; it requires students to trust each other and their teachers. In other words, it depends on relationships. This is particularly important for the liberal arts.

Of course, as Richard Arum and Josipa Roksa's recent study *Academically Adrift* makes clear, there are great variations in what college students are learning. All too often, higher education does not fulfill our aspirations. But none of the problems Arum and Roksa identify are ones that online higher education would solve. As Arum and Roksa make clear, students learn more on campuses where learning is valued and expectations are high. If anything, we need to pay more attention to institutional culture because it matters so much.

10     This does not mean that we should reject technology when it can further learning, as in new computer programs that help diagnose students' specific stumbling blocks. But computers will never replace the inspiring, often unexpected, conversations that happen among students and between students and teachers on campuses. Because computers are not interpretive moral beings, they cannot evaluate assignments in which students are asked to reflect on complicated ideas or come up

with new ones, especially concerning moral questions. Fundamentally, computers cannot cultivate curiosity because machines are not curious.

Technology is a tool, not an end in itself. As the computer scientist Jaron Lanier has written in his book *You Are Not A Gadget*, computers exist to support human endeavors, not the other way around. Many techno-utopists proclaim that computers are becoming smarter, more human, but Lanier wonders whether that is because we tend to reduce our human horizons to interact with our machines. This certainly is one of the dangers of online higher education.

The individualist fallacy applies not just to online advocates' understandings of students, but also their conception of what makes great teachers and scholars. Vedder, for example, echoes Gates in his hope that someday there will be a Wikipedia University, or that the Gates Foundation will start a university in which a few "star professors" are paid to teach thousands of students across the nation and world. Of course, this has been happening since the invention of cassette tapes that offer "the great courses." This is hardly innovative, nor does it a college education make.

Vedder ignores how star professors become great. How do they know what to teach and to write? Their success, like Buffett's, is social: they converse with and read and rely on the work of hundreds, even thousands, of other scholars. Read their articles and books, listen to their lectures, and you can discern how deeply influenced and how dependent they are on the work of their peers. In short, there would be no star professors absent an academy of scholars committed to research.

Schools like the online, Gates Foundation–funded Western Governors University free-ride off the expensive, quality research completed by traditional professors when they rely on open course ware and curricula. Take away the professors, and many online schools will teach material that is out of date or inaccurate or, worse, hand control over to other entities who are not interested in promoting the truth—from textbook companies seeking to maximize sales to coal and pharmaceutical companies offering their own curriculums for "free."

The Web and new technologies are great tools; they have made more 15 information more accessible to more people. This is to be celebrated. Citizens in a democracy should be able to access as much information as freely as possible. A democratic society cannot allow scholars, or anyone else, to be the gatekeepers to knowledge.

Certainly, we will expand online higher education, if for no other reason than because wealthy foundations like Gates and ambitious for-profit entities are putting their money and power behind it. For certain students, especially working adults pursuing clearly defined vocational programs rather than a liberal arts education, online programs may allow opportunities that they would have otherwise foregone. But online higher education will never replace, much less replicate, what happens on college campuses.

Even as we expand online, therefore, we must deepen our commitment to those institutions that cultivate a love of learning in their students, focus on the liberal arts, and produce the knowledge that online and offline teaching requires.

## Responding to Reading

MyWritingLab™

1. What is the importance of "institutional culture" in shaping the way students learn (4)? According to Neem, how does distance learning undercut institutional culture in higher education?
2. What does Neem mean when he says, "Technology is a tool, not an end in itself" (11)? In what sense does he believe that online schools "free-ride off the expensive, quality research completed by traditional professors" (14)?
3. **Rhetorical Analysis** Neem begins his essay by mentioning the "individualist fallacy" (1). What is the meaning of this term? Why does Neem begin his essay with this concept?

## Writing about Reading

MyWritingLab™

1. Do you think students need to be in a traditional classroom to get an education? Why or why not?
2. **Writing with Sources** Many colleges now offer as many courses online as they do in traditional classroom settings. Research online education, and determine its advantages as well as its disadvantages. Then, write a proposal to your college in which you argue for or against more online instruction.

# FOR MORE BALANCE ON CAMPUSES

## Christina Hoff Sommers

### 1950–

*Christina Hoff Sommers, who calls herself an "equity feminist," is currently a resident scholar at the American Enterprise Institute. Sommers is the author of essays in a wide variety of periodicals and has published several books but is best known for* Who Stole Feminism? How Women Have Betrayed Women *(1994) and* The War against Boys: How Misguided Feminism Is Harming Our Young Men *(2000). Her latest book is* Freedom Feminism *(2013). In the following essay, the introduction to a longer essay that appeared in the* Atlantic Monthly, *Sommers makes a plea for more political diversity on America's college campuses.*

Washington—In a recent talk at Haverford College, I questioned the standard women's studies teaching that the United States is a patriarchal society that oppresses women.

For many in the audience, this was their first encounter with a dissident scholar. One student was horrified when I said that the free market had advanced the cause of women by affording them unprecedented economic opportunities. "How can anyone say that capitalism has helped women?" she asked.

Nor did I win converts when I said that the male heroism of special forces soldiers and the firefighters at ground zero should persuade gender scholars to acknowledge that "stereotypical masculinity" had some merit. Later an embarrassed and apologetic student said to me, "Haverford is just not ready for you."

After my talk, the young woman who invited me told me there was little intellectual diversity at Haverford and that she had hoped I would spark debate. In fact, many in the audience were quietly delighted by the exchanges. But two angry students accused her of providing "a forum for hate speech."

As the 2000 election made plain, the United States is pretty evenly    5 divided between conservatives and liberals. Yet conservative scholars have effectively been marginalized, silenced, and rendered invisible on most campuses. This problem began in the late '80s and has become much worse in recent years. Most students can now go through four years of college without encountering a scholar of pronounced conservative views.

Few conservatives make it past the gantlet of faculty hiring in political-science, history, or English departments. In 1998, when a reporter from Denver's *Rocky Mountain News* surveyed the humanities and social sciences at the University of Colorado, Boulder, he found that of 190 professors with party affiliations, 184 were Democrats.

There wasn't a single Republican in the English, psychology, journalism, or philosophy departments. A 1999 survey of history departments found 22 Democrats and 2 Republicans at Stanford. At Cornell and Dartmouth there were 29 and 10 Democrats, respectively, and no Republicans.

The dearth of conservatives in psychology departments is so striking, that one (politically liberal) professor has proposed affirmative-action outreach. Richard Redding, a professor of psychology at Villanova University, writing in a recent issue of *American Psychologist*, notes that of the 31 social-policy articles that appeared in the journal between 1990 and 1999, 30 could be classified as liberal, one as conservative.

The key issue, Professor Redding says, is not the preponderance of Democrats, but the liberal practice of systematically excluding conservatives. Redding cites an experiment in which several graduate departments received mock applications from two candidates nearly identical, except that one "applicant" said he was a conservative Christian. The professors judged the nonconservative to be the significantly better candidate.

Redding asks, rhetorically: "Do we want a professional world    10 where our liberal world view prevents us from considering valuable strengths of conservative approaches to social problems . . . where conservatives are reluctant to enter the profession and we tacitly discriminate against them if they do? That, in fact, is the academic world we now have . . . ."

Campus talks by "politically incorrect" speakers happen rarely; visits are resisted and almost never internally funded. When Dinesh D'Souza, Andrew Sullivan, David Horowitz, or Linda Chavez do appear at a college, they are routinely heckled and sometimes threatened. The academy is now so inhospitable to free expression that conservatives buy advertisements in student newspapers. But most school newspapers won't print them. And papers that do are sometimes vandalized and the editors threatened.

The classical liberalism articulated by John Stuart Mill in his book *On Liberty* is no longer alive on campuses, having died of the very disease Mr. Mill warned of when he pointed out that ideas not freely and openly debated become *dead dogmas*. Mill insisted that the intellectually free person must put himself in the *mental position of those who think differently* adding that dissident ideas are best understood *by hear[ing] them from persons who actually believe them.*

Several groups are working to bring some balance to campus. The Intercollegiate Studies Institute, Young America's Foundation, Clare Boothe Luce Policy Institute, and Accuracy in Academia sponsor lectures by leading conservatives and libertarians. Students can ask these groups for funds to sponsor speakers.

More good news is that David Horowitz's Center for the Study of Popular Culture has launched a "Campaign for Fairness and Inclusion in Higher Education." It calls for university officials to:

1. Establish a zero-tolerance policy for vandalizing newspapers or heckling speakers.
2. Conduct an inquiry into political bias in the allocation of student program funds, including speakers' fees, and seek ways to promote underrepresented perspectives.
3. Conduct an inquiry into political bias in the hiring process of faculty and administrators and seek ways to promote fairness toward—and inclusion of—underrepresented perspectives.

15   Were even one high-profile institution like the University of Colorado to adopt a firm policy of intellectual inclusiveness, that practice would quickly spread, and benighted students everywhere would soon see daylight.

## Responding to Reading

MyWritingLab™

1. According to Sommers, conservatives have been marginalized on most American college campuses. What does she mean? How has this occurred? What evidence does Sommers present to support her claim? Is her evidence persuasive?

2. In Sommers's view, what is the effect of excluding conservatives from the intellectual life of a college or university? What does Sommers say is being done "to bring some balance to campus" (13)?

3. **Rhetorical Analysis** In paragraph 10, Sommers includes a rhetorical question asked by Richard Redding, a professor at Villanova University. What is the point of this question? Why does Sommers insert it where she does?

## Writing about Reading

MyWritingLab™

1. Sommers says that students almost never hear campus talks by "'politically incorrect' speakers" (11). Do you agree with Sommers, or do you believe that at your college or university you are exposed to a cross-section of ideas?

2. **Writing with Sources** Try to determine how politically diverse your school is. First, go online and see if your college is ranked in the *Niche Most Politically Diverse College Rankings*, a site that compares political diversity at more than nine hundred colleges nationwide. Also, interview several of your classmates. Then, write an essay in which you present your findings.

# WE'VE GONE TOO FAR WITH "TRIGGER WARNINGS"

## Jill Filipovic

*A columnist for the* Guardian *and a senior political writer for* Cosmopolitan, *Jill Filipovic writes about feminist issues for the blog* Feministe. *Her work has also appeared in publications such as the* Huffington Post, Women's eNews, *and* Yale Journal of Law & Feminism. *In the following essay, Filipovic explains the problem with "trigger warnings."*

Trigger Warning: this piece discusses trigger warnings. It may also look askance at college students who are now asking that trigger warnings be applied to their course materials.

If you've spent time on feminist blogs lately or in the social-justice-oriented corner of Tumblr, you have likely come across the Trigger Warning (TW): a note to readers that the material following the warning may trigger a post-traumatic stress reaction. In the early days of feminist blogging, trigger warnings were generally about sexual assault, and posted with the understanding that lots of women are sexual assault survivors, lots of women read feminist blogs, and graphic descriptions of rape might lead to panic attacks or other reactions that will really ruin someone's day. Easy enough to give readers a little heads up—a trigger warning—so that they can decide to avoid that material if they know that discussion of rape triggers debilitating reactions.

Trigger warnings in online spaces, though, have expanded widely and become more intricate, detailed, specific and obscure. Trigger warnings, and their cousin the "content note," are now included for a whole slew of potentially offensive or upsetting content, including but not limited to: misogyny, the death penalty, calories in a food item, terrorism, drunk driving, how much a person weighs, racism, gun violence, Stand Your Ground laws,[1] drones, homophobia, PTSD, slavery, victim-blaming, abuse, swearing, child abuse, self-injury, suicide, talk of drug use, descriptions of medical procedures, corpses, skulls, skeletons, needles, discussion of "isms," neuroatypical shaming,[2] slurs (including "stupid" or "dumb"), kidnapping, dental trauma, discussions of sex (even consensual), death or dying, spiders, insects, snakes, vomit, pregnancy, childbirth, blood, scarification,[3] Nazi paraphernalia, slimy things, holes and "anything that might inspire intrusive thoughts in people with OCD.:

It is true that everything on the above list might trigger a PTSD response in someone. The trouble with PTSD, though, is that its triggers are often unpredictable and individually specific—a certain smell, a particular song, being touched in that one way. It's impossible to account for all of them, because triggers are by their nature not particularly rational or universally foreseeable. Some are more common than others, though, which is why it seems reasonable enough for explicitly feminist spaces to include trigger warnings for things like assault and eating disorders.

5    College, though, is different. It is not a feminist blog. It is not a social justice Tumblr.

College isn't exactly the real world either, but it's a space for kinda-sorta adults to wade neck-deep into art, literature, philosophy, and the sciences, to explore new ideas, to expand their knowledge of the cultural canon, to interrogate power and to learn how to make an argument and to read a text. It is, hopefully, a space where the student is challenged and sometimes frustrated and sometimes deeply upset, a place where the student's world expands and pushes them to reach the outer edges —not a place that contracts to meet the student exactly where they are.

Which doesn't mean that individual students should not be given mental health accommodations. It's perfectly reasonable for a survivor of violence to ask a professor for a heads up if the reading list includes a piece with graphic descriptions of rape or violence, for example. But generalized trigger warnings aren't so much about helping people with PTSD as they are about a certain kind of performative feminism: they're a low-stakes way to use the right language to identify yourself as conscious of social justice issues. Even better is demanding a trigger warning—

---

[1] Laws allowing citizens to defend themselves against threats, whether perceived or real. [Eds.]
[2] Shaming the mentally ill. [Eds.]
[3] Scarring the body as a form of adornment. [Eds.]

that identifies you as even more aware, even more feminist, even more solicitous than the person who failed to adequately provide such a warning.

There is real harm in utilizing general trigger warnings in the classroom. Oberlin College recommends that its faculty "remove triggering material when it does not contribute directly to the course learning goals." When material is simply too important to take out entirely, the college recommends trigger warnings. For example, Oberlin says, Chinua Achebe's *Things Fall Apart* is a great and important book, but:

> ... it may trigger readers who have experienced racism, colonialism, religious persecution, violence, suicide, and more.

Students should be duly warned by the professor writing, for example, "Trigger warning: This book contains a scene of suicide."

On its face, that sounds fine (except for students who hate literary spoilers). But a trigger warning for what Oberlin identified as the book's common triggers—racism, colonialism, religious persecution, violence, suicide (and more!)—sets the tone for reading and understanding the book. It skews students' perceptions. It highlights particular issues as necessarily more upsetting than others, and directs students to focus on particular themes that have been singled out by the professor as traumatic.

At Rutgers, a student urged professors to use trigger warnings as a sort of Solomonic baby-splitting between two apparently equally bad choices: banning certain texts or introducing works that may cause psychological distress. Works the student mentioned as particularly triggering include F. Scott Fitzgerald's *The Great Gatsby*, Junot Diaz's *This Is How You Lose Her* and Virginia Woolf's *Mrs. Dalloway*. The warnings would be passage-by-passage, and effectively reach "a compromise between protecting students and defending their civil liberties."

But the space between comfort and freedom is not actually where universities should seek to situate college students. Students should be pushed to defend their ideas and to see the world from a variety of perspectives. Trigger warnings don't just warn students of potentially triggering material; they effectively shut down particular lines of discussion with "that's triggering." Students should—and do—have the right to walk out of any classroom. But students should also accept the challenge of exploring their own beliefs and responding to disagreement. Trigger warnings, of course, don't always shut down that kind of interrogation, but if feminist blogs are any example, they quickly become a way to short-circuit uncomfortable, unpopular or offensive arguments.

That should concern those of us who love literature, but it should particularly trouble the feminist and anti-racist bookworms among us. Trigger warnings are largely perceived as protecting young women and, to a lesser extent, other marginalized groups—people of color,

LGBT people, people with mental illnesses. That the warnings hinge on topics that are more likely to affect the lives of marginalized groups contributes to the general perception of members of those groups as weak, vulnerable and "other."

The kinds of suffering typically imaged and experienced in the white western male realm—war, intra-male violence—are standard. Traumas that impact women, people of color, LGBT people, the mentally ill and other groups whose collective lives far outnumber those most often canonized in the American or European classroom are set apart as different, as particularly *traumatizing*. Trigger warnings imply that our experiences are so unusual the pages detailing our lives can only be turned while wearing kid gloves.

There's a hierarchy of trauma there, as well as a dangerous assumption of inherent difference. There's a reinforcement of the toxic messages young women have gotten our entire lives: that we're inherently vulnerable.

15 And there's something lost when students are warned before they read Achebe or Diaz or Woolf, and when they read those writers first through the lens of trauma and fear.

Then, simply, there is the fact that the universe does not treat its members as if they come hand-delivered in a box clearly marked "fragile." The world can be a desperately ugly place, especially for women. That feminist blogs try to carve out a little section of the world that is a teeny bit safer for their readers is a credit to many of those spaces. Colleges, though, are not intellectual or emotional safe zones. Nor should they be.

Trauma survivors need tools to manage their triggers and cope with every day life. Universities absolutely should prioritize their needs—by making sure that mental health care is adequately funded, widely available and destigmatized.

But they do students no favors by pretending that every piece of potentially upsetting, triggering or even emotionally devastating content comes with a warning sign.

## Responding to Reading

MyWritingLab™

1. What are "trigger warnings"? What does Filipovic mean when she says, "they're a low-stakes way to use the right language to identify yourself as conscious of social issues" (7)?
2. What are Filipovic's concerns about trigger warnings? Why, according to Filipovic, do these warnings "do students no favors" (18)?
3. **Rhetorical Analysis** In paragraph 4, Filipovic concedes the possible advantages of trigger warnings. Does this concession undercut or strengthen her argument? Explain.

## Writing about Reading

MyWritingLab™

1. What is your assessment of trigger warnings? Do they serve a useful purpose, or do they infantilize students?

2. **Writing with Sources** What do instructors think about including trigger warnings in their course syllabi? Research this issue, looking particularly at websites aimed at academics—for example, the American Association of University Professors website and the Inside Higher Education website. On what points do instructors seem to agree? Where do they disagree? Write an essay that presents the results of your research and that takes a stand on this issue.

# WHY I WENT TO COLLEGE
## Martín Espada
### 1957–

*A poet, essayist, and translator, Martín Espada teaches in the English depart-ment at the University of Massachusetts, Amherst. The author of numerous books, including, most recently, the collection* The Meaning of the Shovel *(2014), he is also a Latino rights activist. In the following poem, the speaker considers one reason for attending college.*

If you don't,
my father said,
you better learn
to eat soup
through a straw,
'cause I'm gonna
break your jaw

5

## Responding to Reading

MyWritingLab™

1. How would you characterize the speaker's father?
2. What is the father's attitude toward college? toward his son? How do you know?
3. Espada's poems often deal with people who are marginalized because of their social, economic, and racial status. In what sense does the speaker in "Why I Went to College" fit this description?

## Writing about Reading

MyWritingLab™

Although "Why I Went to College" is humorous, it has a serious purpose. What point is the speaker making about college? about the immigrant experience in the United States?

--- FOCUS ---

### Is a College Education Worth the Money?

© John McPherson/Distributed by Universal Uclick via CartoonStock.com

"Graduating with a total college loan debt of
$120,000, Marissa Kulver... Graduating with a
total debt of $107,000, James Lehman..."

### Responding to the Image

MyWritingLab™

1. The cartoon above addresses the issues of high college tuition and student debt. Who is the cartoon's audience? How can you tell?
2. In what sense is this cartoon ironic? What point do you think the cartoonist wants to make with his use of irony? Do you think he gets his point across? Why or why not?

# IS COLLEGE WORTH IT?
# CLEARLY, NEW DATA SAY

## David Leonhardt

*1973–*

*The editor of the* New York Times *venture* The Upshot, *David Leonhardt analyzes economic and political policy in his work. The winner of the 2011 Pulitzer Prize for commentary, he also published the e-book* Here's the

Deal: How Washington Can Solve the Deficit and Spur Growth *(2013)*.
*In the following essay, Leonhardt argues for the value of a college degree.*

Some newly minted college graduates struggle to find work. Others accept jobs for which they feel overqualified. Student debt, meanwhile, has topped $1 trillion.

It's enough to create a wave of questions about whether a college education is still worth it.

A new set of income statistics answers those questions quite clearly: Yes, college is worth it, and it's not even close. For all the struggles that many young college graduates face, a four-year degree has probably never been more valuable.

The pay gap between college graduates and everyone else reached a record high last year, according to the new data, which is based on an analysis of Labor Department statistics by the Economic Policy Institute in Washington. Americans with four-year college degrees made 98 percent more an hour on average in 2013 than people without a degree. That's up from 89 percent five years earlier, 85 percent a decade earlier and 64 percent in the early 1980s.

There is nothing inevitable about this trend. If there were more college graduates than the economy needed, the pay gap would shrink. The gap's recent growth is especially notable because it has come after a rise in the number of college graduates, partly because many people went back to school during the Great Recession. That the pay gap has nonetheless continued growing means that we're still not producing enough of them.

"We have too few college graduates," says David Autor, an M.I.T. economist, who was not involved in the Economic Policy Institute's analysis. "We also have too few people who are prepared for college."

It's important to emphasize these shortfalls because public discussion today—for which we in the news media deserve some responsibility—often focuses on the undeniable fact that a bachelor's degree does not guarantee success. But of course it doesn't. Nothing guarantees success, especially after 15 years of disappointing economic growth and rising inequality.

When experts and journalists spend so much time talking about the limitations of education, they almost certainly are discouraging some teenagers from going to college and some adults from going back to earn degrees. (Those same experts and journalists are sending their own children to college and often obsessing over which one.) The decision not to attend college for fear that it's a bad deal is among the most economically irrational decisions anybody could make in 2014.

The much-discussed cost of college doesn't change this fact. According to a paper by Mr. Autor published Thursday in the journal *Science*, the true cost of a college degree is about *negative* $500,000. That's right: Over the long run, college is cheaper than free. Not going to college will cost you about half a million dollars.

10    Mr. Autor's paper—building on work by the economists Christopher Avery and Sarah Turner—arrives at that figure first by calculating the very real cost of tuition and fees. This amount is then subtracted from the lifetime gap between the earnings of college graduates and high school graduates. After adjusting for inflation and the time value of money, the net cost of college is negative $500,000, roughly double what it was three decades ago.

This calculation is necessarily imprecise, because it can't control for any pre-existing differences between college graduates and non-graduates—differences that would exist regardless of schooling. Yet other research, comparing otherwise similar people who did and did not graduate from college, has also found that education brings a huge return.

In a similar vein, the new Economic Policy Institute numbers show that the benefits of college don't go just to graduates of elite colleges, who typically go on to earn graduate degrees. The wage gap between people with only a bachelor's degree and people without such a degree has also kept rising.

Tellingly, though, the wage premium for people who have attended college without earning a bachelor's degree—a group that includes community-college graduates—has not been rising. The big economic returns go to people with four-year degrees. Those returns underscore the importance of efforts to reduce the college dropout rate, such as those at the University of Texas, which Paul Tough described in a recent *Times Magazine* article.

But what about all those alarming stories you hear about indebted, jobless college graduates?

15    The anecdotes may be real, yet the conventional wisdom often exaggerates the problem. Among four-year college graduates who took out loans, average debt is about $25,000, a sum that is a tiny fraction of the economic benefits of college. (My own student debt, as it happens, was almost identical to this figure, in inflation-adjusted terms.) And the unemployment rate in April for people between 25 and 34 years old with a bachelor's degree was a mere 3 percent.

I find the data from the Economic Policy Institute especially telling because the institute—a left-leaning research group—makes a point of arguing that education is not the solution to all of the economy's problems. That is important, too. College graduates, like almost everyone else, are suffering from the economy's weak growth and from the disproportionate share of this growth flowing to the very richest households.

The average hourly wage for college graduates has risen only 1 percent over the last decade, to about $32.60. The pay gap has grown mostly because the average wage for everyone else has fallen—5 percent, to about $16.50. "To me, the picture is people in almost every kind of job not being able to see their wages grow," Lawrence Mishel, the institute's president, told me. "Wage growth essentially stopped in 2002."

From the country's perspective, education can be only part of the solution to our economic problems. We also need to find other means for lifting living standards—not to mention ways to provide good jobs for people without college degrees.

But from almost any individual's perspective, college is a no-brainer. It's the most reliable ticket to the middle class and beyond. Those who question the value of college tend to be those with the luxury of knowing their own children will be able to attend it.

Not so many decades ago, high school was considered the frontier of education. Some people even argued that it was a waste to encourage Americans from humble backgrounds to spend four years of life attending high school. Today, obviously, the notion that everyone should attend 13 years of school is indisputable. 20

But there is nothing magical about 13 years of education. As the economy becomes more technologically complex, the amount of education that people need will rise. At some point, 15 years or 17 years of education will make more sense as a universal goal.

That point, in fact, has already arrived.

## Responding to Reading

MyWritingLab™

1. According to Leonhardt, what harm occurs when journalists talk about the "limitations of education" (8)?
2. How does the "conventional wisdom"(15) exaggerate the problems of unemployed college graduates?
3. **Rhetorical Analysis** What kinds of evidence does Leonhardt use to support his thesis? How convincing is this evidence? Explain.

## Writing about Reading

MyWritingLab™

1. What alternatives are there to college? In what instances do you think a four-year college degree may not be worth the cost?
2. **Writing with Sources** Some critics think that in the future, many people will forego a four-year college degree in favor of certification programs lasting a year or less—for example, programs in computer programming and health care. Research this topic, and find out how widespread certification programs are and how likely such programs are to be available in the future. Write an essay in which you report your findings.

# PLAN B: SKIP COLLEGE
## Jacques Steinberg

*The senior vice president of higher education and communications for the nonprofit organization Say Yes to Education, Jacques Steinberg writes about issues in American education. He is the author of* The Gatekeepers: Inside the Admissions Process of a Premier College *(2002) and* You Are an Ironman: How Six Weekend Warriors Chased Their Dream of Finishing the World's Toughest Triathlon *(2011). In the following essay, Steinberg explores "credible alternatives" to a college degree.*

What's the key to success in the United States?

Short of becoming a reality TV star, the answer is rote and, some would argue, rather knee-jerk: Earn a college degree.

The idea that four years of higher education will translate into a better job, higher earnings and a happier life—a refrain sure to be repeated this month at graduation ceremonies across the country—has been pounded into the heads of schoolchildren, parents and educators. But there's an underside to that conventional wisdom. Perhaps no more than half of those who began a four-year bachelor's degree program in the fall of 2006 will get that degree within six years, according to the latest projections from the Department of Education. (The figures don't include transfer students, who aren't tracked.)

For college students who ranked among the bottom quarter of their high school classes, the numbers are even more stark: 80 percent will probably never get a bachelor's degree or even a two-year associate's degree.

5     That can be a lot of tuition to pay, without a degree to show for it.

A small but influential group of economists and educators is pushing another pathway: for some students, no college at all. It's time, they say, to develop credible alternatives for students unlikely to be successful pursuing a higher degree, or who may not be ready to do so.

Whether everyone in college needs to be there is not a new question; the subject has been hashed out in books and dissertations for years. But the economic crisis has sharpened that focus, as financially struggling states cut aid to higher education.

Among those calling for such alternatives are the economists Richard K. Vedder of Ohio University and Robert I. Lerman of American University, the political scientist Charles Murray, and James E. Rosenbaum, an education professor at Northwestern. They would steer some students toward intensive, short-term vocational and career training, through expanded high school programs and corporate apprenticeships.

"It is true that we need more nanosurgeons than we did 10 to 15 years ago," said Professor Vedder, founder of the Center for College Affordability and Productivity, a research nonprofit in Washington. "But the numbers are still relatively small compared to the numbers of nurses' aides we're going to need. We will need hundreds of thousands of them over the next decade."

And much of their training, he added, might be feasible outside the 10 college setting.

College degrees are simply not necessary for many jobs. Of the 30 jobs projected to grow at the fastest rate over the next decade in the United States, only seven typically require a bachelor's degree, according to the Bureau of Labor Statistics.

Among the top 10 growing job categories, two require college degrees: accounting (a bachelor's) and postsecondary teachers (a doctorate). But this growth is expected to be dwarfed by the need for registered nurses, home health aides, customer service representatives and store clerks. None of those jobs require a bachelor's degree.

Professor Vedder likes to ask why 15 percent of mail carriers have bachelor's degrees, according to a 1999 federal study.

"Some of them could have bought a house for what they spent on their education," he said.

Professor Lerman, the American University economist, said some 15 high school graduates would be better served by being taught how to behave and communicate in the workplace.

Such skills are ranked among the most desired—even ahead of educational attainment—in many surveys of employers. In one 2008 survey of more than 2,000 businesses in Washington State, employers said entry-level workers appeared to be most deficient in being able to "solve problems and make decisions," "resolve conflict and negotiate," "cooperate with others" and "listen actively."

Yet despite the need, vocational programs, which might teach such skills, have been one casualty in the push for national education standards, which has been focused on preparing students for college.

While some educators propose a radical renovation of the community college system to teach work readiness, Professor Lerman advocates a significant national investment by government and employers in on-the-job apprenticeship training. He spoke with admiration, for example, about a program in the CVS pharmacy chain in which aspiring pharmacists' assistants work as apprentices in hundreds of stores, with many going on to study to become full-fledged pharmacists themselves.

"The health field is an obvious case where the manpower situation is less than ideal," he said. "I would try to work with some of the major employers to develop these kinds of programs to yield mastery in jobs that do demand high expertise."

20    While no country has a perfect model for such programs, Professor Lerman pointed to a modest study of a German effort done last summer by an intern from that country. She found that of those who passed the Abitur, the exam that allows some Germans to attend college for almost no tuition, 40 percent chose to go into apprenticeships in trades, accounting, sales management, and computers.

"Some of the people coming out of those apprenticeships are in more demand than college graduates," he said, "because they've actually managed things in the workplace."

Still, by urging that some students be directed away from four-year colleges, academics like Professor Lerman are touching a third rail of the education system. At the very least, they could be accused of lowering expectations for some students. Some critics go further, suggesting that the approach amounts to educational redlining, since many of the students who drop out of college are black or non-white Hispanics.

Peggy Williams, a counselor at a high school in suburban New York City with a student body that is mostly black or Hispanic, understands the argument for erring on the side of pushing more students toward college.

"If we're telling kids, 'You can't cut the mustard, you shouldn't go to college or university,' then we're shortchanging them from experiencing an environment in which they might grow," she said.

25    But Ms. Williams said she would be more willing to counsel some students away from the precollege track if her school, Mount Vernon High School, had a better vocational education alternative. Over the last decade, she said, courses in culinary arts, nursing, dentistry and heating and ventilation system repair were eliminated. Perhaps 1 percent of this year's graduates will complete a concentration in vocational courses, she said, compared with 40 percent a decade ago.

There is another rejoinder to the case against college: People with college and graduate degrees generally earn more than those without them, and face lower risks of unemployment, according to figures from the Bureau of Labor Statistics.

Even those who experience a few years of college earn more money, on average, with less risk of unemployment, than those who merely graduate from high school, said Morton Schapiro, an economist who is the president of Northwestern University.

"You get some return even if you don't get the sheepskin," Mr. Schapiro said.

He warned against overlooking the intangible benefits of a college experience—even an incomplete experience—for those who might not apply what they learned directly to their chosen work.

30    "It's not just about the economic return," he said. "Some college, whether you complete it or not, contributes to aesthetic appreciation, better health and better voting behavior."

Nonetheless, Professor Rosenbaum said, high school counselors and teachers are not doing enough to alert students unlikely to earn a college degree to the perilous road ahead.

"I'm not saying don't get the B.A," he said. "I'm saying, let's get them some intervening credentials, some intervening milestones. Then, if they want to go further in their education, they can."

## Responding to Reading

1. Why do some economists and educators believe that there should be alternatives for students who are not likely to succeed in (or are not ready for) college? Do you agree? Does Steinberg?
2. Do you think Steinberg's article makes a more convincing case *for* or *against* encouraging some students to "skip college"? Do you agree with Professors Vedder and Lerman (discussed in paragraphs 7–21) or with the educators quoted in paragraphs 22–31?
3. **Rhetorical Analysis** Where does Steinberg discuss the disadvantages of counseling students not to go to college? What specific disadvantages do his sources identify? Why do you think that he chose to put this discussion where he did?

## Writing about Reading

1. Do you think all students should be encouraged to go to college? Why or why not?
2. **Writing with Sources** Research highly successful people who either did not attend college or dropped out before getting a degree. Then, write an essay in which you make the case that college is not really necessary for success. Make sure that you use the examples that you have found in your research as well as Steinberg's essay to support your points.

# Is College Worth the Money?
## Answers from Six New Graduates

### Liz Dwyer

*In the following article from* GOOD *magazine, education editor Liz Dwyer compiles the responses of six 2011 college graduates to the question examined in this Focus section: Is a college education worth the money? An experienced teacher and an avid blogger, Dwyer writes about educational issues, parenting, and race. Her work has appeared in* Good Housekeeping *magazine, the online publication DivineCaroline, and numerous blogs, including her own, Los Angelista.*

Students are racking up astronomical amounts of debt and moving home with mom and dad after graduation because there are no jobs to be found. PayPal founder Peter Thiel is even encouraging students to drop out and try entrepreneurship instead because, he says, college isn't worth it. So we decided to ask some graduates from the class of 2011 what they think. Almost all of them are worried about paying back their student loan debt, and of those not going on to grad school, none will have traditional full-time jobs. But their answers about the value of college might surprise you.

**1) The Journalist**
**Name:** Sara Fletcher
**Age:** 22
**College:** Northwestern University
**Major:** Journalism
**Post-college plans:** Fletcher's headed to Portland, Oregon, for a public relations internship.
**Is college worth the money?**

"I chose Northwestern's Medill School of Journalism because it is top in the country. The connections here are undeniable and the opportunities for internships and post-grad jobs are better than I could have hoped for had I attended school in-state. I was challenged from the moment I arrived at Medill to basically act as a full-time reporter. Those skills, which I was challenged to develop very independently in and outside of the classroom will be incredibly useful for my work in PR and marketing. That said, I think college, particularly at a top school, is somewhat of a luxury and privilege. It's a chance for a lot of people, myself included, to take four years to really focus ourselves, figure out our passions in life, and gather the skills, critical thinking and connections to live out those passions. Because of the high price, for many that I've met, the luxury of four years at an elite school to 'find yourself' sometimes isn't as immediately justifiable, particularly when a high school grad has the life skills and confidence to enter the working world."

**2) The Dentist**
**Name:** Leah Munson
**Age:** 21
**College:** Binghamton University
**Major:** Biological Sciences
**Post-college plans:** Munson's hoping to get into dental school and be an orthodontist.
**Is college worth the money?**

"I hated college while I was there because I felt like everyone was wasting my time. I have known what I wanted to do since I was 12 and sitting in yet another classroom learning material that only grazed my interest was frustrating. I rushed through my undergraduate work, graduating in 3 years so that I could finally get to where I wanted to be.

Although I have learned a lot in college and looking back I believe that it was very important in shaping who I am today, I hate the fact that I just spent years of my life forcing myself to learn information that I likely won't use again. College is not shaping students for their careers but rather for society. I'm not the person I was when I went to college but not because of anything I learned in a classroom. I'm different because it was a social bootcamp of sorts. Seeing as I already know what I want to do, I took the knowledge with a grain of salt. I was glad to be learning it and found it interesting but I was forced to acknowledge that I would likely never use it again."

### 3) The Startup Guru
**Name:** Ashwin Anandani
**Age:** 22
**College:** Northwestern University
**Major:** Economics
**Post-college plans:** Anandani graduated early, managed to raise some money for a social change startup idea and moved to the Bay Area to pursue it. In the meantime, to keep a roof over his head, he also found a paid part-time job with another startup.
**Is college worth the money?**

"I don't think the value of a college is equal to the sum of its graduates' wages. I paid a couple hundred thousand dollars in total for my (almost) 4 years at university, and while I came out being able to think well, which is what I believe university is really meant to 'teach' you, I can only say that the university contributed a very small share of that ability. Now that I've been out, I'm thinking, 'I really just paid money to be assigned papers and math so I could have a piece of paper that serves as a filtering mechanism for corporations' HR departments?'

I would say my assignments and college requirements were more of a very arduous process of creating a 'fallback plan' so I don't end up on the streets if my startup fails. It's almost a monopoly in terms of options, too—'If you don't go to college, where will you go?'—so we pay the high price to be locked into a degree and we learn how to make standardized documents and take standardized tests. Too bad the world isn't standardized like my degree was."

### 4) The Teacher
**Name:** Alexis Valdez
**Age:** 22
**College:** Holy Cross College
**Major:** Elementary Education, K-6 and ENL (English as a New Language)
**Post-college plans:** Valdez, who is the first in her family to go to college, doesn't yet have a permanent teaching position. She

CHAPTER 4 FOCUS

says she plans to keep submitting applications to all the school districts in her area, and hopes to substitute teach to pay the bills.

**Is college worth the money?**

"I think that even though right now I'm in a tight spot as far as a job and finances go, college was definitely worth the money. In my specific field the job market is particularly sparse, though I wouldn't be as marketable in the teaching world if I hadn't had the opportunity to get real classroom experiences through my college program. I will admit that I'm not pleased to be deep in college debt, but in the long run, I believe that getting a college education was the best choice I could have made for myself to ensure a better future."

### 5) The Entrepreneur
**Name:** Arnela Sulovic
**Age:** 21
**School:** University of Southern California
**Major:** Communication
**Post-college plans:** Sulovic, who immigrated from war-torn Bosnia, is the first in her family to go to college and graduated in three years to save money. She wants to start her own business, but right now she's working as a summer resident adviser for off-campus housing and a sales/partnership intern at Thrillist Rewards. She's still looking for a full-time job.

**Is college worth the money?**

"I strongly believe that college is worth the money. Although everything I learned in the classroom may not be applicable to my career, USC gave me access to unparalleled experiences, introduced me to incredible people and ideas, and broadened my perspective. Furthermore, the extracurricular activities that I participated in helped me build real-world skills and leadership experiences. There are many benefits that one can gain only by experiencing a higher education. If I had known exactly what I wanted to do post-graduation, I could have taken advantage of more opportunities in college. I wish all college classes were hands-on, skill building, and exploratory."

### 6) The Lawyer
**Name:** Beverly Ozowara
**Age:** 21
**College:** University of Notre Dame
**Major:** Psychology & Film, Television, Theatre
**Post-college plans:** Ozowara will be attending Valparaiso Law School and wants to be a family lawyer.

**Is college worth the money?**

"I think that college is definitely worth it, but not because I learned specific things that would be helpful with my career. It was worth it for the valuable resources and connections I formed. It was also worth it because of the priceless undergraduate experience that I couldn't have gotten easily anywhere else. For example, I had the opportunity to travel (for a third of the normal cost) to Brazil with the Notre Dame Concert Band. During the trip, I was able to do things like perform at the oldest concert hall in the Americas and to swim in the Amazon River. I will admit though that I did not learn very many things that are specific to my career. It would have been helpful if there had been a pre-law program or more advising since freshmen year of college geared toward getting internships and familiarizing myself with corporations and the business world."

## Responding to Reading

MyWritingLab™

1. What would the six students change about their undergraduate experiences? What would they keep the same?
2. On which points do these six new graduates seem to agree? On which points do they disagree?
3. **Rhetorical Analysis** This article was presented as six separate interviews. Would it have been better if it were presented as a unified essay with a clear thesis statement? What would have been gained and lost by this approach?

## Writing about Reading

MyWritingLab™

1. Do you think that college should prepare you for life or for a career?
2. **Writing with Sources** Research the state of vocational training in the United States. Then, write an essay in which you argue for or against the advisability of encouraging more high school students to pursue vocational training as opposed to four-year college degrees.

# WIDENING THE FOCUS

## For Critical Reading and Writing

Referring specifically to the three readings in this chapter's Focus section (and possibly to additional sources as well), write an essay in which you answer the question, "Is a College Education Worth the Money?"

## For Further Reading

The following readings can suggest additional perspectives for thinking about the value of a college education.

- Frederick Douglass, "Learning to Read and Write" (p. 132)
- Steven Pinker, "Mind over Mass Media" (p. 195)
- Christina Hoff Sommers, "The War against Boys" (p. 247)

## For Focused Research

As tuition costs continue to rise, students, educators, politicians, and the general public are increasingly asking if a college education is worth the money. In preparation for writing an essay that answers this question, search the Internet for up-to-date statistics on lifetime earnings of college graduates versus nongraduates. Then, write an essay in which you consider how having (or not having) a college degree affects lifetime employment, male versus female earnings, and initial access to the job market. Be sure to support your points with the statistics and examples you find.

## Beyond the Classroom

Interview six adults, three with four-year college degrees and three without. One person in each category should be in his or her 60s, one in his or her 40s, and one a recent college graduate in his or her 20s.

- Ask those without college degrees if they believe they have suffered financially because of their lack of higher education.
- Ask those with college degrees whether they believe the money they spent on college was worth the expense.
- Ask those in both groups to evaluate their professional and economic success.

Then, write an essay that draws some conclusions about the perceived value of a college education for people in different age groups.

— EXPLORING ISSUES AND IDEAS —

## Issues in Education

MyWritingLab™
Visit Chapter 4, "Issues in Education," in MyWritingLab to test your understanding of the chapter objectives.

Write an essay in response to one of the following prompts, which are suitable for assignments that require the use of outside sources as well as for assignments that are not source-based.

1. Many of the readings in this chapter try to define exactly what constitutes a "good" education. Write an essay in which you define a good education.

2. According to Christina Hoff Sommers (p. 94), instructors with conservative political views are being systematically excluded from many American colleges and universities. Write a letter to Sommers in which you agree or disagree with her contentions. Make sure that you address Sommers's specific points and that you use examples from both the essay and your own experience to support your position.

3. In her essay "The Good Immigrant Student" (p. 83), Bich Minh Nguyen discusses the difficulties immigrant students face in American schools. At one point in her essay she says that she has never "gotten over the terror of being called on in class, or the dread in knowing that I'm expected to contribute to class discussion" (89). Assume that you are a tutor in your school's writing center and that you have been asked to write an essay to be included in an orientation booklet. In this essay, your goal is to address the concerns that Nguyen expresses. Be supportive, and give specific advice for overcoming these problems.

4. All the writers in this chapter believe in the power of education to change a person. For many people, this process begins with a teacher who has a profound influence on them. Write an essay in which you discuss such a teacher. What, in your opinion, made this teacher so effective? In what ways did contact with this teacher change you?

5. Write an essay in which you develop a definition of good teaching, considering the relationship of the teacher to the class, the standards teachers should use to evaluate students, and what students should gain from their educational experience. Refer to the ideas of John Holt (p. 78) in your essay.

# 5

# THE POLITICS OF LANGUAGE

*In this chapter, you will learn to*
- analyze readings about the politics of language
- compose essays about the politics of language

During the years he spent in prison, political activist Malcolm X became increasingly frustrated by his inability to express himself in writing, so he began the tedious and often frustrating task of copying words from the dictionary—page by page. The eventual result was that, for the first time, he could pick up a book and read it with understanding: "Anyone who has read a great deal," he says, "can imagine the new world that opened." In addition, by becoming a serious

Malcolm X giving a speech in Washington, D.C., 1961

reader, Malcolm X was able to develop the ideas about race, politics, and economics that he presented so forcefully after he was released from prison.

In our society, language is constantly being manipulated for political ends. This fact should come as no surprise if we consider the potential power of words. Often, the power of a word comes not from its dictionary definition, or *denotation,* but from its *connotations,* the associations that surround it. These connotations can be subtle, giving language the power to confuse and even to harm. For example, whether a doctor who performs an abortion is "terminating a pregnancy" or "murdering a preborn child" is not just a matter of semantics. It is also a political issue, one that has provoked both debate and violence. This potential for misunderstanding, disagreement, deception, and possibly danger makes careful word choice very important.

The Focus section of this chapter (p. 158) addresses the question, "How Free Should Free Speech Be?" As the essays in this section illustrate, the answer to this question is neither straightforward nor simple. In "Shut Up and Play Nice: How the Western World Is Limiting Free Speech," Jonathan Turley discusses the worldwide tendency to limit freedom of expression; in "Kindly Inquisitors, Revisited," Jonathan Rauch defends freedom of expression, no matter how hateful it may be, and in "Should Neo-Nazis Be Allowed Free Speech?" Thane Rosenbaum examines the harm that unbridled free speech can cause.

John F. Kennedy giving a speech in
Berlin, Germany, 1963

## PREPARING TO READ AND WRITE

As you read and prepare to write about the essays in this chapter, you may consider the following questions:

- What assumptions does the writer have about his or her audience? How can you tell?

- What is the writer's primary purpose? For example, is it to analyze ideas about language or to challenge traditional ideas about language use?

- What genre is the writer using? For example, is the reading a memoir? a study of language use? an argument? How do the conventions of this genre influence the writer's choices?

- What appeals does the writer use? For example, does he or she appeal primarily to reason? to emotion? to a combination of the two? Is this the most effective strategy?

- Does the selection deal primarily with written or spoken language?

- Does the writer place more emphasis on the denotations or the connotations of words?

- Does the writer make any distinctions between language applied to males and language applied to females? Do you consider such distinctions valid?

- Does the writer discuss language in the context of a particular culture? Does he or she see language as a unifying or a divisive factor?

- In what ways would the writer like to change or reshape language? What do you see as the possible advantages or disadvantages of such change?

- Does the writer believe that people are shaped by language or that language is shaped by people?

- Does the writer see language as having a particular social or political function? In what sense?

- Does the writer see language as empowering?

- Does the writer make assumptions about people's status on the basis of their use of language? Do these assumptions seem justified?

- Does the writer make a convincing case for the importance of language?

- Is the writer's focus primarily on language's ability to help or its power to harm?

- In what ways are your ideas about the power of words similar to or different from the writer's?

- How is the essay like and unlike other essays in this chapter?

# THE CURIOUS GRAMMAR OF POLICE SHOOTINGS

## Radley Balko

### 1975–

*An opinion blogger for the* Washington Post *blog* The Watch, *Radley Balko writes about issues related to criminal justice, surveillance, and civil liberties. He is the author of* Overkill: The Rise of Paramilitary Police Raids in America *(2006) and* Rise of the Warrior Cop: The Militarization of America's Police Forces *(2013). In the following blog post, Balko dissects the language commonly used to describe police shootings.*

You're probably familiar with the weaselly way politicians tend to apologize when they've been caught red-handed. The most famous example is the use of the line, *mistakes were made.* Use of the passive voice in an admission of wrongdoing has become so common that the political consultant William Schneider suggested a few years ago that it be referred to as the "past exonerative" tense.

You'll often see a similar grammatical device when a police officer shoots someone. Communications officers at policy agencies are deft at contorting the English language to minimize culpability of an officer or of the agency. So instead of ...

... Mayberry Dep. Barney Fife shot and killed a burglary suspect last night ...

You'll see ...

... last night, a burglary suspect was shot and killed in an officer-involved shooting.

It's a way of describing a shooting without assigning responsibility. Most police departments do this. But we can take a few recent examples from the Los Angeles Police Department. Here, for example, is how the LAPD describes a typical shooting that does not involve a police officer:

On February 10, 2014, around 6:10 p.m., the victim was in the parking lot in the 13640 block of Burbank Boulevard, to the rear, when he was confronted by the suspect. The suspect produced a semi-automatic handgun and fired numerous times striking the victim in the torso.

Note the active voice. We have a clear subject, verb, and direct object. Contrast that with how the LAPD has described a few recent shootings by LAPD officers:

When the officers arrived they were confronted by a Hispanic male armed with a sword. The officers attempted to take the suspect into custody by using a taser but it was ineffective. The suspect then ran towards the officers still armed with the sword and an officer-involved-shooting occurred.

– May 2, 2014

The officer exited his police vehicle and began to give commands to the suspect at which time he observed Gomez was armed with a box cutter. Gomez refused to comply with the officers' commands and began to approach him, still armed with the box cutter. The officer deployed his OC spray which did not appear to affect Gomez. When the suspect continued to advance on the officer while refusing to comply with his repeated commands, an officer-involved shooting (OIS) occurred.

– April 28, 2014

While still in a position of cover, the officers encountered a male suspect who was armed with a weapon at which time an officer involved shooting occurred.

–May 12, 2014

5    I'm not questioning whether any of these shootings were justified. I'm just drawing your attention to the language.

There was a particularly egregious example of this with the L.A. Sheriff's Department last April. While responding to reports of a stabbing, LASD deputies shot and killed 30-year-old John Winkler. In an initial press release, the department said Winkler "aggressed the deputies and a deputy-involved shooting occurred." Note that Winkler's actions were put in the active voice, while the officers' actions were put in the passive.

As it turns out, Winkler was innocent. He hadn't "aggressed" the officers at all. Rather, he and another victim, both of whom had been stabbed, were running toward the police to escape their assailant. (The deputies shot the other victim, too.) The press release incorrectly assigned criminal culpability to an innocent stabbing victim, but carefully avoided prematurely assigning responsibility to the deputies who shot him.

One of my favorite examples came in 2011, after the DEA and local police burst into the home of an innocent family during a botched raid. During the raid, a 13-year-old girl was pulled from her bed at gunpoint. She vomited, had an asthma attack, and passed out. The family told a local newspaper that the agents then threatened to kill their dogs unless they stopped them from barking. The DEA later put out a press release apology with this quote from John P. Gilbride, the special agent in charge:

"We sincerely regret that while attempting to execute an arrest warrant for a member of this drug trafficking organization, the innocent McKay family was inadvertently affected by this enforcement operation."

*Inadvertently affected!*

And while *who* was attempting to execute a warrant? The offending parties aren't even mentioned. In fact, Gilbride so butchers the English language here, he nearly suggests that the McKay family conducted the raid themselves.

I bring all of this up because of a more recent example from south-  10
ern Georgia. Last week, a deputy in Coffee County shot a 10-year-old boy in the leg. The deputy was participating in a manhunt for a robbery suspect who had earlier shot a police officer. Here's how a report from Albany, Georgia TV station WALB described the incident:

> The situation of how the child was shot remains unclear. The Georgia Bureau of Investigation in Eastman was called to investigate the shooting. Sheriff Wooten said a deputy, who was not named, was approaching the property when a dog ran up to him. The deputy's gun fired one shot, missing the dog and hitting the child. It was not clear if the gun was accidentally fired by the deputy.

If a kid hadn't been shot in the leg, this would be downright comical. No reasonable person would believe this deputy intentionally sought out and shot a 10-year-old. The most plausible scenario is that the deputy tried to shoot the dog, and mistakenly shot the kid instead. (It certainly wouldn't be the first time a cop has mistakenly shot a citizen, his partner, or himself, while trying to kill a dog.) Perhaps he even mistook the kid for the suspect, or was startled by the kid. It's less plausible, but still possible, that the deputy didn't intend to fire his gun at all, in which case he's still negligent for handling his gun in a way that caused him to accidentally fire it.

What *isn't remotely* plausible is that the deputy's gun jumped out of its holster, walked up to the kid, and shot the kid in the leg. Physics tells us that the gun could not have fired without some sort of intermediary action on the part of the deputy. Yet the sheriff's explanation, at least the way the WALB reporter relays it, leaves open just that possibility.

All of this wouldn't be much more troubling than your typical grammatical ass-covering by other public officials if it weren't for the fact that (a) we're talking about people getting shot and killed, and (b) in most cases, the same police agencies engaging in linguistic gymnastics to publicly deflect responsibility for police shootings will inevitably be in charge of investigating the same officers for the same shootings.

## Responding to Reading

MyWritingLab™

1. What is the passive voice? Why does the political consultant William Schneider call it the "past exonerative" tense (1)?

2. Why does Balko think that the use of the passive voice to report police shootings is important? Do you agree with him?
3. **Rhetorical Analysis**　In paragraph 5, Balko says that he is questioning the language that was used to describe the shootings, not the shootings themselves. Why do you think he makes this distinction? Do you think it is necessary?

## Writing about Reading

1. Do you agree with the points that Balko makes about the use of the passive voice? Do you think it minimizes culpability?
2. **Writing with Sources**　Go online and read newspaper accounts of several recent police shootings. Do these accounts use the passive voice to avoid responsibility? Write an essay in which you analyze the use of the "past exonerative" in several news articles. What do you conclude about this rhetorical strategy and its likely effects on readers?

# IS SOCIAL MEDIA HURTING OUR SOCIAL SKILLS? [INFOGRAPHIC]

## Chase Fleming

*An avid blogger and web strategist, Chase Fleming started the website CommunicationStudies.com, where the following infographic appeared. In it, Fleming illustrates the impact of social media on the quality of our relationships and lives.*

Over the past decade, the Internet has permanently changed the way that the average person communicates with loved ones, friends and colleagues. Some of these changes are positive. People who live abroad can keep in touch with their families, for instance, and people with irregular hours can use websites like Facebook to avoid missing out on conversations with their friends.

However, social media may have a dark side. Education website Schools.com and social website Badoo recently compiled research to create an infographic that shows some of the ways that social media changes the ways that we interact and how we've created a distressingly strong connection with websites like Facebook.

For instance, research shows that worldwide Facebook users as a whole log about 19,963 years on the website every day. That doesn't count mobile users, who log an average of 441 minutes on the website per month in the United States alone.

Overall, 39 percent of Americans spend more time socializing online than in face-to-face interactions. 24 percent of survey respondents said that they had missed a major life event because they were too busy trying to document it for a social media website like Facebook.

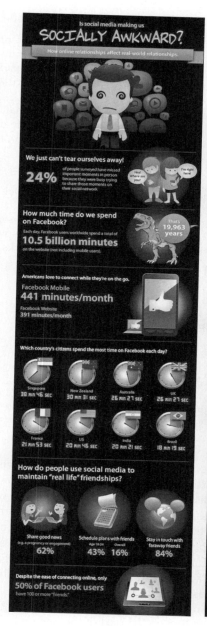

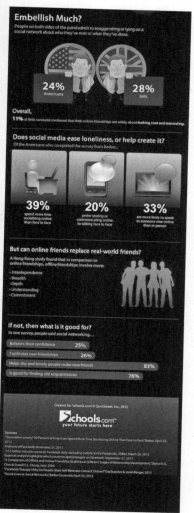

The infographic also notes that social websites make it easier for    5
socially awkward people to make friends and interact. Social networks
are also great for reconnecting with old friends, but social media users
should certainly note that online networks don't always change the
way that we communicate for the better.

## Responding to Reading

1. An **infographic** presents information or data visually. What kind of information does Fleming's infographic present? What would be the advantages and disadvantages of presenting this information in words alone?
2. What is the main point of Fleming's infographic? Write a sentence that summarizes this infographic's thesis.
3. **Rhetorical Analysis** In what order does Fleming present information? Why do you think he chose to arrange his infographic the way he did? Would another order have been more effective? Explain.

## Writing about Reading

1. How has the Internet changed the way you communicate with people? Are these changes positive?
2. **Writing with Sources** Research the ways in which educators and researchers think social media have changed the way people interact. Then, write an essay in which you address Fleming's claim that online networks can negatively affect the way people communicate.

# WILL TEXT MESSAGING DESTROY THE ENGLISH LANGUAGE?

## Dallas Spires

*Author of the blog* Neither Here nor There *Dallas Spires writes for online publications such as* Humanities 360. *In the following essay, Spires considers the historical and rhetorical contexts of texting.*

A new form of written—in this case typed—English has emerged in the last few years that really troubles a lot of people: text messaging. Lately, it has been treated as an entirely new phenomenon, when it has its roots in instant messaging on the internet. This form of "written" language uses different grammatical standards and many abbreviations. In many cases, spelling is ignored (so long as the reader can recognize what word is being sent) and verbs are not conjugated. Those of us who prefer more traditional forms of written English fear for the sanctity of our previous language.

To assume that text messaging will "destroy" the English language shows a certain lack of understanding on the part of the person holding this misconception. Texting is still English. The people using this form of "written" English are still communicating in English. To understand what is being typed, they must have a good understanding of syntax and grammar already. They must be able to recognize speech and sentence patterns, to predict accurately what someone is going to say, especially since the words probably won't be typed out. Unfortunately, for many young people, this understanding is so fundamental that they can't access it in any way other than through texting.

With all the abbreviations and acronyms used in typing text messages, texting reads like some sort of code. This is nothing new. In fact, what you are reading now is a code. It is a code that many of us understand because we have been taught this code by the adults and other people we accept as linguistic authorities. This code relates ideas in the English language. So does Morse code, which is a system of sounds transcribed as dots and dashes that represent messages interpreted as recognizable English by those people who understand the code. However, it doesn't sound or look anything like the code I'm currently using.

The use of codes is widespread, from law enforcement agencies to businesses to criminal organizations. Each one uses a code exclusive to it, except maybe in the case of street gangs. Military groups use codes no one else understands so that ideas in English may be communicated without being easily intercepted. Businesses may use codes simply for ease of communication. Even outside of any code, business communication already uses its own grammatical standards, which can be just as strict as those in English classrooms. Criminal organizations developed codes to deliver messages without being found out. In the case of street gangs, spoken and written codes are used not only to deliver messages within each individual gang but also across enemy lines. The codes they use, of course, are not meant to be understood by the general public but only by the intended audience.

If most of us were to pick up an Old English edition of *Beowulf*, 5 we would swear up and down it was not written in English, when it was. It was written in one of many accepted forms of English used at the time. In fact, what we generally refer to as Old English is actually the West Saxon dialect of Old English. The language was far less uniform during those times than it is today, even with different versions of English appearing more and more within our culture. Only a few years, relatively speaking, after the publication of *Beowulf*, another version of English appeared: Middle English. While Old English contained much Celtic influence, Middle English reflected the French influence at the time. And if a lack of uniform spelling can undermine English, then it's amazing we still speak it after the spelling atrocities committed during the Middle English period. Modern English appeared during Shakespeare's time, which does not look very "modern" for most of us, though it is much easier to understand—even for all its difficulty—than Middle or Old English. The spoken and written forms of English have changed quite a lot during the existence of the language. Even in the last century, there have been many changes and additions made to our understanding of our language.

If we feel that the English language is being undermined simply because the common, accepted written code is falling out of favor, then we need to turn to our teachers, our advertisers, our television stations, where our young people are going to find examples of written or typed English. Our teachers need to put a stronger effort into teaching traditional grammar and mechanics. Currently, in the state of Georgia, it is frowned upon to teach grammar in "isolation," that is, to focus only on grammar instead of putting it in the context of some type of literature (hello, all of the greats stretched or broke the precious rules we hold so dear, so why should we put those rules in context just to confuse our students THAT much more?). This standard of English education in Georgia comes out of the state's response to No Child Left Behind, and many other states have adopted the same standard. Since education is a public issue (public education?), a discussion needs to be opened with the local and state boards if we feel they are not doing their jobs. As for advertisers and the news media, if we feel that the youth are not getting a healthy dose of "good" English, there are ways of letting these agencies know in no uncertain terms that it will no longer be tolerated. The word "boycott" comes to mind.

Texting is a new code used to communicate ideas in English accurately and with ease and efficiency through a specific medium and for an almost exclusive audience. The level to which this code is used seems to depend on the age of the user. Teens seem to be the most proficient at texting, while users in their 20's and 30's seem to use it less and less. Part of the prevalence of this code comes from the fact that the establishment does not like it and cannot read it. While I agree that traditional forms of written and spoken English need to be preserved, I also believe that we all need to understand what is appropriate in different situations.

## Responding to Reading

MyWritingLab™

1. How is texting just like other forms of written English? How is it different? Why does assuming that texting will destroy the English language show "a lack of understanding" (2)?
2. What does Spires mean by saying that texting "is a new code" (7)? In what sense is texting "code"?
3. **Rhetorical Analysis** Spires begins his essay by defining texting. Do you think this extended definition is necessary? Why do you think Spires uses this opening strategy?

## Writing about Reading

MyWritingLab™

1. Do you think that texting has a positive or negative effect on your ability to communicate?
2. **Writing with Sources** Suppose you were asked to debate the question of whether text messaging is destroying the English language. On the one side of this issue are those who say that texting promotes ungrammatical constructions, misspellings, and slang. On the other are those who say that texting enriches communication and forces people to be concise and direct. Investigate this question, and choose a position to support. Then, write an essay that develops your ideas on the issue.

# MOTHER TONGUE

## Amy Tan

### 1952–

*Amy Tan was born to parents who had emigrated from China only a few years earlier. (Her given name is actually An-mei, which means "blessing from America.") A workaholic, Tan began writing stories as a means of personal therapy, and these stories eventually became the highly successful* The Joy Luck Club *(1987), a novel about Chinese-born mothers and their American-born daughters that was later made into a widely praised film. Tan's other books include five more novels, a work of nonfiction, and two illustrated children's books. In the following essay, which was originally delivered as a speech, Tan considers her relationship with her own mother, concentrating on the different "Englishes" they use to communicate with each other and with the world.*

I am not a scholar of English or literature. I cannot give you much more than personal opinions on the English language and its variations in this country or others.

I am a writer. And by that definition, I am someone who has always loved language. I am fascinated by language in daily life. I spend a great deal of my time thinking about the power of language—the way it can evoke an emotion, a visual image, a complex idea, or a simple truth. Language is the tool of my trade. And I use them all—all the Englishes I grew up with.

Recently, I was made keenly aware of the different Englishes I do use. I was giving a talk to a large group of people, the same talk I had already given to half a dozen other groups. The nature of the talk was about my writing, my life, and my book, *The Joy Luck Club.* The talk was going along well enough, until I remembered one major difference that made the whole talk sound wrong. My mother was in the room. And it was perhaps the first time she had heard me give a lengthy speech, using the kind of English I have never used with her. I was saying things like, "The intersection of memory upon imagination" and "There is an aspect of my fiction that relates to thus-and-thus"—a speech filled with carefully wrought grammatical phrases, burdened, it suddenly seemed to me, with nominalized forms, past perfect tenses, conditional phrases, all the forms of standard English that I had learned in school and through books, the forms of English I did not use at home with my mother.

Just last week, I was walking down the street with my mother, and I again found myself conscious of the English I was using, and the English I do use with her. We were talking about the price of new and used furniture and I heard myself saying this: "Not waste money that way." My husband was with us as well, and he didn't notice any switch in my English. And then I realized why. It's because over the twenty years we've been together I've often used that same kind of English with him, and sometimes he even uses it with me. It has become our language of intimacy, a different sort of English that relates to family talk, the language I grew up with.

5      So you'll have some idea of what this family talk I heard sounds like, I'll quote what my mother said during a recent conversation which I videotaped and then transcribed. During this conversation, my mother was talking about a political gangster in Shanghai who had the same last name as her family's, Du, and how the gangster in his early years wanted to be adopted by her family, which was rich by comparison. Later, the gangster became more powerful, far richer than my mother's family, and one day showed up at my mother's wedding to pay his respects. Here's what she said in part:

"Du Yusong having business like fruit stand. Like off the street kind. He is Du like Du Zong—but not Tsung-ming Island people. The local people call putong, the river east side, he belong to that side local people. The man want to ask Du Zong father take him in like become own family. Du Zong father wasn't look down on him, but didn't take seriously, until that man big like become a mafia. Now important person, very hard to inviting him. Chinese way, came only to show respect, don't stay for dinner. Respect for making big celebration, he shows up. Mean gives lots of respect. Chinese custom. Chinese social life that way. If too important won't have to stay too long. He come to my wedding. I didn't see, I heard it. I gone to boy's side, they have YMCA dinner. Chinese age I was nineteen."

You should know that my mother's expressive command of English belies how much she actually understands. She reads the Forbes report, listens to *Wall Street Week*, converses daily with her stockbroker, reads all of Shirley MacLaine's[1] books with ease—all kinds of things I can't begin to understand. Yet some of my friends tell me they understand 50 percent of what my mother says. Some say they understand 80 to 90 percent. Some say they understand none of it, as if she were speaking pure Chinese. But to me, my mother's English is perfectly clear, perfectly natural. It's my mother tongue. Her language, as I hear it, is vivid, direct, full of observation and imagery. That was the language that helped shape the way I saw things, expressed things, made sense of the world.

Lately, I've been giving more thought to the kind of English my mother speaks. Like others, I have described it to people as "broken" or "fractured" English. But I wince when I say that. It has always bothered me that I can think of no way to describe it other than "broken," as if it

---

[1]Actress known for her autobiographical books, in which she traces her many past lives. [Eds.]

were damaged and needed to be fixed, as if it lacked a certain wholeness and soundness. I've heard other terms used, "limited English," for example. But they seem just as bad, as if everything is limited, including people's perceptions of the limited English speaker.

I know this for a fact, because when I was growing up, my mother's "limited" English limited *my* perception of her. I was ashamed of her English. I believed that her English reflected the quality of what she had to say. That is, because she expressed them imperfectly her thoughts were imperfect. And I had plenty of empirical evidence to support me: the fact that people in department stores, at banks, and at restaurants did not take her seriously, did not give her good service, pretended not to understand her, or even acted as if they did not hear her.

My mother has long realized the limitations of her English as well. When I was fifteen, she used to have me call people on the phone to pretend I was she. In this guise, I was forced to ask for information or even to complain and yell at people who had been rude to her. One time it was a call to her stockbroker in New York. She had cashed out her small portfolio and it just so happened we were going to go to New York the next week, our very first trip outside California. I had to get on the phone and say in an adolescent voice that was not very convincing, "This is Mrs. Tan." 10

And my mother was standing in the back whispering loudly, "Why he don't send me check, already two weeks late. So mad he lie to me, losing me money."

And then I said in perfect English, "Yes, I'm getting rather concerned. You had agreed to send the check two weeks ago, but it hasn't arrived."

Then she began to talk more loudly. "What he want, I come to New York tell him front of his boss, you cheating me?" And I was trying to calm her down, make her be quiet, while telling the stockbroker, "I can't tolerate any more excuses. If I don't receive the check immediately, I am going to have to speak to your manager when I'm in New York next week." And sure enough, the following week there we were in front of this astonished stockbroker, and I was sitting there red-faced and quiet, and my mother, the real Mrs. Tan, was shouting at his boss in her impeccable broken English.

We used a similar routine just five days ago, for a situation that was far less humorous. My mother had gone to the hospital for an appointment, to find out about a benign brain tumor a CAT scan had revealed a month ago. She said she had spoken very good English, her best English, no mistakes. Still, she said, the hospital did not apologize when they said they had lost the CAT scan and she had come for nothing. She said they did not seem to have any sympathy when she told them she was anxious to know the exact diagnosis, since her husband and son had both died of brain tumors. She said they would not give her any more information until the next time and she would have to make another appointment for that. So she said she would not leave until the doctor called her daughter. She wouldn't budge. And when the doctor finally called her daughter, me, who spoke in perfect English—lo and behold—we had assurances the CAT scan would be found, promises that a conference call on Monday would be held, and apologies for any suffering my mother had gone through for a most regrettable mistake.

15     I think my mother's English almost had an effect on limiting my possibilities in life as well. Sociologists and linguists probably will tell you that a person's developing language skills are more influenced by peers. But I do think that the language spoken in the family, especially in immigrant families which are more insular, plays a large role in shaping the language of the child. And I believe that it affected my results on achievement tests, IQ tests, and the SAT. While my English skills were never judged as poor, compared to math, English could not be considered my strong suit. In grade school I did moderately well, getting perhaps B's, sometimes B-pluses, in English and scoring perhaps in the sixtieth or seventieth percentile on achievement tests. But those scores were not good enough to override the opinion that my true abilities lay in math and science, because in those areas I achieved A's and scored in the ninetieth percentile or higher.

This was understandable. Math is precise; there is only one correct answer. Whereas, for me at least, the answers on English tests were always a judgment call, a matter of opinion and personal experience. Those tests were constructed around items like fill-in-the-blank sentence completion, such as, "Even though Tom was _____, Mary thought he was _____." And the correct answer always seemed to be the most bland combinations of thoughts, for example, "Even though Tom was shy, Mary thought he was charming," with the grammatical structure "even though" limiting the correct answer to some sort of semantic opposites, so you wouldn't get answers like, "Even though Tom was foolish, Mary thought he was ridiculous." Well, according to my mother, there were very few limitations as to what Tom could have been and what Mary might have thought of him. So I never did well on tests like that.

The same was true with word analogies, pairs of words in which you were supposed to find some sort of logical, semantic relationship— for example, "*Sunset* is to *nightfall* as _____ is to _____." And here you would be presented with a list of four possible pairs, one of which showed the same kind of relationship: *red* is to *stoplight, bus* is to *arrival, chills* is to *fever, yawn* is to *boring*. Well, I could never think that way. I knew what the tests were asking, but I could not block out of my mind the images already created by the first pair, "*sunset* is to *nightfall*"—and I would see a burst of colors against a darkening sky, the moon rising, the lowering of a curtain of stars. And all the other pairs of words—red, bus, stoplight, boring—just threw up a mass of confusing images, making it impossible for me to sort out something as logical as saying: "A sunset precedes nightfall" is the same as "a chill precedes a fever." The only way I would have gotten that answer right would have been to imagine an associative situation, for example, my being disobedient and staying out past sunset, catching a chill at night, which turns into feverish pneumonia as punishment, which indeed did happen to me.

I have been thinking about all this lately, about my mother's English, about achievement tests. Because lately I've been asked, as a writer, why there are not more Asian Americans represented in American literature. Why are there few Asian Americans enrolled in creative writing programs? Why do so many Chinese students go into engineering? Well, these are broad sociological questions I can't begin to answer. But I have noticed in surveys—in fact, just last week—that Asian students, as a whole, always do significantly better on math achievement tests than in English. And this makes me think that there are other Asian-American students whose English spoken in the home might also be described as "broken" or "limited." And perhaps they also have teachers who are steering them away from writing and into math and science, which is what happened to me.

Fortunately, I happen to be rebellious in nature and enjoy the challenge of disproving assumptions made about me. I became an English major my first year in college, after being enrolled as pre-med. I started writing nonfiction as a freelancer the week after I was told by my former boss that writing was my worst skill and I should hone my talents toward account management.

But it wasn't until 1985 that I finally began to write fiction. And at first I wrote using what I thought to be wittily crafted sentences, sentences that would finally prove I had mastery over the English language. Here's an example from the first draft of a story that later made its way into *The Joy Luck Club,* but without this line: "That was my mental quandary in its nascent state." A terrible line, which I can barely pronounce.

Fortunately, for reasons I won't get into today, I later decided I should envision a reader for the stories I would write. And the reader I decided upon was my mother, because these were stories about mothers. So with this reader in mind—and in fact she did read my early drafts—I began to write stories using all the Englishes I grew up with: the English I spoke to my mother, which for lack of a better term might be described as "simple"; the English she used with me, which for lack of a better term might be described as "broken"; my translation of her Chinese, which could certainly be described as "watered down"; and what I imagined to be her translation of her Chinese if she could speak in perfect English, her internal language, and for that I sought to preserve the essence, but neither an English nor a Chinese structure.

I wanted to capture what language ability tests can never reveal: her intent, her passion, her imagery, the rhythms of her speech and the nature of her thoughts.

Apart from what any critic had to say about my writing, I knew I had succeeded where it counted when my mother finished reading my book and gave me her verdict: "So easy to read."

## Responding to Reading                    MyWritingLab™

1. Tan implies that some languages are more expressive than others. Do you agree? Are there some ideas you can express in one language that are difficult or impossible to express in another? Give examples if you can.
2. Do you agree with Tan's statement in paragraph 15 that the kind of English spoken at home can have an effect on a student's performance on IQ tests and the SAT?
3. **Rhetorical Analysis**   Why does Tan begin her essay with the disclaimer, "I am not a scholar of English or literature. I cannot give you much more than personal opinions" (1)? Do these statements add to her credibility or detract from it? Explain.

## Writing about Reading                    MyWritingLab™

1. Do you think the English you speak at home has had a positive or a negative effect on your performance in school?
2. **Writing with Sources**   In paragraph 15 of her essay, Tan says that for immigrant children, the language spoken at home will negatively affect scores on achievement tests, IQ tests, and the SATs. Research this claim, and then write an essay in which you agree or disagree with Tan. Be specific, referring to Tan's essay as well as the information you found in your research.

# LEARNING TO READ AND WRITE

## Frederick Douglass

### 1817–1895

*Frederick Douglass was born a slave in rural Talbot County, Maryland, and later served a family in Baltimore. After escaping to the North in 1838, he settled in Bedford, Massachusetts, where he became active in the abolitionist movement. He recounts these experiences in his most famous work,* Narrative of the Life of Frederick Douglass *(1845). After spending almost two years in England and Europe on a lecture tour, Douglass returned to the United States and purchased his freedom. In 1847, he launched the antislavery newspaper* The North Star *and became a vocal supporter of both Abraham Lincoln and the Civil War. Throughout his life, Douglass believed that the United States Constitution, if interpreted correctly, would enable African Americans to become full participants in the economic, social, and intellectual life of America. In the following excerpt from his* Narrative, *Douglass writes of outwitting his owners to become literate, thereby finding "the pathway from slavery to freedom."*

I lived in Master Hugh's family about seven years. During this time, I succeeded in learning to read and write. In accomplishing this, I was compelled to resort to various stratagems. I had no regular teacher. My mistress, who had kindly commenced to instruct me, had, in compliance with the advice and direction of her husband, not only ceased to instruct, but had set her face against my being instructed by any one else. It is due, however, to my mistress to say of her, that she did not adopt this course of treatment immediately. She at first lacked the depravity indispensable to shutting me up in mental darkness. It was at least necessary for her to have some training in the exercise of irresponsible power, to make her equal to the task of treating me as though I were a brute.

My mistress was, as I have said, a kind and tender-hearted woman; and in the simplicity of her soul she commenced, when I first went to live with her, to treat me as she supposed one human being ought to treat another. In entering upon the duties of a slaveholder, she did not seem to perceive that I sustained to her the relation of a mere chattel,[1] and that for her to treat me as a human being was not only wrong, but dangerously so. Slavery proved as injurious to her as it did to me. When I went there, she was a pious, warm, and tender-hearted woman. There was no sorrow or suffering for which she had not a tear. She had bread for the hungry, clothes for the naked, and comfort for every mourner that came within her reach. Slavery soon proved its ability to divest her of these heavenly qualities. Under its influence, the tender heart became stone, and the lamblike disposition gave way to one of tigerlike fierceness. The first step in her downward course was in her ceasing to instruct me. She now commenced to practice her husband's precepts. She finally became even more violent in her opposition than her husband himself. She was not satisfied with simply doing as well as he had commanded; she seemed anxious to do better. Nothing seemed to make her more angry than to see me with a newspaper. She seemed to think that here lay the danger. I have had her rush at me with a face made all up of fury, and snatch from me a newspaper, in a manner that fully revealed her apprehension. She was an apt woman; and a little experience soon demonstrated, to her satisfaction, that education and slavery were incompatible with each other.

From this time I was most narrowly watched. If I was in a separate room any considerable length of time, I was sure to be suspected of having a book, and was at once called to give an account of myself. All this, however, was too late. The first step had been taken. Mistress, in teaching me the alphabet, had given me the *inch*, and no precaution could prevent me from taking the *ell*.

The plan which I adopted, and the one by which I was most successful, was that of making friends of all the little white boys whom

[1]Property. [Eds.]

I met in the street. As many of these as I could, I converted into teachers. With their kindly aid, obtained at different times and in different places, I finally succeeded in learning to read. When I was sent on errands, I always took my book with me, and by going one part of my errand quickly, I found time to get a lesson before my return. I used also to carry bread with me, enough of which was always in the house, and to which I was always welcome; for I was much better off in this regard than many of the poor white children in our neighborhood. This bread I used to bestow upon the hungry little urchins, who, in return, would give me that more valuable bread of knowledge. I am strongly tempted to give the names of two or three of those little boys, as a testimonial of the gratitude and affection I bear them; but prudence forbids;—not that it would injure me, but it might embarrass them; for it is almost an unpardonable offense to teach slaves to read in this Christian country. It is enough to say of the dear little fellows, that they lived on Philpot Street, very near Durgin and Bailey's ship-yard. I used to talk this matter of slavery over with them. I would sometimes say to them, I wished I could be as free as they would be when they got to be men. "You will be free as soon as you are twenty-one, *but I am a slave for life!* Have not I as good a right to be free as you have?" These words used to trouble them; they would express for me the liveliest sympathy, and console me with the hope that something would occur by which I might be free.

5     I was now about twelve years old, and the thought of being *a slave for life* began to bear heavily upon my heart. Just about this time, I got hold of a book entitled "The Columbian Orator."[2] Every opportunity I got, I used to read this book. Among much of other interesting matter, I found in it a dialogue between a master and his slave. The slave was represented as having run away from his master three times. The dialogue represented the conversation which took place between them, when the slave was retaken the third time. In this dialogue, the whole argument in behalf of slavery was brought forward by the master, all of which was disposed of by the slave. The slave was made to say some very smart as well as impressive things in reply to his master—things which had the desired though unexpected effect; for the conversation resulted in the voluntary emancipation of the slave on the part of the master.

In the same book, I met with one of Sheridan's mighty speeches on and in behalf of Catholic emancipation.[3] These were choice documents to me. I read them over and over again with unabated interest. They gave tongue to interesting thoughts of my own soul, which had frequently flashed through my mind, and died away for want of utterance. The moral which I gained from the dialogue was the power

---

[2]A popular textbook that taught the principles of effective public speaking. [Eds.]

[3]Richard Brinsley Sheridan (1751–1816), British playwright and statesman who made speeches supporting the right of English Catholics to vote. Full emancipation was not granted to Catholics until 1829. [Eds.]

of truth over the conscience of even a slaveholder. What I got from Sheridan was a bold denunciation of slavery, and a powerful vindication of human rights. The reading of these documents enabled me to utter my thoughts, and to meet the arguments brought forward to sustain slavery; but while they relieved me of one difficulty, they brought on another even more painful than the one of which I was relieved. The more I read, the more I was led to abhor and detest my enslavers. I could regard them in no other light than a band of successful robbers, who had left their homes, and gone to Africa, and stolen us from our homes, and in a strange land reduced us to slavery. I loathed them as being the meanest as well as the most wicked of men. As I read and contemplated the subject, behold! that very discontentment which Master Hugh had predicted would follow my learning to read had already come, to torment and sting my soul to unutterable anguish. As I writhed under it, I would at times feel that learning to read had been a curse rather than a blessing. It had given me a view of my wretched condition, without the remedy. It opened my eyes to the horrible pit, but to no ladder upon which to get out. In moments of agony, I envied my fellow-slaves for their stupidity. I have often wished myself a beast. I preferred the condition of the meanest reptile to my own. Any thing, no matter what, to get rid of thinking! It was the everlasting thinking of my condition that tormented me. There was no getting rid of it. It was pressed upon me by every object within sight or hearing, animate or inanimate. The silver trump of freedom had roused my soul to eternal wakefulness. Freedom now appeared, to disappear no more forever. It was heard in every sound, and seen in every thing. It was ever present to torment me with a sense of my wretched condition. I saw nothing without seeing it, I heard nothing without hearing it, and felt nothing without feeling it. It looked from every star, it smiled in every calm, breathed in every wind, and moved in every storm.

I often found myself regretting my own existence, and wishing myself dead; and but for the hope of being free, I have no doubt but that I should have killed myself, or done something for which I should have been killed. While in this state of mind, I was eager to hear any one speak of slavery. I was a ready listener. Every little while, I could hear something about the abolitionists. It was some time before I found what the word meant. It was always used in such connections as to make it an interesting word to me. If a slave ran away and succeeded in getting clear, or if a slave killed his master, set fire to a barn, or did any thing very wrong in the mind of a slaveholder, it was spoken of as the fruit of *abolition*. Hearing the word in this connection very often, I set about learning what it meant. The dictionary afforded me little or no help. I found it was "the act of abolishing"; but then I did not know what was to be abolished. Here I was perplexed. I did not dare to ask any one about its meaning, for I was satisfied that it was something they wanted me to know very little about. After a patient waiting, I got one of our city papers, containing an account of the number of petitions from the north, praying for the abolition of slavery in the District of Columbia, and of the slave trade between the States. From this time I understood the words *abolition* and *abolitionist*, and always drew near when that word was spoken, expecting to hear something of importance to myself and fellow-slaves. The light broke in upon me by degrees. I went one day down on the wharf of Mr. Waters; and seeing two Irishmen unloading a scow of stone, I went, unasked, and helped them. When we had finished, one of them came to me and asked me if I were a slave. I told him I was. He asked, "Are ye a slave for life?" I told him that I was. The good Irishman seemed to be deeply affected by the statement. He said to the other that it was a pity so fine a little fellow as myself should be a slave for life. He said it was a shame to hold me. They both advised me to run away to the north; that I should find friends there, and that I should be free. I pretended not to be interested in what they said, and treated them as if I did not understand them; for I feared they might be treacherous. White men have been known to encourage slaves to escape, and then, to get the reward, catch them and return them to their masters. I was afraid that these seemingly good men might use me so; but I nevertheless remembered their advice, and from that time I resolved to run away. I looked forward to a time at which it would be safe for me to escape. I was too young to think of doing so immediately; besides, I wished to learn how to write, as I might have occasion to write my own pass. I consoled myself with the hope that I should one day find a good chance. Meanwhile, I would learn to write.

The idea as to how I might learn to write was suggested to me by being in Durgin and Bailey's ship-yard, and frequently seeing the ship carpenters, after hewing, and getting a piece of timber ready for use, write on the timber the name of that part of the ship for which it was intended. When a piece of timber was intended for the larboard side, it would be marked thus—"L." When a piece was for the starboard side, it would be marked thus—"S." A piece for the larboard side forward, would be marked thus—"L. F." When a piece was for starboard side forward, it would be marked thus—"S. F." For larboard aft, it would be marked thus—"L. A." For starboard aft, it would be marked thus—"S. A." I soon learned the names of these letters, and for what they were intended when placed upon a piece of timber in the shipyard. I immediately commenced copying them, and in a short time was able to make the four letters named. After that, when I met with any boy who I knew could write, I would tell him I could write as well as he. The next word would be, "I don't believe you. Let me see you try it." I would then make the letters which I had been so fortunate as to learn, and ask him to beat that. In this way I got a good many lessons in writing, which it is quite possible I should never have gotten in any other way. During this time, my copy-book was the board fence, brick wall, and pavement; my pen and ink was a lump of chalk. With these, I learned mainly how to write. I then commenced and continued copying the Italics in Webster's Spelling Book, until I could make them all without looking on the book. By this time, my little Master Thomas had gone to school, and learned how to write, and had written over a number of copy-books. These had been brought home, and shown to some of our near neighbors, and then laid aside. My mistress used to go to class meeting at the Wilk Street meetinghouse every Monday afternoon, and leave me to take care of the house. When left thus, I used to spend the time in writing in the spaces left in Master Thomas's copy-book, copying what he had written. I continued to do this until I could write a hand very similar to that of Master Thomas. Thus, after a long, tedious effort for years, I finally succeeded in learning how to write.

## Responding to Reading

MyWritingLab™

1. What does Douglass mean in paragraph 2 when he says that slavery proved as harmful to his mistress as it did to him? In spite of his owners' actions, what strategies did Douglass use to learn to read?
2. Douglass escaped from slavery in 1838 and became a leading figure in the antislavery movement. How did reading and writing help him develop his ideas about slavery? In what way did language empower him?
3. **Rhetorical Analysis**   Is Douglass addressing primarily a white audience or an audience of African Americans? How do you know?

## Writing about Reading

MyWritingLab™

1. What comment does Douglass's essay make on the condition of African Americans in the mid-nineteenth century? Does this essay, written over 150 years ago, have relevance today? Explain.
2. **Writing with Sources.**   In his narrative, Douglass says that his treatment "was very similar to that of other slave children." Research the living conditions of slaves in the American South. Then, write an essay in which you discuss if Douglass was treated better or worse than other slaves.

# SEXISM IN ENGLISH: EMBODIMENT AND LANGUAGE
## Alleen Pace Nilsen
### *1936–*

*The author of several textbooks and reference works, Alleen Pace Nilsen is an educator and essayist. When Nilsen lived in Afghanistan in the 1960s, she observed the subordinate position of women in that society. When she returned to the United States, she studied American English for its cultural*

*biases toward men and women. Nilsen says of that project, "As I worked my*
*way through the dictionary, I concentrated on the way particular usages,*
*metaphors, slang terms, and definitions reveal society's attitude toward males*
*and females." The following essay is an updated version of Nilsen's findings*
*from her dictionary study.*

During the late 1960s, I lived with my husband and three young children in Kabul, Afghanistan. This was before the Russian invasion, the
Afghan civil war, and the eventual taking over of the country by the
Taleban Islamic movement and its resolve to return the country to a
strict Islamic dynasty, in which females are not allowed to attend school
or work outside their homes.

But even when we were there and the country was considered
moderate rather than extremist, I was shocked to observe how different
were the roles assigned to males and females. The Afghan version of
the *chaderi* [1] prescribed by Moslem women was particularly confining.
Women in religious families were required to wear it whenever they
were outside their family home, with the result being that most of them
didn't venture outside.

The household help we hired were made up of men, because women
could not be employed by foreigners. Afghan folk stories and jokes were
blatantly sexist, as in this proverb: "If you see an old man, sit down and
take a lesson; if you see an old woman, throw a stone."

But it wasn't only the native culture that made me question women's
roles, it was also the American community within Afghanistan.

5    Most of the American women were like myself—wives and mothers
whose husbands were either career diplomats, employees of USAID,
or college professors who had been recruited to work on various contract teams. We were suddenly bereft of our traditional roles: The local
economy provided few jobs for women and certainly none for foreigners; we were isolated from former friends and the social goals we had
grown up with. Some of us became alcoholics, others got very good at
bridge, while still others searched desperately for ways to contribute
either to our families or to the Afghans.

When we returned in the fall of 1969 to the University of Michigan
in Ann Arbor, I was surprised to find that many other women were also
questioning the expectations they had grown up with. Since I had been
an English major when I was in college, I decided that for my part in the
feminist movement I would study the English language and see what
it could tell me about sexism. I started reading a desk dictionary and
making note cards on every entry that seemed to tell something different about male and female. I soon had a dog-eared dictionary, along
with a collection of note cards filling two shoe boxes.

---

[1] A heavily draped cloth covering the entire head and body. [Eds.]

The first thing I learned was that I couldn't study the language without getting involved in social issues. Language and society are as intertwined as a chicken and an egg. The language a culture uses is telltale evidence of the values and beliefs of that culture. And because there is a lag in how fast a language changes—new words can easily be introduced, but it takes a long time for old words and usages to disappear—a careful look at English will reveal the attitudes that our ancestors held and that we as a culture are therefore predisposed to hold. My note cards revealed three main points. While friends have offered the opinion that I didn't need to read a dictionary to learn such obvious facts, the linguistic evidence lends credibility to the sociological observations.

## Women Are Sexy; Men Are Successful

First, in American culture a woman is valued for the attractiveness and sexiness of her body, while a man is valued for his physical strength and accomplishments. A woman is sexy. A man is successful.

A persuasive piece of evidence supporting this view are the eponyms—words that have come from someone's name—found in English. I had a two-and-a-half-inch stack of cards taken from men's names but less than a half-inch stack from women's names, and most of those came from Greek mythology. In the words that came into American English since we separated from Britain, there are many eponyms based on the names of famous American men: Bartlett pear, boysenberry, Franklin stove, Ferris wheel, Gatling gun, mason jar, sideburns, sousaphone, Schick test, and Winchester rifle. The only common eponyms that I found taken from American women's names are Alice blue (after Alice Roosevelt Longworth), bloomers (after Amelia Jenks Bloomer), and Mae West jacket (after the buxom actress). Two out of the three feminine eponyms relate closely to a woman's physical anatomy, while the masculine eponyms (except for "sideburns" after General Burnsides) have nothing to do with the namesake's body, but, instead, honor the man for an accomplishment of some kind.

In Greek mythology women played a bigger role than they did in  10  the biblical stories of the Judeo-Christian cultures, and so the names of goddesses are accepted parts of the language in such place names as Pomona, from the goddess of fruit, and Athens, from Athena, and in such common words as *cereal* from Ceres, *psychology* from Psyche, and *arachnoid* from Arachne. However, there is the same tendency to think of women in relation to sexuality as shown through the eponyms *aphrodisiac* from Aphrodite, the Greek name for the goddess of love and beauty, and *venereal disease* from Venus, the Roman name for Aphrodite.

Another interesting word from Greek mythology is *Amazon*. According to Greek folk etymology, the *a-* means "without," as in *atypical* or *amoral*, while *-mazon* comes from *mazos*, meaning "breast," as still seen in *mastectomy*. In the Greek legend, Amazon women cut off their right breasts so they could better shoot their bows. Apparently, the storytellers had a feeling that for women to play the active, "masculine" role the Amazons adopted for themselves, they had to trade in part of their femininity.

This preoccupation with women's breasts is not limited to the Greeks; it's what inspired the definition and the name for "mammals" (from Indo-European *mammae* for "breasts"). As a volunteer for the University of Wisconsin's *Dictionary of American Regional English (DARE)*, I read a western trapper's diary from the 1830s. I was to make notes of any unusual usages or language patterns. My most interesting finding was that the trapper referred to a range of mountains as "The Teats," a metaphor based on the similarity between the shapes of the mountains and women's breasts. Because today we use the French wording "The Grand Tetons," the metaphor isn't as obvious, but I wrote to mapmakers and found the following listings: Nipple Top and Little Nipple Top near Mount Marcy in the Adirondacks; Nipple Mountain in Archuleta County, Colorado; Nipple Peak in Coke County, Texas; Nipple Butte in Pennington, South Dakota; Squaw Peak in Placer County, California (and many other locations); Maiden's Peak and Squaw Tit (they're the same mountain) in the Cascade Range in Oregon; Mary's Nipple near Salt Lake City, Utah; and Jane Russell Peaks near Stark, New Hampshire.

Except for the movie star Jane Russell, the women being referred to are anonymous—it's only a sexual part of their body that is mentioned. When topographical features are named after men, it's probably not going to be to draw attention to a sexual part of their bodies but instead to honor individuals for an accomplishment.

Going back to what I learned from my dictionary cards, I was surprised to realize how many pairs of words we have in which the feminine word has acquired sexual connotations while the masculine word retains a serious businesslike aura. For example, a callboy is the person who calls actors when it is time for them to go on stage, but a callgirl is a prostitute. Compare sir and madam. *Sir* is a term of respect, while *madam* has acquired the specialized meaning of a brothel manager. Something similar has happened to master and mistress. Would you rather have a painting "by an old master" or "by an old mistress"?

15      It's because the word *woman* had sexual connotations, as in "She's his woman," that people began avoiding its use, hence such terminology as ladies' room, lady of the house, and girl's school or school for young ladies. Those of us who in the 1970s began asking that speakers use the term *woman* rather than *girl* or *lady* were rejecting the idea that *woman* is primarily a sexual term.

I found two-hundred pairs of words with masculine and feminine forms; for example, *heir/heiress, hero/heroine, steward/stewardess, usher/usherette*. In nearly all such pairs, the masculine word is considered the

Gateway Comm College Bkstr
20 Church St RM N109
New Haven, CT 06510
Summer Rent retrn 8/12
(203) 865-5614
www.efollett.com
www.efollett.com

| ITEM | QTY | PRICE | TOTAL |
| --- | --- | --- | --- |

Used
Drugs & Society (w/Access Code
017972599      1    $100.50       $100.50N

Used
Blair Reader (w/out MyCompLab)
017166361      1    $88.00        $88.00N

Sub Total              188.50
Tax                      0.00

Total                 $188.50

Credit Card
Visa                                188.50
Acct# ***********8056
Auth# 005945

Items Purchased: 2
Items Returned:  0

* X 7 9 5 0 9 4 0 3 4 1 5 4 *

Associate:Pedro

Fall 2018
RET/EXCH W/RECPT ONLY
until Sept 14th

4154 0809 403 4              09/05/18  2:16PM

```
*****************************************
*        We want your feedback!         *
*  Go to: www.follettexperience.com     *
*  Get $5 off a minimum $40 purchase    *
*  Validation Code:_____      *
*  Offer expires 30 days from           *
*  purchase date. Exceptions apply,     *
*  see stores for complete details.     *
*****************************************
```

-----------------------------------
TYPE: sale
ACCT: VISA                 INSERTED
     Visa Credit
-----------------------------------
CARD # ***********8056    EXP **/**
DATE/TIME:    09/05/2018   14:16:23
REF #        AUTH #    RESP 00
032137       005945    ISO  00
AID: A0000000031010
TSI: F800 ARC:00  CUR:0840
TVR: 0080008000
APP: Visa Credit
IAD: 060A0A03A02002

                          ------------
Total USD$                     188.50
                          ------------
                Approved
I agree to pay the above total amount
according to the card issuer agreement
(merchant agreement if credit voucher)
             CUSTOMER COPY
4154 0809 403   4      09/05/18 02:16PM

base, with some kind of a feminine suffix being added. The masculine form is the one from which compounds are made; for example, from *king/queen* comes *kingdom* but not *queendom*, from *sportsman/sports-lady* comes *sportsmanship* but not *sportsladyship*. There is one—and only one—semantic area in which the masculine word is not the base or more powerful word. This is in the area dealing with sex, marriage, and motherhood. When someone refers to a virgin, a listener will probably think of a female unless the speaker specifies male or uses a masculine pronoun. The same is true for *prostitute*.

In relation to marriage, linguistic evidence shows that weddings are more important to women than to men. A woman cherishes the wedding and is considered a bride for a whole year, but a man is referred to as a groom only on the day of the wedding. The word *bride* appears in *bridal attendant, bridal gown, bridesmaid, bridal shower,* and even *bridegroom*. *Groom* comes from the Middle English *grom*, meaning "man," and in that sense is seldom used outside of the wedding. With most pairs of male/female words, people habitually put the masculine word first: *Mr. and Mrs., his and hers, boys and girls, men and women, kings and queens, brothers and sisters, guys and dolls,* and *host and hostess*. But it is the bride and groom who are talked about, not the groom and bride.

The importance of marriage to a woman is also shown by the fact that when a marriage ends in death, the woman gets the title of widow. A man gets the derived title of widower. This term is not used in other phrases or contexts, but widow is seen in widowhood, widow's peak, and widow's walk. A widow in a card game is an extra hand of cards, while in typesetting it is a leftover line of type.

Changing cultural ideas bring changes to language, and since I did my dictionary study three decades ago the word *singles* has largely replaced such gender-specific and value-laden terms as *bachelor, old maid, spinster, divorcee, widow,* and *widower*. In 1970 I wrote that when people hear a man called "a professional," they usually think of him as a doctor or a lawyer, but when people hear a woman referred to as "a professional," they are likely to think of her as a prostitute. That's not as true today because so many women have become doctors and lawyers, it's no longer incongruous to think of women in those professional roles.

Another change that has taken place is in wedding announcements. 20 They used to be sent out from the bride's parents and did not even give the name of the groom's parents. Today, most couples choose to list either all or none of the parents' names. Also it is now much more likely that both the bride and groom's picture will be in the newspaper, while twenty years ago only the bride's picture was published on the "Women's" or the "Society" page. In the weddings I have recently attended, the official has pronounced the couple "husband and wife" instead of the traditional "man and wife," and the bride has been asked if she promises to "love, honor, and cherish," instead of to "love, honor, and obey."

## Women Are Passive; Men Are Active

However, other wording in the wedding ceremony relates to a second point that my cards showed, which is that women are expected to play a passive or weak role while men play an active or strong role. In the traditional ceremony, the official asks, "Who gives the bride away?" and the father answers, "I do." Some fathers answer, "Her mother and I do," but that doesn't solve the problem inherent in the question. The idea that a bride is something to be handed over from one man to another bothers people because it goes back to the days when a man's servants, his children, and his wife were all considered to be his property. They were known by his name because they belonged to him, and he was responsible for their actions and their debts.

The grammar used in talking or writing about weddings as well as other sexual relationships shows the expectation of men playing the active role. Men *wed* women while women *become* brides of men. A man *possesses* a woman; he *deflowers* her; he *performs*; he *scores*; he *takes away* her virginity. Although a woman can *seduce* a man, she cannot offer him her virginity. When talking about virginity, the only way to make the woman the actor in the sentence is to say that "she lost her virginity," but people lose things by accident rather than by purposeful actions, and so she's only the grammatical, not the real-life, actor.

The reason that women brought the term Ms. into the language to replace Miss and Mrs. relates to this point. Many married women resent being identified in the "Mrs. Husband" form. The dictionary cards showed what appeared to be an attitude on the part of the editors that it was almost indecent to let a respectable woman's name march unaccompanied across the pages of a dictionary. Women were listed with male names whether or not the male contributed to the woman's reason for being in the dictionary or whether or not in his own right he was as famous as the woman. For example:

Charlotte Brontë = Mrs. Arthur B. Nicholls
Amelia Earhart = Mrs. George Palmer Putnam
Helen Hayes = Mrs. Charles MacArthur
Jenny Lind = Mme. Otto Goldschmit
Cornelia Otis Skinner = daughter of Otis
Harriet Beecher Stowe = sister of Henry Ward Beecher
Dame Edith Sitwell = sister of Osbert and Sacheverell[2]

---

[2]Charlotte Brontë (1816–1855), author of *Jane Eyre*; Amelia Earhart (1898–1937), first woman to fly over the Atlantic; Helen Hayes (1900–1993), actress; Jenny Lind (1820–1887), Swedish soprano; Cornelia Otis Skinner (1901–1979), actress and writer; Harriet Beecher Stowe (1811–1896), author of *Uncle Tom's Cabin*; Edith Sitwell (1877–1964), English poet and critic. [Eds.]

Only a small number of rebels and crusaders got into the dictionary without the benefit of a masculine escort: temperance leaders Frances Elizabeth Caroline Willard and Carry Nation, women's rights leaders Carrie Chapman Catt and Elizabeth Cady Stanton, birth control educator Margaret Sanger, religious leader Mary Baker Eddy, and slaves Harriet Tubman and Phillis Wheatley.

Etiquette books used to teach that if a woman had Mrs. in front of her name, then the husband's name should follow because Mrs. is an abbreviated form of Mistress and a woman couldn't be a mistress of herself. As with many arguments about "correct" language usage, this isn't very logical because Miss is also an abbreviation of Mistress. Feminists hoped to simplify matters by introducing Ms. as an alternative to both Mrs. and Miss, but what happened is that Ms. largely replaced Miss to become a catch-all business title for women. Many married women still prefer the title Mrs., and some even resent being addressed with the term Ms. As one frustrated newspaper reporter complained, "Before I can write about a woman I have to know not only her marital status but also her political philosophy." The result of such complications may contribute to the demise of titles, which are already being ignored by many writers who find it more efficient to simply use names; for example, in a business letter: "Dear Joan Garcia," instead of "Dear Mrs. Joan Garcia," "Dear Ms. Garcia," or "Dear Mrs. Louis Garcia."

Titles given to royalty show how males can be disadvantaged by the 25 assumption that they always play the more powerful role. In British royalty, when a male holds a title, his wife is automatically given the feminine equivalent. But the reverse is not true. For example, a count is a high political officer with a countess being his wife. The same pattern holds true for a duke and a duchess and a king and a queen. But when a female holds the royal title, the man she marries does not automatically acquire the matching title. For example, Queen Elizabeth's husband has the title of prince rather than king, but when Prince Charles married Diana, she became Princess Diana. If they had stayed married and he had ascended to the throne, then she would have become Queen Diana. The reasoning appears to be that since masculine words are stronger, they are reserved for true heirs and withheld from males coming into the royal family by marriage. If Prince Phillip were called "King Phillip," British subjects might forget who had inherited the right to rule.

The names that people give their children show the hopes and dreams they have for them, and when we look at the differences between male and female names in a culture, we can see the cumulative expectations of that culture. In our culture girls often have names taken from small, aesthetically pleasing items; for example, Ruby, Jewel, and Pearl. Esther and Stella mean "star," and Ada means "ornament." One of the few women's names that refers to strength is Mildred, and it means "mild strength." Boys often have names with meanings of power and strength; for example, Neil means "champion"; Martin is from Mars, the God of war; Raymond means "wise protection"; Harold means "chief of the army"; Ira means "vigilant"; Rex means "king"; and Richard means "strong king."

We see similar differences in food metaphors. Food is a passive substance just sitting there waiting to be eaten. Many people have recognized this and so no longer feel comfortable describing women as "delectable morsels." However, when I was a teenager, it was considered a compliment to refer to a girl (we didn't call anyone a "woman" until she was middle-aged) as a cute tomato, a peach, a dish, a cookie, honey, sugar, or sweetie-pie. When being affectionate, women will occasionally call a man honey or sweetie, but in general, food metaphors are used much less often with men than with women. If a man is called "a fruit," his masculinity is being questioned. But it's perfectly acceptable to use a food metaphor if the food is heavier and more substantive than that used for women. For example, pin-up pictures of women have long been known as "cheesecake," but when Burt Reynolds posed for a nude centerfold the picture was immediately dubbed "beefcake," that is, a hunk of meat. That such sexual references to men have come into the language is another reflection of how society is beginning to lessen the differences between their attitudes toward men and women.

Something similar to the fruit metaphor happens with references to plants. We insult a man by calling him a "pansy," but it wasn't considered particularly insulting to talk about a girl being a wallflower, a clinging vine, or a shrinking violet, or to give girls such names as Ivy, Rose, Lily, Iris, Daisy, Camelia, Heather, and Flora. A positive plant metaphor can be used with a man only if the plant is big and strong; for example, Andrew Jackson's nickname of Old Hickory. Also, the phrases *blooming idiots* and *budding geniuses* can be used with either sex, but notice how they are based on the most active thing a plant can do, which is to bloom or bud.

Animal metaphors also illustrate the different expectations for males and females. Men are referred to as studs, bucks, and wolves, while women are referred to with such metaphors as kitten, bunny, beaver, bird, chick, and lamb. In the 1950s, we said that boys went "tom catting," but today it's just "catting around," and both boys and girls do it. When the term foxy, meaning that someone was sexy, first became popular it was used only for females, but now someone of either sex can be described as a fox. Some animal metaphors that are used predominantly with men have negative connotations based on the size and/or strength of the animals; for example, beast, bull-headed, jackass, rat, loanshark, and vulture. Negative metaphors used with women are based on smaller animals; for example, social butterfly, mousey, catty, and vixen. The feminine terms connote action, but not the same kind of large scale action as with the masculine terms.

## Women Are Connected with Negative Connotations; Men with Positive Connotations

The final point that my note cards illustrated was how many positive 30
connotations are associated with the concept of masculinity, while there
are either trivial or negative connotations connected with the corre-
sponding feminine concept. An example from the animal metaphors
makes a good illustration. The word *shrew* taken from the name of a
small but especially vicious animal was defined in my dictionary as
"an ill-tempered scolding woman," but the word *shrewd* taken from the
same root was defined as "marked by clever, discerning awareness"
and was illustrated with the phrase "a shrewd businessman."

Early in life, children are conditioned to the superiority of the masculine role. As child psychologists point out, little girls have much
more freedom to experiment with sex roles than do little boys. If a
little girl acts like a tomboy, most parents have mixed feelings, being
at least partially proud. But if their little boy acts like a sissy (derived
from *sister*), they call a psychologist. It's perfectly acceptable for a little
girl to sleep in the crib that was purchased for her brother, to wear his
hand-me-down jeans and shirts, and to ride the bicycle that he has
outgrown. But few parents would put a boy baby in a white-and-gold
crib decorated with frills and lace, and virtually no parents would
have their little boy wear his sister's hand-me-down dresses, nor
would they have their son ride a girl's pink bicycle with a flower-
bedecked basket. The proper names given to girls and boys show this
same attitude. Girls can have "boy" names—Cris, Craig, Jo, Kelly,
Shawn, Teri, Toni, and Sam—but it doesn't work the other way around.
A couple of generations ago, Beverly, Frances, Hazel, Marion, and
Shirley were common boys' names. As parents gave these names to
more and more girls, they fell into disuse for males, and some older
men who have these names prefer to go by their initials or by such
abbreviated forms as Haze or Shirl.

When a little girl is told to be a lady, she is being told to sit with
her knees together and to be quiet and dainty. But when a little boy is
told to be a man, he is being told to be noble, strong, and virtuous—to
have all the qualities that the speaker looks on as desirable. The concept of manliness has such positive connotations that it used to be a
compliment to call someone a he-man, to say that he was doubly a
man. Today many people are more ambivalent about this term and
respond to it much as they do to the word *macho*. But calling someone
a manly man or a virile man is nearly always meant as a compliment.
Virile comes from the Indo-European *vir*, meaning "man," which is
also the basis of *virtuous*. Consider the positive connotations of both
virile and virtuous with the negative connotations of *hysterical*. The
Greeks took this latter word from their name for uterus (as still seen
in *hysterectomy*). They thought that women were the only ones who

experienced uncontrolled emotional outbursts, and so the condition must have something to do with a part of the body that only women have. But how word meanings change is regularly shown at athletic events where thousands of *virtuous* women sit quietly beside their *hysterical* husbands.

Differences in the connotations between positive male and negative female connotations can be seen in several pairs of words that differ denotatively only in the matter of sex. Bachelor as compared to spinster or old maid has such positive connotations that women try to adopt it by using the term *bachelor-girl* or *bachelorette*. Old maid is so negative that it's the basis for metaphors: pretentious and fussy old men are called "old maids," as are the leftover kernels of unpopped popcorn and the last card in a popular children's card game.

*Patron* and *matron* (Middle English for "father" and "mother") have such different levels of prestige that women try to borrow the more positive masculine connotations with the word *patroness*, literally "female father." Such a peculiar term came about because of the high prestige attached to patron in such phrases as a *patron of the arts* or a *patron saint*. Matron is more apt to be used in talking about a woman in charge of a jail or a public restroom.

35   When men are doing jobs that women often do, we apparently try to pay the men extra by giving them fancy titles. For example, a male cook is more likely to be called a "chef" while a male seamstress will get the title of "tailor." The armed forces have a special problem in that they recruit under such slogans as "The Marine Corps builds men!" and "Join the Army! Become a Man." Once the recruits are enlisted, they find themselves doing much of the work that has been traditionally thought of as "women's work." The solution to getting the work done and not insulting anyone's masculinity was to change the titles as shown below:

> waitress = orderly
> nurse = medic or corpsman
> secretary = clerk-typist
> assistant = adjutant
> dishwasher = KP (kitchen police) or kitchen helper

Compare *brave* and *squaw.* Early settlers in America truly admired Indian men and hence named them with a word that carried connotations of youth, vigor, and courage. But for Indian women they used an Algonquin slang term with negative sexual connotations that are almost opposite to those of brave. Wizard and witch contrast almost as much. The masculine *wizard* implies skill and wisdom combined with magic, while the feminine *witch* implies evil intentions combined with magic. When witch is used for men, as in witch-doctor, many main-stream speakers feel some carry-over of the negative connotations.

Part of the unattractiveness of both witch and squaw is that they have been used so often to refer to old women, something with which our culture is particularly uncomfortable, just as the Afghans were. Imagine my surprise when I ran across the phrases *grandfatherly advice* and *old wives' tales* and realized that the underlying implication is the same as the Afghan proverb about old men being worth listening to while old women talk only foolishness.

Other terms that show how negatively we view old women as compared to young women are *old nag* as compared to *filly, old crow* or *old bat* as compared to *bird,* and being *catty* as compared to being *kittenish.* There is no matching set of metaphors for men. The chicken metaphor tells the whole story of a woman's life. In her youth she is a chick. Then she marries and begins feathering her nest. Soon she begins feeling cooped up, so she goes to hen parties where she cackles with her friends. Then she has her brood, begins to henpeck her husband, and finally turns into an old biddy.

I embarked on my study of the dictionary not with the intention of prescribing language change but simply to see what the language would tell me about sexism. Nevertheless, I have been both surprised and pleased as I've watched the changes that have occurred over the past three decades. I'm one of those linguists who believes that new language customs will cause a new generation of speakers to grow up with different expectations. This is why I'm happy about people's efforts to use inclusive languages, to say "he or she" or "they" when speaking about individuals whose names they do not know. I'm glad that leading publishers have developed guidelines to help writers use language that is fair to both sexes. I'm glad that most newspapers and magazines list women by their own names instead of only by their husbands' names. And I'm so glad that educated and thoughtful people no longer begin their business letters with "Dear Sir" or "Gentlemen," but instead use a memo form or begin with such salutations as "Dear Colleagues," "Dear Reader," or "Dear Committee Members." I'm also glad that such words as *poetess, authoress, conductress,* and *aviatrix* now sound quaint and old-fashioned and that *chairman* is giving way to *chair* or *head, mailman* to *mail carrier, clergyman* to *clergy,* and *stewardess* to *flight attendant.* I was also pleased when the National Oceanic and Atmospheric Administration bowed to feminist complaints and in the late 1970s began to alternate men's and women's names for hurricanes. However, I wasn't so pleased to discover that the change did not immediately erase sexist thoughts from everyone's mind, as shown by a headline about Hurricane David in a 1979 New York tabloid, "David Rapes Virgin Islands." More recently a similar metaphor appeared in a headline in the *Arizona Republic* about Hurricane Charlie, "Charlie Quits Carolinas, Flirts with Virginia."

What these incidents show is that sexism is not something existing independently in American English or in the particular dictionary that

I happened to read. Rather, it exists in people's minds. Language is like an X-ray in providing visible evidence of invisible thoughts. The best thing about people being interested in and discussing sexist language is that as they make conscious decisions about what pronouns they will use, what jokes they will tell or laugh at, how they will write their names, or how they will begin their letters, they are forced to think about the underlying issue of sexism. This is good because as a problem that begins in people's assumptions and expectations, it's a problem that will be solved only when a great many people have given it a great deal of thought.

## Responding to Reading                                              MyWritingLab™

1. What point is Nilsen making about American culture? Does your experience support her conclusions?
2. Many of the connotations of the words Nilsen discusses are hundreds of years old and are also found in languages other than English. Given these widespread and long-standing connotations, do you think attempts by Nilsen and others to change this linguistic situation can succeed?
3. **Rhetorical Analysis**   Does Nilsen use enough examples to support her claims? What other examples can you think of? In what way do her examples—and your own—illustrate the power of language to define the way people think?

## Writing about Reading                                               MyWritingLab™

1. List some words and phrases in your own speaking vocabulary that reinforce the stereotypes Nilsen discusses. What alternatives could you employ? What would be gained and lost if you used these alternatives?
2. **Writing with Sources**   Lately, there has been some push back against the effort to eliminate sexist constructions from English. For example, some charge that this view of language is simplistic and that words can designate gender without being sexist. Research this issue and write a letter to Nilsen in which you agree or disagree with her position.

# THE HUMAN COST OF AN ILLITERATE SOCIETY

## Jonathan Kozol

### 1936–

*In 1964, Jonathan Kozol took a teaching job in the Boston Public Schools System. In 1967, he published his first book,* Death at an Early Age: The Destruction of the Hearts and Minds of Negro Children in the Boston Public Schools. *Based on his experiences as a fourth-grade teacher in an inner-city school, a position from which he was fired for "curriculum deviation," this book won the National Book Award in 1968 and led to a number of specific reforms. Since then, Kozol has divided his time between teaching and social activism. His books include* Illiterate America *(1985),* Savage

*Inequalities (1991),* The Shame of a Nation: The Restoration of Apartheid Schooling in America *(2005), and* The Theft of Memory: Losing
My Father One Day at a Time *(2015). In the following essay, a chapter
from* Illiterate America, *Kozol exposes the problems facing the sixty million
Americans who are unable to read and argues that their plight has important
implications for the nation as a whole.*

PRECAUTIONS. READ BEFORE USING.
Poison: Contains sodium hydroxide (caustic soda-lye).
Corrosive: Causes severe eye and skin damage, may cause blindness.
Harmful or fatal if swallowed.
If swallowed, give large quantities of milk or water.
Do not induce vomiting.
Important: Keep water out of can at all times to prevent contents from
violently erupting ...

—warning on a can of Drano

Questions of literacy, in Socrates' belief, must at length be judged as
matters of morality. Socrates could not have had in mind the moral
compromise peculiar to a nation like our own. Some of our Founding
Fathers did, however, have this question in their minds. One of the
wisest of those Founding Fathers (one who may not have been most
compassionate but surely was more prescient than some of his peers)
recognized the special dangers that illiteracy would pose to basic equity
in the political construction that he helped to shape.

"A people who mean to be their own governors," James Madison
wrote, "must arm themselves with the power knowledge gives. A popular government without popular information or the means of acquir-
ing it, is but a prologue to a farce or a tragedy, or perhaps both."

Tragedy looms larger than farce in the United States today. Illiterate
citizens seldom vote. Those who do are forced to cast a vote of questionable worth. They cannot make informed decisions based on serious print information. Sometimes they can be alerted to their interests
by aggressive voter education. More frequently, they vote for a face, a
smile, or a style, not for a mind or character or body of beliefs.

The number of illiterate adults exceeds by 16 million the entire vote
cast for the winner in the 1980 presidential contest. If even one third
of all illiterates could vote, and read enough and do sufficient math to
vote in their self-interest, Ronald Reagan would not likely have been
chosen president. There is, of course, no way to know for sure. We
do know this: Democracy is a mendacious[1] term when used by those
who are prepared to countenance the forced exclusion of one third
of our electorate. So long as 60 million people are denied significant
participation, the government is neither of, nor for, nor by, the people.
It is a government, at best, of those two thirds whose wealth, skin

[1] Basely dishonest. [Eds.]

color, or parental privilege allows them opportunity to profit from the provocation and instruction of the written word.

5    The undermining of democracy in the United States is one "expense" that sensitive Americans can easily deplore because it represents a contradiction that endangers citizens of all political positions. The human price is not so obvious at first.

Since I first immersed myself within this work I have often had the following dream: I find that I am in a railroad station or a large department store within a city that is utterly unknown to me and where I cannot understand the printed words. None of the signs or symbols is familiar. Everything looks strange: like mirror writing of some kind. Gradually I understand that I am in the Soviet Union. All the letters on the walls around me are Cyrillic. I look for my pocket dictionary but I find that it has been mislaid. Where have I left it? Then I recall that I forgot to bring it with me when I packed my bags in Boston. I struggle to remember the name of my hotel. I try to ask somebody for directions. One person stops and looks at me in a peculiar way. I lose the nerve to ask. At last I reach into my wallet for an ID card. The card is missing. Have I lost it? Then I remember that my card was confiscated for some reason, many years before. Around this point, I wake up in a panic.

This panic is not so different from the misery that millions of adult illiterates experience each day within the course of their routine existence in the U.S.A.

Illiterates cannot read the menu in a restaurant.

They cannot read the cost of items on the menu in the *window* of the restaurant before they enter.

10    Illiterates cannot read the letters that their children bring home from their teachers. They cannot study school department circulars that tell them of the courses that their children must be taking if they hope to pass the SAT exams. They cannot help with homework. They cannot write a letter to the teacher. They are afraid to visit in the classroom. They do not want to humiliate their child or themselves.

Illiterates cannot read instructions on a bottle of prescription medicine. They cannot find out when a medicine is past the year of safe consumption; nor can they read of allergenic risks, warnings to diabetics, or the potential sedative effect of certain kinds of nonprescription pills. They cannot observe preventive health care admonitions. They cannot read about "the seven warning signs of cancer" or the indications of blood-sugar fluctuations or the risks of eating certain foods that aggravate the likelihood of cardiac arrest.

Illiterates live, in more than literal ways, an uninsured existence. They cannot understand the written details on a health insurance form. They cannot read the waivers that they sign preceding surgical procedures. Several women I have known in Boston have entered a slum hospital with the intention of obtaining a tubal ligation and have emerged a few days later after having been subjected to a hysterectomy.[2] Unaware of their rights, incognizant of jargon, intimidated by the unfamiliar air of fear and atmosphere of ether that so many of us find oppressive in the confines even of the most attractive and expensive medical facilities, they have signed their names to documents they could not read and which nobody, in the hectic situation that prevails so often in those overcrowded hospitals that serve the urban poor, had even bothered to explain.

Childbirth might seem to be the last inalienable right of any female citizen within a civilized society. Illiterate mothers, as we shall see, already have been cheated of the power to protect their progeny against the likelihood of demolition in deficient public schools and, as a result, against the verbal servitude within which they themselves exist. Surgical denial of the right to bear that child in the first place represents an ultimate denial, an unspeakable metaphor, a final darkness that denies even the twilight gleamings of our own humanity. What greater violation of our biological, our biblical, our spiritual humanity could possibly exist than that which takes place nightly, perhaps hourly these days, within such over-burdened and benighted institutions as the Boston City Hospital? Illiteracy has many costs; few are so irreversible as this.

Even the roof above one's head, the gas or other fuel for heating that protects the residents of northern city slums against the threat of illness in the winter months become uncertain guarantees. Illiterates cannot read the lease that they must sign to live in an apartment which, too often, they cannot afford. They cannot manage check accounts and therefore seldom pay for anything by mail. Hours and entire days of difficult travel (and the cost of bus or other public transit) must be added to the real cost of whatever they consume. Loss of interest on the check accounts they do not have, and could not manage if they did, must be regarded as another of the excess costs paid by the citizen who is excluded from the common instruments of commerce in a numerate society.

"I couldn't understand the bills," a woman in Washington, D.C., 15 reports, "and then I couldn't write the checks to pay them. We signed things we didn't know what they were."

Illiterates cannot read the notices that they receive from welfare offices or from the IRS. They must depend on word-of-mouth instruction from the welfare worker—or from other persons whom they have good reason to mistrust. They do not know what rights they have, what deadlines and requirements they face, what options they might choose to exercise. They are half-citizens. Their rights exist in print but not in fact.

Illiterates cannot look up numbers in a telephone directory. Even if they can find the names of friends, few possess the sorting skills to

---

[2]A hysterectomy, the removal of the uterus, is a much more radical procedure than a tubal ligation, a method of sterilization that is a common form of birth control. [Eds.]

make use of the yellow pages; categories are bewildering and trade names are beyond decoding capabilities for millions of nonreaders. Even the emergency numbers listed on the first page of the phone book—"Ambulance," "Police," and "Fire"—are too frequently beyond the recognition of nonreaders.

Many illiterates cannot read the admonition on a pack of cigarettes. Neither the Surgeon General's warning nor its reproduction on the package can alert them to the risks. Although most people learn by word of mouth that smoking is related to a number of grave physical disorders, they do not get the chance to read the detailed stories which can document this danger with the vividness that turns concern into determination to resist. They can see the handsome cowboy or the slim Virginia lady lighting up a filter cigarette; they cannot heed the words that tell them that this product is (not "may be") dangerous to their health. Sixty million men and women are condemned to be the unalerted, high-risk candidates for cancer.

Illiterates do not buy "no-name" products in the supermarkets. They must depend on photographs or the familiar logos that are printed on the packages of brand-name groceries. The poorest people, therefore, are denied the benefits of the least costly products.

20    Illiterates depend almost entirely upon label recognition. Many labels, however, are not easy to distinguish. Dozens of different kinds of Campbell's soup appear identical to the nonreader. The purchaser who cannot read and does not dare to ask for help, out of the fear of being stigmatized (a fear which is unfortunately realistic), frequently comes home with something which she never wanted and her family never tasted.

Illiterates cannot read instructions on a pack of frozen food. Packages sometimes provide an illustration to explain the cooking preparations; but illustrations are of little help to someone who must "boil water, drop the food—*within* its plastic wrapper—in the boiling water, wait for it to simmer, instantly remove."

Even when labels are seemingly clear, they may be easily mistaken. A woman in Detroit brought home a gallon of Crisco for her children's dinner. She thought that she had bought the chicken that was pictured on the label. She had enough Crisco now to last a year—but no more money to go back and buy the food for dinner.

Recipes provided on the packages of certain staples sometimes tempt a semiliterate person to prepare a meal her children have not tasted. The longing to vary the uniform and often starchy content of low-budget meals provided to the family that relies on food stamps commonly leads to ruinous results. Scarce funds have been wasted and the food must be thrown out. The same applies to distribution of food-surplus produce in emergency conditions. Government inducements to poor people to "explore the ways" in which to make a tasty meal from tasteless noodles, surplus cheese, and powdered milk are useless to nonreaders. Intended as benevolent advice, such recommendations mock reality and foster deeper feelings of resentment and of inability to cope. (Those, on the other hand, who cautiously refrain from "innovative" recipes in preparation of their children's meals must suffer the opprobrium of "laziness," "lack of imagination... .")

Illiterates cannot travel freely. When they attempt to do so, they encounter risks that few of us can dream of. They cannot read traffic signs and, while they often learn to recognize and to decipher symbols, they cannot manage street names which they haven't seen before. The same is true for bus and subway stops. While ingenuity can sometimes help a man or woman to discern directions from familiar landmarks, buildings, cemeteries, churches, and the like, most illiterates are virtually immobilized. They seldom wander past the streets and neighborhoods they know. Geographical paralysis becomes a bitter metaphor for their entire existence. They are immobilized in almost every sense we can imagine. They can't move up. They can't move out. They cannot see beyond. Illiterates may take an oral test for drivers' permits in most sections of America. It is a questionable concession. Where will they go? How will they get there? How will they get home? Could it be that some of us might like it better if they stayed where they belong?

Travel is only one of many instances of circumscribed existence.  25
Choice, in almost all its facets, is diminished in the life of an illiterate adult. Even the printed TV schedule, which provides most people with the luxury of preselection, does not belong within the arsenal of options in illiterate existence. One consequence is that the viewer watches only what appears at moments when he happens to have time to turn the switch. Another consequence, a lot more common, is that the TV set remains in operation night and day. Whatever the program offered at the hour when he walks into the room will be the nutriment that he accepts and swallows. Thus, to passivity, is added frequency—indeed, almost uninterrupted continuity. Freedom to select is no more possible here than in the choice of home or surgery or food.

"You don't choose," said one illiterate woman. "You take your wishes from somebody else." Whether in perusal of a menu, selection of highways, purchase of groceries, or determination of affordable enjoyment, illiterate Americans must trust somebody else: a friend, a relative, a stranger on the street, a grocery clerk, a TV copywriter.

"All of our mail we get, it's hard for her to read. Settin' down and writing a letter, she can't do it. Like if we get a bill ... we take it over to my sister-in-law ... My sister-in-law reads it."

Billing agencies harass poor people for the payment of the bills for purchases that might have taken place six months before. Utility companies offer an agreement for a staggered payment schedule on a bill past due. "You have to trust them," one man said. Precisely for this reason, you end up by trusting no one and suspecting everyone of possible deceit. A submerged sense of distrust becomes the corollary to a constant need to trust. "They are cheating me ... I have been tricked ... I do not know ..."

*Not knowing:* This is a familiar theme. Not knowing the right word for the right thing at the right time is one form of subjugation. Not knowing the world that lies concealed behind those words is a more terrifying feeling. The longitude and latitude of one's existence are beyond all easy apprehension. Even the hard, cold stars within the firmament above one's head begin to mock the possibilities for self-location. Where am I? Where did I come from? Where will I go?

30   "I've lost a lot of jobs," one man explains. "Today, even if you're a janitor, there's still reading and writing ... They leave a note saying, 'Go to room so-and-so ...' You can't do it. You can't read it. You don't know."

"The hardest thing about it is that I've been places where I didn't know where I was. You don't know where you are ... You're lost."

"Like I said: I have two kids. What do I do if one of my kids starts choking? I go running to the phone ... I can't look up the hospital phone number. That's if we're at home. Out on the street, I can't read the sign. I get to a pay phone. 'Okay, tell us where you are. We'll send an ambulance.' I look at the street sign. Right there, I can't tell you what it says. I'd have to spell it out, letter for letter. By that time, one of my kids would be dead ... These are the kinds of fears you go with, every single day ..."

"Reading directions, I suffer with. I work with chemicals ... That's scary to begin with ..."

"You sit down. They throw the menu in front of you. Where do you go from there? Nine times out of ten you say, 'Go ahead. Pick out something for the both of us.' I've eaten some weird things, let me tell you!"

35   Menus. Chemicals. A child choking while his mother searches for a word she does not know to find assistance that will come too late. Another mother speaks about the inability to help her kids to read: "I can't read to them. Of course that's leaving them out of something they should have. Oh, it matters. You *believe* it matters! I ordered all these books. The kids belong to a book club. Donny wanted me to read a book to him. I told Donny: 'I can't read,' He said: 'Mommy, you sit down. I'll read it to you.' I tried it one day, reading from the pictures. Donny looked at me. He said, 'Mommy, that's not right.' He's only five. He knew I couldn't read ..."

A landlord tells a woman that her lease allows him to evict her if her baby cries and causes inconvenience to her neighbors. The consequence of challenging his words conveys a danger which appears, unlikely as it seems, even more alarming than the danger of eviction. Once she admits that she can't read, in the desire to maneuver for the time in which to call a friend, she will have defined herself in terms of an explicit impotence that she cannot endure. Capitulation in this case is preferable to self-humiliation. Resisting the definition of oneself in terms of what one cannot do, what others take for granted, represents a need so great that other imperatives (even one so urgent as the need to keep one's home in winter's cold) evaporate and fall away in face of fear. Even the loss of home and shelter, in this case, is not so terrifying as the loss of self.

"I come out of school. I was sixteen. They had their meetings. The directors meet. They said that I was wasting their school paper. I was wasting pencils ..."

Another illiterate, looking back, believes she was not worthy of her teacher's time. She believes that it was wrong of her to take up space within her school. She believes that it was right to leave in order that somebody more deserving could receive her place.

Children choke. Their mother chokes another way: on more than chicken bones.

People eat what others order, know what others tell them, strug- 40 gle not to see themselves as they believe the world perceives them. A man in California speaks about his own loss of identity, of self-location, definition:

"I stood at the bottom of the ramp. My car had broke down on the freeway. There was a phone. I asked for the police. They was nice. They said to tell them where I was. I looked up at the signs. There was one that I had seen before. I read it to them: ONE WAY STREET. They thought it was a joke. I told them I couldn't read. There was other signs above the ramp. They told me to try. I looked around for somebody to help. All the cars was going by real fast. I couldn't make them understand that I was lost. The cop was nice. He told me: 'Try once more.' I did my best. I couldn't read. I only knew the sign above my head. The cop was trying to be nice. He knew that I was trapped. 'I can't send out a car to you if you can't tell me where you are.' I felt afraid. I nearly cried. I'm forty-eight years old. I only said: 'I'm on a one-way street ...' "

The legal problems and the courtroom complications that confront illiterate adults have been discussed above. The anguish that may underlie such matters was brought home to me this year while I was working on this book. I have spoken, in the introduction, of a sudden phone call from one of my former students, now in prison for a criminal offense. Stephen is not a boy today. He is twenty-eight years old. He called to ask me to assist him in his trial, which comes up next fall. He will be on trial for murder. He has just knifed and killed a man who first enticed him to his home, then cheated him, and then insulted him—as "an illiterate subhuman."

Stephen now faces twenty years to life. Stephen's mother was illiterate. His grandparents were illiterate as well. What parental curse did not destroy was killed off finally by the schools. Silent violence is repaid with interest. It will cost us $25,000 yearly to maintain this broken soul in prison. But what is the price that has been paid by Stephen's victim? What is the price that will be paid by Stephen?

Perhaps we might slow down a moment here and look at the realities described above. This is the nation that we live in. This is a society that most of us did not create but which our President and other leaders have been willing to sustain by virtue of malign neglect. Do we possess the character and courage to address a problem which so many nations, poorer than our own, have found it natural to correct?

45 The answers to these questions represent a reasonable test of our belief in the democracy to which we have been asked in public school to swear allegiance.

### Responding to Reading

1. According to Kozol, how does illiteracy undermine democracy in the United States? Do you agree with him?
2. Do you think Kozol accurately describes the difficulties illiterates face in their daily lives, or does he seem to be exaggerating? If you think he is exaggerating, what motive might he have?
3. **Rhetorical Analysis** Kozol concludes his essay by asking whether we as a nation have "the character and courage to address" illiteracy (44). He does not, however, offer any concrete suggestions for doing so. Should he have? Why or why not?

### Writing about Reading

1. Keep a log of your activities for a day. Then, discuss which of these activities you could and could not perform if you were illiterate.
2. **Writing with Sources** Some critics have accused Kozol of overstating the problem of illiteracy in the United States. They say that Kozol's numbers are grossly exaggerated and that his definition of *functional illiteracy* is misleading. Research some of Kozol's claims, and then write an essay that addresses the concerns of his critics.

## POEM IN WHICH WORDS HAVE BEEN LEFT OUT

### Charles Jensen

*1977–*

*A poet, educator, and consultant, Charles Jensen is the founding and managing editor of the online poetry magazine LOCUSPOINT and the managing communications editor at the Colburn School in Los Angeles.*

*The author of four poetry chapbooks, he has also published poems in* Columbia Poetry Review, New England Review, *and* Prairie Schooner, *among other publications. In the following poem, the speaker recreates a historical text.*

—The *"Miranda Rights,"*[1] *established 1966*

You have the right to remain
anything you can and will be.

An attorney you cannot afford
will be provided to you.

You have silent will.
You can be against law.
You cannot afford one.

You remain silent. Anything you say                5
will be provided to you.

The right can and will be
against you. The right provided you.

Have anything you say be
right. Anything you say can be right.               10

Say you have the right attorney.
The right remain silent.

Be held. Court the one. Be provided.
You cannot be you.

## Responding to Reading                                    MyWritingLab™

1.  Locate the text of the Miranda rights. What words does the poem leave out?
2.  How does this poem change the meaning of the original text?
3.  What point do you think Jensen is trying to make? Do you think he succeeds?

## Responding in Writing                                     MyWritingLab™

Write a poem based on a different text—for example, part of the Declaration of Independence. Begin by removing words and punctuation to create something new. When you have finished, write an analysis of your poem, telling readers what words you removed and why—in other words, what point you were trying to communicate.

---

[1]The right of criminal suspects in the United States to remain silent before interrogation. [Eds.]

―――――――――― FOCUS ――――――――――

## How Free Should Free Speech Be?

"I am Charlie" demonstration, 2015

### Responding to the Image

MyWritingLab™

1. In 2015, millions rallied around the world to protest the killing of twelve people by Muslim terrorists at the magazine *Charlie Hebdo* in Paris. One reporter described the protest in Paris as "emotional and peaceful, a gesture of unity." In what sense does the image above reflect this assessment?

2. During the protests, many people held signs that said "Je suis Charlie" (French for "I am Charlie.") Why do you think that protesters adopted this slogan? What point were they trying to make?

# SHUT UP AND PLAY NICE: HOW THE WESTERN WORLD IS LIMITING FREE SPEECH

## Jonathan Turley

### *1961–*

*Jonathan Turley is the Shapiro professor of public interest law, director of the Environmental Law Advocacy Center, and executive director of the Project for Older Prisoners at the George Washington University Law School. In the following essay, Turley explains the ways in which free speech is becoming less free.*

Free speech is dying in the Western world. While most people still enjoy considerable freedom of expression, this right, once a near-absolute, has become less defined and less dependable for those espousing controversial social, political or religious views. The decline of free speech has come not from any single blow but rather from thousands of paper cuts of well-intentioned exceptions designed to maintain social harmony.

In the face of the violence that frequently results from anti-religious expression, some world leaders seem to be losing their patience with free speech. After a video called "Innocence of Muslims" appeared on YouTube and sparked violent protests in several Muslim nations last month, U.N. Secretary General Ban Ki-moon warned that "when some people use this freedom of expression to provoke or humiliate some others' values and beliefs, then this cannot be protected."

It appears that the one thing modern society can no longer tolerate is intolerance. As Australian Prime Minister Julia Gillard put it in her recent speech before the United Nations, "Our tolerance must never extend to tolerating religious hatred."

A willingness to confine free speech in the name of social pluralism can be seen at various levels of authority and government. In February, for instance, Pennsylvania Judge Mark Martin heard a case in which a Muslim man was charged with attacking an atheist marching in a Halloween parade as a "zombie Muhammed." Martin castigated not the defendant but the victim, Ernie Perce, lecturing him that "our forefathers intended to use the First Amendment so we can speak with our mind, not to piss off other people and cultures—which is what you did."

Of course, free speech is often precisely about pissing off other people—challenging social taboos or political values.

This was evident in recent days when courts in Washington and New York ruled that transit authorities could not prevent or delay the posting of a controversial ad that says: "In any war between the civilized man and the savage, support the civilized man. Support Israel. Defeat jihad."

When U.S. District Judge Rosemary Collyer said the government could not bar the ad simply because it could upset some Metro riders, the ruling prompted calls for new limits on such speech. And in New York, the Metropolitan Transportation Authority responded by unanimously passing a new regulation banning any message that it considers likely to "incite" others or cause some "other immediate breach of the peace."

Such efforts focus not on the right to speak but on the possible reaction to speech—a fundamental change in the treatment of free speech in the West. The much-misconstrued statement of Justice Oliver Wendell Holmes that free speech does not give you the right to shout fire in a crowded theater is now being used to curtail speech that might provoke a violence-prone minority. Our entire society is being treated as a crowded theater, and talking about whole subjects is now akin to shouting "fire!"

The new restrictions are forcing people to meet the demands of the lowest common denominator of accepted speech, usually using one of four rationales.

## Speech is blasphemous

10  This is the oldest threat to free speech, but it has experienced something of a comeback in the 21st century. After protests erupted throughout the Muslim world in 2005 over Danish cartoons depicting the prophet Muhammad, Western countries publicly professed fealty to free speech, yet quietly cracked down on anti-religious expression. Religious critics in France, Britain, Italy and other countries have found themselves under criminal investigation as threats to public safety. In France, actress and animal rights activist Brigitte Bardot has been fined several times for comments about how Muslims are undermining French culture. And just last month, a Greek atheist was arrested for insulting a famous monk by making his name sound like that of a pasta dish.

Some Western countries have classic blasphemy laws—such as Ireland, which in 2009 criminalized the "publication or utterance of blasphemous matter" deemed "grossly abusive or insulting in relation to matters held sacred by any religion." The Russian Duma recently proposed a law against "insulting religious beliefs." Other countries allow the arrest of people who threaten strife by criticizing religions or religious leaders. In Britain, for instance, a 15-year-old girl was arrested two years ago for burning a Koran.

Western governments seem to be sending the message that free speech rights will not protect you—as shown clearly last month by the images of Nakoula Basseley Nakoula, the YouTube filmmaker, being carted away in California on suspicion of probation violations.

Dutch politician Geert Wilders went through years of litigation before he was acquitted last year on charges of insulting Islam by voicing anti-Islamic views. In the Netherlands and Italy, cartoonists and comedians have been charged with insulting religion through caricatures or jokes.

Even the Obama administration supported the passage of a resolution in the U.N. Human Rights Council to create an international standard restricting some anti-religious speech (its full name: "Combating Intolerance, Negative Stereotyping and Stigmatization of, and Discrimination, Incitement to Violence and Violence Against, Persons Based on Religion or Belief"). Egypt's U.N. ambassador heralded the resolution as exposing the "true nature" of free speech and recognizing that "freedom of expression has been sometimes misused" to insult religion.

At a Washington conference last year to implement the resolution, Secretary of State Hillary Rodham Clinton declared that it would protect both "the right to practice one's religion freely and the right to express one's opinion without fear." But it isn't clear how speech can be protected if the yardstick is how people react to speech—particularly in countries where people riot over a single cartoon. Clinton suggested that free speech resulting in "sectarian clashes" or "the destruction or the defacement or the vandalization of religious sites" was not, as she put it, "fair game."

Given this initiative, President Obama's U.N. address last month 15 declaring America's support for free speech, while laudable, seemed confused—even at odds with his administration's efforts.

## Speech is hateful

In the United States, hate speech is presumably protected under the First Amendment. However, hate-crime laws often redefine hateful expression as a criminal act. Thus, in 2003, the Supreme Court addressed the conviction of a Virginia Ku Klux Klan member who burned a cross on private land. The court allowed for criminal penalties so long as the government could show that the act was "intended to intimidate" others. It was a distinction without meaning, since the state can simply cite the intimidating history of that symbol.

Other Western nations routinely bar forms of speech considered hateful. Britain prohibits any "abusive or insulting words" meant "to stir up racial hatred." Canada outlaws "any writing, sign or visible representation" that "incites hatred against any identifiable group." These laws ban speech based not only on its content but on the reaction of others. Speakers are often called to answer for their divisive or insulting speech before bodies like the Canadian Human Rights Tribunal.

This month, a Canadian court ruled that Marc Lemire, the webmaster of a far-right political site, could be punished for allowing third parties to leave insulting comments about homosexuals and blacks on the site. Echoing the logic behind blasphemy laws, Federal Court Justice Richard Mosley ruled that "the minimal harm caused ... to freedom of expression is far outweighed by the benefit it provides to vulnerable groups and to the promotion of equality."

## Speech is discriminatory

Perhaps the most rapidly expanding limitation on speech is found in anti-discrimination laws. Many Western countries have extended such laws to public statements deemed insulting or derogatory to any group, race or gender.

20        For example, in a closely watched case last year, a French court found fashion designer John Galliano guilty of making discriminatory comments in a Paris bar, where he got into a cursing match with a couple using sexist and anti-Semitic terms. Judge Anne-Marie Sauteraud read a list of the bad words Galliano had used, adding that she found (rather implausibly) he had said "dirty whore" at least 1,000 times. Though he faced up to six months in jail, he was fined.

In Canada, comedian Guy Earle was charged with violating the human rights of a lesbian couple after he got into a trash-talking session with a group of women during an open-mike night at a nightclub. Lorna Pardy said she suffered post-traumatic stress because of Earle's profane language and derogatory terms for lesbians. The British Columbia Human Rights Tribunal ruled last year that since this was a matter of discrimination, free speech was not a defense, and awarded about $23,000 to the couple.

Ironically, while some religious organizations are pushing blasphemy laws, religious individuals are increasingly targeted under anti-discrimination laws for their criticism of homosexuals and other groups. In 2008, a minister in Canada was not only forced to pay fines for uttering anti-gay sentiments but was also enjoined from expressing such views in the future.

## Speech is deceitful

In the United States, where speech is given the most protection among Western countries, there has been a recent effort to carve out a potentially large category to which the First Amendment would not apply. While we have always prosecuted people who lie to achieve financial or other benefits, some argue that the government can outlaw any lie, regardless of whether the liar secured any economic gain.

One such law was the Stolen Valor Act, signed by President George W. Bush in 2006, which made it a crime for people to lie about receiving military honors. The Supreme Court struck it down this year, but at least two liberal justices, Stephen Breyer and Elena Kagan, proposed that such laws should have less of a burden to be upheld as constitutional. The House responded with new legislation that would criminalize lies told with the intent to obtain any undefined "tangible benefit."

The dangers are obvious. Government officials have long labeled 25 whistleblowers, reporters and critics as "liars" who distort their actions or words. If the government can define what is a lie, it can define what is the truth.

For example, in February the French Supreme Court declared unconstitutional a law that made it a crime to deny the 1915 Armenian genocide by Turkey—a characterization that Turkey steadfastly rejects. Despite the ruling, various French leaders pledged to pass new measures punishing those who deny the Armenians' historical claims.

The impact of government limits on speech has been magnified by even greater forms of private censorship. For example, most news organizations have stopped showing images of Muhammad, though they seem to have no misgivings about caricatures of other religious figures. The most extreme such example was supplied by Yale University Press, which in 2009 published a book about the Danish cartoons titled "The Cartoons That Shook the World"—but cut all of the cartoons so as not to insult anyone.

The very right that laid the foundation for Western civilization is increasingly viewed as a nuisance, if not a threat. Whether speech is deemed inflammatory or hateful or discriminatory or simply false, society is denying speech rights in the name of tolerance, enforcing mutual respect through categorical censorship.

As in a troubled marriage, the West seems to be falling out of love with free speech. Unable to divorce ourselves from this defining right, we take refuge instead in an awkward and forced silence.

## Responding to Reading

MyWritingLab™

1. What does Turley mean when he says that there is a willingness to limit free speech "in the name of social pluralism" (4)? How does he support this statement?
2. What limit did Oliver Wendell Holmes put on freedom of speech? According to Turley, how is this limit being misconstrued?
3. **Rhetorical Analysis**  Turley appeals mainly to **logos**—to logic. At what point in the essay does he appeal to emotion (pathos)? How does he establish his credibility (ethos)?

## Writing about Reading

MyWritingLab™

1. What limitations (if any) do you think should be placed on free speech?
2. **Writing with Sources**  In his essay, Turley lists four kinds of speech that some people want banned. Choose one of his categories, and research the pros and cons of prohibiting it. Then, write an essay in which you argue for or against placing restrictions on this type of speech.

CHAPTER 5  FOCUS

# KINDLY INQUISITORS, REVISITED

## Jonathan Rauch

### 1960–

*A contributing editor of* The Atlantic *and* National Journal *and a senior fellow at the Brookings Institution in Washington, D.C., Jonathan Rauch analyzes issues related to culture, politics, and economics. The author of several books, including, most recently,* Gay Marriage: Why It Is Good for Gays, Good for Straights, and Good for America *(2004), he also writes for publications such as the* Chronicle of Higher Education, *the* Economist, Harper's, *the* Los Angeles Times, The New Republic, Reason, *the* New York Times, Slate, U.S. News & World Report, *the* Wall Street Journal, *and the* Washington Post. *Adapted from Rauch's new afterword for the 2013 edition of his book* Kindly Inquisitors *(originally published in 1993), the following essay argues for the cultural value of free speech.*

Twenty years ago, in 1993, Salman Rushdie was a hunted man. Iran had sentenced him to death for writing a novel that allegedly defamed Islam; governments and intellectuals in the West had responded with a measure of defiance, but a larger measure of ambivalence and confusion. Was Rushdie entitled, really, to write a book that he could have anticipated would deeply offend Muslims?

In 1998, as part of an agreement to restore diplomatic relations with Great Britain, the Iranian government formally withdrew its support from the fatwa[1] against Rushdie, and the author resumed public life. But Rushdie's freedom has not put to rest the Rushdie affair. The fatwa's report echoed loudly in 2005 when a Danish newspaper published cartoons, some of them provocative, depicting the Prophet Muhammad. The resulting uproar occasioned, in the West, a chaotic mix of confusion, apology, and defiance, not unlike that which met the Rushdie affair.

The Danish government said, "Freedom of expression is the very foundation of the Danish democracy," but then went on to say, "However, Danish legislation prohibits acts or expressions of a blasphemous or discriminatory nature." When Danish authorities chose not to prosecute the cartoons' publisher, death threats and violent protests around the world led to the murders of several hundred people. In France and Canada, publications that republished the cartoons found themselves under government investigation for inciting hatred or violating human rights. Ultimately, they were not prosecuted. It would be fair to say that the West's defense of intellectual freedom was ringingly ambivalent. The more things change...

Today, what I called in 1993 "the new attacks on free thought" are no longer new. The regulation of speech deemed hateful or discriminatory or harassing has spread internationally and dug in

---

[1]An Islamic legal decision. [Eds.]

domestically. In the United States, hate-speech laws as such are unconstitutional. But indirect, bureaucratic prohibitions have burrowed into workplaces and universities. Federal law holds employers civilly liable for permitting the workplace to become a "hostile environment"—a fuzzy concept which has been stretched to include, for example, a Bible verse printed on a paycheck (could upset an atheist) or a Seventh-Day Adventist's discussion of religion ("religious harassment" because it "depressed" a plaintiff).

Unlike most workplaces, universities are at the heart of intellectual life, and so the bureaucratization of speech controls there is more disturbing. In American universities, the hostile-environment and discriminatory-harassment doctrines have become part of the administrative furniture. "Most colleges and universities in the United States have instituted what are in effect speech codes," write the law professors Arthur Jacobson and Bernhard Schlink, in their contribution to the 2012 collection *The Content and Context of Hate Speech: Rethinking Regulation and Responses.* "The codes range widely in the speech they prohibit," but even the narrower ones "can define harassment more broadly than have the federal courts." Moreover, "colleges and universities are noticeably reticent to afford defendants in campus adjudications procedural protections that in federal and state courts are routine and necessary."

Alas, these sorts of bureaucratic controls have become a background thrum of academic life. They sometimes run into challenges when they go too far in particular cases—as when Brandeis University found a professor guilty of racial harassment for explaining the origin of the word *wetbacks.* But the *idea* that minority rights justify speech codes and quasi-judicial inquisitions is barely controversial among academic administrators. History will someday wonder how the very people who should have been most protective of intellectual freedom took such a wrong turn.

Abroad, without a First Amendment to act as a buffer, direct government restrictions on hate speech have become the norm, enacted by many countries and encouraged by several human rights treaties. Miklós Haraszti, of Columbia University's school of international and public affairs, writes of "a growing, punitive trend that is introducing new speech bans into national criminal codes. Most of them target bad speech specific to the country or to the worries of its ruling parties, the two being practically indistinguishable." The United States and Hungary, according to the British political theorist Bhikhu Parekh, are the only countries which have recently resisted the trend to ban hate speech. (He and Haraszti write in *The Content and Context of Hate Speech.*)

But there is good news, too. Frontal humanitarian and egalitarian attacks on the legitimacy of liberal science—our decentralized, criticism-based global system for developing knowledge—have waned. Arguments for restricting speech in the name of equality and compassion are more sophisticated and concomitantly more modest.

Version 2.0 of the case for bans on speech relies less on metaphorical notions like "words that wound" and "verbal violence," which could mean almost anything. Instead it looks to a narrower hostile-environment doctrine which justifies penalties only in relatively extreme cases, such as when speech seems likely to create a pervasively demeaning or threatening social environment for recently persecuted minorities, denying them (the theory goes) equal status as fully protected citizens. "Offensiveness by itself is not a good reason for legal regulation," writes Jeremy Waldron, a law professor at New York University, in his fine 2012 book, *The Harm in Hate Speech*. "Where there are fine lines to be drawn the law should generally stay on the liberal side of them."

10     I don't think Version 2.0 has succeeded in answering the challenges that I and others have posed. It has not demonstrated that hate speech silences minorities, rather than mobilizing or energizing them; it has not shown that restrictions ameliorate hate or silence haters, rather than intensifying hate and publicizing haters. It has not figured out how to make political authorities interpret and enforce political restrictions apolitically, or how to prevent majorities and authorities from turning restrictions to majoritarian and authoritarian ends. It does not reckon the cost of overdeterrence and of chilling important but controversial conversations; or the cost of stereotyping minorities as vulnerable and defenseless; or the cost of denying the agency of the listener, who, after all, can *choose* how to react to the maunderings of haters. It has yet to enunciate a limiting principle. Why, after all, stop with speech deemed harmful to minorities, when there is so much other socially harmful speech in the world? Doesn't it harm society to let climate-change deniers yammer on?

But save those arguments for another day. I want to try to answer the deepest challenge that Version 2.0 poses. It is an epistemological challenge, and it goes like this:

Some ideas actually *are* false, and at some point the process of checking establishes their falsehood so firmly that to proceed as if they might be true becomes ridiculous. For example, Holocaust denial: Isn't it a stretch to claim we can learn something by debating neo-Nazis about the existence of gas chambers? Fallibilism is all well and good, but come on—enough is enough. In the 21st century, do Jews really need to put up with *The Protocols of the Elders of Zion*, a notorious anti-Semitic fraud? Shouldn't governments at least be allowed to regulate the most injurious of lies in the most blatant of cases?

As for enforcement, it may not be perfect, but what ever is? Even though politicians and courts won't always strike the right balance between free speech and minorities' dignity, they won't always get it wrong, either; the solution is to do a better job of balancing, not to throw away the scales. And we must not overlook the specific effects on minorities; it doesn't seem fair to sacrifice their interests on the altar of free speech. Do gays and Jews benefit from toleration of homophobic or anti-Semitic claptrap?

I believe the answer is yes. Society benefits from the toleration of hate speech, and so do targeted minorities.

Today's narrower, Version 2.0 argument for hate-speech laws asks   15 us to imagine a really hard case: not a society where people say offensive things in random directions now and then (which should be allowed), but one where (in Jeremy Waldron's words) vulnerable groups "have to live and go about in a society festooned with vicious characterizations of them and their kind and with foul denigrations of their status.... [T]he upshot might be that they would avoid much public life or participate in it without the security that the rest of us enjoy; either that, or they would have to summon up (from their own resources) extraordinary reserves of assurance as they went about their business, a burden that is not required of the rest of us." Surely, in so extreme a case, promising to punish violence or discrimination after the fact is not enough; surely, in *this* case, laws preemptively suppressing bigotry are appropriate?

Such societies exist. I grew up in one, because I was born in the United States in 1960, and I am homosexual.

You may remember those days. Gay Americans were forbidden to work for the government; forbidden to obtain security clearances; forbidden to serve in the military. They were arrested for making love, even in their own homes; beaten and killed on the streets; entrapped and arrested by the police for sport; fired from their jobs. They were joked about, demeaned, and bullied as a matter of course; forced to live by a code of secrecy and lies, on pain of opprobrium and unemployment; witch-hunted by anti-Communists, Christians, and any politician or preacher who needed a scapegoat; condemned as evil by moralists and as sick by scientists; portrayed as sinister and simpering by Hollywood; perhaps worst of all, rejected and condemned, at the most vulnerable time of life, by their own parents. America was a society permeated by hate: usually, it's true, hateful ideas and assumptions, not hateful people, but hate all the same. So ubiquitous was the hostility to homosexuality that few gay people ever even dared hold hands in public with the person they loved.

Obviously, passing a hate-speech law to protect homosexuals, much less enforcing one, was not on anyone's agenda. The very idea would have seemed preposterous. Any hate-speech law which might have passed would have targeted gay people (in the name of defending children), not protected us.

The case for hate-speech prohibitions mistakes the cart for the horse, imagining that anti-hate laws are a cause of toleration when they are almost always a consequence. In democracies, minorities do not get fair, enforceable legal protections until after majorities have come around to supporting them. By the time a community is ready to punish intolerance legally, it will already be punishing intolerance culturally. At that point, turning haters into courtroom martyrs is unnecessary and often counterproductive.

Chapter 5 Focus

20    In any case, we can be quite certain that hate-speech laws did not change America's attitude toward its gay and lesbian minority, because there were no hate-speech laws. Today, firm majorities accept the morality of homosexuality, know and esteem gay people, and endorse gay unions and families. What happened to turn the world upside-down?

What happened was this. In 1957, the U.S. Army Map Service fired an astronomer named Franklin Kameny after learning he was gay. Kameny, unlike so many others, did not go quietly. He demanded reinstatement from the U.S. Civil Service Commission and the Congress. When he got nowhere, he filed a Supreme Court brief. "In World War II," he told the Court, "petitioner did not hesitate to fight the Germans, with bullets, in order to help preserve his rights and freedoms and liberties, and those of others. In 1960, it is ironically necessary that he fight the Americans, with words, in order to preserve, against a tyrannical government, some of those same rights, freedoms and liberties, for himself and others."

In 1965, Kameny led dignified gay-rights demonstrations, the first of their kind, in front of the White House and Philadelphia's Independence Hall. (Signs said: "Denial of equality of opportunity is immoral." "We demand that our government confer with us." "Private consenting sexual conduct by adults is NOT the government's concern.")

In 1969, gays rioted against police harassment in New York. In 1970, two gay student activists, Jack Baker and Michael McConnell, walked into a county clerk's office in Minnesota and asked for a marriage license. Much, much more was to come.

In ones and twos at first, then in streams and eventually cascades, gays *talked*. They argued. They explained. They showed. They confronted. If the pervasiveness of bigotry was supposed to silence them, as hate-speech allegedly does, Frank Kameny missed the memo. "If society and I differ on something," he said in 1972, "I'm willing to give the matter a second look. If we still differ, then I am right and society is wrong; and society can go its way so long as it does not get in my way. But, if it does, there's going to be a fight. And I'm not going to be the one who backs down."

25    Kameny and others confronted the psychiatric profession about its irrational pathologizing of homosexuality, bombarded the U.S. Civil Service Commission with demands that it end the ban on gay government employment, and confronted Christians with their hardly Christ-like conduct. "If your god condemns people like me for the crime of loving," Kameny would say, "then your god is a false and bigoted god." In the 1980s and early 1990s, a few visionaries—Andrew Sullivan, Evan Wolfson—argued that gay couples should be allowed to marry, a cause seemingly so hopeless that even many gay people hesitated to endorse it.

Frank Kameny lost every appeal to get his job back; the Supreme Court refused to hear his case. In 1963, he launched a campaign to repeal the District of Columbia's sodomy law and lost (that effort would take three decades). He ran for Congress in 1971 and lost. But at every stage he fired moral imaginations. He and others saw Jerry

Falwell and Anita Bryant[2] not as threats to hide from but as opportunities to be seized: opportunities to rally gays, educate straights, and draw sharp moral comparisons. "Is *that* what you think this country is all about? Really?"

To appeal to a country's conscience, you need an antagonist. Suppression of anti-gay speech and thought, had it been conceivable at the time, would have slowed the country's moral development, not speeded it. It would have given the illusion that the job was finished when, in fact, the job was only beginning. It would have condescended to a people fighting for respect.

I am not naive about the bravery it took for Kameny and others of his generation to step forward. They were hammered. They suffered severely. Kameny lived long enough to be honored by President Obama and, in 2009, to receive an official government apology from the U.S. Office of Personnel Management, which by then was headed by an openly gay man. But most of us are not Kamenys.

Most of us are also not Galileos or Einsteins, or Sakharovs or Kings. The good news is that most of us don't need to be. We need only a few Kamenys—plus a system that is very good at testing and rejecting bad hypotheses and at bringing forward better ones. As gay people stepped forward, liberal science engaged. The old anti-gay dogmas came under critical scrutiny as never before. "Homosexuals molest and recruit children"; "homosexuals cannot be happy"; "homosexuals are really heterosexuals"; "homosexuality is unknown in nature": The canards collapsed with astonishing speed.

What took place was not just empirical learning but also moral 30 learning. How can it be wicked to love? How can it be noble to lie? How can it be compassionate to reject your own children? How can it be kind to harass and taunt? How can it be fair to harp on one Biblical injunction when so many others are ignored? How can it be just to penalize what does no demonstrable harm? Gay people were asking straight people to test their values against logic, against compassion, against life. Gradually, then rapidly, the criticism had its effect.

You cannot be gay in America today and doubt that moral learning is real and that the open society fosters it. And so, 20 years on, I feel more confident than ever that the answer to bias and prejudice is pluralism, not purism. The answer, that is, is not to try to legislate bias and prejudice out of existence or to drive them underground, but to pit biases and prejudices against each other and make them fight in the open. That is how, in the crucible of rational criticism, superstition and moral error are burned away.

I believe the hope of living in a world free of discrimination and prejudice is a utopian pipe dream, and is as anti-human and dangerous as most other utopian pipe dreams. The quest to stamp out

---

[2] Opponents of homosexuality. [Eds.]

discrimination or bigotry or racism wherever it appears is a quest to force all opinion into a single template. I reject the premise—not just the methods—of the 1965 International Convention on the Elimination of All Forms of Racial Discrimination, which calls on signatory countries to prohibit "all dissemination of ideas based on racial superiority or hatred." In my view, if minorities know what is good for us, we should at every turn support pluralism, with all its social messiness and personal hurt. Politicians and activists, however well intentioned, who would shelter us from criticism and debate offer false comfort.

History shows that, over time and probably today more than ever, the more open the intellectual environment, the better minorities will do. It is just about that simple. So here is a reply to advocates of hate-speech regulation who wonder if, today, it really serves any purpose to let people go around touting *The Protocols of the Elders of Zion*. The answer is yes, it does. We cannot fight hate and fraud without seeing them and debunking them. John Stuart Mill, writing in *On Liberty* in 1859, was right. "Wrong opinions and practices gradually yield to fact and argument: but facts and arguments, to produce any effect on the mind, must be brought before it."

Today I fear that many people on my side of the gay-equality question are forgetting our debt to the system that freed us. Some gay people—not all, not even most, but quite a few—want to expunge discriminatory views. "Discrimination is discrimination and bigotry is bigotry," they say, "and they are intolerable whether or not they happen to be someone's religion or moral creed."

35 Here is not the place for an examination of the proper balance between, say, religious liberty and anti-discrimination rules. It is a place, perhaps, for a plea to those of us in the gay-rights movement—and in other minority-rights movements—who now find ourselves in the cultural ascendency, with public majorities and public morality (strange to say it!) on our side. We should be the last people on the planet to demand that anyone be silenced.

Partly the reasons are strategic. Robust intellectual exchange serves our interest. Our greatest enemy is not irrational hate, which is pretty uncommon. It is *rational* hate, hate premised upon falsehood. (If you believe homosexuality poses a threat to your children, you will hate it.) The main way we eliminate hate is not to legislate or inveigh against it, but to replace it—with knowledge, empirical and ethical. That was how Frank Kameny and a few other people, without numbers or law or public sympathy on their side, turned hate on its head. They had arguments, and they had the right to make them.

And partly the reasons are moral. Gay people have lived in a world where we were forced, day in and day out, to betray our consciences and shut our mouths in the name of public morality. Not so long ago, *everybody* thought we were wrong. Now our duty is to protect others' freedom to be wrong, the better to ensure society's odds of being right.

Of course, we can and should correct the falsehoods we hear and, once they are debunked, deny them the standing of *knowledge* in textbooks and professions; but we equally have the responsibility to defend their expression as *opinion* in the public square.

Finding the proper balance is not easy and isn't supposed to be. If a Catholic adoption agency wants to refuse placements to same-sex couples, we will have to argue about where to draw lines. What I am urging is a general proposition: Minorities are the point of the spear defending liberal science. We are the first to be targeted with vile words and ideas, but we are also the leading beneficiaries of a system which puts up with them. The open society is sometimes a cross we bear, but it is also a sword we wield, and we are defenseless without it.

We ought to remember what Frank Kameny never forgot: For politically weak minorities, the best and often only way to effect wholesale change in the world of politics is by effecting change in the world of ideas. Our position as beneficiaries of the open society requires us to serve as guardians of it. Playing that role, not seeking government protections or hauling our adversaries before star chambers, is the greater source of our dignity.

Frank Kameny, an irascible man with a capacious conscience, had it right. In more than 50 years of activism, he never called for silencing or punishing those he disagreed with, but he never cut them any argumentative slack, either. In his spirit, I hope that when gay people—and non-gay people—encounter hateful or discriminatory opinions, we respond not by trying to silence or punish them but by trying to correct them. 40

## Responding to Reading
MyWritingLab™

1.  What is Version 2.0 of the case for banning speech? How is this different from previous efforts to limit certain kinds of speech? What, according to Rauch, is the problem with Version 2.0?
2.  According to Rauch, why should hate speech be tolerated? What does he mean when he says, "For politically weak minorities, the best and often only way to effect wholesale change in the world of politics is by effecting change in the world of ideas" (39)?
3.  **Rhetorical Analysis**  In paragraph 16, Rauch says that he is gay. Why does he include this information? Why does he isolate it in a single paragraph? Does this disclosure strengthen or weaken his argument? Explain.

## Writing about Reading
MyWritingLab™

1.  Do you agree with Rauch that minorities benefit from a free and open society that places few limits on speech?
2.  **Writing with Sources**  As Rauch points out, many colleges and universities have speech codes. Find some of these codes, and read them. What kinds of speech do they limit? How clear are the guidelines for prohibiting speech? What are the penalties for violating these speech codes? Then, write an article for your school newspaper in which you support or argue against the use of speech codes.

# SHOULD NEO-NAZIS BE ALLOWED FREE SPEECH?

## Thane Rosenbaum

### 1960–

*A senior fellow and the director of the Forum on Law, Culture & Society at New York University School of Law, Thane Rosebaum is an essayist and novelist who moderates* The Talk Show, *an annual series of cultural and political talks at the 92nd Street Y. The author of several books, including, most recently,* Payback: The Case for Revenge (2013), *he has also published essays in the* Daily Beast, *the* Huffington Post, *the* New York Times, *the* Wall Street Journal, *and the* Washington Post. *In the following essay, Rosenbaum considers the dangers of free speech.*

Over the past several weeks, free speech has gotten costlier—at least in France and Israel.

In France, Dieudonne M'Bala M'Bala, an anti-Semitic stand-up comic infamous for popularizing the quenelle, an inverted Nazi salute, was banned from performing in two cities. M'Bala M'Bala has been repeatedly fined for hate speech, and this was not the first time his act was perceived as a threat to public order.

Meanwhile, Israel's parliament is soon to pass a bill outlawing the word Nazi for non-educational purposes. Indeed, any slur against another that invokes the Third Reich could land the speaker in jail for six months with a fine of $29,000. The Israelis are concerned about both the rise of anti-Semitism globally, and the trivialization of the Holocaust—even locally.

To Americans, these actions in France and Israel seem positively undemocratic. The First Amendment would never prohibit the quenelle, regardless of its symbolic meaning. And any lover of "Seinfeld" would regard banning the "Soup Nazi" episode as scandalously un-American. After all, in 1977 a federal court upheld the right of neo-Nazis to goose-step right through the town of Skokie, Illinois, which had a disproportionately large number of Holocaust survivors as residents. And more recently, the Supreme Court upheld the right of a church group opposed to gays serving in the military to picket the funeral of a dead marine with signs that read, "God Hates Fags."

5   While what is happening in France and Israel is wholly foreign to Americans, perhaps it's time to consider whether these and other countries may be right. Perhaps America's fixation on free speech has gone too far.

Actually, the United States is an outlier among democracies in granting such generous free speech guarantees. Six European countries, along with Brazil, prohibit the use of Nazi symbols and flags. Many more countries have outlawed Holocaust denial. Indeed, even encouraging racial discrimination in France is a crime. In pluralistic nations like these with clashing cultures and historical tragedies not shared by all, mutual respect and civility helps keep the peace and avoids unnecessary mental trauma.

Yet, even in the United States, free speech is not unlimited. Certain proscribed categories have always existed—libel, slander and defamation, obscenity, "fighting words," and the "incitement of imminent lawlessness"—where the First Amendment does not protect the speaker, where the right to speak is curtailed for reasons of general welfare and public safety. There is no freedom to shout "fire" in a crowded theater. Hate crime statutes exist in many jurisdictions where bias-motivated crimes are given more severe penalties. In 2003, the Supreme Court held that speech intended to intimidate, such as cross burning, might not receive First Amendment protection.

Yet, the confusion is that in placing limits on speech we privilege physical over emotional harm. Indeed, we have an entire legal system, and an attitude toward speech, that takes its cue from a nursery rhyme: "Stick and stones can break my bones but names can never hurt me."

All of us know, however, and despite what we tell our children, names do, indeed, hurt. And recent studies in universities such as Purdue, UCLA, Michigan, Toronto, Arizona, Maryland, and Macquarie University in New South Wales, show, among other things, through brain scans and controlled studies with participants who were subjected to both physical and emotional pain, that emotional harm is equal in intensity to that experienced by the body, and is even more long-lasting and traumatic. Physical pain subsides; emotional pain, when recalled, is relived.

Pain has a shared circuitry in the human brain, and it makes no 10 distinction between being hit in the face and losing face (or having a broken heart) as a result of bereavement, betrayal, social exclusion and grave insult. Emotional distress can, in fact, make the body sick. Indeed, research has shown that pain relief medication can work equally well for both physical and emotional injury.

We impose speed limits on driving and regulate food and drugs because we know that the costs of not doing so can lead to accidents and harm. Why should speech be exempt from public welfare concerns when its social costs can be even more injurious?

In the marketplace of ideas, there is a difference between trying to persuade and trying to injure. One can object to gays in the military without ruining the one moment a father has to bury his son; neo-Nazis can long for the Third Reich without re-traumatizing Hitler's victims; one can oppose Affirmative Action without burning a cross on an African-American's lawn.

CHAPTER 5  FOCUS

Of course, everything is a matter of degree. Juries are faced with similar ambiguities when it comes to physical injury. No one knows for certain whether the plaintiff wearing a neck brace can't actually run the New York Marathon. We tolerate the fake slip and fall, but we feel absolutely helpless in evaluating whether words and gestures intended to harm actually do cause harm. Jurors are as capable of working through these uncertainties in the area of emotional harms as they are in the realm of physical injury.

Free speech should not stand in the way of common decency. No right should be so freely and recklessly exercised that it becomes an impediment to civil society, making it so that others are made to feel less free, their private space and peace invaded, their sensitivities cruelly trampled upon.

## Responding to Reading

MyWritingLab™

1. According to Rosenbaum, why are laws limiting free speech in France and Israel "wholly foreign to Americans" (5)?
2. What kinds of speech are not protected in the United States? Why, according to Rosenbaum, is there confusion about placing limits on free speech?
3. **Rhetorical Analysis**  In paragraph 11, Rosenbaum draws an analogy between limiting speech and limiting driving or regulating food. What are the strengths and weaknesses of this analogy? Is it convincing? Explain.

## Writing about Reading

MyWritingLab™

1. In his conclusion, Rosenbaum says, "Free speech should not stand in the way of common decency." Do you agree that some words are so hurtful they should be banned?
2. **Writing with Sources**  In addition to France and Israel, many countries—for example, Brazil, Canada, and Denmark—place limits on offensive speech. What types of speech do they outlaw? How effective are these prohibitions? Are such laws possible in the United States, or do they violate the First Amendment of the Constitution? Write an essay that answers these questions.

# WIDENING THE FOCUS

### For Critical Reading and Writing

Referring specifically to the three readings in this chapter's Focus section (and possibly to additional sources as well), write an essay in which you answer the question, "How Free Should Free Speech Be?"

### For Further Reading

The following readings can suggest additional perspectives for thinking and writing about freedom of speech.

- Christina Hoff Sommers, "For More Balance on Campuses" (p. 94)
- Jill Filipovic, "We've Gone Too Far with 'Trigger Warnings'" (p. 97)
- Zeynep Tufekci, "After the Protests" (p. 188)

### For Focused Research

Texting presents special challenges to the First Amendment's guarantee of freedom of expression. For example, is the content of a text considered protected speech? Does the government or an employer have the right to access texts? Can certain forms of texting be prohibited—for example, texts that contain explicit sexual material, texts that harass, or texts that encourage others to commit a crime? In preparation for writing an essay about texting and freedom of speech, do a *Google* search using the search terms *texting and freedom of speech*, and then decide what limits, if any, should be placed on texts. In your essay, explain how texting is the same as and different from other forms of communication. Then, identify the areas that you think should (or should not) be limited or possibly prohibited. Make sure to read a cross-section of opinions on this subject and to support your position with examples and evidence from the websites you use.

### Beyond the Classroom

Conduct an email survey of your friends and classmates, asking them the following questions:

- How much time per week do you spend texting? How much time do you spend doing other kinds of writing (such as email and essay writing)?
- What kinds of texts do you send?
- Have you ever received texts that had questionable content? What kind?

Then, write an essay summarizing your findings and taking a position on whether texting should be considered protected speech.

MyWritingLab™

Visit Chapter 5, "The Politics of Language," in MyWritingLab to test your understanding of the chapter objectives.

—————————— EXPLORING ISSUES AND IDEAS ——————————

## The Politics of Language

Write an essay in response to one of the following prompts, which are suitable for assignments that require the use of outside sources as well as for assignments that are not source-based.

1. In "Mother Tongue" (p. 127), Amy Tan distinguishes between the English she speaks to her mother and the English she speaks to the rest of the world. Write an essay in which you describe the various types of English you speak—at home, at school, at work, to your friends, and so on. In what ways are these Englishes alike, and in what ways are they different? What ideas are you able to express best with each type of English?

2. Over fifty years ago, George Orwell wrote an essay in which he discussed how governments use language to control their citizens. Now, control seems to be exerted at times by a desire for political correctness—excessive focus on avoiding language that might offend others because of their politics, race, gender, age, disabilities, or religious beliefs. Write an essay in which you consider the extent to which political correctness is a factor in the language used at your school, in your workplace, and among your friends and family members. Refer to Alleen Pace Nilsen's "Sexism in English: Embodiment and Language" (p. 137) and Thane Rosenbaum's "Should Neo-Nazis Be Allowed Free Speech?" (p. 172) as well as to your own experiences.

3. Both Amy Tan in "Mother Tongue" (p. 127) and Frederick Douglass in "Learning to Read and Write" (p. 132) talk about how education can change one's use of language. Write an essay discussing the effect education has had on your own spoken and written language. What do you think you have gained and lost as your language has changed?

4. Which of your daily activities would you be unable to carry out if, like the people Jonathan Kozol describes in "The Human Cost of an Illiterate Society" (p. 148), you could neither read nor write? Write an article for your local newspaper in which you report on a typical day, being sure to identify specific tasks you could not do. In addition, explain some strategies you would use to hide the fact that you couldn't read or write.

5. A recent study suggests that the population worldwide that has grown up speaking English is shrinking. In the sciences, however, the use of English is expanding. Some researchers warn that this situation could divide the scientific world into the "haves" and "have-nots"—with the "haves" gaining the advantage of being able to publish in prestigious scientific journals and the

"have-nots" unable to achieve access. Do you think this is fair? Write an essay in which you discuss how the privileging of one language over another gives some people advantages and undercuts the ability of others to accomplish their goals. As you write, consider the essays by Frederick Douglass (p. 132), Alleen Pace Nilsen (p. 137), and Jonathan Kozol (p. 148).

6. List some of the words you use to refer to women, minorities, and other groups. Then, write an email to Alleen Pace Nilsen (p. 137) in which you agree or disagree with her assertion that the words people use tell a lot about their values and beliefs. In addition to Nilsen's essay, consider Jonathan Rauch's "Kindly Inquisitors, Revisited" (p. 164).

# 6

# MEDIA AND SOCIETY

*In this chapter, you will learn to*

- analyze readings about media and society
- compose essays about media and society

M any forms of popular media—for example, books, newspapers, and magazines; radio, television, and film—have been around for a long time, and over the years, they have had a powerful impact on our lives. But the popular media have changed dramatically in our lifetimes.

Television is one medium that changed and yet managed to survive, and even thrive. Cable television brought us literally hundreds of stations, along with sitcom reruns that endlessly recycled our childhoods (and our

Fifteenth-century illuminated manuscript depicting the angel
Gabriel speaking to Mary

parents' childhoods). Satellites brought immediacy, delivering news in real time around the clock. Other innovations also appeared on television: home shopping, reality TV, infomercials, music videos. And now, of course, television has become digital and interactive, with viewers no longer tied to a schedule or limited to watching programs on a television set.

Over the years, in response to emerging technology, other forms of media also reinvented themselves. Music evolved from vinyl records to cassettes to CDs to music downloaded onto MP3 players to music streamed on handheld devices. Movies moved from silent to "talkies" and from black and white to color, later enhanced by sophisticated computer animation and special digital effects. Professional journals and popular magazines became available online, and today, portable digital readers permit us to read paperless newspapers and books. In an effort to hold on to readers, newspapers have constructed websites and published online editions, but, despite these innovations, the Internet continues to threaten the survival of the daily newspaper. (Even before the Internet existed, newspaper readership was on the decline; cities that once had several different daily newspapers, with a variety of editorial positions, now have only a few. In fact, over 98 percent of U.S. cities now have just one major daily newspaper.)

Clearly, "new media" is a completely different entity from the media of even a decade ago, and this evolution has had negative as well as positive consequences. In recent years, the increasing power and scope of the Internet, and its ever-increasing ability to enable us to form networks, has changed everything. Today, our access to digital media

Tablet e-reader

has truly made the world into what Canadian cultural critic Marshall McLuhan once called a "global village": a world of nations—and, today, of individuals—that are more and more interconnected and interdependent. The Internet has made available a tremendous amount of information—and the ability to communicate this information almost instantly to millions of people all over the planet. Now, we exchange ideas and images through blogs, chat rooms, bulletin boards, and email as well as through instant messaging, texting, *YouTube*, *Instagram*, *Pinterest*, and *Twitter*. But the development of new media also has a dark side. The same tools that can unite, inform, instruct, entertain, and inspire can also isolate, misinform, frighten, deceive, stereotype, and even brainwash.

In this chapter's Focus section, "Why Are Zombies Invading Our Media?" (p. 206), three writers discuss the zombie phenomenon. In "A Zombie Is a Slave Forever," Amy Wilentz provides background on the origins of zombies and speculates about why they are "returning now to haunt us." In "The Movies That Rose from the Grave," Max Brooks looks at the proliferation of zombies in other media as well as in film. Finally, in "Zombie Studies Gain Ground on College Campuses," Erica E. Phillips surveys some zombie-themed course offerings and explores the implications of this trend.

## PREPARING TO READ AND WRITE

As you read and prepare to write about the essays in this chapter, you may consider the following questions:

- What assumptions does the writer seem to have about his or her audience? How can you tell?

- What is the writer's primary purpose? For example, is it to present information? to persuade? something else?

- What genre is the writer using? For example, is the reading an essay? an op-ed piece? an argument? a work of fiction? How do the conventions of this genre influence the writer's choices?

- What appeals does the writer use? For example, does he or she appeal primarily to emotion or to reason? Is this the most effective appeal?

- Does the essay focus on one particular medium or on the media in general?

- Does the writer discuss traditional media, new media, or both?

- Does the writer see the media as a positive, negative, or neutral force? Why?

- If the writer sees negative effects, where does he or she place blame? Do you agree?

- Does the writer make any recommendations for change? Do these recommendations seem reasonable?

- Is the writer focusing on the media's effects on individuals or on society?

- Does the writer discuss personal observations or experiences? If so, are they similar to or different from your own?

- When was the essay written? Has the situation the writer describes changed since then?

- Which writers' positions on the impact of the media (or on the media's shortcomings) are most alike? Most different? Most like your own?

# EMINEM IS RIGHT

## Mary Eberstadt

*A senior fellow at the Ethics & Public Policy Center in Washington, D.C., Mary Eberstadt is an author of numerous magazine and newspaper articles on various American cultural issues. Her most recent book is* How the West Really Lost God *(2013). Originally published in her 2004 book* Home-Alone America: The Hidden Toll of Day Care, Behavioral Drugs, and Other Parent Substitutes, *the essay excerpted here examines the meanings and social implications of contemporary American popular music.*

If there is one subject on which the parents of America passionately agree, it is that contemporary adolescent popular music, especially the subgenres of heavy metal and hip-hop/rap, is uniquely degraded—and degrading—by the standards of previous generations. At first blush this seems slightly ironic. After all, most of today's baby-boom parents were themselves molded by rock and roll, bumping and grinding their way through adolescence and adulthood with legendary abandon. Even so, the parents are correct: Much of today's music *is* darker and coarser than yesterday's rock. Misogyny, violence, suicide, sexual exploitation, child abuse—these and other themes, formerly rare and illicit, are now as common as the surfboards, drive-ins, and sock hops of yesteryear.

In a nutshell, the ongoing adult preoccupation with current music goes something like this: *What is the overall influence of this deafening, foul, and often vicious-sounding stuff on children and teenagers?* This is a genuinely important question, and serious studies and articles, some concerned particularly with current music's possible link to violence, have lately been devoted to it. In 2000, the American Academy of

Pediatrics, the American Medical Association, the American Psychological Association, and the American Academy of Child & Adolescent Psychiatry all weighed in against contemporary lyrics and other forms of violent entertainment before Congress with a first-ever "Joint Statement on the Impact of Entertainment Violence on Children."

Nonetheless, this is not my focus here. Instead, I would like to turn that logic about influence upside down and ask this question: *What is it about today's music, violent and disgusting though it may be, that resonates with so many American kids?*

As the reader can see, this is a very different way of inquiring about the relationship between today's teenagers and their music. The first question asks what the music *does* to adolescents; the second asks what it *tells* us about them. To answer that second question is necessarily to enter the roiling emotional waters in which that music is created and consumed—in other words, actually to listen to some of it and read the lyrics.

5    As it turns out, such an exercise yields a fascinating and little understood fact about today's adolescent scene. If yesterday's rock was the music of abandon, today's is that of abandon*ment.* The odd truth about contemporary teenage music—the characteristic that most separates it from what has gone before—is its compulsive insistence on the damage wrought by broken homes, family dysfunction, checked-out parents, and (especially) absent fathers. Papa Roach, Everclear, Blink-182, Good Charlotte, Eddie Vedder and Pearl Jam, Kurt Cobain and Nirvana, Tupac Shakur, Snoop Doggy Dogg, Eminem—these and other singers and bands, all of them award-winning top-40 performers who either are or were among the most popular icons in America, have their own generational answer to what ails the modern teenager. Surprising though it may be to some, that answer is: dysfunctional childhood. Moreover, and just as interesting, many bands and singers explicitly link the most deplored themes in music today—suicide, misogyny, and drugs—with that lack of a quasi-normal, intact-home personal past.

To put this perhaps unexpected point more broadly, during the same years in which progressive-minded and politically correct adults have been excoriating Ozzie and Harriet as an artifact of 1950s-style oppression, many millions of American teenagers have enshrined a new generation of music idols whose shared generational signature in song after song is to rage about what *not* having had a nuclear family has done to them. This is quite a fascinating puzzle of the times. The self-perceived emotional damage scrawled large across contemporary music may not be statistically quantifiable, but it is nonetheless among the most striking of all the unanticipated consequences of our home-alone world. . . .

[An] Example of the rage in contemporary music against irresponsible adults—perhaps the most interesting—is that of genre-crossing bad-boy rap superstar Marshall Mathers or Eminem (sometime stage persona "Slim Shady"). Of all the names guaranteed to send a shudder down the parental spine, his is probably the most effective. In fact, Eminem has single-handedly, if inadvertently, achieved the otherwise ideologically impossible: He is the object of a vehemently disapproving public consensus shared by the National Organization for Women, the Gay & Lesbian Alliance Against Defamation, William J. Bennett, Lynne Cheney, Bill O'Reilly, and a large number of other social conservatives as well as feminists and gay activists. In sum, this rapper—"as harmful to America as any al Qaeda fanatic," in O'Reilly's opinion—unites adult polar opposites as perhaps no other single popular entertainer has done.

There is small need to wonder why. Like other rappers, Eminem mines the shock value and gutter language of rage, casual sex, and violence. Unlike the rest, however, he appears to be a particularly attractive target of opprobrium for two distinct reasons. One, he is white and therefore politically easier to attack. (It is interesting to note that black rappers have not been targeted by name anything like Eminem has.) Perhaps even more important, Eminem is one of the largest commercially visible targets for parental wrath. Wildly popular among teenagers these last several years, he is also enormously successful in commercial terms. Winner of numerous Grammys and other music awards and a perpetual nominee for many more, he has also been critically (albeit reluctantly) acclaimed for his acting performance in the autobiographical 2003 movie 8 Mile. For all these reasons, he is probably the preeminent rock/rap star of the last several years, one whose singles, albums, and videos routinely top every chart. His 2002 album, The Eminem Show, for example, was easily the most successful of the year, selling more than 7.6 million copies.

This remarkable market success, combined with the intense public criticism that his songs have generated, makes the phenomenon of Eminem particularly intriguing. Perhaps more than any other current musical icon, he returns repeatedly to the same themes that fuel other success stories in contemporary music: parental loss, abandonment, abuse, and subsequent child and adolescent anger, dysfunction, and violence (including self-violence). Both in his raunchy lyrics as well as in 8 Mile, Mathers's own personal story has been parlayed many times over: the absent father, the troubled mother living in a trailer park, the series of unwanted maternal boyfriends, the protective if impotent feelings toward a younger sibling (in the movie, a baby sister; in real life, a younger brother), and the fine line that a poor, ambitious, and unguided young man might walk between catastrophe and success. Mathers plumbs these and related themes with a verbal savagery that leaves most adults aghast.

Yet Eminem also repeatedly centers his songs on the crypto-traditional notion that children need parents and that *not* having them 10 has made all hell break loose. In the song "8 Mile" from the movie soundtrack, for example, the narrator studies his little sister as she colors one picture after another of an imagined nuclear family, failing to understand that *"mommas got a new man."* *"Wish I could be the daddy that neither one of us had,"* he comments. Such wistful lyrics juxtapose oddly and regularly with Eminem's violent other lines. Even in one of his most infamous songs, "Cleaning Out My Closet (Mama, I'm Sorry)," what drives the vulgar narrative is the insistence on seeing abandonment from a child's point of view. *"My faggot father must have had his panties up in a bunch / 'Cause he split. I wonder if he even kissed me good-bye."*

As with other rappers, the vicious narrative treatment of women in some of Eminem's songs is part of this self-conception as a child victim. Contrary to what critics have intimated, the misogyny in current music does not spring from nowhere; it is often linked to the larger theme of having been abandoned several times—left behind by father, not nurtured by mother, and betrayed again by faithless womankind. One of the most violent and sexually aggressive songs in the last few years is "Kill You" by the popular metal band known as Korn. Its violence is not directed toward just any woman or even toward the narrator's girlfriend; it is instead a song about an abusive stepmother whom the singer imagines going back to rape and murder.

Similarly, Eminem's most shocking lyrics about women are not randomly dispersed; they are largely reserved for his mother and ex-wife, and the narrative pose is one of despising them for not being better women—in particular, better mothers. The worst rap directed at his own mother is indeed gut-wrenching: *"But how dare you try to take what you didn't help me to get? / You selfish bitch, I hope you f— burn in hell for this shit!"* It is no defense of the gutter to observe the obvious: This is not the expression of random misogyny but, rather, of primal rage over alleged maternal abdication and abuse.

Another refrain in these songs runs like this: Today's teenagers are a mess, and the parents who made them that way refuse to get it. In one of Eminem's early hits, for example, a song called "Who Knew," the rapper pointedly takes on his many middle- and upper-middle-class critics to observe the contradiction between their reviling him and the parental inattention that feeds his commercial success. *"What about the make-up you allow your 12 year-old daughter to wear?"* he taunts.

This same theme of AWOL parenting is rapped at greater length in another award-nominated 2003 song called "Sing for the Moment," whose lyrics and video would be recognized in an instant by most teenagers in America. That song spells out Eminem's own idea of what connects him to his millions of fans—a connection that parents, in his view, just don't (or is that won't?) understand. It details the case of one more "problem child" created by *"His f— dad walkin' out."* "Sing for the Moment," like many other songs of Eminem's, is also a popular video.

The "visuals" show clearly what the lyrics depict—hordes of disaffected kids, with flashbacks to bad home lives, screaming for the singer who feels their pain. It concludes by rhetorically turning away from the music itself and toward the emotionally desperate teenagers who turn out for this music by the millions. If the demand of all those empty kids wasn't out there, the narrator says pointedly, then rappers wouldn't be supplying it the way they do.

If some parents still don't get it—even as their teenagers elbow 15 up for every new Eminem CD and memorize his lyrics with psalmist devotion—at least some critics observing the music scene have thought to comment on the ironies of all this. In discussing *The Marshall Mathers LP* in 2001 for *Music Box*, a daily online newsletter about music, reviewer John Metzger argued, "Instead of spewing the hate that he is so often criticized of doing, Eminem offers a cautionary tale that speaks to our civilization's growing depravity. Ironically, it's his teenage fans who understand this, and their all-knowing parents that miss the point." Metzger further specified "the utter lack of parenting due to the spendthrift necessity of the two-income family."[1]

That insight raises the overlooked fact that in one important sense Eminem … would agree with many of today's adults about one thing: The kids *aren't* all right out there after all. Recall, for just one example, Eddie Vedder's rueful observation about what kind of generation would make him or Kurt Cobain its leader. Where parents and entertainers disagree is over who exactly bears responsibility for this moral chaos. Many adults want to blame the people who create and market today's music and videos. Entertainers, Eminem most prominently, blame the absent, absentee, and generally inattentive adults whose deprived and furious children (as they see it) have catapulted today's singers to fame. (As he puts the point in one more in-your-face response to parents: *"Don't blame me when lil' Eric jumps off of the terrace / You shoulda been watchin him—apparently you ain't parents."*)

The spectacle of a foul-mouthed bad-example rock icon instructing the hardworking parents of America in the art of child-rearing is indeed a peculiar one, not to say ridiculous. The single mother who is working frantically because she must and worrying all the while about what her 14-year-old is listening to in the headphones is entitled to a certain fury over lyrics like those. In fact, to read through most rap lyrics is to wonder which adults or political constituencies *wouldn't* take offense. Even so, the music idols who point the finger away from themselves and toward the emptied-out homes of America are telling a truth that some adults would rather not hear. In this limited sense at least, Eminem is right.

To say that today's popular music is uniquely concerned with broken homes, abandoned children, and distracted or incapable parents is

---

[1] John Metzger, review of "Eminem: The Marshall Mathers LP," *Music Box* 8:6 (June 2001).

not to say that this is what all of it is about. Other themes remain a constant, too, although somewhat more brutally than in the alleged golden era recalled by some baby boomers.

Much of today's metal and hip-hop, like certain music of yesterday, romanticizes illicit drug use and alcohol abuse, and much of current hip-hop sounds certain radical political themes, such as racial separatism and violence against the police. And, of course, the most elementally appealing feature of all, the sexually suggestive beat itself, continues to lure teenagers and young adults in its own right—including those from happy homes. Today as yesterday, plenty of teenagers who don't know or care what the stars are raving about find enough satisfaction in swaying to the sexy music. As professor and intellectual Allan Bloom observed about rock in his bestseller, *The Closing of the American Mind* (Simon & Schuster, 1987), the music "gives children, on a silver platter, with all the public authority of the entertaining industry, everything their parents always used to tell them they had to wait for until they grew up and would understand later."

20    Even so, and putting aside such obvious continuities with previous generations, there is no escaping the fact that today's songs are musically and lyrically unlike any before. What distinguishes them most clearly is the fixation on having been abandoned personally by the adults supposedly in charge, with consequences ranging from bitterness to rage to bad, sick, and violent behavior.

And therein lies a painful truth about an advantage that many teenagers of yesterday enjoyed but their own children often do not. Baby boomers and their music rebelled against parents *because* they were parents—nurturing, attentive, and overly present (as those teenagers often saw it) authority figures. Today's teenagers and their music rebel against parents because they are *not* parents—not nurturing, not attentive, and often not even there. This difference in generational experience may not lend itself to statistical measure, but it is as real as the platinum and gold records that continue to capture it. What those records show compared to yesteryear's rock is emotional downward mobility. Surely if some of the current generation of teenagers and young adults had been better taken care of, then the likes of Kurt Cobain, Eminem, Tupac Shakur, and certain other parental nightmares would have been mere footnotes to recent music history rather than rulers of it.

To step back from the emotional immediacy of those lyrics and to juxtapose the ascendance of such music alongside the long-standing sophisticated assaults on what is sardonically called "family values" is to meditate on a larger irony. As today's music stars and their raving fans likely do not know, many commentators and analysts have been rationalizing every aspect of the adult exodus from home—sometimes celebrating it full throttle, as in the example of working motherhood—longer than most of today's singers and bands have been alive.

Nor do they show much sign of second thoughts. Representative sociologist Stephanie Coontz greeted the year 2004 with one more op-ed piece aimed at burying poor metaphorical Ozzie and Harriet for good. She reminded America again that "changes in marriage and family life" are here to stay and aren't "necessarily a problem"; that what is euphemistically called "family diversity" is or ought to be cause for celebration. Many other scholars and observers—to say nothing of much of polite adult society—agree with Coontz. Throughout the contemporary nonfiction literature written of, by, and for educated adults, a thousand similar rationalizations about family "changes" bloom on.

Meanwhile, a small number of emotionally damaged former children, embraced and adored by millions of teenagers like them, rage on in every commercial medium available about the multiple damages of the disappearance of loving, protective, attentive adults—and they reap a fortune for it. If this spectacle alone doesn't tell us something about the ongoing emotional costs of parent–child separation on today's outsize scale, it's hard to see what could.

## Responding to Reading

MyWritingLab™

1. Eberstadt acknowledges in her first paragraph that "contemporary adolescent popular music, especially the subgenres of heavy metal and hip-hop/rap," commonly includes themes of "Misogyny, violence, suicide, sexual exploitation, [and] child abuse. . . ." How does she explain the presence of these themes? In what sense is Eminem "right"?
2. Eberstadt's focus here is not on how music affects adolescents but on what it reveals about them. In paragraph 3, she asks, *What is it about today's music, violent and disgusting though it may be, that resonates with so many American kids?* How does she answer this question? How would you answer it?
3. **Rhetorical Analysis**   In what sense does Eberstadt see today's adolescent music as the music of "abandon*ment*" rather than as the "music of abandon" (5)? How does she believe what she calls "our home-alone world" (6) helps to explain Eminem's violent, misogynistic lyrics? Do you think this essay's primary purpose is to defend the music of performers like Eminem or to attack "irresponsible adults" (7)?

## Writing about Reading

MyWritingLab™

1. Choose two or three contemporary pop songs that you know well, and find their lyrics online. Then, list a few key characteristics of these lyrics. Do your findings support Eberstadt's claims?
2. **Writing with Sources**   Elsewhere in her writing, Eberstadt discusses the lyrics of other musical artists who appeal to today's adolescents, and she argues that their lyrics, like Eminem's, also reveal a preoccupation with family dysfunction and abandonment by parents. Do some research to locate current popular music lyrics that illustrate Eberstadt's claims, and then write an essay explaining how these lyrics support her position. Try to incorporate the views of some contemporary music critics into your discussion.

# AFTER THE PROTESTS
## Zeynep Tufekci

*An assistant professor in the School of Information and Library Science at the University of North Carolina, Chapel Hill, Zeynep Tufekci explores the role of media in social movements. Her work has appeared in* The Atlantic, *the* New York Times, *and her blog* Technosociology. *In the following essay, Tufekci considers the effectiveness of social media in creating lasting change.*

Last Wednesday, more than 100,000 people showed up in Istanbul for a funeral that turned into a mass demonstration. No formal organization made the call. The news had come from Twitter: Berkin Elvan, 15, had died. He had been hit in the head by a tear-gas canister on his way to buy bread during the Gezi protests last June. During the 269 days he spent in a coma, Berkin's face had become a symbol of civic resistance shared on social media from Facebook to Instagram, and the response, when his family tweeted "we lost our son" and then a funeral date, was spontaneous.

Protests like this one, fueled by social media and erupting into spectacular mass events, look like powerful statements of opposition against a regime. And whether these take place in Turkey, Egypt or Ukraine, pundits often speculate that the days of a ruling party or government, or at least its unpopular policies, must be numbered. Yet often these huge mobilizations of citizens inexplicably wither away without the impact on policy you might expect from their scale.

This muted effect is not because social media isn't good at what it does, but, in a way, because it's very good at what it does. Digital tools make it much easier to build up movements quickly, and they greatly lower coordination costs. This seems like a good thing at first, but it often results in an unanticipated weakness: Before the Internet, the tedious work of organizing that was required to circumvent censorship or to organize a protest also helped build infrastructure for decision making and strategies for sustaining momentum. Now movements can rush past that step, often to their own detriment.

In Spain, protesters who called themselves the Indignados (the outraged) took to public squares in large numbers in 2011, yet the austerity policies they opposed are still in effect. Occupy Wall Street filled Lower Manhattan in October 2011, crystallizing the image of the 99 percent versus the 1 percent without forcing a change in the nation's widening inequality. And in Egypt, Tahrir Square protesters in January 2011 used social media to capture the world's attention. Later that year, during clashes in the square, four people in their 20s used Google spreadsheets, mobile communication and Twitter to coordinate supplies for 10 field hospitals that cared for the wounded. But three years later, a repressive military regime is back in power.

Thousands of people turned out in Istanbul last June to defy the 5
government's plan to raze Gezi Park, in spite of the fact that the heavily
censored mass media had all but ignored the initial protests, broadcast-
ing documentaries about penguins instead of the news. Four college
students organized a citizen journalism network that busted censorship 140 characters at a time. I met parents at the protests who were
imploring their children to teach them how to use Twitter as it became a
real-time newswire, an organizing tool and a communication device for
those in the park and its surroundings. One protester told me, "Internet
brings freedom."

But after all that, in the approaching local elections, the ruling party
is expected to retain its dominance.

Compare this with what it took to produce and distribute pamphlets announcing the Montgomery bus boycott in 1955. Jo Ann Robinson, a professor at Alabama State College, and a few students sneaked
into the duplicating room and worked all night to secretly mimeograph
52,000 leaflets to be distributed by hand with the help of 68 African-
American political, religious, educational and labor organizations
throughout the city. Even mundane tasks like coordinating car pools
(in an era before there were spreadsheets) required endless hours of
collaborative work.

By the time the United States government was faced with the March
on Washington in 1963, the protest amounted to not just 300,000 demonstrators but the committed partnerships and logistics required to get
them all there—and to sustain a movement for years against brutally
enforced Jim Crow laws. That movement had the capacity to leverage
boycotts, strikes and demonstrations to push its cause forward. Recent
marches on Washington of similar sizes, including the 50th anniversary
march last year, also signaled discontent and a desire for change, but
just didn't pose the same threat to the powers that be.

Social media can provide a huge advantage in assembling the
strength in numbers that movements depend on. Those "likes" on Facebook, derided as slacktivism or clicktivism, can have long-term consequences by defining which sentiments are "normal" or "obvious"—
perhaps among the most important levers of change. That's one reason
the same-sex marriage movement, which uses online and offline visibility as a key strategy, has been so successful, and it's also why authoritarian governments try to ban social media.

During the Gezi protests, Prime Minister Recep Tayyip Erdogan 10
called Twitter and other social media a "menace to society." More
recently, Turkey's Parliament passed a law greatly increasing the
government's ability to censor online content and expand surveillance,
and Mr. Erdogan said he would consider blocking access to Facebook
and YouTube. It's also telling that one of the first moves by President
Vladimir V. Putin of Russia before annexing Crimea was to shut down
the websites of dissidents in Russia.

Media in the hands of citizens can rattle regimes. It makes it much harder for rulers to maintain legitimacy by controlling the public sphere. But activists, who have made such effective use of technology to rally supporters, still need to figure out how to convert that energy into greater impact. The point isn't just to challenge power; it's to change it.

### Responding to Reading

MyWritingLab™

1. According to Tufekci, what advantages do social media offer for organizing political and social protests?
2. What important limitation of social media does Tufekci identify in paragraph 3?
3. **Rhetorical Analysis**   What is the thesis of Tufekci's essay? Is her primary purpose here to support the use of social media in organizing protests or to warn of its shortcomings?

### Writing about Reading

MyWritingLab™

1. Consider the title of this essay. What does it suggest? What happens "after the protests"?
2. **Writing with Sources**   Research the organization of the 1963 March on Washington (discussed in paragraph 8). What individuals and organizations were involved, and how did they communicate? What kinds of media were used to rally support for the march and to arrange transportation and accommodations for those who attended? Write an essay in which you answer these questions, adding information on the different kinds of media that would be used to organize such a demonstration today.

## CONNECTIVITY AND ITS DISCONTENTS

### Sherry Turkle

*1948–*

*A radio and television media commentator, Sherry Turkle is the Abby Rockefeller Mauzé Professor of the social studies of science and technology at MIT as well as the founder and director of the MIT Initiative on Technology and Self. She is the author of five books, including, most recently,* Alone Together: Why We Expect More from Technology and Less from Each Other *(2011), from which the following is excerpted. In this discussion, Turkle takes a critical look at how technology affects our interpersonal relationships.*

Online connections were first conceived as a substitute for face-to-face contact, when the latter was for some reason impractical: Don't have time to make a phone call? Shoot off a text message. But very quickly, the text message became the connection of choice. We discovered the network—the world of connectivity—to be uniquely suited to the overworked and overscheduled life it makes possible. And now we look to the network to defend us against loneliness even as we use it to control the intensity of our connections. Technology makes it easy to communicate when we wish and to disengage at will.

A few years ago at a dinner party in Paris, I met Ellen, an ambitious, elegant young woman in her early thirties, thrilled to be working at her dream job in advertising. Once a week, she would call her grandmother in Philadelphia using Skype, an Internet service that functions as a telephone with a Web camera, Before Skype, Ellen's calls to her grandmother were costly and brief. With Skype, the calls are free and give the compelling sense that the other person is present—Skype is an almost real-time video link. Ellen could now call more frequently: "Twice a week and I stay on the call for an hour," she told me. It should have been rewarding; instead, when I met her, Ellen was unhappy. She knew that her grandmother was unaware that Skype allows surreptitious multitasking. Her grandmother could see Ellen's face on the screen but not her hands. Ellen admitted to me, "I do my e-mail during the calls. I'm not really paying attention to our conversation."

Ellen's multitasking removed her to another place. She felt her grandmother was talking to someone who was not really there. During their Skype conversations, Ellen and her grandmother were more connected than they had ever been before, but at the same time, each was alone. Ellen felt guilty and confused: she knew that her grandmother was happy, even if their intimacy was now, for Ellen, another task among multitasks.

I have often observed this distinctive confusion: these days, whether you are online or not, it is easy for people to end up unsure if they are closer together or further apart. I remember my own sense of disorientation the first time I realized that I was "alone together." I had traveled an exhausting thirty-six hours to attend a conference on advanced robotic technology held in central Japan. The packed grand ballroom was Wi-Fi enabled: the speaker was using the Web for his presentation, laptops were open throughout the audience, fingers were flying, and there was a sense of great concentration and intensity. But not many in the audience were attending to the speaker. Most people seemed to be doing their e-mail, downloading files, and surfing the Net. The man next to me was searching for a *New Yorker* cartoon to illustrate his upcoming presentation. Every once in a while, audience members gave the speaker some attention, lowering their laptop screens in a kind of curtsy, a gesture of courtesy.

Outside, in the hallways, the people milling around me were looking past me to virtual others. They were on their laptops and their phones, connecting to colleagues at the conference going on around them and to others around the globe. There but not there. Of course, clusters of people chatted with each other, making dinner plans, "networking" in that old sense of the word, the one that implies having a  5 coffee or sharing a meal. But at this conference, it was clear that what people mostly want from public space is to be alone with their personal networks. It is good to come together physically, but it is more important to stay tethered to our devices. I thought of how Sigmund Freud considered the power of communities both to shape and to subvert us, and a psychoanalytic pun came to mind: "connectivity and its discontents."

The phrase comes back to me months later as I interview management consultants who seem to have lost touch with their best instincts for what makes them competitive. They complain about the BlackBerry revolution, yet accept it as inevitable while decrying it as corrosive. They say they used to talk to each other as they waited to give presentations or took taxis to the airport; now they spend that time doing e-mail. Some tell me they are making better use of their "downtime," but they argue without conviction. The time that they once used to talk as they waited for appointments or drove to the airport was never downtime. It was the time when far-flung global teams solidified relationships and refined ideas.

In corporations, among friends, and within academic departments, people readily admit that they would rather leave a voicemail or send an e-mail than talk face-to-face. Some who say "I live my life on my BlackBerry" are forthright about avoiding the "real-time" commitment of a phone call. The new technologies allow us to "dial down" human contact, to titrate its nature and extent. I recently overheard a conversation in a restaurant between two women. "No one answers the phone in our house anymore," the first woman proclaimed with some consternation. "It used to be that the kids would race to pick up the phone. Now they are up in their rooms, knowing no one is going to call them, and texting and going on Facebook or whatever instead." Parents with teenage children will be nodding at this very familiar story in recognition and perhaps a sense of wonderment that this has happened, and so quickly. And teenagers will simply be saying, "Well, what's your point?"

A thirteen-year-old tells me she "hates the phone and never listens to voicemail." Texting offers just the right amount of access, just the right amount of control. She is a modern Goldilocks: for her, texting puts people not too close, not too far, but at just the right distance. The world is now full of modern Goldilockses, people who take comfort in being in touch with a lot of people whom they also keep at bay. A twenty-one-year-old college student reflects on the new balance: "I don't use my phone for calls any more. I don't have the time to just go on and on. I like texting, Twitter, looking at someone's Facebook wall. I learn what I need to know."

Randy, twenty-seven, has a younger sister—a Goldilocks who got her distances wrong. Randy is an American lawyer now working in

California. His family lives in New York, and he flies to the East Coast to see them three or four times a year. When I meet Randy, his sister Nora, twenty-four, had just announced her engagement and wedding date via e-mail to a list of friends and family. "That," Randy says to me bitterly, "is how I got the news." He doesn't know if he is more angry or hurt, "It doesn't feel right that she didn't call," he says. "I was getting ready for a trip home. Couldn't she have told me then? She's my sister, but I didn't have a private moment when she told me in person. Or at least a call, just the two of us. When I told her I was upset, she sort of understood, but laughed and said that she and her fiancé just wanted to do things simply, as simply as possible. I feel very far away from her."

Nora did not mean to offend her brother. She saw e-mail as efficient 10 and did not see beyond. We have long turned to technology to make us more efficient in work; now Nora illustrates how we want it to make us more efficient in our private lives. But when technology engineers intimacy, relationships can be reduced to mere connections. And then, easy connection becomes redefined as intimacy. Put otherwise, cyberintimacies slide into cybersolitudes.

And with constant connection comes new anxieties of disconnection, a kind of panic. Even Randy, who longs for a phone call from Nora on such an important matter as her wedding, is never without his BlackBerry. He holds it in his hands during our entire conversation. Once, he puts it in his pocket. A few moments later, it comes out, fingered like a talisman. In interviews with young and old, I find people genuinely terrified of being cut off from the "grid." People say that the loss of a cell phone can "feel like a death." One television producer in her mid-forties tells me that without her smartphone, "I felt like I had lost my mind." Whether or not our devices are in use, without them we feel disconnected, adrift. A danger even to ourselves; we insist on our right to send text messages while driving our cars and object to rules that would limit the practice.

Only a decade ago, I would have been mystified that fifteen-year-olds in my urban neighborhood, a neighborhood of parks and shopping malls, of front stoops and coffee shops, would feel the need to send and receive close to six thousand messages a month via portable digital devices or that best friends would assume that when they visited, it would usually be on the virtual real estate of Facebook. It might have seemed intrusive, if not illegal, that my mobile phone would tell me the location of all my acquaintances within a ten-mile radius. But these days we are accustomed to all this. Life in a media bubble has come to seem natural. So has the end of a certain public etiquette: on the street, we speak into the invisible microphones on our mobile phones and appear to be talking to ourselves. We share intimacies with the air as though unconcerned about who can hear us or the details of our physical surroundings.

I once described the computer as a second self, a mirror of mind. Now the metaphor no longer goes far enough. Our new devices provide space for the emergence of a new state of the self, itself, split between the screen and the physical real, wired into existence through technology.

Teenagers tell me they sleep with their cell phone, and even when it isn't on their person, when it has been banished to the school locker, for instance, they know when their phone is vibrating. The technology has become like a phantom limb, it is so much a part of them. These young people are among the first to grow up with an expectation of continuous connection: always on, and always on them. And they are among the first to grow up not necessarily thinking of simulation as second best. All of this makes them fluent with technology but brings a set of new insecurities. They nurture friendships on social-networking sites and then wonder if they are among friends. They are connected all day but are not sure if they have communicated. They become confused about companionship. Can they find it in their lives on the screen? Could they find it with a robot? Their digitized friendships—played out with emoticon emotions, so often predicated on rapid response rather than reflection—may prepare them, at times through nothing more than their superficiality, for relationships that could bring superficiality to a higher power, that is, for relationships with the inanimate. They come to accept lower expectations for connection and, finally, the idea that robot friendships could be sufficient unto the day.

15　Overwhelmed by the volume and velocity of our lives, we turn to technology to help us find time. But technology makes us busier than ever and ever more in search of retreat. Gradually, we come to see our online life as life itself. We come to see what robots offer as relationship. The simplification of relationship is no longer a source of complaint. It becomes what we want. These seem the gathering clouds of a perfect storm.

Technology reshapes the landscape of our emotional lives, but is it offering us the lives we want to lead? Many roboticists are enthusiastic about having robots tend to our children and our aging parents, for instance. Are these psychologically, socially, and ethically acceptable propositions? What are our responsibilities here? And are we comfortable with virtual environments that propose themselves not as places for recreation but as new worlds to live in? What do we have, now that we have what we say we want—now that we have what technology makes easy? This is the time to begin these conversations, together.

It is too late to leave the future to the futurists.

## Responding to Reading

MyWritingLab™

1. Relying on extended examples of Skype, texting, and email (and mentioning *Facebook* only in passing), Turkle describes a world in which people are increasingly "unsure if they are closer together or further apart"

(4) and somehow "There but not there" (5). She says, "The world is now full of modern Goldilockses, people who take comfort in being in touch with a lot of people whom they also keep at bay" (8). What does she mean? In what respects do her observations apply to *Facebook* use as well as to the examples she cites?

2. In her conclusion, Turkle says, "It is too late to leave the future to the futurists" (16). Do you think she is right to be alarmed at the trends she identifies? Or, do you think the changes she cites—for example, her statement that "Technology makes it easy to communicate when we wish and to disengage at will" (1)—are, on balance, essentially positive? Explain.

3. **Rhetorical Analysis** What does Turkle mean by the terms *connectivity* (title), *cyberintimacies* and *cybersolitudes* (10), and *robot friendships* (14)? What does her use of these terms tell you about how she sees her audience?

## Writing about Reading

MyWritingLab™

1. Throughout her essay, Turkle cites examples of people she met or interviewed. Do these people's stories seem atypical, or do any of them remind you of people you know? In other words, do the concerns they cite hit home for you? Explain.

2. **Writing with Sources** Conduct some interviews of your own to confirm (or challenge) the conclusions Turkle draws from her conversations and interviews. Then, citing both your own interviews and Turkle's as sources, write an essay in which you take a stand on the issue of whether social networking tends to connect people or keep them apart.

# MIND OVER MASS MEDIA

## Steven Pinker

*1954–*

*A Harvard College professor and the Johnstone Family Professor in the psychology department at Harvard University, Steven Pinker writes about the relationship between language and the brain. A contributor to such publications as the* New Republic, *the* New York Times, *and* Time, *Pinker has written numerous books, including, most recently,* The Sense of Style: The Thinking Person's Guide to Writing in the 21st Century! *(2014). In the following essay, Pinker argues that electronic media can have a positive effect on cognition.*

New forms of media have always caused moral panics: the printing press, newspapers, paperbacks and television were all once denounced as threats to their consumers' brainpower and moral fiber.

So too with electronic technologies. PowerPoint, we're told, is reducing discourse to bullet points. Search engines lower our intelligence, encouraging us to skim on the surface of knowledge rather than dive to its depths. Twitter is shrinking our attention spans.

But such panics often fail basic reality checks. When comic books were accused of turning juveniles into delinquents in the 1950s, crime was falling to record lows, just as the denunciations of video games in the 1990s coincided with the great American crime decline. The decades of television, transistor radios and rock videos were also decades in which I.Q. scores rose continuously.

For a reality check today, take the state of science, which demands high levels of brainwork and is measured by clear benchmarks of discovery. These days scientists are never far from their e-mail, rarely touch paper and cannot lecture without PowerPoint. If electronic media were hazardous to intelligence, the quality of science would be plummeting. Yet discoveries are multiplying like fruit flies, and progress is dizzying. Other activities in the life of the mind, like philosophy, history and cultural criticism, are likewise flourishing, as anyone who has lost a morning of work to the Web site *Arts & Letters Daily* can attest.

5     Critics of new media sometimes use science itself to press their case, citing research that shows how "experience can change the brain." But cognitive neuroscientists roll their eyes at such talk. Yes, every time we learn a fact or skill the wiring of the brain changes; it's not as if the information is stored in the pancreas. But the existence of neural plasticity does not mean the brain is a blob of clay pounded into shape by experience.

Experience does not revamp the basic information-processing capacities of the brain. Speed-reading programs have long claimed to do just that, but the verdict was rendered by Woody Allen after he read *War and Peace* in one sitting: "It was about Russia." Genuine multitasking, too, has been exposed as a myth, not just by laboratory studies but by the familiar sight of an S.U.V. undulating between lanes as the driver cuts deals on his cellphone.

Moreover, as the psychologists Christopher Chabris and Daniel Simons show in their new book *The Invisible Gorilla: And Other Ways Our Intuitions Deceive Us*, the effects of experience are highly specific to the experiences themselves. If you train people to do one thing (recognize shapes, solve math puzzles, find hidden words), they get better at doing that thing, but almost nothing else. Music doesn't make you better at math, conjugating Latin doesn't make you more logical, brain-training games don't make you smarter. Accomplished people don't bulk up their brains with intellectual calisthenics; they immerse themselves in their fields. Novelists read lots of novels, scientists read lots of science.

The effects of consuming electronic media are also likely to be far more limited than the panic implies. Media critics write as if the

STEVEN PINKER • MIND OVER MASS MEDIA 197

brain takes on the qualities of whatever it consumes, the informational equivalent of "you are what you eat." As with primitive peoples who believe that eating fierce animals will make them fierce, they assume that watching quick cuts in rock videos turns your mental life into quick cuts or that reading bullet points and Twitter postings turns your thoughts into bullet points and Twitter postings.

Yes, the constant arrival of information packets can be distracting or addictive, especially to people with attention deficit disorder. But distraction is not a new phenomenon. The solution is not to bemoan technology but to develop strategies of self-control, as we do with every other temptation in life. Turn off e-mail or Twitter when you work, put away your Blackberry at dinner time, ask your spouse to call you to bed at a designated hour.

And to encourage intellectual depth, don't rail at PowerPoint or 10 Google. It's not as if habits of deep reflection, thorough research and rigorous reasoning ever came naturally to people. They must be acquired in special institutions, which we call universities, and maintained with constant upkeep, which we call analysis, criticism and debate. They are not granted by propping a heavy encyclopedia on your lap, nor are they taken away by efficient access to information on the Internet.

The new media have caught on for a reason. Knowledge is increasing exponentially; human brainpower and waking hours are not. Fortunately, the Internet and information technologies are helping us manage, search and retrieve our collective intellectual output at different scales, from Twitter and previews to e-books and online encyclopedias. Far from making us stupid, these technologies are the only things that will keep us smart.

## Responding to Reading

MyWritingLab™

1. Pinker argues that, contrary to claims made by critics of new media, electronic media are not "hazardous to intelligence" (4). How does he support this conclusion?

2. What solutions does Pinker propose for the problem of information overload and to "encourage intellectual depth" (10)? Are these solutions realistic? Explain.

3. **Rhetorical Analysis** Pinker opens his essay by drawing a general analogy between contemporary electronic media and the "new media" of the past. Do you think this is an effective opening strategy? Why or why not?

## Writing about Reading

MyWritingLab™

1. Do you find Pinker's argument convincing? Why or why not?

2. **Writing with Sources** Locate an essay whose position on the topic of new media's "information overload" contradicts Pinker's position. Which argument do you find more convincing? Why? Explain your answer to this question in an essay of your own.

# REALITY IS BROKEN
## Jane McGonigal
### *1977–*

*The director of Games Research & Development at the non-profit research organization Institute for the Future, Jane McGonigal creates games that, as she describes, "are designed to improve real lives and solve real problems." A writer for such publications as the* New Yorker, *the* New York Times, O *magazine, and* Vanity Fair, *McGonigal is the author of* Reality Is Broken: Why Games Make Us Better and How They Can Change the World *(2011), from whose introduction the following argument for the social value of video games is excerpted.*

Anyone who sees a hurricane coming should warn others. I see a hurricane coming.

Over the next generation or two, ever larger numbers of people, hundreds of millions, will become immersed in virtual worlds and online games. While we are playing, things we used to do on the outside, in "reality," won't be happening anymore, or won't be happening in the same way. You can't pull millions of person-hours out of a society without creating an atmospheric-level event.

If it happens in a generation, I think the twenty-first century will see a social cataclysm larger than that caused by cars, radios, and TV, combined. . . . The exodus of these people from the real world, from our normal daily life, will create a change in social climate that makes global warming look like a tempest in a teacup.

—Edward Castronova,
*Exodus to the Virtual World*

Gamers have had enough of reality.

They are abandoning it in droves—a few hours here, an entire weekend there, sometimes every spare minute of every day for stretches at a time—in favor of simulated environments and online games. Maybe you are one of these gamers. If not, then you definitely know some of them.

Who are they? They are the nine-to-fivers who come home and apply all of the smarts and talents that are underutilized at work to plan and coordinate complex raids and quests in massively multiplayer online games like *Final Fantasy XI* and the *Lineage* worlds. They're the music lovers who have invested hundreds of dollars on plastic *Rock Band* and *Guitar Hero* instruments and spent night after night rehearsing, in order to become virtuosos of video game performance.

They're the *World of Warcraft* fans who are so intent on mastering the challenges of their favorite game that, collectively, they've written a quarter of a million wiki articles on the WoWWiki—creating the single largest wiki after Wikipedia. They're the *Brain Age* and *Mario Kart* players who take handheld game consoles everywhere they go, sneaking in short puzzles, races, and minigames as often as possible, and as a result nearly eliminating mental downtime from their lives.

They're the United States troops stationed overseas who dedicate     5
so many hours a week to burnishing their *Halo 3* in-game service record that earning virtual combat medals is widely known as the most popular activity for off-duty soldiers. They're the young adults in China who have spent so much play money, or "QQ coins," on magical swords and other powerful game objects that the People's Bank of China intervened to prevent the devaluation of the yuan, China's real-world currency.

Most of all, they're the kids and teenagers worldwide who would rather spend hours in front of just about any computer game or video game than do anything else.

These gamers aren't rejecting reality entirely. They have jobs, goals, schoolwork, families, commitments, and real lives that they care about. But as they devote more and more of their free time to game worlds, the *real* world increasingly feels like it's missing something.

Gamers want to know: Where, in the real world, is that gamer sense of being fully alive, focused, and engaged in every moment? Where is the gamer feeling of power, heroic purpose, and community? Where are the bursts of exhilarating and creative game accomplishment? Where is the heart-expanding thrill of success and team victory? While gamers may experience these pleasures occasionally in their real lives, they experience them almost constantly when they're playing their favorite games.

The real world just doesn't offer up as easily the carefully designed pleasures, the thrilling challenges, and the powerful social bonding afforded by virtual environments. Reality doesn't motivate us as effectively. Reality isn't engineered to maximize our potential. Reality wasn't designed from the bottom up to make us happy.

And so, there is a growing perception in the gaming community:     10
Reality, compared to games, is broken.

In fact, it is more than a perception. It's a phenomenon. Economist Edward Castronova calls it a "mass exodus" to game spaces, and you can see it already happening in the numbers. Hundreds of millions of people worldwide are opting out of reality for larger and larger chunks of time. In the United States alone, there are 183 million *active gamers* (individuals who, in surveys, report that they play computer or video games "regularly"—on average, thirteen hours a week). Globally, the online gamer community—including console, PC, and mobile phone gaming—counts more than 4 million gamers in the Middle East,

10 million in Russia, 105 million in India, 10 million in Vietnam, 10 million in Mexico, 13 million in Central and South America, 15 million in Australia, 17 million in South Korea, 100 million in Europe, and 200 million in China.

Although a typical gamer plays for just an hour or two a day, there are now more than 6 million people in China who spend at least twenty-two hours a week gaming, the equivalent of a part-time job. More than 10 million "hard-core" gamers in the United Kingdom, France, and Germany spend at least twenty hours a week playing. And at the leading edge of this growth curve, more than 5 million "extreme" gamers in the United States play on average forty-five hours a week.

With all of this play, we have turned digital games—for our computers, for our mobile phones, and for our home entertainment systems—into what is expected to be a $68 billion industry annually by the year 2012. And we are creating a massive virtual silo of cognitive effort, emotional energy, and collective attention lavished on game worlds instead of on the real world.

15      The ever-skyrocketing amounts of time and money spent on games are being observed with alarm by some—concerned parents, teachers, and politicians—and eagerness by others—the many technology industries that expect to profit greatly from the game boom. Meanwhile, they are met with bewilderment and disdain by more than a few nongamers, who still make up nearly half of the U.S. population, although their numbers are rapidly decreasing. Many of them deem gaming a clear waste of time.

As we make these value judgments, hold moral debates over the addictive quality of games, and simultaneously rush to achieve massive industry expansion, a vital point is being missed. The fact that so many people of all ages, all over the world, are choosing to spend so much time in game worlds is a sign of something important, a truth that we urgently need to recognize.

The truth is this: in today's society, computer and video games are fulfilling *genuine human needs* that the real world is currently unable to satisfy. Games are providing rewards that reality is not. They are teaching and inspiring and engaging us in ways that reality is not. They are bringing us together in ways that reality is not.

And unless something dramatic happens to reverse the resulting exodus, we're fast on our way to becoming a society in which a substantial portion of our population devotes its greatest efforts to playing games, creates its best memories in game environments, and experiences its biggest successes in game worlds.

Maybe this sounds hard to believe. To a nongamer, this forecast might seem surreal, or like science fiction. Are huge swaths of civilization really disappearing into game worlds? Are we really rushing headlong into a future where the majority of us use games to satisfy many of our most important needs?

If so, it will not be the first time that such a mass exodus from reality to games has occurred. Indeed, the very first written history of human gameplay, Herodotus' *Histories*, the ancient Greek account of the Persian Wars—dating back more than three thousand years—describes a nearly identical scenario. While the oldest known game is the ancient counting game Mancala—evidence shows it was played during Egypt's age of empires, or the fifteenth to the eleventh centuries BC—it was not until Herodotus that anyone thought to record the origins or cultural functions of these games. And from his ancient text, we can learn a great deal about what's happening today—and what's almost certainly coming next.

It's a bit counterintuitive to think about the future in terms of the past. But as a research director at the Institute for the Future—a non-profit think tank in Palo Alto, California, and the world's oldest future-forecasting organization—I've learned an important trick: to develop foresight, you need to practice hindsight. Technologies, cultures, and climates may change, but our basic human needs and desires—to survive, to care for our families, and to lead happy, purposeful lives—remain the same. So at IFTF we like to say, "To understand the future, you have to look back at least twice as far as you're looking ahead." Fortunately, when it comes to games, we can look even farther back than that. Games have been a fundamental part of human civilization for thousands of years.

In the opening book of *The Histories*, Herodotus writes:

> When Atys was king of Lydia in Asia Minor some three thousand years ago, a great scarcity threatened his realm. For a while people accepted their lot without complaining, in the hope that times of plenty would return. But when things failed to get better, the Lydians devised a strange remedy for their problem. The plan adopted against the famine was to engage in games one day so entirely as not to feel any craving for food ... and the next day to eat and abstain from games. In this way they passed eighteen years, and along the way they invented the dice, knuckle-bones, the ball, and all the games which are common.

What do ancient dice made from sheep's knuckles have to do with the future of computer and video games? More than you might expect.

Herodotus invented history as we know it, and he has described the goal of history as uncovering moral problems and moral truths in the concrete data of experience. Whether Herodotus' story of an eighteen-year famine survived through gameplay is true or, as some modern historians believe, apocryphal, its moral truths reveal something important about the essence of games.

25    We often think of immersive gameplay as "escapist," a kind of passive retreat from reality. But through the lens of Herodotus' history, we can see how games could be a *purposeful* escape, a thoughtful and active escape, and most importantly an extremely helpful escape. For the Lydians, playing together as a nearly full-time activity would have been a behavior highly adaptive to difficult conditions. Games made life bearable. Games gave a starving population a feeling of power in a powerless situation, a sense of structure in a chaotic environment. Games gave them a better way to live when their circumstances were otherwise completely unsupportive and uninhabitable.

Make no mistake: we are no different from the ancient Lydians. Today, many of us are suffering from a vast and primal hunger. But it is not a hunger for food—it is a hunger for more and better engagement from the world around us.

Like the ancient Lydians, many gamers have already figured out how to use the immersive power of play to distract themselves from their hunger: a hunger for more satisfying work, for a stronger sense of community, and for a more engaging and meaningful life.

Collectively, the planet is now spending more than 3 billion hours a week gaming.

We are starving, and our games are feeding us.

## Responding to Reading

MyWritingLab™

1. What central problem does this essay identify? How does McGonigal explain the cause of this problem? Can you offer other explanations?
2. Why does McGonigal quote Herodotus in paragraph 22? How does she answer the question she poses in paragraph 23: "What do ancient dice made from sheep's knuckles have to do with the future of computer and video games?"
3. **Rhetorical Analysis** In paragraphs 3 through 6, McGonigal discusses different kinds of gamers. What point is she making here? Are these paragraphs essential to her essay? Why or why not?

## Writing about Reading

MyWritingLab™

1. In this essay, McGonigal identifies a problem. Do you agree that the situation she identifies actually *is* a problem? Why or why not?
2. **Writing with Sources** This selection is part of the introduction to McGonigal's book *Reality Is Broken*. Later in this introduction, she offers three possible scenarios for the future of gaming: encouraging more and more complex and appealing virtual worlds as alternatives to reality; limiting access to video games in order to encourage a greater focus on reality; or using our knowledge of gaming to help solve the problems of the real world. Which of these three possibilities makes the most sense to you? Which do you think is most likely to occur? Write an essay that answers these questions. Begin by reading some reviews of *Reality Is Broken*, and use these reviews as source material to support your points.

## FICTION

# TELEVISION

## Lydia Davis

### 1947–

*A fiction writer, essayist, and translator, Lydia Davis has published a novel and seven story collections, including* Break It Down *(1986),* Varieties of Disturbance *(2007), and* Can't and Won't *(2014). Like the short-short story that follows, much of her fiction is brief and to the point.*

**1.**

We have all these favorite shows coming on every evening. They say it will be exciting and it always is.

They give us hints of what is to come and then it comes and it is exciting.

If dead people walked outside our windows we would be no more excited.

We want to he part of it all.

We wait to be the people they talk to when they tell us what is to come later in the evening and later in the week.

We listen to the ads until we are exhausted, punished with lists: they want us to buy so much, and we try, but we don't have a lot of money. Yet we can't help admiring the science of it all.

How can we ever be as sure as these people are sure? These women are women in control, as the women in my family are not.

Yet we believe in this world.

We believe these people are speaking to us.

Mother, for example, is in love with an anchorman. And my husband sits with his eyes on a certain young reporter and waits for the camera to draw back and reveal her breasts.

After the news we pick out a quiz show to watch and then a story of detective investigation.

The hours pass. Our hearts go on beating, now slow, now faster.

There is one quiz show which is particularly good. Each week the same man is there in the audience with his mouth tightly closed and tears in his eyes. His son is coming back on stage to answer more questions. The boy stands there blinking at the television camera. They will not let him go on answering questions if he wins the final sum of a hundred and twenty-eight thousand dollars. We don't care much about the boy and we don't like the mother, who smiles and

5

10

shows her bad teeth, but we are moved by the father: his heavy lips, his wet eyes.

And so we turn off the telephone during this program and do not answer the knock at the door that rarely comes. We watch closely, and my husband now presses his lips together and then smiles so broadly that his eyes disappear, and as for me, I sit back like the mother with a sharp gaze, my mouth full of gold.

**2.**

15 It's not that I really think this show about Hawaiian policemen is very good, it's just that it seems more real than my own life.

Different routes through the evening: Channels 2, 2, 4, 7, 9, or channels 13, 13, 13, 2, 2, 4, etc. Sometimes it's the police dramas I want to see, other times the public television documentaries, such as one called *Swamp Critturs*.

It's partly my isolation at night, the darkness outside, the silence outside, the increasing lateness of the hour, that makes the story on television seem so interesting. But the plot, too, has something to do with it: tonight a son comes back after many years and marries his father's wife, (She is not his mother.)

We pay a good deal of attention because these shows seem to be the work of so many smart and fashionable people.

I think it is a television sound beyond the wall, but it's the honking of wild geese flying south in the first dark of the evening.

20 You watch a young woman named Susan Smith with pearls around her neck sing the Canadian National Anthem before a hockey game. You listen to the end of the song, then you change the channel.

Or you watch Pete Seeger's legs bounce up and down in time to his *Reuben E. Lee* song, then change the channel.

It is not what you want to be doing. It is that you are passing the time.

You are waiting until it is a certain hour and you are in a certain condition so that you can go to sleep.

There is some real satisfaction in getting this information about the next day's weather—how fast the wind might blow and from what direction, when the rain might come, when the skies might clear—and the exact science of it is indicated by the words "40 percent" in "40 percent chance."

25 It all begins with the blue dot in the center of the dark screen, and this is when you can sense that these pictures will be coming to you from a long way off.

**3.**

Often, at the end of the day, when I am tired, my life seems to turn into a movie. I mean my real day moves into my real evening, but also moves away from me enough to be strange and a movie. It has by then become so complicated, so hard to understand, that I want to watch a different movie. I want to watch a movie made for TV, which will be simple and easy to understand, even if it involves disaster or disability or disease. It will skip over so much, it will skip over all the complications, knowing we will understand, so that major events will happen abruptly; a man may change his mind though it was firmly made up, and he may also fall in love suddenly. It will skip all the complications because there is not enough time to prepare for major events in the space of only one hour and twenty minutes, which also has to include commercial breaks, and we want major events.

One movie was about a woman professor with Alzheimer's disease; one was about an Olympic skier who lost a leg but learned to ski again. Tonight it was about a deaf man who fell in love with his speech therapist, as I knew he would because she was pretty, though not a good actress, and he was handsome, though deaf. He was deaf at the beginning of the movie and deaf again at the end, while in the middle he heard and learned to speak with a definite regional accent. In the space of one hour and twenty minutes, this man not only heard and fell deaf again but created a successful business through his own talent, was robbed of it through a company man's treachery, fell in love, kept his woman as far as the end of the movie, and lost his virginity, which seemed to be hard to lose if one was deaf and easier once one could hear.

All this was compressed into the very end of a day in my life that as the evening advanced had already moved away from me ...

## Responding to Reading

MyWritingLab™

1. Who is the "we" referred to in this story? Does it include just the narrator and her family, or does it have a wider, more general meaning? When the narrator uses "you," to whom is she referring?
2. This story is divided into three numbered sections. What kind of content is included in each section? What determines where the breaks between sections occur?
3. What role does television actually play in the narrator's life? Do you see it as a cause or an effect?

## Writing about Reading

MyWritingLab™

Imagine the life of the narrator of this story, and write a short character sketch that fills in the information that is missing here. How old is she? Where does she live? Does she have a job? How much television does she watch, and what shows are her favorites?

——————————— FOCUS ———————————

## Why Are Zombies Invading Our Media?

Centers for Disease Control and Prevention public service poster

### Responding to the Image

MyWritingLab™

1. What do you think this image is designed to accomplish? What effect is it supposed to have on its audience? For example, is it supposed to be entertaining? Alarming? How can you tell?

2. Consider the three major elements of this image: the zombies it depicts, the words "Preparedness 101: Zombie Pandemic," and the CDC logo and accompanying source information. Do these three elements all send the same message? Explain.

# A ZOMBIE IS A SLAVE FOREVER
## Amy Wilentz
### 1954–

*A professor of English at the University of California, Irvine, Amy Wilentz is the author of four books, including, most recently,* Farewell, Fred Voodoo *(2013). Her work has appeared in publications such as* Condé Nast Traveler, Harper's, *the* Los Angeles Times, *the* New York Times, Time, Travel + Leisure, *and the* Washington Post. *In the following essay, Wilentz examines the social and political history of the zombie phenomenon.*

Zombies will come to my door on Wednesday night—in rags, eye-sockets blackened, pumping devices that make fake blood run down their faces—asking for candies. There seem to be more and more zombies every Halloween, more zombies than princesses, fairies, ninjas or knights. In all probability, none of them knows what a zombie really is.

Most people think of them as the walking dead, a being without a soul or someone with no free will. This is true. But the zombie is not an alien enemy who's been CGI-ed by Hollywood. He is a New World phenomenon that arose from the mixture of old African religious beliefs and the pain of slavery, especially the notoriously merciless and cold-blooded slavery of French-run, pre-independence Haiti. In Africa, a dying person's soul might be stolen and stoppered up in a ritual bottle for later use. But the full-blown zombie was a very logical offspring of New World slavery.

For the slave under French rule in Haiti—then Saint-Domingue—in the 17th and 18th centuries, life was brutal: hunger, extreme over-work and cruel discipline were the rule. Slaves often could not consume enough calories to allow for normal rates of reproduction; what children they did have might easily starve. That was not of great concern to the plantation masters, who felt that children were a waste of resources, since they weren't able to work properly until they reached 10 or so. More manpower could always be imported from the Middle Passage.

The only escape from the sugar plantations was death, which was seen as a return to Africa, or lan guinée (literally Guinea, or West Africa). This is the phrase in Haitian Creole that even now means heaven. The plantation meant a life in servitude; lan guinée meant freedom. Death was feared but also wished for. Not surprisingly, suicide was a frequent recourse of the slaves, who were handy with poisons and powders. The plantation masters thought of suicide as the worst kind of thievery, since it deprived the master not only of a slave's service, but also of his or her person, which was, after all, the master's property. Suicide was the slave's only way to take control over his or her own body.

5   And yet, the fear of becoming a zombie might stop them from doing so. The zombie is a dead person who cannot get across to lan guinée. This final rest—in green, leafy, heavenly Africa, with no sugarcane to cut and no master to appease or serve—is unavailable to the zombie. To become a zombie was the slave's worst nightmare: to be dead and still a slave, an eternal field hand. It is thought that slave drivers on the plantations, who were usually slaves themselves and sometimes Voodoo priests, used this fear of zombification to keep recalcitrant slaves in order and to warn those who were despondent not to go too far.

In traditional Voodoo belief, in order to get back to lan guinée, one must be transported there by Baron Samedi, the lord of the cemetery and one of the darkest and most complicated of the religion's many complicated gods. Baron is customarily dressed in a business jacket, a top hat and dark glasses; he's foul-mouthed and comic in a low, vicious way. One of Baron's spiritual functions, his most important, is to dig a person's grave and welcome him to the other side. If for some reason a person has thwarted or offended Baron, the god will not allow that person, upon his death, to reach guinée. Then you're a zombie. Some other lucky mortal can control you, it is believed. You'll do the bidding of your master without question.

Haiti's notorious dictator François Duvalier, known as Papa Doc, who controlled Haiti with a viselike grip from 1957 until his death in 1971, well understood the Baron's role. He dressed like Baron, in a black fedora, business suit and heavy glasses or sunglasses. Like Baron at a ceremony, when Duvalier spoke publicly, it was often in a near whisper. His secret police, the Tontons Macoutes, behaved with the complete immorality and obedience of the undead, and were sometimes assumed to be zombies under the dictator's control. I once heard a Haitian radio announcer describe Klaus Barbie, a Nazi known as the Butcher of Lyon, as "youn ansyen Tonton Makout Hitler," or one of Hitler's Tontons Macoutes: a zombie of the Reich.

The only way for a zombie to have his will and soul return is for him to eat salt—a smart boss of a zombie keeps the creature's food tasteless. In the 1980s, with Duvalier's son ousted from power and the moment ripe for reform, the literacy primer put out by the liberation theologians' wing of the Roman Catholic Church in Haiti was called "A Taste of Salt."

There are many reasons the zombie, sprung from the colonial slave economy, is returning now to haunt us. Of course, the zombie is scary in a primordial way, but in a modern way, too. He's the living dead, but he's also the inanimate animated, the robot of industrial dystopias. He's great for fascism: one recent zombie movie (and there have been many) was called "The Fourth Reich." The zombie is devoid of consciousness and therefore unable to critique the system that has entrapped him. He's labor without grievance. He works free and never goes on strike.

You don't have to feed him much. He's a Foxconn[1] worker in China; a maquiladora[2] seamstress in Guatemala; a citizen of North Korea; he's the man, surely in the throes of psychosis and under the thrall of extreme poverty, who, years ago, during an interview, told me he believed he had once been a zombie himself.

So when kids come to your door this Halloween wearing costumes called Child Zombie Doctor or Shopko's Fun World Zombie, offer them a sprinkling of salt along with their candy corn. 10

## Responding to Reading

1. What historical connection do zombies have to slaves? Why was becoming a zombie "the slave's worst nightmare" (5)?
2. Why, according to Wilentz, are zombies "returning now to haunt us" (9) in films and other media? Why are they so frightening?
3. **Rhetorical Analysis** Why does Wilentz frame her essay with introductory and concluding paragraphs about trick-or-treating children? Is this an effective strategy? How does this frame support her essay's main purpose?

## Writing about Reading

1. Write a one-paragraph definition of the word *zombie*.
2. **Writing with Sources** Write an analysis of "Preparedness 101: Zombie Apocalypse," a blog on the website of the Centers for Disease Control and Prevention (CDC). What do you see as the purpose of this blog? Does it achieve this purpose? Is it at all serious? at all useful? In your analysis, evaluate the blog's links and images as well as its content.

# THE MOVIES THAT ROSE FROM THE GRAVE

## Max Brooks

*1972–*

*An author, screenwriter, and actor, Max Brooks often explores the zombie cultural icon in his work. His books include* The Zombie Survival Guide *(2003),* World War Z *(2006), and* The Harlem Hellfighters *(2014). In the following essay, Brooks considers the phenomenon of the "undead explosion" in various kinds of media.*

It will never die! It may disappear for a while, stay out of sight, out of mind, but sooner or later it will rise again, and no matter what we do, or how hard we try, it will never, ever die. A zombie? Hardly, rather our

---

[1] An electronics manufacturing company that supplies products to Apple and other corporations. [Eds.]

[2] A type of factory with usually harsh working conditions. [Eds.]

own fascination with what popular culture now refers to as "the living dead."

Zombies have dominated mainstream horror for more than half a decade. They're everywhere: movies, books, videogames, comics, even a new Broadway musical adaptation of Sam Raimi's *The Evil Dead*. Not only have they replaced previous alpha-monsters such as vampires and werewolves, but they are continuing to generate more interest (and revenue) than almost all other creatures put together. Given that several years ago the living dead were considered an obscure and largely underground sub-genre, it would not be an exaggeration to state that they have enjoyed a spectacular rebirth unlike anything in the history of modern horror.

Where did these creatures come from? Why are they so popular now? And when, if ever, will their reign of terror cease?

Although many cultures have their own myths concerning the raising of the dead (one going as far back as the epic of Gilgamesh), the word "zombie" can trace its origins back to west Africa. The legend involves a "houngan" (wizard) using a magical elixir to transform a living human into a mobile, docile and obedient corpse. The fact that this legend is deeply rooted in reality (Haitian zombie powder was discovered to contain a powerful neuro-toxin that caused a live victim to behave like a resurrected corpse) may explain why, when African slaves were brought to the Americas, European colonists also embraced the notion of the living dead.

5    For several centuries the voodoo zombie remained the staple of tall tales, stage productions, and even early Hollywood movies such as *White Zombie* (1932) and *I Walked With a Zombie* (1943). It wasn't until 1968 that up-and-coming film maker George A. Romero gave us a whole new reason to be afraid. *Night of the Living Dead* replaced the image of a harmless voodoo-created zombie with a hostile, flesh-eating ghoul that swelled its numbers to pandemic proportions. This new ghoul was the result of science, not magic, specifically radiation from a returning space probe. This new ghoul could, likewise, only be dispatched by a scientific solution: destroying the brain or severing it from the rest of the body. This new ghoul obeyed no one, other than its own insatiable craving for living, human flesh. In fact, this new ghoul was only referred to throughout the movie as a ghoul. The word zombie was never mentioned.

Romero's revolutionary creation set the stage for an entirely new genre, the horror-apocalypse or "horocalypse" movie. Zombies would henceforth be associated with the collapse of modern society, a new form of walking plague that threatened to stamp out humanity. Gone were the days of suspense and darkness, of castles and swamps and remote, isolated violence. Zombies would now be waging all-out war across the silver screen, a tradition that has endured for almost 40 years.

Since the premiere of *Night of the Living Dead*, many have sought to capitalise on Romero's initial success. The Italian movie *Night of the Zombie* (1980) mixed a fictional storyline with real-life footage of cannibalism in New Guinea. A similar movie, *Zombi 2*, witnessed a battle between a corpse-like stuntman and an actual man-eating shark. One Japanese film, *Wild Zero*, attempted to combine the living dead with aliens, transsexuals and the Japanese garage band Guitar Wolf. Michael Jackson immortalised dancing zombies with his 1983 music video *Thriller*. And in 1984, Romero's former writing partner, John Russo, released the zombie comedy *The Return of the Living Dead*.

While all of these works enjoyed a loyal fan base, they remained largely a cult sensation until the turn of this century. The rise began slowly at first. Computer games such as *Resident Evil* and *House of the Dead* were becoming successful enough to warrant their development into movies. On the heels of those came Danny Boyle's *28 Days Later* and the remake of Romero's *Dawn of the Dead*, which knocked Mel Gibson's *The Passion of the Christ* off the top spot in the US. Most industry experts predicted this was just a fad. Conventional wisdom predicted a short life for the living dead. Only that didn't happen. More zombie movies were produced, including Romero's own *Land of the Dead*. *Resident Evil* spawned a sequel, as did *House of the Dead*, and *The Return of the Living Dead*.

The literary world was similarly inundated with zombie fiction, as was the world of comics. New videogames such as *Stubbs the Zombie* and the mega-hit *Dead Rising* took their place alongside *Resident Evil* and *House of the Dead*. Even US television could not escape the walking corpses. Last year, Showtime's *Masters of Horror* series broadcast one episode with dead Iraq War veterans rising from their body bags to vote against the politicians that put them there.

Why now? Why such a sudden and ravenous obsession with 10 ghouls? Could it be the zombie authors themselves and the new levels of sophistication they are bringing to the genre? Perhaps. This new generation of writers, directors, illustrators and programmers are the first to have grown up studying the works of Romero and his contemporaries. For them, simply recreating the monsters of their childhood was not enough. Their zombie projects had to . . . be faster, wilder, and, in some cases, even smarter. In some cases, they have surpassed their predecessors in all aspects. But this rise in product quality does nothing to explain society's phenomenal demand for the living dead.

The answer to that question lies not in fiction, but current events. The last six years have witnessed a bombardment of tragic events. Terrorism, war, viral outbreaks and natural disasters have created a global undercurrent of anxiety not seen since the darkest days of the cold war. It seems that just turning on the nightly news either shows some present calamity or one that might potentially befall us any day now.

Zombie movies present people with an outlet for their apocalyptic anxieties without directly confronting them. The living dead are a fictional threat, as opposed to tsunamis or avian flu. No matter how scary or realistic the particular story might be, their unquestionably fictional nature makes them "safe." Someone can watch, say *Dawn of the Dead*, and witness an orgy of graphic violence and destruction, but still know in the back of their minds that, once they switch off the TV, this particular threat will simply cease to exist, something that cannot be said for terrorist docu-drama *Dirty War*, or the classic nuclear nightmare *Threads*. Knowing that zombies can never really rise allows for a feeling of control, a rare and valuable thing these days.

No one can say how long this present undead explosion will be with us. Perhaps they will ebb with the current trend of global chaos. Perhaps, as the dust of this decade settles, and society returns to a semblance of stability, our macabre fascinations will return to more conventional monsters, forsaking flesh-eating ghouls for good old-fashioned werewolves or vampires. No one can say. What is certain is that nothing lasts forever. What else is certain is that the living dead might go away, but they won't be gone forever. They will simply retreat underground again, waiting patiently for the day when they rise again.

## Responding to Reading

MyWritingLab™

1. In paragraph 10, Brooks asks, "Why now? Why such a sudden and ravenous obsession with ghouls?" How does he answer this question? Do you agree with his explanation of the reasons for this trend? What other explanations can you suggest?
2. Does Brooks expect the "undead explosion" (13) to continue? Do you? Why or why not?
3. **Rhetorical Analysis**   How has the portrayal of zombies in film evolved over the years? Is the information Brooks presents about this evolution a necessary part of his essay, or could he have made his case without it? Is all the other information he includes—for example, the origin of the word *zombie*—necessary? Explain.

## Writing about Reading

MyWritingLab™

1. What, if anything, do you find interesting or appealing in tales of the undead? What do you suppose so many others find appealing?
2. **Writing with Sources**   In paragraph 2, Brooks mentions the rise of zombies in a variety of different media, including books. Browse *Amazon. com*, and read the summaries, first pages, and reader reviews of some recently published books with zombie titles and themes. Then, write an essay in which you discuss the needs these books seem to satisfy. Try to incorporate the views of two or three contemporary book critics into your essay.

# Zombie Studies Gain Ground on College Campuses

## Erica E. Phillips

*A reporter for the* Wall Street Journal, *Erica E. Phillips often writes on issues related to the West Coast economy. In "Zombie Studies Gain Ground on College Campuses," Phillips considers the growing popularity of the zombie phenomenon in academia.*

Kyle Bishop figured it was risky when he applied to a University of Arizona Ph.D. program in English eight years ago by proposing a dissertation on zombie movies.

He was dead wrong.

The program approved Mr. Bishop's proposal, and he is now chairman of Southern Utah University's English department. The 40-year-old has been invited to give zombie lectures in Hawaii, Canada and Spain.

"It's clearly now acceptable to study zombies seriously," he says.

Just as zombies—those mythical revived corpses hungry for living human flesh and gray matter—have infiltrated pop culture, they have also gotten their hands on our brainiest reserves: the academy. 5

Mr. Bishop is among an advancing horde of scholars who, compelled by the cultural history and metaphor of the undead, are teaching and conducting research in disciplines from economics to religion to medicine.

The last five years have seen 20 new scholarly books with "zombie" in the title or topic category, according to Baker & Taylor, a distributor of academic and other books; in the 10 prior years, there were 10. JSTOR, an online archive of about 2,000 academic journals, says the journals have run 39 articles invoking the undead since 2005, versus seven in the preceding 10 years.

Mr. Bishop's timing was impeccable. His dissertation coincided with a zombie onslaught that infected television, literature and other media. AMC's TV series *The Walking Dead* is a top-rated cable show, and the 2013 zombie movie *World War Z* grossed $540 million globally.

Mr. Bishop turned his dissertation into a book, *American Zombie Gothic: The Rise and Fall (and Rise) of the Walking Dead in Popular Culture*, which surprised everyone when over 1,000 copies sold. Back when he proposed his dissertation, he says, "nobody would touch the zombie."

Now, zombies thrive on campuses like California State University, 10 East Bay, in Hayward. Christopher Moreman, a philosophy professor there, co-edited a two-volume collection of essays on "the Humanity of the Walking Dead" and "Cross-Cultural Appropriations" of the monsters. The initial plan was for one volume, he says, but over 100 proposals arrived.

When Mr. Moreman worked the theme into a course—"Philosophy 3432: Religion, Monsters and Horror"—he says he drew 55 students vying for 35 spots.

In one class, students read his work examining Buddhist imagery in zombie movies, which echo the religion's meditation on mortality, he says, because "you recognize that everything's temporary and zombies keep going on and on."

Some find the trend ominous. There is a "danger" when scholars probe subjects like zombies, says Mark Bauerlein, an English professor and author of *The Dumbest Generation: How the Digital Age Stupefies Young Americans and Jeopardizes Our Future*.

"They end up invariably turning their attention away from the tradition," he says, "the classics, the works that have survived the test of time."

15    Michael Poliakoff, who directs policy for the American Council of Trustees and Alumni, says the proliferation of undergraduate courses in topics like zombies and vampires is helping ruin American students' brains. Citing various studies, Mr. Poliakoff says many U.S. college graduates still lack proficiency in basic verbal literacy.

"What have we given up in order to dabble in the undead?" he says. "We've given up survival skills."

Last year, some parents objected to an optional reading class at Armand Larive Middle School in Hermiston, Ore., using materials describing a "zombie apocalypse." The district eliminated the material, says Superintendent Dr. Fred Maiocco, and "we extend our regrets to anyone offended."

Zombie scholars say their subject is worthy of study because the living deads' history and ubiquity in modern literature and culture present metaphors ripe for analysis.

Self-described "zombie scholar" Sarah Juliet Lauro, a Clemson University assistant English professor, acknowledges that some think it is silly or inappropriate to study the ghouls.

20    She counters that "it's a deeply important mythology that is specifically about slavery." She is finishing a book tracing zombie folklore to its 18th-century roots in the Haitian Revolution. *Zombis* were field laborers raised from the dead who led a slave rebellion.

Her book, *The Transatlantic Zombie: Slavery, Rebellion and Living Death*, examines how zombies came to represent the struggles of slavery and colonialism.

A former student of Ms. Lauro's, 34-year-old Christopher Schuster, says studying zombies analytically in her class "struck a chord." An Iraq War veteran, he saw parallels to post-traumatic stress disorder. "A single bite changes you from my best friend to someone who's trying to kill me," he says, adding that war "can take a child and turn him into a tormented man."

Zombies are staggering into many fields. Last year, English professor Sherryl Vint at the University of California, Riverside, and a grad student called for submissions to "an edited volume on zombies in comics and graphic novels through the lens of medical discourse."

The editors "seek to move beyond merely identifying the similarities between the etiology[1] of infectious disease and zombie plagues to question how medical discourse constructs and is constructed by popular iconography of the boundaries of life, illness and health."

Other collections due this year include *Economics of the Undead*, [25] which co-editor Glen Whitman, a Cal State Northridge economics professor, says "raises issues of the use of resources" in an apocalyptic event. The work is academic, he says, but might draw readers "with a casual interest in economics."

A media-studies anthology edited by Steve Jones, a senior lecturer at England's Northumbria University, "seeks to investigate zombie sexuality in all its forms and manifestations."

Max Brooks, author of hit pop-culture books like *The Zombie Survival Guide* and *World War Z*—often cited in academic works—is skeptical about exploring the undead theoretically. "It just becomes academics writing papers for other academics," he says.

Instead, he says, "I would want a professor who would dig into the very real questions" that his own books seek to answer—such as, what steps would one take should a zombie apocalypse arrive—and "take that knowledge and apply it to the real world."

## Responding to Reading                                    MyWritingLab™

1. What specific kinds of media does Phillips relate to the zombie phenomenon?
2. How does Phillips account for the appeal zombies have for those writing academic books and dissertations?
3. **Rhetorical Analysis** Consider the language Phillips uses here—for example, words like "infiltrated" (5) and "onslaught" (8). What do such words suggest about her view of the growing influence of zombies in both academia and the media?

## Writing about Reading                                    MyWritingLab™

1. Do you see "zombie studies" as a legitimate academic subject? as a legitimate subject for a critical article or a scholarly book? Why or why not?
2. **Writing with Sources** Research the concept of the "zombie apocalypse" (mentioned in paragraph 17). What are its origins? In what types of media is it depicted? Write an essay in which you define this concept and explain its popularity in various media. You might begin your research by watching the trailer of the 2011 film *Zombie Apocalypse*, browsing sites that describe zombie-apocalypse-themed video games, or reading the Zombie Apocalypse blog on the *Huffington Post* website.

---

[1]Cause. [Eds.]

# WIDENING THE FOCUS

## For Critical Reading and Writing

Referring specifically to the three readings in this chapter's Focus section (and possibly to additional sources as well), write an essay in which you answer the question, "Why Are Zombies Invading Our Media?"

## For Further Reading

The following readings can suggest additional perspectives for reading and writing about why zombies are so prevalent in our media.

- Jill Filipovic, "We've Gone Too Far with Trigger Warnings" (p. 97)
- Thane Rosenbaum, "Should Neo-Nazis Be Allowed Free Speech?" (p. 172)
- Jose Antonio Vargas, "Outlaw: My Life in America as an Undocumented Immigrant" (p. 325)
- Barbara Hurd, "Fracking: A Fable" (p. 409)

 Web Links

## For Focused Research

The zombie phenomenon has infiltrated various kinds of media, from TV shows to public health campaigns. Consider your academic major or a subject you are interested in. What implications do zombie stories have in your field? Do some online research to find what, if anything, writers in your area of study are saying about the zombie phenomenon. Then, write an essay in which you analyze one aspect of this phenomenon as it applies to your field. Use the readings in this chapter's Focus section to spark some ideas.

## Beyond the Classroom

Interview some friends and classmates about the zombie phenomenon. Do they read zombie-themed books or watch TV shows or movies that deal with the undead? What value do they see in these types of media? Take notes on their responses, and then write an essay in which you draw a conclusion about the impact the zombie phenomenon has had on our daily lives.

---------------------- EXPLORING ISSUES AND IDEAS ——

MyWritingLab™
Visit Chapter 6, "Media and Society," in MyWritingLab to test your understanding of the chapter objectives.

## Media and Society

Write an essay in response to one of the following prompts, which are suitable for assignments that require the use of outside sources as well as for assignments that are not source-based.

1.  What do you think the impact of the various media discussed in this chapter will be in the years to come? What trends do you see emerging that you believe will change the way you think or the way you live? Write an essay in which you speculate about future trends and their impact, using the essay in this chapter by Jane McGonigal (p. 198) to support the points you make.

2.  Write an essay in which you consider the representation of a particular ethnic or racial group (or the portrayal of women, the elderly, or people with disabilities) in the media (movies, television, magazine ads, and so on). Do you believe the group you have chosen to write about is adequately represented? Do you think its members are portrayed fairly and accurately, or do you think they are stereotyped? Support your conclusions with specific examples.

3.  Do you think newspapers will survive in their present form, or do you believe that the Internet threatens their survival? Do you believe print newspapers *should* survive—that is, that they are necessary?

4.  To what extent, if any, should explicitly sexual or violent media images be censored? Write an essay in which you take a stand on this issue and explain why you believe such censorship is (or is not) necessary.

5.  What danger, if any, do you see for young people in the seductive messages of the music they listen to? Do you believe that parents and educators are right to be concerned about the effect the messages in rock and rap music have on teenagers and young adults, or do you think they are overreacting? Support your position with quotations from popular music lyrics. If you like, you can also interview friends and relatives and use their responses to help you develop your argument. Before you begin, read Mary Eberstadt's "Eminem Is Right" (p. 181).

6.  Write an analysis of a website, considering the techniques it uses to appeal to its target audience. Who is being addressed, what message is conveyed, and how successfully is this message communicated?

7.  Write an analysis of a current popular reality TV show. Start by describing the program's basic premise, setting, and participants. Then, consider some or all of the following questions:

    • What explains this program's appeal to viewers?

    • What trends in society does the program reflect?

    • Does the program rely on sensationalism?

    • Has the program had any impact on society?

# 7

## GENDER AND IDENTITY

*In this chapter , you will learn to*
- analyze readings about gender and identity
- compose essays about gender and identity

ttitudes about gender have changed dramatically over the past forty years, and they continue to change. For some, these changes have resulted in confusion as well as liberation. One reason for this confusion is that people can no longer rely on fixed gender roles to tell them how to behave in public and how to function within their families. Still, many men and women—uncomfortable with the demands of confining gender roles and unhappy with the expectations

Young boy playing with toy cars

those roles create—yearn for even less rigidity, for an escape from stereotypes into a society where roles are not strictly defined by gender.

In spite of these changes, many people still see men and women in terms of unrealistic stereotypes. Men are strong, tough, and brave, and women are weak, passive, and in need of protection. Men understand mathematics and science and have a natural aptitude for mechanical tasks. They also have the drive, the aggressiveness, the competitive edge, and the power to succeed. They are never sentimental and never cry. Women are better at small, repetitive tasks and shy away from taking bold, decisive actions. They enjoy, and are good at, domestic activities, and they have a natural aptitude for nurturing. Although women may like their jobs, they will leave them to devote themselves to husband and children.

As you read the preceding list of stereotypes, you may react neutrally (or even favorably), or you may react with annoyance; how we react tells us something about our society and something about ourselves. As a number of writers in this chapter point out, however, stereotypes can limit the way people think, the roles they choose to assume, and, ultimately, the positions they occupy in society.

As the Focus section of this chapter, "Who Has It Harder, Girls or Boys?" (p. 244) illustrates, both men and women have problems living up to the images they believe they should conform to and filling the roles that have been set for them. In "The Case against Single-Sex Classrooms" (p. 244), Margaret Talbot questions the rationale for single-sex

Young girl playing with dolls

education; in "The War against Boys" (p. 247), Christina Hoff Sommers makes the case that misguided policies are hurting young men; and in "Men Are from Earth, and So Are Women: It's Faulty Research That Sets Them Apart" (p. 252), Rosalind C. Barnett and Caryl Rivers say that college professors are unwittingly spreading ideas about men and women that are largely unsubstantiated.

## ——————— PREPARING TO READ AND WRITE ———————

As you read and prepare to write about the essays in this chapter , you may consider the following questions:

- What assumptions does the writer have about his or her audience? How can you tell?

- What is the writer's primary purpose? For example, is it to challenge traditional ideas about gender or to support them?

- What genre is the writer using? For example, is the reading an argument or an analysis? How do the conventions of this genre influence the writer's choices?

- What appeals does the writer use? For example, does he or she appeal primarily to reason? to emotion? to a combination of the two? Would another strategy be more effective?

- Is the writer male or female? Can you determine the writer's gender without reading his or her name or the headnote? Does the writer's gender matter?

- Does the writer focus on males, on females, or on both?

- Does the essay's date of publication affect its content?

- Does the essay seem fair? Balanced?

- Does the writer discuss gender as a sexual, political, economic, or social issue?

- What does the writer suggest are the specific advantages or disadvantages of being male? Of being female? Of being gay or straight?

- Does the writer recommend specific societal changes? What are they? Do they seem reasonable or even possible?

- Does the writer think that men and women are fundamentally different? If so, does he or she suggest that these differences can (or should) be overcome, or at least lessened?

- Does the writer think gender differences are the result of environment, heredity, or both?

- Does the essay challenge any of your ideas about male or female roles?

- In what ways is the essay like other essays in this chapter?

# THE M/F BOXES

## E. J. Graff

### 1958–

*A senior fellow at the Schuster Institute for Investigative Journalism and a resident scholar at the Brandeis Women's Studies Research Center, E. J. Graff is a widely published author of articles on gender equality and family issues. She is a contributing editor at the* American Prospect *and the author of two books—*What Is Marriage For? The Strange History of Our Most Intimate Institution *(1999) and, with Evelyn F. Murphy,* Getting Even: Why Women Don't Get Paid Like Men—and What to Do about It *(2005). The following essay questions conventional male/female distinctions and argues that either/or labels falsely prepackage identity and gender.*

A 15-year-old girl is incarcerated in a Chicago mental hospital in 1981 and kept there for three years because she won't wear a dress. A Winn-Dixie truck driver is fired from a job he held for twenty years when his boss learns that he wears women's clothes at home. A small-time hustler in Falls City, Nebraska, is raped and then murdered when he's discovered to be physically female. A woman bleeds to death after a Washington, DC, hit-and-run accident when, after finding male genitals under her clothes, paramedics stand by laughing.

M or F? For most of us that's a simple question, decided while we were in utero. Checking off that box—at the doctor's, on the census, on a driver's license—takes scarcely a thought. But there's an emerging movement of increasingly vocal people whose bodies or behavior unsettle that clear division. They're calling themselves "transgendered": It's a spongy neologism that, at its broadest, absorbs everyone from medically reassigned transsexuals to cross-dressing men to women so masculine that security guards are called to eject them from women's restrooms. Fellow travelers include intersexuals (once called hermaphrodites), whose bodies are both/and rather than either/or. The slash between M/F cuts painfully through these lives.

And so they've started to organize. Brought together by the Internet, inspired by the successes of the gay rights movement, and with national sympathy gained from the movie *Boys Don't Cry*, intersex and transgender activists are starting to get a hearing in organizations ranging from college campuses to city councils, from lesbian and gay rights groups to pediatric conferences. And, like the feminist and gay rights movements before them, the new sex-and-gender activists may force us to rethink, in life and in law, how we define and interpret the basics of sex.

A first clue to how zealously the M/F border is guarded—to how sex is literally constructed—comes at birth. One in 2,000 infants is born with genitalia ambiguous enough to make doctors hem and haw when parents ask that first question: boy or girl? Since the late 1950s/ early 1960s, standard medical procedure has been to lie and obfuscate. Rather than explain that the child is "a mixture of male and female," writes Anne Fausto-Sterling, author of *Sexing the Body*, medical manuals advise physicians to reassign the child surgically to one sex or another, telling parents only that "the gonads were incompletely developed ... and therefore required removal." A large clitoris may be cut down; a micropenis may be removed and a vagina built; a testis or testes are sliced out—sometimes over the parents' explicit objections.

5    Now some of those children have come of age and are telling their stories: severe depression, sexual numbness and a long-time despair at having been folded, spindled and mutilated. The leader of this nascent movement is Cheryl Chase, who in 1993 organized the Intersex Society of North America. ISNA opposes reassignment surgery on intersex infants and advocates raising intersex children as social males or females, educating them about their bodies and letting them choose at puberty whether they'd like surgical assistance or a shift in social sex. ISNA's cause was helped when Johns Hopkins sex researcher and PhD John Money, who wrote the intersex silence-and-reassignment protocol, was profoundly discredited. After a child he called "John" was accidentally castrated soon after birth, Money advised his parents to have him undergo surgery to construct a vagina, raise him as "Joan" and give him female hormones at puberty. Money reported this involuntary sex reassignment as fully successful. But in 1997, both a medical journal report and a *Rolling Stone* article revealed that the reassignment had been a disaster. Despite the insistence of parents, doctors, psychologists and teachers, "Joan" had always insisted that she was "just a boy with long hair in girl's clothes." In adolescence, John took back his manhood.

How did John "know" he was male—and by extension, how do any of us decide we're girls or boys? One theory is that, in utero, John had undergone the androgen bath that turns an undifferentiated fetus— which otherwise becomes female—male, giving him a male identity and masculine behavior. In the other rare cases where XY infants lose penises and are raised as girls, some insist on being boys—but others happily identify as (masculine, lesbian) women, which suggests that things aren't quite so simple. Scientists recognize that our brains and nervous systems are somewhat plastic, developing in response to environmental stimuli. Sexuality—all of it, from identity to presentation to sexual orientation—is no exception; it develops as a biological inter-action between inborn capacities and outside influences. As a result, most of us have a narrow range in which we feel "natural" as we gen-der ourselves daily through clothes, stance, stride, tone. For most, that gendered behavior is consonant with biological sex: Girls present as female, if not feminine, and fall in love with boys; boys present as male or masculine and fall in love with girls. But those in whom gendered behavior is vice versa—feminine boys, highly masculine girls—get treated as unnatural, even though their gendering is just as biological as the rest of ours. What happens to these transgendered folks can be so brutal that the pediatric surgeons who cut off infant clitorises or penises look like merely the advance guard of the M/F border patrol.

Take, for instance, Daphne Scholinski, so masculine that at age 6, strangers chastised her when she tried to use women's restrooms. In her dry, pitiless memoir *The Last Time I Wore a Dress*, Scholinski tells the story of being committed to a mental hospital at 15 for some very real problems, including severe neglect, her father's violence and her own delinquency. The hospital ignored her shocking childhood and instead "treated" her masculinity. Scholinski got demerits if she didn't wear makeup. She was put on a boys' ward, where she was twice raped, to encourage her to be more feminine. Her confinement was so disturbing that she still gets posttraumatic stress flashbacks, including nightmares so terrifying that she wakes up and vomits. And so Scholinski is start-ing an organization dedicated to reforming the diagnosis of childhood GID, or gender identity disorder, under which she was treated.

Or consider the treatment of Darlene Jespersen and Peter Oiler. After working for Harrah's Reno casino for eighteen years, in the summer of 2000, Jespersen was fired from her bar-tending job when Harrah's launched a new policy requiring all its female employees to wear foundation, powder, eye-liner, lipstick and so on. "I tried it," says Jespersen in a plaintive voice, "but I felt so naked." The obverse hap-pened to Peter Oiler, a weathered, middle-aged man with large aviator glasses, a pleasant drawl and a bit of an overbite. After twenty years of being rotated through progressively more responsible jobs in Winn-Dixie's shipping yards, in 1999 Oiler was driving a fifty-foot truck delivering grocery supplies throughout southeastern Louisiana—until Winn-Dixie learned that he called himself "transgendered." Oiler tried to explain that he simply wore women's clothes on the weekends: He wasn't going to become a woman; he didn't want to wear makeup and heels on company time. In January 2000 Oiler was fired.

Jespersen and Oiler are stunned. Jespersen is suing Harrah's. Says Oiler, "I was raised to believe that if you do an honest day's work, you'll get an honest day's pay." The ACLU Lesbian and Gay Rights Project has taken up his case, in part because of the sheer injustice—and in part to get courts to treat discrimination against people who violate sex stereotypes as illegal sex discrimination. If a woman can wear a dress, or if a man can refuse makeup, why not vice versa? In doing so, the ACLU, like the three national lesbian and gay legal organizations, would be building on the 1989 Supreme Court decision *Price Waterhouse v. Ann Hopkins*. Price Waterhouse had told Hopkins that she wasn't going to make partner because she was too masculine—and, in actual written memos, advised her to wear jewelry and makeup, to go to charm school, to be less aggressive. The Supreme Court declared such stereotyping to be sex discrimination.

10     Will judges see Peter Oiler's dismissal as illegal sex stereotyping? There have been some recent hints that they might. In Massachusetts, for instance, the US Court of Appeals for the First Circuit said Lucas Rosa could sue a bank that instructed feminine Rosa, who had shown up to apply for a loan wearing a dress, to go home and come back in men's clothes; a female, after all, would have been considered for the loan. Another Massachusetts judge said that a male student could come to school in a dress, since female students could. A Washington transsexual prisoner raped by a prison guard, and two New York municipal employees harassed for being gay, were allowed to sue when judges ruled they'd been attacked for violating stereotyped expectations of their sex.

Our society has learned to see why women would want masculine privileges like playing soccer and serving on the Supreme Court, but there's been no matching force expanding the world for males. Boys and men still patrol each other's masculinity with a Glengarry Glen Ross level of ridicule and violence that can seem, to women, nearly surreal. Those males who violate the M-box's limits on behavior are quite literally risking their lives.

Which means that, if you're a performing drag queen, a cross-dressing straight man like Peter Oiler, or a transsexual who still has some male ID, do not under any circumstances get stopped by a cop. In New York City, says Pauline Park, a co-founder of NYAGRA (New York Association for Gender Rights Advocacy), even if the police don't actually beat you, "you could be arrested and detained for days or weeks. They don't let people out until they plead guilty to prostitution. They put them in the men's cell, where they're often assaulted and sometimes raped, as a tactic to get people to plead guilty."

And don't turn to emergency medical personnel. In August 1995 Tyra Hunter's car crashed in Washington, DC. When firefighting paramedics cut away her dress and found male genitals, they laughed and mocked her. She bled to death in the hospital. In August 2000 a jury awarded Hunter's mother $1.75 million in a wrongful-death action. Hunter's experience, unfortunately, is not unusual. Once a month, someone transgendered is murdered, and those are just the documented cases. Transgender activists are beginning to mark November 28, the anniversary of another such death, as a Day of Remembrance, with candlelight vigils and a determination to slow the steady drumbeat of murder.

"We're despised. We're pariahs in this society," says Miranda Stevens-Miller, chair of the transgender rights organization It's Time, Illinois, about transsexuals and otherwise transgendered people. Many transsexuals are fired once they begin to transition. Others lose custody and visitation rights, houses, leases. Many are shut out of office and other public restrooms for years—an indignity that cuts to the very core of being human, since every living body needs to pee. And so the most urgent transgender organizing is happening locally, in organizations such as TGNet Arizona, NYAGRA and It's Time, Oregon. They're teaching Trans 101 to local employers, doctors, city councils, lesbian and gay organizations, judges, families, landlords, friends. They're attempting to collect statistics on firings, beatings, murders, bathroom harassment, police abuse. Often these groups are driven by the energy and determination of one or two people who spend their own time and pennies writing and photocopying leaflets, giving workshops for corporate and college groups, and lobbying city councils and lesbian and gay organizations for inclusion in hate-crimes and antidiscrimination laws. Lately, they're having remarkable success at adding "gender identity and expression" to the protected categories in local and state employment nondiscrimination and hate-crimes laws; they've won in locales ranging from Portland, Oregon, to DeKalb, Illinois, to the state of Rhode Island.

Nationally, trans groups are still in the skirmishing phase faced by 15 any new movement, with the inevitable splits over strategy and personality. The group with the most name recognition, GenderPAC, angers some transgender activists by avoiding the "T" word in its advocacy, saying that it aims at gender freedom for everyone; it acts on behalf of such people as Darlene Jespersen and Peter Oiler, or boys called "faggot" for not being noticeably masculine. Currently the most significant transgender organizations nationally are IFGE (International Foundation for Gender Education), GEA (Gender Education and Advocacy) and the Working Group on Trans Equality, a loose network of grass-roots trans activists aiming at a coordinated national presence. Perhaps the biggest success so far is that all the major lesbian and gay organizations and many smaller ones have added transgendered folks to their mission statements as folks who are equally, if differently, queer.

Or is it so different? All of us deviate from what's expected from our sex. While the relationship between transgender activists and lesbian and gay groups has at times been contentious, some lesbian and gay activists, notably Chai Feldblum, Georgetown law professor, are starting to urge that we all organize around our common deviance from sex stereotypes. The differences between homosexual, transgender and transsexual experiences are not that great: All are natural variations on the brain's gendered development that have cropped up throughout human history, from Tiresias to Radclyffe Hall, from Billy Tipton to Quentin Crisp. For the most part, the mainstream sees us on one sliding scale of queerness. And occasionally our struggles and goals intersect quite neatly. For instance, homos can't always tell whether we're harassed at work because someone figures out that we date others of the same sex, or simply because we're too butch or too fey.

And none of us can rely on having our marriages recognized by the institutions around us when we need them—because marriage is one of the last laws on the books that discriminate based on sex. Recently, Joe Gardiner asked a Kansas court to invalidate his dead father's marriage to transwoman (born male, medically and legally reassigned as female) J'Noel Gardiner, saying J'Noel was "really" a man—and therefore could not have legally married a man. The lower court agreed with the son that XY = man, which meant the son would inherit his father's fat estate. But the Kansas appeals judge remanded the case back down for a new trial. Sex, the appeals court declared, isn't decided simply by a chromosome test. Rather, sex is a complex constellation of characteristics that includes not only chromosomes but also "gonadal sex, internal morphologic sex, external morphologic sex, hormonal sex, phenotypic sex, assigned sex and gender of rearing, and sexual identity." The court approvingly quoted Johns Hopkins researcher and medical doctor William Reiner, who wrote, "The organ that appears to be critical to psychosexual development and adaptation is not the external genitalia, but the brain."

## Responding to Reading                              MyWritingLab™

1. How does Graff define the term *transgendered?* What does she mean when she says, "The slash between M/F cuts painfully through these lives" (2)?
2. Graff says that boys and men "patrol each other's masculinity with a … level of ridicule and violence that can seem, to women, nearly surreal" (11). Do you agree with this contention? Do you believe that "males who violate the M-box's limits on behavior are quite literally risking their lives" (11)?
3. **Rhetorical Analysis Graff** begins her essay with a series of examples. Why does she use this strategy? Would another introductory strategy have been more effective? Explain.

## Writing about Reading                               MyWritingLab™

1. In paragraph 3, Graff says, "like the feminist and gay rights movements before them, the new sex-and-gender activists may force us to rethink, in life and in law, how we define and interpret the basics of sex." Do you agree with this statement? How is the situation of transgendered individuals similar to and different from that of women and gays?
2. **Writing with Sources** According to the National Center for Transgender Equality, transgendered people face a disproportionate amount of discrimination. What are the main areas of discrimination that transgenderd people face? In your opinion, has government done enough to ensure transgender equality?

# "BOSSY," THE OTHER B-WORD
## Sheryl Sandberg
*1969–*

## Anna Maria Chávez
*1968–*

*The chief operating officer of Facebook and the founder of the charitable organization LeanIn.org, Sheryl Sandberg is the author of the books* Lean In: Women, Work, and the Will to Lead *(2013) and, with Nell Scovell,* Lean In: For Graduates *(2014). The chief executive officer of Girl Scouts of the USA, Anna Maria Chávez co-launched (with Sandberg) Ban Bossy, a public service campaign that offers leadership advice for girls. In the following essay, Sandberg and Chávez examine the gendered term* bossy.

We were bossy little girls.

*Sheryl:* When my brother and sister describe our childhood, they will say that I never actually *played* as a child but instead just organized other kids' play. At my wedding, they stood up and introduced themselves by explaining, "Hi, we're Sheryl's younger brother and sister… but we're not really her younger brother and sister. We're her first employees—employee No. 1 and employee No. 2."

From a very young age, I liked to organize—the toys in my room, neighborhood play sessions, clubs at school. When I was in junior high and running for class vice president, one of my teachers pulled my best friend aside to warn her not to follow my example: "Nobody likes a *bossy* girl," the teacher warned. "You should find a new friend who will be a better influence on you."

*Anna:* The Latino community of my childhood had clear expectations for each gender: Males made decisions, and females played supporting roles. My brothers and I used to play war with the neighborhood kids. Each child was assigned to a team to prepare for battle. As the only girl, I was always sent to collect ammunition (red berries from nearby trees). One day, I announced that I wanted to lead the battalion. The boys responded, "You are really bossy, Anna, and everyone knows a girl can't lead the troops."

Fortunately, I saw my mother break this mold by running for our 5 local school board. One of the most vivid memories of my childhood was hearing people come up to my father and say that it was inappropriate for his wife to run for office…and having him tell them that he disagreed and was proud of her.

Although the two of us come from different backgrounds, we both heard the same put-down. Call it the other B-word. Whether it is said directly or implied, girls get the message: *Don't be bossy. Don't raise your hand too much. Keep your voice down. Don't lead.*

The word "bossy" has carried both a negative and a female connotation for more than a century. The first citation of "bossy" in the *Oxford English Dictionary* refers to an 1882 article in *Harper's Magazine*, which declared: "There was a lady manager who was dreadfully bossy." A Google Ngram[1] analysis of digitized books over the past 100 years found that the use of "bossy" to describe women first peaked in the Depression-era 1930s, when popular sentiment held that a woman should not "steal" a job from a man, and reached its highest point in the mid-1970s as the women's movement ramped up and more women entered the workforce.

Most dictionary entries for "bossy" provide a sentence showing its proper use, and nearly all focus on women. Examples range from the *Oxford Dictionaries'* "bossy, meddling woman" to *Urban Dictionary*'s "She is bossy, and probably has a pair down there to produce all the testosterone." Ngram shows that in 2008 (the most recent year available), the word appeared in books four times more often to refer to females than to males.

Behind the negative connotations lie deep-rooted stereotypes about gender. Boys are expected to be assertive, confident and opinionated, while girls should be kind, nurturing and compassionate. When a little boy takes charge in class or on the playground, nobody is surprised or offended. We *expect* him to lead. But when a little girl does the same, she is often criticized and disliked.

10      How are we supposed to level the playing field for girls and women if we discourage the very traits that get them there?

Social scientists have long studied how language affects society, and they find that even subtle messages can have a big impact on girls' goals and aspirations. Calling a girl "bossy" not only undermines her ability to see herself as a leader, but it also influences how others treat her. According to data collected by the National Longitudinal Study of Adolescent Health, parents of seventh-graders place more importance on leadership for their sons than for their daughters. Other studies have determined that teachers interact with and call on boys more frequently and allow them to shout out answers more than girls.

It's no surprise that by middle school, girls are less interested in leading than boys are. Sixth- and seventh-grade girls rate being popular and well-liked as more important than being perceived as competent or independent, while boys are more likely to rate competence and independence as more important, according to a report by the American Association of University Women. A 2008 survey by the Girl Scouts of nearly 4,000 boys and girls found that girls between the ages of 8 and 17 avoid leadership roles for fear that they will be labeled "bossy" or disliked by their peers.

---

[1] A tool that determines how often a certain word or word group appears in a source. [Eds.]

And "bossy" is just the beginning. As girls mature, the words may change, but their meaning and impact remain the same. Women who behave assertively are labeled "aggressive," "angry," "shrill" and "overly ambitious." Powerful and successful men are often well liked, but when women become powerful and successful, all of us—both men and women—tend to like them less.

Even our most successful and celebrated female leaders cannot rise above these insults. A foreign-policy adviser once described former British Prime Minister Margaret Thatcher as "the bossy intrusive Englishwoman." Susan Rice, the U.S. national security adviser, was described as having a "bossy demeanor" by a fellow diplomat, while Supreme Court Justice Sonia Sotomayor has been described as "difficult" and "nasty" by lawyers.

The phrase "too ambitious" is leveled at female leaders from Madeleine Albright to Hillary Clinton and perpetuates our most damning stereotypes. Retired Supreme Court Justice Sandra Day O'Connor has a pillow in her California home that declares: "I'm not bossy. I just have better ideas." 15

This doesn't only affect women at the highest levels of power. Over the past year, I (Sheryl) have traveled around the world speaking about my book, *Lean In*. From Beijing to Minneapolis, I have asked groups of men and women to raise their hands if they've been called "too aggressive" at work. Time and again, a small fraction of men raise their hands, while a great majority of women shoot a hand into the air...and sometimes two. At Howard University, I asked a group of female students if they had been called "bossy" during their childhoods. From within the sea of waving hands, one woman shouted, "During my childhood? How about last week!"

These stereotypes become self-fulfilling prophecies. Despite earning the majority of college degrees, women make up just 19% of the U.S. Congress, 5% of Fortune 500 CEOs and 10% of heads of state. Most leadership positions are held by men, so society continues to expect leadership to look and act male and to react negatively when women lead.

The irony, of course, is that so-called bossy women make great leaders. And we need great leaders. Our economic growth depends upon having women fully engaged in the workforce. Our companies perform better with more women in management. And our homes are happier when men and women share responsibilities more equally.

It's time to end the gendered speech that discourages girls from an early age. So the next time you hear a girl called "bossy," do what CBS anchor Norah O'Donnell advised: Smile, take a deep breath and say, "That girl's not bossy. She has *executive leadership skills*."

## Responding to Reading

MyWritingLab™

1. What are the negative connotations of the word *bossy*? How does calling a girl "bossy" undermine "her ability to see herself as a leader" (11)?
2. What do Sandberg and Chávez mean when they say that certain stereotypes become "self-fulfilling prophesies" (17)?
3. **Rhetorical Analysis**   What evidence do Sandberg and Chávez present to support their position? Do they present enough evidence? the right kind of evidence? Is it convincing?

## Writing about Reading

MyWritingLab™

1. What does the word *bossy* mean to you? How is your definition like or unlike the definitions in paragraphs 7 and 8?
2. **Writing with Sources**   In response to Sandberg and Chávez's Ban Bossy campaign, Margaret Talbot writes in *The New Yorker*, "neither banning nor rebranding a single word can accomplish all that much social change." According to Talbot, it's "the acceptance of the behavior that counts." Research the factors that help determine whether a young woman will seek leadership positions. Then, write a response to Sandberg and Chávez's article in which you present your findings.

# WHY I WANT A WIFE

## Judy Brady

*1937–*

*Judy Brady studied art before getting married, having a family, and starting her writing career. A breast cancer survivor, Brady cofounded the Toxic Links Coalition, an environmental advocacy group based in California. She has edited two books about cancer, including* Women and Cancer *(1980) and a collection of essays and poems written by women with cancer titled* One in Three: Women with Cancer Confront an Epidemic *(1991). The following essay, "Why I Want a Wife," appeared in the first issue of* Ms. *magazine in 1972. In this essay, Brady takes a satirical look at what it means to be a wife and mother.*

I belong to that classification of people known as wives. I am A Wife. And, not altogether incidentally, I am a mother.

Not too long ago a male friend of mine appeared on the scene fresh from a recent divorce. He had one child, who is, of course, with his ex-wife. He is looking for another wife. As I thought about him while I was ironing one evening, it suddenly occurred to me that I, too, would like to have a wife. Why do I want a wife?

I would like to go back to school so that I can become economically independent, support myself, and, if need be, support those dependent upon me. I want a wife who will work and send me to school. And while I am going to school I want a wife to take care of my children.

I want a wife to keep track of the children's doctor and dentist appointments. And to keep track of mine, too. I want a wife to make sure my children eat properly and are kept clean. I want a wife who will wash the children's clothes and keep them mended. I want a wife who is a good nurturant attendant to my children, who arranges for their schooling, makes sure that they have an adequate social life with their peers, takes them to the park, the zoo, etc. I want a wife who takes care of the children when they are sick, a wife who arranges to be around when the children need special care, because, of course, I cannot miss classes at school. My wife must arrange to lose time at work and not lose the job. It may mean a small cut in my wife's income from time to time, but I guess I can tolerate that. Needless to say, my wife will arrange and pay for the care of the children while my wife is working.

I want a wife who will take care of *my* physical needs. I want a wife who will keep my house clean. A wife who will pick up after me. I want a wife who will keep my clothes clean, ironed, mended, replaced when need be, and who will see to it that my personal things are kept in their proper place so that I can find what I need the minute I need it. I want a wife who cooks the meals, a wife who is a *good* cook. I want a wife who will plan the menus, do the necessary grocery shopping, prepare the meals, serve them pleasantly, and then do the cleaning up while I do my studying. I want a wife who will care for me when I am sick and sympathize with my pain and loss of time from school. I want a wife to go along when our family takes a vacation so that someone can continue to care for me and my children when I need a rest and change of scene.

I want a wife who will not bother me with rambling complaints 5 about a wife's duties. But I want a wife who will listen to me when I feel the need to explain a rather difficult point I have come across in my course of studies. And I want a wife who will type my papers for me when I have written them.

I want a wife who will take care of the details of my social life. When my wife and I are invited out by friends, I want a wife who will take care of the babysitting arrangements. When I meet people at school that I like and want to entertain, I want a wife who will have the house clean, will prepare a special meal, serve it to me and my friends, and not interrupt when I talk about the things that interest me and my friends. I want a wife who will have arranged that the children are fed and ready for bed before my guests arrive so that the children do not bother us. I want a wife who takes care of the needs of my guests so that they feel comfortable, who makes sure that they have an ashtray, that they are passed the hors d'oeuvres, that they are offered a second helping of the food, that their wine glasses are replenished when necessary, that their coffee is served to them as they like it. And I want a wife who knows that sometimes I need a night out by myself.

I want a wife who is sensitive to my sexual needs, a wife who makes love passionately and eagerly when I feel like it, a wife who makes sure that I am satisfied. And, of course, I want a wife who will not demand sexual attention when I am not in the mood for it. I want a wife who assumes the complete responsibility for birth control, because I do not want more children. I want a wife who will remain sexually faithful to me so that I do not have to clutter up my intellectual life with jealousies. And I want a wife who understands that *my* sexual needs may entail more than strict adherence to monogamy. I must, after all, be able to relate to people as fully as possible.

If, by chance, I find another person more suitable as a wife than the wife I already have, I want the liberty to replace my present wife with another one. Naturally, I will expect a fresh, new life; my wife will take the children and be solely responsible for them so that I am left free.

When I am through with school and have a job, I want my wife to quit working and remain at home so that my wife can more fully and completely take care of a wife's duties.

10

My God, who *wouldn't* want a wife?

## Responding to Reading

MyWritingLab™

1. This essay, written more than forty years ago, has been anthologized many times. To what do you attribute its continued popularity? In what ways, if any, is the essay dated? In what ways is it still relevant?
2. Brady wrote her essay to address a stereotype and a set of social conventions that she thought were harmful to women. Could you make the case that Brady's characterization of a "wife" is harmful both to women and to feminism?
3. **Rhetorical Analysis**   Why does Brady begin her essay by saying that she is both a wife and a mother? How does her encounter with a male friend lead her to decide that she would like to have a wife?

## Writing about Reading

MyWritingLab™

1. What is your definition of a wife? How is it different from (or similar to) Brady's?
2. **Writing with Sources**   Look up the definition of *satire*. Then, write an essay in which you make the case that "Why I Want a Wife" is an example of satire. What point do you think Brady is making with her essay?

# STAY-AT-HOME DADS

## Glenn Sacks

### 1964–

*A media commentator who analyzes men's and fathers' issues, Glenn Sacks is a columnist for the* Chicago Tribune, *the* Los Angeles Times, *Newsday, the* Philadelphia Inquirer, *Insight Magazine, and other publications.*

*Before embarking on a career as a columnist and radio and TV personality, Sacks taught high school, elementary school, and adult education courses in Los Angeles and Miami. In the following essay, Sacks discusses the difficulties men (as well as their wives) face if they want to devote themselves to childrearing and housework.*

The subtext to the wave of concern over the recently announced epidemic of childlessness in successful career women is that women can't have it all after all—and it's men's fault. Why? Because men interfere with their wives' career aspirations by their refusal to become their children's primary caregivers, forcing women to sidetrack their careers if they want children.

Despite the criticism, men generally focus on their careers not out of selfishness but because most women still expect men to be their family's primary breadwinners. For women willing to shoulder this burden themselves, replacing the two-earner couple with a female breadwinner and a stay-at-home dad (SAHD) can be an attractive option. I became a SAHD with the birth of my daughter four years ago, and the arrangement has benefited my family immensely.

My wife and I sometimes remark that if we had met in the era before women had real career opportunities, we'd both be pretty unhappy. As a lone breadwinner I would feel deprived of time with my children. My wife, an ambitious woman who loves her career, would feel stifled as a stay-at-home mom. Since each of us would want to be doing what the other is doing, we would probably resent each other. Instead, the freedom to switch gender roles has allowed each of us to gravitate towards what we really want in life.

Men need not fear a loss of power when they become a SAHD. While SAHDs are sometimes stereotyped as being at the mercy of their stronger wives' commands, in reality, I have more power in the family now than I ever did when I was the family breadwinner. The most important issue in any marriage is deciding how to raise the children. While my wife is an equal partner in any major decision regarding the children, I supervise the children on a day to day basis and I make sure that things are done the way I want them done.

Women also benefit from SAHDs because, with reduced familial 5 responsibilities, they can compete on a level playing field with career-oriented men. For men, it is an opportunity to witness the countless magical, irreplaceable moments of a young child's life, and to enjoy some of the subtle pleasures our fathers never knew, like making dinner with a three-year-old's "help," or putting the baby down for a midday nap in a hammock.

Still, there are adjustments that both men and women will need to make. Women will need to discard the popular yet misguided notion that men "have it all," and understand that being the breadwinner comes with disadvantages as well as advantages.

One disadvantage can be the loss of their primary status with their young children. Mom is #1 not because of biology or God's law but because mom is the one who does most of the child care. This can change when dad becomes the primary caregiver. When my young daughter has a nightmare and cries at 2 AM, my wife is relieved that she's not the one who has to get up and comfort her. The price that my wife has had to accept is that her child insists on being comforted not by her but by "yaddy."

Another disadvantage is that taking on the main breadwinner role reduces a woman's ability to cut back her work schedule or look for a more rewarding job if her career disappoints her. This is one of the reasons many women prefer life as a frazzled two-earner couple—keeping the man on career track as the main breadwinner helps to preserve women's options.

Men will also have to make adjustments. For one, they will have to endure the unconscious hypocrisy of a society which often wrings its hands over the lot of the housewife yet at the same time views SAHDs as freeloaders who have left their working wives holding the bag.

10 SAHDs also have to contend with the societal perception that being a househusband is unmanly. The idea is so pervasive that even I still tend to think "wimp" when I first hear about a SAHD.

Working women sometimes complain that men in the workplace don't take them as seriously as they take men. As a SAHD I have the same complaint. For example, last year I attended a school meeting with my wife, my son's elementary school teacher, and some school officials, most of whom knew that I drove my son to and from school, met with his teachers, and did his spelling words with him every day. Yet the woman who chaired the meeting introduced herself to my wife, began the meeting, and then, only as an afterthought, looked at me and said "and who might you be?"

In addition, while many stay-at-home parents face boredom and social isolation, it can be particularly acute for SAHDs, since there are few other men at home, and connections with stay-at-home moms can be difficult to cultivate.

None of these hurdles are insurmountable, and they pale in comparison to the benefits children derive from having a parent as a primary caregiver—particularly a parent grateful for the once-in-a-lifetime opportunity that he never knew he wanted, and never thought he would have.

## Responding to Reading

MyWritingLab™

1. What are the advantages of being a stay-at-home dad? What does Sacks see as the disadvantages? How practical do you think his solution is?
2. Could you make the argument that Sacks and his wife are simply switching traditional male/female roles? Are there any other models for work

and childcare that Sacks and his wife could consider? Do any of these seem preferable to the one they currently follow?

3. **Rhetorical Analysis** In paragraphs 6–10, Sacks discusses the disadvantages for both men and women of being a stay-at-home dad. Why does he include these disadvantages? Would the essay have been stronger without them? Explain.

## Writing about Reading

MyWritingLab™

1. Would you want your husband to be (or would you want to be) a stay-at-home dad? Why or why not?
2. **Writing with Sources** Recently, the father's rights movement has been growing—especially as it concerns unwed or divorced fathers participating in child rearing. How widespread is this movement? How do its concerns complement the concerns that Sacks discusses in his essay?

# MARKED WOMEN

## Deborah Tannen

### 1945–

*Deborah Tannen, a professor of linguistics at Georgetown University, has written books for both scholarly and popular audiences, with most of her work focusing on communication between men and women. Tannen is best known for her bestseller* You Just Don't Understand: Women and Men in Conversation *(1990); her most recent book is* You Were Always Mom's Favorite!: Sisters in Conversation throughout Their Lives *(2009). The following essay, written in 1993, is a departure from Tannen's usual work. Here she focuses not on different communication styles but on the contrast she finds between the neutral way men in our culture present themselves to the world and the more message-laden way women present themselves.*

Some years ago I was at a small working conference of four women and eight men. Instead of concentrating on the discussion I found myself looking at the three other women at the table, thinking how each had a different style and how each style was coherent.

One woman had dark brown hair in a classic style, a cross between Cleopatra and Plain Jane. The severity of her straight hair was softened by wavy bangs and ends that turned under. Because she was beautiful, the effect was more Cleopatra than plain.

The second woman was older, full of dignity and composure. Her hair was cut in a fashionable style that left her with only one eye, thanks to a side part that let a curtain of hair fall across half her face. As she looked down to read her prepared paper, the hair robbed her of bifocal vision and created a barrier between her and the listeners.

The third woman's hair was wild, a frosted blond avalanche falling over and beyond her shoulders. When she spoke she frequently tossed her head, calling attention to her hair and away from her lecture.

Then there was makeup. The first woman wore facial cover that made her skin smooth and pale, a black line under each eye and mascara that darkened already dark lashes. The second wore only a light gloss on her lips and a hint of shadow on her eyes. The third had blue bands under her eyes, dark blue shadow, mascara, bright red lipstick and rouge; her fingernails flashed red.

I considered the clothes each woman had worn during the three days of the conference: In the first case, man-tailored suits in primary colors with solid-color blouses. In the second, casual but stylish black T-shirts, a floppy collarless jacket and baggy slacks or a skirt in neutral colors. The third wore a sexy jump suit; tight sleeveless jersey and tight yellow slacks; a dress with gaping armholes and an indulged tendency to fall off one shoulder.

Shoes? No. 1 wore string sandals with medium heels; No. 2, sensible, comfortable walking shoes; No. 3, pumps with spike heels. You can fill in the jewelry, scarves, shawls, sweaters—or lack of them.

As I amused myself finding coherence in these styles, I suddenly wondered why I was scrutinizing only the women. I scanned the eight men at the table. And then I knew why I wasn't studying them. The men's styles were unmarked.

The term "marked" is a staple of linguistic theory. It refers to the way language alters the base meaning of a word by adding a linguistic particle that has no meaning on its own. The unmarked form of a word carries the meaning that goes without saying—what you think of when you're not thinking anything special.

The unmarked tense of verbs in English is the present—for example, *visit.* To indicate past, you mark the verb by adding *ed* to yield *visited.* For future, you add a word: *will visit.* Nouns are presumed to be singular until marked for plural, typically by adding *s* or *es*, so *visit* becomes *visits* and *dish* becomes *dishes.*

The unmarked forms of most English words also convey "male." Being male is the unmarked case. Endings like *ess* and *ette* mark words as "female." Unfortunately, they also tend to mark them for frivolousness. Would you feel safe entrusting your life to a doctorette? Alfre Woodard, who was an Oscar nominee for best supporting actress, says she identifies herself as an actor because "actresses worry about eyelashes and cellulite, and women who are actors worry about the characters we are playing." Gender markers pick up extra meanings that reflect common associations with the female gender: not quite serious, often sexual.

Each of the women at the conference had to make decisions about hair, clothing, makeup and accessories, and each decision carried meaning.

Every style available to us was marked. The men in our group had made decisions, too, but the range from which they chose was incomparably narrower. Men can choose styles that are marked, but they don't have to, and in this group none did. Unlike the women, they had the option of being unmarked.

Take the men's hair styles. There was no marine crew cut or oily longish hair falling into eyes, no asymmetrical, two-tiered construction to swirl over a bald top. One man was unabashedly bald; the others had hair of standard length, parted on one side, in natural shades of brown or gray or graying. Their hair obstructed no views, left little to toss or push back or run fingers through and, consequently, needed and attracted no attention. A few men had beards. In a business setting, beards might be marked. In this academic gathering, they weren't.

There could have been a cowboy shirt with string tie or a three-piece suit or a necklaced hippie in jeans. But there wasn't. All eight men wore brown or blue slacks and nondescript shirts of light colors. No man wore sandals or boots; their shoes were dark, closed, comfortable and flat. In short, unmarked.

Although no man wore makeup, you couldn't say the men didn't 15 wear makeup in the sense that you could say a woman didn't wear makeup. For men, no makeup is unmarked.

I asked myself what style we women could have adopted that would have been unmarked, like the men's. The answer was none. There is no unmarked woman.

There is no woman's hair style that can be called standard, that says nothing about her. The range of women's hair styles is staggering, but a woman whose hair has no particular style is perceived as not caring about how she looks, which can disqualify her for many positions, and will subtly diminish her as a person in the eyes of some.

Women must choose between attractive shoes and comfortable shoes. When our group made an unexpected trek, the woman who wore flat, laced shoes arrived first. Last to arrive was the woman in spike heels, shoes in hand and a handful of men around her.

If a woman's clothing is tight or revealing (in other words, sexy), it sends a message—an intended one of wanting to be attractive, but also a possibly unintended one of availability. If her clothes are not sexy, that too sends a message, lent meaning by the knowledge that they could have been. There are thousands of cosmetic products from which women can choose and myriad ways of applying them. Yet no makeup at all is anything but unmarked. Some men see it as a hostile refusal to please them.

Women can't even fill out a form without telling stories about 20 themselves. Most forms give four titles to choose from. "Mr." carries no meaning other than that the respondent is male. But a woman who checks "Mrs." or "Miss" communicates not only whether she has been married but also whether she has conservative tastes in forms of address—and probably other conservative values as well. Checking "Ms." declines to let on about marriage (checking "Mr." declines nothing since nothing was asked), but it also marks her as either liberated or rebellious, depending on the observer's attitudes and assumptions.

I sometimes try to duck these variously marked choices by giving my title as "Dr."—and in so doing risk marking myself as either uppity (hence sarcastic responses like "*Excuse me!*") or an overachiever (hence reactions of congratulatory surprise like "Good for you!").

All married women's surnames are marked. If a woman takes her husband's name, she announces to the world that she is married and has traditional values. To some it will indicate that she is less herself, more identified by her husband's identity. If she does not take her husband's name, this too is marked, seen as worthy of comment: she has done something; she has "kept her own name." A man is never said to have "kept his own name" because it never occurs to anyone that he might have given it up. For him using his own name is unmarked.

A married woman who wants to have her cake and eat it too may use her surname plus his, with or without a hyphen. But this too announces her marital status and often results in a tongue-tying string. In a list (Harvey O'Donovan, Jonathan Feldman, Stephanie Woodbury McGillicutty), the woman's multiple name stands out. It is marked.

I have never been inclined toward biological explanations of gender differences in language, but I was intrigued to see Ralph Fasold bring biological phenomena to bear on the question of linguistic marking in his book *The Sociolinguistics of Language*. Fasold stresses that language and culture are particularly unfair in treating women as the marked case because biologically it is the male that is marked. While two X chromosomes make a female, two Y chromosomes make nothing. Like the linguistic markers *s, es* or *ess*, the Y chromosome doesn't "mean" anything unless it is attached to a root form—an X chromosome.

Developing this idea elsewhere, Fasold points out that girls are born with fully female bodies, while boys are born with modified female bodies. He invites men who doubt this to lift up their shirts and contemplate why they have nipples.

In his book, Fasold notes "a wide range of facts which demonstrates that female is the unmarked sex." For example, he observes that there are a few species that produce only females, like the whiptail lizard. Thanks to parthenogenesis, they have no trouble having as many daughters as they like. There are no species, however, that produce only males. This is no surprise, since any such species would become extinct in its first generation.

Fasold is also intrigued by species that produce individuals not involved in reproduction, like honeybees and leaf-cutter ants. Reproduction is handled by the queen and a relatively few males; the workers are sterile females. "Since they do not reproduce," Fasold says, "there is no reason for them to be one sex or the other, so they default, so to speak, to female."

Fasold ends his discussion of these matters by pointing out that if language reflected biology, grammar books would direct us to use "she" to include males and females and "he" only for specifically male referents. But they don't. They tell us that "he" means "he or she," and that "she" is used only if the referent is specifically female. This use of "he" as the sex-indefinite pronoun is an innovation introduced into English by grammarians in the 18th and 19th centuries, according to Peter Mühlhäusler and Rom Harré in *Pronouns and People*. From at least about 1500, the correct sex-indefinite pronoun was "they," as it still is in casual spoken English. In other words, the female was declared by grammarians to be the marked case.

Writing this article may mark me not as a writer, not as a linguist, not as an analyst of human behavior, but as a feminist—which will have positive or negative, but in any case powerful, connotations for readers. Yet I doubt that anyone reading Ralph Fasold's book would put that label on him.

I discovered the markedness inherent in the very topic of gen-    30
der after writing a book on differences in conversational style based on geographical region, ethnicity, class, age and gender. When I was interviewed, the vast majority of journalists wanted to talk about the differences between women and men. While I thought I was simply describing what I observed—something I had learned to do as a researcher—merely mentioning women and men marked me as a feminist for some.

When I wrote a book devoted to gender differences, in ways of speaking, I sent the manuscript to five male colleagues, asking them to alert me to any interpretation, phrasing or wording that might seem unfairly negative toward men. Even so, when the book came out, I encountered responses like that of the television talk show host who, after interviewing me, turned to the audience and asked if they thought I was male-bashing.

Leaping upon a poor fellow who affably nodded in agreement, she made him stand and asked, "Did what she said accurately describe you?" "Oh, yes," he answered. "That's me exactly." "And what she said about women—does that sound like your wife?" "Oh yes," he responded. "That's her exactly." "Then why do you think she's male-bashing?" He answered, with disarming honesty, "Because she's a woman and she's saying things about men."

To say anything about women and men without marking oneself as either feminist or anti-feminist, male-basher or apologist for men seems as impossible for a woman as trying to get dressed in the morning without inviting interpretations of her character.

Sitting at the conference table musing on these matters, I felt sad to think that we women didn't have the freedom to be unmarked that the men sitting next to us had. Some days you just want to get dressed and go about your business. But if you're a woman, you can't, because there is no unmarked woman.

## Responding to Reading

1. Tannen notes that men "can choose styles that are marked, but they don't have to" (12); however, she believes that women do not have "the option of being unmarked" (12). What does she mean? Can you give some examples of women's styles that you believe are unmarked? (Note that in paragraph 16, Tannen says there are no such styles.)
2. In paragraph 33, Tannen says, "To say anything about women and men without marking oneself as either feminist or anti-feminist, male-basher or apologist for men seems as impossible for a woman as trying to get dressed in the morning without inviting interpretations of her character." Do you agree?
3. **Rhetorical Analysis** In paragraphs 24–28, Tannen discusses Ralph Fasold's book *The Sociolinguistics of Language*. Why does she include this material? Could she have made her point just as effectively without it?

## Writing about Reading

1. Consider the men and women you see every day at school or in your neighborhood. Does their appearance support Tannen's thesis?
2. **Writing with Sources** Do further research into the concept of marked and unmarked in terms of gender identity. Then, look at both the men and women in your classes. Do you agree with Tannen when she says that women do not have "the freedom to be unmarked" (34)?

# THE STORY OF AN HOUR

## Kate Chopin

### *1850–1904*

*Born in St. Louis as Katherine O'Flaherty, Kate Chopin was a short-story writer and novelist well known for her story collections about the Cane River region in Louisiana, including* Bayou Folk *(1894) and* A Night in Arcadie *(1897).* The Awakening *(1899), her final novel about a woman's social and sexual liberation, ignited controversy upon publication and was banned for decades thereafter. The following story, originally published in Vogue magazine in 1894, depicts a particular view of marriage.*

Knowing that Mrs. Mallard was afflicted with a heart trouble, great care was taken to break to her as gently as possible the news of her husband's death.

It was her sister Josephine who told her, in broken sentences; veiled hints that revealed in half concealing. Her husband's friend Richards was there, too, near her. It was he who had been in the newspaper office when intelligence of the railroad disaster was received, with Brently Mallard's name leading the list of "killed." He had only taken the time to assure himself of its truth by a second telegram, and had hastened to forestall any less careful, less tender friend in bearing the sad message.

She did not hear the story as many women have heard the same, with a paralyzed inability to accept its significance. She wept at once, with sudden, wild abandonment, in her sister's arms. When the storm of grief had spent itself she went away to her room alone. She would have no one follow her.

There stood, facing the open window, a comfortable, roomy arm-chair. Into this she sank, pressed down by a physical exhaustion that haunted her body and seemed to reach into her soul.

She could see in the open square before her house the tops of trees 5 that were all aquiver with the new spring life. The delicious breath of rain was in the air. In the street below a peddler was crying his wares. The notes of a distant song which someone was singing reached her faintly, and countless sparrows were twittering in the eaves.

There were patches of blue sky showing here and there through the clouds that had met and piled one above the other in the west facing her window.

She sat with her head thrown back upon the cushion of the chair, quite motionless, except when a sob came up into her throat and shook her, as a child who has cried itself to sleep continues to sob in its dreams.

She was young, with a fair, calm face, whose lines bespoke repression and even a certain strength. But now there was a dull stare in her eyes, whose gaze was fixed away off yonder on one of those patches of blue sky. It was not a glance of reflection, but rather indicated a suspension of intelligent thought.

There was something coming to her and she was waiting for it, fearfully. What was it? She did not know; it was too subtle and elusive to name. But she felt it, creeping out of the sky, reaching toward her through the sounds, the scents, the color that filled the air.

Now her bosom rose and fell tumultuously. She was beginning to 10 recognize this thing that was approaching to possess her, and she was striving to beat it back with her will—as powerless as her two white slender hands would have been.

When she abandoned herself a little whispered word escaped her slightly parted lips. She said it over and over under her breath: "free, free, free!" The vacant stare and the look of terror that had followed it went from her eyes. They stayed keen and bright. Her pulses beat fast, and the coursing blood warmed and relaxed every inch of her body.

She did not stop to ask if it were or were not a monstrous joy that held her. A clear and exalted perception enabled her to dismiss the suggestion as trivial.

She knew that she would weep again when she saw the kind, tender hands folded in death, the face that had never looked save with love upon her, fixed and gray and dead. But she saw beyond that bitter moment a long procession of years to come that would belong to her absolutely. And she opened and spread her arms out to them in welcome.

There would be no one to live for during those coming years; she would live for herself. There would be no powerful will bending hers in that blind persistence with which men and women believe they have a right to impose a private will upon a fellow-creature. A kind intention or a cruel intention made the act seem no less a crime as she looked upon it in that brief moment of illumination.

15   And yet she had loved him—sometimes. Often she had not. What did it matter! What could love, the unsolved mystery, count for in face of this possession of self-assertion which she suddenly recognized as the strongest impulse of her being!

"Free! Body and soul free!" she kept whispering.

Josephine was kneeling before the closed door with her lips to the keyhole, imploring for admission. "Louise, open the door! I beg, open the door—you will make yourself ill. What are you doing Louise? For heaven's sake open the door."

"Go away. I am not making myself ill." No, she was drinking in a very elixir of life through that open window.

Her fancy was running riot along those days ahead of her. Spring days, and summer days, and all sorts of days that would be her own. She breathed a quick prayer that life might be long. It was only yesterday she had thought with a shudder that life might be long.

20   She arose at length and opened the door to her sister's importunities. There was a feverish triumph in her eyes, and she carried herself unwittingly like a goddess of Victory. She clasped her sister's waist, and together they descended the stairs. Richards stood waiting for them at the bottom.

Some one was opening the front door with a latchkey. It was Brently Mallard who entered, a little travel-stained, composedly carrying his grip-sack and umbrella. He had been far from the scene of accident, and did not even know there had been one. He stood amazed at Josephine's piercing cry; at Richards' quick motion to screen him from the view of his wife.

But Richards was too late.

When the doctors came they said she had died of heart disease—of joy that kills.

## Responding to Reading

MyWritingLab™

1. When Mrs. Mallard first hears of her husband's death, she is obviously upset. When she is alone, she begins to react differently. Why?
2. What does "The Story of an Hour" suggest about marriage? Does Chopin's criticism apply to just Mrs. Mallard's marriage (or marriages like hers) or to all marriages? How do you know?
3. *Irony* occurs when a character says one thing but the reader is meant to interpret it differently. In "The Story of an Hour," the doctor says that Mrs. Mallard died because of the overwhelming joy of seeing her husband alive. In what sense is this statement ironic?

## Responding in Writing

MyWritingLab™

Do you think that the view of marriage conveyed in this story is still accurate today?

---
FOCUS
---

## Who Has It Harder, Girls or Boys?

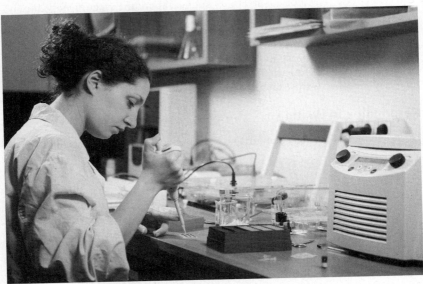

Researcher working in lab

### Responding to the Image

MyWritingLab™

1. What is your reaction to this image? Do you think it reinforces or defies conventional gender stereotypes? Explain.
2. Suppose you were going to use this image in an ad encouraging young women to pursue careers in science. Write two or three lines of text that you could use in your ad. How do the text and the image work together to reinforce your message?

# THE CASE AGAINST SINGLE-SEX CLASSROOMS

## Margaret Talbot

### 1961–

*A staff writer for* The New Yorker, *Margaret Talbot explores social and cultural issues. The author of the book* The Entertainer: Movies, Magic, and My Father's Twentieth Century (2012) *about her father, actor Lyle Talbot, she has published essays in* The Atlantic Monthly, National Geographic, The New Republic, *the* New York Times Book Review, *and the* New York Times Magazine. *In the following essay, Talbot questions the effectiveness of single-sex education.*

A few years ago, when I was looking at middle schools for my daughter, I heard about a school that sounded lovely except for one thing: it had a policy of separating math classes by gender. Having reported on a vogue for single-sex classrooms in the nineties, I knew the rationale: girls and boys distract one another; girls need extra ego boosts and a gentle approach when it comes to studying math and science. I'd never found the arguments especially persuasive. But what really brought me up short was imagining how I would explain the policy to my daughter, whose best friends were boys. Everything I could think of saying sounded offensive or deflating or dumb: math is hard for girls; they—that is, *you*—need special treatment; boys' and girls' brains are different; pre-algebra with boys in the room is just too exciting—you won't know what hit you! If we'd chosen an all-girls' school, that would be one thing. Those schools weren't founded on the premise that men and women have incompatible intellects, but in recognition of what were often limited educational opportunities for women. Their origin stories belonged to the past, and their traditions continued, Hogwarts-like, under their own steam. This was different. This was saying we believe in coeducation, because we live in a coed world, but in this one particular area we're giving up. "Math class is tough!" as that infamous talking Barbie complained.

I remembered all this last week when I read about a new trend toward single-sex classrooms. Only about a dozen public schools were trying them in 2002, but since the Department of Education relaxed its rules on gender-segregated classrooms, in 2006, about five hundred public schools across the country have adopted them, according to an A.P.[1] story. In May, the A.C.L.U.[2] sent cease-and-desist letters to school districts in Alabama, Maine, Mississippi, West Virginia, and Virginia that have been separating boys and girls for academic instruction.

Back in the mid-nineties, when I was reporting on single-sex classrooms, evolutionary psychology was hot, and "hardwired" was the new buzz word, injected like a vitamin shot into weak arguments. Men were hardwired for sleeping around and math, women for monogamy and English. Most people didn't know much about brain science, but that didn't stop them from trotting out vaguely recalled findings based on a handful of M.R.I.s showing that men and women thought differently.

In one way, the fashion in single-sex classrooms has not changed at all. The evidence wasn't very good then for a gap between the genders' learning styles so significant that it would mandate separate instruction, and it hasn't gotten any better. Of course there are psychological and intellectual differences between men and women, but meta-analyses of the best studies show that those differences are relatively

[1]Associated Press, a nonprofit news agency. [Eds.]
[2]American Civil Liberties Union, a nonprofit organization dedicated to protecting civil rights and liberties. [Eds.]

small, that there is a great deal of variability among individuals, and that, as the neuroscientist Lise Eliot writes, "fundamentally, men and women are more similar than different." In an article called, bluntly, "The Pseudoscience of Single-Sex Schooling," which was co-authored by Diane Halpern, a research psychologist at Claremont McKenna college, and published in *Science* magazine this fall, Halpern et al. conclude that "there is no well-designed research showing that single-sex education improves students' academic performance." As Halpern and her co-authors point out, there are some excellent single-sex programs, and some can point to real gains, but often these can be attributed to selection bias—the children involved were more committed students—and to the motivation and sense of mission among teachers and staff. When I was reporting on single-sex education experiments in the nineties, one of the things I noticed was that teaching methods enthusiastically billed as better for girls, like hands-on science demonstrations, or mixing word problems in with more standard equations, would be better for anyone without a natural bent for math or science. A woman whose daughters attend one of the West Virginia middle schools with boys' and girls' classes contributed an article this week to the A.C.L.U. Web site in which she pointed out that her school's all-male classes operated on the humane assumption that many kids concentrate better if they're permitted to move about a bit. In the boys' classes, students could lounge in beanbag chairs and run around outside sometimes to "blow off steam." She thought, reasonably enough, that some girls might benefit from a little of the same freedom.

5     What *has* changed since the nineties is the notion of who single-sex education is supposed to help most. In the nineties, it was girls. The reformers' talk was all about "How Schools Shortchange Girls" (the title of a much-discussed report from the American Association of University Women) or were *Failing at Fairness* (the title of a 1994 book) for young women. Girls were said to be hitting a self-esteem barrier in junior high, when they would droop like Ophelias[3] in need of reviving. But that did not turn out to be the long-term problem. Increasingly, girls have been besting boys' performance across the board: G.P.A.s, school leadership, graduation rates, college attendance. Now segregation by gender is more often an intervention for boys—a switch in target that makes you wonder a little about the reliability of the justifications for the policy. "The goal was to address the struggles boys were having with reading," the A.P. story explains of the effort in an Idaho school. "In the single-sex classes, teachers used microphones that allow them to electronically adjust the tone of their voice to match the level that research suggests is best for boys. When preparing for a test, the boys may go for a run, or engage in some other activity, while the girls are more likely to do calming exercises, such as yoga."

---

[3] A character who dies in the course of William Shakespeare's play *Hamlet*. [Eds.]

And there's the real trouble with this single-sex approach. The presumptions behind it are fusty and often plain silly—which might make them easy for kids who don't conform to them to dismiss, except that their teachers and principals are repeating them so earnestly. Girls thrive on team projects and collaboration; boys on bright lights, loud voices, and competition. Girls like reading; boys don't. Girls do calming exercises; boys run. And on and on. I'll state the obvious: some boys do; some don't. The same goes for girls. Hearing yourself say some of this gobbledygook aloud to your kids, though? That's likely to be good for all of us, regardless of gender. It has a way of sharpening the mind.

## Responding to Reading

MyWritingLab™

1. In paragraph 1, Talbot says that the rationale for single-sex education belongs in the past. Even so, she says, "their traditions continued, Hogwarts-like, under their own steam." What does she mean?
2. According to Talbot, what changed about single-sex education in the nineties? What is your opinion of this change?
3. **Rhetorical Analysis**  Throughout her essay, Talbot references several sources. Why does she do this? Do you think that she could have accomplished her purpose in some other way? If so, how?

## Writing about Reading

MyWritingLab™

1. Do you agree with Talbot's conclusions about single-sex classrooms? Why or why not?
2. **Writing with Sources**  What does the latest research indicate about the effectiveness of single-sex classrooms? Is there general agreement about their usefulness? Write an essay in which you support or challenge Talbot's conclusions.

# THE WAR AGAINST BOYS

## Christina Hoff Sommers

### *1950–*

*In the following, the opening section of a long essay that appeared in* The Atlantic Monthly, *Sommers examines what she calls "the myth of girls in crisis" and demonstrates that, contrary to popular opinion, boys, not girls, are short-changed by today's educational establishment. (See page 94 for Sommers's biography.)*

It's a bad time to be a boy in America. The triumphant victory of the U.S. women's soccer team at the World Cup last summer has come to symbolize the spirit of American girls. The shooting at Columbine High last spring might be said to symbolize the spirit of American boys.

That boys are in disrepute is not accidental. For many years women's groups have complained that boys benefit from a school system that favors them and is biased against girls. "Schools shortchange girls," declares the American Association of University Women. Girls are "undergoing a kind of psychological foot-binding," two prominent educational psychologists say. A stream of books and pamphlets cite research showing not only that boys are classroom favorites but also that they are given to schoolyard violence and sexual harassment.

In the view that has prevailed in American education over the past decade, boys are resented, both as the unfairly privileged sex and as obstacles on the path to gender justice for girls. This perspective is promoted in schools of education, and many a teacher now feels that girls need and deserve special indemnifying consideration. "It is really clear that boys are Number One in this society and in most of the world," says Patricia O'Reilly, a professor of education and the director of the Gender Equity Center, at the University of Cincinnati.

The idea that schools and society grind girls down has given rise to an array of laws and policies intended to curtail the advantage boys have and to redress the harm done to girls. That girls are treated as the second sex in school and consequently suffer, that boys are accorded privileges and consequently benefit—these are things everyone is presumed to know. But they are not true.

5    The research commonly cited to support claims of male privilege and male sinfulness is riddled with errors. Almost none of it has been published in peer-reviewed professional journals. Some of the data turn out to be mysteriously missing. A review of the facts shows boys, not girls, on the weak side of an education gender gap. The typical boy is a year and a half behind the typical girl in reading and writing; he is less committed to school and less likely to go to college. In 1997 college fulltime enrollments were 45 percent male and 55 percent female. The Department of Education predicts that the proportion of boys in college classes will continue to shrink.

Data from the U.S. Department of Education and from several recent university studies show that far from being shy and demoralized, today's girls outshine boys. They get better grades. They have higher educational aspirations. They follow more rigorous academic programs and participate in advanced-placement classes at higher rates. According to the National Center for Education Statistics, slightly more girls than boys enroll in high-level math and science courses. Girls, allegedly timorous and lacking in confidence, now outnumber boys in student government, in honor societies, on school newspapers, and in debating clubs. Only in sports are boys ahead, and women's groups are targeting the sports gap with a vengeance. Girls read more books. They outperform boys on tests for artistic and musical ability. More girls than boys study abroad. More join the Peace Corps. At the same time, more boys than girls are suspended from school. More are held back and more drop out. Boys are three times as likely to receive a diagnosis of attention-deficit hyperactivity disorder. More boys than girls are involved in crime, alcohol, and drugs. Girls attempt suicide more often than boys, but it is boys who more often succeed. In 1997, a typical year, 4,483 young people aged five to twenty-four committed suicide: 701 females and 3,782 males.

In the technical language of education experts, girls are academically more "engaged." Last year an article in *The CQ Researcher* about male and female academic achievement described a common parental observation: "Daughters want to please their teachers by spending extra time on projects, doing extra credit, making homework as neat as possible. Sons rush through homework assignments and run outside to play, unconcerned about how the teacher will regard the sloppy work."

School engagement is a critical measure of student success. The U.S. Department of Education gauges student commitment by the following criteria: "How much time do students devote to homework each night?" and "Do students come to class prepared and ready to learn? (Do they bring books and pencils? Have they completed their homework?)" According to surveys of fourth, eighth, and twelfth graders, girls consistently do more homework than boys. By the twelfth grade boys are four times as likely as girls not to do homework. Similarly, more boys than girls report that they "usually" or "often" come to school without supplies or without having done their homework.

The performance gap between boys and girls in high school leads directly to the growing gap between male and female admissions to college. The Department of Education reports that in 1996 there were 8.4 million women but only 6.7 million men enrolled in college. It predicts that women will hold on to and increase their lead well into the next decade, and that by 2007 the numbers will be 9.2 million women and 6.9 million men.

## Deconstructing the Test-Score Gap

Feminists cannot deny that girls get better grades, are more engaged academically, and are now the majority sex in higher education. They argue, however, that these advantages are hardly decisive. Boys, they point out, get higher scores than girls on almost every significant standardized test—especially the Scholastic Assessment Test and law school, medical school, and graduate school admissions tests. 10

In 1996 I wrote an article for *Education Week* about the many ways in which girl students were moving ahead of boys. Seizing on the test-score data that suggest boys are doing better than girls, David Sadker, a professor of education at American University and a co-author with his wife, Myra, of *Failing at Fairness: How America's Schools Cheat Girls* (1994), wrote, "If females are soaring in school, as Christina Hoff

Sommers writes, then these tests are blind to their flight." On the 1998 SAT boys were thirty-five points (out of 800) ahead of girls in math and seven points ahead in English. These results seem to run counter to all other measurements of achievement in school. In almost all other areas boys lag behind girls. Why do they test better? Is Sadker right in suggesting that this is a manifestation of boys' privileged status?

The answer is no. A careful look at the pool of students who take the SAT and similar tests shows that the girls' lower scores have little or nothing to do with bias or unfairness. Indeed, the scores do not even signify lower achievement by girls. First of all, according to *College Bound Seniors,* an annual report on standardized-test takers published by the College Board, many more "at risk" girls than "at risk" boys take the SAT—girls from lower-income homes or with parents who never graduated from high school or never attended college. "These characteristics," the report says, "are associated with lower than average SAT scores." Instead of wrongly using SAT scores as evidence of bias against girls, scholars should be concerned about the boys who never show up for the tests they need if they are to move on to higher education.

Another factor skews test results so that they appear to favor boys. Nancy Cole, the president of the Educational Testing Service, calls it the "spread" phenomenon. Scores on almost any intelligence or achievement test are more spread out for boys than for girls—boys include more prodigies and more students of marginal ability. Or, as the political scientist James Q. Wilson once put it, "There are more male geniuses and more male idiots."

Boys also dominate dropout lists, failure lists, and learning-disability lists. Students in these groups rarely take college-admissions tests. On the other hand, exceptional boys who take school seriously show up in disproportionately high numbers for standardized tests. Gender-equity activists like Sadker ought to apply their logic consistently: if the shortage of girls at the high end of the ability distribution is evidence of unfairness to girls, then the excess of boys at the low end should be deemed evidence of unfairness to boys.

15    Suppose we were to turn our attention away from the highly motivated, self-selected two fifths of high school students who take the SAT and consider instead a truly representative sample of American schoolchildren. How would girls and boys then compare? Well, we have the answer. The National Assessment of Educational Progress, started in 1969 and mandated by Congress, offers the best and most comprehensive measure of achievement among students at all levels of ability. Under the NAEP program 70,000 to 100,000 students, drawn from forty-four states, are tested in reading, writing, math, and science at ages nine, thirteen, and seventeen. In 1996, seventeen-year-old boys outperformed seventeen-year-old girls by five points in math and eight points in science, whereas the girls outperformed the boys by fourteen points in reading and seventeen points

in writing. In the past few years girls have been catching up in math and science while boys have continued to lag far behind in reading and writing.

In the July, 1995, issue of *Science,* Larry V. Hedges and Amy Nowell, researchers at the University of Chicago, observed that girls' deficits in math were small but not insignificant. These deficits, they noted, could adversely affect the number of women who "excel in scientific and technical occupations." Of the deficits in boys' writing skills they wrote, "The large sex differences in writing . . . are alarming. . . . The data imply that males are, on average, at a rather profound disadvantage in the performance of this basic skill." They went on to warn,

> The generally larger numbers of males who perform near the bottom of the distribution on reading comprehension and writing also have policy implications. It seems likely that individuals with such poor literacy skills will have difficulty finding employment in an increasingly information-driven economy. Thus, some intervention may be required to enable them to participate constructively.

Hedges and Nowell were describing a serious problem of national scope, but because the focus elsewhere has been on girls' deficits, few Americans know much about the problem or even suspect that it exists.

Indeed, so accepted has the myth of girls in crisis become that even teachers who work daily with male and female students tend to reflexively dismiss any challenge to the myth, or any evidence pointing to the very real crisis among boys. Three years ago Scarsdale High School, in New York, held a gender-equity workshop for faculty members. It was the standard girls-are-being-shortchanged fare, with one notable difference. A male student gave a presentation in which he pointed to evidence suggesting that girls at Scarsdale High were well ahead of boys. David Greene, a social-studies teacher, thought the student must be mistaken, but when he and some colleagues analyzed department grading patterns, they discovered that the student was right. They found little or no difference in the grades of boys and girls in advanced-placement social-studies classes. But in standard classes the girls were doing a lot better.

And Greene discovered one other thing: few wanted to hear about his startling findings. Like schools everywhere, Scarsdale High has been strongly influenced by the belief that girls are systematically deprived. That belief prevails among the school's gender-equity committee and has led the school to offer a special senior elective on gender equity. Greene has tried to broach the subject of male underperformance with his colleagues. Many of them concede that in the classes they teach, the girls seem to be doing better than the boys, but they do not see this as part of a larger pattern. After so many years of hearing about silenced, diminished girls, teachers do not take seriously the suggestion that boys are not doing as well as girls even if they see it with their own eyes in their own classrooms.

### Responding to Reading

MyWritingLab™

1. Paragraph 6 of this essay presents a long list of areas in which "girls outshine boys." Do you find this list convincing? What other information could Sommers have provided to support her case?
2. Sommers believes that "the myth of girls in crisis" is so entrenched that "even teachers who work daily with male and female students tend to reflexively dismiss any challenge to the myth" (17). If what she says is true, would you expect this belief among teachers to benefit boys or girls in the long run? Why?
3. **Rhetorical Analysis**   In paragraph 4, Sommers states her essay's thesis: "That girls are treated as the second sex in school and consequently suffer, that boys are accorded privileges and consequently benefit—these are things everyone is presumed to know. But they are not true." Why does she wait so long to state her thesis? Should she have stated it sooner? Explain.

### Writing about Reading

MyWritingLab™

1. Based on your experience, who is more successful in school—girls or boys?
2. **Writing with Sources**   Research the gains in educational achievement that women have made over the past twenty years. To what can these gains be attributed? In what ways do your findings reinforce or contradict Sommers's thesis?

# MEN ARE FROM EARTH, AND SO ARE WOMEN: IT'S FAULTY RESEARCH THAT SETS THEM APART

## Rosalind C. Barnett

*1937–*

## Caryl Rivers

*1937–*

*A senior scientist at Brandeis University's Women's Studies Research Center, Rosalind C. Barnett is a widely published author on gender-related issues. Caryl Rivers, professor of journalism at Boston University, has written numerous books and articles exploring the nature of gender, family, work, and religion. Like Barnett and Rivers's most recent book,* The New Soft War on Women: How the Myth of Female Ascendance Is Hurting Women, Men—and Our Economy *(2013), the following essay reexamines popular (and damaging) beliefs about gender difference.*

Are American college professors unwittingly misleading their students by teaching widely accepted ideas about men and women that are scientifically unsubstantiated?

Why is the dominant narrative about the sexes one of difference, even though it receives little support from carefully designed peer-reviewed studies?

One reason is that findings from a handful of small studies with nonrepresentative samples have often reported wildly overgeneralized but headline-grabbing findings about gender differences. Those findings have then been picked up by the news media—and found their way back into the academy, where they are taught as fact. At the same time, research that tends to debunk popular ideas is often ignored by the news media.

Even worse, many researchers have taken untested hypotheses at face value and used them to plan their studies. Many have also relied exclusively on statistical tests that are designed to find difference, without using tests that would show the degree of overlap between men and women. As a result, findings often suggest—erroneously—that the sexes are categorically different with respect to some specific variable or other.

Yet in the latest edition of its publications manual, the American Psychological Association explicitly asks researchers to consider and report the degree of overlap in statistical studies. For good reason: Even if the mean difference between groups being compared is statistically significant, it may be of trivial consequence if the distributions show a high degree of overlap. Indeed, most studies that do report the size of effects indicate that the differences between the sexes are trivial or slight on a host of personality traits and cognitive and social behaviors.

Because of such serious and pervasive problems, we believe that college students get a distorted picture about the sexes, one that over-states differences while minimizing the more accurate picture—that of enormous overlap and similarity.

It is easy to understand why college professors might spread myths about gender differences. Many of the original studies on which such findings were based have been embraced by both the academy and the wider culture. As Martha T. Mednick, an emerita professor of psychology at Howard University, pointed out in an article some years ago, popular ideas that are intuitively appealing, even if inadequately documented, all too often take on lives of their own. They may have shaky research foundations; they may be largely disproved by later—and better—studies. But bandwagon concepts that have become unhitched from research moorings are rampant in academe, particularly in the classroom. For example:

5

CHAPTER 7 FOCUS

## Women Are Inherently More Caring and More "Relational" than Men

The chief architect of this essentialist idea is Carol Gilligan, the longtime Harvard University psychologist who is now at New York University. In the early 1980s, she laid out a new narrative for women's lives that theorized that women have a unique, caring nature not shared by men. Her ideas have revolutionized the psychology of women and revamped curricula to an unprecedented degree, some observers say. Certainly, almost every student in women's studies and the psychology of women is familiar with Gilligan. But how many are aware of the critics of her theories about women's moral development and the relational self?

Many scholarly reviews of Gilligan's research contend that it does not back up her claims, that she simply created an intriguing hypothesis that needs testing. But the relational self has become near-sacred writ, cited in textbooks, classrooms, and the news media.

10    Anne Alonso, a Harvard psychology professor and director of the Center for Psychoanalytic Studies at Massachusetts General Hospital, told us recently that she is dismayed by the lightning speed at which Gilligan's ideas, based on slender evidence, have been absorbed into psychotherapy. Usually new theories go through a long and rigorous process of publication in peer-reviewed journals before they are accepted by the field. "None of this work has been published in such journals. It's hard to take seriously a whole corpus of work that hasn't been peer-reviewed," Alonso said. The idea of a relational self, she charged, is simply an "idea du jour," one that she called "penis scorn."

## Men Don't Value Personal Relations

According to essentialist theorists, men are uncomfortable with any kind of communication that has to do with personal conflicts. They avoid talking about their problems. They avoid responding too deeply to other people's problems, instead giving advice, changing the subject, making a joke, or giving no response. Unlike women, they don't react to troubles talk by empathizing with others and expressing sympathy. These ideas are often cited in textbooks and in popular manuals, like those written by John Gray, a therapist, and Deborah Tannen, a linguistics professor at Georgetown University. Men are from Mars, women are from Venus, we are told. They just don't understand each other. But systematic research does not support those ideas.

An important article, "The Myth of Gender Cultures: Similarities Outweigh Differences in Men's and Women's Provision of and Responses to Supportive Communication," was published this year in *Sex Roles: A Journal of Research*. Erina L. MacGeorge, of Purdue University, and her colleagues at the University of Pennsylvania find no support for the idea that women and men constitute different "communication cultures." Their article, based on three studies that used questionnaires and interviews, sampled 738 people—417 women and 321 men.

In fact, the authors find, the sexes are very much alike in the way they communicate: "Both men and women view the provision of support as a central element of close personal relationships; both value the supportive communication skills of their friends, lovers, and family members; both make similar judgments about what counts as sensitive, helpful support; and both respond quite similarly to various support efforts."

Yet, MacGeorge and her colleagues point out, we still read in textbooks that:

- "Men's and women's communication styles are startlingly dissimilar"—*The Interpersonal Communication Reader,* edited by Joseph A. DeVito (Allyn and Bacon, 2002).

- "American men and women come from different sociolinguistic subcultures, having learned to do different things with words in a conversation"—a chapter by Daniel N. Maltz and Ruth A. Borker in *Language and Social Identity* (Cambridge University Press, 1982), edited by John J. Gumperz.

- "Husbands and wives, especially in Western societies, come from two different cultures with different learned behaviors and communication styles"—a chapter by Carol J. S. Bruess and Judy C. Pearson in *Gendered Relationships* (Mayfield, 1996), edited by Julia T. Wood.

## Gender Differences in Mate Selection Are Pervasive and Well Established

Evolutionary psychologists like David M. Buss, a professor at the University of Texas at Austin, tell us in such books as *The Evolution of Desire: Strategies of Human Mating* (Basic Books, 1994) that men and women differ widely with respect to the traits they look for in a potential mate. Men, such writers claim, lust after pretty, young, presumably fertile women. Pop culture revels in this notion: Men want young and beautiful mates. There is, it is presumed, a universal female type beloved by men—young, unlined, with features that are close to those of an infant—that signals fertility. If there were a universal male preference for beautiful young women, it would have to be based on a strong correlation between beauty and reproductive success. Sure, Richard Gere chose Julia Roberts in *Pretty Woman* because of her beauty and youth. But would those qualities have assured enhanced fertility?

The answer, according to empirical research, seems to be no. Having a pretty face as a young adult has no relationship to the number of children a woman produces or to her health across the

15

life span. Among married women, physical attractiveness is unrelated to the number of children they produce. If beauty has little to do with reproductive success, why would nature insist that men select for it? It seems more likely that having a young beauty on his arm indicates, instead, that a man is living up to certain cultural and social norms.

According to some who take what we call an ultra-Darwinist stance, there is no mystery about whom women prefer as a mate: The man with resources to feed and protect her future children. The combination of wealth, status, and power (which usually implies an older man) makes "an attractive package in the eyes of the average woman," as Robert Wright, a journalist and author of *The Moral Animal: The New Science of Evolutionary Psychology* (Pantheon, 1994), sums up the argument.

But those who believe that gender roles are shaped at least as much by culture and environment as by biology point out that women's preference for older good providers fits perfectly with the rise of the industrial state. That system, which often called for a male breadwinner and a female working at home, arose in the United States in the 1830s, was dominant until the 1970s, and then declined.

If that is correct, then we should see a declining preference for older men who are good providers, particularly among women with resources. In fact, a study by Alice Eagley, a psychologist at Northwestern University, and Wendy Wood, of Duke University, suggests that as gender equality in society has increased, women have expressed less of a preference for older men with greater earning potential. The researchers have found that when women have access to their own resources, they do not look for age in mates, but prefer qualities like empathy, understanding, and the ability to bond with children. The desire for an older "provider" is evidently not in women's genes. Terri D. Fisher, a psychologist at Ohio State University, told a reporter last year that whenever she teaches her college students the ultra-Darwinian take on the power of youth and beauty, the young men smile and nod and the young women look appalled.

## For Girls, Self-Esteem Plummets at Early Adolescence

20  Girls face an inevitable crisis of self-esteem as they approach adolescence. They are in danger of losing their voices, drowning, and facing a devastating dip in self-regard that boys don't experience. This is the picture that Carol Gilligan presented on the basis of her research at the Emma Willard School, a private girls' school in Troy, N.Y. While Gilligan did not refer to genes in her analysis of girls' vulnerability, she did cite both the "wall of Western culture" and deep early childhood socialization as reasons.

Her theme was echoed in 1994 by the clinical psychologist Mary Pipher's surprise best seller, *Reviving Ophelia* (Putnam, 1994), which spent three years on the *New York Times* best-seller list. Drawing on case studies rather than systematic research, Pipher observed how naturally outgoing, confident girls get worn down by sexist cultural expectations. Gilligan's and Pipher's ideas have also been supported by a widely cited study in 1990 by the American Association of University Women. That report, published in 1991, claimed that teenage girls experience a "free-fall in self-esteem from which some will never recover."

The idea that girls have low self-esteem has by now become part of the academic canon as well as fodder for the popular media. But is it true? No.

Critics have found many faults with the influential AAUW study. When children were asked about their self-confidence and academic plans, the report said 60 percent of girls and 67 percent of boys in elementary school responded, "I am happy the way I am." But by high school, the percentage of girls happy with themselves fell to 29 percent. Could it be that 71 percent of the country's teenage girls were low in self-esteem? Not necessarily. The AAUW counted as happy only those girls who checked "always true" to the question about happiness. Girls who said they were "sometimes" happy with themselves or "sort of" happy with themselves were counted as unhappy.

A sophisticated look at the self-esteem data is far more reassuring than the headlines. A new analysis of all of the AAUW data, and a meta-analysis of hundreds of studies, done by Janet Hyde, a psychologist at the University of Wisconsin at Madison, showed no huge gap between boys and girls. Indeed, Hyde found that the self-esteem scores of boys and girls were virtually identical. In particular there was no plunge in scores for girls during the early teen years—the supposed basis for the idea that girls "lost their voices" in that period. Parents, understandably concerned about noxious, hypersexual media images, may gaze in horror at those images while underestimating the resilience of their daughters, who are able to thrive in spite of them.

## Boys Have a Mathematics Gene, or at Least a Biological Tendency to Excel in Math, That Girls Do Not Possess

Do boys have a mathematics gene—or at least a biological tendency to excel in math—that girls lack, as a popular stereotype has it? Suffice it to say that, despite being discouraged from pursing math at almost every level of school, girls and women today are managing to perform in math at high levels.

25

Do data support arguments for hard-wired gender differences? No. In 2001 Erin Leahey and Guang Guo, then a graduate student and an assistant professor of sociology, respectively, at the University of North Carolina at Chapel Hill, looked at some 20,000 math scores of children ages 4 to 18 and found no differences of any magnitude, even in areas that are supposedly male domains, such as reasoning skills and geometry.

The bandwagon concepts that we have discussed here are strongly held and dangerous. Even though they have been seriously challenged, they continue to be taught by authority figures in the classroom. These ideas are embedded in the curricula of courses in child and adolescent development, moral development, education, moral philosophy, feminist pedagogy, evolutionary psychology, gender studies, and the psychology of women.

Few students have the ability to investigate the accuracy of the claims on their own. And since these ideas resonate with the cultural zeitgeist, students would have little reason to do so in any case. The essentialist perspective has so colored the dialogue about the sexes that there is scant room for any narrative other than difference.

Obviously the difference rhetoric can create harm for both men and women. Men are taught to believe that they are deficient in caring and empathy, while women are led to believe that they are inherently unsuited for competition, leadership, and technological professions. Given how little empirical support exists for essentialist ideas, it's crucial that professors broaden the dialogue, challenging the conventional wisdom and encouraging their students to do so as well.

## Responding to Reading                              MyWritingLab™

1. According to Barnett and Rivers, what problems cause college students to "get a distorted picture about the sexes ..." (6)? In what sense is the view distorted?
2. Why do Barnett and Rivers perceive the "bandwagon concepts" they discuss as dangerous (27)? Why do teachers continue to spread these ideas? What do Barnett and Rivers think should be done about this situation?
3. **Rhetorical Analysis** What specific misleading ideas do Barnett and Rivers identify? How do they challenge these ideas? How effective are their responses to these ideas?

## Writing about Reading                              MyWritingLab™

1. Barnett and Rivers do not specifically address the issue of academic performance in their essay. Do you think they should have?
2. **Writing with Sources** How do you think Barnett and Rivers would respond to the discussion of academic performance in Christina Hoff Sommers's essay "The War against Boys" (p. 247)?

# WIDENING THE FOCUS

## For Critical Reading and Writing

Referring specifically to the three readings in this chapter's Focus section (and possibly to additional sources as well), write an essay in which you answer the question, "Who Has It Harder, Girls or Boys?"

## For Further Reading

The following readings can suggest additional perspectives for thinking and writing about the roles of men and women:

- Alleen Pace Nilsen, "Sexism in English: Embodiment and Language" (p. 137)

- Judith Ortiz Cofer, "The Myth of the Latin Woman: I Just Met a Girl Named Maria" (p. 271)

- Warren Farrell, "Exploiting the Gender Gap" (p. 373)

## For Focused Research

Differences in the ways boys and girls are treated in school remain a contentious discussion topic. In preparation for writing an essay about the gender gap in education, open one of the popular web search engines, and enter the search terms *gender gap and education*. From your search results, select readings about your topic, and use information from these sources to help you develop your essay. You can begin by visiting one or all of the following resources:

- Dockterman, Eliana. "Google Invests $50 Million to Close the Tech Gender Gap." *Time*. June 19, 2014.

- "The Rise of Women: Seven Charts Showing Women's Rapid Gains in Educational Achievement." *Russell Sage Foundation Review*. Feb. 21, 2013.

- Casserly, Meghan. "The Global Gender Gap Is Closing, but the U.S. Is Still Failing Its Women." *Forbes*. Oct. 24, 2012.

## Beyond the Classroom

Interview three female college students majoring in traditionally male fields (business, engineering, math, and so on) and three male students majoring in traditionally female fields (nursing, elementary education, social work, nutrition, and so on). In your interviews, ask the following questions:

- Did your friends, parents, and teachers encourage or discourage your pursuit of this field of study?
- Have you experienced any gender discrimination in the classroom or in any related employment settings?

Based on the responses to these questions, write an essay in which you consider whether educational opportunities are broader or narrower (or the same) for men and for women.

# EXPLORING ISSUES AND IDEAS

## Gender and Identity

MyWritingLab™
Visit Chapter 7, "Gender and Identity," in MyWritingLab to test your understanding of the chapter objectives.

Write an essay in response to one of the following prompts, which are suitable for assignments that require the use of outside sources as well as for assignments that are not source-based.

1. In her well-known work *A Room of One's Own*, novelist and critic Virginia Woolf observes that "any woman born with a great gift in the sixteenth century would certainly have gone crazed, shot herself, or ended her days in some lonely cottage outside the village, half witch, half wizard, feared and mocked at." Write an essay in which you discuss in what respects this statement may still apply to gifted women of your own generation or of your parents' generation. You may want to read Deborah Tannen's "Marked Women" (p. 235) before you plan your essay.

2. List all the stereotypes of women—and of men—identified in the selections you read in this chapter . Then, write an essay in which you discuss those that you think have had the most negative effects. Do you consider these stereotypes just annoying, or actually dangerous? Refer to one or two essays in this chapter  to support your points.

3. Several of the selections in this chapter—for example, "Stay-at-Home Dads" (p. 232) and "Why I Want a Wife" (p. 230)—draw distinctions, implicitly or explicitly, between "men's work" and "women's work." Write an essay in which you consider the extent to which such distinctions exist today, and explain how they have affected your professional goals.

4. Write a letter to Judy Brady in which you update (or challenge) her characterization of a wife in "Why I Want a Wife" (p. 230).

5. A number of the writers in this chapter  examine current ideas about what it means to be male and what it means to be female. Write an essay in which you develop your own definitions of *male* and *female*. You may want to consider E. J. Graff's "The M/F Boxes" (p. 221), Glenn Sacks's "Stay-at-Home Dads" (p. 232), and Deborah Tannen's "Marked Women" (p. 235).

6. Several of the essays in this chapter  deal with gender roles and how they influence relationships between men and women. Write an essay in which you discuss how gender roles have affected you. For example, do you think you have ever been held back or given an unfair advantage because of your gender?

# 8

# CULTURE AND IDENTITY

*In this chapter, you will learn to*
- analyze readings about culture and identity
- compose essays about culture and identity

The word *culture* generally refers to an identity shared by a particular racial, religious, or ethnic group or an identity that is characteristic of a specific geographic region. But in many cases, cultural identity is more complicated, a concept that includes but goes beyond a person's self-identification as an African American or a Muslim or a New Yorker.

For some, cultural identity is determined by shared language or national origin or family history; others may identify with a group on

Gay Pride Parade, New York City

the basis of gender or sexual orientation; still others identify with a particular group because of a shared interest or professional affiliation. Thus, we can talk about computer culture, Wall Street culture, skateboard culture, or football culture as well as about Chinese culture, feminist culture, or gay culture.

Cultural identity can rest on a shared system of deeply held values and beliefs or simply a shared preference in personal style—for example, an affinity for body art or motorcycle gear. But regardless of how we define culture, it is important to remember that cultural identity is not always something we actively choose. For example, sometimes cultural identity is conferred upon us at birth; sometimes we identify with a culture simply out of habit; sometimes a cultural identity is imposed on us by others, determined by how others see us rather than by how we perceive ourselves.

When we examine the idea of cultural identity, we may consider whether it is possible to be loyal to two cultures or how it feels to abandon one culture and take on another. We may also consider how to maintain an individual identity while identifying with one or more groups. Finally, we may consider how loyalty to a particular culture defines an individual—and how the individual helps to define the culture.

In the Focus section of this chapter, "Do Racial Distinctions Still Matter?" (p. 295), three writers consider their own cultures in the context of ethnic and racial identity. In "Which Is It, Hispanic or Latino?"

St. Patrick's Day Parade, South Boston

Cindy Y. Rodriguez examines the relationship between her cultural identity and the terms used to define it; Brent Staples explores his own complex heritage in "Why Race Isn't as 'Black' and 'White' as We Think"; and John H. McWhorter, in "Why I'm Black, Not African American," compares two terms used to define his racial identity.

—————————— PREPARING TO READ AND WRITE ——————————

As you read and prepare to write about the essays in this chapter, you may consider the following questions:

- What assumptions does the writer seem to have about his or her audience? How can you tell?

- What is the writer's primary purpose? To explore his or her own cultural identity? To criticize society's understanding of culture or race? To expose (or come to terms with) cultural stereotypes? Something else?

- What genre is the writer using? For example, is the reading a memoir? a literary work? an argument? How do the conventions of this genre influence the writer's choices?

- What appeals does the writer use? For example, does he or she appeal primarily to emotion or to reason? Is this the most effective appeal?

- Does the writer focus on one particular culture or on culture in general?

- Is the culture the writer discusses defined by race, ethnicity, geography, vocation, or something else?

- Does the writer see his or her own culture in positive, neutral, or negative terms?

- Does the writer explore personal feelings and experiences?

- Would you describe the writer's voice as reflective, angry, resigned, or something else?

- Does the writer identify with the culture he or she discusses or feel like an outsider?

- Does the writer embrace his or her culture or try to maintain a distance from it?

- Does the writer see culture as defining him or her or as only a small part of his or her identity?

- Has the writer chosen to identify with a particular culture, or has his or her cultural identity been determined by how others view him or her?

- Does the writer challenge the way in which a culture is commonly perceived?

- Which of the various writers' ideas about culture and identity are most similar? Which are most like your own?

# Bilingual/Bilingue

## Rhina Espaillat

### 1932–

*Born in the Dominican Republic and raised in New York City, Rhina Espaillat writes poetry in both English and Spanish. She is the author of eleven poetry collections, including, most recently,* Her Place in These Designs *(2008). The following poem considers how bilingualism shapes identity.*

My father liked them separate, one there,
one here (allá y aquí), as if aware
that words might cut in two his daughter's heart
(el corazón) and lock the alien part
to what he was—his memory, his name                                    5
(su nombre)—with a key he could not claim.
"English outside this door, Spanish inside,"
he said, "y basta." But who can divide
the world, the word (mundo y palabra) from
any child? I knew how to be dumb                                        10
and stubborn (testaruda); late, in bed,
I hoarded secret syllables I read
until my tongue (mi lengua) learned to run
where his stumbled. And still the heart was one.
I like to think he knew that, even when,                                15
proud (orgulloso) of his daughter's pen,
he stood outside mis versos, half in fear
of words he loved but wanted not to hear.

## Responding to Reading

MyWritingLab™

1. Is this poem's central figure the speaker or her father? Explain.
2. Spanish words are defined throughout this poem, but no definitions are provided for *y basta* ("and enough"; line 8) or *mis versos* ("my poems"; line 17). Why do you suppose the poet chose not to define these two expressions?
3. What are the "secret syllables" (line 12) the speaker reads when she is in bed at night? Why does she keep them secret?

## Responding in Writing

MyWritingLab™

The speaker's father has a rule: "English outside this door, Spanish inside" (line 7). Do you think the speaker's concept of *bilingual* is different from her father's? If so, how?

# PRAYING FOR COMMON GROUND AT THE CHRISTMAS-DINNER TABLE

## Reza Aslan

### 1972–

*A professor of creative writing at the University of California, Riverside, Reza Aslan is a religion scholar and writer. The founder of the social media network AslanMedia and the cofounder and chief creative officer of the trans-media company BoomGen Studios, he is the author of several books, including, most recently,* Zealot: The Life and Times of Jesus of Nazareth *(2013), which has been translated into twenty-eight languages. In the following essay, Aslan ponders how different religions help build a shared identity.*

The prayer is what tripped us up. It was the first Christmas that my wife and I hosted in our home, and for a good 10 minutes, our two families stood around the dinner table arguing about how to thank God for the meal we were about to eat.

My mother, a born-again Christian, wanted our prayer addressed to Jesus. It was Christmas, after all; we were celebrating Jesus' miraculous birth. "Shouldn't we at least pray to him?" she asked sheepishly.

My little sister, a devout Muslim, loves and admires Jesus as a prophet and messenger of God. But she had no intention of praying to him. She adjusted her hijab[1] and mumbled the Shahada[2] under her breath ("I confess there is no god but God") as a kind of talisman to protect her against my mother's "heresy."

---

[1] A veil worn by some Muslim women. [Eds.]
[2] The Islamic creed that proclaims Muhammad as God's prophet. [Eds.]

My middle sister, a militant atheist, was supremely annoyed with the entire spectacle. She found it hard to believe we were standing around the dinner table, watching the food go cold, as we deliberated which imaginary deity we should pray to before we could start eating. "Why don't we just pray to Santa Claus?" she said. No one else found that funny.

My wife's family, evangelicals from Pittsburgh, was mostly con- 5 fused about why we were serving rice and shish kebabs with our Christmas turkey and mashed potatoes.

Finally, my wife came up with an idea. "Why don't we let Reza decide?" she suggested, volunteering me to be the referee in this prayer match.

I suppose her suggestion made some sense. I am a scholar of religions who has dedicated his life to studying the faith traditions of the world and then teaching those traditions to people who do not share them. For me, this first Christmas at the Aslan household was practically field research. As I watched these people from diverse religious and cultural backgrounds navigate a holiday with quite specific religious and cultural associations, I was tempted to pull out my notebook and begin jotting down my observations.

My family is, in many ways, emblematic of America in the 21st century: multiethnic, multicultural, multireligious. I am a Muslim from Iran. My wife is a Christian from western Pennsylvania. That may seem an incongruous coupling. But when we first met, we realized almost immediately that we shared the same values and worldview, even though we expressed those things in a different spiritual language.

That's all religion is, really: a language made up of symbols and metaphors that allow people to communicate, to themselves and to others, the ineffable experience of faith. I already spoke my wife's spiritual language (Christianity); I taught her mine (Islam). And now we are a spiritually "bilingual" household. Actually, we are multilingual, considering we are committed to teaching our children all the spiritual languages of the world so that they can choose for themselves which ones, if any, they prefer in communicating their own individual faith experience.

But that is also the reason the prayer was tripping us up that first 10 Christmas together. We were having a difficult time understanding one another's spiritual languages, let alone coming to a consensus on which language to use. It reminded me of a Sufi[3] parable about four hungry travelers from different countries who are trying to decide what to buy with the single coin they hold in common. The Persian wants to spend the coin on *angur*; the Turk, on *uzum*; the Arab, on *inab*; and the Greek, on *stafil*. Confusion turns to anger as the four travelers argue among themselves. It takes a passing linguist to explain to them that they are all, in fact, asking for the same thing: grapes.

---

[3]Pertaining to Sufism, Islamic mysticism. [Eds.]

The parable gave me an idea. "Let's skip the formal prayer and just tell each other what we are grateful for," I suggested. "What we are anxious about. What we hope for in the coming year."

We took turns going around the circle: Muslim, Christian, atheist. And, as I expected, we ended up expressing similar dreams and aspirations for ourselves and our loved ones, similar fears and anxieties, similar gratitude for all that we've been given. As with the hapless travelers in the Sufi parable, we realized that we were all feeling the same way; we were just expressing that feeling in different spiritual languages.

Once the prayer was settled, it was time to sit down for a traditional Christmas meal of turkey and kebabs.

### Responding to Reading

MyWritingLab™

1. In paragraph 9, Aslan introduces a definition of *religion* with "That's all religion is, really. . . ." Do you think his definition is accurate? Does it make sense? How would you define *religion*?
2. Do you think Aslan is overly optimistic about the ability of those with different religious beliefs to find common ground? Why or why not?
3. **Rhetorical Analysis**    In paragraph 7, Aslan summarizes his scholarly credentials. Why does he include this information? Is it necessary? Explain.

### Writing about Reading

MyWritingLab™

1. Do all your family members share the same religion? the same general belief system and values? the same political views? If not, what values do they have in common?
2. **Writing with Sources**    Research the beliefs and values of a religion other than yours, and then write an essay in which you identify and discuss the common ground that exists between that religion and your own.

# THE STRUGGLE TO BE AN ALL-AMERICAN GIRL

## Elizabeth Wong

### 1958–

*A playwright and an adjunct assistant professor at the University of Southern California School of Theatre, Elizabeth Wong grew up in Los Angeles's Chinatown. The author of numerous award-winning plays and a former staff writer for the ABC sitcom* All-American Girl, *Wong explores Asian-American culture and identity in her work. In the following essay, she describes the difficult experience of being caught between two cultures.*

It's still there, the Chinese school on Yale Street where my brother and I used to go. Despite the new coat of paint and the high wire fence, the school I knew ten years ago remains remarkably, stoically the same.

Every day at 5 P.M., instead of playing with our fourth- and fifth-grade friends or sneaking out to the empty lot to hunt ghosts and animal bones, my brother and I had to go to Chinese school. No amount of kicking, screaming, or pleading could dissuade my mother, who was solidly determined to have us learn the language of our heritage.

Forcibly, she walked us the seven long, hilly blocks from our home to school, depositing our defiant tearful faces before the stern principal. My only memory of him is that he swayed on his heels like a palm tree, and he always clasped his impatient twitching hands behind his back. I recognized him as a repressed maniacal child killer, and knew that if we ever saw his hands we'd be in big trouble.

We all sat in little chairs in an empty auditorium. The room smelled like Chinese medicine, an imported faraway mustiness. Like ancient mothballs or dirty closets. I hated that smell. I favored crisp new scents. Like the soft French perfume that my American teacher wore in public school.

There was a stage far to the right, flanked by an American flag and the flag of the Nationalist Republic of China, which was also red, white and blue but not as pretty.

Although the emphasis at the school was mainly language—speaking, reading, writing—the lessons always began with an exercise in politeness. With the entrance of the teacher, the best student would tap a bell and everyone would get up, kowtow,[1] and chant, "Sing san ho," the phonetic for "How are you, teacher?"

Being 10 years old, I had better things to learn than ideographs copied painstakingly in lines that ran right to left from the tip of a *moc but*, a real ink pen that had to be held in an awkward way if blotches were to be avoided. After all, I could do the multiplication tables, name the satellites of Mars, and write reports on *Little Women* and *Black Beauty*. Nancy Drew, my favorite book heroine, never spoke Chinese.

The language was a source of embarrassment. More times than not, I had tried to disassociate myself from the nagging loud voice that followed me wherever I wandered in the nearby American supermarket outside Chinatown. The voice belonged to my grandmother, a fragile woman in her seventies who could outshout the best of the street vendors. Her humor was raunchy, her Chinese rhythmless, patternless. It was quick, it was loud, it was unbeautiful. It was not like the quiet, lilting romance of French or the gentle refinement of the American South. Chinese sounded pedestrian. Public.

In Chinatown, the comings and goings of hundreds of Chinese on their daily tasks sounded chaotic and frenzied. I did not want to be thought of as mad, as talking gibberish. When I spoke English, people nodded at me, smiled sweetly, said encouraging words. Even the

---

[1]Kneel and bow in deference. [Eds.]

people in my culture would cluck and say that I'd do well in life. "My, doesn't she move her lips fast," they would say, meaning that I'd be able to keep up with the world outside Chinatown.

10    My brother was even more fanatical than I about speaking English. He was especially hard on my mother, criticizing her, often cruelly, for her pidgin speech—smatterings of Chinese scattered like chop suey in her conversation. "It's not 'What it is,' Mom," he'd say in exasperation. "It's 'What *is* it, what *is* it, what *is* it!'" Sometimes Mom might leave out an occasional "the" or "a," or perhaps a verb of being. He would stop her in mid-sentence: "Say it again, Mom. Say it right." When he tripped over his own tongue, he'd blame it on her: "See, Mom, it's all your fault. You set a bad example."

What infuriated my mother most was when my brother cornered her on her consonants, especially "r." My father had played a cruel joke on Mom by assigning her an American name that her tongue wouldn't allow her to say. No matter how hard she tried, "Ruth" always ended up "Luth" or "Roof."

After two years of writing with a *moc but* and reciting words with multiples of meanings, I finally was granted a cultural divorce. I was permitted to stop Chinese school.

I thought of myself as multicultural. I preferred tacos to egg rolls; I enjoyed Cinco de Mayo more than Chinese New Year.

At last, I was one of you; I wasn't one of them.

15    Sadly, I still am.

## Responding to Reading

MyWritingLab™

1.    In this essay, Wong looks back ten years to her childhood. Why is the Chinese school she remembers still such an important part of her identity? From the vantage point of adulthood, what does she feel she has lost?
2.    What differences does Wong identify between Chinese and American culture? Why, when she was a child, was American culture so much more appealing to her than Chinese culture?
3.    **Rhetorical Analysis**   Evaluate Wong's conclusion. Are her last two sentences an effective conclusion for her essay, or should she have developed a fuller concluding paragraph? Explain.

## Writing about Reading

MyWritingLab™

1.    How would you define an "all-American" boy or girl? Do you think it is possible to preserve one's cultural identity and still be "all-American"?
2.    **Writing with Sources**   Look online for information about schools and programs like Wong's "Chinese school"—schools whose goal is to strengthen the cultural identity of first-generation American children. What, specifically, do these schools hope to achieve, and how? How successful do you think they can be? Are they still necessary in today's multicultural society? Are they more necessary than ever? Write an essay that explores these questions.

# THE MYTH OF THE LATIN WOMAN: I JUST MET A GIRL NAMED MARIA

## Judith Ortiz Cofer

### 1952–

*Born in Hormigueros, Puerto Rico, and raised in Paterson, New Jersey, Judith Ortiz Cofer teaches creative writing at the University of Georgia. She is an award-winning poet and novelist whose books include the novels* The Line of the Sun *(1989) and* Silent Dancing *(1990) as well as a collection of biographical essays. Her most recent book is the memoir* The Cruel Country *(2015). In the following essay from her collection* The Latin Deli: Prose and Poetry *(1993), Cofer describes the stereotypes she has confronted as a Latina.*

On a bus trip to London from Oxford University where I was earning some graduate credits one summer, a young man, obviously fresh from a pub, spotted me and as if struck by inspiration went down on his knees in the aisle. With both hands over his heart he broke into an Irish tenor's rendition of "Maria" from *West Side Story*.[1] My politely amused fellow passengers gave his lovely voice the round of gentle applause it deserved. Though I was not quite as amused, I managed my version of an English smile: no show of teeth, no extreme contortions of the facial muscles—I was at this time of my life practicing reserve and cool. Oh, that British control, how I coveted it. But "Maria" had followed me to London, reminding me of a prime fact of my life: you can leave the island, master the English language, and travel as far as you can, but if you are a Latina, especially one like me who so obviously belongs to Rita Moreno's[2] gene pool, the island travels with you.

This is sometimes a very good thing—it may win you that extra minute of someone's attention. But with some people, the same things can make *you* an island—not a tropical paradise but an Alcatraz, a place nobody wants to visit. As a Puerto Rican girl living in the United States[3] and wanting like most children to "belong," I resented the stereotype that my Hispanic appearance called forth from many people I met.

Growing up in a large urban center in New Jersey during the 1960s, I suffered from what I think of as "cultural schizophrenia." Our life was designed by my parents as a microcosm of their *casas*[4] on the island.

---

[1]A popular Broadway musical, loosely based on *Romeo and Juliet*, about two rival street gangs, one Anglo and one Puerto Rican, in New York City. [Eds.]

[2]Puerto Rico–born actress who won an Oscar for her role in the 1960 movie version of *West Side Story*. [Eds.]

[3]Although it is an island, Puerto Rico is part of the United States (it is a self-governing commonwealth). [Eds.]

[4]Homes. [Eds.]

We spoke in Spanish, ate Puerto Rican food bought at the *bodega*,[5] and practiced strict Catholicism at a church that allotted us a one-hour slot each week for mass, performed in Spanish by a Chinese priest trained as a missionary for Latin America.

As a girl I was kept under strict surveillance by my parents, since my virtue and modesty were, by their cultural equation, the same as their honor. As a teenager I was lectured constantly on how to behave as a proper *señorita*. But it was a conflicting message I received, since the Puerto Rican mothers also encouraged their daughters to look and act like women and to dress in clothes our Anglo friends and their mothers found too "mature" and flashy. The difference was, and is, cultural; yet I often felt humiliated when I appeared at an American friend's party wearing a dress more suitable to a semi-formal than to a playroom birthday celebration. At Puerto Rican festivities, neither the music nor the colors we wore could be too loud.

5      I remember Career Day in our high school, when teachers told us to come dressed as if for a job interview. It quickly became obvious that to the Puerto Rican girls "dressing up" meant wearing their mother's ornate jewelry and clothing, more appropriate (by mainstream standards) for the company Christmas party than as daily office attire. That morning I had agonized in front of my closet, trying to figure out what a "career girl" would wear. I knew how to dress for school (at the Catholic school I attended, we all wore uniforms), I knew how to dress for Sunday mass, and I knew what dresses to wear for parties at my relatives' homes. Though I do not recall the precise details of my Career Day outfit, it must have been a composite of these choices. But I remember a comment my friend (an Italian American) made in later years that coalesced my impressions of that day. She said that at the business school she was attending, the Puerto Rican girls always stood out for wearing "everything at once." She meant, of course, too much jewelry, too many accessories. On that day at school we were simply made the negative models by the nuns, who were themselves not credible fashion experts to any of us. But it was painfully obvious to me that to the others, in their tailored skirts and silk blouses, we must have seemed "hopeless" and "vulgar." Though I now know that most adolescents feel out of step much of the time, I also know that for the Puerto Rican girls of my generation that sense was intensified. The way our teachers and classmates looked at us that day in school was just a taste of the cultural clash that awaited us in the real world, where prospective employers and men on the street would often misinterpret our tight skirts and jingling bracelets as a "come-on."

Mixed cultural signals have perpetuated certain stereotypes—for example, that of the Hispanic woman as the "hot tamale" or sexual

---
[5]Small grocery store. [Eds.]

firebrand. It is a one-dimensional view that the media have found easy to promote. In their special vocabulary, advertisers have designated "sizzling" and "smoldering" as the adjectives of choice for describing not only the foods but also the women of Latin America. From conversations in my house I recall hearing about the harassment that Puerto Rican women endured in factories where the "boss-men" talked to them as if sexual innuendo was all they understood, and worse, often gave them the choice of submitting to their advances or being fired.

It is custom, however, not chromosomes, that leads us to choose scarlet over pale pink. As young girls, it was our mothers who influenced our decisions about clothes and colors—mothers who had grown up on a tropical island where the natural environment was a riot of primary colors, where showing your skin was one way to keep cool as well as to look sexy. Most important of all, on the island, women perhaps felt freer to dress and move more provocatively since, in most cases, they were protected by the traditions, mores, and laws of a Spanish/Catholic system of morality and machismo whose main rule was: *You may look at my sister, but if you touch her I will kill you.* The extended family and church structure could provide a young woman with a circle of safety in her small pueblo on the island; if a man "wronged" a girl, everyone would close in to save her family honor.

My mother has told me about dressing in her best party clothes on Saturday nights and going to the town's plaza to promenade with her girlfriends in front of the boys they liked. The males were thus given an opportunity to admire the women and to express their admiration in the form of *piropos:* erotically charged street poems they composed on the spot. (I have myself been subjected to a few *piropos* while visiting the island, and they can be outrageous, although custom dictates that they must never cross into obscenity.) This ritual, as I understand it, also entails a show of studied indifference on the woman's part; if she is "decent," she must not acknowledge the man's impassioned words. So I do understand how things can be lost in translation. When a Puerto Rican girl dressed in her idea of what is attractive meets a man from the mainstream culture who has been trained to react to certain types of clothing as a sexual signal, a clash is likely to take place. I remember the boy who took me to my first formal dance leaning over to plant a sloppy, over-eager kiss painfully on my mouth; when I didn't respond with sufficient passion, he remarked resentfully: "I thought you Latin girls were supposed to mature early," as if I were expected to *ripen* like a fruit or vegetable, not just grow into womanhood like other girls.

It is surprising to my professional friends that even today some people, including those who should know better, still put others "in their place." It happened to me most recently during a stay at a classy metropolitan hotel favored by young professional couples for weddings. Late one evening after the theater, as I walked toward my room with a colleague (a woman with whom I was coordinating an arts program), a middle-aged man in a tuxedo, with a young girl in satin and lace on his arm, stepped directly into our path. With his champagne glass extended toward me, he exclaimed "Evita!"[6]

10      Our way blocked, my companion and I listened as the man half-recited, half-bellowed "Don't Cry for Me, Argentina." When he finished, the young girl said: "How about a round of applause for my daddy?" We complied, hoping this would bring the silly spectacle to a close. I was becoming aware that our little group was attracting the attention of the other guests. "Daddy" must have perceived this too, and he once more barred the way as we tried to walk past him. He began to shout-sing a ditty to the tune of "La Bamba"—except the lyrics were about a girl named Maria whose exploits rhymed with her name and gonorrhea. The girl kept saying "Oh, Daddy" and looking at me with pleading eyes. She wanted me to laugh along with the others. My companion and I stood silently waiting for the man to end his offensive song. When he finished, I looked not at him but at his daughter. I advised her calmly never to ask her father what he had done in the army. Then I walked between them and to my room. My friend complimented me on my cool handling of the situation, but I confessed that I had really wanted to push the jerk into the swimming pool. This same man—probably a corporate executive, well-educated, even worldly by most standards—would not have been likely to regale an Anglo woman with a dirty song in public. He might have checked his impulse by assuming that she could be somebody's wife or mother, or at least *somebody* who might take offense. But, to him, I was just an Evita or a Maria: merely a character in his cartoon-populated universe.

Another facet of the myth of the Latin woman in the United States is the menial, the domestic—Maria the housemaid or countergirl. It's true that work as domestics, as waitresses, and in factories is all that's available to women with little English and few skills. But the myth of the Hispanic menial—the funny maid, mispronouncing words and cooking up a spicy storm in a shiny California kitchen—has been perpetuated by the media in the same way that "Mammy" from *Gone with the Wind* became America's idea of the black woman for generations. Since I do not wear my diplomas around my neck for all to see, I have on occasion been sent to that "kitchen" where some think I obviously belong.

One incident has stayed with me, though I recognize it as a minor offense. My first public poetry reading took place in Miami, at a restaurant where a luncheon was being held before the event. I was nervous and excited as I walked in with notebook in hand. An older woman

---

[6]A Broadway musical, later made into a movie, about Eva Duarte de Perón, the former first lady of Argentina. [Eds.]

motioned me to her table, and thinking (foolish me) that she wanted me to autograph a copy of my newly published slender volume of verse, I went over. She ordered a cup of coffee from me, assuming that I was the waitress. (Easy enough to mistake my poems for menus, I suppose.) I know it wasn't an intentional act of cruelty. Yet of all the good things that happened later, I remember that scene most clearly, because it reminded me of what I had to overcome before anyone would take me seriously. In retrospect I understand that my anger gave my reading fire. In fact, I have almost always taken any doubt in my abilities as a challenge, the result most often being the satisfaction of winning a convert, of seeing the cold, appraising eyes warm to my words, the body language change, the smile that indicates I have opened some avenue for communication. So that day as I read, I looked directly at that woman. Her lowered eyes told me she was embarrassed at her faux pas, and when I willed her to look up at me, she graciously allowed me to punish her with my full attention. We shook hands at the end of the reading and I never saw her again. She has probably forgotten the entire incident, but maybe not.

Yet I am one of the lucky ones. There are thousands of Latinas without the privilege of an education or the entrees into society that I have. For them life is a constant struggle against the misconceptions perpetuated by the myth of the Latina. My goal is to try to replace the old stereotypes with a much more interesting set of realities. Every time I give a reading, I hope the stories I tell, the dreams and fears I examine in my work, can achieve some universal truth that will get my audience past the particulars of my skin color, my accent, or my clothes.

I once wrote a poem in which I called all Latinas "God's brown daughters." This poem is really a prayer of sorts, offered upward, but also, through the human-to-human channel of art, outward. It is a prayer for communication and for respect. In it, Latin women pray "in Spanish to an Anglo God/with a Jewish heritage," and they are "fervently hoping/that if not omnipotent,/at least He be bilingual."

## Responding to Reading                        MyWritingLab™

1.  In paragraph 1, Cofer says, "you can leave [Puerto Rico], master the English language, and travel as far as you can, but if you are a Latina, . . . the island travels with you." What does she mean? Do you think this is also true of people from other ethnic groups (and other nations)? Can you think of any groups whose culture and ethnicity is *not* likely to travel with them?

2.  Throughout this essay, Cofer speaks of the "cultural schizophrenia" (3) she felt, describing the "conflicting message" (4), the "cultural clash" (5), and the "mixed cultural signals" (6) she received from the two worlds she inhabited. Do you see this kind of "schizophrenia" as inevitable, or do you think it can be overcome? Do you think it *should* be overcome? Explain.

3.  **Rhetorical Analysis**  Evaluate the title of Cofer's essay. Is the subtitle necessary? What exactly is the "myth of the Latin woman"?

## Writing about Reading

1. What stereotypes are associated with your own ethnic group? Do you see these stereotypes as benign or harmful?
2. **Writing with Sources**  Locate some sources that discuss stereotypes—past and present—associated with your own racial, ethnic, or religious group. How did these stereotypes originate? How have they been used? What do you conclude about the impact (and dangers) of such stereotypes? Write an essay that explores these questions.

# MUSLIM IN AMERICA
## Jeffery Sheler
## Michael Betzold

*Author of three books on religious issues, Jeffery Sheler is a contributing editor at* U.S. News & World Report *and a correspondent for PBS's* Religion & Ethics NewsWeekly *television news program. Freelance writer Michael Betzold has written several articles and nonfiction books as well as a novel. In the following essay, Sheler and Betzold explore what it means to be a Muslim in America.*

Inside a storefront on West Warren Avenue, a gritty Dearborn, Mich., neighborhood of modest shops with hand-painted Arabic signs, a handful of men respond to the high-pitched chant of the muezzin[1] and form a line facing Mecca. They bow, sit, and prostrate on colorful rugs in a mostly silent rendition of the salat, the daily prayers Muslims have recited for nearly 1,400 years. In a smaller room, a cluster of women with head coverings also recite the prayers in response to the voice of the imam, which they can hear from across the hall. Most of the worshipers are recent refugees from Iraq who want a link to the country they still consider home. "They thank God they are here" in America, says Imam Hushan Al-Husainy, the mosque leader. "But their heart is back home with their loved ones who are suffering."

Meanwhile, 68 miles away, beneath a gleaming white dome and twin minarets that tower over the Ohio cornfields southwest of Toledo, hundreds of families assemble for worship—a largely upper-middle-class flock that represents some 22 nationalities, most U.S. citizens and some second- or third-generation Americans. Few of the women wear head coverings outside of the prayer hall, where only a 3-foot-high partition separates men and women, side by side. After prayers, they all gather for a potluck. The Toledo center, says its president, Cherrefe Kadri, represents a "progressive and middle-of-the-road" brand of Islam that, she says, is "very much at home in Middle America."

---

[1]At a mosque, the person who leads the call to prayer. [Eds.]

This, then, is American Islam: The modern Islamic Center of Greater Toledo and the traditionalist Karbala Islamic Education Center are but two examples of its wide-ranging diversity. And even though it is the nation's fastest-growing faith, with an estimated 7 million adherents here—nearly double from a decade ago—Islam remains widely misunderstood in this country. The religion of more than a fifth of the world's population is viewed by many Americans as foreign, mysterious, even threatening to the nation's "Judeo-Christian heritage"—certainly no less so since the events of September 11—despite the fact that it shares common roots with Christianity and Judaism and has been present in North America for centuries.

**The rules.** Indeed, Islam embraces the monotheism of Christianity and Judaism, accepts the Hebrew Bible, and venerates Jesus as a prophet. It is centered on the Koran—the Islamic scriptures, which Muslims believe were revealed to the prophet Mohammed—which commands five basic devotional duties, called the "Five Pillars": a declaration of belief that "there is no God but Allah [Arabic for "the God"] and Mohammed is his prophet"; prayers offered five times a day; daytime fasting during the month of Ramadan; charitable giving; and at least one pilgrimage to Mecca. Muslims are forbidden to consume alcohol, illicit drugs, pork, or any meat that is not halal—the Islamic equivalent of kosher. Premarital sex and extramarital sex are sternly prohibited, as are most forms of unchaperoned dating. Emphasis on public modesty prompts many Muslims to cover themselves from the wrists to the ankles. Muslims also may not gamble or pay or accept interest on loans or savings accounts. It is a regimen that often runs in conflict with the dominant culture. Most American Muslims have no choice but to break the prohibition on usury to buy homes and automobiles, for example.

But if the intense scrutiny focused on world Islam since September 11 has revealed anything, it is that the faith is no monolith. While there is much that binds the world's 1.2 billion Muslims together, there is no authoritative hierarchy—no pope, no central group of elders—that speaks to them or for them. And American Islam, it emerges, is its own special brand. A recent study sponsored by the Council on American-Islamic Relations [CAIR] in cooperation with the Hartford Institute for Religion Research found that American Muslims generally are more accepting of differences, less inclined to fundamentalism, and more at home in a secular society than most Muslims elsewhere. They are also ethnically diverse: Most are immigrants or their descendants from Islamic countries in Asia, Africa, and the Middle East. About a third are African-Americans, and a small number are whites of European descent.

**Connections?** But while diversity may naturally include the extremes, the question on many people's minds has been what exactly the relationship is between American Islam and the kind of terror and anti-Americanism that came so horribly into focus last month under the guise of religious zealotry. One moderate American Islamic leader, Sheik Muhammad Hisham Kabbani, told a State Department forum in 1999 that 80 percent of the nation's mosques are headed by clerics who espouse "extremist ideology"—which Kabbani associates with Wahhabism, an Islamic fundamentalist movement that began in Saudi Arabia in the 18th century. But Kabbani, head of the Islamic Supreme Council of America, a Washington, D.C.–based advocacy group, added that "a majority of American Muslims do not agree" with the extremist ideology.

Other American Muslim leaders say Kabbani's estimate of Wahhabi influence in U.S. mosques is exaggerated. "I don't know where he came up with that," says Ingrid Mattson, a Hartford Seminary professor and vice president of the Islamic Society of North America [ISNA]. African-Americans alone account for a third of the mosques, she notes, "and they clearly are not Wahhabis." The CAIR-Hartford study found that about 20 percent of mosques say they interpret the Koran literally, but 7 in 10 follow a more nuanced, nonfundamentalist approach.

Scholars say the democratic structure and autonomy of many American mosques protect them from extremist takeovers. Modern Islamic centers, like the one in Toledo, are "less likely to be dominated by a single teacher or viewpoint," says Frederick Denny, a scholar of Islam at the University of Colorado. That describes at least 60 percent of American mosques, according to the CAIR-Hartford study. Those that are more fundamentalist, he says, often are smaller, with transient members, such as those that "cater to foreign students who want something that feels like home." Even where fundamentalism exists, says Mattson, "there is a huge distinction between fundamentalist ideology and support of terrorism."

What divides American Muslims most often, says Denny, "is not liberal-versus-conservative ideology but how best to domesticate Islam in a Western society without doing violence to either." What, for example, are American Muslims to do with sharia, the Islamic legal and ethical codes that tradition says should undergird Islamic society? Radical clerics say it is a Muslim's duty to impose sharia throughout the world, by force if necessary. But moderates argue that Islamic law must be internalized. "It shouldn't be taken literally," says Imam Farooq Aboelzahab of the Toledo mosque. "The way sharia was applied 1,400 years ago may not always fit. It must be applied to the place and time where you live."

10    One indication that many Muslims are feeling more at home in America is their growing involvement in the nation's public life. During the past five years, Islamic leaders and groups have become increasingly outspoken on social- and foreign-policy issues. Groups like CAIR, ISNA, the American Muslim Council, and the Islamic Institute maintain a high-visibility Washington presence, working to

rally Muslim political activism and acting as media watchdogs. While American Islamic groups were virtually unanimous in condemning the terrorist attacks on New York and Washington, they remain vociferous critics of U.S. policy in the Middle East.

Stronger rhetoric, of course, has its price in this country. In late September, a prominent imam at a Cleveland mosque nearly lost his job over anti-Jewish remarks he had made in a speech 10 years ago. The board at the Islamic Center of Cleveland voted to keep Fawaz Damra after he apologized for the remarks, which appeared on a tape that surfaced recently, but local Jewish leaders are still upset.

**Incendiary rhetoric.** Meanwhile, a leading Muslim teacher in Northern California has apologized for his own rhetorical excesses. Hamza Yusuf, who was invited to the White House to pray with President Bush after the attacks, later came under criticism for saying in a speech two days before the attacks that the United States "stands condemned" and faced "a terrible fate" because of rampant immorality and injustice in its treatment of minorities. While their causes may be just, says Yusuf, "the rhetoric of some Muslim leaders has been too incendiary—I myself have been guilty of it." September 11, he says, "was a wake-up call to me. I don't want to contribute to the hate in any shape or form."

A decade ago, Sulayman Nyang, professor of African studies at Howard University in Washington, D.C., warned in a speech that Islam will be accepted in America only when Muslims fully take their place alongside other citizens, participating in the nation's civic life, and when what the Islamic faith can offer Western culture is recognized widely as something of value. Neither, he says, will be easy to accomplish. But in times like these, such hard work is more important than ever.

## Responding to Reading

MyWritingLab™

1. According to Sheler and Betzold, how is Islam like other widely followed U.S. religions? How is it different?
2. In paragraph 5, the writers assert that the Muslim faith is "no monolith." What do they mean? What evidence do they offer to support this claim?
3. **Rhetorical Analysis** This essay appeared in a newsmagazine on October 29, 2001, just weeks after the 9/11 terrorist attacks. What do you suppose the writers' primary purpose was? How can you tell?

## Writing about Reading

MyWritingLab™

1. What do you think it would take for Muslims to truly feel "at home in America" (10)? What elements of their culture might they have to sacrifice? Is this sacrifice worth making?
2. **Writing with Sources** Do some research about U.S. Muslims who are immigrants or first-generation Americans. What are their major concerns? What goals do they have for themselves and for their children? How are their goals and expectations like and unlike those of other Americans?

# THE GAYEST ONE

## Brett Krutzsch

*A Ph.D. student in religion at Temple University, Brett Krutzsch explores
the connections between religion and LGBT (lesbian, gay, bisexual, and
transgender) issues. He received the 2014–15 LGBT Religious History
Award for his dissertation excerpt titled "The Martyrdom of Matthew
Shepard." His work has appeared in the* New York Blade *and* New York
Press. *In the following essay, Krutzsch considers the nuances of gay identity
from a personal perspective.*

"Everyone agreed that you're the gayest person in the department," my
best friend from work said to me as we strolled through SoHo. Sara was
recapping a conversation from a happy hour I missed because I had
been at a book reading by Paula Deen, the eccentric Southern woman
on the Food Network.

"What does that mean?" I asked.

"Nobody gave any reasons. Someone asked who was the biggest
homosexual, people looked around, and Matt said your name. Everybody agreed."

I was immediately irritated and annoyed. Out of the 50 individuals who work in my division at NYU, 11 of us are gay men. How could
I so quickly and unanimously be considered the fruitiest of the bunch?

5      Sara changed the topic to her upcoming wedding. As she talked
about whether or not to keep her hair straight or curly, I recalled a
friend's birthday party a year ago. We were at a straight bar near Union
Square, and an attractive woman, probably in her late 20s, repeatedly
glanced my way the entire night. Eventually, she approached me and
asked, "Are you here for Craig's party?"

"Yes, I am," I said, as I watched her eyes get big and the color drain
from her face.

"Oh, you're gay," she interjected.

I had said three words. Three very little words. Each with one
syllable. That was all it took for her to know my sexual orientation.

"I am," I said with an awkward laugh, realizing that she had
wanted to hit on me.

10      "Oh, I thought. I mean, I'm sorry," she mumbled, and then ran off,
looking embarrassed.

I turned around and told my friends what happened, and they
burst out laughing. I wasn't amused. I left the party soon after that and
walked home, feeling sorry for myself.

Still talking about her wedding. Sara decided she should keep her
hair curly since she was having an outdoor ceremony in July. "After
all," she said. "It could never be completely straight anyway."

Apparently, with a voice like mine, neither could I.

That week I couldn't stop fixating on the idea of me as the biggest queen at work. I tried thinking of stereotypes I fit, but things still didn't make sense. Of all the gay men in my department, I was the only one in a long-term relationship. My boyfriend and I lived together, had joint finances, and shared holidays with each other's families. We were boringly monogamous. Our nights usually concluded with *Seinfeld*, not sex. So it couldn't be that I embodied the stereotype of the promiscuous gay man with a wild night life. I hadn't set foot in a gay club in three years. Of all the queer men I worked with, my homelife seemed the most heterosexual.

OK, my interests and hobbies were never particularly manly. I'd    15
much rather be at a Broadway show than at a Yankees game. Given a choice, I always picked a day at the spa over a day of camping. I've typically been more comfortable at brunches with women chatting about sample sales than out having beers with the guys talking about cars or the stock market.

Not long ago I was walking down Third Avenue with my friend Lauren. It was raining and we shared an umbrella. We passed a homeless man sprawled out on the sidewalk who yelled to Lauren, "Hey, gorgeous, want to get married?"

"Sorry, I'm taken," Lauren said, looking up at me.

The homeless man screamed back, "Yeah, to a homo."

I wasn't singing "It's Raining Men" under the umbrella. I was just walking. Even the homeless man had enough gay-dar to know I wasn't heterosexual.

I assumed that I was decreed the gayest at my job because I was    20
the least likely to pass as straight. I wore form-fitting Burberry polos, openly raved about Kelly Clarkson, and bought expensive Kiehl's skin care products even though I was only 28. If I were put in a lineup, it probably wouldn't take someone with Nancy Drew's investigative skills to finger me as the boy who likes boys. Nevertheless, I was still perplexed by people's need to ask, "Who among us is the biggest fairy?" I doubt straight guys ever sat around saying: "Bob, you're definitely the straightest one here." "No way, Harry. You're totally straighter."

When I moved to Manhattan four years ago I thought I was relocating to the gay mecca, as if the mother ship were calling me home. On my first outing to the bars of Chelsea and subsequent walks along Eighth Avenue I quickly observed that I didn't look like other gay men in the area. Standing six feet tall and weighing 140 pounds, I was a skinny Jewish bookworm who had no interest in going to the gym to become one of the musclemen who ruled the New York City gayborhoods. They paid little attention to me, so at that point in my life I felt like I wasn't gay enough.

I never believed my sexuality was a choice, but how I presented myself to the world was. Until I came out of the closet my senior year at Emory University, I wore oversized T-shirts and pretended to have a crush on Jennifer Aniston, like many of the straight, beer-drinking guys my age, never letting on that my lust was actually for Brad Pitt. I've since learned that I wasn't fooling anyone—my family members and friends have said they always assumed I was gay.

Growing up in Indiana, the boys in my school constantly asked why I talked like a girl. I didn't understand what they meant until I was in third grade, when I heard myself on an answering machine. I sounded just like my friend Liz, so each night I prayed for my voice to deepen and be like my dad's. After puberty, when I thought my prayers had been answered, the same boys asked why I talked like Michael Jackson. I always felt my voice was a reminder that I was different, a freak, and less than a real man.

When I came out at 22, my shrink said it could take several years to fully accept my sexuality. Six years have passed, and I'm now sharing my life with an incredible partner, but I still struggle, because I think of myself as a liberal Jewish pseudo-intellectual, not an über-homosexual. I know it isn't a bad thing to be the gayest one. I'm just not sure how to accept the title or if I'm ready to wear the tiara and sash.

## Responding to Reading                                    MyWritingLab™

1. Despite his apparent comfort with and acceptance of his gay identity, Krutzsch objects to being so easily recognized as gay—and to being characterized as the "gayest person in the department" (1). Why?
2. How, according to Krutzsch, is gay culture stereotyped? In what respects does he believe he does not fit that stereotype?
3. **Rhetorical Analysis**   In paragraph 22, Krutzsch says, "I never believed my sexuality was a choice, but how I presented myself to the world was." What distinction is he making here? How do you think he wants readers to perceive him? Does he achieve his goal?

## Writing about Reading                                    MyWritingLab™

1. Do you think Krutzsch should take steps to present himself to the world differently? If so, what specific steps should he take?
2. **Writing with Sources**   Attitudes about gays and lesbians have changed dramatically in the past forty years or so, and so has the social, political, and economic landscape for these groups. Search for information about the 1969 Stonewall riots. Then, write an essay in which you explore changing attitudes about gay marriage, gays in the military, gays on college campuses or in the workplace, or a similar topic since Stonewall. What has changed, and what has stayed the same? Be sure to read articles in gay and lesbian publications and websites as well as in mainstream sources.

# ON THE MEANING OF PLUMBING
# AND POVERTY
## Melanie Scheller

*Melanie Scheller is the author of the children's book* My Grandfather's Hat *(1992) and the writer and director of the short film* No Where, USA *(2009). In the following essay, Scheller explores the cultural identity of the rural poor.*

Several years ago I spent some time as a volunteer on the geriatric ward of a psychiatric hospital. I was fascinated by the behavior of one of the patients, an elderly woman who shuffled at regular intervals to the bathroom, where she methodically flushed the toilet. Again and again she carried out her sacred mission as if summoned by some supernatural force, until the flush of the toilet became a rhythmic counterpoint for the ward's activity. If someone blocked her path or if, God forbid, the bathroom was in use when she reached it, she became agitated and confused.

Obviously, that elderly patient was a sick woman. And yet I felt a certain kinship with her, for I too have suffered from an obsession with toilets. I spent much of my childhood living in houses without indoor plumbing, and while I don't feel compelled to flush a toilet at regular intervals, I sometimes feel that toilets, or the lack thereof, have shaped my identity in ways that are painful to admit.

I'm not a child of the Depression,[1] but I grew up in an area of the South that had changed little since the day of the New Deal.[2] My mother was a widow with six children to support, not an easy task under any circumstances, but especially difficult in rural North Carolina during the 1960s. To her credit, we were never seriously in danger of going hungry. Our vegetable garden kept us stocked with tomatoes and string beans. We kept a few chickens and sometimes a cow. Blackberries were free for the picking in the fields nearby. Neighbors did their good Christian duty by bringing us donations of fresh fruit and candy at Christmastime. But a roof over our heads—that wasn't so easily improvised.

Like rural Southern gypsies, we moved from one dilapidated Southern farmhouse to another in a constant search for a decent place to live. Sometimes we moved when the rent increased beyond the 30 or 40 dollars my mother could afford. Or the house burned down, not an unusual occurrence in substandard housing. One year when we were

---

[1]Great Depression (1929–1939). [Eds.]

[2]Economic relief and reform program implemented by the U.S. government between 1933–1939. [Eds.]

gathered together for Thanksgiving dinner, a stranger walked in without knocking and announced that we were being evicted. The house had been sold without our knowledge and the new owner wanted to start remodeling immediately. We tried to finish our meal with an attitude of thanksgiving while he worked around us with his tape measure.

5      Usually we rented from farm families who'd moved from the old home place to one of the brick boxes that are now the standard in rural Southern architecture. The old farmhouse wasn't worth fixing up with a septic tank and flush toilet, but it was good enough to rent for a few dollars a month to families like mine. The idea of tenants' rights hadn't trickled down yet from the far reaches of the liberal North. It never occurred to us to demand improvements in the facilities. The ethic of the land said we should take what we could get and be grateful for it.

Without indoor plumbing, getting clean is a tiring and time consuming ritual. At one point I lived in a five-room house with six or more people, all of whom congregated in the one heated room to eat, do homework, watch television, dress and undress, argue, wash dishes. During cold weather we dragged mattresses from the unheated rooms and slept huddled together on the floor by the woodstove. For my bathing routine, I first pinned a sheet to a piece of twine strung across the kitchen. That gave me some degree of privacy from the six other people in the room. At that time our house had an indoor cold-water faucet, from which I filled a pot of water to heat on the kitchen stove. It took several pots of hot water to fill the metal washtub we used.

Since I was a teenager and prone to sulkiness if I didn't get special treatment, I got to take the first bath while the water was still clean. The others used the water I left behind, freshened up with hot water from the pot on the stove. Then the tub had to be dragged to the door and the bath water dumped outside. I longed to be like the woman in the Calgon bath oil commercials, luxuriating in a marble tub full of scented water with bubbles piled high and stacks of thick, clean towels nearby.

People raised in the land of the bath-and-a-half may wonder why I make such a fuss about plumbing. Maybe they spent a year in the Peace Corps, or they back-packed across India, or they worked at a summer camp and, gosh, using a latrine isn't all that bad. And of course it's *not* that bad. Not when you can catch the next plane out of the country, or pick up your duffel bag and head for home, or call mom and dad to come and get you when things get too tedious. A sojourn in a Third World country, where everyone shares the same primitive facilities, may cause some temporary discomfort, but the experience is soon converted into amusing anecdotes for cocktail-party conversation. It doesn't corrode your self-esteem with a sense of shame the way a childhood spent in chronic, unrelenting poverty can.

In the South of my childhood, not having indoor plumbing was the indelible mark of poor white trash. The phrase "so poor they didn't

have a pot to piss in" said it all. Poor white trash were viciously stereotyped, and never more viciously than on the playground. White-trash
children had cooties—everybody knew that. They had ringworm and
pinkeye—don't get near them or you might catch it. They picked their
noses. They messed in their pants. If a white-trash child made the mistake of catching a softball during recess, the other children made an
elaborate show of wiping it clean before they would touch it.

Once a story circulated at school about a family whose infant 10
daughter had fallen into the "slop jar" and drowned. When I saw the
smirks and heard the laughter with which the story was told, I felt sick
and afraid in the pit of my stomach. A little girl had died, but people
were laughing. What had she done to deserve that laughter? I could
only assume that using a chamber pot was something so disgusting, so
shameful, that it made a person less than human.

My family was visibly and undeniably poor. My clothes were obviously hand-me-downs. I got free lunches at school. I went to the health
department for immunizations. Surely it was equally obvious that we
didn't have a flush toilet. But like an alcoholic who believes no one will
know he has a problem as long as he doesn't drink in public, I convinced myself that no one knew my family's little secret. It was a form
of denial that would color my relationships with the outside world for
years to come.

Having a friend from school spend the night at my house was
out of the question. Better to be friendless than to have my classmates
know my shameful secret. Home visits from teachers or ministers left
me in a dither of anticipatory anxiety. As they chattered on and on with
Southern small talk about tomato plants and relish recipes, I sat on the
edge of my seat, tensed against the dreaded words, "May I use your
bathroom, please?" When I began dating in high school, I'd lie in wait
behind the front door, ready to dash out as soon as my date pulled in
the driveway, never giving him a chance to hear the call of nature while
on our property.

With the help of a scholarship I was able to go away to college,
where I could choose from dozens of dormitory toilets and take as
many hot showers as I wanted, but I could never openly express my joy
in using the facilities. My roommates, each a pampered only child from
a well-to-do family, whined and complained about having to share a
bathroom. I knew that if I expressed delight in simply having a bathroom, I would immediately be labeled as a hick. The need to conceal
my real self by stifling my emotions created a barrier around me and
I spent my college years in a vacuum of isolation.

Almost 20 years have passed since I first tried to leave my family's
chamber pot behind. For many of those years it followed behind me—
the ghost of chamber pots past—clanging and banging and threatening
to spill its humiliating contents at any moment. I was convinced that

everyone could see it, could smell it even. No college degree or job title seemed capable of banishing it.

15    If finances had permitted, I might have become an Elvis Presley or a Tammy Faye Bakker, easing the pain of remembered poverty with gold-plated bathtub fixtures and leopard-skinned toilet seats. I feel blessed that gradually, ever so gradually, the shame of poverty has begun to fade. The pleasures of the present now take priority over where a long-ago bowel movement did or did not take place. But for many Southerners, chamber pots and outhouses are more than just memories.

In North Carolina alone, 200,000 people still live without indoor plumbing.[3] People who haul their drinking water home from a neighbor's house or catch rainwater in barrels. People who can't wash their hands before handling food, the way restaurant employees are required by state law to do. People who sneak into public restrooms every day to wash, shave, and brush their teeth before going to work or to school. People who sacrifice their dignity and self-respect when forced to choose between going homeless and going to an outhouse. People whose children think they deserve the conditions in which they live and hold their heads low to hide the shame. But they're not the ones who should feel ashamed. No, they're not the ones who should feel ashamed.

## Responding to Reading                                         MyWritingLab™

1. In paragraph 2, Scheller says, "I sometimes feel that toilets, or the lack thereof, have shaped my identity in ways that are painful to admit." Exactly how has the issue of indoor plumbing shaped her identity?
2. What specific problems, apart from the lack of indoor plumbing, did Scheller and her family face because they were poor? Why do you think she focuses on toilets instead of on another problem?
3. **Rhetorical Analysis**  How does Scheller see herself as different from those who were "raised in the land of the bath-and-a-half" (8)? How do you think she expects readers to react to this characterization?

## Writing about Reading                                          MyWritingLab™

1. The culture of rural poverty Scheller describes in this essay is not a culture that is generally freely chosen. How do you suppose their shared experiences and memories might nevertheless create a sense of cultural identity for the rural poor?
2. **Writing with Sources**  In this essay, Scheller discusses living conditions for poor rural Southerners in the 1960s. What has changed for them since her childhood? What has stayed the same? Write an essay exploring the progress (or lack of progress) in one rural community.

---

[3]According to the North Carolina Housing Coalition, more than 16,000 homes in the state are still without indoor plumbing. [Eds.]

# "WHAT ARE YOU GOING TO BE?"

## Steven Korbar

### *1967–*

*A playwright and actor based in Los Angeles, Steven Korbar has produced plays throughout the United States and Canada. His work has appeared in* The Best Ten-Minute Plays 2010 *and* 2013 *as well as in the 2013 Queer Theatre Festival in Washington, D.C. The following ten-minute play reveals the cultural significance of the clothes and costumes we wear.*

CHARACTERS:
    GREG: thirties to forties
    CAROL: thirties to forties
    NATALIE: an adolescent girl

SETTING: An upper middle class home—decorated for Halloween.

TIME: Early evening

> *Lights come up to find CAROL seated in a living room setting. She is very still and appears rather stunned. After a moment GREG enters. He is carrying a grocery bag and is in high spirits.*

GREG: Okay, don't get mad at me, but I broke my promise—I bought more Halloween candy! I know we already have a ton but A) they were having an incredible sale and B) and most importantly . . . they're "Junior Mints"! I figure we can just put them in the back of the cupboard and conveniently forget them till Trick or Treating is over tomorrow night. Oh don't be all angry. "Junior Mints"! . . . What's the matter?

CAROL: *(A choked voice)* . . . Natalie . . .

GREG: *(Stricken)* What? . . . What!?

> *Quickly becoming hysterical. Dropping the bag*
> Oh God! Natalie. NATALIE! Where is she, where . . .

CAROL: No. No, she's fine. She's not hurt or sick or anything.

GREG: Then why did you . . . Oh my God! What is wrong with you!?   5
    Why did you say 'Natalie' like something horrible happened?

CAROL: *(Flatly)* I'm sorry.

GREG: You scared the living . . . you don't joke around like that—you took ten years off my life, you, you made me drop my "Junior Mints".

CAROL: I'm very sorry. I should have phrased what I had to say differently.

GREG: What could you have to say that was worth giving me a cardiac infarction?

10 CAROL: Natalie . . . finally decided what she's going to be for Halloween.

GREG: *(A beat)* Her Halloween costume. Carol, what is the point of all this family therapy if you're just going to keep overreacting to every little thing? You know what Dr. Penelope told you; perspective is what we have to strive for. If you just take a step back and a deep cleansing breath; pretty soon you're going to see that what seemed so dire really wasn't such a terrible . . .

> *NATALIE enters. We assume she is a normal adolescent girl, though it is hard to tell as she is dressed in the burka[1] of a Muslim woman from the Middle East. Her costume is heavy, black and very constricting. GREG stares at her for a long moment. He looks at CAROL and then back to NATALIE, Trying desperately not to overreact.*

. . . Hey princess.

NATALIE: Hi Dad

GREG: What'cha doing?

NATALIE: Just trying on my Halloween costume.

15 GREG: So you decided against the ballerina?

NATALIE: Yeah. I'm going to be a Muslim woman from the Middle East instead.

GREG: Why . . . did you decide to be that?

NATALIE: Cause I wanted a costume not a lot of other girls would have.

GREG: . . . Good job.

20 NATALIE: There isn't any reason you don't want me wearing this . . . is there?

GREG: I . . . can't think of any.

NATALIE: Good. Well, I'm going to go back to my room, figure out which way is Mecca[2] and practice lying face down on the floor.

> *NATALIE exits*

GREG: *(A long beat. Trying desperately to sound reasonable)* Well . . . we said no Lady Gaga.

CAROL: This is not my fault. I am a good mother—there are no preservatives in anything I feed that girl.

---

[1] A veil worn by some Muslim women. [Eds.]
[2] An Islamic holy city in Saudi Arabia. [Eds.]

GREG: This is not about fault. This can be an opportunity; to learn more about our daughter and try to understand her thought process. 25

NATALIE: *(OFF STAGE)* I can hear every word your saying.

GREG: *(Yelling towards the direction of her room)* Well then shut your door Missy!

> *To CAROL. More quietly*

Let's just try to discuss this quietly. Now, where did she get the . . .

CAROL: Burka is the word you're trying to sound casual saying. And I don't know where she got it—I was too terrified to look through her browsing history.

GREG: There is no reason to be terrified. There is nothing wrong with being Middle Eastern. We cannot let her feel we have a problem with that. Muslims are human beings just like you and me—we see them every day on "Anderson Cooper". We just have to figure out why Natalie wants to dress like one.

CAROL: I know why—to destroy me. She's rejecting everything I've ever taught her about being a modern, post-feminist woman and chosen the most subservient, oppressed female role model she could find. My God, she might as well just be dressing up as my mother for Halloween! 30

GREG: Those are a completely different set of issues. What matters now is that if we decide it's better for her not to wear this costume, she doesn't think it's because we have any sort of discriminatory . . .

> *NATALIE enters*

NATALIE: Hey mom, can I have a needle and thread to fix my costume; I think too much of my face is showing.

GREG: You know sweetie, we actually wanted to talk to you about your costume and what you'll be wearing tomorrow night.

NATALIE: I'll be wearing this.

GREG: Maybe . . . but your mom and I would like you to be aware of all your options. For instance, you could reexamine the whole line of Disney princesses—there's Jasmine from "Aladdin". All the same ethnicity and you could look so pretty. 35

NATALIE: No. Nobody my age is going to wear a princess costume. And even if I did it sure wouldn't be Jasmine—she's a total infidel. Anyway, who cares what I wear, it's just a costume and the costumes we wear shouldn't matter . . . right Dad?

GREG: Right! . . . right.

CAROL: Natalie, it's just that we feel it might seem disrespectful to people of the Muslim faith for you to be wearing this as a costume for Halloween.

GREG: *(Impressed with CAROL'S ruse)* Good!

> *Immediately to NATALIE. Earnestly*

Right. Halloween is more of a secular holiday and it's just better to keep religion out of it.

40 CAROL: Remember how the Davis's passed out bible quotes instead of candy last Halloween; their house got TP'd for four straight nights.

NATALIE: *(Suspiciously)* Tell me the truth; this really isn't because the two of you have got some weird thing against Islam, is it?

GREG: No!

CAROL: No!

GREG: No!

45 CAROL: No!

GREG: It's just: you don't want to belittle anyone's faith sweetie. I mean, you wouldn't run around asking for candy dressed as a Catholic nun, would you?

CAROL: Well honey, some people do go out dressed as nuns. It's a costume: they go out dressed as slutty nuns.

GREG: . . . Those are slutty nurses.

NATALIE!: No, she's right. Some are nurses but a lot of them are slutty nuns too.

50 GREG: Okay, fine. There are slutty nun costumes; but you wouldn't go out dressed in one would you?

NATALIE: No. I already know two girls who are going as that.

GREG: *(More frustrated)* I think it is just culturally insensitive to these people as a group. And by these people I do not mean . . . *(Catching himself and making air quotes)* 'These People'. I just, I don't feel comfortable with you dressing this way.

NATALIE: When Lauren Nakamura went dressed as a geisha last year, the two of you wouldn't stop gushing about how adorable she looked.

GREG: That is completely different.

55 NATALIE: Why, because Arabs frighten you but you find Asians all cute and non-threatening?

GREG: Absolutely not!

CAROL: No!

GREG: Do not put words in my mouth! The image of the passive Asian is nothing but a ridiculous, antiquated racial stereotype!

CAROL: Of course it is.

60 GREG: Just look at Pearl Harbor.

> *After realizing what he's said, putting a discrete hand over his mouth*

CAROL: What your father means is he would like you to find another costume to wear.

NATALIE: What would he like me to be; a white, male, Protestant who can prove he's straight?

> GREG *instinctively moves to attack NATALIE—muttering something like "You miserable little . . . ". Carol restrains him.*

CAROL: This is not a judgment on anyone's religion or race.

NATALIE: Then why is Dad getting all freaked out?

GREG: I am not getting freaked out: nobody ever even mentioned 65 terrorism.

NATALIE: What!?

GREG: I mean; it is wrong to ascribe the worst in human nature to any one particular people. And anybody who does that is ignorant and we should just feel sorry for them.

NATALIE: Then I can go like this?

GREG: I will lock you in the crawl space first.

NATALIE: Well my friend Lele really is Muslim and she likes this 70 costume and she's totally cool with me wearing it.

GREG: I don't care what your friend thinks. You are not wearing that costume. It is inappropriate; it's thoughtless and wearing it would just be plain insulting to the people and culture of Islam!

NATALIE: Is that what all of your Muslim friends say Dad?

*GREG tries to answer but is left with his mouth open. NATALIE stares at him for a beat, turns and exits in triumphant silence*

GREG: *(A beat, then erupting in frustration)* What is going on here! I don't understand, why is she doing this to us!

NATALIE: *(Off stage)* I can still hear you!

75

GREG: I am going to remove that door from its hinges!

NATALIE: *(Off stage)* That doesn't even make sense—I could hear you better then!

GREG: I know that!

> *Moving to CAROL. Whispering*
She used to be so sweet when she was little.

CAROL: I told you we shouldn't have let her have all those inoculations.

GREG: We could just cram her into a stuffed pumpkin and that was her 80 costume.

CAROL: Polio and Rubella; fine. But she was never right again after that Smallpox vaccine.

GREG: *(Humiliated)* I said terrorist.

CAROL: And Pearl Harbor.

GREG: Since the day she was born I've tried to teach her to respect diversity. She has been to every church, heard every philosophy; we introduced her to that school friend of yours who's a Wiccan[3] and a Lesbian. I've taken that girl to so many Bat mitzvahs[4] in the last year I could practically poach a salmon all by myself. I paid $125.00 for a dress so she could look right at her friend's quinceanera[5] and another $15.00 to the gardener to learn how to pronounce quinceanera! What in the hell more do I have to do—she wouldn't go with me to the Tyler Perry movie!

CAROL: If you ask me this whole place is just crawling with Radon.

85    GREG: Will you stop blaming everything on hazardous materials.

CAROL: Well I told you; it's not me. I breast fed that kid for fourteen months and stayed gluten free the whole time—I did my part.

GREG: Well all I know is I left a peaceful home this morning, worked hard all day for my family and when I walked back through the front door this evening suddenly it's a Jihad![6] Where did that come from?

CAROL: Well not my side of the family—she didn't inherit any of that gamy, exotic blood from me.

GREG: . . . And what in the hell is that supposed to mean?

>    CAROL *does not respond*

I'm part Dutch, part Scots/Irish and 1/8th Armenian.

>    CAROL *points at him as if to say 'Bingo'*

Armenia is in Europe.

90    CAROL: Oh no it's not. Not real Europe. Not "Sound of Music" Europe. You've always had a little smudge of the Third World on you; I knew it the first time I saw that dusky little mother of yours—I mean, no offence, but the woman's always looked like she just finished carrying a jug of water on her head.

GREG: Are you out of your mind?

CAROL: And there's another trail that's straight out of the Casbah[7]—your condescending manner towards women. So archaic and primitive—it's down right patriarchal.

GREG: Oh really, is that what your Wiccan friend would call it?

CAROL: And a homophobe to boot.

95    GREG: You are making me very angry!

---

[3] A believer in Wicca, a religion based in magic and nature. [Eds.]
[4] A rite of passage for Jewish girls passing into womanhood. [Eds.]
[5] A rite of passage for Hispanic girls passing into womanhood. [Eds.]
[6] An Islamic holy war. [Eds.]
[7] A fortress or native sector in North Africa. [Eds.]

CAROL: Oh boy, start gathering up your stones everybody: I feel an honor killing coming on!

GREG: Do you even understand the sociopolitical implications of what you're saying? This is the kind of thinking that fostered colonialism for the last two centuries.

*NATALIE enters no longer wearing the burka*

NATALIE: Okay, okay, okay—just stop the arguing, alright! If this is what it's going to do to you, fine; I won't wear the stupid costume. If my parents can't handle somebody dressing a little different then I guess I was just expecting too much! Everyone has their secret little hates and prejudices, even my own mother and father. That's just how it is. So I'll just do what you want. I'll go back to wearing my original Lady Gaga costume . . . unless you have something against her religion too?

*CAROL and GREG simultaneously shake their heads*

Okay then. Thai's how it's going to be and we won't even talk about it anymore.

I'm not a baby—it's not like I can't stand disappointment. I guess I have to start getting used to it sometime, don't I?

GREG: *(Earnestly)* Natalie . . . I want you to know I think you've shown a lot of maturity tonight. And maturity is a rare thing at any age.

NATALIE: Thanks Dad—I bet that's just how Anderson Cooper would have put it. 100

*NATALIE exits. There is a silence.*

GREG: Well, I think it all worked out for the best.

CAROL: In the long run I think so.

GREG: It's good she made the decision by herself.

CAROL: It wouldn't have been right if we'd had to force her.

GREG: These are volatile times; it's just better not to broach certain 105 subjects.

GREG: *(Suddenly aware)* . . . Did she just play us?

CAROL: Played us like a violin.

GREG: She was never going to wear that as a costume, was she?

CAROL: She was going as Lady Gaga if she'd had to slit our throats.

GREG: We really did kind of raise a terrorist, didn't we? 110

CAROL: Utterly remorseless.

GREG: It's just stunning. How she manipulated us. The way she preyed on our irrational fears and exploited our ingrained prejudices. And for no other reason but to get what she wanted from us.

CAROL: I always did tell her she could be the first woman president of the United States.

GREG: Well, she sure had my number. If anyone asks me, I guess I know what I'm going to be for Halloween.

115  CAROL: Your own adolescent daughters little bitch?

GREG: I was going to say a hypocrite. How can I ever look another Arab American in the eye again?

CAROL: Well, since I don't think there are any in our 'Emotional Eating' class, I doubt it will be a problem. Anyway, Halloween will be over and done with tomorrow night, and if we're lucky we can just put the whole horrible thing behind us.

GREG: Can we? Christmas is only two months away.

CAROL: (*Remembering a horrible fact*) . . . Oh my God.

120  GREG: She's still got her heart set on that puppy.

CAROL: Oh no! The dander . . . the dander. We can't have it in the house!

GREG: (*Low and fatalistic*) We may not have a choice Carol. We may not have a choice.

> (*A distraught beat. Then yelling in the direction of NATALIE'S bedroom*)

I know you can hear me!

> NATALIE *is heard laughing Off Stage. CAROL and GREG cower together.*

### End Of Play

## Responding to Reading
MyWritingLab™

1. Why is Carol so upset about her daughter's Halloween costume?
2. What is Greg's main concern about Natalie's choice? Why doesn't he feel comfortable with her wearing a burka?
3. What stereotypes of Muslims are explored in this play? What stereotypes of other groups are identified? What do these stereotypes reveal about Carol and Greg?

## Responding in Writing
MyWritingLab™

Why do you think Natalie chose a burka for her costume? To get attention? To "destroy" Carol by choosing "the most subservient, oppressed female role model she could find"? To wear "a costume not a lot of other girls would have"? For some other reason (or combination of reasons)?

--- FOCUS ---

## Do Racial Distinctions Still Matter?

→ **NOTE: Please answer BOTH Question 8 about Hispanic origin and Question 9 about race. For this census, Hispanic origins are not races.**

**8. Is Person 1 of Hispanic, Latino, or Spanish origin?**

☐ **No,** not of Hispanic, Latino, or Spanish origin
☐ Yes, Mexican, Mexican Am., Chicano
☐ Yes, Puerto Rican
☐ Yes, Cuban
☐ Yes, another Hispanic, Latino, or Spanish origin — *Print origin, for example, Argentinean, Colombian, Dominican, Nicaraguan, Salvadoran, Spaniard, and so on.* ⃕

☐☐☐☐☐☐☐☐☐☐☐☐☐☐☐☐☐☐☐☐

**9. What is Person 1's race?** *Mark* [X] *one or more boxes.*

☐ White
☐ Black, African Am., or Negro
☐ American Indian or Alaska Native — *Print name of enrolled or principal tribe.* ⃕

☐☐☐☐☐☐☐☐☐☐☐☐☐☐☐☐☐☐☐☐

☐ Asian Indian      ☐ Japanese      ☐ Native Hawaiian
☐ Chinese            ☐ Korean         ☐ Guamanian or Chamorro
☐ Filipino           ☐ Vietnamese     ☐ Samoan
☐ Other Asian — *Print race, for example, Hmong, Laotian, Thai, Pakistani, Cambodian, and so on.* ⃕      ☐ Other Pacific Islander — *Print race, for example, Fijian, Tongan, and so on.* ⃕

☐☐☐☐☐☐☐☐☐☐☐☐☐☐☐☐☐☐☐☐

☐ Some other race — *Print race.* ⃕

☐☐☐☐☐☐☐☐☐☐☐☐☐☐☐☐☐☐☐☐

Two questions on 2010 census form

## Responding to the Image

MyWritingLab™

1. Do you think questions 8 and 9 on the census form offer enough choices? Do you think these questions offer *too many* choices? Explain.
2. Which box (or boxes) would you check to describe your own racial and ethnic identity? Why?

# WHICH IS IT, HISPANIC OR LATINO?

## Cindy Y. Rodriguez

*A lecturer of journalism and media studies at Rutgers University's School of Communication and Information, Cindy Y. Rodriguez writes about issues pertaining to Latino culture and identity, media, and politics. She is a senior editor for CafeMom's Vivala, an online space for Latinas to chat and collaborate. In the following essay, Rodriguez describes the complexities of Latino culture.*

If there's one thing everyone should know about Hispanics in the United States, it's that this rapidly growing minority has an undefined identity crisis.

Why? Because of the confusion surrounding what to call people whose ethnic background is from Latin American and Spanish-speaking countries. Some even feel 100% American or 100% Latino—or Hispanic, depending to whom you're talking.

How do you know which term to use? "Hispanic" and "Latino" are often used interchangeably and aim to describe the same group of people, but technically they do not mean the same thing.

What's more, within Hispanic communities in the United States, most people identify with their country of origin and often use hyphens to represent their loyalties to both cultures: like "Mexican-American."

5       We're constantly having to straddle two worlds: the one where our families came from and where we've chosen to live.

To make matters even more complicated, all that can change depending on where Latinos are in any given moment.

When I'm in my parents' native country of Peru, I'm American with Peruvian parents and that's that. No matter how hard I've tried to be "Peruvian enough" to my fellow Peruvians, I might as well be a gringa[1] in their eyes.

And, when I'm back in United States, someone will inevitably ask me where I'm from in a way that suggests I'm not from the good ol' U.S. of A.

In other words, imagine having to constantly tell people that you're made of two colors: blue and yellow, but all people see is green, and you constantly have to go in the light and show them you are made of both colors.

10      Identifying as Hispanic or Latino comes with its ups and downs. But perhaps breaking down what these terms mean and how they're used within this diverse community of 54 million Latinos can help shed some light on our experience.

---

[1]Female foreigner. [Eds.]

## Hispanic or Latino?

Years ago, I attended a media networking event hoping to meet more established journalists.

I remember saying something along the lines of, "Ah, the joys of being Hispanic," and an older Latina woman turned around and said, "No, sweetie, you are a Latina. Don't refer to yourself as Hispanic. The government invented that word for us."

Um, OK. I think I hit a nerve.

Then, a younger Latino man snickered and asked her to not take those labels so seriously. She quickly turned to him and, judging by her wide eyes and stiff demeanor, she clearly did not agree. Her eyes then met with mine and she looked at me as if I had to make a choice: Hispanic or Latino? What's it going to be?

The room immediately felt as if it divided into two uncomfortable 15 teams.

I could feel the warm embrace from the "Hispanic team," which was easygoing and used both terms interchangeably, and imagined them saying to me, "Come on over! Hispanic? Latino? Whatever you feel is best."

But the looming eyes of "Latino team" made me feel obligated to side with them and take some kind of political stance on the term. Using Latino had a slight "sticking it to the man" feel.

I wasn't sure how I felt about identifying with either term, so I decided to hold my tongue, take a deep breath and smile.

Even though this woman I had never met tried to impose her label on me, she was partially right.

The term Hispanic was first used by the U.S. government in the 20 1970s in an attempt to count people from Mexico, Cuba and Central and South America but what she failed to mention was that the term has existed for centuries.

Back then, there wasn't a private or public sector that had a uniform way of collecting data on the Hispanic community, so a committee was formed and it opted not to use Latino because, if taken literally, it could include Europeans of Latin origin.

The goal was to accurately account for this growing and discriminated against population so laws could be implemented to help with their needs as well as trace their accomplishments.

The term Latino finally came to fruition in the 2000 census as a more inclusive way to include mixed races known as "mestizo" or "mulato" in Central and South America.

In short, Hispanic refers to language and Latino refers to geography.

One reason for my ambivalence with both these terms is that I 25 didn't grow up using either one.

I was born and raised in New Jersey by my Peruvian immigrant parents in a predominantly Hispanic community where everyone identified

CHAPTER 8 FOCUS

with their family's country of origin. I was Peruvian for the better half of my life and it's perhaps why I use the terms interchangeably and have no preference.

I'm not alone.

Most Hispanics in the United States prefer to use their country of origin to describe themselves most often. About half said they have no preference for either term but for those who did, Hispanic was preferred over "Latino," according to the Pew Research Center.

"For example, in California, the state with the largest Hispanic population, 30% say they prefer 'Hispanic' and 17% say they prefer the term 'Latino,'" according to Pew. The results were similar in Florida and New York.

30   The only exception is Texas where there was an overwhelming preference for "Hispanic." Among Hispanic Texans, 46% prefer the term Hispanic, while 8% say they prefer Latino.

But this wasn't always the case.

"There was a time when Latino was primarily used in the West Coast and Hispanic on the East Coast," said Mark Hugo Lopez, director of Hispanic Research at the Pew Research Center.

The use of both pan-ethnic terms are unique to the United States, Lopez added, as is the ongoing identity debate on which term to use.

## Latino vs. Hispanic on social media

Latinos are the most active of all ethnic groups on social media networking sites—Hispanic adults topping at 72%, followed by African Americans at 68% and whites at 65%—and CNN recently looked into which term was used more often and in what state across the country.

35   Even though Pew found that Hispanic was preferred over Latino when it came to identity, in the past year, CNN found that Latino was mentioned more on Twitter than Hispanic.

\* \* \*

"From what I've seen, the term Hispanic inspires more rage than Latino," said Adrian Carrasquillo, former social media manager at NBC Latino and now editor of Latino coverage for BuzzFeed.

"For a long time the Latino community has been fragmented, but now they are starting to have more cohesion and the rise of Latino is bringing people together more," he added.

The term's popularity may also have to do with the sudden surge of niche sites that contain the term, like Fox *New Latino* or The Huffington Post's *LatinoVoices* or two new magazines: *Cosmopolitan for Latinas* and *Glam Belleza Latina*.

CNN found the states where Google users searched the most for the term Latino from 2011–2014 were Virginia, California, Texas, Florida, Arizona and New York. The states with the highest Google searches for

Hispanic were New Mexico, Texas, District of Columbia, Florida and Arizona.

Google searches for Hispanic have declined over the past 10 years, 40 while searches for Latino have remained steady and even seen an uptick in the past two to three years. The only exception each year was during Hispanic Heritage Month.

"Groups like Latinos in Social Media and niche Latino sites that have launched recently have a lot to do with Latino being used more than Hispanic, but Latino refers to flavors, people and music. You don't hear people say 'Hispanic music,' they say 'Latino music,' " said Joe Kutchera, author of *Latino Link: Building Brands Online with Hispanic Communities and Content.*

"Latino media outlets have turned to Latino more because the term feels more inclusive, but that can always change. Younger generations are generally more accepting and don't care as much about these labels," Kutchera added.

Such was the case for Lance Rios when he started the popular Latino-based community Facebook page Being Latino. He said he realized Latino held more weight than Hispanic because it was a term embraced within the community.

"Twenty years ago Chicanos[2] were Chicanos, and Boricuas[3] were Boricuas but now it's different," Rios said. "Latino encompasses many more who can identify with having parents from different parts of Latin America."

## That annoying question: Where are you from?

Marco Perez, founder of the United Latino Professionals, has developed 45 a good-natured sense of humor when he is asked a question that many Latinos often hear: Where are you from?

Perez said the question doesn't bother him much anymore.

"I just say I was born in Guatemala but was raised in New York since I was toddler so I identify myself more with 'American' culture," Perez said.

It's clearly not a one-word answer for Perez but not as complicated as some make it out to be.

"Their reaction always depends on who it is, their level of education and what part of the country I'm in. But I get reactions such as, 'No, I mean ethnic origin,' but in many cases they simply leave it at an awkward, 'Oh OK,'" Perez said.

There are a couple of reasons why this question is irritating to many 50 Latinos. It implies that the person being asked is a foreigner when he or she, or his or her family, could have easily been in the United States for several generations.

[2]Mexican Americans. [Eds.]
[3]Puerto Ricans. [Eds.]

It also inevitably puts Latinos in a box, making them feel singled out and forced to justify their American-ness.

Before I knew any better, the question also made me feel foreign, so I always had my Americana spiel ready to go: "Yes, I'm Peruvian but I was born and raised in New Jersey. And, I went to Rutgers, and watched 'Full House' and 'Saved by the Bell' growing up. I love apple pie and spend Fourth of July weekend down the shore, etc."

The only time I feel like I'm identifying with the Hispanic or Latino label is when I'm around non-Latinos or filling out the census survey.

## Living in two worlds

With all the "Latino boom" talk, I realized I am a part of the population that isn't just part of the changing face of America but that also is altering its economic landscape.

55    You've heard the statistics: Latinos have a $1 trillion buying power only expected to grow. The Latino vote helped Obama get elected in 2008 and 2012. They're one out of every six people, one out of every four babies born each year.

The Hispanic population accounted for more than half of the country's growth in the past decade as well as 95% of the teen population growth through 2020. And, by 2050, Latinos are projected to make up 30% of the U.S. population.

That's what Hispanic marketing expert Chiqui Cartagena calls the duality of the Latino reality.

"From the grocery aisle where you pick up your Corona beer and your dulce de leche ice cream, to the Billboard charts where Pitbull, Marc Anthony and Jennifer Lopez routinely dominate, to the lunch you order at Chipotle...the Latino effect is everywhere," wrote Cartagena, the vice president of corporate marketing for Univision Cartagena, in an op-ed for CNN.

When companies talk about the Hispanic market, they are referring to the bilingual Latino who has embraced both cultures, eats pizza and tacos, and the growing share of Hispanics who prefer to consume their news in English from television, print, radio and Internet outlets.

60    But Pew also found that most Latinos acknowledge the importance of speaking Spanish and found that more than 34 million Hispanics ages 5 and older spoke Spanish at home, which may be the reason why English and Spanish have influenced each other so much.

Language isn't the only aspect of Latino culture to keep in mind when speaking to this growing community in the United States. It's also important to know that Latinos are not a monolithic culture.

While a large percentage of the Hispanic market is of Mexican origin, there are still two dozen other nationalities that make up America's Latino population. Also, Latinos come in all shapes, complexions and sizes.

Glenda Guevara has little patience for stereotypes these days.

"I now take the 'where are you from?' as a teaching moment," said Guevara, who was born in El Salvador. "But I do get furious when I'm told that I can't be from El Salvador because I don't fit the 'look.'"

Without completely losing her cool, Guevara continually responds 65 by asking, "What exactly does an El Salvadoran look like? Please tell me what my people should look like?"

Latin America's diverse racial demographics are the result of a mixed-race background of European, African and indigenous cultures.

All the attention Latinos have gotten over the years has come with its fair share of stereotypes and misconceptions, some I'm able to laugh off and some I wish I could wave a magic wand and change immediately, like:

Being asked to say something in Spanish (Nope, I'm not here solely for your entertainment.), to explain where exactly Peru is (Don't admit the little geography you know.), if I know someone you once met in Peru (It's a big country, the chances are impossible.), if I'm a U.S. citizen (That's never, ever appropriate.), and—my personal favorite—introducing me to your friend from a Latin American country because you believe we will hit it off. (Common backgrounds don't necessarily mean you are introducing me to my future bestie.)

These awkward and often staggering encounters only confirm how ambiguous Latinos' collective identity is to those on the outside.

But if waving that wand meant having to alter who I am or how I 70 move seamlessly between two worlds, then I'd hold back. I can only hope that as the Hispanic community continues to grow, so will a more defined identity.

## Responding to Reading

MyWritingLab™

1. According to Rodriguez, what traits do Latinos share?
2. What differences among Latinos does Rodriguez identify? How does she explain why these differences exist?
3. **Rhetorical Analysis** In paragraphs 11 through 33, Rodriguez explains why some groups prefer *Hispanic* while others prefer *Latino*. Summarize the two groups' positions. Do you think Rodriguez should have explained why she uses the term *Latino* in this essay? What do you think John H. McWhorter (p. 305) might think of her use of this term?

## Writing about Reading

MyWritingLab™

1. Given all the differences among Latinos that Rodriguez identifies, do you think there is really a distinctive "Latino culture"? Why or why not?
2. **Writing with Sources** Research the history of the US government's decision to adopt the term *Hispanic* and the reactions of various Latino groups and individuals to this term. Based on what you find in your research, do you think there can (or should be) one term to describe all people of Latino heritage? If so, what term, and why? If not, why not?

CHAPTER 8 FOCUS

# WHY RACE ISN'T AS "BLACK" AND "WHITE" AS WE THINK

## Brent Staples

### 1951–

*After earning a Ph.D. in psychology from the University of Chicago in 1977, Brent Staples turned to journalism, writing for the* Chicago Sun-Times *and the* New York Times. *In 1990, he joined the editorial board of the* New York Times, *where his columns now appear regularly. His memoir* Parallel Time *(1994), which was inspired by his brother's murder in a dispute over a cocaine deal, describes Staples's own internal struggles. In the following essay, he considers the ways in which we live in a post-racial society.*

People have occasionally asked me how a black person came by a "white" name like Brent Staples. One letter writer ridiculed it as "an anchorman's name" and accused me of making it up. For the record, it's a British name—and the one my parents gave me. "Staples" probably arrived in my family's ancestral home in Virginia four centuries ago with the British settlers.

The earliest person with that name we've found—Richard Staples—was hacked to death by Powhatan Indians not far from Jamestown in 1622. The name moved into the 18th century with Virginians like John Staples, a white surveyor who worked in Thomas Jefferson's home county, Albemarle, not far from the area where my family was enslaved.

The black John Staples who married my paternal great-great-grandmother just after Emancipation—and became the stepfather of her children—could easily have been a Staples family slave. The transplanted Britons who had owned both sides of my family had given us more than a preference for British names. They had also given us their DNA. In what was an almost everyday occurrence at the time, my great-great-grandmothers on both sides gave birth to children fathered by white slave masters.

I've known all this for a long time, and was not surprised by the results of a genetic screening performed by DNAPrint Genomics, a company that traces ancestral origins to far-flung parts of the globe. A little more than half of my genetic material came from sub-Saharan Africa—common for people who regard themselves as black—with slightly more than a quarter from Europe.

The result that knocked me off my chair showed that one-fifth of my    5
ancestry is Asian. Poring over the charts and statistics, I said out loud,
"This has got to be a mistake."

That's a common response among people who are tested. Ostensibly white people who always thought of themselves as 100 percent European find they have substantial African ancestry. People who regard themselves as black sometimes discover that the African ancestry is a minority portion of their DNA.

These results are forcing people to re-examine the arbitrary calculations our culture uses to decide who is "white" and who is "black."

As with many things racial, this story begins in the slave-era South, where sex among slaves, masters and mistresses got started as soon as the first slave ship sailed into Jamestown Harbor in 1619. By the time of the American Revolution, there was a visible class of light-skinned black people who no longer looked or sounded African. Free mulattos, emancipated by guilt-ridden fathers, may have accounted for up to three-quarters of the tiny free-black population before the Revolution.

By the eve of the Civil War, the swarming numbers of mixed-race slaves on Southern plantations had become a source of constant anguish to planters' wives, who knew quite well where those racially ambiguous children were coming from.

Faced with widespread fear that racial distinctions were losing sig-    10
nificance, the South decided to define the problem away. People with any ascertainable black ancestry at all were defined as black under the law and stripped of basic rights. The "one drop" laws defined as black even people who were blond and blue-eyed and appeared white.

Black people snickered among themselves and worked to subvert segregation at every turn. Thanks to white ancestry spread throughout the black community, nearly every family knew of someone born black who successfully passed as white to get access to jobs, housing and public accommodations that were reserved for white people only. Black people who were not quite light enough to slip undetected into white society billed themselves as Greek, Spanish, Portuguese, Italian, South Asian, Native American—you name it. These defectors often married into ostensibly white families at a time when interracial marriage was either illegal or socially stigmatized.

Those of us who grew up in the 1950's and 60's read black-owned magazines and newspapers that praised the racial defectors as pioneers while mocking white society for failing to detect them. A comic newspaper column by the poet Langston Hughes—titled "Why Not Fool Our White Folks?"—typified the black community's sense of smugness about knowing the real racial score. In keeping with this history, many black people I know find it funny when supposedly white Americans profess shock at the emergence of blackness in the family tree. But genetic testing holds plenty of surprises for black folks, too.

CHAPTER 8 FOCUS

Which brings me back to my Asian ancestry. It comes as a surprise, given that my family's oral histories contain not a single person who is described as Asian. More testing on other family members should clarify the issue, but for now, I can only guess. This ancestry could well have come through a 19th-century ancestor who was incorrectly described as Indian, often a catchall category at the time.

The test results underscore what anthropologists have said for eons: racial distinctions as applied in this country are social categories and not scientific concepts. In addition, those categories draw hard, sharp distinctions among groups of people who are more alike than they are different. The ultimate point is that none of us really know who we are, ancestrally speaking. All we ever really know is what our parents and grandparents have told us.

## Responding to Reading                     MyWritingLab™

1. What do the following pieces of information lead you to conclude about Staples's racial heritage?

   - Two of his great-great-grandmothers had children by white slave masters.

   - About half of his genetic material is from sub-Saharan Africa.

   - About a quarter of his genetic material is from Europe.

   - Twenty percent of his ancestry is Asian.

2. In his conclusion, Staples points out that "racial distinctions as applied in this country are social categories and not scientific concepts" (14). Do you think his conclusion suggests an optimistic or pessimistic view of future race relations? Explain.

3. **Rhetorical Analysis**   Given what we learn about Staples's roots, do you think *black* is the most appropriate term he could use to describe his racial identity? On what grounds would John H. McWhorter (p. 305) agree with this choice?

## Writing about Reading                     MyWritingLab™

1. In paragraph 7, Staples says that results of DNA analysis are "forcing people to re-examine the arbitrary calculations our culture uses to decide who is 'white' and who is 'black.'" Do you agree that the re-examination he refers to is actually occurring, or do you believe the "arbitrary calculations" will continue to rule?

2. **Writing with Sources**   What can you find out about your own racial, religious, and cultural heritage? Interview several older relatives, and consult family genealogical records or other documents if available. Then, write an essay in which you trace your heritage and define your identity.

# WHY I'M BLACK, NOT AFRICAN AMERICAN
## John H. McWhorter
### 1965–

*A Manhattan Institute scholar and a contributing editor to the Institute's* City Journal, *John H. McWhorter teaches linguistics at the Center for American Studies at Columbia University. McWhorter is also a contributing editor at the* New Republic *and* TheRoot.com *and the author of numerous books on language, race, culture, and music, including, most recently,* The Language Hoax: Why the World Looks the Same in Any Language *(2014). His work has appeared in numerous publications, such as the* Chronicle of Higher Education, *the* Los Angeles Times, New York *magazine, the* New York Times, *the* Wall Street Journal, *and the* Washington Post. *In the following essay, McWhorter considers the cultural significance of the terms we use to define racial identity.*

It's time we descendants of slaves brought to the United States let go of the term "African American" and go back to calling ourselves Black—with a capital B.

Modern America is home now to millions of immigrants who were born in Africa. Their cultures and identities are split between Africa and the United States. They have last names like Onwughalu and Senkofa. They speak languages like Wolof, Twi, Yoruba and Hausa, and speak English with an accent. They were raised on African cuisine, music, dance and dress styles, customs and family dynamics. Their children often speak or at least understand their parents' native language.

Living descendants of slaves in America neither knew their African ancestors nor even have elder relatives who knew them. Most of us worship in Christian churches. Our cuisine is more southern U.S. than Senegalese. Starting with ragtime and jazz, we gave America intoxicating musical beats based on African conceptions of rhythm, but with melody and harmony based on Western traditions.

Also, we speak English. Black Americans' home speech is largely based on local dialects of England and Ireland. Africa echoes in the dialect only as a whisper, in certain aspects of sound and melody. A working-class black man in Cincinnati has more in common with a working-class white man in Providence than with a Ghanaian.

With the number of African immigrants in the U.S. nearly tripling since 1990, the use of "African American" is becoming increasingly strained. For example, Alan Keyes, the Republican Senate candidate in Illinois, has claimed that as a descendant of slaves, he is the "real" African American, compared with his Democratic rival, Barack Obama, who has an African father and white mother. And the reason Keyes and others are making arguments such as this is rather small, the idea being that "African American" should refer only to people with a

5

history of subordination in this country—as if African immigrants such as Amadou Diallo, who was killed by police while reaching for his wallet, or Caribbean ones such as torture victim Abner Louima have found the U.S. to be the Land of Oz.

We are not African to any meaningful extent, but we are not white either—and that is much of why Jesse Jackson's presentation of the term "African American" caught on so fast. It sets us apart from the mainstream. It carries an air of standing protest, a reminder that our ancestors were brought here against their will, that their descendants were treated like animals for centuries, and that we have come a long way since then.

But we need a way of sounding those notes with a term that, first, makes some sense and, second, does not insult the actual African Americans taking their place in our country. And our name must also celebrate our history here, in the only place that will ever be our home. To term ourselves as part "African" reinforces a sad implication: that our history is basically slave ships, plantations, lynching, fire hoses in Birmingham, and then South Central,[1] and that we need to look back to Mother Africa to feel good about ourselves.

But what about the black business districts that thrived across the country after slavery was abolished? What about Frederick Douglass, Ida B. Wells, W.E.B. Du Bois, Gwendolyn Brooks, Richard Wright and Thurgood Marshall, none born in Africa and all deeply American people? And while we're on Marshall, what about the civil rights revolution, a moral awakening that we gave to ourselves and the nation. My roots trace back to working-class Black people—Americans, not foreigners—and I'm proud of it. I am John Hamilton McWhorter the Fifth. Four men with my name and appearance, doing their best in a segregated America, came before me. They and their dearest are the heritage that I can feel in my heart, and they knew the sidewalks of Philadelphia and Atlanta, not Sierra Leone.

So, we will have a name for ourselves—and it should be Black. "Colored" and "Negro" had their good points but carry a whiff of *Plessy v. Ferguson* and Bull Connor[2] about them, so we will let them lie. "Black" isn't perfect, but no term is.

10    Meanwhile, the special value of "Black" is that it carries the same potent combination of pride, remembrance and regret that "African American" was designed for. Think of what James Brown meant with "Say it loud, I'm Black and I'm proud." And then imagine: "Say it loud, I'm African American and I'm proud."

Since the late 1980s, I have gone along with using "African American" for the same reason that we throw rice at a bride—because everybody else was doing it. But no more. From now on, in my writings on race

---

[1]The 1992 South Central Los Angeles race riots. [Eds.]

[2]The Birmingham, Alabama, Commissioner of Public Safety (1897–1973) who, in 1963, ordered police officers to use police dogs and fire hoses to break up civil rights demonstrations. [Eds.]

I will be returning to the word I grew up with, which reminds me of my true self and my ancestors who worked here to help make my life possible: Black.

## Responding to Reading

1. Why does McWhorter believe that *African American* is an inappropriate term for black Americans?
2. According to McWhorter, what negative associations does the term *African American* have? What positive connotations does he associate with *black*? Does he make a convincing argument for his characterization of these two terms?
3. **Rhetorical Analysis** Throughout this essay, McWhorter capitalizes the word *black* but not the word *white*. Why? What is your reaction to this stylistic decision?

## Writing about Reading

1. What different terms are used to identify the ethnic or racial group from which you draw your primary cultural identity? Which term do you prefer, and why?
2. **Writing with Sources** In paragraph 8, McWhorter lists six prominent men and women. Research the life and career of one of these people. Then, write an essay in which you apply McWhorter's criteria to help you decide whether the individual you chose should be considered *black* or *African American*.

# WIDENING THE FOCUS

## For Critical Reading and Writing

Referring specifically to the three readings in this chapter's Focus section (and possibly to additional sources as well), write an essay in which you answer the question, "Do Racial Distinctions Still Matter?"

## For Further Reading

The following readings can suggest additional perspectives for thinking and writing about the role of race and culture in American society.

- Linda Hogan, "Heritage" (p. 34)
- Laila Lalami, "My Fictional Grandparents" (p. 50)
- Brent Staples, "Just Walk On By" (p. 313)
- Henry Louis Gates, Jr., "Delusions of Grandeur" (p. 370)
- Martin Luther King, Jr., "Letter from Birmingham Jail" (p. 411)

Web Links

## For Focused Research

The diverse cultural makeup of the United States has defined the country since its inception. Today, the population of some cultural groups, such as Asian Americans and Hispanics, is growing exponentially. To gain greater insight into the various cultural groups in the United States, consult the PewResearchCenter's *Hispanic Trends* website as well as the website for Brigham Young University's McKay School of Education, which contains information on specific cultural groups. Then, write an essay about the fastest-growing cultural groups in the United States. Who is in the majority now, and who will be in the majority in 25 or 50 years? How do you think the growing population of these groups will change the United States? Support your points with information from the online resources you use.

## Beyond the Classroom

Survey ten classmates representing several different races, and ask them the following questions:

- Would you date a person of another race? Why or why not?
- Would you marry a person of another race? Why or why not?
- How would your parents react in each case?

Compare the responses you get from people of different races. Based on this very limited sample, do the respondents from one background seem more open to interracial dating and marriage than the respondents from another background? If so, how do you account for these differences? Write an essay that summarizes your conclusions.

## EXPLORING ISSUES AND IDEAS

MyWritingLab™
Visit Chapter 8, "Culture and Identity," in MyWritingLab to test your understanding of the chapter objectives.

### Culture and Identity

Write an essay in response to one of the following prompts, which are suitable for assignments that require the use of outside sources as well as for assignments that are not source-based.

1. Write an essay in which you define your cultural identity. With which group or groups do you identify most strongly, and why? Begin your essay by analyzing how one writer in this chapter views his or her personal cultural identity. Then, discuss how your own attitudes toward culture are like and unlike those held by the writer you chose.

2. Do you think there is a distinctly "American" culture? If so, what are its key characteristics? Do you think that this "American" culture will endure? Write an essay in which you answer these questions, using information from readings in this chapter to support your points.

3. Some writers represented in this chapter (for example, Judith Ortiz Cofer, p. 271) feel pulled in two directions, torn between their own culture and the "American" society in which they live. Do you believe this conflict can ever be resolved, or do you think first-generation Americans (and perhaps their children and even their children's children) will always feel torn?

4. Is it possible to identify equally with two cultures—for example, black and Latino, Christian and Asian, urban and Native American? Write an essay that answers this question, referring to one or more essays in this chapter as well as to your own experiences.

5. Write an extended definition of a culture that is not based on race, ethni-city, or religion—for example, business culture; hockey culture; or rural, suburban, or urban culture.

6. Many people believe that a "culture of poverty" exists in our nation. Define this culture, enumerating its features, and explain how and why members of this culture are set apart from mainstream culture. Refer to Melanie Scheller's essay (p. 283) in your discussion.

# 9

## THE AMERICAN DREAM

*In this chapter, you will learn to*
- analyze readings about the American Dream
- compose essays about the American Dream

The American Dream—a term popularized by James Truslow Adams in his 1931 book *The Epic of America*—today encompasses everything from political and religious freedom to equal access to education and equal opportunity in the workplace. For immigrants, particularly those escaping difficult or even dangerous conditions in their native countries, the dream has also meant political and religious freedom, freedom from discrimination and persecution, and a guarantee of safety. For generations, it has also meant the possibility of upward

African-American man at "colored" drinking fountain, Oklahoma City, OK, 1939

mobility, financial success, and, eventually, economic prosperity. However, for many Americans today, burdened by student loans, mortgage debt, medical bills, and unemployment, the dream can seem elusive. Middle-class wages are stagnating while the very rich get richer, and many feel they can no longer hope for a financially secure retirement. In fact, a 2014 survey revealed that 64 percent of Americans said they no longer believe in the American Dream.

Still, we pursue the American Dream. For some, this pursuit means struggling to overcome their status as newcomers or outsiders: to fit in, to belong, to be accepted. As they work toward their goals, however, some of these individuals must make painful decisions, for full participation in American society may mean assimilating: giving up language, custom, and culture and becoming more like others. Thus, although the American Dream may ultimately mean winning something, it can sometimes mean losing something as well.

For many people, an important part of the American Dream is the chance to reinvent themselves—the opportunity to become someone different, someone better. From Benjamin Franklin to Malcolm X, Americans have a long tradition of reinvention, which can involve anything from undertaking a program of self-improvement to undergoing a complete change of social identity.

In a free and mobile society, people can (theoretically, at least) become whatever they want to be. In the United States, reinvention has often come about through education and hard work, but Americans have also been able to change who they are and how they are perceived

President-elect Barack Obama saluted by US Capitol Police guards at his inauguration in January 2009

by changing their professions, their associations, or their places of residence. Along with this process of reinvention comes a constant self-analysis, as we Americans continue to question who we are and what we can become.

In this chapter's Focus section, "Is the American Dream Still Attainable?" (p. 338), Michael W. Kraus, Shai Davidai, and A. David Nussbaum, in "American Dream? Or Mirage?" discuss the relationship between upward mobility and the American Dream; Neal Gabler, in "The New American Dream," examines how the dream has changed for middle- and upper-middle-class Americans; and Robert D. Putnam, in "Crumbling American Dreams," considers whether the dream can be sustained in the future.

## —————— PREPARING TO READ AND WRITE ——————

As you read and prepare to write about the essays in this chapter , you may consider the following questions:

- What assumptions does the writer seem to have about his or her audience? How can you tell?

- Is the writer's primary purpose to define the American Dream? to explain his or her dream to others? to explore his or her own place in American society? to persuade readers to take action? something else?

- What genre is the writer using? For example, is the reading a proposal? a poem? a speech? How do the conventions of this genre influence the writer's choices?

- What appeals does the writer use? For example, does he or she appeal primarily to emotion or to reason? Is this the most effective appeal?

- What does the American Dream mean to the writer? Is the American Dream defined in social, political, economic, or cultural terms?

- Has the writer been able to achieve the American Dream? If so, by what means? If not, why not?

- What are the greatest obstacles that stand between the writer and the American Dream? Would you characterize these obstacles as primarily cultural, social, political, racial, economic, religious, or educational?

- Who do you think has the easiest access to the American Dream? For whom is access most difficult? Why?

- Is the writer looking at the United States from the point of view of an insider or an outsider?

- Does the writer want to change his or her status? to change the status of others? What steps, if any, does he or she take to do so? What additional steps could he or she take?

- Does the writer focus on his or her own pursuit of the American Dream or on what the dream means to a particular group—or to the nation?

- Does the writer speak as an individual or as a representative of a particular group?

- Which writers' views of the American Dream are most similar? most different? most like your own?

# JUST WALK ON BY

## Brent Staples

### 1951–

*Originally published in Ms. in 1986, the following essay conveys Staples's reactions to white people's images of black men. (See page 302 for Staples's biography.)*

My first victim was a woman—white, well dressed, probably in her early twenties. I came upon her late one evening on a deserted street in Hyde Park, a relatively affluent neighborhood in an otherwise mean, impoverished section of Chicago. As I swung onto the avenue behind her, there seemed to be a discreet, uninflammatory distance between us. Not so. She cast back a worried glance. To her, the youngish black man—a broad six feet two inches with a beard and billowing hair, both hands shoved into the pockets of a bulky military jacket—seemed menacingly close. After a few more quick glimpses, she picked up her pace and was soon running in earnest. Within seconds she disappeared into a cross street.

That was more than a decade ago. I was 22 years old, a graduate student newly arrived at the University of Chicago. It was in the echo of that terrified woman's footfalls that I first began to know the unwieldy inheritance I'd come into—the ability to alter public space in ugly ways. It was clear that she thought herself the quarry of a mugger, a rapist, or worse. Suffering a bout of insomnia, however, I was stalking sleep, not defenseless wayfarers. As a softy who is scarcely able to take a knife to a raw chicken—let alone hold it to a person's throat—I was surprised, embarrassed, and dismayed all at once. Her flight made me feel like an accomplice in tyranny. It also made it clear that I was indistinguishable from the muggers who occasionally seeped into the area from the surrounding ghetto. That first encounter, and those that followed, signified that a vast, unnerving gulf lay between nighttime pedestrians—particularly women—and me. And I soon gathered that being perceived as dangerous is a hazard in itself. I only needed to turn a corner into a dicey situation, or crowd some frightened, armed person in a foyer somewhere, or make an errant move after being pulled over by a policeman. Where fear and weapons meet—and they often do in urban America—there is always the possibility of death.

In that first year, my first away from my hometown, I was to become thoroughly familiar with the language of fear. At dark, shadowy intersections in Chicago, I could cross in front of a car stopped at a traffic light and elicit the *thunk, thunk, thunk, thunk* of the driver—black, white, male, or female—hammering down the door locks. On less traveled streets after dark, I grew accustomed to but never comfortable with people who crossed to the other side of the street rather than pass me. Then there were the standard unpleasantries with police, doormen, bouncers, cab drivers, and others whose business it is to screen out troublesome individuals *before* there is any nastiness.

I moved to New York nearly two years ago and I have remained an avid night walker. In central Manhattan, the near-constant crowd cover minimizes tense one-on-one street encounters. Elsewhere—visiting friends in SoHo, where sidewalks are narrow and tightly spaced buildings shut out the sky—things can get very taut indeed.

5      Black men have a firm place in New York mugging literature. Norman Podhoretz in his famed (or infamous) 1963 essay, "My Negro Problem—And Ours," recalls growing up in terror of black males; they "were tougher than we were, more ruthless," he writes—and as an adult on the Upper West Side of Manhattan, he continues, he cannot constrain his nervousness when he meets black men on certain streets. Similarly, a decade later, the essayist and novelist Edward Hoagland extols a New York where once "Negro bitterness bore down mainly on other Negroes." Where some see mere panhandlers, Hoagland sees "a mugger who is clearly screwing up his nerve to do more than just *ask* for money." But Hoagland has "the New Yorker's quickhunch posture for broken-field maneuvering," and the bad guy swerves away.

I often witness that "hunch posture," from women after dark on the warrenlike streets of Brooklyn where I live. They seem to set their faces on neutral and, with their purse straps strung across their chests bandolier style, they forge ahead as though bracing themselves against being tackled. I understand, of course, that the danger they perceive is not a hallucination. Women are particularly vulnerable to street violence, and young black males are drastically overrepresented among the perpetrators of that violence. Yet these truths are no solace against the kind of alienation that comes of being ever the suspect, against being set apart, a fearsome entity with whom pedestrians avoid making eye contact.

It is not altogether clear to me how I reached the ripe old age of 22 without being conscious of the lethality nighttime pedestrians attributed to me. Perhaps it was because in Chester, Pennsylvania, the small, angry industrial town where I came of age in the 1960s, I was scarcely noticeable against a backdrop of gang warfare, street knifings, and murders. I grew up one of the good boys, had perhaps a half-dozen fist fights. In retrospect, my shyness of combat has clear sources.

Many things go into the making of a young thug. One of those things is the consummation of the male romance with the power to intimidate. An infant discovers that random flailings send the baby bottle flying out of the crib and crashing to the floor. Delighted, the joyful babe repeats those motions again and again, seeking to duplicate the feat. Just so, I recall the points at which some of my boyhood friends were finally seduced by the perception of themselves as tough guys. When a mark cowered and surrendered his money without resistance, myth and reality merged—and paid off. It is, after all, only manly to embrace the power to frighten and intimidate. We, as men, are not supposed to give an inch of our lane on the highway; we are to seize the fighter's edge in work and in play and even in love; we are to be valiant in the face of hostile forces.

Unfortunately, poor and powerless young men seem to take all this nonsense literally. As a boy, I saw countless tough guys locked away; I have since buried several, too. They were babies, really—a teenage cousin, a brother of 22, a childhood friend in his mid-twenties—all gone down in episodes of bravado played out in the streets. I came to doubt the virtues of intimidation early on. I chose, perhaps even unconsciously, to remain a shadow—timid, but a survivor.

The fearsomeness mistakenly attributed to me in public places of- 10 ten has a perilous flavor. The most frightening of these confusions occurred in the late 1970s and early 1980s when I worked as a journalist in Chicago. One day, rushing into the office of a magazine I was writing for with a deadline story in hand, I was mistaken for a burglar. The office manager called security and, with an ad hoc posse, pursued me through the labyrinthine halls, nearly to my editor's door. I had no way of proving who I was. I could only move briskly toward the company of someone who knew me.

Another time I was on assignment for a local paper and killing time before an interview. I entered a jewelry store on the city's affluent Near North Side. The proprietor excused herself and returned with an enormous red Doberman pinscher straining at the end of a leash. She stood, the dog extended toward me, silent to my questions, her eyes bulging nearly out of her head. I took a cursory look around, nodded, and bade her good night. Relatively speaking, however, I never fared as badly as another black male journalist. He went to nearby Waukegan, Illinois, a couple of summers ago to work on a story about a murderer who was born there. Mistaking the reporter for the killer, police hauled him from his car at gunpoint and but for his press credentials would probably have tried to book him. Such episodes are not uncommon. Black men trade tales like this all the time.

In "My Negro Problem—And Ours," Podhoretz writes that the hatred he feels for blacks makes itself known to him through a variety of avenues—one being his discomfort with that "special brand of paranoid touchiness" to which he says blacks are prone. No doubt he is speaking here of black men. In time, I learned to smother the rage I felt at so often being taken for a criminal. Not to do so would surely have led to madness—via that special "paranoid touchiness" that so annoyed Podhoretz at the time he wrote the essay.

I began to take precautions to make myself less threatening. I move about with care, particularly late in the evening. I give a wide berth to nervous people on subway platforms during the wee hours, particularly when I have exchanged business clothes for jeans. If I happen to be entering a building behind some people who appear skittish, I may walk by, letting them clear the lobby before I return, so as not to seem to be following them. I have been calm and extremely congenial on those rare occasions when I've been pulled over by the police.

And on late-evening constitutionals along streets less traveled by, I employ what has proved to be an excellent tension-reducing measure: I whistle melodies from Beethoven and Vivaldi and the more popular classical composers. Even steely New Yorkers hunching toward nighttime destinations seem to relax, and occasionally they even join in the tune. Virtually everybody seems to sense that a mugger wouldn't be warbling bright, sunny selections from Vivaldi's *Four Seasons*. It is my equivalent of the cowbell that hikers wear when they know they are in bear country.

## Responding to Reading

MyWritingLab™

1. In paragraph 13, Staples suggests some strategies that he believes make him "less threatening." What else, if anything, do you think he could do? Do you believe he *should* adopt such strategies?

2. Although Staples says he arouses fear in others, he also admits that he himself feels fearful. Why? Do you think he has reason to be fearful? What does this sense of fear say about his access to the American Dream?

3. **Rhetorical Analysis**   Staples speaks quite matter-of-factly about the fear he inspires. Why do you think he chose to use a direct, measured tone here? What other options did he have? Was this the best choice?

## Writing about Reading

MyWritingLab™

1. Does your experience support Staples's assumption that black men have the "ability to alter public space" (2)? Explain. Do you believe white men also have this ability?

2. **Writing with Sources**   Research various American cities' "stop and frisk" laws and the objections to (as well as support for) these laws. What connection do you see between such ordinances and Staples's comments about people's view of him as threatening? What is your view of these laws?

# DR. KING'S RIGHTEOUS FURY

## Jonathan Rieder

*A sociology professor at Barnard College, Jonathan Rieder is the author of three books:* Canarsie: The Jews and Italians of Brooklyn against Liberalism *(1985),* The Word of the Lord Is upon Me: The Righteous Performance of Martin Luther King, Jr. *(2008), and* Gospel of Freedom: Martin Luther King, Jr.'s Letter from Birmingham Jail and the Struggle That Changed a Nation *(2013). His work has appeared in publications such as the* Huffington Post, *the* Los Angeles Times, The New Yorker, *the* New York Times, *the* New York Times Book Review, Slate, *and the* Washington Post. *In the following essay, Rieder considers what the American Dream has meant to King and to other African Americans.*

Chris Rock caused a stir last Fourth of July when he tweeted, "Happy white peoples independence day the slaves weren't free but I'm sure they enjoyed fireworks." Mr. Rock's tweet may not have topped the Rev. Jeremiah A. Wright Jr.'s "God damn America" sermon, but both sentiments are of a piece, and both seem a far cry from the Rev. Dr. Martin Luther King Jr.'s appeal to the American dream and his embrace of "the magnificent words of the Constitution and the Declaration of Independence."

But this view of King as an ardent proponent of American exceptionalism fails to capture a significant part of his thinking, a set of ideas embodied in one of his most famous works, "Letter from Birmingham Jail." What we remember today as a stirring piece about freedom and justice was also a furious reading of American history and an equally indignant attitude toward King's white contemporaries.

Arrested on April 12, 1963, during an epic struggle to desegregate Birmingham, Ala., King was in jail when he read the statement of eight white moderate clergymen who criticized the demonstrations as "untimely," branded King "extreme" and chided the protesters for precipitating violence.

King's letter, written on scraps of paper smuggled out of the jail and first made public on April 16, 1963, began as irate jottings of rebuttal. In its final form, though, the indignation was not evident in every sentence: the opening words, "My dear fellow clergymen," brimmed with precious gentility.

Later, King offered reasoned justifications for civil disobedience and rarefied nods to the theologians Martin Buber and Paul Tillich. And he evoked universalism with the proclamation, "Injustice anywhere is a threat to justice everywhere." 5

Yet black anger, not fancy philosophy, was the driving force behind the letter. You don't have to be a literary critic to sense the cold fury:

"For years now, I have heard the word 'Wait!' It rings in the ear of every Negro with piercing familiarity."

In a line worthy of Malcolm X decrying white "tricknology," King savaged what he saw as white mendacity: "This 'Wait!' has almost always meant 'Never.' " His target was not the Ku Klux Klan, but a vast majority of "moderate" Americans, including the Kennedy administration, who had urged him to postpone the protests. Presumably, they meant never, too.

Hardly naïve about the power of moral appeal to stir the white conscience, King flirted with the idea that whites were virtually incapable of empathizing with the black plight. "I should have realized that few members of the oppressor race can understand the deep groans or passionate yearnings of the oppressed race."

In a mass meeting just days after getting out of jail, he depicted blacks as alone in an indifferent nation: "Don't you ever think that anything is going to be given to us in this struggle."

10      Toward the end of the letter, King wrote, "I have no fear about the outcome of our struggle in Birmingham." Where did he find such certainty? Ultimately, it was rooted in his belief, stated elsewhere, that "the Lord will make a way out of no way" and "there is a balm in Gilead."[1] Yet in his letter King offered none of this. It was as if he viewed the white ministers as unworthy of spiritual sharing. (In a mass meeting a few weeks later, he would gibe, "They are all pitiful.")

Nor did King draw confidence from the idea that America was destined for democracy. While he did mention that "we will reach the goal of freedom in Birmingham…because the goal of America is freedom," this is a brief aside and not his central point. Rather, King found optimism in his deep faith in black people. At its core, the "Letter" was a proclamation of black self-sufficiency.

King began his paean to black majesty with the line "abused and scorned though we may be," a reference to the slavery-era spiritual "'Buked and Scorned," which evokes the slaves' suffering and their conviction that "Jesus died to set me free."

It was a touchstone for King, a link to his revered forebears, and one he referenced repeatedly. "Abused and scorned though we may be, our destiny is tied up with America's destiny. Before the Pilgrims landed at Plymouth we were here. Before the pen of Jefferson etched across the pages of history the mighty words of the Declaration of Independence, we were here."

Reading those lines on paper barely hints at the force of those stanzas as King usually spoke them: a defiant assertion of a black right to belong that rested on something more primal than, and prior to, the nation's official documents and civic heroes.

---

[1] A Biblical reference signifying a medicinal cure or salvation through Jesus Christ; also a traditional African American spiritual. [Eds.]

In the "Letter," King immediately sidled from the "we were here" 15
refrain into another of his favorite passages of ancestor worship: "For
more than two centuries our forebears labored in this country without
wages; they made cotton king; they built the homes of their masters
while suffering gross injustice and shameful humiliation. And yet out
of a bottomless vitality they continued to thrive and develop. If the
inexpressible cruelties of slavery could not stop us, the opposition we
now face will surely fail."

It is a mistake, then, to make too much of King's occasional references to the American dream. He read American history in the light
of the black experience of it. The labor of a slave was not the labor of
a lonely individual who sought the pristine state of American nature,
worked the land and acquired property. The story of the slaves was
of a people in "exile," King said, whose skin color and forced labor
made for a different kind of "exceptionalism": They were other people's property, the instruments of somebody else's dream.

King continued with this theme to the end of his life. "They kept
us in slavery 244 years in this country, and they said they freed us from
slavery," King recalled in a 1968 speech, shortly before he was killed,
"but they didn't give us any land...And they haven't given us anything! After making our foreparents work and labor for 244 years—for
nothing! Didn't pay 'em a cent."

"We hold these truths to be self-evident, that all men are endowed
by their creator with inalienable rights. That's a beautiful creed,"
King told his crowd. It is easy to read such sentences in "Letter from
Birmingham Jail" and other works by King and leave it at that. But it
is vital to read what he said next: "America has never lived up to it."

## Responding to Reading
MyWritingLab™

1. Rieder opens his essay with a quotation by Chris Rock. Is this an effective
   introduction to the argument that follows? Why or why not?
2. In paragraph 16, Rieder says, "It is a mistake, ... to make too much of
   King's occasional references to the American Dream." Why does Rieder
   believe that this is "a mistake"? How do you suppose Rieder would expect
   King to have defined the American Dream?
3. **Rhetorical Analysis**   Rieder's primary purpose in this essay is to correct
   what he believes is a common misconception about King's "Letter from
   Birmingham Jail." What is this misconception? What do you think Rieder
   hopes to achieve by re-examining King's writing?

## Writing about Reading
MyWritingLab™

1. Look through the text of "Letter from Birmingham Jail" (p. 411), and
   choose a passage to analyze closely. Do you see the passage as "a stirring
   piece about freedom and justice" or as "a furious reading of American
   history" (2)?

2. **Writing with Sources**   Watch Jeremiah A. Wright's sermon (mentioned in paragraph 1) on YouTube, and read a transcript of his words. Then, do the same with Martin Luther King, Jr.'s famous "I Have a Dream" speech. In an essay, analyze the similarities and differences between the two speeches, focusing on their content, rhetorical strategies, and delivery.

# THE DECLARATION OF INDEPENDENCE

## Thomas Jefferson

### *1743–1826*

*Thomas Jefferson—lawyer, statesman, diplomat, architect, scientist, politician, writer, education theorist, and musician—graduated from William and Mary College in 1762 and went on to lead an impressive political life. Jefferson served as a member of the Continental Congress, governor of Virginia, secretary of state to George Washington, and vice president to John Adams and also served two terms as the U.S. president (1801–1809), during which he oversaw the Louisiana Purchase. After retiring from public office, Jefferson founded the University of Virginia in 1819. He was an avid collector of books and owned nearly ten thousand, which later became the foundation of the Library of Congress. A firm believer in reason and the natural rights of individuals, Jefferson drafted the Declaration of Independence, which was later amended by the Continental Congress. In this document, he presents the colonists' grievances in order to justify their decision to declare their independence from England.*

## In Congress, July 4, 1776: The Unanimous Declaration of the Thirteen United States of America

When in the Course of human events it becomes necessary for one people to dissolve the political bands which have connected them with another, and to assume among the powers of the earth, the separate and equal station to which the Laws of Nature and of Nature's God entitle them, a decent respect to the opinions of mankind requires that they should declare the causes which impel them to the separation.

We hold these truths to be self-evident, that all men are created equal, that they are endowed by their Creator with certain unalienable Rights, that among these are Life, Liberty and the pursuit of Happiness. That to secure these rights, Governments are instituted among Men, deriving their just powers from the consent of the governed. That whenever any Form of Government becomes destructive of these ends, it is the Right of the People to alter or to abolish it, and to institute new Government, laying its foundation on such principles and organizing its powers in such form, as to them shall seem most likely to effect their Safety and Happiness. Prudence, indeed, will dictate that Governments long established should not be changed for light and transient causes; and accordingly all experience hath shewn, that mankind are more disposed to suffer, while evils are sufferable, than to right themselves by abolishing the forms to which they are accustomed. But when a long train of abuses and usurpations, pursuing invariably the same Object, evinces a design to reduce them under absolute Despotism, it is their right, it is their duty, to throw off such Government, and to provide new Guards for their future security. Such has been the patient sufferance of these Colonies; and such is now the necessity which constrains them to alter their former Systems of Governors. The history of the present King of Great Britain is a history of repeated injuries and usurpations, all having in direct object the establishment of an absolute Tyranny over these States. To prove this, let Facts be submitted to a candid world.

He has refused his Assent to Laws, the most wholesome and necessary for the public good.

He has forbidden his Governors to pass laws of immediate and pressing importance, unless suspended in their operation till his Assent should be obtained; and when so suspended, he has utterly neglected to attend to them.

He has refused to pass other Laws for the accommodation of large districts of people, unless those people would relinquish the right of Representation in the Legislature, a right inestimable to them and formidable to tyrants only.

He has called together legislative bodies at places unusual, uncomfortable, and distant from the depository of their Public Records, for the sole purpose of fatiguing them into compliance with his measures.

He has dissolved Representative Houses repeatedly, for opposing with manly firmness his invasions on the rights of the people.

He has refused for a long time, after such dissolutions, to cause others to be elected; whereby the Legislative Powers, incapable of Annihilation, have returned to the People at large for their exercise; the State remaining in the mean time exposed to all the dangers of invasion from without, and convulsions within.

He has endeavored to prevent the population of these States; for that purpose obstructing the Laws for Naturalization of Foreigners; refusing to pass others to encourage their migration hither, and raising the conditions of new Appropriations of Lands.

He has obstructed the Administration of Justice, by refusing his Assent to Laws for establishing Judiciary Powers.

He has made Judges dependent on his Will alone, for the tenure of their offices, and the amount and payment of their salaries.

He has erected a multitude of New Offices, and sent hither swarms of Officers to harass our people, and eat out their substance.

He has kept among us, in times of peace, Standing Armies without the Consent of our legislatures.

He has affected to render the Military independent of and superior to the Civil Power.

15    He has combined with others to subject us to a jurisdiction foreign to our constitution, and unacknowledged by our laws; giving his Assent to their Acts of pretended Legislation: For quartering large bodies of armed troops among us: For protecting them, by a mock Trial, from punishment for any Murders which they should commit on the Inhabitants of these States: For cutting off our Trade with all parts of the world: For imposing Taxes on us without our Consent: For depriving us in many cases, of the benefits of Trial by Jury; For transporting us beyond Seas to be tried for pretended offenses: For abolishing the free System of English Laws in a neighboring Province, establishing therein an Arbitrary government, and enlarging its Boundaries so as to render it at once an example and fit instrument for introducing the same absolute rule into these Colonies: For taking away our Charters, abolishing our most valuable Laws and altering fundamentally the Forms of our Governments: For suspending our own Legislatures, and declaring themselves invested with power to legislate for us in all cases whatsoever.

He has abdicated Government here, by declaring us out of his Protection and waging War against us.

He has plundered our seas, ravaged our Coasts, burnt our towns, and destroyed the lives of our people.

He is at this time transporting large Armies of foreign Mercenaries to complete the works of death, desolation and tyranny, already begun with circumstances of Cruelty & Perfidy scarcely paralleled in the most barbarous ages, and totally unworthy the Head of a civilized nation.

He has constrained our fellow Citizens taken Captive on the high Seas to bear Arms against their Country, to become the executioners of their friends and Brethren, or to fall themselves by their Hands.

20    He has excited domestic insurrections amongst us, and has endeavored to bring on the inhabitants of our frontiers, the merciless Indian Savages, whose known rule of warfare, is an undistinguished destruction of all ages, sexes, and conditions.

In every stage of these Oppressions We have Petitioned for Redress in the most humble terms: Our repeated Petitions have been answered only by repeated injury. A Prince, whose character is thus marked by every act which may define a Tyrant, is unfit to be the ruler of a free people.

Nor have We been wanting in attention to our British brethren. We have warned them from time to time of attempts by their legislature to extend an unwarrantable jurisdiction over us. We have reminded them of the circumstances of our emigration and settlement here. We have appealed to their native justice and magnanimity, and we have conjured them by the ties of our common kindred to disavow these usurpations, which would inevitably interrupt our connections and correspondence. They too have been deaf to the voice of justice and of consanguinity. We must, therefore, acquiesce in the necessity, which denounces our Separation, and hold them, as we hold the rest of mankind, Enemies in War, in Peace Friends.

We, therefore, the Representatives of the United States of America, in General Congress, Assembled, appealing to the Supreme Judge of the world for the rectitude of our intentions, do, in the Name, and by Authority of the good People of these Colonies, solemnly publish and declare, That these United Colonies are, and of Right ought to be free and independent states; that they are Absolved from all Allegiance to the British Crown, and that all political connection between them and the State of Great Britain, is and ought to be totally dissolved; and that as Free and Independent States, they have full Power to levy War, conclude Peace, contract Alliances, establish Commerce, and to do all other Acts and Things which Independent States may of right do. And for the support of this Declaration, with a firm reliance on the protection of Divine Providence, we mutually pledge to each other our Lives, our Fortunes, and our sacred Honor.

## Responding to Reading

MyWritingLab™

1. The Declaration of Independence was written in the eighteenth century, a time when logic and reason were thought to be the supreme achievements of human beings. Do you think this document appeals just to reason, or does it also appeal to the emotions?
2. Do you think it is fair, as some have done, to accuse the framers of the Declaration of Independence of being racist? of being sexist?
3. **Rhetorical Analysis**  Paragraphs 3–20 consist of a litany of grievances, expressed in parallel language. What did Jefferson hope to achieve with this use of parallelism for these grievances? Do you think he achieved this goal?

## Writing about Reading

MyWritingLab™

1. Rewrite five or six sentences from paragraphs 3–20 of the Declaration of Independence in modern English, substituting contemporary examples for the injustices Jefferson enumerates.
2. **Writing with Sources**  Look online for Elizabeth Cady Stanton's Declaration of Sentiments and Resolutions, presented in 1848 at the Women's Rights Convention in Seneca Falls, NY. Then, write an essay in which you compare this document with the Declaration of Independence in terms of content, goals, and rhetorical strategies.

# THE GETTYSBURG ADDRESS
## Abraham Lincoln
### *1809–1865*

*The sixteenth president of the United States, Abraham Lincoln led the Union to victory in the American Civil War. Known as the "Great Emancipator," Lincoln freed the slaves of the Confederacy with the Emancipation Proclamation, which was issued on January 1, 1863. On November 19, 1863, Lincoln delivered the Gettysburg Address during the dedication of the National Cemetery at Gettysburg, Pennsylvania, where the Battle of Gettysburg had claimed more than 40,000 Union and Confederate lives in July of that year.*

Four score and seven years ago our fathers brought forth on this continent, a new nation, conceived in Liberty, and dedicated to the proposition that all men are created equal.

Now we are engaged in a great civil war, testing whether that nation, or any nation so conceived and so dedicated, can long endure. We are met on a great battle-field of that war. We have come to dedicate a portion of that field, as a final resting place for those who here gave their lives that that nation might live. It is altogether fitting and proper that we should do this.

But, in a larger sense, we can not dedicate—we can not consecrate—we can not hallow—this ground. The brave men, living and dead, who struggled here, have consecrated it, far above our poor power to add or detract. The world will little note, nor long remember what we say here, but it can never forget what they did here. It is for us the living, rather, to be dedicated here to the unfinished work which they who fought here have thus far so nobly advanced. It is rather for us to be here dedicated to the great task remaining before us—that from these honored dead we take increased devotion to that cause for which they gave the last full measure of devotion—that we here highly resolve that these dead shall not have died in vain—that this nation, under God, shall have a new birth of freedom—and that government of the people, by the people, for the people, shall not perish from the earth.

## Responding to Reading

MyWritingLab™

1. To Lincoln and his audience, what is the "great task remaining before us" (3)?
2. In paragraph 3, Lincoln says, "The world will little note, nor long remember what we say here, but it can never forget what they [the brave soldiers] did here." Is he correct? Explain.
3. **Rhetorical Analysis** The first paragraph of this speech looks back, the second paragraph describes the present, and the third paragraph looks ahead. Using contemporary conversational style, write a one-sentence summary of each of these paragraphs. What makes this structure so effective?

## Writing about Reading

1.  What "great tasks" do you believe still face our nation's leaders? Which of these do you think will still be a challenge in fifty years? Why?
2.  **Writing with Sources**  What was Lincoln's purpose when he delivered the Gettysburg Address in 1863? How was the speech received at the time? How have more recent scholars and historians assessed its content and its impact? Write an essay that traces the influence of this famous speech over the years.

# OUTLAW: MY LIFE IN AMERICA AS AN UNDOCUMENTED IMMIGRANT

## Jose Antonio Vargas

### 1981–

*Jose Antonio Vargas is a Filipino journalist and a former reporter for the* Washington Post. *Vargas was a member of the team of journalists who won the Pulitzer Prize in 2008 for breaking news reporting about the Virginia Tech campus shootings. He also started the online project* Define American *to promote "a new conversation about immigration." In the following essay, originally published in 2011 in the* New York Times Magazine, *Vargas reveals himself as an "undocumented immigrant" who has been living illegally in the United States since he was twelve years old.*

One August morning nearly two decades ago, my mother woke me and put me in a cab. She handed me a jacket. "*Baka malamig doon*" were among the few words she said. ("It might be cold there.") When I arrived at the Philippines' Ninoy Aquino International Airport with her, my aunt and a family friend, I was introduced to a man I'd never seen. They told me he was my uncle. He held my hand as I boarded an airplane for the first time. It was 1993, and I was 12.

My mother wanted to give me a better life, so she sent me thousands of miles away to live with her parents in America—my grand-father (*Lolo* in Tagalog[1]) and grandmother (*Lola*). After I arrived in Mountain View, Calif., in the San Francisco Bay Area, I entered sixth grade and quickly grew to love my new home, family

---

[1]Official language of the Philippines. [Eds.]

and culture. I discovered a passion for language, though it was hard to learn the difference between formal English and American slang. One of my early memories is of a freckled kid in middle school asking me, "What's up?" I replied, "The sky," and he and a couple of other kids laughed. I won the eighth-grade spelling bee by memorizing words I couldn't properly pronounce. (The winning word was "indefatigable.")

One day when I was 16, I rode my bike to the nearby D.M.V. office to get my driver's permit. Some of my friends already had their licenses, so I figured it was time. But when I handed the clerk my green card as proof of U.S. residency, she flipped it around, examining it. "This is fake," she whispered. "Don't come back here again."

Confused and scared, I pedaled home and confronted Lolo. I remember him sitting in the garage, cutting coupons. I dropped my bike and ran over to him, showing him the green card. *"Peke ba ito?"* I asked in Tagalog. ("Is this fake?") My grandparents were naturalized American citizens—he worked as a security guard, she as a food server—and they had begun supporting my mother and me financially when I was 3, after my father's wandering eye and inability to properly provide for us led to my parents' separation. Lolo was a proud man, and I saw the shame on his face as he told me he purchased the card, along with other fake documents, for me. "Don't show it to other people," he warned.

5    I decided then that I could never give anyone reason to doubt I was an American. I convinced myself that if I worked enough, if I achieved enough, I would be rewarded with citizenship. I felt I could earn it.

I've tried. Over the past 14 years, I've graduated from high school and college and built a career as a journalist, interviewing some of the most famous people in the country. On the surface, I've created a good life. I've lived the American dream.

But I am still an undocumented immigrant. And that means living a different kind of reality. It means going about my day in fear of being found out. It means rarely trusting people, even those closest to me, with who I really am. It means keeping my family photos in a shoebox rather than displaying them on shelves in my home, so friends don't ask about them. It means reluctantly, even painfully, doing things I know are wrong and unlawful. And it has meant relying on a sort of 21st-century underground railroad of supporters, people who took an interest in my future and took risks for me.

Last year I read about four students who walked from Miami to Washington to lobby for the Dream Act, a nearly decade-old immigration bill that would provide a path to legal permanent residency for young people who have been educated in this country. At the risk of deportation—the Obama administration has deported almost

800,000 people in the last two years—they are speaking out. Their courage has inspired me.[2]

There are believed to be 11 million undocumented immigrants in the United States. We're not always who you think we are. Some pick your strawberries or care for your children. Some are in high school or college. And some, it turns out, write news articles you might read. I grew up here. This is my home. Yet even though I think of myself as an American and consider America my country, my country doesn't think of me as one of its own.

My first challenge was the language. Though I learned English 10 in the Philippines, I wanted to lose my accent. During high school, I spent hours at a time watching television (especially *Frasier, Home Improvement* and reruns of *The Golden Girls*) and movies (from *Goodfellas* to *Anne of Green Gables*), pausing the VHS to try to copy how various characters enunciated their words. At the local library, I read magazines, books and newspapers—anything to learn how to write better. Kathy Dewar, my high-school English teacher, introduced me to journalism. From the moment I wrote my first article for the student paper, I convinced myself that having my name in print—writing in English, interviewing Americans—validated my presence here.

The debates over "illegal aliens" intensified my anxieties. In 1994, only a year after my flight from the Philippines, Gov. Pete Wilson was re-elected in part because of his support for Proposition 187, which prohibited undocumented immigrants from attending public school and accessing other services. (A federal court later found the law unconstitutional.) After my encounter at the D.M.V. in 1997, I grew more aware of anti-immigrant sentiments and stereotypes: *they don't want to assimilate, they are a drain on society.* They're not talking about me, I would tell myself. I have something to contribute.

To do that, I had to work—and for that, I needed a Social Security number. Fortunately, my grandfather had already managed to get one for me. Lolo had always taken care of everyone in the family. He and my grandmother emigrated legally in 1984 from Zambales, a province in the Philippines of rice fields and bamboo houses, following Lolo's sister, who married a Filipino-American serving in the American military. She petitioned for her brother and his wife to join her. When they got here, Lolo petitioned for his two children—my mother and her younger brother—to follow them. But instead of mentioning that my mother was a married woman, he listed her as single. Legal residents can't petition for their married children. Besides, Lolo didn't care for my father. He didn't want him coming here too.

But soon Lolo grew nervous that the immigration authorities reviewing the petition would discover my mother was married, thus

---

[2]In 2011, the Obama administration instituted a policy that would generally not deport undocumented immigrants unless they posed a threat of some kind. [Eds.]

derailing not only her chances of coming here but those of my uncle as well. So he withdrew her petition. After my uncle came to America legally in 1991, Lolo tried to get my mother here through a tourist visa, but she wasn't able to obtain one. That's when she decided to send me. My mother told me later that she figured she would follow me soon. She never did.

The "uncle" who brought me here turned out to be a coyote,[3] not a relative, my grandfather later explained. Lolo scraped together enough money—I eventually learned it was $4,500, a huge sum for him—to pay him to smuggle me here under a fake name and fake passport. (I never saw the passport again after the flight and have always assumed that the coyote kept it.) After I arrived in America, Lolo obtained a new fake Filipino passport, in my real name this time, adorned with a fake student visa, in addition to the fraudulent green card.

15　　Using the fake passport, we went to the local Social Security Administration office and applied for a Social Security number and card. It was, I remember, a quick visit. When the card came in the mail, it had my full, real name, but it also clearly stated: "Valid for work only with I.N.S. authorization."

When I began looking for work, a short time after the D.M.V. incident, my grandfather and I took the Social Security card to Kinko's, where he covered the "I.N.S. authorization" text with a sliver of white tape. We then made photocopies of the card. At a glance, at least, the copies would look like copies of a regular, unrestricted Social Security card.

Lolo always imagined I would work the kind of low-paying jobs that undocumented people often take. (Once I married an American, he said, I would get my real papers, and everything would be fine.) But even menial jobs require documents, so he and I hoped the doctored card would work for now. The more documents I had, he said, the better.

While in high school, I worked part time at Subway, then at the front desk of the local Y.M.C.A., then at a tennis club, until I landed an unpaid internship at the *Mountain View Voice*, my hometown newspaper. First I brought coffee and helped around the office; eventually I began covering city-hall meetings and other assignments for pay.

For more than a decade of getting part-time and full-time jobs, employers have rarely asked to check my original Social Security card. When they did, I showed the photocopied version, which they accepted. Over time, I also began checking the citizenship box on my federal I-9 employment eligibility forms. (Claiming full citizenship was actually easier than declaring permanent resident "green card" status, which would have required me to provide an alien registration number.)

---

[3]Someone who smuggles undocumented immigrants into the United States. [Eds.]

This deceit never got easier. The more I did it, the more I felt like an  20
impostor, the more guilt I carried—and the more I worried that I would
get caught. But I kept doing it. I needed to live and survive on my own,
and I decided this was the way.

Mountain View High School became my second home. I was
elected to represent my school at school-board meetings, which gave
me the chance to meet and befriend Rich Fischer, the superintendent for
our school district. I joined the speech and debate team, acted in school
plays and eventually became co-editor of the *Oracle*, the student newspaper. That drew the attention of my principal, Pat Hyland. "You're
at school just as much as I am," she told me. Pat and Rich would soon
become mentors, and over time, almost surrogate parents for me.

After a choir rehearsal during my junior year, Jill Denny, the choir
director, told me she was considering a Japan trip for our singing group.
I told her I couldn't afford it, but she said we'd figure out a way. I hesitated, and then decided to tell her the truth. "It's not really the money,"
I remember saying. "I don't have the right passport." When she assured
me we'd get the proper documents, I finally told her. "I can't get the
right passport," I said. "I'm not supposed to be here."

She understood. So the choir toured Hawaii instead, with me in
tow. (Mrs. Denny and I spoke a couple of months ago, and she told me
she hadn't wanted to leave any student behind.)

Later that school year, my history class watched a documentary on
Harvey Milk, the openly gay San Francisco city official who was assassinated. This was 1999, just six months after Matthew Shepard's body
was found tied to a fence in Wyoming. During the discussion, I raised
my hand and said something like: "I'm sorry Harvey Milk got killed for
being gay ....I've been meaning to say this... . I'm gay."

I hadn't planned on coming out that morning, though I had known  25
that I was gay for several years. With that announcement, I became
the only openly gay student at school, and it caused turmoil with my
grandparents. Lolo kicked me out of the house for a few weeks. Though
we eventually reconciled, I had disappointed him on two fronts. First,
as a Catholic, he considered homosexuality a sin and was embarrassed
about having *"ang apo na bakla"* ("a grandson who is gay"). Even worse,
I was making matters more difficult for myself, he said. I needed to
marry an American woman in order to gain a green card.

Tough as it was, coming out about being gay seemed less daunting
than coming out about my legal status. I kept my other secret mostly
hidden.

While my classmates awaited their college acceptance letters,
I hoped to get a full-time job at the *Mountain View Voice* after graduation. It's not that I didn't want to go to college, but I couldn't apply for
state and federal financial aid. Without that, my family couldn't afford
to send me.

But when I finally told Pat and Rich about my immigration "problem"—as we called it from then on—they helped me look for a solution. At first, they even wondered if one of them could adopt me and fix the situation that way, but a lawyer Rich consulted told him it wouldn't change my legal status because I was too old. Eventually they connected me to a new scholarship fund for high-potential students who were usually the first in their families to attend college. Most important, the fund was not concerned with immigration status. I was among the first recipients, with the scholarship covering tuition, lodging, books and other expenses for my studies at San Francisco State University.

As a college freshman, I found a job working part time at the *San Francisco Chronicle*, where I sorted mail and wrote some freelance articles. My ambition was to get a reporting job, so I embarked on a series of internships. First I landed at the *Philadelphia Daily News*, in the summer of 2001, where I covered a drive-by shooting and the wedding of the 76ers star Allen Iverson. Using those articles, I applied to the *Seattle Times* and got an internship for the following summer.

30    But then my lack of proper documents became a problem again. The *Times*'s recruiter, Pat Foote, asked all incoming interns to bring certain paperwork on their first day: a birth certificate, or a passport, or a driver's license plus an original Social Security card. I panicked, thinking my documents wouldn't pass muster. So before starting the job, I called Pat and told her about my legal status. After consulting with management, she called me back with the answer I feared: I couldn't do the internship.

This was devastating. What good was college if I couldn't then pursue the career I wanted? I decided then that if I was to succeed in a profession that is all about truth-telling, I couldn't tell the truth about myself.

After this episode, Jim Strand, the venture capitalist who sponsored my scholarship, offered to pay for an immigration lawyer. Rich and I went to meet her in San Francisco's financial district.

I was hopeful. This was in early 2002, shortly after Senators Orrin Hatch, the Utah Republican, and Dick Durbin, the Illinois Democrat, introduced the Dream Act—Development, Relief and Education for Alien Minors. It seemed like the legislative version of what I'd told myself: If I work hard and contribute, things will work out.

But the meeting left me crushed. My only solution, the lawyer said, was to go back to the Philippines and accept a 10-year ban before I could apply to return legally.

35    If Rich was discouraged, he hid it well. "Put this problem on a shelf," he told me. "Compartmentalize it. Keep going."

And I did. For the summer of 2003, I applied for internships across the country. Several newspapers, including the *Wall Street Journal*, the *Boston Globe* and the *Chicago Tribune*, expressed interest. But when the

*Washington Post* offered me a spot, I knew where I would go. And this time, I had no intention of acknowledging my "problem."

The Post internship posed a tricky obstacle: It required a driver's license. (After my close call at the California D.M.V., I'd never gotten one.) So I spent an afternoon at the Mountain View Public Library, studying various states' requirements. Oregon was among the most welcoming—and it was just a few hours' drive north.

Again, my support network came through. A friend's father lived in Portland, and he allowed me to use his address as proof of residency. Pat, Rich and Rich's longtime assistant, Mary Moore, sent letters to me at that address. Rich taught me how to do three-point turns in a parking lot, and a friend accompanied me to Portland.

The license meant everything to me—it would let me drive, fly and work. But my grandparents worried about the Portland trip and the Washington internship. While Lola offered daily prayers so that I would not get caught, Lolo told me that I was dreaming too big, risking too much.

I was determined to pursue my ambitions. I was 22, I told them, responsible for my own actions. But this was different from Lolo's driving a confused teenager to Kinko's. I knew what I was doing now, and I knew it wasn't right. But what was I supposed to do? 40

I was paying state and federal taxes, but I was using an invalid Social Security card and writing false information on my employment forms. But that seemed better than depending on my grandparents or on Pat, Rich and Jim—or returning to a country I barely remembered. I convinced myself all would be O.K. if I lived up to the qualities of a "citizen": hard work, self-reliance, love of my country.

At the D.M.V. in Portland, I arrived with my photocopied Social Security card, my college I.D., a pay stub from the *San Francisco Chronicle* and my proof of state residence—the letters to the Portland address that my support network had sent. It worked. My license, issued in 2003, was set to expire eight years later, on my 30th birthday, on Feb. 3, 2011. I had eight years to succeed professionally, and to hope that some sort of immigration reform would pass in the meantime and allow me to stay.

It seemed like all the time in the world.

My summer in Washington was exhilarating. I was intimidated to be in a major newsroom but was assigned a mentor—Peter Perl, a veteran magazine writer—to help me navigate it. A few weeks into the internship, he printed out one of my articles, about a guy who recovered a long-lost wallet, circled the first two paragraphs and left it on my desk. "Great eye for details—awesome!" he wrote. Though I didn't know it then, Peter would become one more member of my network.

At the end of the summer, I returned to the *San Francisco Chronicle*. My plan was to finish school—I was now a senior—while I worked for 45 the *Chronicle* as a reporter for the city desk. But when the *Post* beckoned again, offering me a full-time, two-year paid internship that I could start when I graduated in June 2004, it was too tempting to pass up. I moved back to Washington.

About four months into my job as a reporter for the *Post*, I began feeling increasingly paranoid, as if I had "illegal immigrant" tattooed on my forehead—and in Washington, of all places, where the debates over immigration seemed never-ending. I was so eager to prove myself that I feared I was annoying some colleagues and editors—and worried that any one of these professional journalists could discover my secret. The anxiety was nearly paralyzing. I decided I had to tell one of the higher-ups about my situation. I turned to Peter.

By this time, Peter, who still works at the *Post*, had become part of management as the paper's director of newsroom training and professional development. One afternoon in late October, we walked a couple of blocks to Lafayette Square, across from the White House. Over some 20 minutes, sitting on a bench, I told him everything: the Social Security card, the driver's license, Pat and Rich, my family.

Peter was shocked. "I understand you 100 times better now," he said. He told me that I had done the right thing by telling him, and that it was now our shared problem. He said he didn't want to do anything about it just yet. I had just been hired, he said, and I needed to prove myself. "When you've done enough," he said, "we'll tell Don and Len together." (Don Graham is the chairman of the Washington Post Company; Leonard Downie Jr. was then the paper's executive editor.) A month later, I spent my first Thanksgiving in Washington with Peter and his family.

In the five years that followed, I did my best to "do enough." I was promoted to staff writer, reported on video-game culture, wrote a series on Washington's H.I.V./AIDS epidemic and covered the role of technology and social media in the 2008 presidential race. I visited the White House, where I interviewed senior aides and covered a state dinner—and gave the Secret Service the Social Security number I obtained with false documents.

50      I did my best to steer clear of reporting on immigration policy but couldn't always avoid it. On two occasions, I wrote about Hillary Clinton's position on driver's licenses for undocumented immigrants. I also wrote an article about Senator Mel Martinez of Florida, then the chairman of the Republican National Committee, who was defending his party's stance toward Latinos after only one Republican presidential candidate—John McCain, the co-author of a failed immigration bill—agreed to participate in a debate sponsored by Univision, the Spanish-language network.

It was an odd sort of dance: I was trying to stand out in a highly competitive newsroom, yet I was terrified that if I stood out too much,

I'd invite unwanted scrutiny. I tried to compartmentalize my fears, distract myself by reporting on the lives of other people, but there was no escaping the central conflict in my life. Maintaining a deception for so long distorts your sense of self. You start wondering who you've become, and why.

In April 2008, I was part of a *Post* team that won a Pulitzer Prize for the paper's coverage of the Virginia Tech shootings a year earlier. Lolo died a year earlier, so it was Lola who called me the day of the announcement. The first thing she said was, "*Anong mangyayari kung malaman ng mga tao?*"

What will happen if people find out?

I couldn't say anything. After we got off the phone, I rushed to the bathroom on the fourth floor of the newsroom, sat down on the toilet and cried.

In the summer of 2009, without ever having had that follow-up talk 55 with top *Post* management, I left the paper and moved to New York to join the *Huffington Post*. I met Arianna Huffington at a Washington Press Club Foundation dinner I was covering for the *Post* two years earlier, and she later recruited me to join her news site. I wanted to learn more about Web publishing, and I thought the new job would provide a useful education.

Still, I was apprehensive about the move: many companies were already using E-Verify, a program set up by the Department of Homeland Security that checks if prospective employees are eligible to work, and I didn't know if my new employer was among them. But I'd been able to get jobs in other newsrooms, I figured, so I filled out the paperwork as usual and succeeded in landing on the payroll.

While I worked at the *Huffington Post*, other opportunities emerged. My H.I.V./AIDS series became a documentary film called *The Other City*, which opened at the Tribeca Film Festival last year and was broadcast on Showtime. I began writing for magazines and landed a dream assignment: profiling Facebook's Mark Zuckerberg for the *New Yorker*.

The more I achieved, the more scared and depressed I became. I was proud of my work, but there was always a cloud hanging over it, over me. My old eight-year deadline—the expiration of my Oregon driver's license—was approaching.

After slightly less than a year, I decided to leave the *Huffington Post*. In part, this was because I wanted to promote the documentary and write a book about online culture—or so I told my friends. But the real reason was, after so many years of trying to be a part of the system, of focusing all my energy on my professional life, I learned that no amount of professional success would solve my problem or ease the sense of loss and displacement I felt. I lied to a friend about why I couldn't take a weekend trip to Mexico. Another time I concocted an excuse for why I couldn't go on an all-expenses-paid trip to Switzerland. I have been unwilling, for years, to be in a long-term relationship because I never wanted anyone to get too close and ask too many questions. All the while, Lola's question was stuck in my head: What will happen if people find out?

60      Early this year, just two weeks before my 30th birthday, I won a small reprieve: I obtained a driver's license in the state of Washington. The license is valid until 2016. This offered me five more years of acceptable identification—but also five more years of fear, of lying to people I respect and institutions that trusted me, of running away from who I am.

I'm done running. I'm exhausted. I don't want that life anymore.

So I've decided to come forward, own up to what I've done, and tell my story to the best of my recollection. I've reached out to former bosses and employers and apologized for misleading them—a mix of humiliation and liberation coming with each disclosure. All the people mentioned in this article gave me permission to use their names. I've also talked to family and friends about my situation and am working with legal counsel to review my options. I don't know what the consequences will be of telling my story.

I do know that I am grateful to my grandparents, my Lolo and Lola, for giving me the chance for a better life. I'm also grateful to my other family—the support network I found here in America—for encouraging me to pursue my dreams.

It's been almost 18 years since I've seen my mother. Early on, I was mad at her for putting me in this position, and then mad at myself for being angry and ungrateful. By the time I got to college, we rarely spoke by phone. It became too painful; after a while it was easier to just send money to help support her and my two half-siblings. My sister, almost 2 years old when I left, is almost 20 now. I've never met my 14-year-old brother. I would love to see them.

65      Not long ago, I called my mother. I wanted to fill the gaps in my memory about that August morning so many years ago. We had never discussed it. Part of me wanted to shove the memory aside, but to write this article and face the facts of my life, I needed more details. Did I cry? Did she? Did we kiss goodbye?

My mother told me I was excited about meeting a stewardess, about getting on a plane. She also reminded me of the one piece of advice she gave me for blending in: If anyone asked why I was coming to America, I should say I was going to Disneyland.

## Responding to Reading

MyWritingLab™

1. List the specific illegal acts Vargas's grandfather (and Vargas himself) committed to hide the fact that Vargas was in the United States illegally. What motivated each of these acts? How does Vargas justify them? What finally motivated Vargas to (in his words) "come forward, own up to what I've done, and tell my story" (62)?

2. What obstacles did Vargas face because of his immigration status? How did he overcome them? How did his "support network" (38) help him? Do you think these people did the right thing by helping him?
3. **Rhetorical Analysis**   How do you think Vargas expected readers to respond to each of the following statements?

   • "I convinced myself that if I worked enough, if I achieved enough, I would be rewarded with citizenship." (5)

   • "Tough as it was, coming out about being gay seemed less daunting than coming out about my legal status." (26)

   • "I decided then that if I was to succeed in a profession that is all about truth-telling, I couldn't tell the truth about myself." (31)

Do you think Vargas is being completely honest with himself in each case? Do you see any irony in his words?

## Writing about Reading                                    MyWritingLab™

1. What different connotations do the terms *undocumented immigrants* and *illegal aliens* have (11)? Which terms do you think should be used to refer to Vargas and others in his situation? Why?
2. **Writing with Sources**   Search online for information about Vargas since 2011, when this essay was published. Then, read the text of the executive order on immigration enacted by President Obama in 2014 as well as any national immigration laws passed since 2011. Using this research to support your points, write an essay in which you evaluate the strengths and weaknesses of Vargas's arguments. Do you see him as an "outlaw" or as someone with a legitimate grievance? Do you believe he deserves amnesty?

POETRY

# THE NEW COLOSSUS

## Emma Lazarus

*1849–1887*

*Born to a wealthy family in New York City and educated by private tutors, Emma Lazarus became one of the foremost poets of her day. Today, she is remembered solely for her poem "The New Colossus," a sonnet written in 1883 as part of an effort to raise funds for the Statue of Liberty. The poem was later inscribed on the statue's base, and it remains a vivid reminder of the immigrant's American dream.*

Not like the brazen giant of Greek fame,
With conquering limbs astride from land to land;
Here at our sea-washed, sunset gates shall stand

A mighty woman with a torch, whose flame
5   Is the imprisoned lightning, and her name
Mother of Exiles. From her beacon-hand
Glows world-wide welcome; her mild eyes command
The air-bridged harbor that twin cities frame.
"Keep, ancient lands, your storied pomp!" cries she
10   With silent lips. "Give me your tired, your poor,
Your huddled masses yearning to breathe free,
The wretched refuse of your teeming shore.
Send these, the homeless, tempest-tost to me,
I lift my lamp beside the golden door!"

## Responding to Reading                      MyWritingLab™

1. The Colossus of Rhodes, an enormous statue of the Greek god Apollo, was
   considered one of the seven wonders of the ancient world. It stood at the
   mouth of the harbor at Rhodes. Why do you think this poem is called "The
   New Colossus"?
2. Who is the poem's speaker? Who is being addressed?
3. What is the "golden door" to which the poem's last line refers? What aspects of the American Dream does this poem express?

## Responding in Writing                      MyWritingLab™

Find some photographs of the Statue of Liberty. What elements of the Statue
has Lazarus captured in this poem? What characteristics, if any, has she failed
to capture?

## FOCUS

## Is the American Dream Still Attainable?

1960s family outside suburban home

### Responding to the Image

MyWritingLab™

1. Write a new caption for the image above, inventing names, ages, and family roles for the people pictured.
2. In a few sentences, describe the neighborhood you think this family lives in.
3. How is this family, and their home, like and unlike your own? How do you account for any differences you identify?

# AMERICAN DREAM? OR MIRAGE?

## Michael W. Kraus
## Shai Davidai
## A. David Nussbaum

*An assistant professor of psychology at the University of Illinois, Urbana-Champaign, Michael W. Kraus studies issues related to social hierarchy and power. An adjunct associate professor of behavioral science at the University of Chicago Booth School of Business, A. David Nussbaum researches the challenges we face in maintaining a coherent self-image. Shai Davidai is a graduate student in social psychology at Cornell University. In "American Dream? Or Mirage?" the writers consider the psychology behind the American Dream.*

Economic inequality in the United States is at its highest level since the 1930s, yet most Americans remain relatively unconcerned with the issue. Why?

One theory is that Americans accept such inequality because they overestimate the reality of the "American dream"—the idea that any American, with enough resolve and determination, can climb the economic ladder, regardless of where he starts in life. The American dream implies that the greatest economic rewards rightly go to society's most hard-working and deserving members.

Recently, studies by two independent research teams (each led by an author of this article) found that Americans across the economic spectrum did indeed severely misjudge the amount of upward mobility in society. The data also confirmed the psychological utility of this mistake: Overestimating upward mobility was self-serving for rich and poor people alike. For those who saw themselves as rich and successful, it helped justify their wealth. For the poor, it provided hope for a brighter economic future.

In studies by one author of this article, Shai Davidai, and the Cornell psychologist Thomas Gilovich, published earlier this year in *Perspectives on Psychological Science*, more than 3,000 respondents viewed a graph of the five income quintiles in American society and were asked to estimate the likelihood that a randomly selected person born to the bottom quintile would move to each of the other income quintiles in his lifetime. These estimates were compared with actual mobility trends documented by the Pew Research Center. Participants in the survey overshot the likelihood of rising from the poorest quintile to one of the three top quintiles by nearly 15 percentage points. (On average, only 30 percent of individuals make that kind of leap.)

Studies by another author of this article, the University of Illinois psychologist Michael W. Kraus, and his colleague Jacinth J.X. Tan, to be published in next month's issue of the *Journal of Experimental Social Psychology*, found a similar pattern: When asked to estimate how many college students came from families in the bottom 20 percent of income, respondents substantially misjudged, estimating that those from the lowest income bracket attended college at a rate five times greater than the actual one documented by the Current Population Survey.

One experiment by Professors Kraus and Tan demonstrated the self-serving nature of these errant upward mobility estimates. As with the studies above, participants were asked to estimate the ease of moving up the economic ladder. This time, however, they were also asked to estimate upward mobility for people who were similar to them "in terms of goals, abilities, talents and motivations." In this case, respondents were even more likely to overestimate upward mobility. We believe unduly in our own capacity to move up the economic ladder, and these beliefs increase our mobility overestimates more generally.

For those lower in income or educational attainment, lower standing was associated with greater overestimation of upward mobility. Those with the most room to move up were more likely to think that such movement was possible.

However, when people were asked to explicitly state how high up the economic ladder they felt, after accounting for their actual economic standing, the reverse pattern emerged: The higher up people said they were, the more they overestimated the likelihood of upward mobility. Being aware of your position at the top of a low-mobility hierarchy can be uncomfortable, because without mobility, sitting at the top is the result of luck, rather than merit.

Some Americans were better than others when it came to judging economic mobility. Across both sets of studies, political liberals were less likely to overestimate upward mobility relative to conservatives— a finding consistent with other research suggesting that conservatives see our society as more merit-based than do liberals.

In addition, studies by Professor Gilovich and Mr. Davidai found that members of ethnic minority groups tended to overestimate upward mobility more than did European Americans. This result indicated that those with the most to gain from believing in an upwardly mobile society tended to believe so more strongly.

Taken together, these sets of studies suggest that belief in the American dream is woefully misguided when compared with objective reality. Addressing the rising economic gap between rich and poor in society, it seems, will require us to contend not only with economic and political issues, but also with biases of our psychology.

5

10

CHAPTER 9 FOCUS

## Responding to Reading

1. According to the writers, what is "one theory" (2) that explains why Americans are not concerned about economic equality? Do the writers believe Americans *should* be concerned about this issue? Explain.
2. What do the writers conclude about the relationship between how Americans see the American Dream and "objective reality" (11)? Given that conclusion, do you see this article as optimistic, pessimistic, or neutral? Why?
3. **Rhetorical Analysis**　The writers mention several times that one or more of them authored each of the published or soon-to-be-published studies that they discuss here. Why do they point out this? How does their authorship of the studies they discuss affect your response to the article?

## Writing about Reading

1. How much economic mobility do you believe you have? What factors do you think will enable you to "climb the economic ladder" (2), and what might limit your ability to move up?
2. **Writing with Sources**　Locate a good definition of the term *upward mobility*, and search for information about Horatio Alger, a nineteenth-century writer known for his stories of young people—mostly boys—who achieve success through hard work (and luck). Then, read one of Alger's "rags to riches" novels, available at the *Horatio Alger Society* website, and write an essay analyzing the book's characterization of the American Dream.

# THE NEW AMERICAN DREAM

## Neal Gabler

### *1950–*

*A professor in the film program at Stony Brook University, Southampton, Neal Gabler is a journalist, cultural historian, political commentator, and film critic. He has authored and coauthored several books, including, most recently,* Walt Disney: The Triumph of the American Imagination *(2006). His work has appeared in such publications as the* Boston Globe, Esquire, *the* Los Angeles Times, New York *magazine, the* New York Times, Salon, Us, *and* Vogue. *In the following essay, Gabler defines the "new American Dream."*

A disgruntled New York mother recently filed a lawsuit against her 4-year-old daughter's preschool, charging that the school had reneged on its promise to adequately prepare the girl for an Ivy League education. Apparently the kids were playing with blocks when they should have been discussing Wittgenstein.[1] Understandably the suit was met with ridicule as another example of overbearing parenting, but it is also an example of how many of us, especially in the middle and upper-middle classes, not only aspire to be perfect; we *expect* perfection.

Though Americans have always been cockeyed optimists, they didn't necessarily think they would find nirvana on earth. The American Dream, as it was devised in the late 19th century, referred to opportunity. The idea was that anyone in this pragmatic, un-class-conscious society of ours could, by dint of hard work, rise to the level of his aspiration.

But over the past 50 years, the American Dream has been revised. It is no longer about seizing opportunity but about realizing perfection. Many Americans have come to feel that the lives they always imagined for themselves are not only attainable; those lives are now transcendable, as if our imaginations were inadequate to the possibilities. In short, many Americans have come to believe in their own perfectibility.

It was historian Daniel Boorstin who wrote in the early 1960s that his was the first generation to live within its illusions. This was a time when Americans had assimilated images from movies and television, books, and advertising as part of their consciousness. They saw fabulous worlds and wanted to enter them. As Boorstin said of the movie star: "His mere existence proves the perfectibility of any man or woman." To want to enter these worlds wasn't entirely novel. What was novel was the conviction that we could. In effect, America had become the first country to democratize dreams.

What Boorstin couldn't have foreseen was that perfectionism was encouraged not just by the media, popular culture, and an expansive post-war economy but by the country's political institutions. Ronald Reagan, as much as any single individual, promoted the idea that the only limit to our success was our own inadequacies—a bromide, to be sure, but one that came with an unsettling corollary: To be less than perfect was to be inadequate. And this corollary also had a patriotic corollary of its own: Anything less than perfection was both a personal failure and a national affront since Americans weren't inadequate. We owed it to the nation to live perfectly.

It is difficult to say whether the overstuffed 1980s fed this attitude or this attitude fed the 1980s, but whichever it was, success was redefined from personal satisfaction to public vindication. There was a great national competition in which many Americans felt they had to prove their value to everyone else. And the best measure of that value was not just wealth or a glowing career or a trophy wife or a beautiful family. It was all of it. If anything, that competition has only intensified since.

---

[1]Ludwig Wittgenstein (1889–1951), an Austrian-British philosopher. [Eds.]

Thus not only have the terms of success changed but also the very terms of life. For a person who can live within his illusions, the career has to be perfect, the wife has to be perfect, the children have to be perfect, the home has to be perfect, the car has to be perfect, the social circle has to be perfect. We agonize a lot over perfection, and we dedicate a lot of time, energy, and money to it—everything from plastic surgery to gated communities of McMansions to the professionalization of our children's activities like soccer and baseball to pricey preschools that prepare 4-year-olds for Harvard. After all, we are all on the Ivy League track now.

Or else. And that's another thing that a perfectionist society has engendered. It has removed failure as an option because we realize that there are no second chances, that mistakes are usually irrevocable, and that you have to assume there are other people out there—*your competition!*—whose wives will always be beautifully coiffed and dressed or whose husbands will be power brokers, whose children will score 2,400 on their SATs and who will be playing competitive-level tennis, whose careers will be skyrocketing, whose fortunes will be growing. In a world in which perfection is expected, you must be perfect. Otherwise you are second rate.

Not that this is easy. To live within your illusions is also to live within the pressure to sustain them, which is the pressure of middle-class America today. It is to say that the birthright of a 4-year-old girl in New York is to be a rich, beautiful, brilliant, powerful, Ivy League-educated Mistress of the Universe who will live not just the good life but the perfect one. That's the new American Dream.

## Responding to Writing

MyWritingLab™

1. Gabler claims that many Americans today dream not just of opportunity but of perfection. Whom or what does he blame for this situation?
2. What is a *cockeyed optimist* (2)? What is *nirvana* (2)? What is a *trophy wife* (6)? What does Gabler's use of these expressions tell you about how he perceives his audience?
3. **Rhetorical Analysis** Gabler, an upper-middle-class male, clearly expects his audience to be composed of people like himself. How can you tell? Do you think this narrow focus is the most effective strategy?

## Writing about Reading

MyWritingLab™

1. Do you agree with Gabler that Americans now "expect perfection"(1)? Do you think his characterization could apply to lower-middle-class Americans as well as to the middle- and upper-middle-class readers he is addressing?
2. **Writing with Sources** Research the history of suburban "McMansions" (7). What is a McMansion? Is this term's connotation positive, neutral, or negative? In what sense does the McMansion represent the culmination of the American Dream? In what sense could it be seen as a corruption of that dream? Write an essay in which you address these questions.

# CRUMBLING AMERICAN DREAMS
## Robert D. Putnam
### *1941–*

*The Peter and Isabel Malkin Professor of public policy at Harvard University's John F. Kennedy School of Government, Robert D. Putnam is the author of numerous books, including, most recently,* Our Kids: The American Dream in Crisis *(2015). "Crumbling American Dreams" appeared in the* New York Times *blog* Opinionator *as part of "The Great Divide" series about inequality in America. In this essay, Putnam considers the complex failure of the American Dream.*

My hometown—Port Clinton, Ohio, population 6,050—was in the 1950s a passable embodiment of the American dream, a place that offered decent opportunity for the children of bankers and factory workers alike.

But a half-century later, wealthy kids park BMW convertibles in the Port Clinton High School lot next to decrepit "junkers" in which homeless classmates live. The American dream has morphed into a split-screen American nightmare. And the story of this small town, and the divergent destinies of its children, turns out to be sadly representative of America.

Growing up, almost all my classmates lived with two parents in homes their parents owned and in neighborhoods where everyone knew everyone else's first name. Some dads worked in the local auto-part factories or gypsum mines, while others, like my dad, were small businessmen. In that era of strong unions and full employment, few families experienced joblessness or serious economic insecurity. Very few P.C.H.S. students came from wealthy backgrounds, and those few made every effort to hide that fact.

Half a century later, my classmates, now mostly retired, have experienced astonishing upward mobility. Nearly three-quarters of them surpassed their parents in education and in that way advanced economically as well. One-third of my classmates came from homes with parents who had not completed high school and, of that group, nearly half went to college.

Low costs at public and private colleges across Ohio were supplemented by locally raised scholarships—from the Rotary Club, the United Automobile Workers, the Junior Women's Club and the like. Although the only two black students in my class encountered racial prejudice in town and none of their parents had finished grade school, both reached graduate school. Neither for them nor for our white classmates was family background the barrier to upward mobility that it would become in the next century.

Our (white) star quarterback, whom I will call J, grew up on the poor side of town. His dad, who had an eighth-grade education, worked two jobs to keep the family afloat—on the line at Port Clinton Manufacturing from 7 to 3, then at the canning factory from 3:30 to 11. Despite his 70-plus-hour workweek, J's dad made it to J's games. Unable to afford a car, J's family hitched rides with neighbors to church every week and ate a lot of hash. Despite their modest background, J's parents urged him to aim for college, and he chose the college-prep track at P.C.H.S., finishing in the top quarter of our class. His minister pointed him toward a downstate Lutheran institution and made a phone call to help find him financial aid. J graduated debt-free and continued on to seminary and a successful career as a Lutheran minister, coaching high school football on the side.

J's rise from a well-knit but modest working-class family to a successful professional career was not atypical, as a recent survey of my classmates revealed. My classmates describe our youth in strikingly similar terms: "We were poor, but we didn't know it." In fact, however, in the breadth and depth of the social support we enjoyed, we were rich, but we didn't know it.

As we graduated, none of us had any inkling that Port Clinton would change anytime soon. While almost half of us headed off to college, those who stayed in town had reason to expect a steady job (if they were male), marriage and a more comfortable life than their parents'.

But just beyond the horizon a national economic, social and cultural whirlwind was gathering force that would radically transform the life chances of the children and grandchildren of the graduates of the P.C.H.S. class of 1959. The change would be jaw dropping and heart wrenching, for Port Clinton turns out to be a poster child for changes that have engulfed America.

10   The manufacturing foundation of Port Clinton's modest prosperity in the 1950s and 1960s began to tremble in the 1970s. The big Standard Products factory at the east end of town provided nearly 1,000 steady, good-paying blue-collar jobs in the 1950s, but the payroll was more than halved in the 1970s. After two more decades of layoffs and "give backs," the plant gates on Maple Street finally closed in 1993, leaving a barbed-wire-encircled ruin now graced with Environmental Protection Agency warnings of toxicity. But that was merely the most visible symbol of the town's economic implosion.

Manufacturing employment in Ottawa County plummeted from 55 percent of all jobs in 1965 to 25 percent in 1995 and kept falling. By 2012 the average worker in Ottawa County had not had a real raise for four decades and, in fact, is now paid roughly 16 percent less in inflation-adjusted dollars than his or her grandfather in the early 1970s. The local population fell as P.C.H.S. graduates who could escape increasingly did. Most of the downtown shops of my youth stand empty and derelict, driven out of business by gradually shrinking paychecks and the Walmart on the outskirts of town.

The social impact of those economic hammer blows was initially cushioned by the family and community bonds that had been so strong in my youth. But as successive graduating P.C.H.S. classes entered an ever worsening local economy, the social fabric of the 1950s and 1960s was gradually shredded. Juvenile-delinquency rates began to skyrocket in the 1980s and were triple the national average by 2010. Not surprisingly, given falling wages and loosening norms, single-parent households in Ottawa County doubled from 10 percent in 1970 to 20 percent in 2010, while the divorce rate more than quadrupled. In Port Clinton itself, the epicenter of the local economic collapse in the 1980s, the rate of births out of wedlock quadrupled between 1978 and 1990, topping out at about 40 percent, nearly twice the race-adjusted national average (itself rising rapidly).

Unlike working-class kids in the class of 1959, many of their counterparts in Port Clinton today are, despite toil and talent, locked into troubled, even hopeless lives. R, an 18-year-old white woman, is almost the same age as my grandchildren. Her grandfather could have been one of my classmates. But when I went off to college on a scholarship from a local employer, he skipped college in favor of a well-paid, stable blue-collar job. Then the factories closed, and good, working-class jobs fled. So while my kids, and then my grandchildren, headed off to elite colleges and successful careers, his kids never found steady jobs, were seduced by drugs and crime, and burned through a string of impermanent relationships.

His granddaughter R tells a harrowing tale of loneliness, distrust and isolation. Her parents split up when she was in preschool and her mother left her alone and hungry for days. Her dad hooked up with a woman who hit R, refused to feed her and confined R to her room with baby gates. She says her only friend was a yellow mouse who lived in her apartment. Caught trafficking drugs in high school, R spent several months in a juvenile detention center and failed out of high school, finally eking out a diploma online. Her experiences left her with a deep-seated mistrust of anyone and everyone, embodied by the scars on her arms where a boyfriend injured her in the middle of the night. R wistfully recalls her stillborn baby, born when she was 14. Since breaking up with the baby's dad, who left her for someone else, and with a second fiancé, who cheated on her after his release from prison, R is currently dating an older man with two infants born to different mothers—and, despite big dreams, she is not sure how much she should hope for.

R's story is heartbreaking. But the story of Port Clinton over the last half-century—like the history of America over these decades—is not simply about the collapse of the working class but also about the birth

15

of a new upper class. In the last two decades, just as the traditional economy of Port Clinton was collapsing, wealthy professionals from major cities in the Midwest have flocked to Port Clinton, building elaborate mansions in gated communities along Lake Erie and filling lagoons with their yachts. By 2011, the child poverty rate along the shore in upscale Catawba was only 1 percent, a fraction of the 51 percent rate only a few hundred yards inland. As the once thriving middle class disappeared, adjacent real estate listings in the Port Clinton News Herald advertised near-million-dollar mansions and dilapidated double-wides.

The contrast with the egalitarian ethos and reality of the 1950s—the contrast between the upward mobility experienced by J and the bleak prospects of R—vividly captures Port Clinton's transformation in the last half-century, much like that of the rest of the country. My research team has talked with dozens of R's from Austin, Tex., to Duluth, Minn., and from Atlanta to Orange County, Calif.

The crumbling of the American dream is a purple problem, obscured by solely red or solely blue lenses. Its economic and cultural roots are entangled, a mixture of government, private sector, community and personal failings. But the deepest root is our radically shriveled sense of "we." Everyone in my parents' generation thought of J as one of "our kids," but surprisingly few adults in Port Clinton today are even aware of R's existence, and even fewer would likely think of her as "our kid." Until we treat the millions of R's across America as our own kids, we will pay a major economic price, and talk of the American dream will increasingly seem cynical historical fiction.

## Responding to Reading                                    MyWritingLab™

1. In paragraph 2, Putnam says, "The American dream has morphed into a split-screen American nightmare." What exactly does he mean?
2. How and why did Putnam's hometown of Port Clinton, Ohio, change? How are the stories of "J" and "R" different?
3. **Rhetorical Analysis**  Evaluate Putnam's conclusion. What does he mean by "The crumbling of the American dream is a purple problem … "? How do you suppose he expects his readers to feel when they finish reading his essay? Explain.

## Writing about Reading

1. Does the town or neighborhood in which you grew up (or live now) also exemplify the "split-screen nightmare" that Putnam describes? If so, how? If not, how is your community different from his?

2. **Writing with Sources** Research the socio-economic development of your own community over the last half-century. Then, write an essay in which you discuss the upward mobility (and the obstacles to that upward mobility) of your own "J" and "R."

# WIDENING THE FOCUS

## For Critical Reading and Writing

Referring specifically to the three readings in this chapter's Focus section (and possibly to additional sources as well), write an essay in which you answer the question, "Is the American Dream Still Attainable?"

## For Further Reading

The following readings can suggest additional perspectives for thinking and writing about the feasibility of the American Dream:

- Gary Shteyngart, "Sixty-Nine Cents" (p. 53)

- Bich Minh Nguyen, "The Good Immigrant Student" (p. 83)

- David Leonhardt, "Is College Worth It? Clearly, New Data Say" (p. 102)

- Andrew Curry, "Why We Work" (p. 353)

## For Focused Research

As the essays in this chapter's Focus section illustrate, Americans' views of the American Dream are as varied as are their cultural backgrounds. Search online for different perspectives of the American Dream. Start with the American RadioWorks program *A Better Life*, or search for the *Forbes* series "The American Dream" and locate the more than sixty responses by well-known people to the question, "What is the American Dream?" Consider the similarities and differences among these views and how they relate to the readings in this chapter . Then, write an essay that compares at least three views of the American Dream. Include in your essay your own definition of the American Dream that synthesizes the various perspectives you discuss. Be sure to document the online sources you use.

## Beyond the Classroom

Interview a first-generation American, a second-generation American, and a third-generation American. How are their views of the American Dream different? How are they like and unlike the dreams of various writers represented in this chapter ? Write an essay summarizing your findings.

## EXPLORING ISSUES AND IDEAS

### The American Dream

MyWritingLab™

Visit Chapter 9, "The American Dream," in MyWritingLab to test your understanding of the chapter objectives.

Write an essay in response to one of the following prompts, which are suitable for assignments that require the use of outside sources as well as for assignments that are not source-based.

1. In an excerpt from his book *The Audacity of Hope*, President Barack Obama writes, "I believe that part of America's genius has always been its ability to absorb newcomers, to forge a national identity out of the disparate lot that arrived on our shores." Write an essay in which you support the idea that the strength of the United States comes from its ability to assimilate many different groups. In your essay, discuss specific contributions your own ethnic group and others have made to American society.

2. "Outlaw: My Life in America as an Undocumented Immigrant" (p. 325) deals with the uniquely American concept of reinventing oneself, taking on a new identity. Write an essay in which you outline the options available to new-comers to the United States who wish to achieve this kind of transformation. Whenever possible, give examples from the readings in this chapter .

3. In his keynote speech at the 2012 Democratic National Convention, Júlian Castro, the mayor of San Antonio, observed, "the American Dream is not a sprint, or even a marathon, but a relay." What do you think he meant? Do you think he is right? How do you think some of the other writers in this chapter would react to this statement?

4. Using the readings in this chapter as source material, write a manifesto that sets forth the rights and responsibilities of all Americans. You might begin by reading President John F. Kennedy's inaugural address (p. 462).

5. Discouraged by the racism they experienced in the United States, Richard Wright, James Baldwin, and other prominent black writers left their country and lived the rest of their lives as expatriates in Paris. Under what circumstances could you imagine leaving the United States and living forever in another country?

# 10

# WHY WE WORK

*In this chapter, you will learn to*
- analyze readings about why we work
- compose essays about why we work

Although work has always been a part of the human experience, the nature of work has evolved considerably—especially over the last two hundred years. During the Middle Ages and the Renaissance, work was often done by family units. Whether it involved planting and harvesting crops, tending livestock, or engaging in the manufacture of goods, parents, grandparents, and children (and possibly an apprentice or two) worked together, at home. With the Industrial Revolution, however, the nature of work changed. Manufacturing

Auto workers making car radiators on assembly line, circa 1915

became centralized in factories, and tasks that were formerly divided among various members of a family were now carried out more efficiently by machines. People worked long hours—in many cases twelve to fifteen hours a day, six and sometimes seven days a week—and could be fired for any reason. By the middle of the nineteenth century, most of the great manufacturing cities of Europe were overcrowded and polluted, teeming with unskilled factory workers. It is no wonder that labor unions became increasingly popular as they organized workers to fight for job security, shorter workdays, and minimum safety standards.

Thanks to the labor struggles of the past, many workers today have pension plans, health insurance, sick leave, paid vacations, life insurance, and other benefits. In spite of these advances, however, there is a dark side to this situation. American workers—like all workers—are subject to unpredictable changes in both the national and the global economies. As a result, during good times workers experience low unemployment and receive high wages, and during economic downturns—such as the one that began in 2008—workers experience higher unemployment and receive lower wages. Add to this situation the tendency of American companies to move manufacturing and high-tech jobs overseas and to see employees as entities whose jobs can be phased out as the need arises, and it is no surprise that workers are often stressed, insecure, and unhappy. The result is that many of today's workers question the role that work plays in their lives and wonder if it is in their best interest to invest so much time and energy in their jobs.

Welding robots on a contemporary car assembly line

The essays in the Focus section of this chapter (p. 377) address the question, "Is Every Worker Entitled to a Living Wage?" These essays ask important questions about the nature of both work and compensation. In "Measuring the Full Impact of Minimum and Living Wage Laws," Jeannette Wicks-Lim discusses the beneficial effects of paying a living wage; in "If a Business Won't Pay a Living Wage, It Shouldn't Exist," the Daily Take Team takes an extreme position on the living wage; and in "The Minimum Wage Delusion, and the Death of Common Sense," James Dorn examines the belief that raising the wages of low-wage workers helps their job prospects.

## PREPARING TO READ AND WRITE

As you read and prepare to write about the selections in this chapter, you may consider the following questions:

- What assumptions does the writer have about his or her audience? How can you tell?

- What is the writer's primary purpose? For example, is it to reinforce traditional ideas about work? to point out inequities? to offer new insights?

- What genre is the writer using? For example, is the reading an analysis? an argument? How do the conventions of this genre influence the writer's choices?

- What appeals does the writer use? For example, does he or she appeal primarily to reason? to emotion? to a combination of the two? Is this the most effective strategy?

- What do you know about the writer? In what way does the writer's economic and social position affect his or her definition of work?

- Is the writer male or female? Does the writer's gender affect his or her attitude toward work?

- When was the selection written? Does the date of publication affect its content?

- Does the selection seem fair? Balanced? Does the writer have any preconceived ideas about work and its importance?

- Is the writer generally sympathetic or unsympathetic toward workers?

- Does the writer have a realistic or unrealistic view of work?

- On what specific problems does the writer focus?

- What specific solutions does the writer suggest? Are these solutions feasible?

- Is your interpretation of the problem the same as or different from the interpretation presented in the reading?
- Are there any aspects of the problem that the writer ignores?
- Does the reading challenge any of your ideas about work?
- In what ways is the selection like other selections in this chapter?

# WHY WE WORK

## Andrew Curry

*1976–*

*Currently a freelance writer and editor, Andrew Curry was an associate editor for* U.S. News and World Report. *"Why We Work" was the cover story of the February 24, 2003, issue. In this essay, Curry examines the nature of work and explains why many workers today feel unfulfilled.*

In 1930, W. K. Kellogg made what he thought was a sensible decision, grounded in the best economic, social, and management theories of the time. Workers at his cereal plant in Battle Creek, Mich., were told to go home two hours early. Every day. For good.

The Depression-era move was hailed in *Factory and Industrial Management* magazine as the "biggest piece of industrial news since [Henry] Ford announced his five-dollar-a-day policy." President Herbert Hoover summoned the eccentric cereal magnate to the White House and said the plan was "very worthwhile." The belief: Industry and machines would lead to a workers' paradise where all would have less work, more free time, and yet still produce enough to meet their needs.

So what happened? Today, work dominates Americans' lives as never before, as workers pile on hours at a rate not seen since the Industrial Revolution. Technology has offered increasing productivity and a higher standard of living while bank tellers and typists are replaced by machines. The mismatch between available work and those available to do it continues, as jobs go begging while people beg for jobs. Though Kellogg's six-hour day lasted until 1985, Battle Creek's grand industrial experiment has been nearly forgotten. Instead of working less, our hours have stayed steady or risen—and today many more women work so that families can afford the trappings of suburbia. In effect, workers chose the path of consumption over leisure.

But as today's job market shows so starkly, that road is full of potholes. With unemployment at a nine-year high and many workers worried about losing their jobs—or forced to accept cutbacks in pay and benefits—work is hardly the paradise economists once envisioned.

5      Instead, the job market is as precarious today as it was in the early 1980s, when business began a wave of restructurings and layoffs to maintain its competitiveness. Many workers are left feeling unsecure, unfulfilled, and underappreciated. It's no wonder surveys of today's workers show a steady decline in job satisfaction. "People are very emotional about work, and they're very negative about it," says David Rhodes, a principal at human resource consultants Towers Perrin. "The biggest issue is clearly workload. People are feeling crushed."

The backlash comes after years of people boasting about how hard they work and tying their identities to how indispensable they are. Ringing cellphones, whirring faxes, and ever present E-mail have blurred the lines between work and home. The job penetrates every aspect of life. Americans don't exercise, they work out. We manage our time and work on our relationships. "In reaching the affluent society, we're working longer and harder than anyone could have imagined," says Rutgers University historian John Gillis. "The work ethic and identifying ourselves with work and through work is not only alive and well but more present now than at any time in history."

## Stressed Out

It's all beginning to take a toll. Fully one third of American workers— who work longer hours than their counterparts in any industrialized country—felt overwhelmed by the amount of work they had to do, according to a 2001 Families and Work Institute survey. "Both men and women wish they were working about 11 hours [a week] less," says Ellen Galinsky, the institute's president. "A lot of people believe if they do work less they'll be seen as less committed, and in a shaky economy no one wants that."

The modern environment would seem alien to pre-industrial laborers. For centuries, the household—from farms to "cottage" craftsmen—was the unit of production. The whole family was part of the enterprise, be it farming, blacksmithing, or baking. "In pre-industrial society, work and family were practically the same thing," says Gillis.

The Industrial Revolution changed all that. Mills and massive iron smelters required ample labor and constant attendance. "The factory took men, women and children out of the workshops and homes and put them under one roof and timed their movements to machines," writes Sebastian de Grazia in *Of Time, Work and Leisure*. For the first time, work and family were split. Instead of selling what they produced, workers sold their time. With more people leaving farms to move to cities and factories, labor became a commodity, placed on the market like any other.

10     Innovation gave rise to an industrial process based on machinery and mass production. This new age called for a new worker. "The only safeguard of order and discipline in the modern world is a standardized

worker with interchangeable parts," mused one turn-of-the-century writer.

Business couldn't have that, so instead it came up with the science of management. The theories of Frederick Taylor, a Philadelphia factory foreman with deep Puritan roots, led to work being broken down into component parts, with each step timed to coldly quantify jobs that skilled craftsmen had worked a lifetime to learn. Workers resented Taylor and his stopwatch, complaining that his focus on process stripped their jobs of creativity and pride, making them irritable. Long before anyone knew what "stress" was, Taylor brought it to the workplace—and without sympathy. "I have you for your strength and mechanical ability, and we have other men paid for thinking," he told workers.

## Long Hours

The division of work into components that could be measured and easily taught reached its apex in Ford's River Rouge plant in Dearborn, Mich., where the assembly line came of age. "It was this combination of a simplification of tasks ... with moving assembly that created a manufacturing revolution while at the same time laying waste human potential on a massive scale," author Richard Donkin writes in *Blood, Sweat and Tears.*

To maximize the production lines, businesses needed long hours from their workers. But it was no easy sell. "Convincing people to work 9 to 5 took a tremendous amount of propaganda and discipline," says the University of Richmond's Joanne Ciulla, author of *The Working Life: The Promise and Betrayal of Modern Work.* Entrepreneurs, religious leaders, and writers like Horatio Alger created whole bodies of literature to glorify the work ethic.

Labor leaders fought back with their own propaganda. For more than a century, a key struggle for the labor movement was reducing the amount of time workers had to spend on the job. "They were pursuing shorter hours and increased leisure. In effect, they were buying their time," says University of Iowa Prof. Benjamin Hunnicutt, author of *Work Without End: Abandoning Shorter Hours for the Right to Work.*

The first labor unions were organized in response to the threat of    15
technology, as skilled workers sought to protect their jobs from mechanization. Later, semi- and unskilled workers began to organize as well, agitating successfully for reduced hours, higher wages, and better work conditions. Unions enjoyed great influence in the early 20th century, and at their height in the 1950s, 35 percent of U.S. workers belonged to one.

Union persistence and the mechanization of factories gradually made shorter hours more realistic. Between 1830 and 1930, work hours were cut nearly in half, with economist John Maynard Keynes famously predicting in 1930 that by 2030 a 15-hour workweek would be standard. The Great Depression pressed the issue, with job sharing proposed as a serious solution to widespread unemployment. Despite business and religious opposition over worries of an idle populace, the Senate passed a bill that would have mandated a 30-hour week in 1933; it was narrowly defeated in the House.

Franklin Delano Roosevelt struck back with a new gospel that lives to this very day: consumption. "The aim ... is to restore our rich domestic market by raising its vast consuming capacity," he said. "Our first purpose is to create employment as fast as we can." And so began the modern work world. "Instead of accepting work's continuing decline and imminent fall from its dominant social position, businessmen, economists, advertisers, and politicians preached that there would never be 'enough,'" Hunnicutt writes in *Kellogg's Six-Hour Day*. "The entrepreneur and industry could invent new things for advertising to sell and for people to want and work for indefinitely."

The New Deal dumped government money into job creation, in turn encouraging consumption. World War II fueled the fire, and American workers soon found themselves in a "golden age"—40-hour workweeks, plenty of jobs, and plenty to buy. Leisure was the road not taken, a path quickly forgotten in the postwar boom of the 1950s and 1960s.

## Discontent

Decades of abundance, however, did not bring satisfaction. "A significant number of Americans are dissatisfied with the quality of their working lives," said the 1973 report "Work in America" from the Department of Health, Education and Welfare. "Dull, repetitive, seemingly meaningless tasks, offering little challenge or autonomy, are causing discontent among workers at all occupational levels." Underlying the dissatisfaction was a very gradual change in what the "Protestant work ethic" meant. Always a source of pride, the idea that hard work was a calling from God dated to the Reformation and the teachings of Martin Luther. While work had once been a means to serve God, two centuries of choices and industrialization had turned work into an end in itself, stripped of the spiritual meaning that sustained the Puritans who came ready to tame the wilderness.

20   By the end of the '70s, companies were reaching out to spiritually drained workers by offering more engagement while withdrawing the promise of a job for life, as the American economy faced a stiff challenge from cheaper workers abroad. "Corporations introduced feel-good programs to stimulate jaded employees with one hand while taking away the elements of a 'just' workplace with the other," says Andrew Ross, author of *No Collar: The Humane Workplace and Its Hidden Costs*. Employees were given more control over their work and

schedules, and "human relations" consultants and motivational speakers did a booming business. By the 1990s, technology made working from home possible for a growing number of people. Seen as a boon at first, telecommuting and the rapidly proliferating "electronic leash" of cellphones made work inescapable, as employees found themselves on call 24/7. Today, almost half of American workers use computers, cellphones, E-mail, and faxes for work during what is supposed to be nonwork time, according to the Families and Work Institute. Home is no longer a refuge but a cozier extension of the office.

The shift coincided with a shortage of highly skilled and educated workers, some of whom were induced with such benefits as stock options in exchange for their putting the company first all the time. But some see a different explanation for the rise in the amount of time devoted to work. "Hours have crept up partly as a consequence of the declining power of the trade-union movement," says Cornell University labor historian Clete Daniel. "Many employers find it more economical to require mandatory overtime than hire new workers and pay their benefits." Indeed, the trend has coincided with the steady decline in the percentage of workers represented by unions, as the labor movement failed to keep pace with the increasing rise of white-collar jobs in the economy. Today fewer than 15 percent of American workers belong to unions.

## Nirvana?

The Internet economy of the '90s gave rise to an entirely new corporate climate. The "knowledge worker" was wooed with games, gourmet chefs, and unprecedented freedom over his schedule and environment. Employees at Intuit didn't have to leave their desks for massages; Sun Microsystems offered in-house laundry, and Netscape workers were offered an on-site dentist. At first glance, this new corporate world seemed like nirvana. But "for every attractive feature, workers found there was a cost," says Ross. "It was both a worker's paradise and a con game."

When the stock market bubble burst and the economy fell into its recent recession, workers were forced to re-evaluate their priorities. "There used to be fat bonuses and back rubs, free bagels and foosball tables—it didn't really feel like work," says Allison Hemming, who organizes "pink-slip parties" for laid-off workers around the country and has written *Work It! How to Get Ahead, Save Your Ass, and Land a Job in Any Economy*. "I think people are a lot wiser about their choices now. They want a better quality of life; they're asking for more flextime to spend with their families."

In a study of Silicon Valley culture over the past decade, San Jose State University anthropologist Jan English-Lueck found that skills learned on the job were often brought home. Researchers talked to families with mission statements, mothers used conflict-resolution buzzwords with their squabbling kids, and engineers used flowcharts to organize Thanksgiving dinner. Said one participant: "I don't live life; I manage it."

25     In some ways, we have come full circle. "Now we're seeing the return of work to the home in terms of telecommuting," says Gillis. "We may be seeing the return of households where work is the central element again."

But there's still the question of fulfillment. In a recent study, human resources consultants Towers Perrin tried to measure workers' emotions about their jobs. More than half of the emotion was negative, with the biggest single factor being workload but also a sense that work doesn't satisfy their deeper needs. "We expect more and more out of our jobs," says Hunnicutt. "We expect to find wonderful people and experiences all around us. What we find is Dilbert."

## Responding to Reading

MyWritingLab™

1. Why does "work dominate Americans' lives as never before" (3)? According to Curry, what toll does this situation take on American workers?
2. How did the Industrial Revolution change the nature of work? What effect did Frederick Taylor have on work? According to Curry, why were the first labor unions formed? Why was the New Deal the "golden age" for workers (18)?
3. **Rhetorical Analysis** Curry thinks that today's workers are unfulfilled. What evidence does he provide to support this contention? Does he provide enough evidence? the right kind of evidence? Explain.

## Writing about Reading

MyWritingLab™

1. Why do the people you know work? Do their motives support or challenge Curry's conclusion?
2. **Writing with Sources** Examine the question of why people work. Then, write an essay in which you discuss your findings in light of Curry's essay. Does your research support Curry's conclusions? Are there issues he should have examined but did not?

# CRASHING INTO CEILINGS: A REPORT FROM THE NINE-TO-FIVE SHIFT

## Debora L. Spar

*1963–*

*The president of Barnard College and the founder of the Athena Center for Leadership Studies, Debora L. Spar is committed to the education and advancement of women worldwide. She is the author of several books, including, most recently,* Wonder Women: Sex, Power, and the Quest for Perfection *(2013), from which the following essay was excerpted. Here, Spar considers the professional struggles women continue to face.*

At every women's conference, in every think tank report, at every celebration of Women's History Month or International Women's Day, the same data are repeated. I've said them so many times myself that I can reel them off from memory. But they are crucial, and they bear repeating once again. Only twenty-one companies on the Fortune 500 list are run by female chief executives. Only 16.6 percent of these companies' board members are women. Women account for only 16 percent of partners at the largest law firms in the United States, and only 19 percent of the country's surgeons. Across the board, women earn on average twenty-three cents less than men for every dollar that they earn.

Two things, of course, leap out from this rather depressing list. First, that the numbers are so similar across even hugely different industries (movie directors and accountants, for instance). And second, that the vast bulk of them seem stubbornly cemented at around 16 percent. It's as if some evil grim reaper came regularly to mow down any female who dared to peek her head above the mandated allotment. *Women? Yes, we love them. Please, give us more. Oh, no; no, wait. Not that many more ... there seems to be a mistake ... BEGONE!*

What makes this accounting even more dismal is that it is no longer credible to blame the proverbial pipeline. For decades, after all, the dearth of women at the top of organizations could easily be explained by the dearth of women anywhere in the organization. No female surgeons? Well, of course not, if there are no women in medical school. No female law partners? Wholly predictable if there are no female associates. But the pipeline to the top has been full now, or at least plentiful, for over twenty years. In 1984, the year I entered graduate school, 31 percent of graduating physicians were female, as were 36 percent of graduating lawyers and 37 percent of newly minted Ph.D.s. By 1994, women constituted fully 50 percent of graduating physicians, 46 percent of graduating lawyers, and 48 percent of Ph.D.s. Theoretically, all of these women have now been in the workforce for somewhere between fifteen and twenty-five years, more than enough time for them to have soared, crawled, or shouldered their way to the top. But they haven't. Instead, as the oft-repeated numbers show, women's position in the ranks of power has hardly surged ahead. Think about it. In 1980, there were eighteen women in Congress (3 percent) and two in state governorships. Now there are ninety-eight (18 percent) and five, respectively. In 1980, there were 58 female mayors of major American cities; now there are 217. Yes, women ran (unsuccessfully) for both president and vice president in 2008, but women also ran (unsuccessfully) for president in 1964, and vice president in 1984. Without question, women have advanced professionally since the days of the feminist revolution, but that advance has been slower—much, much slower—than anyone really expected.

To get a more nuanced sense of where, and how, women are getting stuck, it's useful to look at a few fields where the deceleration has been most pronounced. In law, for instance, women seem particularly prone to being jammed into the 16 percent cranny. Since the 1980s, as noted above, women have been filing into law schools, accounting for more than 40 percent of law degrees by 1986. Yet the percentage of female partners at major law firms has remained stubbornly set at around 16 percent, and the average compensation of a male partner is still almost $90,000 higher than that of his female counterpart. As a result, according to Judge Judith Kaye, the first female chief judge of the State of New York, "what the profession still lacks is a critical mass of women to mentor junior associates approaching pivotal points in their careers, to ensure not only implementation of diversity programs but also accountability with regard to these programs, or to influence firm-wide decisions from the management ranks. The statistics tell us that we are definitely not there yet." Similarly, while women have prolifer-ated across the lower and middle tiers of finance, they show few signs of achieving anything close to equal representation at the top: only 2.7 percent of CEOs, 16.6 percent of executive officers, and 18 percent of board directors. When I asked Ina Drew, former chief investment officer at JPMorgan Chase, and one of the banking sector's highest-ranking and longest-serving women, how to explain this discrepancy, her answer was succinct: "The top echelons of finance still lack mentors that women desperately need … If women remain unfulfilled by their positions without the potential for growth and discouraged by male aggression, the discrepancies will persist."

5    My friend Jill is a case in point. Born on a farm outside Lincoln, Nebraska, Jill attended college on a full ROTC[1] scholarship. She stud-ied Chinese as an undergraduate, earned a black belt in karate, and eventually became an ordnance officer in the Army. For four years, she dismantled bombs, and managed troops, and served on security detail for the White House. Needless to say, this is not a woman who scares easily, or who shies away from hardship. Jill married Paul, a classmate from ROTC, and helped support him through medical school. Then she entered law school, moved to Michigan, and gave birth to three kids—all in fairly rapid succession. For a while, it worked. Paul put in long hours as a newly minted orthopedic surgeon; Jill opened a small private law practice; and they hired a nanny they liked. Slowly, though, the troubles crept in. Paul was on call many nights and weekends, leaving Jill to juggle the kids, the errands, and the housework. Her cases were intriguing, but limited by her inability to bring on additional partners or devote more than fifty hours a week to the job. Their parents lived far away, and Jill never quite found the energy to put three toddlers in the back of the car and make the long drive back to Lincoln. So she slowly wound the practice down, throwing herself into volunteer work and her sons' tennis teams. Now the boys have graduated, though, and the

---

[1] The Reserve Officers' Training Corps. [Eds.]

big house is empty. Jill travels some, and works out, and tends to her increasingly far-flung family. But she rues the career she didn't have, and the regrets that hound her frequently. "This isn't what they gave me a degree for," she confided recently. "Somewhere, I screwed up."

My friend Shireen's regrets, meanwhile, are of a different sort. Petite and vivacious, she is one of those rare women who always manage to look both casually dressed and meticulously put together. Shireen went to business school in the early 1980s, when women were still rare among the ranks of MBAs. She graduated near the top of her class and took a fast-paced job in media marketing. She also met and married a fellow student, a hardworking son of Mexican immigrants who joined a media conglomerate as well. Shireen and Miguel worked happily together through the first few years of their marriage, grabbing takeout, skipping weekends, and sharing stories. They worked through the arrival of baby number one, and baby number two. After about eight years, however, and the arrival of baby number three, Miguel's career march accelerated. Suddenly, he was working hundred-hour weeks and shuttling back and forth among the company's expanded global operations. Without much fanfare, Shireen quietly stepped down. "What was I going to do?" she recalls. "Leave the kids with nannies around the clock?" So she took on all the child care, and the housework, and the increasingly large role of becoming a corporate wife. Today, even with her kids now grown and out of the house, Shireen maintains a breakneck schedule. She serves on several nonprofit boards and is involved with a score of local charities. She and Miguel have a strong and happy marriage. But she wears a veneer of wariness, a wariness that stems from suspecting what others want of her, and why. "People always say that they want me for my brains or my energy," she says with a smile. "But I know what they mean. They want Miguel's money. And the funny thing is," she continues, "that I really do have a lot of brains and energy. Or at least I once did."

Where women have made significant strides, for better or worse, is at the lower end of the pay scale and professional spectrum, in areas such as nursing, hairdressing, and middle school teaching, where women wholly dominate men. As reported in the 2009 Shriver Report, fully half of all workers in the United States are now female, and mothers contribute to their family's earnings in nearly two-thirds of American households. Mothers are the primary breadwinners, in fact, in four out of every ten households; and half of these mothers are single. These are important facts to consider, and complicated to think through. Because what does it really mean to have a household run by a single mother earning, on average, only $36,000 a year? Or to have two working-class parents holding down jobs and struggling to afford day care for their kids? The good news is that millions of women—black, white, Latina, and Asian—are financially independent, working in full- or part-time jobs to support themselves and their families. The bad news, though, is that many of these women are only barely hanging on, operating along the bottom of the social and economic pyramid, where women have long struggled and from which they were supposed to have escaped.

And certainly, some have. In 2009, women entrepreneurs ran more than 10 million businesses with combined sales of $1.1 trillion. As of 2007, firms owned by women in the United States employed 7.6 million people. But the aggregate numbers—that darned list of statistics again—make clear that most positions of power in this country (and indeed, around the world) are still persistently held by men. Women are flocking into college, into graduate programs, into entry-level and midlevel positions across every conceivable industry—but they are falling out well before they reach the top.

Why?

10      It isn't legalized prejudice anymore. It isn't barriers on the way in. And it's not just men being mean. Indeed, most men in visible positions of power today are almost desperate to have some reasonable number of women in their ranks. So what accounts for the bottleneck? For the clogged pipeline, the glass ceiling, the pervasive code words meant to capture the reality that women are simply getting stuck?

Clearly, painfully, they're getting stuck because so many of them are choosing to stop. Women are not getting fired from midlevel positions at accounting or law firms; they are not disproportionately being denied tenure at major research universities. They are deciding, like Jill and Shireen, that they need to stay at home, or work part time, or step away from the fast track. Individually, each of these women's moves may make great sense. Together, though, they have created a landscape where women are still scarce, and where the clashing visions between what is and what was expected to be makes them feel scarcer still.

## Responding to Reading

MyWritingLab™

1. At the beginning of paragraph 4, Spar says, "women are getting stuck." How does she explain why they are "getting stuck"?
2. What reasons does Spar give to explain why women seem to be underrepresented in top organizations? Why else could women be underrepresented?
3. **Rhetorical Analysis**   In paragraphs 5 and 6, Spar presents two long narrative examples. How convincing are they? Do they rely on logic, emotion, or the credibility of the writer? Do you think Spar's use of "My friend" to introduce these two examples is effective?

## Writing about Reading

MyWritingLab™

1. When referring to the reasons for the underrepresentation of women in high positions, Spar says, "It isn't legalized prejudice anymore" (10). Do you agree?
2. **Writing with Sources**   The term *glass ceiling* refers to the invisible barrier that keeps women (as well as certain minorities) from advancing to

the higher levels of corporations. Research the concept of the glass ceiling. Then, write an essay to Spar in which you explain why you agree or disagree with her conclusion. Make sure you explore a wide range of opinions.

# WHEN WORK IS A GAME, WHO WINS?

## Ben Mauk

*A regular online contributor to* The New Yorker, *Ben Mauk writes about a range of issues related to work and art. He has written for publications such as* The American Reader, The Believer, *the* Los Angeles Review of Books, The Paris Review Daily, *the* Sun, *and* Vice. *In the following essay, Mauk examines the role of "gamification" in the workplace.*

This summer, *Der Spiegel* ran several stories revealing the extent of the N.S.A.'s[1] large-scale monitoring of European communications. At the agency's European Cryptologic Center, in Hesse, the paper reported, agents learned to use the controversial XKeyscore software to mine Web users' private e-mails, online chats, and browsing histories with no prior authorization. One element stands out as particularly surreal: "To create additional motivation," according to *Der Spiegel*, "the NSA incorporated various features from computer games into the program." For instance, analysts who excelled at an XKeyscore training program could acquire "skilz" points and "unlock achievements."

For many readers, the existence of such games confirmed suspicions of the N.S.A.'s cavalier attitude toward online privacy. On the technology blog Gizmodo, Adam Clark Estes wrote, "Did analysts level up when they identified American citizens who were talking with targets? Or get extra lives for intercepting messages between citizens that include mention of one of these targets?" Other bloggers recalled Pentagon's Plan X, a coordinated effort between game designers, animators, and security experts to make waging "cyber offense" more like a video game.

Yet despite the uneasy reactions to *Der Spiegel*'s report, the argument that work should feel more like a video game—complete with points, instant performance feedback, and flashy graphics—has, in the past decade, become a common refrain in Silicon Valley, and the so-called gamification of work is already under way in many industries. For some offices, that means designing sales competitions with sports-themed graphics and points systems to emulate ESPN-style action. For others, it means simulating cyber attacks to promote teamwork among a company's security staff. Still others might use merit badges to reward employees for meeting new co-workers or even for eating healthfully.

---

[1]The National Security Agency. [Eds.]

* * *

In 1959, a Duke sociologist named Donald F. Roy joined a group of machine-line workers in Chicago to study how menial laborers, working twelve-hour shifts, coped with their factory conditions—in particular, the problem of monotony. The study, titled "Banana Time: Job Application and Informal Interaction," describes how the workers consciously broke up their day with food breaks ("peach time," "fish time," "coke time"); self-imposed, if meaningless, benchmarks ("stamp a thousand green shapes in a row"); and even practical jokes, such as a daily ritual in which one employee stole and ate another's banana, precipitating a volley of "protests and denunciations" from the victim—who nevertheless always made sure to bring another banana to work the next day. Through this kind of ritualized fun, Roy found, "the 'beast of boredom' was gentled to the harmlessness of a kitten."

5    Roy was among a group of mid-century sociologists who were trying to figure out why factory workers did not rise up in protest against their low pay and horrible conditions, Ethan Mollick, a professor at the Wharton School of Business at the University of Pennsylvania, told me. One researcher, who happened to return to Roy's Chicago factory many years after "Banana Time," found that the workers there had become obsessed with a factory-wide competition to beat individual production quotas. What's more, employees were more enthralled by the game itself than by the modest cash prize for which they were competing. Games, the researcher concluded, could divert factory workers' energies away from collective bargaining and toward internal competition. In doing so, they encouraged workers to consent to the factory owners' production goals.

"At a certain point, there was a transition from viewing games as something that hurt production to a tacit realization that maybe games are doing us a service," Mollick told me. People realized that games could be "built on top of the goals of management."

When researchers study what spurs people to work harder, they look at both "intrinsic" motivators—enjoyment of the work itself—or "extrinsic" rewards, such as money, benefits, and social events, said Nancy Rothbard, also a professor at Wharton. Increasingly, researchers have come to think of games as yet another extrinsic reward, like company picnics or managerial praise.

"What well-designed games do is to create challenges and well-measured rewards for those challenges that give frequent positive feedback, designed to make workers feel more positively," Rothbard said. In other words, turning work into a game can make employees more satisfied and, potentially, more productive—all under the guise of having fun.

Hey, you know what kind of games are fun? Video games, which evolved around the same time as modern industrial psychology, and have since incentivized millions of children and adults to save princesses, steal cars, solve puzzles, build cities, and wage merciless wars in virtual worlds, with fun being pretty much the only salient reward. Today, some gurus in the burgeoning field of "game studies" argue that video games, in particular, can be powerful motivators.

In her influential 2012 book *Reality Is Broken*, Jane McGonigal—a 10 game designer and TED Talk favorite—writes that this is because the non-game world falls short of our expectations and desires in ways that games never do. "The real world just doesn't offer up as easily the carefully designed pleasures, the thrilling challenges, and the powerful social bonding afforded by virtual environments." McGonigal, seeming like the world's most cheerful existentialist, itemizes reality's many flaws—that it is "hopeless," "depressing," and "trivial"—and suggests that games like World of Warcraft and Rock Band hold the cure. Instead of continuing to suffer in a world without meaning, she writes, "imagine a near future in which most of the real world works more like a game."

* * *

That may not be a stretch. Today, you can track your cross-training with Nike+, become mayor of your coffee shop with Foursquare, win badges for energy conservation with Opower, level up in German, Spanish, or Italian on Duolingo, out-clean your spouse in ChoreWars, or try some of the hundreds of other apps and sites that use gaming features to help you lose weight, balance your budget, or just gamify your entire life. By 2016, M2 Research predicts that gamification will be a $2.8 billion industry.

The research firm further predicts that workplace gamification will see the greatest growth. To understand how that would look, consider Zillow, the real-estate Web site, whose salespeople win points by making cold calls and closing sales, and account managers get ahead by earning positive surveys from customers or convincing them to return for more business. If you're a Zillow worker and a customer gives you some nice feedback, for example, TV screens across the company will light up with graphics, videos, and your own head shot—all themed according to whatever sport is in season. (Right now, it's football.)

"The TVs are pervasive throughout the office, so that even when you're on a call you can look over and see the screen," Tony Small, a Zillow vice-president, told me. Workers, he said, are constantly in competition to rise to the top of each so-called leader board.

In fact, most examples of workplace gamification are competitive in nature, relying on points, badges, and leader boards to motivate performance. In the past few years, venders with names like Busification, Leaderboarded, Hoopla, and the dystopian-sounding Dopamine have emerged to offer these features. (Hoopla's motto: "Put Fun to Work.")

15    "Imagine if you're watching a football game on TV and someone scores a touchdown," said Small. "It looks like that. Our sales teams are competitive, and they happen to like sports. So when we found a channel that ESPN-izes what workers do, they really liked it."

One can imagine how gamification software can be adapted to any metric. If you're trying to limit unnecessary e-mails or shorten meeting times, for instance, you could dock employees points for sending an e-mail, or reward managers with a badge for ending a meeting early.

\* \* \*

Not all designers are unruffled by the way games have transitioned into the workplace. Ian Bogost, a game designer and professor at the Georgia Institute of Technology, is among the industry's most vocal critics. In a 2011 speech, "Gamification Is Bullshit," he said gamification, having nothing to do with the pleasure of gaming, should instead be called "exploitationware," which opportunists have "pursued to capitalize on a cultural moment, through services about which they have questionable expertise, to bring about results meant to last only long enough to pad their bank accounts before the next bullshit trend comes along."

Bogost told me he is not inherently opposed to the use of game-like tools to quantify employee performance, especially in the salesroom. But he worries about potential misuse in other fields: "The question is, do we want to apply this to every single job? Food workers? Public-transit drivers?" He went on, "I'm opposed to the idea that you can give workers sugar pills, instead of pay and benefits—instead of the courtesy of being treated like a human being."

That idea—and the debate over it—predates the gamification trend by many decades, and remains a contentious topic in industrial psychology: To what degree can non-remunerative features of a workplace compensate for work that is not, in itself, rewarding? If your job is dull, menial, or unpleasant, will any number of free gym memberships, weekend retreats, or gamified work environments satisfy you?

20    And then there's another question: Is there something inherently un-fun about being forced by your boss to play a video game? While most research on workplace games has concerned itself with spontaneous, employee-generated play, one forthcoming study—authored by Mollick, the Wharton professor, and his colleague Nancy Rothbard—is among the first to consider the effect on workers of "managerially imposed" exercises that mimic video games. The researchers found that some sales workers at a start-up were more satisfied—although not more productive—when they were given a basketball-themed "gamified" environment. But, crucially, the effect worked only for those employees who said they felt that the game was fair, coherent,

and a legitimate activity to associate with work. Those in the gamified environment who felt the game was unfair, confusing, or just inappropriate—about half of the workers in the group—were significantly less satisfied in their work, and slightly less productive. To improve workers' satisfaction through games, the authors determined, you need their consent.

The study, which is currently under review at a peer-reviewed journal, is a reminder that, while consumers can choose whether they want to play a game, workers can't opt out of their jobs. The result is a paradox the researchers define as "mandatory fun."

Mollick hopes to do more experiments to see how rates of consent might be improved. And yet, while gamification with proper consent may help to motivate employees, it does not seem likely that a veneer of play will create new meaning in the workplace. Nor will it fix a work culture that is fundamentally broken. Instead, gamification—like the old-fashioned games of an earlier era—could end up encouraging competition among workers who, decades earlier, might have found another activity to share: uniting as a single team to demand higher pay, better benefits, and more meaningful work.

## Responding to Reading

MyWritingLab™

1. Although Mauk refers to various things that businesses can do to make work like a game, he never defines *game*. Is this definition needed? Why or why not?
2. According to Mauk, what are the possible benefits of making work more like a video game?
3. **Rhetorical Analysis**   Mauk concludes his essay by discussing some of the problems of "gamification." Why does he include this information? Does this strategy strengthen or weaken his argument? Explain.

## Writing about Reading

MyWritingLab™

1. Think of a job you had, and consider how making that job like a video game could create additional motivation.
2. **Writing with Sources**   Go online and research the features that well-designed video games should have. Then, "gamify" another job with which you are familiar. How could you convince workers to participate in the game? What positive effects do you think this mandated play would have on workers? Why? What negative effects of "gamification" might occur?

# It's Not about You
## David Brooks
### 1961–

*The following essay describes the particular challenges facing today's college graduates as they look for work. (See page 64 for Brooks's biography.)*

Over the past few weeks, America's colleges have sent another class of graduates off into the world. These graduates possess something of inestimable value. Nearly every sensible middle-aged person would give away all their money to be able to go back to age 22 and begin adulthood anew.

But, especially this year, one is conscious of the many ways in which this year's graduating class has been ill served by their elders. They enter a bad job market, the hangover from decades of excessive borrowing. They inherit a ruinous federal debt.

More important, their lives have been perversely structured. This year's graduates are members of the most supervised generation in American history. Through their childhoods and teenage years, they have been monitored, tutored, coached and honed to an unprecedented degree.

Yet upon graduation they will enter a world that is unprecedentedly wide open and unstructured. Most of them will not quickly get married, buy a home and have kids, as previous generations did. Instead, they will confront amazingly diverse job markets, social landscapes and lifestyle niches. Most will spend a decade wandering from job to job and clique to clique, searching for a role.

5    No one would design a system of extreme supervision to prepare people for a decade of extreme openness. But this is exactly what has emerged in modern America. College students are raised in an environment that demands one set of navigational skills, and they are then cast out into a different environment requiring a different set of skills, which they have to figure out on their own.

Worst of all, they are sent off into this world with the whole babyboomer theology ringing in their ears. If you sample some of the commencement addresses being broadcast on C-Span these days, you see that many graduates are told to: Follow *your* passion, chart *your* own course, march to the beat of *your* own drummer, follow *your* dreams and find *your*self. This is the litany of expressive individualism, which is still the dominant note in American culture.

But, of course, this mantra misleads on nearly every front.

College grads are often sent out into the world amid rapturous talk of limitless possibilities. But this talk is of no help to the central business of adulthood, finding serious things to tie yourself down to. The successful young adult is beginning to make sacred commitments—to a spouse, a community and calling—yet mostly hears about freedom and autonomy.

Today's graduates are also told to find their passion and then pursue their dreams. The implication is that they should find themselves first and then go off and live their quest. But, of course, very few people at age 22 or 24 can take an inward journey and come out having discovered a developed self.

Most successful young people don't look inside and then plan a   10 life. They look outside and find a problem, which summons their life. A relative suffers from Alzheimer's and a young woman feels called to help cure that disease. A young man works under a miserable boss and must develop management skills so his department can function. Another young woman finds herself confronted by an opportunity she never thought of in a job category she never imagined. This wasn't in her plans, but this is where she can make her contribution.

Most people don't form a self and then lead a life. They are called by a problem, and the self is constructed gradually by their calling.

The graduates are also told to pursue happiness and joy. But, of course, when you read a biography of someone you admire, it's rarely the things that made them happy that compel your admiration. It's the things they did to court unhappiness—the things they did that were arduous and miserable, which sometimes cost them friends and aroused hatred. It's excellence, not happiness, that we admire most.

Finally, graduates are told to be independent-minded and to express their inner spirit. But, of course, doing your job well often means suppressing yourself. As Atul Gawande mentioned during his countercultural address last week at Harvard Medical School, being a good doctor often means being part of a team, following the rules of an institution, going down a regimented checklist.

Today's grads enter a cultural climate that preaches the self as the center of a life. But, of course, as they age, they'll discover that the tasks of a life are at the center. Fulfillment is a byproduct of how people engage their tasks, and can't be pursued directly. Most of us are egotistical and most are self-concerned most of the time, but it's nonetheless true that life comes to a point only in those moments when the self dissolves into some task. The purpose in life is not to find yourself. It's to lose yourself.

## Responding to Reading

MyWritingLab™

1. What does Brooks mean when he says that today's young people are victims of "extreme supervision" (5)?
2. What is the "baby-boomer theology" to which Brooks refers in paragraph 6? In what sense does he think this philosophy reverses life's priorities? Why does it create problems for new college graduates?
3. **Rhetorical Analysis**  Brooks begins his conclusion by speaking of "today's grads." He then shifts to "most of us" and ends by saying, "The purpose in

life is not to find yourself." Why does he make these shifts? How do they help him make his point?

## Writing about Reading

1. Do you think Brooks is correct when he characterizes you and your peers as members "of the most supervised generation in American history" (3)?

2. **Writing with Sources** According to Brooks, most successful people don't look inside themselves and plan their lives. Instead, they "find a problem, which summons their life" (10). Interview several people between the ages of twenty-two and twenty-four and find out if what Brooks contends is borne out by the facts. Then, write an essay in which you agree or disagree with Brooks's essay.

# DELUSIONS OF GRANDEUR

## Henry Louis Gates, Jr.

### *1950–*

*Henry Louis Gates, Jr., earned a Ph.D. (1979) in English literature from Clare College at the University of Cambridge, where he was the first African American to do so. At age thirty, he received a MacArthur Foundation Genius Grant (1980). He has taught at Yale, Cornell, Duke, and Harvard. One of Gates's best-known works is* Loose Canons: Notes on the Culture Wars *(1992), in which he discusses gender, literature, and multiculturalism in American arts and letters. His latest book is* Finding Your Roots: The Official Companion to the PBS Series *(2014). He is general editor of the first (1996) second (2003), and third (2014) editions of* The Norton Anthology of African American Literature; *a contributor to* The New Yorker; *and the author of essays, reviews, and profiles in many other publications. In the following essay, Gates points out how few African Americans actually succeed as professional athletes and argues that the schools should do more to encourage young black men to pursue more realistic goals.*

Standing at the bar of an all-black VFW post in my hometown of Piedmont, W.Va., I offered five dollars to anyone who could tell me how many African-American professional athletes were at work today. There are 35 million African-Americans, I said.

"Ten million!" yelled one intrepid soul, too far into his cups.

"No way ... more like 500,000," said another.

"You mean *all* professional sports," someone interjected, "including golf and tennis, but not counting the brothers from Puerto Rico?" Everyone laughed.

5    "Fifty thousand, minimum," was another guess.

Here are the facts:

There are 1,200 black professional athletes in the U.S.
There are 12 times more black lawyers than black athletes.
There are 2¹/₂ times more black dentists than black athletes.
There are 15 times more black doctors than black athletes.

Nobody in my local VFW believed these statistics; in fact, few people would believe them if they weren't reading them in the pages of *Sports Illustrated*. In spite of these statistics, too many African-American youngsters still believe that they have a much better chance of becoming another Magic Johnson or Michael Jordan than they do of matching the achievements of Baltimore Mayor Kurt Schmoke or neurosurgeon Dr. Benjamin Carson, both of whom, like Johnson and Jordan, are black.

In reality, an African-American youngster has about as much chance of becoming a professional athlete as he or she does of winning the lottery. The tragedy for our people, however, is that few of us accept that truth.

Let me confess that I love sports. Like most black people of my generation—I'm 40—I was raised to revere the great black athletic heroes, and I never tired of listening to the stories of triumph and defeat that, for blacks, amount to a collective epic much like those of the ancient Greeks: Joe Louis's demolition of Max Schmeling; Satchel Paige's dazzling repertoire of pitches; Jesse Owens's in-your-face performance in Hitler's 1936 Olympics; Willie Mays's over-the-shoulder basket catch; Jackie Robinson's quiet strength when assaulted by racist taunts; and a thousand other grand tales.

Nevertheless, the blind pursuit of attainment in sports is having a devastating effect on our people. Imbued with a belief that our principal avenue to fame and profit is through sport, and seduced by a win-at-any-cost system that corrupts even elementary school students, far too many black kids treat basketball courts and football fields as if they were classrooms in an alternative school system. "O.K., I flunked English," a young athlete will say. "But I got an A plus in slamdunking." 10

The failure of our public schools to educate athletes is part and parcel of the schools' failure to educate almost everyone. A recent survey of the Philadelphia school system, for example, stated that "more than half of all students in the third, fifth and eighth grades cannot perform minimum math and language tasks." One in four middle school students in that city fails to pass to the next grade each year. It is a sad truth that such statistics are repeated in cities throughout the nation. Young athletes—particularly young black athletes—are especially ill-served. Many of them are functionally illiterate, yet they are passed along from year to year for the greater glory of good old Hometown High. We should not be surprised to learn, then, that only 26.6% of black athletes at the collegiate level earn their degrees. For every successful educated black professional athlete, there are thousands of dead and wounded. Yet young blacks continue to aspire to careers as athletes, and it's no wonder why; when the University of North Carolina recently commissioned a sculptor to create archetypes of its student body, guess which ethnic group was selected to represent athletes?

Those relatively few black athletes who do make it in the professional ranks must be prevailed upon to play a significant role in the education of all of our young people, athlete and nonathlete alike. While some have done so, many others have shirked their social obligations: to earmark small percentages of their incomes for the United Negro College Fund; to appear on television for educational purposes rather than merely to sell sneakers; to let children know the message that becoming a lawyer, a teacher or a doctor does more good for our people than winning the Super Bowl; and to form productive liaisons with educators to help forge solutions to the many ills that beset the black community. These are merely a few modest proposals.

A similar burden falls upon successful blacks in all walks of life. Each of us must strive to make our young people understand the realities. Tell them to cheer Bo Jackson but to emulate novelist Toni Morrison or businessman Reginald Lewis or historian John Hope Franklin or Spelman College president Johnetta Cole—the list is long.

Of course, society as a whole bears responsibility as well. Until colleges stop using young blacks as cannon fodder in the big-business wars of so-called nonprofessional sports, until training a young black's mind becomes as important as training his or her body, we will continue to perpetuate a system akin to that of the Roman gladiators, sacrificing a class of people for the entertainment of the mob.

## Responding to Reading

MyWritingLab™

1. What does Gates mean when he says, "The failure of our public schools to educate athletes is part and parcel of the schools' failure to educate almost everyone" (11)? Do you agree? In addition to the public schools, who or what else could be responsible for the situation Gates describes?
2. What does Gates mean when he says that colleges are using young blacks as "cannon fodder" (14)? According to Gates, how are young black athletes like Roman gladiators? Do you think that this comparison is accurate? fair?
3. **Rhetorical Analysis**  Why does Gates begin his essay with an anecdote? What does this story reveal about African Americans' assumptions about sports? What other introductory strategy could he have used? What are the advantages and disadvantages of each?

## Writing about Reading

MyWritingLab™

1. What were your reactions to the statistics presented in paragraph 6?
2. **Writing with Sources**  Find some other statistics about African American job participation. Then, write the text of a children's book designed to convey this information to preschoolers.

# EXPLOITING THE GENDER GAP

## Warren Farrell

### 1943–

*Described as "the Gloria Steinem of Men's Liberation," Warren Farrell teaches and writes about men's and women's issues. He is the chair of the Commission to Create a White House Council on Boys to Men and has taught at the School of Medicine at the University of California, San Diego, as well as at Georgetown University, Rutgers University, and American University. The author of numerous books, Farrell is currently coauthoring* Boys to Men *with John Gray. In the following essay, Farrell examines the wage disparity between men and women.*

Nothing disturbs working women more than the statistics often mentioned on Labor Day showing that they are paid only 76 cents to men's dollar for the same work. If that were the whole story, it should disturb all of us; like many men, I have two daughters and a wife in the work force.

When I was on the board of the National Organization for Women in New York City, I blamed discrimination for that gap. Then I asked myself, "If an employer has to pay a man one dollar for the same work a woman would do for 76 cents, why would anyone hire a man?"

Perhaps, I thought, male bosses undervalue women. But I discovered that in 2000, women without bosses—who own their own businesses—earned only 49 percent of male business owners. Why? When the Rochester Institute of Technology surveyed business owners with M.B.A.'s from one top business school, they found that money was the primary motivator for only 29 percent of the women, versus 76 percent of the men. Women put a premium on autonomy, flexibility (25- to 35-hour weeks and proximity to home), fulfillment and safety.

After years of research, I discovered 25 differences in the work-life choices of men and women. All 25 lead to men earning more money, but to women having better lives.

High pay, as it turns out, is about tradeoffs. Men's tradeoffs include working more hours (women work more around the home); taking more dangerous, dirtier and outdoor jobs (garbage collecting, construction, trucking); relocating and traveling; and training for technical jobs with less people contact (like engineering). 5

Is the pay gap, then, about the different choices of men and women? Not quite. It's about parents' choices. Women who have never been married and are childless earn 117 percent of their childless male counterparts. (This comparison controls for education, hours worked and age.) Their decisions are more like married men's, and never-married men's decisions are more like women's in general (careers in arts, no weekend work, etc.).

Does this imply that mothers sacrifice careers? Not really. Surveys of men and women in their 20's find that both sexes (70 percent of men, and 63 percent of women) would sacrifice pay for more family time. The next generation's discussion will be about who gets to be the primary parent.

Don't women, though, earn less than men in the same job? Yes and no. For example, the Bureau of Labor Statistics lumps together all medical doctors. Men are more likely to be surgeons (versus general practitioners) and work in private practice for hours that are longer and less predictable, and for more years. In brief, the same job is not the same. Are these women's choices? When I taught at a medical school, I saw that even my first-year female students eyed specialties with fewer and more predictable hours.

But don't female executives also make less than male executives? Yes. Discrimination? Let's look. The men are more frequently executives of national and international firms with more personnel and revenues, and responsible for bottom-line sales, marketing and finances, not human resources or public relations. They have more experience, relocate and travel overseas more, and so on.

10    Comparing men and women with the "same jobs," then, is to compare apples and oranges. However, when all 25 choices are the same, the great news for women is that then the women make more than the men. Is there discrimination against women? Yes, like the old boys' network. And sometimes discrimination against women becomes discrimination against men: in hazardous fields, women suffer fewer hazards. For example, more than 500 marines have died in the war in Iraq. All but two were men. In other fields, men are virtually excluded—try getting hired as a male dental hygienist, nursery school teacher, cocktail waiter.

There are 80 jobs in which women earn more than men—positions like financial analyst, speech-language pathologist, radiation therapist, library worker, biological technician, motion picture projectionist. Female sales engineers make 143 percent of their male counterparts; female statisticians earn 135 percent.

I want my daughters to know that people who work 44 hours a week make, on average, more than twice the pay of someone working 34 hours a week. And that pharmacists now earn almost as much as doctors. But only by abandoning our focus on discrimination against women can we discover these opportunities for women.

## Responding to Reading

MyWritingLab™

1. How does Farrell explain the wage disparity that exists between men and women? Do you think his explanation makes sense?
2. What does Farrell mean when he concludes, "Comparing men and women with the 'same jobs,' then, is to compare apples and oranges" (10)? Do you think this analogy is accurate? Is it fair?
3. **Rhetorical Analysis**   In paragraph 1, Farrell mentions that he has "two daughters and a wife in the work force." In paragraph 2, he points out that he was on the board of the New York chapter of the National Organization for Women. Why do you think he includes this information? What assumptions is he making about his readers?

## Writing about Reading

MyWritingLab™

1. Do you think Farrell is oversimplifying the issue of wage discrimination when he says, "But only by abandoning our focus on discrimination against women can we discover these opportunities for women" (12)? Explain.
2. **Writing with Sources**   Clearly, not everyone would agree with Farrell's analysis. Look at essays on both sides of this issue. Which side do you think makes better arguments? Then, write an e-mail to Farrell in which you respond to his central thesis.

POETRY

# I HEAR AMERICA SINGING

## Walt Whitman

### *1819—1892*

*A journalist, editor, printer, teacher, and government clerk, Walt Whitman is one of America's most important and widely read poets. He is the author of numerous prose and poetry collections, including* Leaves of Grass, *which Whitman published in several editions and in which "I Hear America Singing" appeared. In this poem, Whitman celebrates work as a kind of song.*

I hear America singing, the varied carols I hear,
Those of mechanics, each one singing his as it should be blithe and strong,
The carpenter singing his as he measures his plank or beam,
The mason singing his as he makes ready for work, or leaves off work,
The boatman singing what belongs to him in his boat, the deckhand singing on the steamboat deck,

5

The shoemaker singing as he sits on his bench, the hatter singing as he stands,
The wood-cutter's song, the ploughboy's on his way in the morning, or at noon intermission or at sundown,
The delicious singing of the mother, or of the young wife at work, or of the girl sewing or washing,
Each singing what belongs to him or her and to none else,
10    The day what belongs to the day—at night the party of young fellows, robust, friendly,
Singing with open mouths their strong melodious songs.

## Responding to Reading                                    MyWritingLab™

1. What attitude toward America is Whitman trying to convey in this poem? How can you tell?
2. Whitman includes a catalog of workers in this poem. What does he want to illustrate through this range of jobs? Is he successful?
3. What does this poem say about work? about people who work? about America? In what sense can the Americans in this poem be said to be singing?

## Responding in Writing                                    MyWritingLab™

Write your updated version of "I Hear America Singing." Make sure you include a variety of present-day occupations in your poem.

—————————— FOCUS ——————————

## Is Every Worker Entitled to a Living Wage?

McDonald's worker striking for a $15 hourly wage, Los Angeles, August 29, 2013

### Responding to the Image

MyWritingLab™

1. The photo above shows a man holding a sign. What point is the photo making?
2. At what audience do you think the photo is aimed? Explain.
3. *Visual irony* occurs when two contrasting elements are placed side by side in a visual. In the photo above, find some examples of visual irony. How do they help the photo achieve its purpose?

# MEASURING THE FULL IMPACT OF MINIMUM AND LIVING WAGE LAWS

## Jeannette Wicks-Lim

*1970–*

*An assistant research professor at the Political Economy Research Institute at the University of Massachusetts, Amherst, Jeannette Wicks-Lim specializes in labor economics and the political economy of race. She coauthored the book* A Measure of Fairness: The Economics of Living Wages and Minimum Wages in the United States *(2008) and coedited the essay col-lection* Capitalism on Trial: Explorations in the Tradition of Thomas E. Weisskopf *(2013). In the following essay, Wicks-Lim analyzes the effects of minimum- and living-wage laws.*

Raising the minimum wage is quickly becoming a key political issue for this fall's midterm elections.[1] In the past, Democratic politicians have shied away from the issue while Republicans have openly opposed a higher minimum wage. But this year is different. Community activists are forcing the issue by campaigning to put state minimum-wage pro-posals before the voters this fall in Arizona, Colorado, Ohio, and Mis-souri. No doubt inspired by the 100-plus successful local living-wage campaigns of the past ten years, these activists are also motivated by a federal minimum wage that has stagnated for the past nine years. The $5.15 federal minimum is at its lowest value in purchasing-power terms in more than 50 years; a single parent with two children, work-ing full-time at the current minimum wage, would fall $2,000 below the poverty line.

Given all the political activity on the ground, the Democrats have decided to make the minimum wage a central plank in their party plat-form. Former presidential candidate John Edwards has teamed up with Sen. Edward Kennedy (D-Mass.) and ACORN, a leading advocacy group for living wage laws, to push for a $7.25 federal minimum. Even some Republicans are supporting minimum wage increases. In fact, a bipartisan legislative coalition unexpectedly passed a state minimum wage hike in Michigan this March.

Minimum-wage and living-wage laws have always caused an up-roar in the business community. Employers sound the alarm about the dire consequences of a higher minimum wage both for themselves and for the low-wage workers these laws are intended to benefit: Minimum wage mandates, they claim, will cause small-business owners to close shop and lay off their low-wage workers. A spokesperson for the Na-tional Federation of Independent Business (NFIB), commenting on a proposal to raise Pennsylvania's minimum wage in an interview with the *Philadelphia Inquirer*, put it this way: "That employer may as well be handing out pink slips along with the pay raise."

What lies behind these bleak predictions? Mark Shaffer, owner of Shaffer's Park Supper Club in Crivitz, Wisc., provided one explana-tion to the *Wisconsin State Journal*: "...increasing the minimum wage would create a chain reaction. Every worker would want a raise to keep pace, forcing up prices and driving away customers." In other words, employers will not only be forced to raise the wages of those workers

---

[1]This essay was published in May 2006. [Eds.]

earning below the new minimum wage, but also the wages of their co-workers who earn somewhat more. The legally required wage raises are difficult enough for employers to absorb, they claim; these other raises—referred to as ripple effect raises—aggravate the situation. The result? "That ripple effect is going to lay off people."

Ripple effects represent a double-edged sword for minimum-wage and living-wage proponents. Their extent determines how much low-wage workers will benefit from such laws. If the ripple effects are small, then a higher minimum (or living) wage would benefit only a small class of workers, and boosting the minimum wage might be dismissed as an ineffective antipoverty strategy. If the ripple effects are large, then setting higher wage minimums may be seen as a potent policy tool to improve the lives of the working poor. But at the same time, evidence of large ripple effects provides ammunition to employers who claim they cannot afford the costs of a higher wage floor.

So what is the evidence on ripple effects? Do they bloat wage bills and overwhelm employers? Do they expand the number of workers who get raises a little or a lot? It's difficult to say because the research on ripple effects has been thin. But getting a clear picture of the full impact of minimum and living wage laws on workers' wages is critical to evaluating the impact of these laws. New research provides estimates of the scope and magnitude of the ripple effects of both minimum-wage and living-wage laws. This evidence is crucial for analyzing both the full impact of this increasingly visible policy tool and the political struggles surrounding it.

## Why Do Employers Give Ripple-Effect Raises?

Marge Thomas, CEO of Goodwill Industries in Maryland, explains in an interview with *The Gazette* (Md.): "There will be a ripple effect [in response to Maryland's recent minimum wage increase to $6.15], since it wouldn't be fair to pay people now making above the minimum wage at the same level as those making the new minimum wage." That is, without ripple effects, an increase in the wage floor will worsen the relative wage position of workers just above it. If there are no ripple effects, workers earning $6.15 before Maryland's increase would not only see their wages fall to the bottom of the wage scale, but also to the same level as workers who had previously earned inferior wages (i.e., workers who earned between $5.15 and $6.15).

Employers worry that these workers would view such a relative decline in their wages as unfair, damaging their morale—and their productivity. Without ripple effect raises, employers fear, their disgruntled staff will cut back on hard-to-measure aspects of their work such as responding to others cheerfully and taking initiative in assisting customers.

Chapter 10 Focus

So employers feel compelled to preserve some consistency in their wage scales. Workers earning $6.15 before the minimum increase, for example, may receive a quarter raise, to $6.40, to keep their wages just above the new $6.15 minimum. That employers feel compelled to give non-mandated raises to some of their lowest-paid workers because it is the "fair" thing to do may appear to be a dubious claim. Perhaps so, but employers commonly express anxiety about the costs of minimum-wage and living-wage laws for this very reason.

## The Politics of Ripple Effects

10    Inevitably, then, ripple effects come into play in the political battles around minimum-wage and living-wage laws—but in contradictory ways for both opponents and supporters. Opponents raise the specter of large ripple effects bankrupting small businesses. At the same time, though, they argue that minimum-wage laws are not effective in fighting poverty because they do not cover many workers—and worse, because those who are covered are largely teens or young-adult students just working for spending money. If ripple effects are small, this shores up opponents' assertions that minimum-wage laws have a limited impact on poverty. Evidence of larger ripple effects, on the other hand, would mean that the benefits of minimum-wage laws are larger than previously understood, and that these laws have an even greater potential to reduce poverty among the working poor.

The political implications are complicated further in the context of living-wage laws, which typically call for much higher wage floors than state and federal minimum-wage laws do. The living-wage movement calls for wage floors to be set at rates that provide a "livable income," such as the federal poverty level for a family of four, rather than at the arbitrary—and very low—level current minimum-wage laws set. The difference is dramatic: the living-wage ordinances that have been passed in a number of municipalities typically set a wage floor twice the level of federal and state minimum wages.

So the mandated raises under living-wage laws are already much higher than under even the highest state minimum-wage laws. If living-wage laws have significant ripple effects, opponents have all the more ammunition for their argument that the costs of these laws are unsustainable for employers.

## How Big Are Ripple Effects?

My answer is a typical economists' response: it depends. In a nutshell, it depends on how high the wage minimum is set. The reason for this is simple. Evidence from the past 20 years of changes to state and federal minimum wages suggests that while there is a ripple effect, it doesn't extend very far beyond the new minimum. So, if the wage minimum is set high, then a large number of workers are legally due raises and, relatively speaking, the number of workers who get ripple-effect raises is small. Conversely, if the wage minimum is set low, then a small number of workers are legally due raises and, relatively speaking, the number of workers who get ripple-effect raises is large.

In the case of minimum-wage laws, the evidence suggests that ripple effects do dramatically expand their impact. Minimum wages are generally set low relative to the wage distribution. Because so many more workers earn wages just above the minimum wage compared to those earning the minimum, even a small ripple effect increases considerably the number of workers who benefit from a rise in the minimum wage. And even though the size of these raises quickly shrinks the higher the worker's wage rate, the much greater number of affected workers translates into a significantly larger increase in the wage bills of employers.

For example, my research shows that the impact of the most recent federal minimum-wage increase, from $4.75 to $5.15 in 1997, extended to workers earning wages around $5.75. Workers earning between the old and new minimums generally received raises to bring their wages in line with the new minimum—an 8% raise for those who started at the old minimum. Workers earning around $5.20 (right above the new minimum of $5.15) received raises of around 2%, bringing their wages up to about $5.30. Finally, those workers earning wages around $5.75 received raises on the order of 1%, bringing their wages up to about $5.80.

This narrow range of small raises translates into a big overall impact. Roughly 4 million workers (those earning between $4.75 and $5.15) received mandated raises in response to the 1997 federal minimum wage increase. Taking into account the typical work schedules of these workers, these raises translated into a $741 million increase to employers' annual wage bills. Now add in ripple effects: Approximately 11 million workers received ripple-effect raises, adding another $1.3 billion to employers' wage bills. In other words, ripple-effect raises almost quadrupled the number of workers who benefited from the minimum-wage increase and almost tripled the over-all costs associated with it.

Dramatic as these ripple effects are, the real impact on employers can only be gauged in relation to their capacity to absorb the higher wage costs. Here, there is evidence that businesses are not overwhelmed by the costs of a higher minimum wage, even including ripple effects. For example, in a study I co-authored with University of Massachusetts economists Robert Pollin and Mark Brenner on the Florida ballot measure to establish a $6.15 state minimum wage (which passed overwhelmingly in 2004), we accounted for ripple-effect costs of roughly this same magnitude. Despite almost tripling the number of affected

15

workers (from almost 300,000 to over 850,000) and more than doubling the costs associated with the new minimum wage (from $155 million to $410 million), the ripple effects, combined with the mandated wage increases, imposed an average cost increase on employers amounting to less than one-half of 1% of their sales revenue. Even for employers in the hotel and restaurant industry, where low-wage workers tend to be concentrated, the average cost increase was less than 1% of their sales revenue. In other words, a 1% increase in prices for hotel rooms or restaurant meals could cover the increased costs associated with both legally mandated raises and ripple-effect raises.

The small fraction of revenue that these raises represent goes a long way toward explaining why economists generally agree that minimum-wage laws are not "job killers," as opponents claim. According to a 1998 survey of economists, a consensus seems to have been reached that there is minimal job loss, if any, associated with minimum-wage increases in the ranges that we've seen.

Just as important, this new research revises our understanding of who benefits from minimum wage laws. Including ripple-effect raises expands the circle of minimum-wage beneficiaries to include more adult workers and fewer teenage or student workers. In fact, accounting for ripple effects decreases the prevalence of teenagers and traditional-age students (age 16 to 24) among workers likely to be affected by a federal minimum-wage increase from four out of ten to three out of ten. In other words, adult workers make up an even larger majority of likely minimum-wage beneficiaries when ripple effects are added to the picture.

## The Case of Living-Wage Laws

20 With living-wage laws, the ripple effect story appears to be quite different, however—primarily because living wage laws set much higher wage minimums.

To understand why living-wage laws might generate far less of a ripple effect than minimum-wage hikes, it is instructive to look at the impact of raising the minimum wage on the retail trade industry. About 15% of retail trade workers earn wages at or very close to the minimum wage, compared to 5% of all workers. As a result, a large fraction of the retail trade industry workforce receives legally mandated raises when the minimum wage is raised, which is just what occurs across a broader group of industries and occupations when a living-wage ordinance is passed.

My research shows that the relative impact of the ripple effect that accompanies a minimum-wage hike is much smaller within retail trade than across all industries. Because a much larger share of workers in retail receive legally required raises when the minimum wage is raised, this reduces the relative number of workers receiving ripple effect raises, and, in turn, the relative size of the costs associated with ripple effects. This analysis suggests that the ripple effects of living wage laws will likewise be smaller than those found with minimum-wage laws.

To be sure, the ripple effect in the retail trade sector may underestimate the ripple effect of living-wage laws for a couple of reasons. First, unlike minimum-wage hikes, living-wage laws may have ripple effects that extend across firms as well as up the wage structure within firms. Employers who do not fall under a living-wage law's mandate but who are competing for workers within the same local labor market as those that do may be compelled to raise their own wages in order to retain their workers. Second, workers just above living-wage levels are typically higher on the job ladder and may have more bargaining power than workers with wages just above minimum-wage levels and, as a result, may be able to demand more significant raises when living-wage laws are enacted.

However, case studies of living-wage ordinances in Los Angeles and San Francisco do suggest that the ripple effect plays a smaller role in the case of living-wage laws than in the case of minimum-wage laws. These studies find that ripple effects add less than half again to the costs of mandated raises—dramatically less than the almost tripling of costs by ripple effects associated with the 1997 federal minimum-wage increase. In other words, the much higher wage floors set by living-wage laws appear to reverse the importance of legally required raises versus ripple-effect raises.

Do the costs associated with living-wage laws—with their higher wage floors—overwhelm employers, even if their ripple effects are small? To date, estimates suggest that within the range of existing living-wage laws, businesses are generally able to absorb the cost increases they face. For example, Pollin and Brenner studied a 2000 proposal to raise the wage floor from $5.75 to $10.75 in Santa Monica, Calif. They estimated that the cost increase faced by a typical business would be small, on the order of 2% of sales revenue, even accounting for both mandated and ripple-effect raises. Their estimates also showed that some hotel and restaurant businesses might face cost increases amounting to up to 10% of their sales revenue—not a negligible sum. However, after examining the local economy, Pollin and Brenner concluded that even these cost increases would not be likely to force these businesses to close their doors. Moreover, higher productivity and lower turnover rates among workers paid a living wage would also reduce the impact of these costs.

Ultimately, the impact of ripple-effect raises appears to depend crucially on the level of the new wage floor. The lower the wage floor, as in the case of minimum-wage laws, the more important the role of ripple-effect raises. The higher the wage floor, as in the case of living-wage laws, the less important the role of ripple-effect raises.

25

## Making the Case

The results of this new research are generally good news for proponents of living- and minimum-wage laws. Ripple effects do not portend dire consequences for employers from minimum and living wage laws; at the same time, ripple-effect raises heighten the effectiveness of these laws as antipoverty strategies.

In the case of minimum-wage laws, because the cost of legally mandated raises relative to employer revenues is small, even ripple effects large enough to triple the cost of a minimum-wage increase do not represent a large burden for employers. Moreover, ripple effects enhance the somewhat anemic minimum-wage laws to make them more effective as policy tools for improving the lot of the working poor. Accounting for ripple effects nearly quadruples the number of beneficiaries of a minimum-wage hike and expands the majority of those beneficiaries who are adults—in many instances, family breadwinners.

However, ripple effects do not appear to overwhelm employers in the case of the more ambitious living-wage laws. The strongest impact from living-wage laws appears to come from legally required raises rather than from ripple-effect raises. This reinforces advocates' claims that paying a living wage is a reasonable, as well as potent, way to fight poverty.

SOURCES Fairris, D. et al. *Examining the evidence: The impact of the Los Angeles living wage ordinance on workers and businesses.* (Los Angeles Alliance for a New Economy, 2005); Fuchs, V. et al. "Economists' Views About Parameters, Values and Policies: Survey Results in Labor and Public Economics," *Journal of Economic Literature* (Sept. 1998); Pollin, R., Brenner, M. and Wicks-Lim, J. "Economic Analysis of the Florida Minimum Wage Proposal" (Center for American Progress, 2004); Pollin, R. and Brenner, M. "Economic Analysis of the Santa Monica Living Wage Proposal," (Political Economy Research Institute, 2000); Reich, M. et al. *Living wages and economic performance.* (Institute of Industrial Relations, 2003); Wicks-Lim, J. "Mandated wage floors and the wage structure: Analyzing the ripple effects of minimum and prevailing wage laws." (Ph.D. dissertation, University of Massachusetts-Amherst, 2005).

## Responding to Reading

MyWritingLab™

1. What is "the ripple effect"? According to Wicks-Lim, what effect does an increase in the minimum wage have on those who make above the minimum wage? on employers who must pay higher wages?
2. Why is there less of a ripple effect with living-wage laws than with minimum-wage laws?
3. **Rhetorical Analysis**   Wicks-Lim never defines "minimum wage," "living wage," or "ripple effect." Should she have? What does the failure to define these terms suggest about how she views her readers?

## Writing about Reading

1. Do you think all Americans are entitled to a living wage? Why or why not?
2. **Writing with Sources**   Research the debate over enacting living-wage legislation. What are the advantages and disadvantages of such legislation? Write an essay in which you present your findings and take a stand on this issue.

# IF A BUSINESS WON'T PAY A LIVING WAGE, IT SHOULDN'T EXIST

## The Daily Take Team, the *Thom Hartmann Program*

*The Daily Take Team writes for the* Thom Hartmann Program, *a progressive radio talk show hosted by entrepreneur and author Thom Hartmann. Hartmann has published numerous books, including, most recently,* Death in the Pines: An Oakley Tyler Novel *(2015). The following essay argues for the necessity of a living wage for all workers.*

Last week,[1] thousands of fast food workers from across the country walked off their jobs to demand a living wage of $15 an hour. Ever since, the Republican talking point machine has been running on all cylinders.

According to pundits on the right, giving fast food workers or any other workers, for that matter, a $7 or $8 bump to their hourly wages would cut so much into the bottom lines of "job-creators" that business owners would have to either pass the cost of a living-wage onto consumers or simply stop hiring new workers altogether.

But lost among all the noise on the right is one very, very important point: getting tax preferences and limitations on liability to do business in the United States is a privilege, not a right. It's a privilege that we as a society offer to budding entrepreneurs and big business alike in exchange for goods, services, and jobs.

Look at it this way: when someone opens up a business, they're entitled to all sorts of special tax breaks that most people can't get. They can write off fancy meals; they can write off nights stayed at five-star hotels; they can write off airfare to anywhere in the world they do business, or even might do business; and they can even write off any legal expenses they incur when they get busted for breaking the law. Drug dealers who push pot can't write off their lawyer's fees, but drug dealers at Big Pharma,[2] even when they lie and break the law in ways that kill people, can—all because they're incorporated.

---

[1]This essay was published on August 8, 2013. [Eds.]
[2]A nickname for the pharmaceutical industry. [Eds.]

5      All these breaks come in exchange for the company receiving these benefits giving society something back in return. Besides a useful service like selling meals or a good product like a well-made car, the single most important thing a business owner can give back to society is a well-paying job with benefits.

       A job that pays a living wage isn't just good for the workers who get to take home a livable paycheck, it's good for other business owners and the economy as a whole. Businesses need people with a reasonable income to buy their goods. When workers are paid so little that they can barely afford to eat, they can't spend additional money and as a result, the entire economy suffers. This is economics 101.

       That implicit contract between society and the business owner used to be common knowledge in this country and, until the Reagan Revolution,[3] was kept intact by businesses. Now, however, corporate America has thrown it out the window.

       Walmart is the most egregious example. The nation's largest employer is one big corporate welfare scheme for the company's executives and the billionaire Walton family.

       Walmart makes nearly $35,000 in profit every minute and, as of 2012, its average annual sales stood at $405 billion dollars.

10     According to *Mother Jones*, the six Waltons, whose money comes from Walmart, control an estimated $115 billion dollar fortune. In total, that's more than a staggering 42% of Americans combined.

       And where did they get all that money? They took it out of the business instead of paying their workers a living wage.

       Thus, at the same time that Walmart executives are raking in the millions and the Walton family's fortune is ballooning, Walmart employees struggle to get by.

       The average Walmart employee makes about $9 per hour, and would have to work over 7 million years at that rate to accumulate as much wealth as the Waltons have. To make matters worse, only some of the company's employees qualify for its very minimal health insurance plan.

       As a result, you and me—and the rest of America's taxpayers—are subsidizing Walmart by paying for the healthcare costs, housing, and food of Walmart employees. In fact, Walmart employees are the single largest group of Medicaid recipients in the United States.

15     A report released earlier this year by Congressional Democrats showed how much taxpayers subsidize the billionaire Walton Family at just one Walmart store in Wisconsin.

       That report found that just that one Wisconsin store "costs taxpayers at least $904,542 per year and could cost taxpayers up to $1,744,590 per year."

---

[3]The presidency of Ronald Reagan (1981–1989). [Eds.]

That's $1.7 million that could be used to build a new school for kids, patch up one of our country's many crumbling bridges, or build a community health center. Instead, the Walton billionaires are taking that $1.7 million as dividends and they even get their own special low tax rate—about half of what working people pay—because it's dividend income.

Walmart isn't living up to its end of the American business bargain. It gets billions of dollars in taxpayer subsidies while its employees need government assistance to survive. If we're going to give businesses, like Walmart, the privileges and tax breaks associated with running a business, they should at the very least conduct themselves in ways that benefit society, rather than hurt it.

Fortunately, there is an alternative. Costco, a wholesale distributor and one of Walmart's major competitors, is among America's most successful companies. In the first quarter of 2013 alone, its profits "jumped 19 percent to $459 million," beating out its rivals K-Mart, Target, and, of course, Walmart. Since 2009, its stocks have doubled in value and profits are up 15 percent. But unlike Walmart, Costco pays its workers a living wage, and then some. The average Costco employee makes a little over $20 an hour and takes home, on average, around $45,000 a year. By comparison, the average yearly pay of an employee at Walmart's wholesale unit, Sam's Club, is only about $17,500.

But that's not even the best part. Costco offers customers cheap 20 prices that are comparable to or even better than those offered at Walmart, all while paying its workers a decent wage and giving almost 90 percent of them company-subsidized health care plans.

So what's the difference between the two chain stores? Costco's founders, Jeffrey Brotman and James Sinegal, aren't among the world's super rich like the Walton family. The Walton billionaires bleed their workers dry and it makes them one of the richest families in the world. The guys who started and the executives who run Costco are merely multi-millionaires.

The point here is that it *is* possible for companies to pay their workers a living wage, make money, and give their customers an excellent product, all at the same time. The idea that we have to choose between paying workers well and having successful businesses is just false. That choice only exists when the owners insist on squeezing billions out of their workers.

A living wage isn't just something corporations owe their workers, it's something corporations owe America.

If a corporation won't pay a living wage, then it shouldn't have the right to exist. Period. End of story.

CHAPTER 10  FOCUS

## Responding to Reading

1. According to the writers, "Walmart isn't living up to its end of the American business bargain" (18). What is that bargain? Why is Walmart not living up to it?
2. List the major claim the writers make in this essay. What evidence do they present to support this claim? Do they present enough evidence? the right kind of evidence?
3. **Rhetorical Analysis** *Hyperbole* is the use of exaggerated claims that are not intended to be taken literally. Can you find any examples of hyperbole in this essay? Do you think they strengthen the essay? Why or why not?

## Writing about Reading

1. According to the writers, "the single most important thing a business owner can give back to society is a well-paying job with benefits" (5). Do you agree?
2. **Writing with Sources** In 2015, Walmart raised the minimum wage of its lowest-paid workers to $9.00 and hour, $1.75 above the federal minimum wage. Research the reasons why Walmart decided to make this change. Then, write an essay in which you discuss how Walmart's action affects this essay's main point.

# THE MINIMUM WAGE DELUSION, AND THE DEATH OF COMMON SENSE

## James Dorn

*A regular online contributor to* Forbes, *James Dorn writes about issues related to global economic policy and monetary reform. The vice president for monetary studies, the editor of the* Cato Journal, *and a senior fellow at the Cato Institute in Washington, D.C., he is also the editor or coeditor of numerous books, including, most recently,* Peter Bauer and the Economics of Prosperity *(2009). In the following essay, Dorn considers the negative effects of raising the minimum wage.*

Senator Edward Kennedy once called the minimum wage "one of the best antipoverty programs we have." Jared Bernstein, former chief economist to Vice President Joe Biden, thinks "it raises the pay of low-wage workers without hurting their job prospects." And Ralph Nader[1] thinks low-wage workers deserve a pay increase—and the government should provide it.

Why do those beliefs persist in the face of common economic sense? No legislator has ever overturned the law of demand, which says that when the price of labor rises, the quantity demanded will fall (assuming

---

[1]American political activist (1934– ). [Eds.]

other things are constant). That same law tells us that quantity demanded (i.e., the number of jobs for low-skilled workers) will decrease more in the long run than in the short run, as employers switch to labor-saving methods of production—and unemployment will increase.

The belief that increasing the minimum wage is socially beneficial is a delusion. It is short-sighted and ignores evident reality. Workers who retain their jobs are made better off but only at the expense of unskilled, mostly young, workers who either lose their jobs or can't find a job at the legal minimum.

A higher minimum wage attracts new entrants but does not guarantee them a job. What happens on the demand side of the market is not surprising: if the minimum wage exceeds the prevailing market wage (determined by supply and demand), some workers will lose their jobs or have their hours cut. There is abundant evidence that a 10 percent increase in the minimum wage leads to a 1 to 3 percent *decrease* in employment of low-skilled workers (using teens as a proxy) in the short run, and to a larger decrease in the long run, along with rising unemployment.

Employers have more flexibility in the long run and will find ways to economize on the higher-priced labor. New technology will be introduced along with labor-saving capital investment, and skilled workers will tend to replace unskilled workers. Those substitutions will occur even before an increase in the minimum wage, if employers believe such an increase is imminent. There will be fewer jobs for low-skilled workers and higher unemployment rates—especially for minorities— and participation rates will fall as workers affected by the minimum wage drop out of the formal labor market.

The minimum wage violates the principle of freedom by limiting the range of choices open to workers, preventing them from accepting jobs at less than the legal minimum. It also prohibits employers from hiring those workers, even if both parties would be better off. Thus, contrary to the claims of minimum-wage proponents, the government does not increase opportunities for low-skilled workers by increasing the minimum wage. If a worker loses her job or can't find one, her income is zero. Employers will not pay a worker $9 per hour if that worker cannot produce at least that amount.

Politicians promise low-skilled workers a higher wage, but that promise cannot be kept if employers cannot profit from retaining those workers or hiring similar workers. Jobs will be lost, not created; and unemployment will rise as more workers search for jobs but can't find any at the above-market wage.

Most employers cannot simply raise prices to cover the higher minimum wage, particularly in the competitive services sector. And if they do increase prices, consumers will buy less or have less money to spend on other things, meaning fewer jobs on net. Moreover, if the

5

minimum wage cuts into profits, there will be less capital investment and job growth will slow.

A recent study by Jonathan Meer and Jeremy West, economists at Texas A&M University, found that "the most prominent employment effect of minimum wage laws is a decline in the hiring of new employees." That effect takes place over time as employers shift to labor-saving methods of production. Since the minimum wage has the largest impact on the least-skilled workers who have few alternatives, their lifetime earnings will be adversely affected by delaying entry into the work force and losing valuable job experience.

10     Proponents of the minimum wage such as John Schmitt, a senior fellow at the Center for Economic and Policy Research in Washington, like to argue that the mean effect of the minimum wage on jobs for low-skilled workers is close to zero. But a preponderance of evidence has shown that there are *no positive effects* on employment of low-skilled workers that offset the negative effects from an increase in the minimum wage. The trick is to control for other factors ("confounding variables") affecting the demand for labor and to make sure the data and research design are valid. The focus should be on those workers adversely affected by the minimum wage—namely, younger individuals with little education and few skills.

In a recent case study that controls for confounding factors that make it difficult to isolate the impact of an increase in the minimum wage on employment for low-skilled workers, Joseph Sabia, Richard Burkhauser, and Benjamin Hansen find that when New York State increased the minimum wage from $5.15 to $6.75 per hour, in 2004–06, there was a "20.2 to 21.8 percent reduction in the employment of younger less-educated individuals," with the greatest impact on 16-to-24 year olds.

Advocates of the minimum wage like to point to the "natural experiment" that David Card and Alan Krueger conducted to see whether a minimum wage hike in New Jersey adversely affected employment in the fast-food industry compared to Pennsylvania, which did not increase its minimum wage. Based on telephone surveys, the authors concluded that the minimum wage hike significantly increased jobs for low-skilled, fast-food workers in New Jersey. Not surprisingly, their results were overturned by more careful research that found an adverse effect on employment (see David Neumark and William Wascher, *American Economic Review*, 2000).

It should be obvious that limiting one's study to franchise restaurants like McDonald's ignores smaller independents that are harmed by increases in the minimum wage and can't compete with their larger rivals. No one interviewed those workers who lost their jobs or could not find a job at the higher minimum wage. Proponents of the minimum wage focus on workers who retain their jobs and get a higher wage, but ignore those who lose their jobs and get a lower wage or none at all. Using econometrics to pretend that the law of demand is dead is a dangerous delusion.

If one gets empirical results that go against the grain of long-held economic laws, one should be very wary of advocating policies based on those results. One should also not stop with the short-run effects of the minimum wage but trace out the longer-run effects on the number of jobs and unemployment rates for affected workers.

Today black teen unemployment is more than 40 percent; nearly double that for white teens. In 2007, prior to the Great Recession, the black teen unemployment rate was about 29 percent. There is no doubt the increase in the federal minimum wage from $5.15 to $7.25 per hour contributed to the higher unemployment rate. If Congress passes a new minimum wage law that makes it illegal for employers to pay less than $9 per hour, and for workers to accept less than that amount, we can expect further erosion of the market for unskilled workers, especially black teens.

With so many young, unskilled workers looking for work, employers can pick and choose. They can cut benefits and hours; and they can substitute more-skilled workers for less-skilled workers. Recent studies based on data for contiguous counties across state borders have ignored labor-labor substitution and wrongly concluded that higher minimum wages do not adversely affect employment.

Arindrajit Dube, T. William Lester, and Michael Reich, for example, use county-level data over a 16.5 year period to examine the impact of local differences in minimum wages on employment in restaurants, which primarily hire low-skilled workers. Based on their analysis and assumptions, they "find no adverse employment effects."

Proponents of a higher minimum wage have rested their case on Dube et al. and related studies—such as Sylvia Allegretto, Dube, and Reich, who conclude that "minimum wage increases—in the range that have been implemented in the United States—do not reduce employment among teens." Neumark, Salas, and Wascher, in a new study for the National Bureau of Economic Research, argue that "neither the conclusions of these studies nor the methods they use are supported by the data." Indeed, Dube et al. admit that their data prevent them from testing "whether restaurants respond to minimum wage increases by hiring more skilled workers and fewer less-skilled ones."

Existing evidence supports labor-labor substitution in response to a higher minimum wage—especially over the longer run. Employers have a strong incentive to retain better-educated teens and train them, and to hire skilled workers to operate labor-saving equipment. Contrary to the claims of Bernstein and others who support the minimum wage, a higher minimum (other things constant) will *decrease* employment opportunities for the least-skilled workers. Workers who retain

15

CHAPTER 10 FOCUS

their jobs will be higher productivity workers—not low-wage workers in low-income families. Minimum wage laws harm the very workers they are intended to help.

20 Small businesses are already laying off low-skilled workers and investing in self-service tablets, robotics, and other labor-saving devices in anticipation of a higher minimum wage; and hours are being cut. Those trends will continue, especially if the minimum wage is indexed for inflation.

Advocates of higher minimum wages confuse cause and effect. They think a higher minimum wage causes incomes to go up for low-skilled workers and doesn't destroy jobs. Workers are assumed to have higher wages and retain their jobs as a result of government policy—even though they have done nothing to improve their job skills. But if a worker is producing $5.15 per hour and now the employer must pay $9 per hour, there will be little incentive to retain her. There will also be little incentive to hire new workers. Without an increase in the demand for labor—that is, an increase in labor productivity due to better technology, more capital per worker, or additional education—a higher minimum wage will simply price some workers (the least productive) out of the market, and their incomes will be zero.

The minimum wage is not a panacea for poverty. Indeed, Neumark, Schweitzer, and Wascher examine the evidence and conclude that "the net effect of higher minimum wages is ... to increase the proportion of families that are poor and near-poor" (*Journal of Human Resources*, 2005). Thus, the minimum wage tends to increase, not decrease, the poverty rate.

The best antipoverty program is not the minimum wage but economic freedom that expands workers' choices and allows entrepreneurs to freely hire labor without the government dictating the terms of the exchange, except to prevent fraud and violence. When entrepreneurs adopt new technology and make capital investments autonomously—that is, without being induced to do so because of government mandated increases in wage rates—there is a boost in worker productivity, jobs, and incomes. But when the government increases the minimum wage above the prevailing market wage for low-skilled workers, firms will have an incentive to substitute labor-saving production techniques that destroy jobs for low-productivity workers, especially minorities, and prevent workers from moving up the income ladder.

Unions are key advocates of higher minimum wages because the demand for union workers tends to increase along with wage rates after an increase in the minimum wage. Likewise, large retailers and franchise restaurants already paying more than the minimum wage may support an increase in the legal minimum because it helps protect their businesses from smaller competitors. Poverty advocates also favor the minimum wage because it is a "feel good" policy and they believe it will lead to higher incomes for low-wage workers, without seeing the longer-run consequences on jobs and unemployment.

Ignoring the law of demand to adopt a higher minimum wage in 25 the hope of helping low-wage workers is a grand delusion. The persistence of this false belief ignores economic reality. It is a red herring that diverts attention from alternative policies that would increase economic freedom and prosperity for all workers.

## Responding to Reading MyWritingLab™

1. According to Dorn, "The belief that increasing the minimum wage is socially beneficial is a delusion" (3). Why? What evidence does he offer to support this statement?
2. In paragraph 21, Dorn says, "Advocates of higher minimum wages confuse cause and effect." What does he mean? Do you think he is right?
3. **Rhetorical Analysis**   At what points in his essay does Dorn introduce arguments against his position? How effectively does he refute (argue against) these counterarguments?

## Writing about Reading MyWritingLab™

1. Dorn asserts that the minimum wage "diverts attention from alternative policies that would increase economic freedom and prosperity for all workers" (25). Other than increasing the minimum wage, what do you think the government (or private business) could do to help low-skilled workers earn more money?
2. **Writing with Sources**   According to some critics, the minimum wage is not supposed to be a living wage. It is intended for unskilled workers in entry-level jobs, who are promoted once they gain experience. Research this subject, concentrating on the types of workers who earn the minimum wage. How accurate is the position taken by these critics of the minimum wage? What types of workers earn the minimum wage? How long do they typically stay in entry-level positions? Do they, as these critics claim, tend to move up to higher-paying jobs, or do many of them remain minimum-wage workers? Write an essay in which you present your findings, and take a position on the issue of whether the minimum wage should be a living wage.

# WIDENING THE FOCUS

## For Critical Reading and Writing

Referring specifically to the three readings in this chapter's Focus section (and possibly to additional sources as well), write an essay in which you answer the question, "Is Every Worker Entitled to a Living Wage?"

## For Further Reading

The following readings can suggest additional perspectives for thinking and writing about work and compensation.

- Lynda Barry, "The Sanctuary of School" (p. 75)
- Melanie Scheller, "On the Meaning of Plumbing and Poverty" (p. 283)
- Robert D. Putnam, "Crumbling American Dreams" (p. 343)

## For Focused Research

Child labor is a topic that has sparked debate around the globe. In the United States, for example, students at several colleges and universities have protested their bookstores' sale of merchandise made in foreign sweatshops by child laborers who receive little or no pay and who work in dismal conditions. To gain greater insight into worldwide child labor, visit the website for the International Programme on the Elimination of Child Labour (IPEC). Then, write an essay that examines child labor in various countries, considering such factors as the pay and working conditions of child laborers as well as the kinds of industries that use child labor. What alternatives are available to the children in these countries? What happens to the children who do not get these jobs? Could an argument be made in defense of child labor?

## Beyond the Classroom

Assemble a group of friends and classmates, and lead a discussion about fair wages, gathering opinions based on personal experiences and observations. (You will want to record this group session so you can listen to the responses later.) Then, write an essay summarizing the group's opinions, quoting individual group members to illustrate various points of view. Then develop your own conclusions about whether all workers are entitled to a living wage.

# EXPLORING ISSUES AND IDEAS

MyWritingLab™

Visit Chapter 10, "Why We Work," in MyWritingLab to test your understanding of the chapter objectives.

## Why We Work

Write an essay in response to one of the following prompts, which are suitable for assignments that require the use of outside sources as well as for assignments that are not source-based.

1. Write an essay in which you describe in detail the worst job you ever had.

2. Considering the essays in this chapter—especially "Why We Work" (p. 353), "When Work Is a Game, Who Wins?" (p. 363), and "It's Not about You" (p. 368)—write an essay in which you discuss what you believe the purpose of work should be. For example, should it be to earn money, or should it be to gain personal satisfaction and fulfillment? Are these two goals mutually exclusive? Does the way we work in this country help people achieve these goals?

3. In "It's Not about You" (p. 368), David Brooks sees working in positive terms—as the way a person achieves his or her full potential as a human being. In "Why We Work" (p. 353), however, Andrew Curry makes the point that most workers dislike their jobs. Which of these two views of work do you hold? Write an essay in which you give the reasons for your belief. Illustrate your points with your own experiences as well as with references to the essays by Brooks and Curry.

4. Imagine that you have been asked by your former high school to address students in this year's graduating class about how to get part-time and summer jobs to offset the high cost of college. Write a speech that is inspirational but also offers specific advice.

5. In his essay "Delusions of Grandeur" (p. 370), Henry Lewis Gates, Jr. points out that "only 26% of African-American athletes at the collegiate level earn their degrees" (11). According to Gates, colleges should stop using African-American athletes "as cannon fodder in the big-business wars" of non-professional sports (14). Do you agree with Gates that colleges are exploiting African American athletes? Do you think these student-athletes would be better off preparing themselves for careers in the workplace?

# 11

## MAKING ETHICAL CHOICES

*In this chapter , you will learn to*
- analyze readings about making ethical choices
- compose essays about making ethical choices

As Robert Frost suggests in his poem "The Road Not Taken" (p. 399), making choices is fundamental to our lives. The ability—and, in fact, the need—to make complex decisions is part of what makes us human. On a practical level, we choose friends, mates, careers, and places to live. On a more abstract level, we struggle to make the moral and ethical choices that people have struggled with over the years.

Many times, complex questions have no easy answers; occasionally, they have no answers at all. For example, should we obey a law that we

Diamond wedding engagement ring

believe to be morally wrong? Should we stand up to authority even if our stand puts us at risk? Should we help less fortunate individuals if such help threatens our own social or economic status? Should we strive to do well or to do good? Should we tell the truth even if the truth may hurt us—or hurt someone else? Which road should we take, the easy one or the more difficult one?

Most of the time, the choice we (and the writers whose works appear in this chapter ) face is the same: to act or not to act. To make a decision, we must understand both the long- and short-term consequences of acting in a particular way or of choosing not to act. We must struggle with the possibility of compromise—and with the possibility of making a morally or ethically objectionable decision. And, perhaps most important, we must learn to take responsibility for our decisions.

In the context of the pressure on today's college students to make the right ethical choices, the Focus section of this chapter, "What Has Happened to Academic Integrity?" (p. 441), considers the erosion of academic integrity and the persistence of plagiarism. In "The Truth about Plagiarism," Richard A. Posner defines and explains the concept of plagiarism, noting how it is different from "real theft" and other crimes; in "Student Plagiarism in an Online World," Julie R. C. H. Ryan considers some of the challenges faced by students and their instructors in the digital age; and in "A Better Way to Prevent Cheating: Appeal to Fairness," David Callahan suggests that cheating should be considered "an issue of justice.

Diamond miners, South Africa

---

## PREPARING TO READ AND WRITE

As you read and prepare to write about the selections in this chapter, you may consider the following questions:

- What assumptions does the writer seem to have about his or her audience? How can you tell?

- What is the writer's primary purpose? To explain an ethical dilemma of his or her own? to expose a lack of ethics in society or in certain individuals? to recommend a course of action? something else?

- What genre is the writer using? For example, is the reading a proposal? a news article? a poem? an argument? a memoir? How do the conventions of this genre influence the writer's choices?

- What appeals does the writer use? For example, does he or she appeal primarily to reason or to emotion?

- On what specific choice or choices does the selection focus? Is the decision to be made moral? ethical? political? practical?

- Does the writer introduce a **dilemma**, a choice between equally problematic alternatives?

- Does the choice the writer presents apply only to one specific situation or case, or does it also have a wider application?

- Is the writer emotionally involved with the issue he or she is discussing? Does this involvement (or lack of involvement) affect the effectiveness of the writer's argument?

- What social, political, or religious ideas influence the writer? How can you tell? Are these ideas similar to or different from your own views?

- Does the choice being considered lead the writer to examine his or her own values? The values of others? The values of the society at large? Does the writer lead you to examine your own values?

- Does the writer offer a solution to a problem? If so, do you find this solution reasonable?

- Does the choice the writer advocates require sacrifice? If so, does the sacrifice seem worth it?

- Which writers' views seem most alike? Which seem most different?

# THE ROAD NOT TAKEN
## Robert Frost
### *1874–1963*

*Robert Frost, four-time Pulitzer Prize–winning poet of rural New England, lived most of his life in New Hampshire and taught at Amherst College, Harvard University, and Dartmouth College. His subjects at first seem familiar and comfortable, as does his language, but the symbols, allusions, and underlying meanings in many of his poems are quite complex. Some of Frost's most famous poems are "Birches," "Mending Wall," and "Stopping by Woods on a Snowy Evening." In the poem that follows, the speaker hesitates before making a choice.*

Two roads diverged in a yellow wood,
And sorry I could not travel both
And be one traveller, long I stood
And looked down one as far as I could
To where it bent in the undergrowth;                                5

Then took the other, as just as fair,
And having perhaps the better claim,
Because it was grassy and wanted wear;
Though as for that the passing there
Had worn them really about the same,                                10

And both that morning equally lay
In leaves no step had trodden black.
Oh, I kept the first for another day!
Yet knowing how way leads on to way,
I doubted if I should ever come back.                               15

I shall be telling this with a sigh
Somewhere ages and ages hence:
Two roads diverged in a wood, and I—
I took the one less travelled by,
And that has made all the difference.                               20

## Responding to Reading                          MyWritingLab™

1. What is the difference between the two paths Frost's speaker considers? Why does he make the choice he does?

2. Is "The Road Not Taken" simply about two paths in the wood, or does it suggest more? What makes you think so? To what larger choices might the speaker be alluding?
3. What does the speaker mean by "that has made all the difference" (line 20)?

## Responding in Writing

MyWritingLab™

In your own words, write a short prose summary of this poem. Use first person and past tense (as Frost does).

# ETHICS

## Linda Pastan

### *1932–*

*The winner of numerous prizes for her poetry, Linda Pastan often focuses on the complexity of domestic life, using intense imagery to bring a sense of mystery to everyday matters. She has been a lecturer at the Breadloaf Writers Conference in Vermont and an instructor at American University, and she has published numerous collections of poetry, including* Waiting for My Life *(1981),* PM/AM: New and Selected Poems *(1983),* Carnival Evening: New and Selected Poems 1968–1998 *(1998),* The Last Uncle: Poems *(2002),* Queen of a Rainy Country *(2006), and* Traveling Light: Poems *(2011). In "Ethics," from* Waiting for My Life, *the speaker introduces an ethical dilemma.*

In ethics class so many years ago
our teacher asked this question every fall:
if there were a fire in a museum
which would you save, a Rembrandt painting
5    or an old woman who hadn't many
years left anyhow? Restless on hard chairs
caring little for pictures or old age
we'd opt one year for life, the next for art
and always half-heartedly. Sometimes
10   the woman borrowed my grandmother's face
leaving her usual kitchen to wander
some drafty, half imagined museum.
One year, feeling clever, I replied
why not let the woman decide herself?
15   Linda, the teacher would report, eschews
the burdens of responsibility.

This fall in a real museum I stand
before a real Rembrandt, old woman,
or nearly so, myself. The colors
within this frame are darker than autumn,                    20
darker even than winter—the browns of earth,
though earth's most radiant elements burn
through the canvas. I know now that woman
and painting and season are almost one
and all beyond saving by children.                           25

## Responding to Reading

MyWritingLab™

1. What choice actually confronts Pastan's speaker? What answer do you think the teacher expects the students to give?
2. Do you agree with the teacher that refusing to choose means avoiding responsibility? Does Frost's speaker (p. 399) have the option not to choose? Explain.
3. When the speaker says that "woman / and painting and season are almost one" (lines 23–24), what does she mean? Does she imply that the teacher's question really has no answer? that the children who would "opt one year for life, the next for art" (line 8) are right?

## Responding in Writing

MyWritingLab™

Confronted with the choice facing the speaker, would you save the Rembrandt painting or the elderly woman? Why? Would you find this a difficult choice to make?

# THE UNACKNOWLEDGED ETHICISTS ON CAMPUSES

## David A. Hoekema

*A philosophy professor at Calvin College, David A. Hoekema specializes in political philosophy, African philosophy, and aesthetics. He is the author or editor of five published books and one forthcoming book,* Picking Up Pieces and Making Peace: The Role of Churches in the Northern Uganda Conflict. *In the following essay, Hoekema examines possible sources of ethical guidance for college students.*

Catalogs and presidential speeches assure us repeatedly that the study of the liberal arts strengthens morality and instills virtue, but they do not tell us how. If virtue can indeed be taught, where can we find its teachers? College study is widely assumed to foster a deeper sense of moral conviction, but scarcely a trace of moral instruction remains anywhere in the curriculum.

One of the distinctive features of the university environment is the openness of students to new ideas and challenges. What, then, are the dominant influences on students' thinking concerning moral choices? Who, and where, are the ethics experts on campuses? And is it possible for them to instill a more rigorous and more demanding vision of the moral life than that of the surrounding culture?

We can find the answers to such questions primarily by understanding the influence of three distinct groups. None of the groups bear a close resemblance to a 19th-century college president holding forth on moral philosophy to assembled seniors. But each plays a vital role in shaping students' sense of what is expected of them as responsible adults.

The first and most prominent group consists of the professors standing in front of their classrooms. Whether consciously or unconsciously, whether systematically or haphazardly, they serve as moral guides to students. Many professors would deny if asked that this has anything to do with their responsibilities or their function as members of the faculty. But it is a role that all faculty members do in fact occupy, and which contributes one of the most important elements of the moral atmosphere on any campus. It is not just professors in humanities disciplines like religion, philosophy, and history who play this role but also those in social sciences and sciences. Even if only a few courses explicitly deal with ethical questions, every class is to some degree a class in ethics.

5　For it is not so much the content as the conduct of classroom discourse that shapes students' conceptions of how to lead their lives. Students learn what it means to disagree forcefully but respectfully, and they observe how much or how little concern their instructors show when a student is unable to grasp critical concepts. Professors teach students about morality by the ways in which they grade tests, structure assignments, and respond to student complaints.

Further, only a minority of students envision their future selves following the same vocation as their professors, but they all are influenced by what they see in their instructors' understanding of their own vocation. They can see the difference between a dedicated teacher and one who is merely earning a paycheck, between an insincere and a genuine commitment to students' intellectual and personal welfare. They can distinguish between a scholar engaged in passionate pursuit of deeper understanding and a status seeker always trying to climb the ladder to a more prestigious institution. Those differences inform students' reflections on their vocational plans and shape students' sense of what it means to do one's life work with integrity and commitment.

A smaller but equally influential army of ethics teachers can be found in the student-life staff. It is not just when students do something foolish and shortsighted, and then face disciplinary sanctions, that such administrators become involved in students' personal and moral lives. From the first days of orientation through senior-week activities, they help students learn who they are and decide what they value.

And what sort of guidance do they offer? At best, student-life administrators challenge students to advance to a deeper level of critical awareness of their own choices through conversations, programmed activities, and interactions related to campus discipline. They emphasize that compliance with campus rules is only a small part of the important task of developing a strong sense of moral direction and personal integrity. Discipline for misbehavior becomes the occasion for serious reflection on why a student has fallen short, not just of college expectations, but also of the expectations other students have of her—and indeed that she has of herself.

Whether student-life administrators see themselves as having the authority to offer any specific moral guidance to students varies widely from campus to campus and person to person, and their influence is often implicit and indirect. Yet on every campus, we will find some student-life administrators who are deeply engaged in the most serious and searching moral inquiry with the students. No other group exercises so profound an influence over students' moral growth.

A subset of the student-life community includes those who coordinate religious life. The relationship between a campus pastor and a student involved in worship leadership may be as close as any relationship between adults and students on a campus. But at most institutions, the scope of such relationships is limited to a relatively small group of the student population. 10

The third major group of ethics experts are the student leaders of major campus organizations. Adolescents, we know, are profoundly influenced by the examples and opinions of their peers and are particularly likely to admire and emulate those who have risen to high levels of visibility and responsibility. Which students play the most important role depends on the specifics of each campus's history and culture, but captains and star players on sports teams, student-government leaders, and student journalists are usually among them. The relationship of student leaders to the members of their organizations is likely to involve little explicit discussion of matters of morality and personal responsibility, but beneath the surface a great deal of ethical instruction takes place. Indeed, some of the most influential teachers of ethics on our campuses, in the long run, are probably other students—people whom we as faculty and staff members tend to see as recipients rather than sources of instruction.

It is clear that serious and sustained problems of student conduct, particularly in upholding academic integrity and taking responsibility for destructive and self-destructive behaviors, are present at every college. For example, the prevalence of cheating on assignments and tests is notoriously difficult to measure accurately, but anyone who asserts that it is absent from his campus is kidding himself. Still, there are teachers of ethics on our campuses: the professoriate, the student-life staff, and the leadership of student organizations and activities.

But do the members of any of these groups really believe that they have something of substance to teach? Many do not. Professors believe they have the duty and authority to convey to students a deeper understanding of history or biology or accounting, but not of morality. They hold themselves responsible for preparing engaging lectures, setting challenging assignments, and keeping their own intellects continually sharpened by research and scholarship. How students conduct their lives outside class, however, is considered to lie wholly outside the faculty's concerns.

Meanwhile, members of the second group, student-life administrators, see their role as settling conflicts, enforcing serious campus rules, and helping everyone get along better. But, not wanting to appear judgmental, they usually scrupulously avoid applying moral categories to students. And those who make up the third group, student leaders, are themselves often in need of moral guidance as they learn to shoulder adult responsibilities.

15      If few of those potential teachers of virtue have anything that they believe they can teach, from whom will students learn? In the end, students will learn from one another, without any systematic assistance in learning what it means to grow morally—to critique, challenge, and refine a vision of what makes a life worthwhile. Offered no coherent or articulate ethical framework beyond the encouragement to fit in and enjoy their lives, students will model themselves on peers and adults whom they admire. In good times they will make themselves comfortable and get along. But in times of crisis and conflict, when hard choices arise and it takes a keen eye for moral nuance and a courageous heart to move forward, they will be woefully unprepared.

And what will be the outcome? That is a question that should trouble the sleep of anyone involved in higher education today. The absence of any effective ethical content in the curriculum may produce a future generation of parents and corporate leaders who are no better prepared to solve the urgent problems of the day than physicians would be to perform surgery if they had learned medicine from their friends and conferred their own diplomas.

We need to adjust our expectations of both students and faculty members in ways that will enhance, not impede, more-effective relationships of moral guidance and effective ethical modeling. For the resources needed for a renewed sense of the ethical core of liberal education are already in place on every campus. Neglect of moral issues has arisen not from ignorance of what morality is, but rather from the conviction that morality is no longer the business of the university. Yet there remain some faculty members, and many campus-life staff members and campus chaplains, who hold to a more integrated vision of students' lives. They are ready to engage more thoughtfully and intensively in the moral formation of their students.

When we make room in our academic institutions for all to relate to one another as thoughtful and responsible moral agents, we will find that we can actually teach each other a great deal. There are lots of ethicists in the house. We need only to build institutional structures and expectations that will encourage them to get to work.

## Responding to Reading

MyWritingLab™

1. According to Hoekema, if the three groups he identifies are unwilling or unable to teach ethics and morals to students, students will have to "learn from one another" (15). Do you think students can learn ethics and morals from one another? Does Hoekema?
2. In paragraph 4, Hoekema says, "Even if only a few courses explicitly deal with ethical questions, every class is to some degree a class in ethics." Do you agree?
3. **Rhetorical Analysis**   Hoekema identifies the contributions of three groups of "unacknowledged ethicists." What determines the order in which he discusses the three groups? Is this the most effective order? Why or why not?

## Writing about Reading

MyWritingLab™

1. Do you think that formal, systematic "moral instruction" and "ethical content" (16) should be a required part of the college curriculum? If so, what form should this instruction take, and where (and by whom) should it be taught? If not, why not?
2. **Writing with Sources**   Interview at least one ethicist on your campus from each category Hoekema identifies. What kinds of personal traits, training, and experience does each ethicist have? Write an essay based on your interviews in which you explain what qualifies someone to be an effective ethicist.

# How Not to Be Alone

## Jonathan Safran Foer

### 1977–

*A visiting professor in the creative writing program at New York University, Jonathan Safran Foer is the author of the novels* Everything Is Illuminated *(2002) and* Extremely Loud & Incredibly Close *(2005) as well as the nonfiction book* Eating Animals *(2009). His work appears in publications such as the* Guardian, The New Yorker, *and the* New York Times. *The following essay, which was adapted from Foer's 2013 commencement speech at Middlebury College, considers the fate of compassion in the digital age.*

A couple of weeks ago, I saw a stranger crying in public. I was in Brooklyn's Fort Greene neighborhood, waiting to meet a friend for breakfast. I arrived at the restaurant a few minutes early and was sitting on the bench outside, scrolling through my contact list. A girl, maybe 15 years old, was sitting on the bench opposite me, crying into her phone. I heard her say, "I know, I know, I know" over and over.

What did she know? Had she done something wrong? Was she being comforted? And then she said, "Mama, I know," and the tears came harder.

What was her mother telling her? Never to stay out all night again? That everybody fails? Is it possible that no one was on the other end of the call, and that the girl was merely rehearsing a difficult conversation?

"Mama, I know," she said, and hung up, placing her phone on her lap.

5      I was faced with a choice: I could interject myself into her life, or I could respect the boundaries between us. Intervening might make her feel worse, or be inappropriate. But then, it might ease her pain, or be helpful in some straightforward logistical way. An affluent neighborhood at the beginning of the day is not the same as a dangerous one as night is falling. And I was me, and not someone else. There was a lot of human computing to be done.

It is harder to intervene than not to, but it is vastly harder to choose to do either than to retreat into the scrolling names of one's contact list, or whatever one's favorite iDistraction happens to be. Technology celebrates connectedness, but encourages retreat. The phone didn't make me avoid the human connection, but it did make ignoring her easier in that moment, and more likely, by comfortably encouraging me to forget my choice to do so. My daily use of technological communication has been shaping me into someone more likely to forget others. The flow of water carves rock, a little bit at a time. And our personhood is carved, too, by the flow of our habits.

Psychologists who study empathy and compassion are finding that unlike our almost instantaneous responses to physical pain, it takes time for the brain to comprehend the psychological and moral dimensions of a situation. The more distracted we become, and the more emphasis we place on speed at the expense of depth, the less likely and able we are to care.

Everyone wants his parent's, or friend's, or partner's undivided attention—even if many of us, especially children, are getting used to far less. Simone Weil[1] wrote, "Attention is the rarest and purest form of generosity." By this definition, our relationships to the world, and to one another, and to ourselves, are becoming increasingly miserly.

---

[1]French philosopher (1909–1943). [Eds.]

Most of our communication technologies began as diminished substitutes for an impossible activity. We couldn't always see one another face to face, so the telephone made it possible to keep in touch at a distance. One is not always home, so the answering machine made a kind of interaction possible without the person being near his phone. Online communication originated as a substitute for telephonic communication, which was considered, for whatever reasons, too burdensome or inconvenient. And then texting, which facilitated yet faster, and more mobile, messaging. These inventions were not created to be improvements upon face-to-face communication, but a declension of acceptable, if diminished, substitutes for it.

But then a funny thing happened: we began to prefer the diminished substitutes. It's easier to make a phone call than to schlep to see someone in person. Leaving a message on someone's machine is easier than having a phone conversation—you can say what you need to say without a response; hard news is easier to leave; it's easier to check in without becoming entangled. So we began calling when we knew no one would pick up. 10

Shooting off an e-mail is easier, still, because one can hide behind the absence of vocal inflection, and of course there's no chance of accidentally catching someone. And texting is even easier, as the expectation for articulateness is further reduced, and another shell is offered to hide in. Each step "forward" has made it easier, just a little, to avoid the emotional work of being present, to convey information rather than humanity.

The problem with accepting—with preferring—diminished substitutes is that over time, we, too, become diminished substitutes. People who become used to saying little become used to feeling little.

With each generation, it becomes harder to imagine a future that resembles the present. My grandparents hoped I would have a better life than they did: free of war and hunger, comfortably situated in a place that felt like home. But what futures would I dismiss out of hand for my grandchildren? That their clothes will be fabricated every morning on 3-D printers? That they will communicate without speaking or moving?

Only those with no imagination, and no grounding in reality, would deny the possibility that they will live forever. It's possible that many reading these words will never die. Let's assume, though, that we all have a set number of days to indent the world with our beliefs, to find and create the beauty that only a finite existence allows for, to wrestle with the question of purpose and wrestle with our answers.

We often use technology to save time, but increasingly, it either 15 takes the saved time along with it, or makes the saved time less present, intimate and rich. I worry that the closer the world gets to our fingertips, the further it gets from our hearts. It's not an either/or—being "anti-technology" is perhaps the only thing more foolish than being unquestioningly "pro-technology"—but a question of balance that our lives hang upon.

Most of the time, most people are not crying in public, but everyone is always in need of something that another person can give, be it undivided attention, a kind word or deep empathy. There is no better use of a life than to be attentive to such needs. There are as many ways to do this as there are kinds of loneliness, but all of them require attentiveness, all of them require the hard work of emotional computation and corporeal compassion. All of them require the human processing of the only animal who risks "getting it wrong" and whose dreams provide shelters and vaccines and words to crying strangers.

We live in a world made up more of story than stuff. We are creatures of memory more than reminders, of love more than likes. Being attentive to the needs of others might not be the point of life, but it is the work of life. It can be messy, and painful, and almost impossibly difficult. But it is not something we give. It is what we get in exchange for having to die.

### Responding to Reading

MyWritingLab™

1. What does Foer mean when he says, "Technology celebrates connectedness, but encourages retreat" (6)? Is this statement accurate, or is Foer oversimplifying a complicated subject?
2. What is a "diminished substitute" (10)? Do you agree with Foer's observation, "The problem with accepting—with preferring—diminished substitutes is that over time, we, too, become diminished substitutes" (12)?
3. **Rhetorical Analysis**  Foer begins his essay with an anecdote about a stranger crying in public. He indicates that he faced a choice: he could have either intervened in her life or respected the boundaries between them. He never tells readers what he decided to do, however. Should he have done so? What do you think he decided?

### Writing about Reading

MyWritingLab™

1. How would you have reacted to the stranger crying in the park? Why?
2. **Writing with Sources**  Research the effects (negative as well as positive) of texting, email, and social media in general on personal communication. Also, look at Sherry Turkle's essay in Chapter 6. After deciding how you feel about this issue, write an essay in which you agree or disagree with Foer's statements in paragraph 13.

# FRACKING: A FABLE

## Barbara Hurd

*An essayist and poet, Barbara Hurd teaches in the MFA in writing program at the Vermont College of Fine Arts. Writing about various issues related to natural history, she is the author of several books, including, most recently,* Listening to the Savage: River Notes and Half-Heard Melodies *(2016). In "Fracking: A Fable," Hurd imagines what the impact of fracking, a kind of drilling for natural gas, might be.*

*for our grandchildren, with apologies*

In the past, everything took forever.

Rain fell for centuries, and millions of years after that, the ancient Appalachian Basin just west of what is now the East Coast spent even more millennia becoming a sprawling, shallow bowl. And then nothing much happened. Another million years passed. Mountain ranges slowly rose and receded, and continents wandered into each other and eventually the basin began to fill with seawater and for another million years, the surrounding mountains slid wetly down the slopes of themselves and settled into the bottom sludge of the basin.

More tens of thousands of centuries passed while the water sloshed and the undersea mud thickened, and in all that time, no human ever stood on its shores, no blue crab ever scurried in the ooze. There were no witnesses. And even if there had been, who could have stood the boredom of watching that slow, barely breathing world? The only testimony ever made to that languid time was locked in the mud.

For yet another several million years, it piled up—thick, black, and putrid. Over the next millennia, miniscule creatures evolved: phytoplankton, blue-green algae. They floated in the shallow seas until they died and drifted down to be entombed in the ooze that lay fifty, one hundred, two hundred feet deep.

Then came more mountains moving. A few continents collided, some peaks rose, some valleys sank. Meanwhile, down in the black ooze, remnants of those tiny creatures that had been held in the mud were shoved more tightly together, packed side by side with sludged-in sediment, cemented together, cooked by the heat deep in the earth, and converted into hydrocarbons. Layer after layer of crammed-together particles and silt began to sink under the accumulating weight of the mountains that grew above. Wrung of its moisture, its pliability, its flow, the mud slowly, slowly, over millions of years, turned into gas-rich rock.

And there it lay, miles under the surface, as the old basin above it emptied and rose and more continents meandered into each other

5

and finally the sun dried the Appalachians, which eroded and softened, and three hundred million years after the first mud settled on the bottom of that basin, humans appeared. We developed with lightning speed—geologically speaking—our brains and vision and hands, our fast and furious tools, our drills and ingenuity, and all the while that ooze-become-rock lay locked and impenetrable, deep in the earth, farther than anything, including anyone's imagination, reached, until in the split second that is humankind's history on this planet we pushed a drill with a downhole mud-motor a mile deep and made it turn sideways and snaked it into that ancient rock speckled with evidence of another eon, and a few minutes later we detonated small explosives and blasted millions of gallons of slick water—sand and water and a bit of biocide in case anything was alive down there—into what hadn't seen water or light for four hundred million years.

The shale shattered, the black rock spider-webbed with skinny fissures as the above world inserted its tendrils, and into those tiny rifts we rammed more sand to keep them wedged open wider.

And then—remember the blue-green algae?—the gas that had been locked in that stony underworld for almost four hundred million years suddenly had an exit. It flowed through the intricate shudderings of brand new fissures and up the borehole through the limestone that had been laid down millions of years after the mud, and up through the bedrock just below someone's pasture and out into a world with air and fresh water where we humans, fur-less and in need of fuel to stay warm, exercised our resourceful minds.

And then in another split-second's time—geologically speaking— we drilled another thousand wells, fracked another million tons of stony earth a mile beneath our feet.

10   And when the slick water was withdrawn from the fissures and small slither-spaces and that prehistoric bedrock was lickety-split forever changed, no one could predict the impact, not even we inventive humans whose arrival on this planet is so recent, whose footprints, so conspicuous and large, often obliterate cautionary tales.

And soon the unpredictable, as always, occurred.

And now, in no time at all, not everything takes forever any longer.

## Responding to Reading

MyWritingLab™

1.  A *fable* is a short tale that teaches a moral lesson. In what sense is this a fable? What moral lesson does it try to teach? Is it successful?
2.  At the end of her fable, Hurd implies that something unexpected occurred because of fracking. Should she have been more specific? Why do you think she is so vague?
3.  **Rhetorical Analysis**   Hurd ends her fable with a one-sentence conclusion. How does this conclusion reinforce her main point? Is it enough?

## Writing about Reading

1. Write your own fable about an issue that you care about. Make sure your fable teaches a moral lesson.
2. **Writing with Sources**   Currently, Pennsylvania allows fracking, and New York does not. Examine the debates that are still taking place in these states. Then, write a letter to the governor of one of the states in which you argue against the position on fracking that is currently in place.

# LETTER FROM BIRMINGHAM JAIL
# Martin Luther King, Jr.

### 1929–1968

*One of the greatest civil rights leaders and orators of the last century, Baptist minister Martin Luther King, Jr., earned a B.A. degree from Morehouse College (1948), a B.D. degree from Crozer Theological Seminary in Pennsylvania (1951), and a Ph.D. from Boston University (1955). Influenced by Thoreau and Gandhi, King altered the spirit of African American protest in the United States by advocating nonviolent civil disobedience to achieve racial equality. King was arrested more than twenty times and assaulted at least four times for his activities, but he also was awarded five honorary degrees, was named Man of the Year by* Time *magazine in 1963, and the following year was awarded the Nobel Peace Prize. His books include* Letter from Birmingham Jail *(1963) and* Where Do We Go from Here: Chaos or Community? *(1967). King was assassinated on April 4, 1968, in Memphis, Tennessee. The following letter, written by King in 1963, is his eloquent and impassioned response to a public statement by eight fellow clergymen in Birmingham, Alabama, who appealed to the citizenry of that city to "observe the principles of law and order and common sense" rather than join in the principled protests that King was leading.*

## My Dear Fellow Clergymen:[1]

While confined here in the Birmingham city jail, I came across your recent statement calling my present activities "unwise and untimely." Seldom do I pause to answer criticism of my work and ideas. If I sought to answer all the criticisms that cross my desk, my secretaries would have little time for anything other than such correspondence in the course of the day, and I would have no time for constructive work. But

---

[1]This response to a published statement by eight fellow clergymen from Alabama (Bishop C. C. J. Carpenter, Bishop Joseph A. Durick, Rabbi Milton L. Grafman, Bishop Paul Hardin, Bishop Holan B. Harmon, the Reverend George M. Murray, the Reverend Edward V. Ramage and the Reverend Earl Stallings) was composed under somewhat constricting circumstances. Begun on the margins of the newspaper in which the statement appeared while I was in jail, the letter was continued on scraps of writing paper supplied by a friendly Negro trusty, and concluded on a pad my attorneys were eventually permitted to leave me. Although the text remains in substance unaltered, I have indulged in the author's prerogative of polishing it for publication.

since I feel that you are men of genuine good will and that your criticisms are sincerely set forth, I want to try to answer your statement in what I hope will be patient and reasonable terms.

I think I should indicate that I am here in Birmingham, since you have been influenced by the view which argues against "outsiders coming in." I have the honor of serving as president of the Southern Christian Leadership Conference, an organization operating in every southern state, with headquarters in Atlanta, Georgia. We have some eighty-five affiliated organizations across the South, and one of them is the Alabama Christian Movement for Human Rights. Frequently we share staff, educational, and financial resources with our affiliates. Several months ago the affiliate here in Birmingham asked us to be on call to engage in a non-violent direct-action program if such were deemed necessary. We readily consented, and when the hour came we lived up to our promise. So I, along with several members of my staff, am here because I was invited here. I am here because I have organizational ties here.

But more basically, I am in Birmingham because injustice is here. Just as the prophets of the eighth century B.C. left their villages and carried their "thus saith the Lord" far beyond the boundaries of their home towns, and just as the Apostle Paul left his village of Tarsus and carried the gospel of Jesus Christ to the far corners of the Greco-Roman world, so am I compelled to carry the gospel of freedom beyond my own home town. Like Paul, I must constantly respond to the Macedonian call for aid.

Moreover, I am cognizant of the interrelatedness of all communities and states. I cannot sit idly by in Atlanta and not be concerned about what happens in Birmingham. Injustice anywhere is a threat to justice everywhere. We are caught in an inescapable network of mutuality, tied in a single garment of destiny. Whatever affects one directly, affects all indirectly. Never again can we afford to live with the narrow, provincial "outside agitator" idea. Anyone who lives inside the United States can never be considered an outsider anywhere within its bounds.

5     You deplore the demonstrations taking place in Birmingham. But your statement, I am sorry to say, fails to express a similar concern for the conditions that brought about the demonstrations. I am sure that none of you would want to rest content with the superficial kind of social analysis that deals merely with effects and does not grapple with underlying causes. It is unfortunate that demonstrations are taking place in Birmingham, but it is even more unfortunate that the city's white power structure left the Negro community with no alternative.

In any nonviolent campaign there are four basic steps: collection of the facts to determine whether injustices exist; negotiation; self-purification; and direct action. We have gone through all these steps in Birmingham. There can be no gainsaying the fact that racial injustice engulfs this community. Birmingham is probably the most thoroughly segregated city in the United States. Its ugly record of brutality is widely known. Negroes have experienced grossly unjust treatment in the courts. There have been more unsolved bombings of Negro homes and churches in Birmingham than in any other city in the nation. These are the hard, brutal facts of the case. On the basis of these conditions, Negro leaders sought to negotiate with the city fathers. But the latter consistently refused to engage in good-faith negotiation.

Then, last September, came the opportunity to talk with leaders of Birmingham's economic community. In the course of the negotiations, certain promises were made by the merchants—for example, to remove the stores' humiliating racial signs. On the basis of these promises, the Reverend Fred Shuttlesworth and the leaders of the Alabama Christian Movement for Human Rights agreed to a moratorium on all demonstrations. As the weeks and months went by, we realized that we were the victims of a broken promise. A few signs, briefly removed, returned; the others remained.

As in so many past experiences, our hopes had been blasted, and the shadow of deep disappointment settled upon us. We had no alternative except to prepare for direct action, whereby we would present our very bodies as a means of laying our case before the conscience of the local and the national community. Mindful of the difficulties involved, we decided to undertake a process of self-purification. We began a series of workshops on nonviolence, and we repeatedly asked ourselves: "Are you able to accept blows without retaliating?" "Are you able to endure the ordeal of jail?" We decided to schedule our direct-action program for the Easter season, realizing that except for Christmas, this is the main shopping period of the year. Knowing that a strong economic-withdrawal program would be the by-product of direct action, we felt that this would be the best time to bring pressure to bear on the merchants for the needed change.

Then it occurred to us that Birmingham's mayoral election was coming up in March, and we speedily decided to postpone action until after election day. When we discovered that the Commissioner of Public Safety, Eugene "Bull" Connor,[2] had piled up enough votes to be in the run-off, we decided again to postpone action until the day after the run-off so that the demonstrations could not be used to cloud the issues. Like many others, we wanted to see Mr. Connor defeated, and to this end we endured postponement after postponement. Having aided in this community need, we felt that our direct-action program could be delayed no longer.

You may well ask, "Why direct action? Why sit-ins, marches, and so forth? Isn't negotiation a better path?" You are quite right in calling for negotiation. Indeed, this is the very purpose of direct action. Nonviolent direct action seeks to create such a crisis and foster such a tension that a community which has constantly refused to negotiate is forced to confront the issue. It seeks so to dramatize the issue that it can

10

---

[2]An ardent segregationist, Connor ordered police officers to use police dogs and fire hoses to break up civil rights demonstrations. (Conner lost his bid for mayor.) [Eds.]

no longer be ignored. My citing the creation of tension as part of the work of the nonviolent-resister may sound rather shocking. But I must confess that I am not afraid of the word "tension." I have earnestly opposed violent tension, but there is a type of constructive, nonviolent tension which is necessary for growth. Just as Socrates felt that it was necessary to create a tension in the mind so that individuals could rise from the bondage of myths and half-truths to the unfettered realm of creative analysis and objective appraisal, so must we see the need for nonviolent gadflies to create the kind of tension in society that will help men rise from the dark depths of prejudice and racism to the majestic heights of understanding and brotherhood.

The purpose of our direct-action program is to create a situation so crisis-packed that it will inevitably open the door to negotiation. I therefore concur with you in your call for negotiation. Too long has our beloved Southland been bogged down in a tragic effort to live in monologue rather than dialogue.

One of the basic points in your statement is that the action that I and my associates have taken in Birmingham is untimely. Some have asked: "Why didn't you give the new city administration time to act?" The only answer that I can give to this query is that the new Birmingham administration must be prodded about as much as the outgoing one, before it will act. We are sadly mistaken if we feel that the election of Albert Boutwell as mayor will bring the millennium to Birmingham. While Mr. Boutwell is a much more gentle person than Mr. Connor, they are both segregationists, dedicated to maintenance of the status quo. I have hoped that Mr. Boutwell will be reasonable enough to see the futility of massive resistance to desegregation. But he will not see this without pressure from devotees of civil rights. My friends, I must say to you that we have not made a single gain in civil rights without determined legal and nonviolent pressure. Lamentably, it is an historical fact that privileged groups seldom give up their privileges voluntarily. Individuals may see the moral light and voluntarily give up their unjust posture; but, as Reinhold Niebuhr[3] has reminded us, groups tend to be more immoral than individuals.

We know through painful experience that freedom is never voluntarily given by the oppressor; it must be demanded by the oppressed. Frankly, I have yet to engage in a direct-action campaign that was "well timed" in the view of those who have not suffered unduly from the disease of segregation. For years now I have heard the word "Wait!" It rings in the ear of every Negro with piercing familiarity. This "Wait!" has almost always meant "Never." We must come to see, with one of our distinguished jurists, that "justice too long delayed is justice denied."[4]

---

[3]American religious and social thinker (1892–1971). [Eds.]
[4]Attributed to British statesman William Ewart Gladstone (1809–1898), a stalwart of the Liberal Party who also said, "You cannot fight the future. Time is on our side." [Eds.]

We have waited for more than 340 years for our constitutional and God-given rights. The nations of Asia and Africa are moving with jet-like speed toward gaining political independence, but we still creep at horse-and-buggy pace toward gaining a cup of coffee at a lunch counter. Perhaps it is easy for those who have never felt the stinging darts of segregation to say, "Wait." But when you have seen vicious mobs lynch your mothers and fathers at will and drown your sisters and brothers at whim; when you have seen hate-filled policemen curse, kick, and even kill your black brothers and sisters; when you see the vast majority of your twenty million Negro brothers smothering in an airtight cage of poverty in the midst of an affluent society; when you suddenly find your tongue twisted and your speech stammering as you seek to explain to your six-year-old daughter why she can't go to the public amusement park that has just been advertised on television, and see tears welling up in her eyes when she is told that Funtown is closed to colored children, and see ominous clouds of inferiority beginning to form in her little mental sky, and see her beginning to distort her personality by developing an unconscious bitterness toward white people; when you have to concoct an answer for a five-year-old son who is asking, "Daddy, why do white people treat colored people so mean?"; when you take a cross-country drive and find it necessary to sleep night after night in the uncomfortable corners of your automobile because no motel will accept you; when you are humiliated day in and day out by nagging signs reading "white" and "colored"; when your first name becomes "nigger," your middle name becomes "boy" (however old you are) and your last name becomes "John," and your wife and mother are never given the respected title "Mrs."; when you are harried by day and haunted by night by the fact that you are a Negro, living constantly at tiptoe stance, never quite knowing what to expect next, and are plagued with inner fears and outer resentments; when you are forever fighting a degenerating sense of "nobodiness"—then you will understand why we find it difficult to wait. There comes a time when the cup of endurance runs over, and men are no longer willing to be plunged into the abyss of despair. I hope, sirs, you can understand our legitimate and unavoidable impatience.

You express a great deal of anxiety over our willingness to break    15
laws. This is certainly a legitimate concern. Since we so diligently urge people to obey the Supreme Court's decision of 1954 outlawing segregation in the public schools, at first glance it may seem rather paradoxical for us consciously to break laws. One may well ask: "How can you advocate breaking some laws and obeying others?" The answer lies in the fact that there are two types of laws: just and unjust. I would be the first to advocate obeying just laws. One has not only a legal but a moral responsibility to obey just laws. Conversely, one has a moral

responsibility to disobey unjust laws. I would agree with St. Augustine[5] that "an unjust law is no law at all."

Now, what is the difference between the two? How does one determine whether a law is just or unjust? A just law is a man-made code that squares with the moral law or the law of God. An unjust law is a code that is out of harmony with the moral law. To put it in the terms of St. Thomas Aquinas:[6] An unjust law is a human law that is not rooted in eternal law and natural law. Any law that uplifts human personality is just. Any law that degrades human personality is unjust. All segregation statutes are unjust because segregation distorts the soul and damages the personality. It gives the segregator a false sense of superiority and the segregated a false sense of inferiority. Segregation, to use the terminology of the Jewish philosopher Martin Buber,[7] substitutes an "I-it" relationship for an "I-thou" relationship and ends up relegating persons to the status of things. Hence segregation is not only politically, economically, and sociologically unsound, it is morally wrong and sinful. Paul Tillich[8] has said that sin is separation. Is not segregation an existential expression of man's tragic separation, his awful estrangement, his terrible sinfulness? Thus it is that I can urge men to obey the 1954 decision of the Supreme Court, for it is morally right; and I can urge them to disobey segregation ordinances, for they are morally wrong.

Let us consider a more concrete example of just and unjust laws. An unjust law is a code that a numerical or power majority group compels a minority group to obey but does not make binding on itself. This is *difference* made legal. By the same token, a just law is a code that a majority compels a minority to follow and that it is willing to follow itself. This is *sameness* made legal.

Let me give another explanation. A law is unjust if it is inflicted on a minority that, as a result of being denied the right to vote, had no part in enacting or devising the law. Who can say that the legislature of Alabama which set up that state's segregation laws was democratically elected? Throughout Alabama all sorts of devious methods are used to prevent Negroes from becoming registered voters, and there are some counties in which, even though Negroes constitute a majority of the population, not a single Negro is registered. Can any law enacted under such circumstances be considered democratically structured?

Sometimes a law is just on its face and unjust in its application. For instance, I have been arrested on a charge of parading without a permit. Now, there is nothing wrong in having an ordinance which requires a permit for a parade. But such an ordinance becomes unjust

---

[5]Italian-born missionary and theologian (?–c. 604). [Eds.]
[6]Italian philosopher and theologian (1225–1274). [Eds.]
[7]Austrian existentialist philosopher and Judaic scholar (1878–1965). [Eds.]
[8]American philosopher and theologian (1886–1965). [Eds.]

when it is used to maintain segregation and to deny citizens the First-Amendment privilege of peaceful assembly and protest.

I hope you are able to see the distinction I am trying to point out. In no sense do I advocate evading or defying the law, as would the rabid segregationist. That would lead to anarchy. One who breaks an unjust law must do so openly, lovingly, and with a willingness to accept the penalty. I submit that an individual who breaks a law that conscience tells him is unjust, and who willingly accepts the penalty of imprisonment in order to arouse the conscience of the community over its injustice, is in reality expressing the highest respect for law.

Of course, there is nothing new about this kind of civil disobedience. It was evidenced sublimely in the refusal of Shadrach, Meshach, and Abednego to obey the laws of Nebuchadnezzar, on the ground that a higher moral law was at stake.[9] It was practiced superbly by the early Christians, who were willing to face hungry lions and the excruciating pain of chopping blocks rather than submit to certain unjust laws of the Roman Empire. To a degree, academic freedom is a reality today because Socrates practiced civil disobedience.[10] In our own nation, the Boston Tea Party represented a massive act of civil disobedience.

We should never forget that everything Adolf Hitler did in Germany was "legal" and everything the Hungarian freedom fighters[11] did in Hungary was "illegal." It was "illegal" to aid and comfort a Jew in Hitler's Germany. Even so, I am sure that, had I lived in Germany at the time, I would have aided and comforted my Jewish brothers. If today I lived in a Communist country where certain principles dear to the Christian faith are suppressed, I would openly advocate disobeying that country's anti-religious laws.

I must make two honest confessions to you, my Christian and Jewish brothers. First, I must confess that over the past few years I have been gravely disappointed with the white moderate. I have almost reached the regrettable conclusion that the Negro's great stumbling block in his stride toward freedom is not the White Citizen's Counciler or the Ku Klux Klanner, but the white moderate, who is more devoted to "order" than to justice; who prefers a negative peace which is the absence of tension to a positive peace which is the presence of justice; who constantly says, "I agree with you in the goal you seek, but I

20

[9]In the book of Daniel, Nebuchadnezzar commanded the people to worship a golden statue or be thrown into a furnace of blazing fire. When Shadrach, Meshach, and Abednego refused to worship any god but their own, they were bound and thrown into a blazing furnace, but the fire had no effect on them. Their escape led Nebuchadnezzar to make a decree forbidding blasphemy against their god. [Eds.]

[10]The ancient Greek philosopher Socrates was tried by the Athenians for corrupting their youth through his use of questions to teach. When he refused to change his methods of teaching, he was condemned to death. [Eds.]

[11]The Hungarian anti-Communist uprising of 1956 was quickly crushed by the army of the USSR. [Eds.]

cannot agree with your methods of direct action"; who paternalistically believes he can set the timetable for another man's freedom; who lives by a mythical concept of time and who constantly advises the Negro to wait for a "more convenient season." Shallow understanding from people of good will is more frustrating than absolute misunderstanding from people of ill will. Lukewarm acceptance is much more bewildering than outright rejection.

I had hoped that the white moderate would understand that law and order exist for the purpose of establishing justice and that when they fail in this purpose they become the dangerously structured dams that block the flow of social progress. I had hoped that the white moderate would understand that the present tension in the South is a necessary phase of the transition from an obnoxious negative peace, in which the Negro passively accepted his unjust plight, to a substantive and positive peace, in which all men will respect the dignity and worth of human personality. Actually, we who engage in nonviolent direct action are not the creators of tension. We merely bring to the surface the hidden tension that is already alive. We bring it out in the open, where it can be seen and dealt with. Like a boil that can never be cured so long as it is covered up but must be opened with all its ugliness to the natural medicines of air and light, injustice must be exposed, with all the tension its exposure creates, to the light of human conscience and the air of national opinion, before it can be cured.

25    In your statement you assert that our actions, even though peaceful, must be condemned because they precipitate violence. But is this a logical assertion? Isn't this like condemning a robbed man because his possession of money precipitated the evil act of robbery? Isn't this like condemning Socrates because his unswerving commitment to truth and his philosophical inquiries precipitated the act by the misguided populace in which they made him drink hemlock? Isn't this like condemning Jesus because his unique God-consciousness and never-ceasing devotion to God's will precipitated the evil act of crucifixion? We must come to see that, as the federal courts have consistently affirmed, it is wrong to urge an individual to cease his efforts to gain his basic constitutional rights because the quest may precipitate violence. Society must protect the robbed and punish the robber.

I had also hoped that the white moderate would reject the myth concerning time in relation to the struggle for freedom. I have just received a letter from a white brother in Texas. He writes: "All Christians know that the colored people will receive equal rights eventually, but it is possible that you are in too great a religious hurry. It has taken Christianity almost two thousand years to accomplish what it has. The teachings of Christ take time to come to earth." Such an attitude stems from a tragic misconception of time, from the strangely irrational notion that there is something in the very flow of time that will inevitably cure all ills. Actually, time itself is neutral; it can be used either destructively or constructively. More and more I feel that the people of ill will have used time much more effectively than have the people of good will. We will have to repent in this generation not merely for the hateful words and actions of the bad people, but for the appalling silence of the good people. Human progress never rolls in on wheels of inevitability; it comes through the tireless efforts of men willing to be co-workers with God, and without this hard work, time itself becomes an ally of the forces of social stagnation. We must use time creatively, in the knowledge that the time is always ripe to do right. Now is the time to make real the promise of democracy and transform our pending national elegy into a creative psalm of brotherhood. Now is the time to lift our national policy from the quicksand of racial injustice to the solid rock of human dignity.

You speak of our activity in Birmingham as extreme. At first I was rather disappointed that fellow clergymen would see my nonviolent efforts as those of an extremist. I began thinking about the fact that I stand in the middle of two opposing forces in the Negro community. One is a force of complacency, made up in part of Negroes who, as a result of long years of oppression, are so drained of self-respect and a sense of "somebodiness" that they have adjusted to segregation; and in part of a few middle-class Negroes who, because of a degree of academic and economic security and because in some ways they profit by segregation, have become insensitive to the problems of the masses. The other force is one of bitterness and hatred, and it comes perilously close to advocating violence. It is expressed in the various black nationalist groups that are springing up across the nation, the largest and best-known being Elijah Muhammad's Muslim movement. Nourished by the Negro's frustration over the continued existence of racial discrimination, this movement is made up of people who have lost faith in America, who have absolutely repudiated Christianity, and who have concluded that the white man is an incorrigible "devil."

I have tried to stand between these two forces, saying that we need emulate neither the "do-nothingism" of the complacent nor the hatred and despair of the black nationalist. For there is the more excellent way of love and nonviolent protest. I am grateful to God that, through the influence of the Negro church, the way of nonviolence became an integral part of our struggle.

If this philosophy had not emerged, by now many streets of the South would, I am convinced, be flowing with blood. And I am further convinced that if our white brothers dismiss as "rabblerousers" and "outside agitators" those of us who employ nonviolent direct action, and if they refuse to support our nonviolent efforts, millions of Negroes will, out of frustration and despair, seek solace and security in black-nationalist ideologies—a development that would inevitably lead to a frightening racial nightmare.

30     Oppressed people cannot remain oppressed forever. The yearning for freedom eventually manifests itself, and that is what has happened to the American Negro. Something within has reminded him of his birthright of freedom, and something without has reminded him that it can be gained. Consciously or unconsciously, he has been caught up by the *Zeitgeist*,[12] and with his black brothers of Africa and his brown and yellow brothers of Asia, South America, and the Caribbean, the United States Negro is moving with a sense of great urgency toward the promised land of racial justice. If one recognizes this vital urge that has engulfed the Negro community, one should readily understand why public demonstrations are taking place. The Negro has many pent-up resentments and latent frustrations, and he must release them. So let him march; let him make prayer pilgrimages to the city hall; let him go on freedom rides—and try to understand why he must do so. If his repressed emotions are not released in nonviolent ways, they will seek expression through violence; this is not a threat but a fact of history. So I have not said to my people, "Get rid of your discontent." Rather, I have tried to say that this normal and healthy discontent can be channeled into the creative outlet of nonviolent direct action. And now this approach is being termed extremist.

But though I was initially disappointed at being categorized as an extremist, as I continued to think about the matter I gradually gained a measure of satisfaction from the label. Was not Jesus an extremist for love: "Love your enemies, bless them that curse you, do good to them that hate you, and pray for them which despitefully use you, and persecute you." Was not Amos an extremist for justice: "Let justice roll down like waters and righteousness like an ever-flowing stream." Was not Paul an extremist for the Christian gospel: "I bear in my body the marks of the Lord Jesus." Was not Martin Luther an extremist: "Here I stand; I cannot do otherwise, so help me God." And John Bunyan: "I will stay in jail to the end of my days before I make a butchery of my conscience." And Abraham Lincoln: "This nation cannot survive half slave and half free." And Thomas Jefferson: "We hold these truths to be self-evident, that all men are created equal … . " So the question is not whether we will be extremists, but what kind of extremists we will be. Will we be extremists for hate or for love? Will we be extremists for the preservation of injustice or for the extension of justice? In that dramatic scene on Calvary's hill three men were crucified. We must never forget that all three were crucified for the same thing—the crime of extremism. Two were extremists for immorality, and thus fell below their environment. The other, Jesus Christ, was an extremist for love, truth, and goodness, and thereby rose above his environment. Perhaps the South, the nation, and the world are in dire need of creative extremists.

---

[12]German for *the spirit of the times*. [Eds.]

I had hoped that the white moderate would see this need. Perhaps I was too optimistic; perhaps I expected too much. I suppose I should have realized that few members of the oppressor race can understand the deep groans and passionate yearnings of the oppressed race, and still fewer have the vision to see that injustice must be rooted out by strong, persistent, and determined action. I am thankful, however, that some of our white brothers in the South have grasped the meaning of this social revolution and committed themselves to it. They are still all too few in quantity, but they are big in quality. Some—such as Ralph McGill, Lillian Smith, Harry Golden, James McBridge Dabbs, Ann Braden, and Sarah Patton Boyle—have written about our struggle in eloquent and prophetic terms. Others have marched with us down nameless streets of the South. They have languished in filthy, roach-infested jails, suffering the abuse and brutality of policemen who view them as "dirty nigger-lovers." Unlike so many of their moderate brothers and sisters, they have recognized the urgency of the moment and sensed the need for powerful "action" antidotes to combat the disease of segregation.

Let me take note of my other major disappointment. I have been so greatly disappointed with the white church and its leadership. Of course, there are some notable exceptions. I am not unmindful of the fact that each of you has taken some significant stands on this issue. I commend you, Reverend Stallings, for your Christian stand on this past Sunday, in welcoming Negroes to your worship service on a nonsegregated basis. I commend the Catholic leaders of this state for integrating Spring Hill College several years ago.

But despite these notable exceptions, I must honestly reiterate that I have been disappointed with the church. I do not say this as one of those negative critics who can always find something wrong with the church. I say this as a minister of the gospel, who loves the church; who was nurtured in its bosom; who has been sustained by its spiritual blessings and who will remain true to it as long as the cord of life shall lengthen.

When I was suddenly catapulted into the leadership of the bus protest in Montgomery, Alabama, a few years ago, I felt we would be supported by the white church. I felt that the white ministers, priests, and rabbis of the South would be among our strongest allies. Instead, some have been outright opponents, refusing to understand the freedom movement and misrepresenting its leaders; all too many others have been more cautious than courageous and have remained silent behind the anesthetizing security of stained glass windows.

In spite of my shattered dreams, I came to Birmingham with the hope that the white religious leadership of this community would see the justice of our cause and, with deep moral concern, would serve as the channel through which our just grievances could reach the power

35

structure. I had hoped that each of you would understand. But again I have been disappointed.

I have heard numerous southern religious leaders admonish their worshipers to comply with a desegregation decision because it is the law, but I have longed to hear white ministers declare: "Follow this decree because integration is morally right and because the Negro is your brother." In the midst of blatant injustices inflicted upon the Negro, I have watched white churchmen stand on the sideline and mouth pious irrelevancies and sanctimonious trivialities. In the midst of a mighty struggle to rid our nation of racial and economic injustice, I have heard many ministers say: "Those are social issues, with which the gospel has no real concern." And I have watched many churches commit themselves to a completely otherworldly religion which makes a strange, un-Biblical distinction between body and soul, between the sacred and the secular.

I have traveled the length and breadth of Alabama, Mississippi, and all the other southern states. On sweltering summer days and crisp autumn mornings I have looked at the South's beautiful churches with their lofty spires pointing heavenward. I have beheld the impressive outlines of her massive religious-education buildings. Over and over I have found myself asking: "What kind of people worship here? Who is their God? Where were their voices when the lips of Governor Barnett[13] dripped with words of interposition and nullification? Where were they when Governor Wallace[14] gave a clarion call for defiance and hatred? Where were their voices of support when bruised and weary Negro men and women decided to rise from the dark dungeons of complacency to the bright hills of creative protest?"

Yes, these questions are still in my mind. In deep disappointment I have wept over the laxity of the church. But be assured that my tears have been tears of love. There can be no deep disappointment where there is not deep love. Yes, I love the church. How could I do otherwise? I am in the rather unique position of being the son, the grandson, and the great-grandson of preachers. Yes, I see the church as the body of Christ. But, oh! How we have blemished and scarred that body through social neglect and through fear of being nonconformists.

40        There was a time when the church was very powerful—in the time when the early Christians rejoiced at being deemed worthy to suffer for what they believed. In those days the church was not merely a thermometer that recorded the ideas and principles of popular opinion; it was a thermostat that transformed the mores of society. Whenever the

---

[13]Ross Barnett, segregationist governor of Mississippi, who strongly resisted the integration of the University of Mississippi in 1962. [Eds.]

[14]George Wallace, segregationist governor of Alabama, best known for standing in the doorway of a University of Alabama building to block the entrance of two black students who were trying to register. [Eds.]

early Christians entered a town, the people in power became disturbed and immediately sought to convict the Christians for being "disturbers of the peace" and "outside agitators." But the Christians pressed on, in the conviction that they were "a colony of heaven," called to obey God rather than man. Small in number, they were big in commitment. They were too God-intoxicated to be "astronomically intimidated." By their effort and example they brought an end to such ancient evils as infanticide and gladiatorial contests.

Things are different now. So often the contemporary church is a weak, ineffectual voice with an uncertain sound. So often it is an arch-defender to the status quo. Far from being disturbed by the presence of the church, the power structure of the average community is consoled by the church's silent—and often even vocal—sanction of things as they are.

But the judgment of God is upon the church as never before. If today's church does not recapture the sacrificial spirit of the early church, it will lose its authenticity, forfeit the loyalty of millions, and be dismissed as an irrelevant social club with no meaning for the twentieth century. Every day I meet young people whose disappointment with the church has turned into outright disgust.

Perhaps I have once again been too optimistic. Is organized religion too inextricably bound to the status quo to save our nation and the world? Perhaps I must turn my faith to the inner spiritual church, the church within the church, as the true *ekklesia*[15] and the hope of the world. But again I am thankful to God that some noble souls from the ranks of organized religion have broken loose from the paralyzing chains of conformity and joined us as active partners in the struggle for freedom. They have left their secure congregations and walked the streets of Albany, Georgia, with us. They have gone down the highways of the South on tortuous rides for freedom. Yes, they have gone to jail with us. Some have been dismissed from their churches, have lost the support of their bishops and fellow ministers. But they have acted in the faith that right defeated is stronger than evil triumphant. Their witness has been the spiritual salt that has preserved the true meaning of the gospel in these troubled times. They have carved a tunnel of hope through the dark mountain of disappointment.

I hope the church as a whole will meet the challenge of this decisive hour. But even if the church does not come to the aid of justice, I have no despair about the future. I have no fear about the outcome of our struggle in Birmingham, even if our motives are at present misunderstood. We will reach the goal of freedom in Birmingham and all over the nation, because the goal of America is freedom. Abused and scorned though we may be, our destiny is tied up with America's

---

[15]The Greek word for the early Christian church. [Eds.]

destiny. Before the pilgrims landed at Plymouth, we were here. Before the pen of Jefferson etched the majestic words of the Declaration of Independence across the pages of history, we were here. For more than two centuries our forebears labored in this country without wages; they made cotton king; they built the homes of their masters while suffering gross injustice and shameful humiliation—and yet out of a bottomless vitality they continued to thrive and develop. If the inexpressible cruelties of slavery could not stop us, the opposition we now face will surely fail. We will win our freedom because the sacred heritage of our nation and the eternal will of God are embodied in our echoing demands.

45    Before closing I feel impelled to mention one other point in your statement that has troubled me profoundly. You warmly commended the Birmingham police force for keeping "order" and "preventing violence." I doubt that you would have so warmly commended the police force if you had seen its dogs sinking their teeth into unarmed, nonviolent Negroes. I doubt that you would so quickly commend the policemen if you were to observe their ugly and inhumane treatment of Negroes here in the city jail; if you were to watch them push and curse old Negro women and young Negro girls; if you were to see them slap and kick old Negro men and young boys; if you were to observe them, as they did on two occasions, refuse to give us food because we wanted to sing our grace together. I cannot join you in your praise of the Birmingham police department.

It is true that the police have exercised a degree of discipline in handling the demonstrators. In this sense they have conducted themselves rather "nonviolently" in public. But for what purpose? To preserve the evil system of segregation. Over the past few years I have consistently preached that nonviolence demands that the means we use must be as pure as the ends we seek. I have tried to make clear that it is wrong to use immoral means to attain moral ends. But now I must affirm that it is just as wrong, or perhaps even more so, to use moral means to preserve immoral ends. Perhaps Mr. Connor and his policemen have been rather nonviolent in public, as was Chief Pritchett in Albany, Georgia, but they have used the moral means of nonviolence to maintain the immoral end of racial injustice. As T. S. Eliot[16] has said, "The last temptation is the greatest treason: To do the right deed for the wrong reason."

I wish you had commended the Negro sit-inners and demonstrators of Birmingham for their sublime courage, their willingness to suffer, and their amazing discipline in the midst of great provocation. One day the South will recognize its real heroes. They will be the James Merediths,[17] with the noble sense of purpose that enables them to face

---

[16]American-born British poet (1888–1965), winner of the 1948 Nobel Prize in Literature. [Eds.]

[17]First African American to enroll at the University of Mississippi, after federal troops were brought in to control demonstrators protesting his enrollment. [Eds.]

jeering and hostile mobs, and with the agonizing loneliness that characterizes the life of the pioneer. They will be old, oppressed, battered Negro women, symbolized in a seventy-two-year-old woman in Montgomery, Alabama, who rose up with a sense of dignity and with her people decided not to ride segregated buses, and who responded with ungrammatical profundity to one who inquired about her weariness: "My feets is tired, but my soul is at rest." They will be the young high school and college students, the young ministers of the gospel and a host of their elders, courageously and nonviolently sitting in at lunch counters and willingly going to jail for conscience' sake. One day the South will know that when these disinherited children of God sat down at lunch counters, they were in reality standing up for what is best in the American dream and for the most sacred values in our Judaeo-Christian heritage, thereby bringing our nation back to those great wells of democracy which were dug deep by the founding fathers in their formulation of the Constitution and the Declaration of Independence.

Never before have I written so long a letter. I'm afraid it is much too long to take your precious time. I can assure you that it would have been much shorter if I had been writing from a comfortable desk, but what else can one do when he is alone in a narrow jail cell, other than write long letters, think long thoughts, and pray long prayers?

If I have said anything in this letter that overstates the truth and indicates an unreasonable impatience, I beg you to forgive me. If I have said anything that understates the truth and indicates my having a patience that allows me to settle for anything less than brotherhood, I beg God to forgive me.

I hope this letter finds you strong in the faith. I also hope that circumstances will soon make it possible for me to meet each of you, not as an integrationist or a civil-rights leader but as a fellow clergyman and a Christian brother. Let us all hope that the dark clouds of racial prejudice will soon pass away and the deep fog of misunderstanding will be lifted from our fear-drenched communities, and in some not too distant tomorrow the radiant stars of love and brotherhood will shine over our great nation with all their scintillating beauty.     50

Yours for the cause of Peace and Brotherhood,

MARTIN LUTHER KING, JR.

## Responding to Reading                    MyWritingLab™

1. Do you believe King would have been justified in arguing that he had no alternative other than protest? Would you accept this argument?
2. In paragraph 30, King says, "Oppressed people cannot remain oppressed forever." Do you think world events of the last few years confirm or contradict this statement?
3. **Rhetorical Analysis**  Throughout this letter, King uses elaborate diction and complex rhetorical strategies. He addresses his audience directly;

makes frequent use of balance and parallelism, understatement, and meta-phor; and makes many historical and religious allusions. What effect do you think King intended these rhetorical strategies to have on the letter's original audience of clergymen? Does King's elaborate style enhance his argument, or does it just get in the way?

## Writing about Reading

MyWritingLab™

1. Write a short manifesto advocating civil disobedience for a cause you strongly believe in. To inspire others to follow the course of action you propose, explain the goal you are seeking, and identify the opposing forces that you believe make civil disobedience necessary. Then, outline the form you expect your peaceful protest to take.
2. **Writing with Sources**  Find the text of Henry David Thoreau's "On the Duty of Civil Disobedience" and some writings by Mahatma Gandhi on-line. Then, write an essay identifying similarities between King's ideas about peaceful nonviolent protest and the ideas of Thoreau and Gandhi.

# DOG LAB
# Claire McCarthy
## *1963–*

*A graduate of Harvard Medical School, Claire McCarthy is now an assis-tant in medicine and a pediatrician at Boston Children's Hospital as well as an assistant professor of pediatrics at Harvard Medical School. During her medical training, she kept detailed journals, which provided the basis for her books* Learning How the Heart Beats: The Making of a Pediatrician *(1995) and* Everyone's Children: A Pediatrician's Story of an Inner-City Practice *(1998). In the following essay, a chapter from* Learning How the Heart Beats, *McCarthy recalls her reluctance to attend an optional lab lesson in which students studied the cardiovascular system of a sedated living dog, which was then euthanized.*

When I finished college and started medical school, the learning changed fundamentally. Whereas in college I had been learning mostly for learning's sake, learning in order to know something, in medical school I was learning in order to *do* something, do the thing I wanted to do with my life. It was exhilarating and at the same time a little scary. My study now carried responsibility.

The most important course in the first year besides Anatomy was Physiology, the study of the functions and processes of the human body. It was the most fascinating subject I had ever studied. I found the intri-cacies of the way the body works endlessly intriguing and ingenious: the way the nervous system is designed to differentiate a sharp touch from a soft one; the way muscles move and work together to throw a ball; the wisdom of the kidneys, which filter the blood and let pass out only waste products and extra fluid, keeping everything else carefully within. It was magical to me that each organ and system worked so beautifully and in perfect concert with the rest of the body.

The importance of Physiology didn't lie just in the fact that it was fascinating, however. The other courses I was taking that semester, like Histology and Biochemistry, were fascinating, too. But because Physiology was the study of how the body actually works, it seemed the most pertinent to becoming a physician. The other courses were more abstract. Physiology was practical, and I felt that my ability to master Physiology would be a measure of my ability to be a doctor.

When the second-year students talked about Physiology, they always mentioned "dog lab." They mentioned it briefly but significantly, sharing knowing looks. I gathered that it involved cutting dogs open and that it was controversial, but that was all I knew. I didn't pursue it, I didn't ask questions. That fall I was living day to day, lecture to lecture, test to test. My life was organized around putting as much information into my brain as possible, and I didn't pay much attention to anything else.

I would get up around six, make coffee, and eat my bowl of cereal while I sat at my desk. There was nowhere else to sit in my dormitory room, and if I was going to sit at my desk, I figured I might as well study, so I always studied as I ate. I had a small refrigerator and a hot plate so that I could fix myself meals. After breakfast it was off to a morning of lectures, back to the room at lunchtime for a yogurt or soup and more studying, then afternoon lectures and labs. Before dinner I usually went for a run or a swim; although it was necessary for my sanity and my health, I always felt guilty that I wasn't studying instead. I ate dinner at my desk or with other medical students at the cafeteria in Beth Israel Hospital. We sat among the doctors, staff, and patients, eating our food quickly. Although we would try to talk about movies, current affairs, or other "nonmedical" topics, sooner or later we usually ended up talking about medicine; it was fast becoming our whole life. After dinner it was off to the eerie quiet of the library, where I sat surrounded by my textbooks and notes until I got tired or frustrated, which was usually around ten-thirty. Then I'd go back to the dorm, maybe chat with the other students on my floor, maybe watch television, probably study some more, and then fall asleep so that I could start the routine all over again the next morning.

My life had never been so consuming. Sometimes I felt like a true student in the best sense of the word, wonderfully absorbed in learning; other times I felt like an automaton. I was probably a combination of the two. It bothered me sometimes that this process of teaching me to take care of people was making me live a very study-centered, self-centered life. However, it didn't seem as though I had a choice.

One day at the beginning of a physiology lecture the instructor announced that we would be having a laboratory exercise to study the cardiovascular system, and that dogs would be used. The room was quickly quiet; this was the infamous "dog lab." The point of the exercise, he explained, was to study the heart and blood vessels in vivo[1] to learn the effects of different conditions and chemicals by seeing them rather than just by reading about them. The dogs would be sedated and the changes in their heart rates, respiratory rates, and blood pressure would be monitored with each experiment. As the last part of the exercise the sleeping dogs' chests would be cut open so we could actually watch the hearts and lungs in action, and then the dogs would be killed, humanely. We would be divided up into teams of four, and each team would work with a teaching assistant. Because so many teaching assistants were required, the class would be divided in half, and the lab would be held on two days.

The amphitheater buzzed.

The lab was optional, the instructor told us. We would not be marked off in any way if we chose not to attend. He leaned against the side of the podium and said that the way he saw it there was a spectrum of morality when it came to animal experimentation. The spectrum, he said, went from mice or rats to species like horses or apes, and we had to decide at which species we would draw our lines. He hoped, though, that we would choose to attend. It was an excellent learning opportunity, and he thought we ought to take advantage of it. Then he walked behind the podium and started the day's lecture.

10      It was all anyone could talk about: should we do dog lab or shouldn't we? We discussed it endlessly.

There were two main camps. One was the "excellent learning opportunity" camp, which insisted that dog lab was the kind of science we came to medical school to do and that learning about the cardiovascular system on a living animal would make it more understandable and would therefore make us better doctors.

Countering them was the "importance of a life" camp. The extreme members of this camp insisted that it was always wrong to murder an animal for experimentation. The more moderate members argued that perhaps animal experimentation was useful in certain kinds of medical research, but that dog lab was purely an exercise for our education and didn't warrant the killing of a dog. We could learn the material in other ways, they said.

On and on the arguments went, with people saying the same things over and over again in every conceivable way. There was something very important about this decision. Maybe it was because we were just beginning to figure out how to define ourselves as physicians—were

---

[1]Latin phrase for "in the living being." [Eds.]

we scientists, eager for knowledge, or were we defenders of life? The dog lab seemed to pit one against the other. Maybe it was because we thought that our lives as physicians were going to be filled with ethical decisions, and this was our first since entering medical school. It was very important that we do the right thing, but the right thing seemed variable and unclear.

I was quiet during these discussions. I didn't want to kill a dog, but I certainly wanted to take advantage of every learning opportunity offered me. And despite the fact that the course instructor had said our grades wouldn't be affected if we didn't attend the lab, I wasn't sure I believed him, and I didn't want to take any chances. Even if he didn't incorporate the lab report into our grades, I was worried that there would be some reference to it in the final exam, some sneaky way that he would bring it up. Doing well had become so important that I was afraid to trust anyone; doing well had become more important than anything.

I found myself waiting to see what other people would decide. I was ashamed not to be taking a stand, but I was stuck in a way I'd never been before. I didn't like the idea of doing the lab; it felt wrong. Yet for some reason I was embarrassed that I felt that way, and the lab seemed so important. The more I thought about it, the more confused I became.    15

Although initially the students had appeared divided more or less evenly between the camps, as the lab day drew nearer the majority chose to participate. The discussions didn't stop, but they were fewer and quieter. The issue seemed to become more private.

I was assigned to the second lab day. My indecision was becoming a decision since I hadn't crossed my name off the list. I can still change my mind, I told myself. I'm not on a team yet, nobody's counting on me to show up. One of my classmates asked me to join his group. I hedged.

The day before group lists had to be handed in, the course instructor made an announcement. It was brief and almost offhand: he said that if any of us wished to help anesthetize the dogs for the lab, we were welcome to do so. He told us where to go and when to be there for each lab day. I wrote the information down.

Somehow, this was what I needed. I made my decision. I would do the lab, but I would go help anesthetize the dogs first.

Helping with the anesthesia, I thought, would be taking full responsibility for what I was doing, something that was very important    20
to me. I was going to *face* what I was doing, see the dogs awake with their tails wagging instead of meeting them asleep and sort of pretending they weren't real. I also thought it might make me feel better to know that the dogs were treated well as they were anesthetized and to be there, helping to do it gently. Maybe in part I thought of it as my penance.

The day of the first lab came. Around five o'clock I went down to the Friday afternoon "happy hour" in the dormitory living room to talk to the students as they came back. They came back singly or in pairs, quiet, looking dazed. They threw down their coats and backpacks and made their way to the beer and soda without talking to anyone. Some, once they had a cup in their hands, seemed to relax and join in conversations; others took their cups and sat alone on the couches. They all looked tired, worn out.

"Well?" I asked several of them. "What was it like?"

Most shrugged and said little. A few said that it was interesting and that they'd learned a lot, but they said it without any enthusiasm. Every one of them said it was hard. I thought I heard someone say that their dog had turned out to be pregnant. Nobody seemed happy.

The morning of my lab was gray and dreary. I overslept, which I hardly ever do. I got dressed quickly and went across the street to the back entrance of the lab building. It was quiet and still and a little dark. The streets were empty except for an occasional cab. I found the open door and went in.

25    There was only one other student waiting there, a blond-haired woman named Elise. I didn't know her well. We had friends in common, but we'd never really talked. She was sweet and soft-spoken; she wore old jeans and plaid flannel shirts and hung out with the activist crowd. She had always intimidated me. I felt as though I weren't political enough when I was around her. I was actually a little surprised that she was doing the lab at all, as many of her friends had chosen not to.

We greeted each other awkwardly, nodding hello and taking our places leaning against the wall. Within a few minutes one of the teaching assistants came in, said good morning, pulled out some keys, and let us into a room down the hall. Two more teaching assistants followed shortly.

The teaching assistants let the dogs out of cages, and they ran around the room. They were small dogs; I think they were beagles. They seemed happy to be out of their cages, and one of them, white with brown spots, came over to me with his tail wagging. I leaned over to pet him, and he licked my hand, looking up at me eagerly. I stood up again quickly.

The teaching assistant who had let us in, a short man with tousled brown hair and thick glasses, explained that the dogs were to be given intramuscular injections of a sedative that would put them to sleep. During the lab they would be given additional doses intravenously as well as other medications to stop them from feeling pain. We could help, he said, by holding the dogs while they got their injections. Elise and I nodded.

So we held the dogs, and they got their injections. After a few minutes they started to stumble, and we helped them to the floor. I remember that Elise petted one of the dogs as he fell asleep and that she cried. I didn't cry, but I wanted to.

When we were finished, I went back to my room. I sat at my desk, drank my coffee, and read over the lab instructions again. I kept thinking about the dogs running around, about the little white one with the brown spots, and I felt sick. I stared at the instructions without really reading them, looking at my watch every couple of minutes. At five minutes before eight I picked up the papers, put them in my backpack with my books, and left.

The lab was held in a big open room with white walls and lots of windows. The dogs were laid out on separate tables lined up across the room; they were on their backs, tied down. They were all asleep, but some of them moved slightly, and it chilled me.

We walked in slowly and solemnly, putting our coats and backpacks on the rack along the wall and going over to our assigned tables. I started to look for the dog who had licked my hand, but I stopped myself. I didn't want to know where he was.

Our dog was brown and black, with soft floppy ears. His eyes were shut. He looked familiar. We took our places, two on each side of the table, laid out our lab manuals, and began.

The lab took all day. We cut through the dog's skin to find an artery and vein, into which we placed catheters. We injected different drugs and chemicals and watched what happened to the dog's heart rate and blood pressure, carefully recording the results. At the end of the day, when we were done with the experiments, we cut open the dog's chest. We cut through his sternum and pulled open his rib cage. His heart and lungs lay in front of us. The heart was a fist-size muscle that squeezed itself as it beat, pushing blood out. The lungs were white and solid and glistening under the pleura that covered them. The instructor pointed out different blood vessels, like the aorta and the superior vena cava. He showed us the stellate ganglion, which really did look like a star. I think we used the electrical paddles of a defibrillator and shocked the dog's heart into ventricular fibrillation, watching it shiver like Jell-O in front of us. I think that's how we killed them—or maybe it was with a lethal dose of one of the drugs. I'm not sure. It's something I guess I don't want to remember.

Dan was the anesthesiologist, the person assigned to making sure that the dog stayed asleep throughout the entire procedure. Every once in a while Dan would get caught up in the experiment and the dog would start to stir. I would nudge Dan, and he would quickly give more medication. The dog never actually woke up, but every time he moved even the slightest bit, every time I had to think about him being a real dog who was never going to wag his tail or lick anyone's hand again because of us, I got so upset that I couldn't concentrate. In fact, I had trouble concentrating on the lab in general. I kept staring at the dog.

As soon as we were finished, or maybe a couple of minutes before, I left. I grabbed my coat and backpack and ran down the stairs out into the dusk of the late afternoon. It was drizzling, and the medical school looked brown and gray. I walked quickly toward the street.

I was disappointed in the lab and disappointed in myself for doing it. I knew now that doing the lab was wrong. Maybe not wrong for everyone—it was clearly a complicated and individual choice—but wrong for me. The knowledge I had gained wasn't worth the life of a dog to me. I felt very sad.

The drizzle was becoming rain. I slowed down; even though it was cold, the rain felt good. A couple of people walking past me put up their umbrellas. I let the rain fall on me. I wanted to get wet.

From the moment you enter the field of medicine as a medical student, you have an awareness that you have entered something bigger and more important than you are. Doctors are different from other people, we are told implicitly, if not explicitly. Medicine is a way of life, with its own values and guidelines for daily living. They aren't bad values; they include things like the importance of hard work, the pursuit of knowledge, and the preservation of life—at least human life. There's room for individuality and variation, but that's something I realized later, much later. When I started medical school I felt that not only did I have to learn information and skills, I had to become a certain kind of person, too. It was very important to me to learn to do the thing that a doctor would do in a given situation. Since the course instructor, who represented Harvard Medical School to me, had recommended that we do the lab, I figured that a doctor would do it. That wasn't the only reason I went ahead with the lab, but it was a big reason.

40    The rain started to come down harder and felt less pleasant. I walked more quickly, across Longwood Avenue into Vanderbilt Hall. I could hear familiar voices coming from the living room, but I didn't feel like talking to anyone. I ducked into the stairwell.

I got to my room, locked the door behind me, took off my coat, and lay down on my bed. The rain beat against my window. It was the time I usually went running, but the thought of going back out in the rain didn't appeal to me at all. I was suddenly very tired.

As I lay there I thought about the course instructor's discussion of the spectrum of morality and drawing lines. Maybe it's not a matter of deciding which animals I feel comfortable killing, I thought. Maybe it's about drawing different kinds of lines: drawing the lines to define how much of myself I will allow to change. I was proud of being a true student, even if it did mean becoming a little like an automaton. But I still needed to be the person I was before; I needed to be able to make some decisions without worrying about what a doctor would do.

I got up off the bed, opened a can of soup, and put it in a pan on the hot plate to warm. I got some bread and cheese out of the refrigerator, sat down at my desk, and opened my Biochemistry text.

Suddenly I stopped. I closed the text, reached over, and turned on the television, which sat on a little plastic table near the desk. There would be time to study later. I was going to watch television, read a newspaper, and call some friends I hadn't called since starting medical school. It was time to make some changes, some changes back.

## Responding to Reading

MyWritingLab™

1. Summarize the two main schools of thought about whether or not to participate in "dog lab." Why did McCarthy decide to help anesthetize the dogs? Did she really have a choice? Explain.
2. Does McCarthy believe that the knowledge she gained was worth the sacrifice of the dog? Do you agree with her? Do you think her experience in "dog lab" changed her? Do you think it made her a better doctor?
3. **Rhetorical Analysis**  Why do you think McCarthy decided to write this essay? Do you think her primary purpose was to explain two different viewpoints? to justify her own decision? something else?

## Responding in Writing

MyWritingLab™

1. Do you see a difference in the relative value of the lives of a laboratory animal, an animal in the wild, and a pet? Or, do you think the lives of all three kinds of animals have equal value? Explain your beliefs.
2. **Writing with Sources**  Visit the website of the American Association for Laboratory Animal Science (AALAS) to find information about this organization's views on using animals in laboratory settings. Then, write an essay in which you take a position on this issue, citing the AALAS site as well as McCarthy's essay.

# A MODEST PROPOSAL

## Jonathan Swift

### *1667–1745*

*Jonathan Swift was an Irish essayist, satirist, and poet. He wrote numerous works, many of which dealt with Irish/British political tensions and religious issues. His best-known works include* A Tale of a Tub *(1704),* Gulliver's Travels *(1726), and "A Modest Proposal" (1729), which follows. In this essay, Swift proposes a satirical solution to a social and ethical problem.*

It is a melancholy object to those, who walk through this great town, or travel in the country, when they see the streets, the roads and cabbin-doors crowded with beggars of the female sex, followed by three, four, or six children, all in rags, and importuning every passenger for an alms. These mothers instead of being able to work for their honest livelihood, are forced to employ all their time in stroling to beg sustenance for their helpless infants who, as they grow up, either turn thieves for want of work, or leave their dear native country, to fight for the Pretender in Spain,[1] or sell themselves to the Barbadoes.

I think it is agreed by all parties, that this prodigious number of children in the arms, or on the backs, or at the heels of their mothers, and frequently of their fathers, is in the present deplorable state of the kingdom, a very great additional grievance; and therefore whoever could find out a fair, cheap and easy method of making these children sound and useful members of the common-wealth, would deserve so well of the publick, as to have his statue set up for a preserver of the nation.

But my intention is very far from being confined to provide only for the children of professed beggars: it is of a much greater extent, and shall take in the whole number of infants at a certain age, who are born of parents in effect as little able to support them, as those who demand our charity in the streets.

As to my own part, having turned my thoughts for many years, upon this important subject, and maturely weighed the several schemes of our projectors, I have always found them grossly mistaken in their computation. It is true, a child just dropt from its dam, may be supported by her milk, for a solar year, with little other nourishment: at most not above the value of two shillings, which the mother may certainly get, or the value in scraps, by her lawful occupation of begging; and it is exactly at one year old that I propose to provide for them in such a manner, as, instead of being a charge upon their parents, or the parish, or wanting food and raiment for the rest of their lives, they shall, on the contrary, contribute to the feeding, and partly to the cloathing of many thousands.

5      There is likewise another great advantage in my scheme, that it will prevent those voluntary abortions, and that horrid practice of women murdering their bastard children, alas! too frequent among us, sacrificing the poor innocent babes, I doubt, more to avoid the expence than the shame, which would move tears and pity in the most savage and inhuman breast.

The number of souls in this kingdom being usually reckoned one million and a half, of these I calculate there may be about two hundred thousand couple whose wives are breeders; from which number I subtract thirty thousand couple, who are able to maintain their own children, (although I apprehend there cannot be so many, under the present distresses of the kingdom) but this being granted, there will

---

[1]The descendant of King James II (1644–85), who, as a Catholic, was an exile in Spain. [Eds.]

remain an hundred and seventy thousand breeders. I again subtract fifty thousand, for those women who miscarry, or whose children die by accident or disease within the year. There only remain an hundred and twenty thousand children of poor parents annually born. The question therefore is, How this number shall be reared, and provided for? which, as I have already said, under the present situation of affairs, is utterly impossible by all the methods hitherto proposed. For we can neither employ them in handicraft or agriculture; we neither build houses, (I mean in the country) nor cultivate land: they can very seldom pick up a livelihood by stealing till they arrive at six years old; except where they are of towardly parts, although I confess they learn the rudiments much earlier; during which time they can however be properly looked upon only as probationers: As I have been informed by a principal gentleman in the county of Cavan, who protested to me, that he never knew above one or two instances under the age of six, even in a part of the kingdom so renowned for the quickest proficiency in that art.

I am assured by our merchants, that a boy or a girl before twelve years old, is no saleable commodity, and even when they come to this age, they will not yield above three pounds, or three pounds and half a crown at most, on the exchange; which cannot turn to account either to the parents or kingdom, the charge of nutriments and rags having been at least four times that value.

I shall now therefore humbly propose my own thoughts, which I hope will not be liable to the least objection.

I have been assured by a very knowing American of my acquaintance in London, that a young healthy child well nursed, is, at a year old, a most delicious nourishing and wholesome food, whether stewed, roasted, baked, or boiled; and I make no doubt that it will equally serve in a fricasie, or a ragoust.

I do therefore humbly offer it to publick consideration, that of the hundred and twenty thousand children, already computed, twenty thousand may be reserved for breed, whereof only one fourth part to be males; which is more than we allow to sheep, black cattle, or swine, and my reason is, that these children are seldom the fruits of marriage, a circumstance not much regarded by our savages, therefore, one male will be sufficient to serve four females. That the remaining hundred thousand may, at a year old, be offered in sale to the persons of quality and fortune, through the kingdom, always advising the mother to let them suck plentifully in the last month, so as to render them plump, and fat for a good table. A child will make two dishes at an entertainment for friends, and when the family dines alone, the fore or hind quarter will make a reasonable dish, and seasoned with a little pepper or salt, will be very good boiled on the fourth day, especially in winter.

I have reckoned upon a medium, that a child just born will weigh 12 pounds, and in a solar year, if tolerably nursed, encreaseth to 28 pounds.

I grant this food will be somewhat dear, and therefore very proper for landlords, who, as they have already devoured most of the parents, seem to have the best title to the children.

Infant's flesh will be in season throughout the year, but more plentiful in March, and a little before and after; for we are told by a grave author,[2] an eminent French physician, that fish being a prolifick dyet, there are more children born in Roman Catholick countries about nine months after Lent, the markets will be more glutted than usual, because the number of Popish infants, is at least three to one in this kingdom, and therefore it will have one other collateral advantage, by lessening the number of Papists among us.

I have already computed the charge of nursing a beggar's child (in which list I reckon all cottagers, labourers, and four-fifths of the farmers) to be about two shillings per annum, rags included; and I believe no gentleman would repine to give ten shillings for the carcass of a good fat child, which, as I have said, will make four dishes of excellent nutritive meat, when he hath only some particular friend, or his own family to dine with him. Thus the squire will learn to be a good landlord, and grow popular among his tenants, the mother will have eight shillings neat profit, and be fit for work till she produces another child.

15  Those who are more thrifty (as I must confess the times require) may flea the carcass; the skin of which, artificially dressed, will make admirable gloves for ladies, and summer boots for fine gentlemen.

As to our City of Dublin, shambles may be appointed for this purpose, in the most convenient parts of it, and butchers we may be assured will not be wanting; although I rather recommend buying the children alive, and dressing them hot from the knife, as we do roasting pigs.

A very worthy person, a true lover of his country, and whose virtues I highly esteem, was lately pleased, in discoursing on this matter, to offer a refinement upon my scheme. He said, that many gentlemen of this kingdom, having of late destroyed their deer, he conceived that the want of venison might be well supply'd by the bodies of young lads and maidens, not exceeding fourteen years of age, nor under twelve; so great a number of both sexes in every country being now ready to starve for want of work and service: And these to be disposed of by their parents if alive, or otherwise by their nearest relations. But with due deference to so excellent a friend, and so deserving a patriot, I cannot be altogether in his sentiments; for as to the males, my American acquaintance assured me from frequent experience, that their flesh was generally tough and lean, like that of our school-boys, by continual exercise, and their taste disagreeable, and to fatten them would not answer the charge. Then as to the females, it would, I think, with humble submission, be a loss to the publick, because they soon would become

---

[2]François Rabelais (1494–1553?). [Eds.]

breeders themselves: And besides, it is not improbable that some scrupulous people might be apt to censure such a practice, (although indeed very unjustly) as a little bordering upon cruelty, which, I confess, hath always been with me the strongest objection against any project, how well soever intended.

But in order to justify my friend, he confessed, that this expedient was put into his head by the famous Salmanaazor,[3] a native of the island Formosa, who came from thence to London, above twenty years ago, and in conversation told my friend, that in his country, when any young person happened to be put to death, the executioner sold the carcass to persons of quality, as a prime dainty; and that, in his time, the body of a plump girl of fifteen, who was crucified for an attempt to poison the Emperor, was sold to his imperial majesty's prime minister of state, and other great mandarins of the court in joints from the gibbet, at four hundred crowns. Neither indeed can I deny, that if the same use were made of several plump young girls in this town, who without one single groat to their fortunes, cannot stir abroad without a chair, and appear at a play-house and assemblies in foreign fineries which they never will pay for; the kingdom would not be the worse.

Some persons of a desponding spirit are in great concern about that vast number of poor people, who are aged, diseased, or maimed; and I have been desired to employ my thoughts what course may be taken, to ease the nation of so grievous an incumbrance. But I am not in the least pain upon that matter, because it is very well known, that they are every day dying, and rotting, by cold and famine, and filth, and vermin, as fast as can be reasonably expected. And as to the young labourers, they are now in almost as hopeful a condition. They cannot get work, and consequently pine away from want of nourishment, to a degree, that if at any time they are accidentally hired to common labour, they have not strength to perform it, and thus the country and themselves are happily delivered from the evils to come.

I have too long digressed, and therefore shall return to my subject. 20 I think the advantages by the proposal which I have made are obvious and many, as well as of the highest importance.

For first, as I have already observed, it would greatly lessen the number of Papists, with whom we are yearly over-run, being the principal breeders of the nation, as well as our most dangerous enemies, and who stay at home on purpose with a design to deliver the kingdom to the Pretender, hoping to take their advantage by the absence of so many good Protestants, who have chosen rather to leave their country, than stay at home and pay tithes against their conscience to an episcopal curate.

---

[3]George Psalmanazar (1679?–1763), a Frenchman who fraudulently claimed to come from Formosa (now Taiwan), which he wrote about in a book. [Eds.]

Secondly, The poorer tenants will have something valuable of their own, which by law may be made liable to a distress, and help to pay their landlord's rent, their corn and cattle being already seized, and money a thing unknown.

Thirdly, Whereas the maintainance of an hundred thousand children, from two years old, and upwards, cannot be computed at less than ten shillings a piece per annum, the nation's stock will be thereby encreased fifty thousand pounds per annum, besides the profit of a new dish, introduced to the tables of all gentlemen of fortune in the kingdom, who have any refinement in taste. And the money will circulate among our selves, the goods being entirely of our own growth and manufacture.

Fourthly, The constant breeders, besides the gain of eight shillings sterling per annum by the sale of their children, will be rid of the charge of maintaining them after the first year.

25  Fifthly, This food would likewise bring great custom to taverns, where the vintners will certainly be so prudent as to procure the best receipts for dressing it to perfection; and consequently have their houses frequented by all the fine gentlemen, who justly value themselves upon their knowledge in good eating; and a skilful cook, who understands how to oblige his guests, will contrive to make it as expensive as they please.

Sixthly, This would be a great inducement to marriage, which all wise nations have either encouraged by rewards, or enforced by laws and penalties. It would encrease the care and tenderness of mothers towards their children, when they were sure of a settlement for life to the poor babes, provided in some sort by the publick, to their annual profit instead of expence. We should soon see an honest emulation among the married women, which of them could bring the fattest child to the market. Men would become as fond of their wives, during the time of their pregnancy, as they are now of their mares in foal, their cows in calf, or sow when they are ready to farrow; nor offer to beat or kick them (as is too frequent a practice) for fear of a miscarriage.

Many other advantages might be enumerated. For instance, the addition of some thousand carcasses in our exportation of barrel'd beef: the propagation of swine's flesh, and improvement in the art of making good bacon, so much wanted among us by the great destruction of pigs, too frequent at our tables; which are no way comparable in taste or magnificence to a well grown, fat yearly child, which roasted whole will make a considerable figure at a Lord Mayor's feast, or any other publick entertainment. But this, and many others, I omit, being studious of brevity.

Supposing that one thousand families in this city, would be constant customers for infants flesh, besides others who might have it at merry meetings, particularly at weddings and christenings, I compute that Dublin would take off annually about twenty thousand carcasses; and the rest of the kingdom (where probably they will be sold somewhat cheaper) the remaining eighty thousand.

I can think of no one objection, that will possibly be raised against this proposal, unless it should be urged, that the number of people will be thereby much lessened in the kingdom. This I freely own, and 'twas indeed one principal design in offering it to the world. I desire the reader will observe, that I calculate my remedy for this one individual Kingdom of Ireland, and for no other that ever was, is, or, I think, ever can be upon Earth. Therefore let no man talk to me of other expedients: Of taxing our absentees at five shillings a pound: Of using neither cloaths, nor houshold furniture, except what is of our own growth and manufacture: Of utterly rejecting the materials and instruments that promote foreign luxury: Of curing the expensiveness of pride, vanity, idleness, and gaming in our women: Of introducing a vein of parsimony, prudence and temperance: Of learning to love our country, wherein we differ even from Laplanders, and the inhabitants of Topinamboo: Of quitting our animosities and factions, nor acting any longer like the Jews, who were murdering one another at the very moment their city was taken: Of being a little cautious not to sell our country and consciences for nothing: Of teaching landlords to have at least one degree of mercy towards their tenants. Lastly, of putting a spirit of honesty, industry, and skill into our shop-keepers, who, if a resolution could now be taken to buy only our native goods, would immediately unite to cheat and exact upon us in the price, the measure, and the goodness, nor could ever yet be brought to make one fair proposal of just dealing, though often and earnestly invited to it.

Therefore I repeat, let no man talk to me of these and the like expedients, 'till he hath at least some glympse of hope, that there will ever be some hearty and sincere attempt to put them into practice. 30

But, as to my self, having been wearied out for many years with offering vain, idle, visionary thoughts, and at length utterly despairing of success, I fortunately fell upon this proposal, which, as it is wholly new, so it hath something solid and real, of no expence and little trouble, full in our own power, and whereby we can incur no danger in disobliging England. For this kind of commodity will not bear exportation, and flesh being of too tender a consistence, to admit a long continuance in salt, although perhaps I could name a country, which would be glad to eat up our whole nation without it.

After all, I am not so violently bent upon my own opinion, as to reject any offer, proposed by wise men, which shall be found equally innocent, cheap, easy, and effectual. But before something of that kind shall be advanced in contradiction to my scheme, and offering a better, I desire the author or authors will be pleased maturely to consider two points. First, As things now stand, how they will be able to find food and raiment for a hundred thousand useless mouths and backs. And secondly, There being a round million of creatures in humane figure throughout this kingdom, whose whole subsistence put into a common stock, would leave them in debt two million of pounds sterling, adding those who are beggars by profession, to the bulk of farmers, cottagers and labourers, with their wives and children, who are beggars in effect; I desire those politicians who dislike my overture, and may perhaps be so bold to attempt an answer, that they will first ask the parents of these mortals, whether they would not at this day think it a great happiness to have been sold for food at a year old, in the manner I prescribe, and thereby have avoided such a perpetual scene of misfortunes, as they have since gone through, by the oppression of landlords, the impossibility of paying rent without money or trade, the want of common sustenance, with neither house nor cloaths to cover them from the inclemencies of the weather, and the most inevitable prospect of intailing the like, or greater miseries, upon their breed for ever.

I profess, in the sincerity of my heart, that I have not the least personal interest in endeavouring to promote this necessary work, having no other motive than the publick good of my country, by advancing our trade, providing for infants, relieving the poor, and giving some pleasure to the rich. I have no children, by which I can propose to get a single penny; the youngest being nine years old, and my wife past child-bearing.

## Responding to Reading

MyWritingLab™

1. In this essay, Swift identifies a serious problem. What is this problem? How would his "modest proposal" solve it?
2. Find a definition of *satire*. How does "A Modest Proposal" fit this definition?
3. **Rhetorical Analysis** In what respects does Swift believe that the British government's treatment of the Irish is unethical? Do you think his purpose in this essay is just to get readers to think more deeply about this problem, or do you think he expects them to take some kind of action?

## Writing about Reading

MyWritingLab™

1. Write your own satirical "modest proposal" for solving a problem on your college campus—for example, academic cheating, student debt, or binge drinking.
2. **Writing with Sources** Write a serious proposal for solving a problem on your college campus. Research this problem by interviewing students, faculty, and staff and by reading back issues of your school newspaper.

---

## FOCUS

## What Has Happened to Academic Integrity?

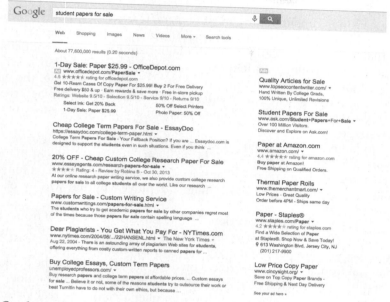

*Google* search results for "student papers for sale"

## Responding to the Image

MyWritingLab™

1. What, if anything, does the list pictured above tell you about the state of academic integrity in the 21st century? Could you argue that the availability of papers for sale is irrelevant to the way students view plagiarism?
2. Do your own search for "student papers for sale," click on one of the links listed, and evaluate the site it leads you to. Do you think this site makes an effective appeal to its intended audience? Why or why not? (Remember to evaluate the site's language as well as its content and appearance.)
3. Some term paper sites include a disclaimer stating that they assume users will not hand in the papers they purchase but will rather use them as research sources. What is your response to such disclaimers?

# THE TRUTH ABOUT PLAGIARISM

## Richard A. Posner

### 1939–

*A judge of the US Court of Appeals for the Seventh Circuit and a senior lecturer at the University of Chicago Law School, Richard A. Posner is a legal expert whose work focuses on the economics of intellectual property and health policy. He has written numerous academic articles, book reviews, and books, including the book* Divergent Paths: The Academy and the Judiciary *(2016). In the following essay, Posner considers the difference between plagiarism and theft.*

Plagiarism is considered by most writers, teachers, journalists, scholars and even members of the general public to be the capital intellectual crime. Being caught out in plagiarism can blast a politician's career, earn a college student expulsion and destroy a writer's, scholar's or journalist's reputation. In recent days, for example, the *New York Times* has referred to "widespread fabrication and plagiarism" by reporter Jayson Blair as "a low point in the 152-year history of the newspaper."

In James Hynes' splendid satiric novella of plagiarism, *Casting the Runes*, the plagiarist, having by black magic murdered one of the historians whom he plagiarized and tried to murder a second, is himself killed by the very same black magic, deployed by the widow of his murder victim.

There is a danger of overkill. Plagiarism can be a form of fraud, but it is no accident that, unlike real theft, it is not a crime. If a thief steals your car, you are out the market value of the car, but if a writer copies material from a book you wrote, you don't have to replace the book. At worst, the undetected plagiarist obtains a reputation that he does not deserve (that is the element of fraud in plagiarism). The real victim of his fraud is not the person whose work he copies, but those of his competitors who scruple to enhance their own reputations by such means.

The most serious plagiarisms are by students and professors, whose undetected plagiarisms disrupt the system of student and scholarly evaluation. The least serious are those that earned the late Stephen Ambrose and Doris Kearns Goodwin such obloquy last year. Popular historians, they jazzed up their books with vivid passages copied from previous historians without quotation marks, though with footnote attributions that made their "crime" easy to detect.

5  (One reason that plagiarism, like littering, is punished heavily, even though an individual act of plagiarism usually does little or no harm, is that it is normally very difficult to detect—but not in the case of Ambrose and Goodwin.) Competing popular historians might have been injured, but I'm not aware of anyone actually claiming this.

Confusion of plagiarism with theft is one reason plagiarism engenders indignation; another is a confusion of it with copyright infringement. Wholesale copying of copyrighted material is an infringement of a property right, and legal remedies are available to the copyright holder. But the copying of brief passages, even from copyrighted materials, is permissible under the doctrine of "fair use," while wholesale copying from material that is in the public domain—material that never was copyrighted, or on which the copyright has expired—presents no copyright issue at all.

Plagiarism of work in the public domain is more common than otherwise. Consider a few examples: *West Side Story* is a thinly veiled copy (with music added) of *Romeo and Juliet*, which in turn plagiarized Arthur Brooke's *The Tragicall Historye of Romeo and Juliet*, published in 1562, which in turn copied from several earlier Romeo and Juliets, all of which were copies of Ovid's story of Pyramus and Thisbe.

*Paradise Lost* plagiarizes the book of Genesis in the Old Testament. Classical musicians plagiarize folk melodies (think only of Dvorak, Bartok, and Copland) and often "quote" (as musicians say) from earlier classical works. Edouard Manet's most famous painting, *Dejeuner sur l'herbe*, copies earlier paintings by Raphael, Titian, and Courbet, and *My Fair Lady* plagiarized Shaw's play *Pygmalion*, while Woody Allen's movie *Play It Again, Sam* "quotes" a famous scene from *Casablanca*. Countless movies are based on books, such as *The Thirty-Nine Steps* on John Buchan's novel of that name or *For Whom the Bell Tolls* on Hemingway's novel.

Many of these "plagiarisms" were authorized, and perhaps none was deceptive; they are what Christopher Ricks in his excellent book *Allusions to the Poets* helpfully terms *allusion* rather than *plagiarism*. But what they show is that copying with variations is an important form of creativity, and this should make us prudent and measured in our condemnations of plagiarism.

Especially when the term is extended from literal copying to the 10 copying of ideas. Another phrase for copying an idea, as distinct from the form in which it is expressed, is dissemination of ideas. If one needs a license to repeat another person's idea, or if one risks ostracism by one's professional community for failing to credit an idea to its originator, who may be forgotten or unknown, the dissemination of ideas is impeded.

I have heard authors of history textbooks criticized for failing to document their borrowing of ideas from previous historians. This is an absurd criticism. The author of a textbook makes no claim to originality; rather the contrary—the most reliable, if not necessarily the most exciting, textbook is one that confines itself to ideas already well accepted, not at all novel.

It would be better if the term *plagiarism* were confined to literal copying, and moreover literal copying that is not merely unacknowledged but deceptive. Failing to give credit where credit is due should be regarded as a lesser, indeed usually merely venial, offense.

The concept of plagiarism has expanded, and the sanctions for it, though they remain informal rather than legal, have become more severe, in tandem with the rise of individualism. Journal articles are no longer published anonymously, and ghostwriters demand that their contributions be acknowledged.

CHAPTER 11   FOCUS

Individualism and a cult of originality go hand in hand. Each of us supposes that our contribution to society is unique rather than fungible and so deserves public recognition, which plagiarism clouds.

15     This is a modern view. We should be aware that the high value placed on originality is a specific cultural, and even field-specific, phenomenon, rather than an aspect of the universal moral law.

Judges, who try to conceal rather than to flaunt their originality, far from crediting their predecessors with original thinking like to pretend that there is no original thinking in law, that judges are just a transmission belt for rules and principles laid down by the framers of statutes or the Constitution.

Resorting to plagiarism to obtain a good grade or a promotion is fraud and should be punished, though it should not be confused with "theft." But I think the zeal to punish plagiarism reflects less a concern with the real injuries that it occasionally inflicts than with a desire on the part of leaders of professional communities, such as journalists and historians, to enhance their profession's reputation.

Journalists (like politicians) have a bad reputation for truthfulness, and historians, in this "postmodernist" era, are suspected of having embraced an extreme form of relativism and of having lost their regard for facts. Both groups hope by taking a very hard line against plagiarism and fabrication to reassure the public that they are serious diggers after truth whose efforts, a form of "sweat equity," deserve protection against copycats.

Their anxieties are understandable; but the rest of us will do well to keep the matter in perspective, realizing that the term *plagiarism* is used loosely and often too broadly; that much plagiarism is harmless and (when the term is defined broadly) that some has social value.

## Responding to Reading

MyWritingLab™

1. In paragraph 3, Posner says, "There is a danger of overkill. Plagiarism can be a form of fraud, but it is no accident that, unlike real theft, it is not a crime." How do you think David Callahan (p. 452) would react to this statement?
2. According to Posner, what is the difference between plagiarism and theft? Between plagiarism and copyright infringement? Between plagiarism and allusion? Do you see these distinctions as valid in cases of academic plagiarism? Why or why not?
3. **Rhetorical Analysis** Evaluate Posner's concluding paragraph. Does his statement that "much plagiarism is harmless" adequately sum up his essay's position? What else, if anything, do you think he should address in this paragraph?

## Writing about Reading

MyWritingLab™

1. Do you agree with Posner that "much plagiarism is harmless" (19)? Under what circumstances, if any, do you think academic cheating is "harmless"?

2. **Writing with Sources**  In paragraph 4, Posner states, "The most serious plagiarisms are by students and professors … ." Do you agree, or do you believe plagiarism on the part of professional writers and scholars—or politicians—is more serious? Research incidents of plagiarism by historians Stephen Ambrose and Doris Kearns Goodwin—or by political leaders or news reporters—and discuss the issue of student plagiarism with students on your campus. Then, write an essay in which you explain why you agree or disagree with Posner's statement.

# STUDENT PLAGIARISM IN AN ONLINE WORLD
## Julie J. C. H. Ryan

*An associate professor of engineering management and systems engineering at George Washington University, Julie J. C. H. Ryan specializes in information security. She coauthored the book* Defending Your Digital Assets against Hackers, Crackers, Spies, and Thieves *(2000) and edited the book* Leading Issues in Information Warfare and Security Research *(2011). The following essay, which was published in 1998, considers the changing nature of academic integrity in the Internet Age. Although some of the websites Ryan mentions are now obsolete, her thesis about plagiarism is all the more meaningful today.*

In academe, the consequences of plagiarism are clear: Using someone else's words or ideas without attribution is grounds for failed assignments, suspension, or expulsion. For some students, however, breaking the rules seems to be an irresistible challenge. And so the game goes: Students continually look for (and find) ways to cheat, and teachers remain on the alert for purloined paragraphs, pages, and even entire papers.

Plagiarized work used to be generated through frat house recycling efforts, purchased from local ghost writers, or simply copied from campus library reference materials—all clumsy efforts readily detectable by educators familiar with their course material. But the World Wide Web and other electronic resources have changed the game and left educators scrambling to keep abreast of plagiarists' new methods.

### [Abusing Electronic Media]

Before the world was linked by the Internet, hard-to-detect plagiarism required ingenuity and skill. But today, with the click of a mouse, even technologically inept students have access to vast information resources in cyberspace without having to leave the comfort of their dorm rooms.

A few words typed into a Web search engine can lead a student to hundreds, sometimes thousands, of relevant documents, making it easy to "cut and paste" a few paragraphs from here and a few more from there until the student has an entire paper-length collection. Or a student can find a research paper published in one of the hundreds of new journals that have gone online over the past few years, copy the entire text, turn it into a new document, and then offer it up as an original work without having to type anything but a cover page. Even recycling efforts and ghost writers have gone global, with Web sites offering professionally or student-written research papers for sale, some even with a money back guarantee against detection.

## Facing the New Plagiarism Reality

5 I ran headlong into these new practices during the fall 1997 semester as my husband and I each taught an introductory information security concepts course for George Washington University. When students turned in their required research papers, we were initially surprised at how well they seemed to have mastered the course material. But when we looked closer, we realized that in many cases we were not looking at original student work.

Consider the following extract from one of the student-submitted papers:

> Both the government and the healthcare unions agree that electronic health records must be at least as well protected as paper ones; the Data Protection Act makes physicians and others responsible for the security of personal health information that they collect; and a recent Directive obliges the government to prohibit the processing of health data except where the data subject has given his explicit consent, and in certain other circumstances.

The level of erudition, education, and sophistication evidenced in this extract (and the entire document) made it immediately suspect—the student was, after all, taking an introductory course in information security concepts. To satisfy his curiosity, my husband asked me to research the paper content for possible plagiarism. I did so using the tool most readily available, the Internet. It didn't take me long to find an exact match.

I used the AltaVista Search engine to conduct a search for specific phrases (or strings) in the paper. To search for an exact match, I used quotation marks around the string. If quotations marks are not used, the results will include Web pages that contain some or all of the words in the string.

I also could have performed a category search using one of the comprehensive listing services that index Web sites by category. Yahoo! is one of the most popular sites of this type. Comprehensive list sites give you two search options. You can choose a category from the site's standing lists, or you can type a few words into the search box and the site's internal search engine will retrieve a list of categories and Web site that include the words in your search parameters. I found the following extract in an online journal article by Ross J. Anderson, a distinguished University of Cambridge computer researcher. The differences from the previous extract are underlined:

> Both the government and the healthcare unions **are** agreed that electronic health records must be at least as well protected as paper ones; the Data Protection Act makes **GPs** and others responsible for the security of personal health information that they collect; and a recent **EU** Directive obliges the government to prohibit the processing of health data except where the data subject has given his explicit consent, and in certain other circumstances **[EU95]** .

It took me five minutes on the Internet to determine the probable source of the paper, and another 10 minutes to confirm word-for-word plagiarism. The entire paper, including the title, table of contents, and bibliography, was plagiarized. An open-and-shut case.

Once I caught the first plagiarism, I decided to check every paper. I discovered that seven of 42 students plagiarized most or all of their papers, and four others turned in papers with footnotes that could charitably be called substandard.

In the spring 1998 semester I discovered that the same percentage of students—one out of every six—plagiarized their entire papers. Also, as in the previous semester, several students' papers had inadequate footnotes.

## [To Catch a Plagiarist]

The World Wide Web provides plagiarists with a rich library of material from which to gather information, but it also provides professors with a powerful tool to check sources and catch the word thieves.

The laziness that prompts students to cheat can also prompt them to do a terrible job with their plagiarism. Being able to copy electronic source material rids them of the chore of retyping the paper, and some students don't even bother to proofread the results. These halfhearted efforts can easily be detected if you know what to look for.

### Context Change.

Students try to camouflage copying by changing the context of the original paper. For example, I received a paper purported to be a draft information security policy for an institute in Korea. The references to Massachusetts law were, therefore, somewhat startling. It turned out that the paper was an almost complete copy of Harvard University's information security policy.

10

CHAPTER 11   FOCUS

## Missing Footnotes.

One technique that seems to appeal to plagiarists is to skip footnotes altogether. This is presumably done with the notion that when challenged, the student can point to a bibliography and claim ignorance regarding proper footnoting procedure. I have, in fact, had students try this defense. To counter this, sit down with the student and ask him or her about the subject matter of the paper and the cited bibliographic references. If the student doesn't understand or can't discuss the ideas presented in the paper, or doesn't know the subject matter of the books referenced, then it's safe to assume the student didn't write the paper.

## False References.

Citing nonexistent books or journal articles, or referring to sources unrelated to the subject matter is also common. Usually sparsely identified, these references tend to list overview or general subject texts, as opposed to the much more specific sources found in legitimate papers.

For example, a false footnote from a spring 1998 paper:

*Pfleeger, Charles P. (1997) Security in Computing. New Jersey*

A real footnote from a legitimate paper that same semester:

*Denning, Dorothy E., Encryption Policy and Market Trends, http://www. cs.georgetown.edu/~denning/crypto, March 14, 1998.*

True footnotes explain the source of data or some technicality in the text, while false footnotes may stand out because of their placement.

An example from a spring 1998 paper:

*Encryption systems fall into two broad classes (Fites & Kratz, 1993). Conventional or symmetric cryptosystems—those in which an entity with the ability to encrypt also has the ability to decrypt and vice versa—are the systems under consideration in this paper … . All known public key cryptosystems, however, are subject to shortcut attacks and must therefore use keys ten or more times the length of those discussed here to achieve an equivalent level of security.*

Note several things about the reference—it is placed where it appears to substantiate the purported fact that there are two broad classes of encryption systems. However, this is a widely held piece of knowledge that does not warrant footnoting except by the most compulsive of students. The sentences following that, however, are quite different. They do, in fact, warrant footnoting in that they convey specific information that is not in the realm of what may be purported to be common knowledge. And yet there is no footnote.

15    Further, an examination of the Fites & Katz reference reveals it to be a general purpose text of some age (in an era when information

technology turns over generationally every 18 months or so, even a few years can have dramatic effects on the content of a text). As referenced: *Fites, Philip & Kratz, Martin P. J., (1993). Information Systems Security. New York.*

Online bookstores provide book descriptions and reviews, and information on availability, all of which can be used to make sure a reference book is appropriate for the subject matter. Using the online bookstore Amazon.com revealed that the true title of the above-mentioned text to be *Information Systems Security: A Practitioner's Reference*, and that it is out of print. A search on the Internet using the AltaVista search engine revealed a source with more information on the subject matter of the text:

> *Information Systems Security: A Practitioner's Reference. Philip Fites and Martin P. J. Kratz*
>
> *You will refer to this valuable resource again and again. There are chapters on countermeasures, designing secure systems, software, accounting and auditing controls. Operations and physical security in fire prevention, libraries and database protection, waste disposal and storage are all discussed. All-encompassing and up-to-date, it's a vital reference tool! 471 pp., 1993 SCVR (http://www.asisonline.org/catcomputer.html#infosecurity, 13 May 1998)*

Clearly the text, while useful, is not a cryptography reference. In this case, the false footnote actually highlighted the suspect nature of the text. Other suspect elements of this passage include the reference to "systems under consideration in this paper." As the paper was purportedly an analysis on electronic terrorism, this phrase seemed odd.

A string search on the Internet, again using the AltaVista search engine, revealed the true source of the material:

> *Minimal Key Lengths for Symmetric Ciphers to Provide Adequate Commercial Security: A Report by an Ad Hoc Group of Cryptographers and Computer Scientists, January 1996, by Matt Blaze et al.*

This paper is published on the Internet at multiple locations.

## Cyberspace Cooperation

While AltaVista and other search engines are excellent resources, they are of little or no use if the source text was not electronically published. In this case, an investigator can occasionally find clues in a paper that can point to the true author. An example of this occurred in a paper that appeared to be scanned in from a source text. The following is a quote from that student-submitted paper:

> *NetBill, a system under development at Carnegie Mellon University (CMU), Pittsburgh, in joint action with Mellon Bank Corp., also in Pittsburgh, is*

*accelerated for delivering such information goods as text, images, and software over the Internet. Its developers, including the author, have stressed the significance of securing that consumers receive the information they pay for. For that reason, consumers are not charged until the information has actually been delivered to them.*

This paper initially frustrated me, because I had a very strong suspicion that it was plagiarized but couldn't find the source of this text using either a string or category search.

However, the conjunction of references to "the author" and to what seemed to be a proprietary product of Carnegie Mellon University—NetBill—led me to the Carnegie Mellon University Web site. I used the site's internal search engine to find references to NetBill. In doing so, I discovered that Marvin Sirbu is leader of the NetBill project. The search also provided Sirbu's e-mail address.

20   I immediately sent an e-mail to Sirbu, inquiring as to whether he found that text extract familiar. Sirbu's reply included both the source identification and a URL from which the original document was available. When I compared the original with the student paper, I discovered that the entire paper was plagiarized, including the section headings.

If the Carnegie Mellon site had not provided Sirbu's e-mail address, I could have tried a string search of his name or used one of the many "phone book"-type search engines to hunt down the information.

These search tools may be new to you, but all are relatively easy to use. Most Web search sites have "Help" sections that provide information on using their specific search engines, and there are several sites dedicated to search instruction, including Search Insider.

## [Why cheating still matters]

The papers that are the subject of this article were out-and-out forgeries, with inadequate, nonexistent, or false footnotes. In many cases the plagiary attempts were so patently obvious they were insulting.

20   The attempted deception is particularly disturbing because the class was an overview of information security concepts and practices. The curriculum focused on the value and protection of information, and specific readings and lectures addressed copyright law and other relevant topics. These students will go on to computer-related careers where they have to deal with information security issues on a regular basis, yet they showed no regard for information's basic value.

Also disturbing was students' reactions when caught. Instead of expressing shame or remorse, reactions included denial (even in the face of overwhelming evidence) and defiance. One student even exclaimed: "You can't do this to me—I'm on a scholarship!" A response from another student caught plagiarizing is immortalized in the following e-mail:

*Hi prof.*

*I just wanted to tell you something. I called all my friends and asked them how they usually do their papers. Most of them told me that they do the same thing. They didn't know it is illegal and they can't do that. Can you believe it?*

*Anyway, I told some of them what I did and what happened to me and they were shocked. They didn't know that what they do is wrong …*

*That's why, I did that without knowing it's wrong. Also, I talked to my advisor in the writing center who reviewed my paper. He told me that he didn't notice that, even though I gave him all the articles I used in my paper … All I want to say is that I wanted to get an A in your class and I wanted to give you a good paper ….*

Several other students made similar ignorance pleas when confronted, despite the fact that we emphasized acceptable footnoting practices for research papers during both semesters. In spring 1998, the emphasis on proper procedure was naturally even higher than it had been in fall 1997, and the repercussions from the preceding semester were still a subject of gossip within the student population. Thus it was quite startling to yet again see students attempt to pass off other people's works as their own.

## [Conclusion]

Often lost in the discussion of plagiarism is the interest of the students who don't cheat. They do legitimate research and write their own papers. They work harder (and learn more) than the plagiarists, yet their grades may suffer when their papers are judged and graded against papers that are superior but stolen material. Students have a right to expect fairness in the classroom. When teachers turn a blind eye to plagiarism, it undermines that right and denigrates grades, degrees, and even institutions.

Plagiarism is alive and well on campuses and in cyberspace. But educators should take some solace in the fact that while the Internet is a useful resource for plagiarists, it is also an excellent tool to use against them.

## Responding to Reading                    MyWritingLab™

1. Is Ryan addressing students or instructors? How do you know? What is her purpose in writing this essay?
2. Writing in 1998, Ryan notes that electronic resources have already "changed the game" (2). How? At that time, what Internet tools enabled instructors to identify plagiarists? What clues alerted instructors to the possibility of Internet plagiarism?
3. **Rhetorical Analysis**   How does Ryan establish her credibility? Does she provide enough information to convince readers that she is someone worth listening to?

## Writing about Reading

1. When you do research, do you find it difficult to keep track of online sources? What steps do you take to make sure that you do not unintentionally commit plagiarism?

2. **Writing with Sources**   What guidelines does your school give concerning Internet plagiarism? Research the guidelines provided by two other schools in your area, and compare them to those at your school. What do all these guidelines have in common? How do they differ? Write your own set of guidelines that clearly conveys to students the need to follow ethical practices when using Internet sources.

# A BETTER WAY TO PREVENT CHEATING: APPEAL TO FAIRNESS

## David Callahan

### 1965–

*The founder and editor of the website* Inside Philanthropy, *and a radio and television commentator, David Callahan explores issues related to finances and ethics. He is the author of eight books, including, most recently,* Fortunes of Change: The Rise of the Liberal Rich and the Remaking of America *(2010). His articles have appeared in such publications as the* Nation, *the* New York Times, *and the* Washington Post. *In the following essay, Callahan offers suggestions to help prevent cheating in college.*

As professors sit down to grade mid-term exams, it's time for some to play their least favorite role: cop. With surveys finding that up to three-quarters of college students cheat, faculty and administrators are making a bigger push for integrity. What most still lack, however, is a compelling moral argument against cheating.

A growing number of universities have enacted honor codes, but many of these codes—along with campus efforts to publicize them—fail to make a strong case for why cheating is wrong. Often they invoke fuzzy ideals of honor or, conversely, dwell on the negative consequences for cheaters who are caught. Neither approach gets very far, not these days.

Honor, with its emphasis on doing the right thing for its own sake, is no match for the anxious cynicism of many college students. This point was driven home to me by a junior I met in North Carolina. Why not cheat, he argued, given how many of America's most successful people cut corners to get where they are? Cheating is how the real world works, he said. Look at the politicians who lie or the sluggers who take steroids, or the CEOs who cook the books. The student also pointed to the hurdles he faced as he tried to get ahead: high tuition costs, heavy student loans, low-paying jobs without benefits. America wasn't a fair place for kids like him, so it made sense to try to level the playing field by bending a few rules.

Many young people take this bleak view. A 2008 poll of high school students found that 59 percent agreed that "successful people do what they have to do to win, even if others consider it cheating." Young people believe in honor and value integrity; they also worry that living by these beliefs could mean ending up as a loser. In justifying her cheating, one student told a researcher: "Good grades can make the difference between going to medical school and being a janitor." Few professors have a ready retort to this logic.

Appeals to self-interest only worsen the problem. If you tell a student    5
that she shouldn't cheat because she might get caught, or that she's "just cheating herself" by not learning the material, or that integrity is an asset in life to be cultivated, she might respond—as the student I met in North Carolina did—by spelling out the ways that successful cheating could advance one's self-interest, especially if "everybody else" is doing it.

Students with a strong sense of right and wrong, learned early in life, may be more willing to sacrifice personal advancement for the sake of their values. Some research has shown, for instance, that students with a theistic outlook are less likely to cheat. But most colleges aren't in the position to reshape students' character at this level. Likewise, our universities have limited influence over the broader socioeconomic trends that help fuel cheating, such as rising economic inequality and increasing middle-class insecurity.

What can faculty and administrators do to stem epidemic cheating? Their best hope is to cast cheating as an issue of justice.

Students may be cynical about what it takes to succeed these days, but they do care about fairness. And cheating is nothing if not unfair. Cheaters get rewards they don't deserve, like scholarships, admission to college or grad school, internships, and jobs. Cheating is the antithesis of equal opportunity: the notion that we all should have a fair shot at success and that the people who get rewarded are the people who deserve those rewards because they worked the hardest.

Many students understand that the ideal of equal opportunity is threatened in an era of rising inequality. Quite a few say they want to do something about this. Anticheating efforts offer a way to build, on campus, a microcosm of the kind of society they want to live in—one with a level playing field for all. I've met many students who see this and many who are organizing to fight cheating.

Maybe academic integrity will never become a great campus cause.    10
But if faculty can cast this issue as a matter of justice, and empower students to take action, perhaps some day they won't have to spend so much time playing cop.

## Responding to Reading

MyWritingLab™

1. What practical objections does Callahan have to the kind of appeals to students that stress the idea of "doing the right thing for its own sake" (3)? to what he calls "appeals to self-interest" (5)? Do his objections make sense to you?

2. Evaluate the following two statements (the first by a student, the second by Callahan).

   • "Cheating is how the real world works …. " (3)
   • "Students may be cynical about what it takes to succeed these days, but they do care about fairness." (8)

Given your assessments of these two statements, do you think Callahan's recommendations for how to prevent cheating are unrealistically optimistic?

3. **Rhetorical Analysis**  Reread Callahan's criticisms of college honor codes in paragraph 2. Why does he locate this discussion here? Should he have developed this material further? Why or why not? What do you suppose Richard Posner (p. 441) would think of honor codes?

## Writing about Reading

MyWritingLab™

1. Do you think professors should take on the role of "cops" when it comes to uncovering cheating and other forms of academic dishonesty? Why or why not?

2. **Writing with Sources**  Write a proposal to your school's administration in which you make recommendations of your own for preventing cheating. Acknowledging the suggestions by Callahan and others you find in your research, tailor the recommendations specifically to the students at your college or university. (If you like, you can focus on one major or even one class at your school.)

# WIDENING THE FOCUS

## For Critical Reading and Writing

Referring specifically to the three readings in this chapter's Focus section (and possibly to additional sources as well), write an essay in which you answer the question, "What Has Happened to Academic Integrity?"

## For Further Reading

The following readings can suggest additional perspectives for thinking and writing about the issue of academic integrity:

- Amy Chua, adapted from *Battle Hymn of the Tiger Mother* (p. 59)

- John Holt, "School Is Bad for Children" (p. 78)

- Christina Hoff Sommers, "The War against Boys" (p. 247)

- David A. Hoekema, "The Unacknowledged Ethicists on Campuses" (p. 401)

## For Focused Research

Web Links

Honor codes are an integral part of the academic policies at many colleges and universities across the United States. However, not all honor codes are alike: they vary considerably from school to school. In preparation for writing an essay about higher-education honor codes, do a *Google* search using the search terms *honor codes and US colleges,* and read information about the honor codes at various schools. In your essay, explain the range of honor codes at US colleges and universities and what these schools hope to accomplish by enforcing them. Are honor codes a good solution to the problems created by the decline of academic integrity? Support your points with examples and evidence from the school websites you use.

## Beyond the Classroom

Interview the following people: several professors (in different fields), one student from every year at your school, and two college librarians. Ask each of them if they think plagiarism and other forms of academic dishonesty are on the rise—and, if so, why. Then, ask them what solutions they propose to address the problems they identify. Write an essay in the form of a proposal that summarizes the recommendations you have gathered.

——————————— EXPLORING ISSUES AND IDEAS ———————

## Making Ethical Choices

MyWritingLab™

Visit Chapter 11, "Making Ethical Choices," in MyWritingLab to test your understanding of the chapter objectives.

Write an essay in response to one of the following prompts, which are suitable for assignments that require the use of outside sources as well as for assignments that are not source-based.

1. Martin Luther King, Jr. (p. 411) considers the difficulties of resisting majority rule, standing up to authority, and protesting against established rules and laws. Choose a law or practice that you consider unjust, and write an essay in which you explain why you believe it should be challenged (or even disobeyed).

2. Do you believe it is possible both to do good (that is, to help others) and to do well (that is, to be financially successful), or do you believe these two goals are mutually exclusive? Write an essay in which you answer this question, citing examples of people you know as well as public figures who have (or have not) managed both to do good and to do well.

3. Do you think that people can be guided by a moral and ethical code that is strictly secular, or do you believe it is only possible to live a moral, ethical life if one believes in a higher power and follows the guidelines set by a particular religion? Write an essay that explains your position.

4. Do you believe that decisions about what steps to take to preserve the environment are essentially ethical choices? Or, do you think a person's behavior in situations like this has nothing to do with ethics or morals?

5. Imagine that you are in charge of an almost-full lifeboat and can take on only one additional passenger. Which of the following people would you choose, and why?

- A healthy three-year-old
- An elderly Nobel Prize winner
- A single father of two young children
- A thirty-year-old decorated combat veteran
- A middle-aged doctor who has performed life-saving surgery

Write an essay in which you consider which of the candidates most deserves to be saved (not which one can be of most practical help to the others in the lifeboat). Before you focus on the person you would save, evaluate the pros and cons of saving each of the others.

# 12

## FACING THE FUTURE

*In this chapter, you will learn to*
- analyze readings about life in the future
- compose essays about life in the future

In the early part of the twentieth century, people envisioned the future as a place of infinite possibilities, where human intellect would create a society in which technology and industry could solve all the world's problems. War would be a thing of the past, and so would famine and disease. Soon, however, two World Wars (and many small ones) revealed the folly of these forecasts. Instead of creating a utopia,

View of a future city from the 1927 science fiction movie *Metropolis*

technology enabled human beings to create destruction on a scale never witnessed before in human history.

Of course, the new developments were not all bad. In the early part of the twentieth century, people traveled mainly on foot, by horse, or by train. By the middle of the century, the automobile and the jet plane enabled them to travel great distances in hours instead of weeks. In 1969, the same rocket technology that had enabled Nazi Germany to launch V2 rockets against England in 1944 also enabled the United States to send astronauts to the moon. Throughout the twentieth century, medicine made advances that enabled doctors to cure diseases—such as polio, typhus, and cholera—that had decimated human populations for centuries. With the inventions of the telephone, radio, and television, people were able to transmit and receive information instantly, regardless of distance. And the computer gave people access to information on a scale that earlier generations could never have imagined.

Now, in the second decade of the twenty-first century, people understandably wonder what is in store for them.

- Will the family look much as it does today, or will *family* be defined differently?

- Will education as we know it endure, or will online education replace face-to-face classroom instruction?

Contemporary view of the Brooklyn Bridge and the Manhattan skyline at night

- How will social media affect our language?

- Will cultural identity become more or less important?

- Will technology bring people closer together or push them further apart?

- How will gender roles change? Will these changes be for the better?

- How will the nature of work and workers' roles change? What new jobs will emerge?

- Will more people realize the American Dream, or will it remain out of reach for many?

- What new ethical dilemmas will the future bring?

- Finally, will the future be benign or harmful? Will human beings achieve the society that they have always wished for, or will this century be as destructive as the last one?

The three college commencement speeches in the Focus section of this chapter (p. 492) address the question "What Comes Next?" and reflect the hopes, fears, and mood of the speakers, the nation, and the graduates. The speeches deal with traditional themes, such as success, happiness, personal fulfillment, and service, as well as more contemporary issues, such as saving the environment, continuing the work of fighting racism, and dealing with the state of the economy.

## ———————— PREPARING TO READ AND WRITE ————————

As you read and prepare to write about the selections in this chapter, you may consider the following questions:

- What assumptions does the writer seem to have about his or her audience? How can you tell?

- What is the writer's primary purpose? To predict a future event or situation? To comment on a trend or tendency in today's world? To analyze a problem or propose a solution? To issue a warning? Something else?

- What genre is the writer using? For example, is the reading a literary work? a speech? an argument? How do the conventions of this genre influence the writer's choices?

- On what specific issue does the writer focus?

- Is the writer optimistic, pessimistic, or ambivalent about the future?

- Does the writer believe that the future he or she envisions is inevitable, or does he or she believe that people can influence future events?

- Does the writer identify a specific problem? Does he or she think the problem can be solved?

- Is the writer emotionally involved with the issue he or she is discussing? Does this involvement (or lack of involvement) affect the writer's credibility?

- What social or political ideas influence the writer's view of the future? How can you tell? Are these ideas similar to or different from your own ideas?

- Does the predicted future cause the writer to examine his or her own values? The values of society? Does the writer lead you to examine your own values?

- Which writers' views of the future seem most similar? Which seem most different?

- Which writer's view of the future seems the most plausible? Which seems the least plausible?

## POETRY

# DOVER BEACH

## Matthew Arnold

### *1822–1888*

*Matthew Arnold was an English Victorian poet, literary and social critic, essayist, and lecturer. In addition to his poetry, Arnold is known for such works as* Essays in Criticism *(1865) and* Culture and Anarchy *(1869). Considered one of the most influential Victorian poets, Arnold explained that his poems portray "the main movement of mind over the last quarter of a century." The following famous poem conveys a vision of the future.*

The sea is calm to-night.
The tide is full, the moon lies fair
Upon the straits; on the French coast the light
Gleams and is gone; the cliffs of England stand;
5   Glimmering and vast, out in the tranquil bay.
Come to the window, sweet is the night-air!

Only, from the long line of spray
Where the sea meets the moon-blanched land,
Listen! you hear the grating roar
Of pebbles which the waves draw back, and fling,        10
At their return, up the high strand,
Begin, and cease, and then again begin,
With tremulous cadence slow, and bring
The eternal note of sadness in.

Sophocles[1] long ago                                   15
Heard it on the Aegean,[2] and it brought
Into his mind the turbid ebb and flow
Of human misery; we
Find also in the sound a thought,
Hearing it by this distant northern sea.                20

The Sea of Faith
Was once, too, at the full, and round earth's shore
Lay like the folds of a bright girdle furled.
But now I only hear
Its melancholy, long, withdrawing roar,                 25
Retreating, to the breath
Of the night-wind, down the vast edges drear
And naked shingles of the world.
Ah, love, let us be true
To one another! for the world, which seems              30
To lie before us like a land of dreams,
So various, so beautiful, so new,
Hath really neither joy, nor love, nor light,
Nor certitude, nor peace, nor help for pain;
And we are here as on a darkling plain                  35
Swept with confused alarms of struggle and flight,
Where ignorant armies clash by night.

## Responding to Reading                      MyWritingLab™

1. How would you describe the mood of the poem? How does the poem's mood reflect its subject?
2. The poem's first stanza opens with a description of the calm night sea. In the second stanza, the sea is said to remind Sophocles of "the turbid ebb and flow of human misery." In the third stanza, the sea is called the "sea of faith," but the speaker hears its "melancholy, long, withdrawing roar." What is the significance of these changing characterizations of the sea?
3. Who are the "ignorant armies" (line 37)? Why do they "clash by night"?

---

[1]Ancient Greek dramatist (c. 496 BC–406 BC). [Eds.]
[2]Aegean Sea. [Eds.]

## Writing about Reading

What vision of the future is presented in the poem's last stanza?

# INAUGURAL ADDRESS

## John F. Kennedy

### 1917–1963

*Born in Brookline, Massachusetts, John Fitzgerald Kennedy received a bachelor's degree from Harvard University and served in the navy during World War II as a PT boat commander in the South Pacific. A charismatic politician, he was elected to the United States House of Representatives in 1947 and to the Senate in 1953. In 1960, defeating Republican candidate (and later president) Richard Nixon, Kennedy became the youngest man and the first Catholic to be elected president. During his tenure, he supported policies promoting racial equality, aid to the poor and to education, and increased availability of medical care; he also conceived of the idea of the Peace Corps. However, Kennedy was also responsible for involving the country further in the doomed Vietnam conflict. He was assassinated in November of 1963, a year before the end of his first term.*

Vice President Johnson, Mr. Speaker, Mr. Chief Justice, President Eisenhower, Vice President Nixon, President Truman, Reverend Clergy, fellow citizens:

We observe today not a victory of party but a celebration of freedom—symbolizing an end as well as a beginning—signifying renewal as well as change. For I have sworn before you and Almighty God the same solemn oath our forebears prescribed nearly a century and three-quarters ago.

The world is very different now. For man holds in his mortal hands the power to abolish all forms of human poverty and all forms of human life. And yet the same revolutionary beliefs for which our forebears fought are still at issue around the globe—the belief that the rights of man come not from the generosity of the state but from the hand of God.

We dare not forget today that we are the heirs of that first revolution. Let the word go forth from this time and place, to friend and foe alike, that the torch has been passed to a new generation of Americans—born in this century, tempered by war, disciplined by a hard and bitter peace, proud of our ancient heritage—and unwilling to witness or permit the slow undoing of those human rights to which this nation has always been committed, and to which we are committed today at home and around the world.

Let every nation know, whether it wishes us well or ill, that we 5 shall pay any price, bear any burden, meet any hardship, support any friend, oppose any foe to assure the survival and the success of liberty.

This much we pledge—and more.

To those old allies whose cultural and spiritual origins we share, we pledge the loyalty of faithful friends. United there is little we cannot do in a host of cooperative ventures. Divided there is little we can do— for we dare not meet a powerful challenge at odds and split asunder.

To those new states whom we welcome to the ranks of the free, we pledge our word that one form of colonial control shall not have passed away merely to be replaced by a far more iron tyranny. We shall not always expect to find them supporting our view. But we shall always hope to find them strongly supporting their own freedom—and to remember that, in the past, those who foolishly sought power by riding the back of the tiger ended up inside. To those people in the huts and villages of half the globe struggling to break the bonds of mass misery, we pledge our best efforts to help them help themselves, for whatever period is required—not because the communists may be doing it, not because we seek their votes, but because it is right. If a free society can- not help the many who are poor, it cannot save the few who are rich.

To our sister republics south of our border, we offer a special pledge—to convert our good words into good deeds—in a new alliance for progress—to assist free men and free governments in casting off the chains of poverty. But this peaceful revolution of hope cannot become the prey of hostile powers. Let all our neighbors know that we shall join with them to oppose aggression or subversion anywhere in the Amer- icas. And let every other power know that this Hemisphere intends to remain the master of its own house.

To that world assembly of sovereign states, the United Nations, our 10 last best hope in an age where the instruments of war have far outpaced the instruments of peace, we renew our pledge of support—to prevent it from becoming merely a forum for invective—to strengthen its shield of the new and the weak—and to enlarge the area in which its writ may run.

Finally, to those nations who would make themselves our adver- sary, we offer not a pledge but a request: that both sides begin anew the quest for peace, before the dark powers of destruction unleashed by science engulf all humanity in planned or accidental self-destruction.

We dare not tempt them with weakness. For only when our arms are sufficient beyond doubt can we be certain beyond doubt that they will never be employed.

But neither can two great and powerful groups of nations take com- fort from our present course—both sides overburdened by the cost of modern weapons, both rightly alarmed by the steady spread of the deadly atom, yet both racing to alter that uncertain balance of terror that stays the hand of mankind's final war.

So let us begin anew—remembering on both sides that civility is not a sign of weakness, and sincerity is always subject to proof. Let us never negotiate out of fear. But let us never fear to negotiate.

15   Let both sides explore what problems unite us instead of belaboring those problems which divide us.

Let both sides, for the first time, formulate serious and precise proposals for the inspection and control of arms and bring the absolute power to destroy other nations under the absolute control of all nations.

Let both sides seek to invoke the wonders of science instead of its terrors. Together let us explore the stars, conquer the deserts, eradicate disease, tap the ocean depths and encourage the arts and commerce.

Let both sides unite to heed in all corners of the earth the command of Isaiah—to "undo the heavy burdens . . . (and) let the oppressed go free."

And if a beachhead of cooperation may push back the jungle of suspicion, let both sides join in creating a new endeavor, not a new balance of power, but a new world of law, where the strong are just and the weak secure and the peace preserved.

20   All this will not be finished in the first one hundred days. Nor will it be finished in the first one thousand days, nor in the life of this Administration, nor even perhaps in our lifetime on this planet. But let us begin.

In your hands, my fellow citizens, more than mine, will rest the final success or failure of our course. Since this country was founded, each generation of Americans has been summoned to give testimony to its national loyalty. The graves of young Americans who answered the call to service surround the globe.

Now the trumpet summons us—again not as a call to bear arms, though arms we need—not as a call to battle, though embattled we are—but a call to bear the burden of a long twilight struggle, year in and year out, "rejoicing in hope, patient in tribulation"—a struggle against the common enemies of man: tyranny, poverty, disease and war itself. Can we forge against these enemies a grand and global alliance, North and South, East and West, that can assure a more fruitful life for all mankind? Will you join in that historic effort?

In the long history of the world, only a few generations have been granted the role of defending freedom in its hour of maximum danger. I do not shrink from this responsibility—I welcome it. I do not believe that any of us would exchange places with any other people or any other generation. The energy, the faith, the devotion which we bring to this endeavor will light our country and all who serve it—and the glow from that fire can truly light the world. And so, my fellow Americans: ask not what your country can do for you—ask what you can do for your country. My fellow citizens of the world: ask not what America will do for you, but what together we can do for the freedom of man.

Finally, whether you are citizens of America or citizens of the world, ask of us here the same high standards of strength and sacrifice which we ask of you. With a good conscience our only sure reward, with history the final judge of our deeds, let us go forth to lead the land we love, asking His blessing and His help, but knowing that here on earth God's work must truly be our own.

## Responding to Reading

MyWritingLab™

1. What are Kennedy's hopes for the future? What problems does he think the United States must solve? Has the United States solved the problems that Kennedy mentions in his speech, or have they yet to be fully addressed?
2. Near the end of his speech, Kennedy says, "And so, my fellow Americans: ask not what your country can do for you—ask what you can do for your country" (23). What does this famous, often-quoted passage actually mean in practical terms? Do you think this call to action is realistic? Do you think it is fair? Explain.
3. **Rhetorical Analysis**   At the beginning of his speech, Kennedy alludes to the "revolutionary beliefs" of Thomas Jefferson and asserts, "We are the heirs of that first revolution" (3-4). What does he mean? Is this a good opening strategy?

## Writing about Reading

MyWritingLab™

1. Exactly what do you expect America to do for you, and what do you expect to do for your country?
2. **Writing with Sources**   Do some research online, and find out how Americans reacted to Kennedy's speech at the time it was delivered. Then, find out how they evaluate it today. Write an essay in which you account for the differences.

# THE OBLIGATION TO ENDURE

## Rachel Carson

### 1907–1964

*Naturalist and environmentalist Rachel Carson was a specialist in marine biology. She won the National Book Award for* The Sea Around Us *(1951), which, like her other books, appeals to scientists and nonscientists alike. While working as an aquatic biologist for the U.S. Fish and Wildlife Service, Carson became concerned about ecological hazards and wrote* Silent Spring *(1962), in which she warned readers about the indiscriminate use of pesticides. This book influenced President John F. Kennedy to begin investigations into this and other environmental problems. Recently, however, critics have challenged the accuracy of Carson's science and questioned the validity of her conclusions concerning the dangers of DDT. In the excerpt from* Silent Spring *that follows, Carson urges readers to question the use of chemical pesticides.*

The history of life on earth has been a history of interaction between living things and their surroundings. To a large extent, the physical form and the habits of the earth's vegetation and its animal life have been molded by the environment. Considering the whole span of earthly time, the opposite effect, in which life actually modifies its surroundings, has been relatively slight. Only within the moment of time represented by the present century has one species—man—acquired significant power to alter the nature of his world.

During the past quarter century this power has not only increased to one of disturbing magnitude but it has changed in character. The most alarming of all man's assaults upon the environment is the contamination of air, earth, rivers, and sea with dangerous and even lethal materials. This pollution is for the most part irrecoverable; the chain of evil it initiates not only in the world that must support life but in living tissues is for the most part irreversible. In this now universal contamination of the environment, chemicals are the sinister and little-recognized partners of radiation in changing the very nature of the world—the very nature of its life. Strontium 90, released through nuclear explosions into the air, comes to earth in rain or drifts down in fallout, lodges in soil, enters into the grass or corn or wheat grown there, and in time takes up its abode in the bones of a human being, there to remain until his death. Similarly, chemicals sprayed on croplands or forests or gardens lie long in soil, entering into living organisms, passing from one to another in a chain of poisoning and death. Or they pass mysteriously by underground streams until they emerge and, through the alchemy of air and sunlight, combine into new forms that kill vegetation, sicken cattle, and work unknown harm on those who drink from once pure wells. As Albert Schweitzer[1] has said, "Man can hardly even recognize the devils of his own creation."

It took hundreds of millions of years to produce the life that now inhabits the earth—eons of time in which that developing and evolving and diversifying life reached a state of adjustment and balance with its surroundings. The environment, rigorously shaping and directing the life it supported, contained elements that were hostile as well as supporting. Certain rocks gave out dangerous radiation; even within the light of the sun, from which all life draws its energy, there were short-wave radiations with power to injure. Given time—time not in years but in millennia—life adjusts, and a balance has been reached. For time is the essential ingredient; but in the modern world there is no time.

The rapidity of change and the speed with which new situations are created follow the impetuous and heedless pace of man rather than the deliberate pace of nature. Radiation is no longer merely the background radiation of rocks, the bombardment of cosmic rays, the ultraviolet of

---

[1]French theologian (1875-1965) honored for his work as a scientist, humanitarian, musician, and religious thinker. In 1952, he was awarded the Nobel Peace Prize. [Eds.]

the sun that have existed before there was any life on earth; radiation is now the unnatural creation of man's tampering with the atom. The chemicals to which life is asked to make its adjustment are no longer merely the calcium and silica and copper and all the rest of the minerals washed out of the rocks and carried in rivers to the sea; they are the synthetic creations of man's inventive mind, brewed in his laboratories, and having no counterparts in nature.

To adjust to these chemicals would require time on the scale that is   5 nature's; it would require not merely the years of a man's life but the life of generations. And even this, were it by some miracle possible, would be futile, for the new chemicals come from our laboratories in an endless stream; almost five hundred annually find their way into actual use in the United States alone. The figure is staggering and its implications are not easily grasped—500 new chemicals to which the bodies of men and animals are required somehow to adapt each year, chemicals totally outside the limits of biologic experience.

Among them are many that are used in man's war against nature. Since the mid-1940s over 200 basic chemicals have been created for use in killing insects, weeds, rodents, and other organisms described in the modern vernacular as "pests"; and they are sold under several thousand different brand names.

These sprays, dusts, and aerosols are now applied almost universally to farms, gardens, forests, and homes—nonselective chemicals that have the power to kill every insect, the "good" and the "bad," to still the songs of birds and the leaping of fish in the streams, to coat the leaves with a deadly film, and to linger on in soil—all this though the intended target may be only a few weeds or insects. Can anyone believe it is possible to lay down such a barrage of poisons on the surface of the earth without making it unfit for all life? They should not be called "insecticides," but "biocides."

The whole process of spraying seems caught up in an endless spiral. Since DDT was released for civilian use, a process of escalation has been going on in which ever more toxic materials must be found. This has happened because insects, in a triumphant vindication of Darwin's principle of the survival of the fittest, have evolved super races immune to the particular insecticide used, hence a deadlier one has always to be developed—and then a deadlier one than that. It has happened also because, for reasons to be described later, destructive insects often undergo a "flare-back" or resurgence, after spraying in numbers greater than before. Thus the chemical war is never won, and all life is caught in its violent crossfire.

Along with the possibility of the extinction of mankind by nuclear war, the central problem of our age has therefore become the contamination of man's total environment with such substances of incredible potential for harm—substances that accumulate in the tissues of plants and animals and even penetrate the germ cells to shatter or alter the very material of heredity upon which the shape of the future depends.

10     Some would-be architects of our future look toward a time when it will be possible to alter the human germ plasm by design. But we may easily be doing so now by inadvertence, for many chemicals, like radiation, bring about gene mutations. It is ironic to think that man might determine his own future by something so seemingly trivial as the choice of an insect spray.

All this has been risked—for what? Future historians may well be amazed by our distorted sense of proportion. How could intelligent beings seek to control a few unwanted species by a method that contaminated the entire environment and brought the threat of disease and death even to their own kind? Yet this is precisely what we have done. We have done it, moreover, for reasons that collapse the moment we examine them. We are told that the enormous and expanding use of pesticides is necessary to maintain farm production. Yet is our real problem not one of *overproduction?* Our farms, despite measures to remove acreages from production and to pay farmers *not* to produce, have yielded such a staggering excess of crops that the American taxpayer in 1962 is paying out more than one billion dollars a year as the total carrying cost of the surplus-food storage program. And is the situation helped when one branch of the Agriculture Department tries to reduce production while another states, as it did in 1958, "It is believed generally that reduction of crop acreages under provisions of the Soil Bank will stimulate interest in use of chemicals to obtain maximum production on the land retained in crops."

All this is not to say there is no insect problem and no need of control. I am saying, rather, that control must be geared to realities, not to mythical situations, and that the methods employed must be such that they do not destroy us along with the insects.

The problem whose attempted solution has brought such a train of disaster in its wake is an accomplishment of our modern way of life. Long before the age of man, insects inhabited the earth—a group of extraordinarily varied and adaptable beings. Over the course of time since man's advent, a small percentage of the more than half a million species of insects have come into conflict with human welfare in two principal ways: as competitors for the food supply and as carriers of human disease.

Disease-carrying insects become important where human beings are crowded together, especially under conditions where sanitation is poor, as in time of natural disaster or war or in situations of extreme poverty and deprivation. Then control of some sort becomes necessary. It is a sobering fact, however, as we shall presently see, that the method of massive chemical control has had only limited success, and also threatens to worsen the very conditions it is intended to curb.

Under primitive agricultural conditions the farmer had few insect    15
problems. These arose with the intensification of agriculture—the devotion of immense acreages to a single crop. Such a system set the stage
for explosive increases in specific insect populations. Single-crop farming does not take advantage of the principles by which nature works;
it is agriculture as an engineer might conceive it to be. Nature has introduced great variety into the landscape, but man has displayed a passion for simplifying it. Thus he undoes the built-in checks and balances
by which nature holds the species within bounds. One important natural check is a limit on the amount of suitable habitat for each species.
Obviously then, an insect that lives on wheat can build up its population to much higher levels on a farm devoted to wheat than on one in
which wheat is intermingled with other crops to which the insect is not
adapted.

The same thing happens in other situations. A generation or more
ago, the towns of large areas of the United States lined their streets with
the noble elm tree. Now the beauty they hopefully created is threatened
with complete destruction as disease sweeps through the elms, carried
by a beetle that would have only limited chance to build up large populations and to spread from tree to tree if the elms were only occasional
trees in a richly diversified planting.

Another factor in the modern insect problem is one that must be
viewed against a background of geologic and human history: the
spreading of thousands of different kinds of organisms from their
native homes to invade new territories. This worldwide migration has
been studied and graphically described by the British ecologist Charles
Elton in his recent book *The Ecology of Invasions*. During the Cretaceous
Period, some hundred million years ago, flooding seas cut many land
bridges between continents and living things found themselves confined in what Elton calls "colossal separate nature reserves." There,
isolated from others of their kind, they developed many new species.
When some of the land masses were joined again, about 15 million
years ago, these species began to move out into new territories—a
movement that is not only still in progress but is now receiving considerable assistance from man.

The importation of plants is the primary agent in the modern
spread of species, for animals have almost invariably gone along with
the plants, quarantine being a comparatively recent and not completely
effective innovation. The United States Office of Plant Introduction
alone has introduced almost 200,000 species and varieties of plants
from all over the world. Nearly half of the 180 or so major insect enemies of plants in the United States are accidental imports from abroad,
and most of them have come as hitchhikers on plants.

In new territory, out of reach of the restraining hand of the natural enemies that kept down its numbers in its native land, an

invading plant or animal is able to become enormously abundant. Thus it is no accident that our most troublesome insects are introduced species.

20      These invasions, both the naturally occurring and those dependent on human assistance, are likely to continue indefinitely. Quarantine and massive chemical campaigns are only extremely expensive ways of buying time. We are faced, according to Dr. Elton, "with a life-and-death need not just to find new technological means of suppressing this plant or that animal"; instead we need the basic knowledge of animal populations and their relations to their surroundings that will "promote an even balance and damp down the explosive power of outbreaks and new invasions."

Much of the necessary knowledge is now available but we do not use it. We train ecologists in our universities and even employ them in our governmental agencies but we seldom take their advice. We allow the chemical death rain to fall as though there were no alternative, whereas in fact there are many, and our ingenuity could soon discover many more if given opportunity.

Have we fallen into a mesmerized state that makes us accept as inevitable that which is inferior or detrimental, as though having lost the will or the vision to demand that which is good? Such thinking, in the words of the ecologist Paul Shepard, "idealizes life with only its head out of water, inches above the limits of toleration of the corruption of its own environment. . . . Why should we tolerate a diet of weak poisons, a home in insipid surroundings, a circle of acquaintances who are not quite our enemies, the noise of motors with just enough relief to prevent insanity? Who would want to live in a world which is just not quite fatal?"

Yet such a world is pressed upon us. The crusade to create a chemically sterile, insect-free world seems to have engendered a fanatic zeal on the part of many specialists and most of the so-called control agencies. On every hand there is evidence that those engaged in spraying operations exercise a ruthless power. "The regulatory entomologists . . . function as prosecutor, judge and jury, tax assessor and collector and sheriff to enforce their own orders," said Connecticut entomologist Neely Turner. The most flagrant abuses go unchecked in both state and federal agencies.

It is not my contention that chemical insecticides must never be used. I do contend that we have put poisonous and biologically potent chemicals indiscriminately into the hands of persons largely or wholly ignorant of their potentials for harm. We have subjected enormous numbers of people to contact with these poisons, without their consent and often without their knowledge. If the Bill of Rights contains no guarantee that a citizen shall be secure against lethal poisons distributed either by private individuals or by public officials, it is surely only because our forefathers, despite their considerable wisdom and foresight, could conceive of no such problem.

I contend, furthermore, that we have allowed these chemicals to be 25 used with little or no advance investigation of their effect on soil, water, wildlife, and man himself. Future generations are unlikely to condone our lack of prudent concern for the integrity of the natural world that supports all life.

There is still very limited awareness of the nature of the threat. This is an era of specialists, each of whom sees his own problem and is unaware of or intolerant of the larger frame into which it fits. It is also an era dominated by industry, in which the right to make a dollar at whatever cost is seldom challenged. When the public protests, confronted with some obvious evidence of damaging results of pesticide applications, it is fed little tranquilizing pills of half truth. We urgently need an end to these false assurances, to the sugar coating of unpalatable facts. It is the public that is being asked to assume the risks that the insect controllers calculate. The public must decide whether it wishes to continue on the present road, and it can do so only when in full possession of the facts. In the words of Jean Rostand, "The obligation to endure gives us the right to know."

## Responding to Reading

MyWritingLab™

1. In paragraph 9, Carson says, "Along with the possibility of the extinction of mankind by nuclear war, the central problem of our age has . . . become the contamination of man's total environment with such substances of incredible potential for harm. . . . " Do you think she makes a good point, or do you think she overstates her case?
2. What future scenario does Carson predict if the use of pesticides is not curtailed? Does she provide enough evidence to support her prediction? Explain.
3. **Rhetorical Analysis**   In paragraph 24, Carson attempts to address critics' objections by saying that she does not believe insecticides "must never be used." Is she successful? Do you think she should have discussed the problems that could result if the use of insecticides such as DDT were reduced or eliminated?

## Writing about Reading

MyWritingLab™

1. Since Carson wrote her book, DDT has been banned. Recently, however, some scientists have said that it should be reintroduced on a limited basis because some insects have developed resistance to safer insecticides. Do you think this information strengthens or weakens Carson's position?
2. **Writing with Sources**   How accurate are Carson's claims about the detrimental effects of the widespread use of pesticides? After doing some research, write an essay in which you assess the validity of her ideas.

# THE CHANGING DEMOGRAPHICS OF AMERICA
## Joel Kotkin

*A presidential fellow in urban futures at Chapman University, Joel Kotkin is an executive editor of* www.newgeography.com *and a columnist for* Forbes.com *and* Politico.com. *His work has appeared in such publications as* Newsweek, *the* New York Times, *the* Wall Street Journal, *and the* Washington Post. *He is the author of several books, including, most recently,* The New Class Conflict (2014). *The following essay was adapted from his 2010 book* The Next Hundred Million: America in 2050.

Estimates of the U.S. population at the middle of the 21st century vary, from the U.N.'s 404 million to the U.S. Census Bureau's 422 to 458 million. To develop a snapshot of the nation at 2050, particularly its astonishing diversity and youthfulness, I use the nice round number of 400 million people, or roughly 100 million more than we have today.

The United States is also expected to grow somewhat older. The portion of the population that is currently at least 65—13 percent—is expected to reach about 20 percent by 2050. This "graying of America" has helped convince some commentators of the nation's declining eminence. For example, international relations expert Parag Khanna envisions a "shrunken America" lucky to eke out a meager existence between a "triumphant China" and a "retooled Europe." Morris Berman, a cultural historian, says America "is running on empty."

But even as the baby boomers age, the population of working and young people is also expected to keep rising, in contrast to most other advanced nations. America's relatively high fertility rate—the number of children a woman is expected to have in her lifetime—hit 2.1 in 2006, with 4.3 million total births, the highest levels in 45 years. That's thanks largely to recent immigrants, who tend to have more children than residents whose families have been in the United States for several generations. Moreover, the nation is on the verge of a baby boomlet, when the children of the original boomers have children of their own.

Between 2000 and 2050, census data suggest, the U.S. 15-to-64 age group is expected to grow 42 percent. In contrast, because of falling fertility rates, the number of young and working-age people is expected to decline elsewhere: by 10 percent in China, 25 percent in Europe, 30 percent in South Korea and more than 40 percent in Japan.

5    Within the next four decades, most of the developed countries in Europe and East Asia will become veritable old-age homes: A third or more of their populations will be over 65. By then, the United States is likely to have more than 350 million people under 65.

The prospect of an additional 100 million Americans by 2050 worries some environmentalists. A few have joined traditionally conservative xenophobes and anti-immigration activists in calling for a national policy to slow population growth by severely limiting immigration. The U.S. fertility rate—50 percent higher than that of Russia, Germany and Japan and well above that of China, Italy, Singapore, South Korea and virtually all the rest of Europe—has also prompted criticism.

Colleen Heenan, a feminist author and environmental activist, says Americans who favor larger families are not taking responsibility for "their detrimental contribution" to population growth and "resource shortages." Similarly, Peter Kareiva, the chief scientist at the Nature Conservancy, compared different conservation measures and concluded that not having a child is the most effective way of reducing carbon emissions and becoming an "eco hero."

Such critiques don't seem to take into account that a falling population and a dearth of young people may pose a greater threat to the nation's well-being than population growth. A rapidly declining population could create a society that doesn't have the work force to support the elderly and, overall, is less concerned with the nation's long-term future.

The next surge in growth may be delayed if tough economic times continue, but over time the rise in births, producing a generation slightly larger than the boomers, will add to the work force, boost consumer spending and generate new entrepreneurial businesses. And even with 100 million more people, the United States will be only one-sixth as crowded as Germany is today.

Immigration will continue to be a major force in U.S. life. The    10 United Nations estimates that 2 million people a year will move from poorer to developed nations over the next 40 years, and more than half of those will come to the United States, the world's preferred destination for educated, skilled migrants. In 2000, according to the Organization for Economic Co-operation and Development, an association of 30 democratic, free-market countries, the United States was home to 12.5 million skilled immigrants, equaling the combined total for Germany, France, the United Kingdom, Australia, Canada and Japan.

If recent trends continue, immigrants will play a leading role in our future economy. Between 1990 and 2005, immigrants started one out of four venture-backed public companies. Large American firms are also increasingly led by people with roots in foreign countries, including 15 of the Fortune 100 CEOs in 2007.

For all these reasons, the United States of 2050 will look different from that of today: Whites will no longer be in the majority. The U.S. minority population, currently 30 percent, is expected to exceed 50 percent before 2050. No other advanced, populous country will see such diversity.

In fact, most of America's net population growth will be among its minorities, as well as in a growing mixed-race population. Latino and Asian populations are expected to nearly triple, and the children of immigrants will become more prominent. Today in the United States,

25 percent of children under age 5 are Hispanic; by 2050, that percentage will be almost 40 percent.

Growth places the United States in a radically different position from that of Russia, Japan and Europe. Russia's low birth and high mortality rates suggest its overall population will drop 30 percent by 2050, to less than a third of the United States'. While China's population will continue to grow for a while, it may begin to experience decline as early as 2035, first in work force and then in actual population, mostly because of the government's one-child mandate, instituted in 1979 and still in effect. By 2050, 31 percent of China's population will be older than 60. More than 41 percent of Japanese will be that old.

15 Political prognosticators say China and India pose the greatest challenges to American predominance. But China, like Russia, lacks the basic environmental protections, reliable legal structures, favorable demographics and social resilience of the United States. India still has an overwhelmingly impoverished population and suffers from ethnic, religious and regional divisions. The vast majority of the Indian population remains semiliterate and lives in poor rural villages.

Suburbia will continue to be a mainstay of American life. Despite criticisms that suburbs are culturally barren and energy-inefficient, most U.S. metropolitan population growth has taken place in suburbia, confounding oft-repeated predictions of its decline.

Some aspects of suburban life—notably long-distance commuting and heavy reliance on fossil fuels—will have to change. The new suburbia will be far more environmentally friendly—what I call "greenurbia." The Internet, wireless phones, video conferencing and other communication technologies will allow more people to work from home: At least one in four or five will do so full time or part time, up from roughly one in six or seven today.

A new landscape may emerge, one that resembles the network of smaller towns characteristic of 19th-century America. The nation's landmass is large enough—about 3 percent is currently urbanized—to accommodate this growth, while still husbanding critical farmland and open space.

In other advanced nations where housing has become both expensive and dense—Japan, Germany, South Korea and Singapore—birthrates have fallen, partly because of the high cost of living, particularly for homes large enough to comfortably raise children. Preserving suburbs may therefore be critical for U.S. demographic vitality.

20 A 2009 study by the Brookings Institution found that between 1998 and 2006, jobs shifted away from the center and to the periphery in 95 out of 98 leading metropolitan regions—from Dallas and Los Angeles to Chicago and Seattle. Walter Siembab, a planning consultant, calls the process of creating sustainable work environments on the urban periphery "smart sprawl."

Super-fuel-efficient cars of the future are likely to spur smart sprawl. They may be a more reasonable way to meet environmental needs than shifting back to the mass-transit-based models of the industrial age; just 5 percent of the U.S. population uses mass transit on a daily basis.

Suburbs epitomize much of what constitutes the American dream for many people. Minorities, once largely associated with cities, tend to live in the suburbs; in 2008 they were a majority of residents in Texas, New Mexico, California and Hawaii. Nationwide, about 25 percent of suburbanites are minorities; by 2050 immigrants, their children and native-born minorities will become an even more dominant force in shaping suburbia.

The baby boom generation is poised for a large-scale "back to the city" movement, according to many news reports. But Sandra Rosenbloom, a University of Arizona gerontology professor, says roughly three-quarters of retirees in the first bloc of boomers appear to be sticking close to the suburbs, where the vast majority reside.

"Everybody in this business wants to talk about the odd person who moves downtown," Rosenbloom observes. "[But] most people retire in place. When they move, they don't move downtown, they move to the fringes."

To be sure, there will be 15 million to 20 million new urban dwellers 25 by 2050. Many will live in what Wharton business professor Joseph Gyourko calls "superstar cities," such as San Francisco, Boston, Manhattan and western Los Angeles—places adapted to business and recreation for the elite and those who work for them. By 2050, Seattle, Portland and Austin could join their ranks.

But because these elite cities are becoming too expensive for the middle class, the focus of urban life will shift to cities that are more spread out and, by some standards, less attractive. They're what I call "cities of aspiration," such as Phoenix, Houston, Dallas, Atlanta and Charlotte. They'll facilitate upward mobility, as New York and other great industrial cities once did, and begin to compete with the superstar cities for finance, culture and media industries, and the amenities that typically go along with them.

What the United States does with its demographic dividend—its relatively young working-age population—is critical. Simply to keep pace with the growing U.S. population, the nation needs to add 125,000 jobs a month, the New America Foundation estimates. Without robust economic growth but with an expanding population, the country will face a massive decline in living standards.

Entrepreneurs, small businesses and self-employed workers will become more common. Between 1980 and 2000 the number of self-employed individuals expanded, to about 15 percent of the work force. More workers will live in an economic environment like that of Hollywood or Silicon Valley, with constant job hopping and changes in alliances among companies.

For much of American history, race has been the greatest barrier to a common vision of community. Race still remains all too synonymous with poverty: Considerably higher poverty rates for blacks and Hispanics persist. But the future will most likely see a dimming of economic distinctions based on ethnic origins.

30    The most pressing social problem facing mid-21st-century America will be fulfilling the historic promise of upward mobility. In recent decades, certain high-end-occupation incomes grew rapidly, while wages for lower-income and middle-class workers stagnated. Even after the 2008 economic downturn, largely brought on by Wall Street, it was primarily middle-class homeowners and jobholders who bore the brunt, sometimes losing their residences.

Most disturbingly, the rate of upward mobility has stagnated overall, as wages have largely failed to keep up with the cost of living. It is no easier for poor and working-class people to move up the socioeconomic ladder today than it was in the 1970s; in some ways, it's more difficult. The income of college-educated younger people, adjusted for inflation, has been in decline since 2000.

To reverse these trends, I think Americans will need to attend to the nation's basic investments and industries, including manufacturing, energy and agriculture. This runs counter to the fashionable assertion that the American future can be built around a handful of high-end creative jobs and will not require reviving the old industrial economy.

A more competitive and environmentally sustainable America will rely on technology. Fortunately, no nation has been more prodigious in its ability to apply new methods and techniques to solve fundamental problems; the term "technology" was invented in America in 1829. New energy finds, unconventional fuel sources and advanced technology are likely to ameliorate the long-prophesied energy catastrophe.

And technology can ease or even reverse the environmental costs of growth. With a population of 300 million, the United States has cleaner air and water now than 40 years ago, when the population was 200 million.

35    The America of 2050 will most likely remain the one truly transcendent superpower in terms of society, technology and culture. It will rely on what has been called America's "civil religion"—its ability to forge a unique common national culture amid great diversity of people and place. We have no reason to lose faith in the possibilities of the future.

## Responding to Reading

MyWritingLab™

1. How does Kotkin respond to those who say that the United States is in decline? How does he respond to those who encourage American families to have fewer children? Do you find his arguments convincing?

2. What effect will the demographic trends Kotkin describes have on cities? on suburbs? on workers? What does Kotkin think will be the most pressing social problem facing mid-twenty-first-century America?

3. **Rhetorical Analysis**   For the most part, Kotkin uses statistics to support his points. What other kinds of evidence could he have used? Should he have included other types of evidence in his essay? Explain.

## Writing about Reading

MyWritingLab™

1. Overall, do you think Kotkin's view of the United States is optimistic or pessimistic?

2. **Writing with Sources**   Examine the demographic trends in the United States since 2010, when Kotkin's essay appeared. Write an essay in which you evaluate Kotkin's essay in light of these trends.

# THE ELUSIVE BIG IDEA

## Neal Gabler

### 1950–

*A senior fellow at the University of Southern California's Annenberg Norman Lear Center, Neal Gabler is a journalist, cultural historian, political commentator, and film critic. He has authored and coauthored several books, including* Walt Disney: The Triumph of the American Imagination *(2006). His work has appeared in such publications as* Esquire, *the* Los Angeles Times, New York *magazine, the* New York Times, Salon, Us, *and* Vogue. *Gabler is currently writing a biography of the late senator Edward M. Kennedy. In the following essay, Gabler considers the future of ideas.*

The July/August issue of the *Atlantic* trumpets the "14 Biggest Ideas of the Year." Take a deep breath. The ideas include "The Players Own the Game" (No. 12), "Wall Street: Same as it Ever Was" (No. 6), "Nothing Stays Secret" (No. 2), and the very biggest idea of the year, "The Rise of the Middle Class—Just Not Ours," which refers to growing economies in Brazil, Russia, India and China.

Now exhale. It may strike you that none of these ideas seem particularly breathtaking. In fact, none of them are ideas. They are more on the order of observations. But one can't really fault the *Atlantic* for mistaking commonplaces for intellectual vision. Ideas just aren't what they used to be. Once upon a time, they could ignite fires of debate, stimulate other thoughts, incite revolutions and fundamentally change the ways we look at and think about the world.

They could penetrate the general culture and make celebrities out of thinkers—notably Albert Einstein, but also Reinhold Niebuhr, Daniel Bell, Betty Friedan, Carl Sagan and Stephen Jay Gould, to name a few. The ideas themselves could even be made famous: for instance, for "the end of ideology," "the medium is the message," "the feminine mystique," "the Big Bang theory," "the end of history." A big idea could capture the cover of *Time*—"Is God Dead?"—and intellectuals like Norman Mailer, William F. Buckley Jr. and Gore Vidal would even occasionally be invited to the couches of late-night talk shows. How long ago that was.

If our ideas seem smaller nowadays, it's not because we are dumber than our forebears but because we just don't care as much about ideas as they did. In effect, we are living in an increasingly post-idea world—a world in which big, thought-provoking ideas that can't instantly be monetized are of so little intrinsic value that fewer people are generating them and fewer outlets are disseminating them, the Internet notwithstanding. Bold ideas are almost passé.

5   It is no secret, especially here in America, that we live in a post-Enlightenment age in which rationality, science, evidence, logical argument and debate have lost the battle in many sectors, and perhaps even in society generally, to superstition, faith, opinion and orthodoxy. While we continue to make giant technological advances, we may be the first generation to have turned back the epochal clock—to have gone backward intellectually from advanced modes of thinking into old modes of belief. But post-Enlightenment and post-idea, while related, are not exactly the same.

Post-Enlightenment refers to a style of thinking that no longer deploys the techniques of rational thought. Post-idea refers to thinking that is no longer done, regardless of the style.

The post-idea world has been a long time coming, and many factors have contributed to it. There is the retreat in universities from the real world, and an encouragement of and reward for the narrowest specialization rather than for daring—for tending potted plants rather than planting forests.

There is the eclipse of the public intellectual in the general media by the pundit who substitutes outrageousness for thoughtfulness, and the concomitant decline of the essay in general-interest magazines. And there is the rise of an increasingly visual culture, especially among the young—a form in which ideas are more difficult to express.

But these factors, which began decades ago, were more likely harbingers of an approaching post-idea world than the chief causes of it. The real cause may be information itself. It may seem counterintuitive that at a time when we know more than we have ever known, we think about it less.

We live in the much vaunted Age of Information. Courtesy of the [10]
Internet, we seem to have immediate access to anything that anyone
could ever want to know. We are certainly the most informed generation in history, at least quantitatively. There are trillions upon trillions
of bytes out there in the ether—so much to gather and to think about.

And that's just the point. In the past, we collected information not
simply to know things. That was only the beginning. We also collected
information to convert it into something larger than facts and ultimately more useful—into ideas that made sense of the information. We
sought not just to apprehend the world but to truly comprehend it,
which is the primary function of ideas. Great ideas explain the world
and one another to us.

Marx pointed out the relationship between the means of production and our social and political systems. Freud taught us to explore
our minds as a way of understanding our emotions and behaviors.
Einstein rewrote physics. More recently, McLuhan theorized about the
nature of modern communication and its effect on modern life. These
ideas enabled us to get our minds around our existence and attempt to
answer the big, daunting questions of our lives.

But if information was once grist for ideas, over the last decade it
has become competition for them. We are like the farmer who has too
much wheat to make flour. We are inundated with so much information
that we wouldn't have time to process it even if we wanted to, and most
of us don't want to.

The collection itself is exhausting: what each of our friends is doing
at that particular moment and then the next moment and the next one;
who Jennifer Aniston is dating right now; which video is going viral on
YouTube this hour; what Princess Letizia or Kate Middleton is wearing
that day. In effect, we are living within the nimbus of an informational
Gresham's law[1] in which trivial information pushes out significant
information, but it is also an ideational Gresham's law in which information, trivial or not, pushes out ideas.

We prefer knowing to thinking because knowing has more immedi- [15]
ate value. It keeps us in the loop, keeps us connected to our friends and
our cohort. Ideas are too airy, too impractical, too much work for too
little reward. Few talk ideas. Everyone talks information, usually personal information. Where are you going? What are you doing? Whom
are you seeing? These are today's big questions.

It is certainly no accident that the post-idea world has sprung up
alongside the social networking world. Even though there are sites and
blogs dedicated to ideas, Twitter, Facebook, Myspace, Flickr, etc., the
most popular sites on the Web, are basically information exchanges,
designed to feed the insatiable information hunger, though this is

---

[1]Economics law that states devalued money makes more valuable forms of money obsolete over time.
[Eds.]

hardly the kind of information that generates ideas. It is largely useless except insofar as it makes the possessor of the information feel, well, informed. Of course, one could argue that these sites are no different than conversation was for previous generations, and that conversation seldom generated big ideas either, and one would be right.

But the analogy isn't perfect. For one thing, social networking sites are the primary form of communication among young people, and they are supplanting print, which is where ideas have typically gestated. For another, social networking sites engender habits of mind that are inimical to the kind of deliberate discourse that gives rise to ideas. Instead of theories, hypotheses and grand arguments, we get instant 140-character tweets about eating a sandwich or watching a TV show. While social networking may enlarge one's circle and even introduce one to strangers, this is not the same thing as enlarging one's intellectual universe. Indeed, the gab of social networking tends to shrink one's universe to oneself and one's friends, while thoughts organized in words, whether online or on the page, enlarge one's focus.

To paraphrase the famous dictum, often attributed to Yogi Berra, that you can't think and hit at the same time, you can't think and tweet at the same time either, not because it is impossible to multitask but because tweeting, which is largely a burst of either brief, unsupported opinions or brief descriptions of your own prosaic activities, is a form of distraction or anti-thinking.

The implications of a society that no longer thinks big are enormous. Ideas aren't just intellectual playthings. They have practical effects.

20    An artist friend of mine recently lamented that he felt the art world was adrift because there were no longer great critics like Harold Rosenberg and Clement Greenberg to provide theories of art that could fructify the art and energize it. Another friend made a similar argument about politics. While the parties debate how much to cut the budget, he wondered where were the John Rawlses and Robert Nozicks who could elevate our politics.

One could certainly make the same argument about economics, where John Maynard Keynes remains the center of debate nearly 80 years after propounding his theory of government pump priming. This isn't to say that the successors of Rosenberg, Rawls and Keynes don't exist, only that if they do, they are not likely to get traction in a culture that has so little use for ideas, especially big, exciting, dangerous ones, and that's true whether the ideas come from academics or others who are not part of elite organizations and who challenge the conventional wisdom. All thinkers are victims of information glut, and the ideas of today's thinkers are also victims of that glut.

But it is especially true of big thinkers in the social sciences like the cognitive psychologist Steven Pinker, who has theorized on everything from the source of language to the role of genetics in human nature, or the biologist Richard Dawkins, who has had big and controversial ideas on everything from selfishness to God, or the psychologist Jonathan Haidt, who has been analyzing different moral systems and drawing fascinating conclusions about the relationship of morality to political beliefs. But because they are scientists and empiricists rather than generalists in the humanities, the place from which ideas were customarily popularized, they suffer a double whammy: not only the whammy against ideas generally but the whammy against science, which is typically regarded in the media as mystifying at best, incomprehensible at worst. A generation ago, these men would have made their way into popular magazines and onto television screens. Now they are crowded out by informational effluvium.

No doubt there will be those who say that the big ideas have migrated to the marketplace, but there is a vast difference between profit-making inventions and intellectually challenging thoughts. Entrepreneurs have plenty of ideas, and some, like Steven P. Jobs of Apple, have come up with some brilliant ideas in the "inventional" sense of the word.

Still, while these ideas may change the way we live, they rarely transform the way we think. They are material, not ideational. It is thinkers who are in short supply, and the situation probably isn't going to change anytime soon.

We have become information narcissists, so uninterested in any- 25 thing outside ourselves and our friendship circles or in any tidbit we cannot share with those friends that if a Marx or a Nietzsche were suddenly to appear, blasting his ideas, no one would pay the slightest attention, certainly not the general media, which have learned to service our narcissism.

What the future portends is more and more information—Everests of it. There won't be anything we won't know. But there will be no one thinking about it.

Think about that.

## Responding to Reading                        MyWritingLab™

1. Gabler says that we live in "an increasingly post-idea world" (4), noting that the most popular social networking sites on the Web are "information exchanges" that do little to "generate ideas" (16). What does he mean? Do you agree?

2. What does Gabler mean when he says that entrepreneurs like Steve Jobs have ideas in the "'inventional' sense of the word" (23)? Why do their ideas "rarely transform the way we think" (24)? What are the implications of this situation for the future?

3. **Rhetorical Analysis**   Much of this essay is a comparison. What two things is Gabler comparing? How does this comparison help to support his argument?

## Writing about Reading

1. Do you agree with Gabler's assertion that we live in a culture that has "little use for ideas, especially big, exciting, dangerous ones . . . " (21)?
2. **Writing with Sources** Find information about the "thinkers" Gabler mentions in paragraph 3 and elsewhere in this essay. Then, choose one of these thinkers, and investigate what his or her "big idea" was. Finally, write an essay in which you explain how this idea changed people's thinking at the time.

# THE NEXT AMERICAN FRONTIER

## Michael S. Malone

### 1954–

*Michael S. Malone writes about a range of topics related to business and technology. He is the author of several books, including, most recently,* The Intel Trinity: How Robert Noyce, Gordon Moore, and Andy Grove Built the World's Most Important Company *(2014). His work has appeared in such publications as the* Economist, *the* New York Times, *and the* Wall Street Journal. *In the following essay, Malone considers "new American frontiers."*

The entire world seems to be heading toward points of inflection. The developing world is embarking on the digital age. The developed world is entering the Internet era. And the United States, once again at the vanguard, is on the verge of becoming the world's first Entrepreneurial Nation.

At the Chicago World's Fair in 1893, Frederick Jackson Turner delivered a paper to the American Historical Association—the most famous ever by an American historian. In "The Significance of the Frontier in American History," he noted that, according to the most recent U.S. census, so much of the nation had been settled that there was no longer an identifiable western migration. The very notion of a "frontier" was obsolete.

For three centuries the frontier had defined us, tantalized us with the perpetual chance to "light out for the territories" and start our lives over. It was the foundation of those very American notions of "federalism" and "rugged individualism." But Americans had crossed an invisible line in history, entering a new world with a new set of rules.

What Turner couldn't guess was that the unexplored prairie would become the uninvented new product, the unexploited new market and the untried new business plan.

5      The great new American frontiers proved to be those of business, science and technology. In the course of the 20th century, Americans

invented more milestone technologies and inventions, created more wealth and leisure time, and reorganized their institutions more times than any country had ever done before—despite a massive economic depression and two world wars. It all reached a crescendo in the magical year of 1969, with the creation of the Internet, the invention of the microprocessor and, most of all, a man walking on the moon.

Along with genetic engineering, we are still busily spinning out the implications of these marvels. Yet it is becoming increasingly apparent that the cultural underpinnings of these activities have changed in some fundamental way.

We still have schools, but a growing number of our children are studying at home or attending private schools—and those in public schools are doing ever more amounts of their class work on the Internet.

We still have companies and corporations, but now they are virtualized, with online work teams handing off assignments to each other 24/7 around the world. Men and women go to work, but the office is increasingly likely to be in the den. In 2005, an Intel survey of its employees found that nearly 20% of its professionals had never met their boss face-to-face. Half of them never expected to. Last summer, when the Media X institute at Stanford extended that survey to IBM, Sun, HP, Microsoft and Cisco, the percentages turned out to be even greater.

Newspapers are dying, networks are dying, and if teenage boys playing GTA 4 and World of Warcraft have any say about it, so is television. More than 200 million people now belong to just two social networks: MySpace and Facebook. And there are more than 80 million videos on YouTube, all put there by the same individual initiative.

The most compelling statistic of all? Half of all new college gradu- 10 ates now believe that self-employment is more secure than a full-time job. Today, 80% of the colleges and universities in the U.S. now offer courses on entrepreneurship; 60% of Gen Y business owners consider themselves to be serial entrepreneurs, according to *Inc.* magazine. Tellingly, 18 to 24-year-olds are starting companies at a faster rate than 35 to 44-year-olds. And 70% of today's high schoolers intend to start their own companies, according to a Gallup poll.

An upcoming wave of new workers in our society will never work for an established company if they can help it. To them, having a traditional job is one of the biggest career failures they can imagine.

Much of childhood today is spent, not in organized sports or organizations, but in ad hoc teams playing online games such as Half Life, or competing in robotics tournaments, or in constructing and decorating MySpace pages. Without knowing it, we have been training a whole generation of young entrepreneurs.

And who is going to dissuade them? Mom, who is a self-employed consultant working out of the spare bedroom? Or Dad, who is at Starbucks working on the spreadsheet of his new business plan?

In the past there have been trading states like Venice, commercial regions like the Hanseatic League, and even so-called nations of shopkeepers. But there has never been a nation in which the dominant paradigm is entrepreneurship. Not just self-employment or sole proprietorship, but serial company-building, entire careers built on perpetual change, independence and the endless pursuit of the next opportunity.

15   Without noticing it, we have once again discovered, and then raced off to settle, a new frontier. Not land, not innovation, but ourselves and a growing control over our own lives and careers.

And why not? Each step in the development of American society has been towards an ever-greater level of independence, freedom and personal liberty. And as the rest of the world catches up to where we were, we've already moved on to the next epoch in the national story.

But liberty exacts its own demands. Entrepreneurial America is likely to become even more innovative than it is today. And that innovation is likely to spread across society, not just as products and inventions, but new ways of living and new types of organizations.

The economy will be much more volatile and much more competitive. In the continuous fervor to create new institutions, it will become increasingly difficult to sustain old ones. New political parties, new social groupings, thousands of new manias and movements and millions of new companies will pop up over the next few decades. Large corporations that don't figure out how to combine permanence with perpetual change will be swept away.

This higher level of anarchy will be exciting, but it will also sometimes be very painful. Entire industries will die almost overnight, laying off thousands, while others will just as suddenly appear, hungry for employees. Continuity and predictability will become the rarest of commodities. And if the entrepreneurial personality honors smart failures, by the same token it has little pity for weakness. That fraction of Americans—10%, 20%—who still dream of the gold watch or the 30-year pin will suffer the most . . . and unless their needs are somehow met as well, they will remain a perpetually open wound in our society.

20   Scary, exciting, liberating, frustrating, infinitely ambitious and thoroughly amnesic. If you live in a high-tech community like Silicon Valley or Redmond or Austin, you already live in this world. It's hard to imagine more exciting places to be.

For all of our fears about privacy and security, for all the added pressures that will be created by heightened competition and clashing ambitions, America as an entrepreneurial nation will reward each of us with greater independence—and perhaps even greater happiness—

than ever before. It waits out there for each of us. Being good entrepreneurs, it's time to look ahead, develop a good plan, and then bet everything on ourselves.

## Responding to Reading                                    MyWritingLab™

1. According to Malone, what are "the great new American frontiers" (5)? Why was 1969 a "magical year" (5)?
2. In paragraph 15, Malone says that the new frontier we are settling is "Not land, not innovation, but ourselves and a growing control of our own lives and careers." What does he mean? What are the implications for the future of Malone's new frontier? Do you agree?
3. **Rhetorical Analysis**  Why does Malone begin his essay by talking about Frederick Jackson Turner? How do Turner's ideas set the stage for the rest of the essay?

## Writing about Reading                                     MyWritingLab™

1. In paragraph 11, Malone says that "new workers in our society" consider getting "a traditional job" with an "established company" to be "one of the biggest career failures" they can imagine. Why? Do you think these workers have a point?
2. **Writing with Sources**  Malone's essay is generally very optimistic. Research the success rate of business start-ups, and then write a response to Malone in which you challenge his positive assessment of "America as an entrepeneureal nation" (21).

# INNOVATION STARVATION

## Neal Stephenson

### *1959–*

*Neal Stephenson writes science fiction and essays with an emphasis on technology and the future. He is the author of several novels, including, most recently,* Seveneves *(2015). His work has also appeared in* Wired *magazine,* World Policy Journal, *and other publications. In the following essay, Stephenson considers the future of creativity.*

My lifespan encompasses the era when the United States of America was capable of launching human beings into space. Some of my earliest memories are of sitting on a braided rug before a hulking black-and-white television, watching the early Gemini missions. This summer, at the age of 51—not even old—I watched on a flatscreen as the last Space Shuttle lifted off the pad. I have followed the dwindling of the space program with sadness, even bitterness. Where's my donut-shaped space station? Where's my ticket to Mars? Until recently, though, I have kept my feelings to myself. Space exploration has always had its detractors. To complain about its demise is to expose oneself to attack from those who have no sympathy that an affluent, middle-aged white American has not lived to see his boyhood fantasies fulfilled.

Still, I worry that our inability to match the achievements of the 1960s space program might be symptomatic of a general failure of our society to get big things done. My parents and grandparents witnessed the creation of the airplane, the automobile, nuclear energy, and the computer to name only a few. Scientists and engineers who came of age during the first half of the 20th century could look forward to building things that would solve age-old problems, transform the landscape, build the economy, and provide jobs for the burgeoning middle class that was the basis for our stable democracy.

The Deepwater Horizon oil spill of 2010 crystallized my feeling that we have lost our ability to get important things done. The OPEC oil shock was in 1973—almost 40 years ago. It was obvious then that it was crazy for the United States to let itself be held economic hostage to the kinds of countries where oil was being produced. It led to Jimmy Carter's proposal for the development of an enormous synthetic fuels industry on American soil. Whatever one might think of the merits of the Carter presidency or of this particular proposal, it was, at least, a serious effort to come to grips with the problem.

Little has been heard in that vein since. We've been talking about wind farms, tidal power, and solar power for decades. Some progress has been made in those areas, but energy is still all about oil. In my city, Seattle, a 35-year-old plan to run a light rail line across Lake Washington is now being blocked by a citizen initiative. Thwarted or endlessly delayed in its efforts to build things, the city plods ahead with a project to paint bicycle lanes on the pavement of thoroughfares.

5    In early 2011, I participated in a conference called Future Tense, where I lamented the decline of the manned space program, then pivoted to energy, indicating that the real issue isn't about rockets. It's our far broader inability as a society to execute on the big stuff. I had, through some kind of blind luck, struck a nerve. The audience at Future Tense was more confident than I that science fiction [SF] had relevance—even utility—in addressing the problem. I heard two theories as to why:

1. The Inspiration Theory. SF inspires people to choose science and engineering as careers. This much is undoubtedly true, and somewhat obvious.
2. The Hieroglyph Theory. Good SF supplies a plausible, fully thought-out picture of an alternate reality in which some sort of compelling innovation has taken place. A good SF universe has a coherence and internal logic that makes sense to scientists

and engineers. Examples include Isaac Asimov's robots, Robert Heinlein's rocket ships, and William Gibson's cyberspace. As Jim Karkanias of Microsoft Research puts it, such icons serve as hieroglyphs—simple, recognizable symbols on whose significance everyone agrees.

Researchers and engineers have found themselves concentrating on more and more narrowly focused topics as science and technology have become more complex. A large technology company or lab might employ hundreds or thousands of persons, each of whom can address only a thin slice of the overall problem. Communication among them can become a mare's nest of email threads and Powerpoints. The fondness that many such people have for SF reflects, in part, the usefulness of an over-arching narrative that supplies them and their colleagues with a shared vision. Coordinating their efforts through a command-and-control management system is a little like trying to run a modern economy out of a Politburo.[1] Letting them work toward an agreed-on goal is something more like a free and largely self-coordinated market of ideas.

## Spanning the Ages

SF has changed over the span of time I am talking about—from the 1950s (the era of the development of nuclear power, jet airplanes, the space race, and the computer) to now. Speaking broadly, the techno-optimism of the Golden Age of SF has given way to fiction written in a generally darker, more skeptical and ambiguous tone. I myself have tended to write a lot about hackers—trickster archetypes who exploit the arcane capabilities of complex systems devised by faceless others.

Believing we have all the technology we'll ever need, we seek to draw attention to its destructive side effects. This seems foolish now that we find ourselves saddled with technologies like Japan's ramshackle 1960's-vintage reactors at Fukushima when we have the possibility of clean nuclear fusion on the horizon. The imperative to develop new technologies and implement them on a heroic scale no longer seems like the childish preoccupation of a few nerds with slide rules. It's the only way for the human race to escape from its current predicaments. Too bad we've forgotten how to do it.

"You're the ones who've been slacking off!" proclaims Michael Crow, president of Arizona State University (and one of the other speakers at Future Tense). He refers, of course, to SF writers. The scientists and engineers, he seems to be saying, are ready and looking for things to do. Time for the SF writers to start pulling their weight and supplying big visions that make sense. Hence the Hieroglyph project,

---

[1]Communist political committee. [Eds.]

an effort to produce an anthology of new SF that will be in some ways a conscious throwback to the practical techno-optimism of the Golden Age.

## Spaceborne Civilizations

10   China is frequently cited as a country now executing on Big Stuff, and there's no doubt they are constructing dams, high-speed rail systems, and rockets at an extraordinary clip. But those are not fundamentally innovative. Their space program, like all other countries' (including our own), is just parroting work that was done 50 years ago by the Soviets and the Americans. A truly innovative program would involve taking risks (and accepting failures) to pioneer some of the alternative space launch technologies that have been advanced by researchers all over the world during the decades dominated by rockets.

Imagine a factory mass-producing small vehicles, about as big and complicated as refrigerators, which roll off the end of an assembly line, are loaded with space-bound cargo, and topped off with non-polluting liquid hydrogen fuel, then exposed to intense concentrated heat from an array of ground-based lasers or microwave antennas. Heated to temperatures beyond what can be achieved through a chemical reaction, the hydrogen erupts from a nozzle on the base of the device and sends it rocketing into the air. Tracked through its flight by the lasers or microwaves, the vehicle soars into orbit, carrying a larger payload for its size than a chemical rocket could ever manage, but the complexity, expense, and jobs remain grounded. For decades, this has been the vision of such researchers as physicists Jordin Kare and Kevin Parkin. A similar idea, using a pulsed ground-based laser to blast propellant from the backside of a space vehicle, was being talked about by Arthur Kantrowitz, Freeman Dyson, and other eminent physicists in the early 1960s.

If that sounds too complicated, then consider the 2003 proposal of Geoff Landis and Vincent Denis to construct a 20-kilometer-high tower using simple steel trusses. Conventional rockets launched from its top would be able to carry twice as much payload as comparable ones launched from ground level. There is even abundant research, dating all the way back to Konstantin Tsiolkovsky, the father of astronautics beginning in the late 19th century, to show that a simple tether—a long rope, tumbling end-over-end while orbiting the earth—could be used to scoop payloads out of the upper atmosphere and haul them up into orbit without the need for engines of any kind. Energy would be pumped into the system using an electrodynamic process with no moving parts.

All are promising ideas—just the sort that used to get an earlier generation of scientists and engineers fired up about actually building something.

But to grasp just how far our current mindset is from being able to attempt innovation on such a scale, consider the fate of the space shuttle's external tanks [ETs]. Dwarfing the vehicle itself, the ET was the largest and most prominent feature of the space shuttle as it stood on the pad. It remained attached to the shuttle—or perhaps it makes as much sense to say that the shuttle remained attached to it—long after the two strap-on boosters had fallen away. The ET and the shuttle remained connected all the way out of the atmosphere and into space. Only after the system had attained orbital velocity was the tank jettisoned and allowed to fall into the atmosphere, where it was destroyed on re-entry.

At a modest marginal cost, the ETs could have been kept in orbit    15
indefinitely. The mass of the ET at separation, including residual propellants, was about twice that of the largest possible Shuttle payload. Not destroying them would have roughly tripled the total mass launched into orbit by the Shuttle. ETs could have been connected to build units that would have humbled today's International Space Station. The residual oxygen and hydrogen sloshing around in them could have been combined to generate electricity and produce tons of water, a commodity that is vastly expensive and desirable in space. But in spite of hard work and passionate advocacy by space experts who wished to see the tanks put to use, NASA—for reasons both technical and political—sent each of them to fiery destruction in the atmosphere. Viewed as a parable, it has much to tell us about the difficulties of innovating in other spheres.

## Executing the Big Stuff

Innovation can't happen without accepting the risk that it might fail. The vast and radical innovations of the mid-20th century took place in a world that, in retrospect, looks insanely dangerous and unstable. Possible outcomes that the modern mind identifies as serious risks might not have been taken seriously—supposing they were noticed at all—by people habituated to the Depression, the World Wars, and the Cold War, in times when seat belts, antibiotics, and many vaccines did not exist. Competition between the Western democracies and the communist powers obliged the former to push their scientists and engineers to the limits of what they could imagine and supplied a sort of safety net in the event that their initial efforts did not pay off. A grizzled NASA veteran once told me that the Apollo moon landings were communism's greatest achievement.

In his recent book *Adapt: Why Success Always Starts with Failure*, Tim Harford outlines Charles Darwin's discovery of a vast array of distinct species in the Galapagos Islands—a state of affairs that contrasts with the picture seen on large continents, where evolutionary experiments tend to get pulled back toward a sort of ecological consensus by interbreeding. "Galapagan isolation" vs. the "nervous corporate hierarchy" is the contrast staked out by Harford in assessing the ability of an organization to innovate.

Most people who work in corporations or academia have witnessed something like the following: A number of engineers are sitting together in a room, bouncing ideas off each other. Out of the discussion emerges a new concept that seems promising. Then some laptop-wielding person in the corner, having performed a quick Google search, announces that this "new" idea is, in fact, an old one—or at least vaguely similar—and has already been tried. Either it failed, or it succeeded. If it failed, then no manager who wants to keep his or her job will approve spending money trying to revive it. If it succeeded, then it's patented and entry to the market is presumed to be unattainable, since the first people who thought of it will have "first-mover advantage" and will have created "barriers to entry." The number of seemingly promising ideas that have been crushed in this way must number in the millions.

What if that person in the corner hadn't been able to do a Google search? It might have required weeks of library research to uncover evidence that the idea wasn't entirely new—and after a long and toilsome slog through many books, tracking down many references, some relevant, some not. When the precedent was finally unearthed, it might not have seemed like such a direct precedent after all. There might be reasons why it would be worth taking a second crack at the idea, perhaps hybridizing it with innovations from other fields. Hence the virtues of Galapagan isolation.

20    The counterpart to Galapagan isolation is the struggle for survival on a large continent, where firmly established ecosystems tend to blur and swamp new adaptations. Jaron Lanier, a computer scientist, composer, visual artist, and author of the recent book *You Are Not a Gadget: A Manifesto,* has some insights about the unintended consequences of the Internet—the informational equivalent of a large continent—on our ability to take risks. In the pre-net era, managers were forced to make decisions based on what they knew to be limited information. Today, by contrast, data flows to managers in real time from countless sources that could not even be imagined a couple of generations ago, and powerful computers process, organize, and display the data in ways that are as far beyond the hand-drawn graph-paper plots of my youth as modern video games are to tic-tac-toe. In a world where decision-makers are so close to being omniscient, it's easy to see risk as a quaint artifact of a primitive and dangerous past.

The illusion of eliminating uncertainty from corporate decision-making is not merely a question of management style or personal preference. In the legal environment that has developed around publicly traded corporations, managers are strongly discouraged from shouldering any risks that they know about—or, in the opinion of some future jury, should have known about—even if they have a hunch that the gamble might pay off in the long run. There is no such thing as "long run" in industries driven by the next quarterly report. The possibility of some innovation making money is just that—a mere possibility that will not have time to materialize before the subpoenas from minority shareholder lawsuits begin to roll in.

Today's belief in ineluctable certainty is the true innovation-killer of our age. In this environment, the best an audacious manager can do is to develop small improvements to existing systems—climbing the hill, as it were, toward a local maximum, trimming fat, eking out the occasional tiny innovation—like city planners painting bicycle lanes on the streets as a gesture toward solving our energy problems. Any strategy that involves crossing a valley—accepting short-term losses to reach a higher hill in the distance—will soon be brought to a halt by the demands of a system that celebrates short-term gains and tolerates stagnation, but condemns anything else as failure. In short, a world where big stuff can never get done.

## Responding to Reading

MyWritingLab™

1. Do you think Stephenson's career as a science fiction writer gives him special insight into his subject? What references to science fiction does he make in his essay? How do these references help to reinforce his essay's central point?
2. What is the difference between "Galapagan isolation" and the "nervous corporate hierarchy" (17)? According to Stephenson, how do these two concepts help explain the ability (or inability) of an organization to innovate?
3. **Rhetorical Analysis**  Stephenson says that he wonders if our failure "to match the achievements of the 1960s space program" is symptomatic of our general inability "to get big things done" (2). What does he mean? What evidence does he present to support this concern? Does he make a convincing case?

## Writing about Reading

MyWritingLab™

1. Do you, like Stephenson, worry that we will not be able to match the scientific and technical achievements of the past? Or, do you believe our greatest achievements in these areas are yet to come?
2. **Writing with Sources**  In the numbered list in paragraph 5 of his essay, Stephenson mentions "The Hieroglyph Theory." Since this essay appeared, Stephenson has been working on the Hieroglyph project. Research the Hieroglyph project, and then write an essay in which you outline the project's goals and explain whether you think these goals are feasible.

---

## FOCUS

### What Comes Next?

Hillary Rodham at her Wellesley College graduation, 1969

## Responding to the Image

MyWritingLab™

1. The photo above shows Hillary Rodham Clinton (then Hillary D. Rodham) at her 1969 graduation, where she delivered a commencement speech to her class. In her speech, she mentions that her fellow students have always questioned the basic assumptions underlying their education and that this questioning forced Wellesley to make certain changes. How much influence do you think students should have concerning academic policy decisions?

2. Elsewhere in her speech, Clinton says, "We're searching for [a] more immediate, ecstatic and penetrating mode of living. And so our questions, our questions about our institutions, about our colleges, about our churches, about our government continue." When you think about the future—after you graduate—what specific questions do you have? Which questions do you think you will be able to answer? Which do you think will remain unanswered?

3. Toward the end of her speech, Clinton says, "I was talking to [a] woman who said that she wouldn't want to be me for anything in the world. She wouldn't want to live today and look ahead to what it is she sees because she's afraid. Fear is always with us but we just don't have time for it. Not now." If Clinton were graduating this year (instead of 1969), do you think that she would express the same optimism about the future? Explain.

# COMMENCEMENT SPEECH, LOS ANGELES CITY COLLEGE, 2010

## Hilda L. Solis

### *1957–*

*Hilda L. Solis is the current Supervisor for the First District of Los Angeles County and formerly served as the United States Secretary of Labor in the Obama administration. In 2010, she coauthored the book* Reinvesting in America's Youth: Lessons from the 2009 Recovery Act Summer Youth Employment Initiative. *Solis delivered the following commencement address at Los Angeles City College in 2010.*

Good morning Los Angeles City College 2010 graduates! Thank you Dr. (Jamillah) Moore for your warm introduction. It's great to see you again. Dr. Moore and I have known each other from our days in the California State Assembly. Dr. Moore's passion for community colleges is evident as her leadership extends to issues at both the state and federal levels. And I think that we can all agree that she always puts her students and those in most need at the forefront of everything she does.

I want to acknowledge and thank the faculty and staff that are present. I also want to welcome your City Controller Wendy Gruel and Assemblyman Warren Furatani for joining us as well.

It's an honor to speak at the 2010 Los Angeles City College graduation ceremony! I think that now is the appropriate time to say . . . congratulations class of 2010! You deserve a big round of applause.

I know many family members are here. . . . I want to congratulate all the parents, grandparents, wives, husbands and children. Today, we also celebrate all of the support you gave these graduates during their time here at Los Angeles City College. Even if it was just that delicious breakfast your mom made you or that $50.00 your grandfather gave you for your textbook. Or that tender hug you received from your spouse after your exam! Your family played an important role in your education!

And at this time, I want to extend a special welcome and congratulate the nineteen U.S. veterans who are graduating today. I thank each and every one of you for your sacrifice and service to our country! 5

I must say, from where I'm standing the class of 2010 looks like they are going to conquer the world!

Standing here in front of you reminds me of the moment I was in your place . . . boy was it challenging . . . especially to have been the first in the family to go to college. I understand that 50% of today's graduates are the first in their family to graduate from college. Graduates, this is a remarkable accomplishment and you are setting a wonderful example for your families and community.

CHAPTER 12  FOCUS

Who would have thought that one day this farm land—once the original campus for UCLA—would become an institution that would prepare generations of professionals? In September of 1929 Los Angeles City College opened its doors to 1,300 students, with close to 60 teachers on staff. Fast-track to 2010 and you have more than 17,000 students enrolled here! Today 1,600 degrees and certificates will be awarded, which is the most since 1985. This is a remarkable milestone and Dr. Moore, I congratulate you and your staff!

Great minds and great students do come out of community colleges. That is why I began my career in public service as a Board Member of the Rio Hondo Community College Board of Trustees. And, as I look around, I am filled with a sense of pride and excitement for this graduating class. We are here to celebrate your achievements and your hard work. You've put in your time and it has paid off. Yes, some days I'm sure were more difficult than others, but you always found a solution. You've learned from one another; you've helped each other . . . regardless of where you come from, your paths have crossed here at this campus and today we celebrate the finish line for this part of your life.

10 One day, many of you will be behind this podium telling your story. With all honesty, I never imagined a moment like this would come in my life. You want to know why? Because in high school a counselor told me I was not the type of person that could go to college. He told me I should settle for a secretarial job. Apparently, he thought I had a bright future as an office assistant. I guess he could predict the future because I did become a secretary, the Secretary of Labor.

Students, I tell you, it's easy to give up, especially when we come from a family with financial difficulties and when our parents don't fully understand the educational system in this country. In my case, my mother migrated from Nicaragua and my father came from Mexico . . . both worked hard and barely earned the minimum wage. They worked to provide for us, sacrificing their health along the way to make sure we had a roof over our heads and food on our table. But that did not matter because we had things more valuable than money; we had love, dignity and respect in our home.

And one thing I will never forget: my father taught me to not be afraid to ask questions. So I started to ask a lot of questions. I wanted to know how people obtained Pell Grants, Cal Grants, Financial Aid, work-study . . . all of those things . . . I asked and I found out.

Soon, I was working at the bookstore and then at the public library; I was earning money while going to school . . . just like many of you did. My siblings realized the opportunities too . . . and today, my twin sisters are engineers and another sister has a PhD in public health.

You still have a road to travel . . . and it won't be easy, but you are determined to make your dreams a reality. Just remember that the steps you take after today will be extremely important for your future.

Don't wait around too long to think about what you're going to do next because the clock is ticking. Go out and take risks . . . find mentors, network, set goals for yourself, learn about other cultures and issues. Little did I know that the people I was meeting in high school and college were shaping the person I am today!

My education and involvement with the community made me aware of the social and civic turmoil taking place in my own neighborhood. I grew up in La Puente, about 30 minutes from here. You want to know who and what inspired me to pursue the field that I am in today? It was the people around me . . . my community! 15

The more I learned about the issues affecting my immediate environment, the more reasons I had to stand up on behalf of a united voice. It broke my heart to learn that people were being mistreated at the workplace. Some were facing discrimination, some were not getting paid for their work, and many were exposed to toxic chemicals and landfills. I wanted to do something about it. That was my calling . . . a calling for me to take action and help to be a voice and champion for my community's most vulnerable citizens!

My first task as a public servant would be to help community colleges increase the diversity among minorities and women. Following that, I worked to improve community colleges' vocational job training programs. When I became a legislator, I tackled other important issues like health care, domestic violence . . . and veterans needed a voice too . . . I saw the need for representation in different places. Also, during the late 90's, I noticed that polluting projects were operating here in Los Angeles . . . and primarily in minority and low-income neighborhoods!

The 90210 zip code was not touched or polluted that's for sure, but the poor were breathing harmful air. I went against the businesses that were profiting from this tragedy and other politicians refused to stand with me. I always think that "fighting for what is just is not always popular but it is necessary." And that's exactly what I did. As a result, in 1999 Governor Gray Davis signed into law Senate Bill 115, the first of its kind. This law was defined as "the fair treatment of all races, cultures, and incomes with respect to the development, adoption, implementation, and enforcement of environmental laws."

I would soon be surprised with a prestigious award for my environmental work. I was the first woman to receive the John F. Kennedy Profile in Courage Award—for my courage to stand and fight on behalf of disadvantaged communities. But my work did not stop in the California State Senate and Legislature! During my eight years in Congress I worked to help ease the burden of working families:

- I fought to allow immigrant students to attend state colleges at in-state tuition rates;

- I have proudly supported the Dream Act;

- I pressed for legislation to help reduce teen pregnancy within Latinas and African Americans; and

- I helped pass legislation to fund domestic violence programs.

20   Now, as your Secretary of Labor, it is my obligation to help American workers and all of you prepare for jobs in the 21st century economy. An education can fortify you against the uncertainties of a 21st century economy. And your education is even more important now that you're entering a tough job market. You're accepting your degrees as international competition increases, and with an economy that's still rebounding. In the words of President Obama—"let there be no doubt—the future belongs to the nation that best educates its citizens."

With your degree and certificates in hand, you're in a stronger position to outcompete workers around the globe. Workers with more technical expertise and critical thinking capacity will be best positioned to secure the higher wage jobs of the future. Today, the reality is that African-Americans and Latinos are not entering fields related to science, technology, engineering, and math! STEM jobs as they call it. Even fewer women are bound to go into those careers.

And along that field of work will be "green jobs." Green jobs are more than a job; they are the future careers of the 21st century economy. The President and I strongly believe that green jobs will be a key driver behind America's economic recovery. These clean energy jobs are available to anyone willing to upgrade their skills. However, the bigger question is . . . who will lead the world in making the fuel-efficient vehicles, wind turbines, solar panels and other technologies of tomorrow? Let me tell you who will . . . American workers will and many of you here today.

This Administration's number one priority in confronting the economic crisis is to put Americans back to work. Therefore, the Labor Department is making the necessary investments for workers and as of now . . . we are:

- investing $720 million in job training programs that focus on careers in allied health, clean and renewable energy and information technology.

- enforcing our labor laws, so that you are paid fairly and have a safe workplace.

- protecting vulnerable workers, because no one should be subject to workplace discrimination.

In essence, we are preparing the next generation of the U.S. labor force and I want to make sure you're part of it.

Class of 2010, the opportunities for a better life and a better tomorrow are all in your hands. Let this be "only" the beginning of the great things you have yet to accomplish. Ask yourself . . . what will I do after today? Will you take the easy path from here? Or, will you be ready for the next challenge? "Let us think of education as the means of developing our greatest abilities, because in each of us there is a private hope and dream which, fulfilled, can be translated into benefit for everyone and greater strength for our Nation." Those were the words of President John F. Kennedy.

Starting today, your dreams and aspirations will continue to fuel 25 the next generation of scholars. Your education will benefit your families, communities and ultimately our country because you are the future of our nation.

So, class of 2010, many great opportunities await you . . . it's up to you to go after them!

It was an honor to be here with you on this very important day. Congratulations . . . you deserve to celebrate!

Felicidades y si se puede![1]

## Responding to Reading

MyWritingLab™

1.  In her speech, Solis tells about a high school counselor who advised her to become a secretary. What lesson does this story teach about success? About failure?
2.  Solis delivered her speech to graduates who were about to enter a very difficult job market. What advice does she give them? In light of the economic situation, do you think her advice is useful? Explain.
3.  **Rhetorical Analysis**   Solis's speech has two parts. In the first part, she tells listeners about herself. In the second part, she discusses her role as Secretary of Labor. How do these two parts complement each other? Are both topics relevant to her audience? Explain.

## Writing about Reading

MyWritingLab™

1.  If you were giving a speech to the graduates of Los Angeles City College today, what advice would you give them?
2.  **Writing with Sources**   Review a variety of commencement addresses from fifty years ago. How are the personal and professional backgrounds of the speakers different from Solis's? Write an essay in which you examine these differences and explain what they indicate about how American society has changed.

---

[1]Spanish for *Congratulations and yes you can!* [Eds.]

# COMMENCEMENT SPEECH, UNIVERSITY OF PORTLAND, 2009

## Paul Hawken

*1946–*

*An environmentalist and entrepreneur, Paul Hawken is the founder of the Natural Capital Institute, a research organization devoted to the environment and social justice. Hawken is the author of numerous books, including, most recently,* Blessed Unrest: How the Largest Movement in the World Came into Being, and Why No One Saw It Coming *(2007). He has published articles in* BioScience, *the* Boston Globe, Esquire, Harvard Business Review, Inc., Mother Jones, Nation's Business, Orion, *the* San Francisco Chronicle, Sierra, *and* Utne Reader. *Hawken delivered the following commencement address at the University of Portland in 2009.*

When I was invited to give this speech, I was asked if I could give a simple short talk that was "direct, naked, taut, honest, passionate, lean, shivering, startling, and graceful." No pressure there.

Let's begin with the startling part. Class of 2009: you are going to have to figure out what it means to be a human being on earth at a time when every living system is declining, and the rate of decline is accelerating. Kind of a mind-boggling situation . . . but not one peer-reviewed paper published in the last thirty years can refute that statement. Basically, civilization needs a new operating system, you are the programmers, and we need it within a few decades.

This planet came with a set of instructions, but we seem to have misplaced them. Important rules like don't poison the water, soil, or air, don't let the earth get overcrowded, and don't touch the thermostat have been broken. Buckminster Fuller[1] said that spaceship earth was so ingeniously designed that no one has a clue that we are on one, flying through the universe at a million miles per hour, with no need for seatbelts, lots of room in coach, and really good food—but all that is changing.

There is invisible writing on the back of the diploma you will receive, and in case you didn't bring lemon juice to decode it, I can tell you what it says: You are Brilliant, and the Earth is Hiring. The earth couldn't afford to send recruiters or limos to your school. It sent you rain, sunsets, ripe cherries, night blooming jasmine, and that unbelievably cute person you are dating. Take the hint. And here's the deal: Forget that this task of planet-saving is not possible in the time required. Don't be put off by people who know what is not possible. Do what needs to be done, and check to see if it was impossible only after you are done.

---

[1] American engineer and architect (1895–1983). [Eds.]

When asked if I am pessimistic or optimistic about the future, my 5
answer is always the same: If you look at the science about what is
happening on earth and aren't pessimistic, you don't understand the
data. But if you meet the people who are working to restore this earth
and the lives of the poor, and you aren't optimistic, you haven't got a
pulse. What I see everywhere in the world are ordinary people willing
to confront despair, power, and incalculable odds in order to restore
some semblance of grace, justice, and beauty to this world. The poet
Adrienne Rich wrote, "So much has been destroyed I have cast my lot
with those who, age after age, perversely, with no extraordinary power,
reconstitute the world." There could be no better description. Humanity is coalescing. It is reconstituting the world, and the action is taking
place in schoolrooms, farms, jungles, villages, campuses, companies,
refugee camps, deserts, fisheries, and slums.

You join a multitude of caring people. No one knows how many
groups and organizations are working on the most salient issues of our
day: climate change, poverty, deforestation, peace, water, hunger, conservation, human rights, and more. This is the largest movement the
world has ever seen. Rather than control, it seeks connection. Rather
than dominance, it strives to disperse concentrations of power. Like
Mercy Corps,[2] it works behind the scenes and gets the job done. Large
as it is, no one knows the true size of this movement. It provides hope,
support, and meaning to billions of people in the world. Its clout resides in idea, not in force. It is made up of teachers, children, peasants,
businesspeople, rappers, organic farmers, nuns, artists, government
workers, fisherfolk, engineers, students, incorrigible writers, weeping
Muslims, concerned mothers, poets, doctors without borders, griev-
ing Christians, street musicians, the President of the United States of
America, and as the writer David James Duncan would say, the Creator,
the One who loves us all in such a huge way.

There is a rabbinical teaching that says if the world is ending and
the Messiah arrives, first plant a tree, and then see if the story is true.
Inspiration is not garnered from the litanies of what may befall us; it
resides in humanity's willingness to restore, redress, reform, rebuild,
recover, reimagine, and reconsider. "One day you finally knew what
you had to do, and began, though the voices around you kept shouting
their bad advice," is Mary Oliver's[3] description of moving away from
the profane toward a deep sense of connectedness to the living world.

Millions of people are working on behalf of strangers, even if
the evening news is usually about the death of strangers. This kind-
ness of strangers has religious, even mythic origins, and very specific
eighteenth-century roots. Abolitionists were the first people to create a
national and global movement to defend the rights of those they did not

---

[2]Global aid organization. [Eds.]
[3]American poet (1935–). [Eds.]

know. Until that time, no group had filed a grievance except on behalf of itself. The founders of this movement were largely unknown—Granville Sharp, Thomas Clarkson, Josiah Wedgwood—and their goal was ridiculous on the face of it: at that time three out of four people in the world were enslaved. Enslaving each other was what human beings had done for ages. And the abolitionist movement was greeted with incredulity. Conservative spokesmen ridiculed the abolitionists as liberals, progressives, do-gooders, meddlers, and activists. They were told they would ruin the economy and drive England into poverty. But for the first time in history a group of people organized themselves to help people they would never know, from whom they would never receive direct or indirect benefit. And today tens of millions of people do this every day. It is called the world of non-profits, civil society, schools, social entrepreneurship, non-governmental organizations, and companies who place social and environmental justice at the top of their strategic goals. The scope and scale of this effort is unparalleled in history.

The living world is not "out there" somewhere, but in your heart. What do we know about life? In the words of biologist Janine Benyus, life creates the conditions that are conducive to life. I can think of no better motto for a future economy. We have tens of thousands of abandoned homes without people and tens of thousands of abandoned people without homes. We have failed bankers advising failed regulators on how to save failed assets. We are the only species on the planet without full employment. Brilliant. We have an economy that tells us that it is cheaper to destroy earth in real time rather than renew, restore, and sustain it. You can print money to bail out a bank but you can't print life to bail out a planet. At present we are stealing the future, selling it in the present, and calling it gross domestic product. We can just as easily have an economy that is based on healing the future instead of stealing it. We can either create assets for the future or take the assets of the future. One is called restoration and the other exploitation. And whenever we exploit the earth we exploit people and cause untold suffering. Working for the earth is not a way to get rich, it is a way to be rich.

10    The first living cell came into being nearly 40 million centuries ago, and its direct descendants are in all of our bloodstreams. Literally you are breathing molecules this very second that were inhaled by Moses, Mother Teresa, and Bono. We are vastly interconnected. Our fates are inseparable. We are here because the dream of every cell is to become two cells. And dreams come true. In each of you are one quadrillion cells, 90 percent of which are not human cells. Your body is a community, and without those other microorganisms you would perish in hours. Each human cell has 400 billion molecules conducting millions of processes between trillions of atoms. The total cellular activity in one human body is staggering: one septillion actions at any one moment, a one with twenty-four zeros after it. In a millisecond, our body has

undergone ten times more processes than there are stars in the universe, which is exactly what Charles Darwin foretold when he said science would discover that each living creature was a "little universe, formed of a host of self-propagating organisms, inconceivably minute and as numerous as the stars of heaven."

So I have two questions for you all: First, can you feel your body? Stop for a moment. Feel your body. One septillion activities going on simultaneously, and your body does this so well you are free to ignore it, and wonder instead when this speech will end. You can feel it. It is called life. This is who you are. Second question: Who is in charge of your body? Who is managing those molecules? Hopefully not a political party. Life is creating the conditions that are conducive to life inside you, just as in all of nature. Our innate nature is to create the conditions that are conducive to life. What I want you to imagine is that collectively humanity is evincing a deep innate wisdom in coming together to heal the wounds and insults of the past.

Ralph Waldo Emerson once asked what we would do if the stars only came out once every thousand years. No one would sleep that night, of course. The world would create new religions overnight. We would be ecstatic, delirious, made rapturous by the glory of God. Instead, the stars come out every night and we watch television.

This extraordinary time when we are globally aware of each other and the multiple dangers that threaten civilization has never happened, not in a thousand years, not in ten thousand years. **Each of us is as complex and beautiful as all the stars in the universe. We have done great things and we have gone way off course in terms of honoring creation.** You are graduating to the most amazing, stupefying challenge ever bequeathed to any generation. The generations before you failed. They didn't stay up all night. They got distracted and lost sight of the fact that life is a miracle every moment of your existence. Nature beckons you to be on her side. You couldn't ask for a better boss. The most unrealistic person in the world is the cynic, not the dreamer. Hope only makes sense when it doesn't make sense to be hopeful. This is your century. Take it and run as if your life depends on it.

## Responding to Reading

MyWritingLab™

1. In paragraph 6, Hawken tells graduating students, "You join a multitude of caring people." Do you think the optimism about the future that this statement reveals is justified? Explain.
2. What is Hawken's actual message to the graduating class of University of Portland? Do you think his message is both realistic and appropriate? Does this 2009 message seem dated in any way?
3. **Rhetorical Analysis**  Hawken begins his speech by stating that "every living system is declining, and the rate of decline is accelerating" (2). What evidence does he offer to support this claim? How convincing is this supporting evidence?

## Writing about Reading

1. In paragraph 9, Hawken says, "Working for the earth is not a way to get rich, it is a way to be rich." What does he mean? Do you agree with this sentiment?
2. **Writing with Sources**   Research Hawken's business ventures. Then, write an essay in which you discuss whether his entrepreneurial accomplishments reflect the ideals expressed in his commencement speech.

# COMMENCEMENT SPEECH, HOWARD UNIVERSITY, 1994

## Colin Powell

### 1937–

*Colin Powell was the first African-American chairman of the United States Joint Chiefs of Staff, serving from 1989 to 1993, and United States Secretary of State, serving from 2001 to 2005. He is the author of numerous books, including, most recently,* It Worked for Me: In Life and Leadership *(2012). Powell delivered the following commencement address at Howard University in 1994.*

The real challenge in being a commencement speaker is figuring out how long to speak. The graduating students want a short speech, five to six minutes and let's get it over. They are not going to remember who their commencement speaker was anyway. P O W E L L.

Parents are another matter. Arrayed in all their finery they have waited a long time for this day, some not sure it would ever come, and they want it to last. So go on and talk for two or three hours. We brought our lunch and want our money's worth.

The faculty member who suggested the speaker hopes the speech will be long enough to be respectable, but not so long that he has to take leave for a few weeks beginning Monday.

So the poor speaker is left figuring out what to do. My simple rule is to respond to audience reaction. If you are appreciative and applaud a lot early on, you get a nice, short speech. If you make me work for it, we're liable to be here a long time.

5    You know, the controversy over Howard's speaking policy has its positive side. It has caused the university to go through a process of self-examination, which is always a healthy thing to do. Since many people have been giving advice about how to handle this matter, I thought I might as well too.

First, I believe with all my heart that Howard must continue to serve as an institute of learning excellence where freedom of speech is strongly encouraged and rigorously protected. That is at the very essence of a great university and Howard is a great university.

And freedom of speech means permitting the widest range of views to be present for debate, however controversial those views may be. The First Amendment right of free speech is intended to protect the controversial and even outrageous word, and not just comforting platitudes, too mundane to need protection.

Some say that by hosting controversial speakers who shock our sensibilities, Howard is in some way promoting or endorsing their message. Not at all. Howard has helped put their message in perspective while protecting their right to be heard. So that the message can be exposed to the full light of day.

I have every confidence in the ability of the administration, the faculty and the students of Howard to determine who should speak on this campus. No outside help needed, thank you.

I also have complete confidence in the students of Howard to make   10
informed, educated judgments about what they hear.

But for this freedom to hear all views, you bear a burden to sort out wisdom from foolishness. There is great wisdom in the message of self reliance, of education, of hard work, and of the need to raise strong families. There is utter foolishness, evil, and danger in the message of hatred, or of condoning violence, however cleverly the message is packaged or entertainingly it is presented. We must find nothing to stand up and cheer about or applaud in a message of racial or ethnic hatred.

I was at the inauguration of President Mandela in South Africa earlier this week. You were there too by television and watched that remarkable event. Together, we saw what can happen when people stop hating and begin reconciling. DeKlerk the jailer became DeKlerk the liberator, and Mandela the prisoner became Mandela the president. Twenty seven years of imprisonment did not embitter Nelson Mandela. He invited his three jail keepers to the ceremony. He used his liberation to work his former tormentors to create a new South Africa and to eliminate the curse of apartheid from the face of the earth. What a glorious example! What a glorious day it was!

Last week you also saw Prime Minister Rabin and PLO Chairman Arafat sign another agreement on their still difficult, long road to peace, trying to end hundreds of years of hatred and two generations of violence. Palestinian authorities have now begun entering Gaza and Jericho.

In these two historic events, intractable enemies of the past have shown how you can join hands to create a force of moral authority more powerful than any army and which can change the world.

Although there are still places of darkness in the world where the   15
light of reconciliation has not penetrated, these two beacons of hope show what can be done when men and women of goodwill work together for peace and for progress.

There is a message in these two historic events for us assembled here today. As the world goes forward, we cannot start going backward. African Americans have come too far and we have too far yet to go to take a detour into the swamp of hatred. We, as a people who have suffered so much from the hatred of others must not now show tolerance for any movement or philosophy that has at its core the hatred of Jews or anyone else. Our future lies in the philosophy of love and understanding and caring and building. Not of hatred and tearing down.

We know that. We must stand up for it and speak up for it! We must not be silent if we would live up to the legacy of those who have gone before us from this campus.

I have no doubt that this controversy will pass and Howard University will emerge even stronger, even more than ever a symbol of hope, of promise, and of excellence. That is Howard's destiny!

Ambassador Annenberg, one of your honorees today, is a dear friend of mine and is one of America's leading businessmen and greatest philanthropists. You have heard of his recent contribution to American education and his generous gift to Howard. A few years ago I told Mr. Annenberg about a project I was involved in to build a memorial to the Buffalo Soldiers, those brave black cavalrymen of the West whose valor had long gone unrecognized. Ambassador Annenberg responded immediately, and with his help the memorial now stands proudly at Fort Leavenworth, Kansas.

20    The Buffalo Soldiers were formed in 1867, at the same time as Howard University. It is even said that your mascot, the bison, came from the bison, or buffalo, soldiers. Both Howard and the Buffalo Soldiers owe their early success to the dedication and faith of white military officers who served in the Civil War. In Howard's case, of course, it was your namesake, Major General Oliver Howard.

For the 10th Cavalry Buffalo Soldiers, it was Colonel Benjamin Grierson who formed and commanded that regiment for almost twenty five years. And he fought that entire time to achieve equal status for his black comrades.

Together, Howard University and the Buffalo Soldiers showed what black Americans were capable of when given the education and opportunity; and when shown respect and when accorded dignity.

I am a direct descendant of those Buffalo Soldiers, of the Tuskegee Airmen, and of the Navy's Golden Thirteen, and Montfort Point Marines, and all the black men and women who served this nation in uniform for over three hundred years. All of whom served in their time and in their way and with whatever opportunity existed then to break down the walls of discrimination and racism to make the path easier for those of us who came after them.

I climbed on their backs and stood on their shoulders to reach the top of my chosen profession to become chairman of the American Joint

Chiefs of Staff. I will never forget my debt to them and to the many white "Colonel Griersons" and "General Howards" who helped me over the thirty five years of my life as a soldier. They would say to me now, "Well done. And now let others climb up on your shoulders."

Howard's Buffalo Soldiers did the same thing, and on their shoulders now stand governors and mayors and congressmen and generals and doctors and artists and writers and teachers and leaders in every segment of American society. And they did it for the class of 1994. So that you can now continue climbing to reach the top of the mountain, while reaching down and back to help those less fortunate.

You face "Great Expectations." Much has been given to you and much is expected from you. You have been given a quality education, presented by a distinguished faculty who sit here today in pride of you. You have inquiring minds and strong bodies given to you by God and by your parents, who sit behind you and pass on to you today their still unrealized dreams and ambitions. You have been given citizenship in a country like none other on earth, with opportunities available to you like nowhere else on earth, beyond anything available to me when I sat in a place similar to this thirty six years ago.

What will be asked of you is hard work. Nothing will be handed to you. You are entering a life of continuous study and struggle to achieve your goals. A life of searching to find that which you do well and love doing. Never stop seeking.

I want you to have faith in yourselves. I want you to believe to the depth of your soul that you can accomplish any task that you set your mind and energy to. I want you to be proud of your heritage. Study your origins. Teach your children racial pride and draw strength and inspiration from the cultures of our forebears.

Not as a way of drawing back from American society and its European roots. But as a way of showing that there are other roots as well. African and Caribbean roots that are also a source of nourishment for the American family tree. To show that African Americans are more than a product of our slave experience. To show that our varied backgrounds are as rich as that of any other American—not better or greater, but every bit as equal.

Our black heritage must be a foundation stone we can build on, not a place to withdraw into. I want you to fight racism. But remember, as Dr. King and Dr. Mandela have taught us, racism is a disease of the racist. Never let it become yours. White South Africans were cured of the outward symptoms of the disease by President Mandela's inauguration, just as surely as black South Africans were liberated from apartheid. Racism is a disease you can help cure by standing up for your rights and by your commitment to excellence and to performance. By being ready to take advantage of your rights and the opportunities that will come from those rights.

Never let the dying hand of racism rest on your shoulder, weighing you down. Let racism always be someone else's burden to carry. As you seek your way in the world, never fail to find a way to serve your community. Use your education and your success in life to help those still trapped in cycles of poverty and violence. Above all, never lose faith in America. Its faults are yours to fix, not to curse.

America is a family. There may be differences and disputes in the family, but we must not allow the family to be broken into warring factions. From the diversity of our people, let us draw strength and not cause weakness. Believe in America with all your heart and soul and mind. It remains the "last best hope of Earth." You are its inheritors and its future is today placed in your hands.

Go forth from this place today inspired by those who went before you. Go forth with the love of your families and the blessings of your teachers.

Go forth to make this a better country and society. Prosper, raise strong families, remembering that all you will leave behind is your good works and your children.

35      Go forth with my humble congratulations.

And let your dreams be your only limitations. Now and forever.

Thank you and God bless you.

Have a great life!

## Responding to Reading

MyWritingLab™

1.  In his speech, Powell refers to the inauguration of Nelson Mandela as President of South Africa as well as to the signing of peace accords by Yitzhak Rabin, former Prime Minister of Israel, and Yasser Arafat, former Chairman of the PLO. What do these two events show? What message does Powell think they send to his listeners?
2.  What does Powell mean in paragraph 30 when he says, "Our black heritage must be a foundation stone we can build on, not a place to withdraw into"?
3.  **Rhetorical Analysis**   Powell delivered his speech at Howard University, a school that has allowed some highly controversial individuals to speak on campus. Why do you think Powell begins his speech by addressing this situation? Is this an effective strategy?

## Writing about Reading

MyWritingLab™

1.  Speaking over twenty years ago, Powell says, "America is a family. There may be differences and disputes in the family, but we must not allow the family to be broken into warring factions" (32). How do you think he would characterize America today?
2.  **Writing with Sources**   Like most commencement speeches, Powell's speech is optimistic. Identify a few troubling recent events—for example, the shootings that gave rise to the Black Lives Matter movement—and then write an essay in which you consider whether Powell's optimism is still justified.

# WIDENING THE FOCUS

## For Critical Reading and Writing

Referring specifically to the three speeches in this chapter's Focus section, write an essay in which you answer the question, "What Comes Next?"

## For Further Reading

The following readings can suggest additional perspectives for thinking and writing about the issues that society will face in the future:

- Tao Lin, "When I Moved Online" (p. 57)
- Jill Filipovic, "We've Gone Too Far with Trigger Warnings" (p. 97)
- Dallas Spires, "Will Text Messaging Destroy the English Language" (p. 124)
- Brent Staples, "Why Race Isn't as 'Black' and 'White' as We Think" (p. 302)
- Barbara Hurd, "Fracking: A Fable" (p. 409)

## For Focused Research

This Focus section offers three examples of commencement addresses. Consider the similarities and differences among these addresses. Then, do a *Google* search for additional examples of commencement addresses from the past thirty years, and write an essay that considers the following questions: What dominant themes are present in the addresses over the years? What changes do you see in the subject matter of commencement addresses over time, and how do these changes reflect changes in society? Quote from key commencement addresses to support your points.

## Beyond the Classroom

Choose two or three classic science fiction movies that are set in a future that is close to our own time—for example, *2001: A Space Odyssey* (made in 1968 and set in 2001), *Blade Runner* (made in 1982 and set in 2019), and *Back to the Future Part II* (made in 1989 and set in 2015). After viewing the movies, write an essay in which you report how accurate their predictions are. What did the movies get right? What did they get wrong? What conclusions can you draw about Hollywood's ability to predict the future?

CHAPTER 12   FOCUS

MyWritingLab™

Visit Chapter 12,
"Facing the Future," in
MyWritingLab to test
your understanding of the
chapter objectives.

———————————— EXPLORING ISSUES AND IDEAS ————

## Facing the Future

Write an essay in response to one of the following prompts, which are suitable for assignments that require the use of outside sources as well as for assignments that are not source-based.

1. How do you think higher education will change in the future? Will it be widely available or limited to a privileged few? Will traditional instruction be replaced by technology? Will students be offered more practical options than they currently have? Read a few essays in Chapter 4, "Issues in Education," and Michael S. Malone's "The Next American Frontier" (p. 482). Then, incorporating the information in these essays, write an essay in which you present your ideas on this issue.

2. Over the past fifty years, gender roles in the workplace and in society in general have changed considerably. Read Cheryl Sandberg and Anna Maria Chavez's "'Bossy,' The other B-Word" (p. 227), Debora Spar's "Crashing into Ceilings: A Report from the Nine-to-Five Shift" (p. 358), and Glenn Sacks's "Stay-at-Home Dads" (p. 232). Then, write an essay in which you discuss how equal (or unequal) male/female roles will be twenty years from now. Be specific, and refer to the essays you read for this assignment.

3. In his poem "Dover Beach" (p. 460), Matthew Arnold paints a dark picture of a world without religious faith. What do you see as the future of religion in the United States? Do you think that the United States is a country in which religious faith is declining or is increasing? In addition to considering the ideas explored in Arnold's poem use material from Colin Powell's Commencement Speech.

4. Write an essay in which you examine where you expect to be ten years after you graduate. Before you write, read "Why We Work" by Andrew Curry (p. 353), "The Next American Frontier" by Michael Malone (p. 482), and the three commencement speeches in this chapter's Focus section.

5. Overall, are you optimistic or pessimistic about the future? Do you think human beings will achieve the society that they have always wished for, or do you think this century will be as destructive as the last one? Write an essay in which you answer these questions. To support your position, refer to two or three of the readings in this chapter.

# APPENDIX

# Appendix

# MLA Documentation

When you write an essay that incorporates research, you need to **document** your sources—identify words and ideas that are not your own. If you do not document your sources, you will be committing **plagiarism**—using the words or ideas of others without giving proper credit. With so many online sources that can be readily copied and pasted, it is easy to lose track of your sources and plagiarize without intending to. To avoid unintentionally committing plagiarism, take careful notes, and be sure to identify all words and ideas that are not your own.

When you begin writing your essay and start incorporating research, you should use the documentation style required by your instructor. Modern Language Association (MLA) style (shown below) is the documentation style used by many instructors in liberal arts and the humanities.

MLA-style documentation requires *in-text citations*, in the form of parenthetical references, along with a *works-cited list* at the end of your essay, which includes the complete information for all of the sources you have used throughout your essay.

## In-Text Citations

In-text citations, which include signal phrases and parenthetical references, contain the information necessary to direct your readers to the full source citation in the works-cited list at the end of your essay. Usually a parenthetical reference includes the author's last name and the page number: (Covert 5). Notice there is no comma after the name and no "p." before the page number. MLA recommends that you try to introduce quoted, paraphrased, or summarized material with a phrase that names the author. When you do so, you include only the page number in parentheses at the end of the sentence, before the final punctuation.

> Bryce Covert claims that contrary to the popular argument that raising the minimum wage amount will reduce the number of jobs, actually "employment is unlikely to suffer from a higher wage" (5).

Following are some examples of parenthetical references that can cause problems because they do not follow this basic format.

## Citing a work within an anthology or a collection

Include the name of the author of the work (not the editor of the anthology or collection) and the page numbers from the anthology or collection.

In a narrative of her early childhood experiences, Lynda Barry describes what school was for her, an environment that was "secure, warm and stable" (76).

## Citing a work without page numbers

For print and online sources that lack page numbers, include only the author's last name.

As a *New York Times* contributor states, "The era dominated by consumer electronics—what most of us call gadgets—is in turmoil" (Manjoo).

## Citing a work with no listed author

When there is no listed author, include the full title. Shorten long titles to the first two or three words of the original title.

Income inequality is on the rise; in fact, "the income gap" is at "its widest point in at least three decades" ("Fix Education").

## Citing two or more works by the same author

When citing multiple works by the same author, identify the author in a signal phrase. Then, in the parenthetical reference, include both the shortened title and the page number.

William Zinsser claims that good writing is uncluttered, free of jargon and verbosity (*On Writing Well* 6) and encourages educators to teach their students this kind of writing, despite the vague and wordy writing style of most academics (*Writing to Learn* 12).

## Citing common literature

Common literary works, such as novels, stories, poems, and plays, are often available in different editions, so you should include additional information (such as part, line, or chapter numbers) that will allow readers to find the borrowed material in any edition.

In fact, Dickens alludes to the difficulty of describing his years spent at the factory several times within the autobiographical fragment, writing at one point, "How much I suffered, it is, as I have said already, utterly beyond my power to tell" (770; pt. 18, ch. 55).

## Works Cited

The works-cited page appears at the end of your essay after the last page of text. For example, if the last page of your essay is page 8, your list of works cited would begin on page 9. Center the title *Works Cited* at the top of the page. (This title should not be italicized, underlined, or placed in quotation marks.)

Like the rest of your essay, the works-cited list should be double-spaced. Entries should be alphabetized by the author's last name or, if there is no listed author, by the first main word of the title. The first line of each entry should begin at the left margin; second and subsequent lines should be indented one-half inch. Generally, each section of the entry (author name, title, etc.) should be followed by a period and one space.

### *Works-cited entries*

### An article in a scholarly journal

Include the author's name, the title of the article (in quotation marks), the title of the journal (italicized), the volume and issue numbers (unspaced), the year of publication, the page numbers (or *n. pag.* if no page numbers are given), and the medium (*Print* or *Web*). For an online journal, include the date of access following the medium.

> Mani, B. Venkat. "Borrowing Privileges: Libraries and the Institutionalization of World Literature." *Modern Language Quarterly* 74.2 (2013): 239–60. Print.

> Dowling, David. "Escaping the Shallows: Deep Reading's Revival in the Digital Age." *Digital Humanities Quarterly* 8.2 (2014): n. pag. Web. 9 Jan. 2015.

### An article in a newspaper

Include the author's name, the article title (in quotation marks), the newspaper title (italicized), the date of publication, the page numbers (if in print), and the medium (*Print* or *Web*). For an online article, include the sponsor of the site after the title of the newspaper and the date of access following the medium.

> Belkin, Douglas. "Colleges Turn to Personality Assessments to Find Successful Students." *Wall Street Journal* 9 Jan. 2015: A3. Print.

> Manjoo, Farhad. "In a World of Phones, Gadgets Must Adapt." *New York Times.* New York Times, 7 Jan. 2015. Web. 29 Jan. 2015.

### An article in a magazine

> Covert, Bryce. "Does the Minimum Wage Kill Jobs?" *The Nation* 27 Oct.
>
> 2014: 5. Print.

> Paterniti, Michael. "The Dogs of War." *National Geographic*. National
>
> Geographic Society, Jun. 2014. Web. 12 Nov. 2014.

### An editorial

> Sauerbrey, Anna. "Germany Is Not Turning Backward." Editorial. *New York*
>
> *Times* 23 Jan. 2015: A27. Print.

> "Fix Education, Fix Income Inequality." Editorial. *Houston Chronicle*. Hearst
>
> Newspapers, 19 Dec. 2014. Web. 12 Jan. 2015.

### A print article in an online database

Follow the guidelines for the print version of the periodical type (journal, newspaper, magazine). Also include the name of the online database (italicized) before the medium (*Web*), and the date of access.

> Irimies, Cosmin. "Effective Communication: An Essential Step Towards Public
>
> Success." *Journal of Media Research* 6.1 (2013): 37–42. *Communication*
>
> *& Mass Media Complete*. Web. 12 Dec. 2014.

### A book by a single author

Include the author name(s), title (italicized), edition number (if not the first), city of publication, publisher, year of publication, and medium.

> Hemeyer, Julia Corbett. *Religion in America*. 6th ed. New York: Pearson,
>
> 2010. Print.

### A book by two or more authors

The first author should appear last name first. Second and subsequent authors appear first name followed by last name.

> Aronson, Marc, and Marina Budhos. *Sugar Changed the World: A Story of*
>
> *Magic, Spice, Slavery, Freedom, and Science*. New York: Houghton,
>
> 2010. Print.

## A work in an anthology

Begin with the author and title of the selection, followed by the title of the anthology (italicized), the abbreviation *Ed.*, and the name(s) of the editor(s).

> Barry, Lynda. "The Sanctuary of School." *The Blair Reader: Exploring Issues and Ideas*. Ed. Laurie G. Kirszner and Stephen R. Mandell. 9th ed. Boston: Pearson, 2017. 75–77. Print.

## An online book/e-book

Include the name of the website (italicized), the medium (*Web*), and the access date.

> Wilkins, W. J. *Hindu Mythology, Vedic and Puranic*. London: W. Thacker, 1900. *Internet Sacred Text Archive*. Web. 11 Nov. 2014.

## A web page

Include the name of the author or editor of the site, the title of the site (italicized), the name of the sponsor (or *N.p.* if there is no sponsor), the date of publication, the medium (*Web*), and the date of access.

> Balk, Alex, and Choire Sicha, eds. *The Awl*. N.p., 2009. Web. 10 Jan. 2015.

## A blog post

Include the author's name and the title of the post (in quotation marks), the title of the blog (italicized), the sponsor of the blog (or *N.p.* if there isn't one), the date of the last update, the medium (*Web*), and the date of access.

> Gallagher, Jillian. "Writing Resolutions." *Looks & Books: Literary Fashion, Fashionable Lit*. N.p., 23 Dec. 2014. Web. 2 Jan. 2015.

## A tweet

Begin with the writer's name, if known. Include the user name in parentheses if different from the writer's name. If only the user name is known, begin with that. Include the full tweet (in quotation marks), followed by the date and time of the tweet along with the medium (*Tweet*).

> Lamott, Anne. "Reality & truth if you want to be a writer. Reality is not NPR & Oprah. Reality: it takes forever, goes slowly, makes you nuts. Jump in." 10 Jan. 2015, 7:48 a.m. Tweet.

## A Facebook post

Include the name of the writer, business, or organization followed by the type and date of posting and the medium (*Facebook posting*).

> Dogs Helping Veterans. Status update. 11 Jan. 2015. Facebook posting.

## An email message

Include the name of the writer, the subject line of the email (in quotation marks), the words "message to" and the recipient's name, the date of the message, and the medium (*E-mail*).

> Rogers, Marcia. "Presentation Topics." Message to students. 9 Jan. 2015.
> E-mail.

## A brochure, pamphlet, or press release

> Environmental Working Group. "New Bill Aims to Bring More Effective
> Sunscreens to Market." Washington: Environmental Working Group,
> 15 July 2014. Web. 15 Jan. 2015.

## A government publication

If an author is named, begin with that. If not, begin with the government name and the agency. End with the publication information.

> Ortman, Jennifer M., Victoria A. Velkoff, and Howard Hogan. "An Aging
> Nation: The Older Population in the United States." 6 May 2014.
> *United States Census Bureau.* Web. 15 Sept. 2014.

## A film or sound recording

For a film, begin with the title, followed by the director, the writers or major performers, and the distributor. When citing a DVD, include that label along with the film's original release date. When citing a film viewed on a website, give the site's name, the medium (*Web*), and the date of access. For sound recordings, follow the same format, except the medium would be *MP3 file, CD,* or *LP*.

> *Schooled: The Price of College Sports.* Dir. Ross Finkel, Trevor Martin, and
> Jonathan Paley. Perf. Sam Rockwell. Epix, 2013. *Netflix.* Web.
> 8 Nov. 2014.

## A TV show

"Other People's Children." *Modern Family*. Writ. Christopher Lloyd, Steven Levitan, and Megan Ganz. Dir. James Alan Hensz. ABC. WABC, New York, 12 Mar. 2014. Television.

## A literary work

Nye, Naomi Shihab. "The Art of Disappearing." *Words under the Words: Selected Poems*. Portland: Eighth Mountain, 1994. 29. Print.

## A visual: cartoon, comic strip, or advertisement

Begin with the artist's name, followed by the title (if any), the label (*Cartoon, Comic strip, Advertisement*), and the publication information for either a print or an online source.

Dator, Joe. Cartoon. *New Yorker*. Condé Nast, 15 Jan. 2015. Web. 17 Jan. 2015.

## An interview

Raine, Mina. Personal interview. 12 June 2014.
Vaccaro, Karen. Telephone interview. 18 Sept. 2014.

## A speech

Include the speaker's name, the title (or the label *Speech* if there is no title), the sponsor and place (or other publication information), and the date.

Radjou, Navi. "Creative Problem-Solving in the Face of Extreme Limits." *TED Talks*. TED Talks, Oct. 2014. Web. 7 Dec. 2014.

# CREDITS

Arnold, Matthew, "Dover Beach" from *New Poems*, Issue 4. London: Macmillan and Company, 1867, p. 112.

Aslan, Reza, "Praying for Common Ground at the Christmas-Dinner Table." *The New York Times*, December 21, 2014.

Balko, Radley, "The Curious Grammar of Police Shootings." *The Washington Post*, July 14, 2014.

Barnett, Rosalind C., and Caryl Rivers, "Men Are from Earth, and So Are Women: It's Faulty Research That Sets Them Apart." *The Chronicle of Higher Education*. Reprinted with permission.

Barry, Lynda, "The Sanctuary of School" from *The New York Times*, January 5, 1992. Copyright © 1992 by Lynda Barry. All rights reserved. Used with permission.

Brady, Judy, "I Want a Wife." Reprinted with permission.

Brooks, David, "Amy Chua Is a Wimp." *The New York Times*, January 17, 2011.

Brooks, David, "It's Not About You." *The New York Times*, May 30, 2011.

Brooks, Max, "The Movies That Rose from the Grave." *The Guardian*, November 10, 2006. Copyright Guardian News & Media Ltd 2006.

Callahan, David, "A Better Way to Prevent Cheating: Appeal to Fairness." *The Christian Science Monitor*, May 8, 2006.

Carson, Rachel, "The Obligation to Endure" from *Silent Spring*. Copyright © 1962 by Rachel L. Carson. Copyright © renewed 1990 by Roger Christie. Reprinted by permission of Houghton Mifflin Harcourt Publishing Company. All rights reserved. [Electronic/Audio Rights: from *Silent Spring* by Rachel Carson. Copyright © 1962 by Rachel L. Carson, Copyright © renewed 1990 by Roger Christie. Reprinted by permission of Frances Collin, Trustee. All copying, including electronic, or re-distribution of this text, is expressly forbidden.]

Chavez, Anna Maria, and Sheryl Sandberg, "Bossy, the other B-word." *The Wall Street Journal*. Reprinted with permission.

Chopin, Kate, "Story of an Hour." *St. Louis Life*, January 5, 1895.

Chua, Amy, "Why Chinese Mothers are Superior." *The Wall Street Journal*, June 8, 2011.

Cofer, Judith Ortiz, "The Myth of the Latin Woman: I Just Met a Girl Named Maria." The University of Georgia Press. Reprinted with permission.

Curry, Andrew, "Why We Work," *U.S. News and World Report*. Reprinted with permission.

The Daily Take Team, the *Thom Hartmann Program*, "If a Business Won't Pay a Living Wage, It Shouldn't Exist." TruthOut.org

Davis, Lydia, "Television." Reprinted by permission Farrar, Straus and Giroux, LLC: "Television" from *Varieties of Disturbance*. Copyright © 2007 by Lydia Davis. [Electronic/Audio: "Television" by Lydia Davis. Copyright © 2007 by Lydia Davis in *Varieties of Disturbance*, published by Farrar, Straus, and Giroux. Reprinted with permission of the Denise Shannon Literary Agency, Inc. All rights reserved.]

Dorn, James, "The Minimum Wage Delusion, And the Death Of Common Sense." *Forbes*, May 7, 2013.

Douglass, Frederick, *Narrative of the Life of Frederick Douglass, An American Slave*. Boston: Anti-Slavery Office, 1845.

Dwyer, Liz, "Is College Worth the Money?" Reprinted from *GOOD Magazine*, by L. Dwyer, 2011. Retrieved from http://magazine.good.is/articles/is-college-worth-the-money-reflections-from-six-graduates-of-the-class-of-2011. Copyright 2011 by GOOD Worldwide, Inc. Reprinted with permission.

Eberstadt, Mary, "Eminem Is Right." *Policy Review*, December 1, 2004. Reprinted with permission.

Espada, Martín, "Why I Went to College." From *A Mayan Astronomer in Hell's Kitchen*. Copyright © 2000 by Martín Espada. Used by permission of the author and W. W. Norton & Company, Inc.

Espaillat, Rhina, "Bilingual/Bilingue." Originally published in *Where Horizons Go*, by Rhina Espalliat (Truman State University Press, 1998).

Farrell, Warren, "Exploiting the Gender Gap." *The New York Times*, September 5, 2005.

Filopovic, Jill, "We've Gone Too Far with 'Trigger Warnings.'" Copyright Guardian News & Media Ltd 2014.

Fleming, Chase, "Is Social Media Hurting Our Social Skills?" *Communication Studies*, June 21, 2012. Reprinted with permission of the author.

Foer, Jonathan Safran, "How Not to Be Alone." *The New York Times*, June 9, 2013.

Frost, Robert, "The Road Not Taken." *Mountain Interval*. New York: Henry Holt and Company, 1916.

Gabler, Neal, "The Elusive Big Idea." *The New York Times*, August 13, 2011.

Gabler, Neal, *The New American Dream*. Reprinted with permission.

Gates, Henry Louis Jr., "Delusions of Grandeur." Copyright © 1991 by Henry Louis Gates, Jr. Originally published in *Sports Illustrated*. Reprinted by permission of the author.

Google search results for "student papers for sale." Google Inc., Screenshot

Graff, E. J., "The M/F Boxes," © E. J. Graff, first published in *The Nation*, December 17, 2001. Reprinted with permission from the author.

Hayden, Robert, "Those Winter Sundays." © 1966 by Robert Hayden, from *Collected Poems of Robert Hayden*, edited by Frederick Glaysher. Used by permission of Liveright Publishing Corporation.

Hawken, Paul, "The Earth Is Hiring" Commencement Speech, University of Portland, May 3, 2009. Reprinted with permission.

Hoekema, David A., "Unacknowledged Ethicists on Campus." Reprinted with permission.

Hogan, Linda, "Heritage" from *Red Clay* (Greenfield Center, NY: Greenfield Review Press, 1994). Copyright © 1994 by Linda Hogan. Reprinted with the permission of The Permissions Company, Inc., on behalf of the author, www.permissionscompany.com

Holt, John, "Schools Are Bad Places for Kids." Reproduced from *The Underachieving School*, by John Holt, with permission of Sentient Publications, LLC.

Hurd, Barbara, "Fracking: A Fable." *Brevity Magazine*, March 3, 2013.

"Is Social Media Hurting Our Social Skills?" [INFOGRAPHIC] Provided by Schools.com, a division of QuinStreet, Inc.

Jefferson, Thomas, *The Declaration of Independence*, 1776.

Jensen, Charles, "Poem in Which Words Have Been Left Out." Originally published in *Poem-a-Day* by The Academy of American Poets. Reprinted with permission.

Kennedy, John F., President Inaugural Address, Washington, DC, January 20, 1961.

King, Martin Luther Jr., "Letter from Birmingham Jail." © 1963 Dr. Martin Luther King Jr., © renewed 1991 Coretta Scott King.

Putnam, Robert D., "Crumbling American Dreams." *The New York Times*, August 4, 2013.

Rauch, Jonathan, *Kindly Inquisitors: The New Attacks on Free Thought*. Chicago: University of Chicago Press, 2014.

Rieder, Jonathan, "Dr. King's Righteous Fury." *The New York Times*, April 16, 2013.

Rodríguez, Cindy Y., "Which Is It, Hispanic or Latino?" CNN, May 3, 2014.

Rosenbaum, Thane, "Should Neo-Nazis Be Allowed Free Speech?" *The Daily Beast*, January 30, 2014. Copyright © 2014 Thane Rosenbaum. All rights reserved.

Rubenfeld, Sophia Chua, "Why I Love My Strict Chinese Mom." *New York Post*, January 18, 2011.

Ryan, Julie J. C. H., "Student Plagiarism in an Online World," *ASEE Prism Magazine*. Reprinted courtesy of PRISM Magazine and the American Society for Engineering Education.

Sacks, Glenn, "Stay at Home Dads." *Newsday*. Reprinted with permission.

Scheller, Melanie, "On the Meaning of Plumbing and Poverty." Copyright Melanie Scheller. Originally published in *The Independent Weekly*.

Sheler, Jeffery, "Muslim in America," *U.S. News and World Report*. Reprinted with permission.

Shteyngart, Gary, "Sixty-Nine Cents." Copyright © 2007 by Gary Shteyngart. First appeared in *The New Yorker*. Reprinted with permission of the Denise Shannon Literary Agency, Inc. All rights reserved.

Solis, Hilda L., from Remarks by Secretary of Labor Hilda L. Solis, Los Angeles City College Graduation, June 8, 2010.

Sommers, Christina Hoff, "For More Balance on Campuses." The Young America's Foundation Speakers Program, May 6, 2002. Reprinted with permission.

Sommers, Christina Hoff, "The War Against Boys." *The Atlantic Monthly*, May 1, 2000. Reprinted with permission.

Spar, Debora L., "Crashing into Ceilings: A Report from the Nine-to-Five Shift." Reprinted by permission Farrar, Straus and Giroux, LLC: Excerpt from *Wonder Women: Sex, Power, and the Quest for Perfection* by Debora L. Spar. Copyright © 2013 by Debora L. Spar.

Spires, Dallas, "Will Text Messaging Destroy the English Language?" Dallas Spires is an insurance salesman and freelance writer based in Macon, GA. Reprinted with permission.

Staples, Brent, "Just Walk on By: Black Men and Public Spaces." Reprinted with permission from Brent Staples.

Staples, Brent, "Why Race Isn't as 'Black' and 'White' as We Think." *The New York Times*, October 31, 2005.

Steinberg, Jacques, "Plan B: Skip College." *The New York Times*, May 15, 2010.

Stephenson, Neal, "Innovation Starvation." Originally published in *World Policy Journal*, Fall 2011. Collected in *Some Remarks* published by William Morrow, 2012. All rights reserved. Used with permission.

Swift, Jonathan, "A Modest Proposal." London: S Harding, 1729.

Talbot, Margaret, "The Case against Single-Sex Classrooms." Margaret Talbot/*The New Yorker*.

Tan, Amy, "Mother Tongue." Copyright © 1990 by Amy Tan. First appeared in *The Threepenny Review*. Reprinted by permission of the author and the Sandra Dijkstra Literary Agency.

Tannen, Deborah, "Marked Women." From "Wears Jump Suit. Sensible Shoes. Uses Husband's Last Name." *The New York Times Magazine*, June 20, 1993. Originally titled "Marked Women, Unmarked Men." Copyright Debora

Tannen. Adapted from *Talking from 9 to 5: Women and Men at Work*, HarperCollins. Reprinted with Permission.

Tannen, Deborah, "The Triumph of the Yell." *The New York Times*, January 14, 1994. Copyright Deborah Tannen. Reprinted with permission.

Tufekci, Zeynep, "After the Protests." *The New York Times*, March 20, 2014.

Turkle, Sherry, "Connectivity and Its Discontents." From *Alone Together: Why We Expect More from Technology and Less from Each Other*, copyright © 2011. Reprinted by permission of Basic Books, a member of The Perseus Books Group. [Audio: Courtesy of Tantor Media, Inc.]

Turley, Jonathan, "Shut Up and Play Nice: How the Western World is Limiting Free Speech." *The Washington Post*, October 12, 2012.

Vargas, Jose Antonio, "My Life as an Undocumented Immigrant." *The New York Times*, June 22, 2011.

White, E. B., "Once More to the Lake," from *One Man's Meat*, text copyright ©1941 by E. B. White. Copyright renewed. Reprinted by permission of Tilbury House, Publishers, Thomaston, Maine. [Electronic: "Once More to the Lake" © [1941] by EB White. Used by Permission. All rights reserved.]

Whitman, Walt, "I Hear America Singing." *Leaves of Grass*. Brooklyn: Fulton Street Printing, 1855.

Wicks-Lim, Jeannette, "Measuring the Full Impact of Minimum and Living Wage Laws." Reprinted by permission of *Dollars & Sense*, a progressive economics magazine www.dollarsandsense.org.

Wilentz, Amy, "A Zombie Is a Slave Forever." *The New York Times*, October 31, 2012.

Wong, Elizabeth, "The Struggle to Be an All-American Girl." *Los Angeles Times*. Reprinted with permission of the Author, www.elizabethwong.net

## PHOTO CREDITS

**Page 13:** Image reprinted with permission from Adbusters Media Foundation; **page 31:** Courtesy of White Literary LLC; **page 32:** Image provided courtesy of Kristin Ohlson, reprinted with permission; **page 59:** Gail Albert Halaban/ Corbis Outline/Corbis; **page 72:** Chippix/Shutterstock; **page 73:** Age fotostock/Alamy; **page 102:** John McPherson/Distributed by Universal Uclick/CartoonStock; **page 116:** Eve Arnold/Magnum Photos; **page 117:** Heinz-J/Rgen G/Ttert/Picture-alliance/dpa/Newscom; **page 123:** Provided by Schools.com, a division of QuinStreet, Inc.; **page 177:** Emeric Fohlen/ NurPhoto/Sipa USA/Newscom; **page 178:** Geoff Dann © Dorling Kindersley, Courtesy of the Museum of the Order of St John, London; **page 179:** StockWERK/Fotolia; **page 206:** Centers for Disease Control and Prevention/ AP Photo; **page 218:** Zurijeta/Shutterstock/Pearson Asset Library; **page 219:** Petro Feketa/Fotolia; **page 244:** Nikesidoroff/Fotolia; **page 262:** Sean Pavone/ Alamy; **page 263:** Della Huff/Alamy; **page 310:** Bettmann/Corbis; **page 311:** Damon Winter/The New York Times/Redux; **page 330:** H.Armstrong Robert/ Alamy; **page 350:** Edwin Levick/Hulton Archive/Getty Images; **page 351:** Betastock/Shutterstock; **page 377:** JIM RUYMEN/UPI/Newscom; **page 396:** Poplasen/Fotolia; **page 397:** Alan Gignoux/Alamy; **page 457:** Photos 12/ Alamy; **page 458:** Shutterstock; **page 492:** Sygma/Corbis

# INDEX OF AUTHORS AND TITLES